Die geheime Kunst des Polsterns
BESESSEN
DEEP-SEATED
The Secret Art of Upholstery

arnoldsche

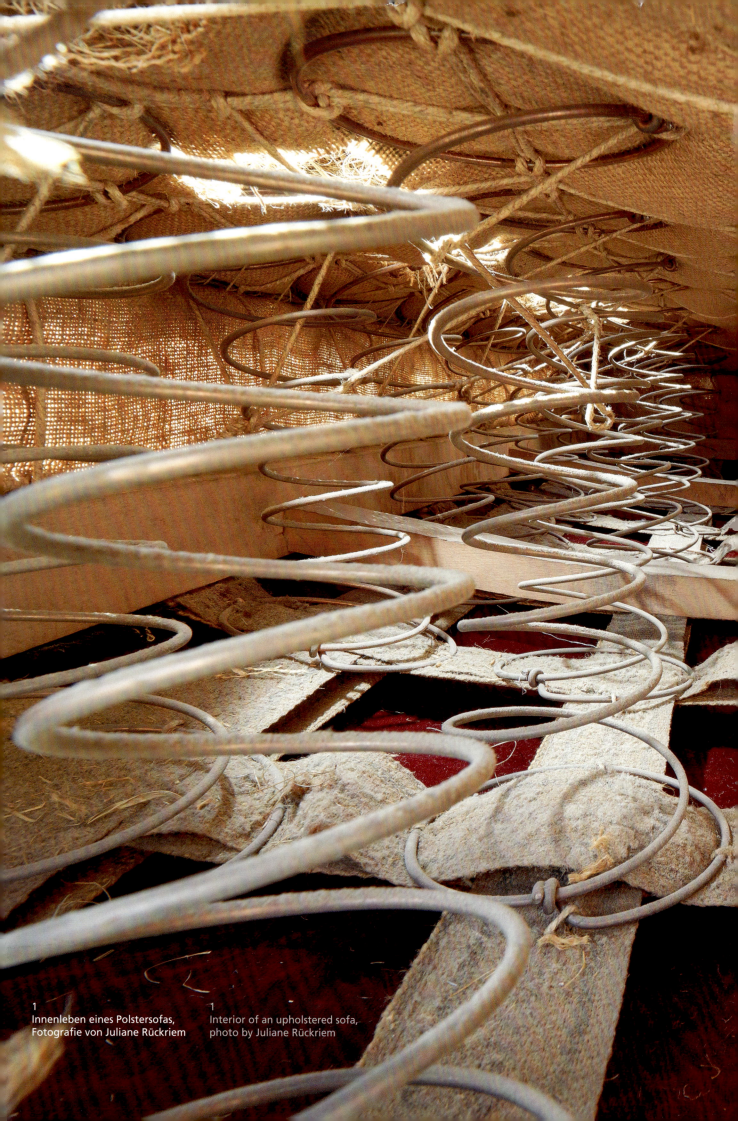

1 Innenleben eines Polstersofas, Fotografie von Juliane Rückriem

1 Interior of an upholstered sofa, photo by Juliane Rückriem

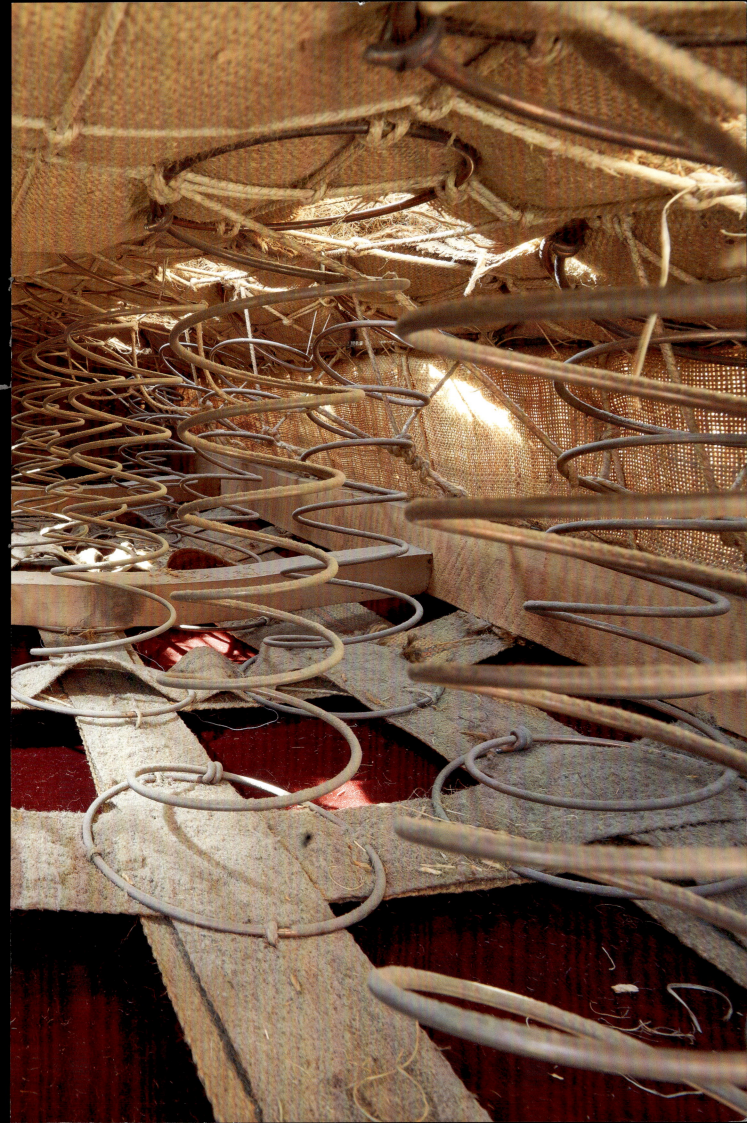

2
Konzeptzeichnung von Thomas Schriefers

2
Conceptual drawing by Thomas Schriefers

Inhalt | Contents

Vorwort / *Olaf Thormann*	7	Preface / *Olaf Thormann*
Einleitung / *Thomas Schriefers*	13	Introduction / *Thomas Schriefers*
Renaissance – Barock – Rokoko / *Thomas Schriefers*	16	Renaissance – Baroque – Rococo / *Thomas Schriefers*
Werkzeug und Spiralfedern / *Thomas Schriefers*	37	Tools and springs / *Thomas Schriefers*
Das Chamber Horse – Ein federndes Fitnessgerät des 18. Jahrhunderts / *Cordula Fink*	42	The chamber horse – Sprung fitness equipment of the eighteenth century / *Cordula Fink*
Spielarten des Klassizismus / *Xenia Schürmann*	53	Variations of Classicism / *Xenia Schürmann*
Polsteraufbau eines klassizistischen Stuhls / *Thomas Schriefers*	67	Upholstery of a Classicist chair / *Thomas Schriefers*
Wohnformen im ersten Drittel des 19. Jahrhunderts / *Thomas Rudi*	71	Dwelling in the first third of the nineteenth century / *Thomas Rudi*
Historismus und Jugendstil / *Thomas Schriefers*	76	Historicism and Jugendstil / *Thomas Schriefers*
Andere Ansprüche – Neue Ideen / *Thomas Schriefers*	102	Different demands – New ideas / *Thomas Schriefers*
Mit fulminanter Wirkung – Eine Sitzgruppe nach dem Entwurf von Ernst Max Jahn aus dem Jahr 1928 / *Thomas Andersch*	156	With brilliant effect – A seating group designed by Ernst Max Jahn in 1928 / *Thomas Andersch*
Konventionen / *Thomas Schriefers*	162	Conventions / *Thomas Schriefers*
Nach 1945 / *Thomas Schriefers*	166	After 1945 / *Thomas Schriefers*
Umdenken / *Thomas Schriefers*	221	Rethinking / *Thomas Schriefers*
Hören, Schauen, Fühlen, Sitzen / *Thomas Schriefers*	227	Listening, seeing, touching, sitting / *Thomas Schriefers*
500 Jahre Textilien für Polstermöbel / *Stefanie Seeberg*	242	500 years of furnishing textiles for upholstered furniture / *Stefanie Seeberg*
Filigrane Kunstwerke: Borten und Quasten / *Stefanie Seeberg*	272	Delicate artworks: Braids and tassels / *Stefanie Seeberg*
Armlehn- und Rückenlehnpolster / *Maximilian Busch*	293	Upholstering arm- and backrests / *Maximilian Busch*
Kissen / *Maximilian Busch*	301	Cushions / *Maximilian Busch*
Glossar: Fachbegriffe, Materialien, Arbeitstechniken	305	Glossary: Technical terms, materials, techniques
Objekt und Bild	326	Objects and images
Anmerkungen	371	Notes
Literaturverzeichnis	381	Bibliography
Abbildungsnachweis	389	List of illustrations
Impressum	390	Imprint

3
Illustration von Saul Steinberg, in: *The Art of Living*,
New York 1949

3
Illustration by Saul Steinberg, in: *The Art of Living*,
New York 1949

Vorwort
Olaf Thormann

Während die potentielle Kunstfertigkeit von Goldschmieden, Töpfern oder Glasbläsern der Allgemeinheit plausibel ist, haben viele Menschen heute von der Arbeit der Polsterer ungleich vagere Vorstellungen. In Ausstellungen und Schaufenstern sind deren Erzeugnisse wesentlich seltener zu sehen. Oft glaubt man, dass die Übermacht der Industrie nur noch wenig Bedarf für solche Tätigkeit zulasse. Dabei steht natürlich außer Frage, dass wir alle den Komfort des guten Sitzens und Liegens schätzen. Schon unsere frühen Kindheitserinnerungen speichern häufig das erstaunliche Federn alter Sofapolster, die haptische Erfahrung bestimmter Bezugsstoffe, aber auch die vielfältigen Abnutzungsspuren, denen Polstermöbel im Gebrauch nun einmal unterliegen und die einer Dauerhaftigkeit ihrer ursprünglichen Erscheinung nicht förderlich sind.

Hat ein gepolstertes Möbel erst einmal eine „Auffrischung" erfahren, so verändert das nicht selten seinen Charakter extrem, manchmal bis zur Unkenntlichkeit. Ich erinnere mich gut an einen ins Jahr 1994 zu datierenden Besuch bei einer alten Leipziger Dame, die noch in einer in den späten 1920er Jahren von einem Innenarchitekten individuell im Art déco entworfenen Wohnung lebte. Teile der Einrichtung, so ein heute in unserer Ständigen Ausstellung präsentiertes Speisezimmer, waren nahezu unverändert über die Zeiten gekommen. Andere der Möbel jedoch hatten in den 1960er Jahren unter veränderten ästhetischen Paradigmen eine Erneuerungskur erhalten, die sie drei Jahrzehnte später, 1994 bei unserem Besuch, tendenziell unscheinbar und wenig interessant erscheinen ließen. Der Fund alter Fotos der Wohnungseinrichtung offenbarte jedoch ein gänzlich anderes Bild ihres ursprünglichen Aussehens, das von gewagter Farbigkeit und großflächigen textilen Musterungen bestimmt wurde. Beflügelt von der Hoffnung, diesen Möbeln irgendwann wieder ihre eigentliche Anmutung zurückgeben zu können, haben wir sie im Auge behalten und gehegt. 2021 gelang dann Thomas Andersch die Restaurierung, die er in einem Beitrag dieser Publikation detailliert beschreibt.

Der Blick auf die eigene Museumsgeschichte zeigt, dass schon früh die Bedeutung aller Komponenten der Möbelkunst erkannt wurde – eifrig sammelte man Relikte alter Bezugsstoffe, Posamente, Fransen, Kordeln etc. Er lehrt aber bedauerlicherweise auch, wie unsensibel Institutionen, die Kulturgut bewahren sollten, mit diesem umgehen. In den Nachkriegsjahrzehnten angestellte Tapezierer haben gnadenlos etliche aus damaliger Betrachtung unansehnlich gewordene Polster durch in keinem Bezug zu den Originalen stehende moderne ersetzt, ohne auch nur die geringste Dokumentation zu hinterlassen. Dies ist kein Einzelfall. In vielen öffentlichen Sammlungen sind hinsichtlich der Authentizität des Erscheinungsbildes ausgestellter Möbel Fragezeichen geboten.

Publikationen und fachwissenschaftliche Expertise zum Thema sind eher rar. Dabei verhält es sich doch bei einem

Preface
Olaf Thormann

While the potential craftsmanship of goldsmiths, potters and glass blowers is conceivable to the general public, many people have much vaguer ideas about the work of an upholsterer. In exhibitions and window displays their works are displayed much less frequently. Often it is believed that the predominance of industry leaves little need for such an occupation. At the same time, it is without question that all of us value being able to sit and lounge comfortably. Even our early childhood memories often recall the astonishing cushions of old upholstered sofas, the tactile experience of particular cover fabrics but also the many traces of wear and tear that upholstered furniture is subjected to and which are not conducive to the durability of its original appearance.

Once a piece of upholstered furniture has been 'refreshed', its character changes dramatically, more often than not to the point of becoming unrecognisable. I recall a visit in 1994 to an old lady in Leipzig who still lived in an apartment that had been custom-designed in Art Deco style by an interior architect in the late 1920s. Parts of the furnishings, such as the dining room presented in our permanent exhibition, had been preserved almost unaltered. Other pieces of furniture, on the contrary had been refreshed during the 1960s according to contemporary aesthetic paradigms, which at the time of our visit three decades later in 1994 made them appear rather unimpressive and less interesting. Old photographs of the interior revealed an entirely different original appearance dominated by daring colours and large textile patterns. Motivated by the hope to restore the original character of these pieces of furniture, we kept an eye on them and preserved them. In 2021, Thomas Andersch succeeded in restoring them, which he describes in detail in an article in this publication.

Taking a look at our own museum history reveals that the importance of all components of the art of furniture was understood early on – relics of old textile covers, passementerie, fringes, cords, etc. were collected eagerly. At the same time, this unfortunately also teaches us how institutions that are meant to preserve objects of cultural heritage treat them with insensitivity. Upholsterers employed in the post-war period mercilessly replaced upholstery that had become unappealing in the eyes of the time with modern ones that bore no relation to the originals, without leaving any documentation. This is not an individual case. In many public institutions, the authenticity of the appearance of exhibited furniture should be questioned.

Publications and academic expertise on the subject are comparatively rare. Yet, a piece of furniture is no different from a painting, for example: it requires complex examination and research and precise reconstruction or approximation if one wants to determine and convey its value.

Möbel nicht anders als etwa bei einem Gemälde: Es verlangt komplexe Untersuchung und Betrachtung und sorgfältige Wiederherstellung oder Annäherung, wenn man seinen Wert ermessen und vermitteln will.

Die Fachgruppe der Restauratoren im Handwerk e.V., Fachbereich Raumausstatter-Handwerk, die in dieser Hinsicht vorbildliche Arbeit leistet, hat dankenswerterweise den Impuls für unser Ausstellungs- und Publikationsprojekt eingebracht. Dr. Thomas Schriefers hat es als Spiritus Rector mit größtem Elan, unermüdlicher Kreativität und ebensolcher Kundigkeit geformt. Dabei konnte er sich sowohl auf ein aktives Netzwerk hoch engagierter externer Partner als auch die mit Herzblut involvierten Kolleginnen und Kollegen unseres Hauses stützen.

Ohne großzügige Leihgaben verschiedener Institutionen und Privatpersonen – allem voran die aus der großartigen Sammlung von Werner Löffler in Reichenschwand – wäre die Ausstellung undenkbar. Gleichermaßen gilt dies für alle Förderer, namentlich für die Sächsische Landesstelle für Museumswesen. Mein herzlicher Dank gilt allen Unterstützern, allen auf verschiedenen Ebenen Beteiligten, den Autorinnen und Autoren und dem Verlag. Die Vielzahl der zu würdigenden Namen ist untenstehend und im Impressum benannt.

Unsere Hoffnung ist, mit Ausstellung und Katalogband ein neues, tiefergehendes Verständnis für die noch immer „geheime", weil unterschätzte und doch für die Geschichte unseres Wohnens so substantielle Kunst des Polsterns zu schaffen. Ich bin mir sicher, dass die ausgesuchte Qualität der Exponate Besucher und Leser fesseln und für eine neue, differenzierte Sichtweise sensibilisieren wird.

The Fachgruppe der Restauratoren im Handwerk e.V., Fachbereich Raumausstatter-Handwerk, which carries out exemplary work in this respect, thankfully provided the impulse for this exhibition and publication project. Dr Thomas Schriefers shaped it as the driving force with great élan, untiring creativity and just as much expertise. In his efforts he was able to rely both on an active network of highly motivated external partners as well as colleagues from our institution who were involved with their heart and soul.

Without the generous loans from various institutions and private individuals – especially from the magnificent collection of Werner Löffler in Reichenschwand – this exhibition could not have been realised. The same is true for all sponsors, namely the Sächsische Landesstelle für Museumswesen. I thank all supporters, everyone involved at various levels, the authors as well as the publishers. The multitude of names of lenders and conservators to be recognised is listed below as well as in the imprint.

It is our hope that the exhibition and the catalogue will create a new, deeper understanding for the still "secret", because underrated and yet for our history of living so substantial art of upholstery. I am sure that the quality of exhibits will captivate visitors and readers and sensitise them to a new, differentiated point of view.

Beteiligte Restaurator*innen im Raumausstatterhandwerk e. V. |
Participating conservators
Astrid Boeck, Waabs / Maximilian Busch, Berlin / Volker Engels, Schalksmühle / Edmund Graf, Lorsch / Alexander Hahlbeck, Lübeck / Rolf Hegenbart, Kleinmachnow / Bernd Lehmkuhl, Glandorf / Wolfgang Nerge, Obernkirchen / Doris Nolting, Löhne / Stefan Oswald, Hersbruck / Torsten Otto, Markkleeberg / Reinhardt Roßberg, Markkleeberg / Karin Semkowicz, Steinheim-Bergheim / Bernhard Ziegler, Gundelsheim

Leihgeber*innen | Lenders
Astrid Boeck, Waabs / Maximilian Busch, Berlin / Volker Engels, Schalksmühle / Dr. Cordula Fink, Köln / Edmund Graf, Lorsch / Rolf Hegenbart, Kleinmachnow / Wolfgang Nerge, Obernkirchen / Doris Nolting, Löhne / Stefan Oswald, Hersbruck / Torsten Otto, Markkleeberg / Reinhardt Roßberg, Markkleeberg / Caroline Scarbata / Dr. Thomas Schriefers, Köln / Karin Semkowicz, Steinheim-Bergheim / Bernhard Ziegler, Gundelsheim / Deutsches Stuhlbaumuseum Rabenau e.V. / die LÜBECKER MUSEEN – St. Annen-Museum / Germanisches Nationalmuseum Nürnberg / LÖFFLER COLLECTION, Reichenschwand / Museum für Kunst und Kulturgeschichte Schloss Gottorf, Landesmuseen Schleswig-Holstein / Museumslandschaft Hessen Kassel, Schloss Wilhelmshöhe

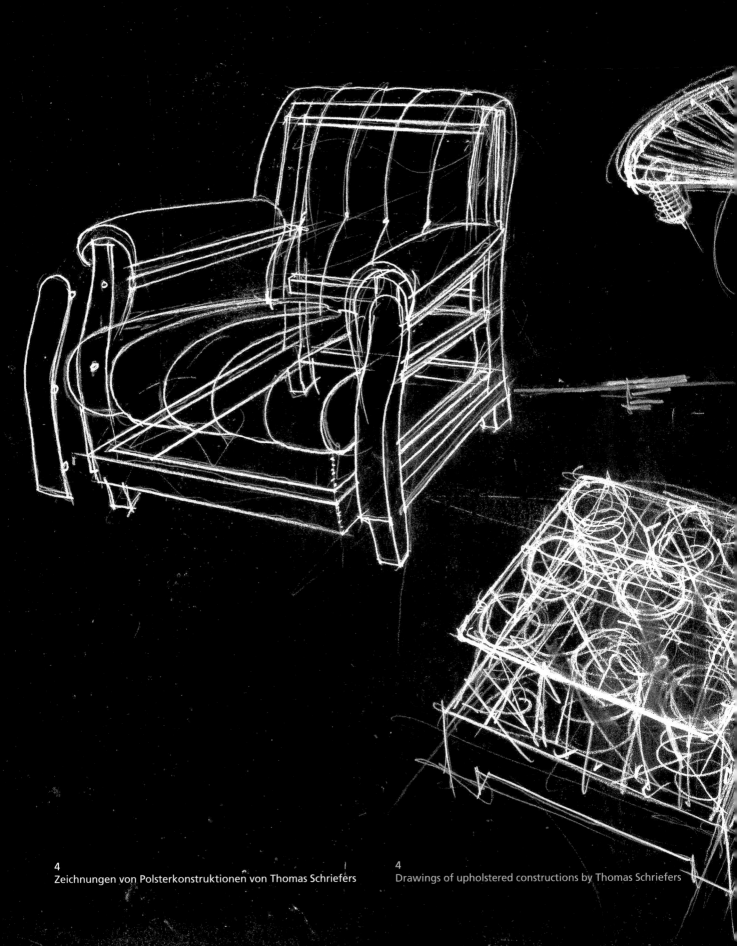

4
Zeichnungen von Polsterkonstruktionen von Thomas Schriefers

4
Drawings of upholstered constructions by Thomas Schriefers

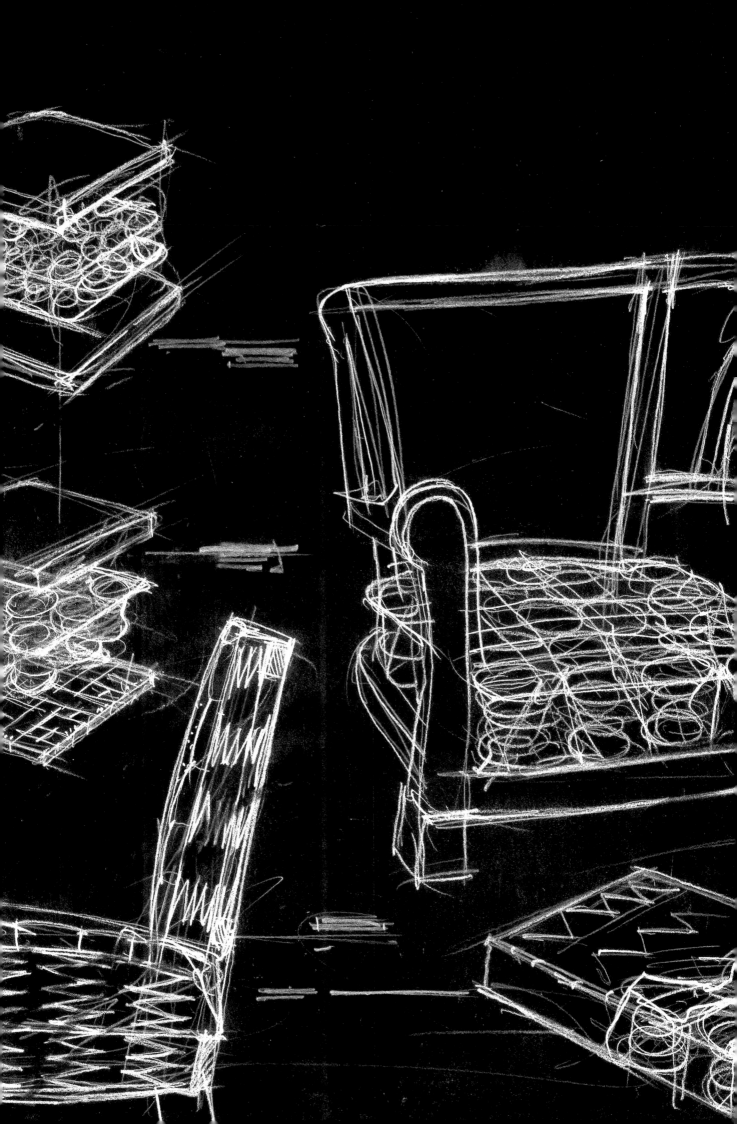

Einleitung

Thomas Schriefers

Gepolsterte Sitzmöbel, ob neu erworben oder ererbt, geschenkt oder getauscht, sind uns allen vertraut als mehr oder weniger beständige, geliebte Begleiter des Alltags. Polster sind behaglich, sie vermitteln Geborgenheit und versprechen Komfort, sie besitzen ein spezifisches Design, behaupten oder schaffen Status und erzählen Geschichte(n). Über ihr Innenleben machen wir uns kaum Gedanken. Dabei ist ein Einblick ins verborgene Innere der Stühle und Sessel eine Reise zu den Geheimnissen der geschnürten und gefederten Konstruktionen, die sich als unbekannte, zu entdeckende handwerkliche Meisterwerke erweisen.

Die Ausstellung BESESSEN. *Die geheime Kunst des Polsterns* spürt den Möbeln und ihrem Innenleben durch die letzten 400 Jahre bis in unsere Tage nach, erzählt Geschichten, vermittelt spielerisch und sinnlich Wissen und erklärt, warum das Polstern immer auch Teil einer Kultur- und Sozialgeschichte ist und zu den nachhaltigsten Handwerken gehört.

In der Ausstellung korrespondieren im ersten Teil Polstermöbel herausragender Gestalter mit handwerklichen Schnittmodellen, Textilien und Bilddokumenten. Sie stellen die Entwicklungsgeschichte des Polsterns dar. Die Besucher*innen erhalten hier Einblick in die üblicherweise nicht sichtbare Polstertechnologie und verfolgen deren Entwicklung vom Kissen und Flachpolster über erste Formen des Hochpolsters mit Federn bis zu experimentellen Konstruktionsformen und modernen Schaumstoffen, bevor sie im Dialogbereich Polster ausprobieren und sich zu den eigenen Ansprüchen für ein bequemes Sitzen selbst äußern können. In der Orangerie zeigen dann von der LÖFFLER COLLECTION zur Verfügung gestellte Stuhlikonen, wie vielfältig sich Polstersitzen im 20. Jahrhundert entwickelte.

Den innovativen Ideen der Polster-Meister nachspüren zu wollen erfordert, die Stuhltektonik in Hinblick auf ihre konstruktiven und formalen Eigenschaften zu betrachten und über das Spannungsverhältnis von *Hülle und Verhülltem*[1] zu reflektieren. Soziale Faktoren sind ebenso einzubeziehen wie die in bestimmten Epochen vorherrschenden Vorlieben. Je nach Temperament und Befindlichkeit offenbart dann das Erscheinungsbild eines Wohnraums den Wunsch der Bewohner nach Harmonie, vermittelt Spannung durch Gegensätze, zeigt sich angefüllt oder leer, bewusst komponiert, liebevoll arrangiert oder in Gleichgültigkeit vernachlässigt. Dem entspricht die Stellung des Polstermöbels, das von den einen zum unübersehbaren Mittelpunkt einer hedonistischen Lebenswelt erkoren wird, während es andere als überkommenes Relikt aus alter Zeit betrachten und aus ihren Räumen verbannen. Ob das gebrauchte Polstermöbel auf dem Dachboden abgestellt, dem Zeitgeschmack angepasst oder entsorgt wird, ist eine Frage des Wertes, welchen wir ihm beimessen. Heute spielen dabei auch Fragen wie die nach der Verträglichkeit bestimmter Materialien, deren ökologische Unbedenklichkeit und die Recycelbarkeit eine große Rolle.

Im Rahmen der 1979 in Wien veranstalteten Ausstellung *Vorsicht Polstermöbel!*[2] rückte Robert Maria Stieg erstmals das Thema ökologischer Verantwortung ins Zentrum der

Introduction

Thomas Schriefers

Upholstered seating furniture, whether newly acquired or inherited, gifted or exchanged, is familiar to all of us as a more or less constant, beloved companion of everyday life. Upholstery is cosy, it conveys security and promises comfort, it has a specific design, asserts or creates status and tells a (hi)story. We hardly give much thought to its inner life. Yet a glimpse into the hidden interior of chairs and armchairs is a journey into the secrets of lashed and sprung constructions, turn out to be unknown masterpieces of craftsmanship ready to be discovered.

The exhibition *DEEP-SEATED: The Secret Art of Upholstery* traces furniture and its inner life through the last 400 years to our own day it tells stories, imparts knowledge in a playful and sensory way and explains why upholstery is always part of a cultural and social history and why it is one of the most sustainable crafts.

In the first part of the exhibition, upholstered furniture by outstanding designers is put in context using sectional models, textiles and images. They present the history of the development of upholstery. Visitors are given an insight into the usually invisible upholstery techniques and can follow their development from cushions and simple unsprung padding over the first forms of high, sprung upholstery, to experimental forms of construction and modern foams, before trying out upholstery in the dialogue area and expressing their own expectations of what comfortable seating should be. In the Orangerie, iconic chairs from the Löffler Collection then show the diverse ways in which upholstered seating progressed during the twentieth century.

Tracing the innovative ideas of the master upholsterers requires looking at chair tectonics in terms of their constructive and formal characteristics and reflecting on the tension between the *cover and the covered*.[1] Social factors must be considered as well as the preferences prevailing during certain periods. Depending on temperament and mood, the appearance of a living space then reveals the inhabitants' desire for harmony, creates interest through contrasts, shows itself filled or empty, consciously composed, lovingly arranged or neglected in indifference. This corresponds to the position of the upholstered furniture piece, which is chosen by some as the conspicuous centre of a hedonistic living space, while others regard it as an outdated relic of old times and banish it from their rooms. Whether the used upholstered furniture is put in the attic, adapted to contemporary taste or disposed of is a question of the value we attach to it. Today, issues such as the compatibility of certain materials, their ecological safety and recyclability also play a major role.

In the context of the exhibition *Vorsicht: Polstermöbel!*,[2] held in Vienna in 1979, Robert Maria Stieg was the first to bring the issue of ecological responsibility to the centre of attention: *Who asks about the lifespan of a product, whether it can be repaired or reupholstered,*

Betrachtung: *Wer fragt nach der Lebensdauer eines Produktes, nach dessen Reparier- oder Neubeziehbarkeit, nach der Qualität der Werkstoffe? Wer weiß schon, was sich unter dem so hübschen, oft dünnen Kleidchen eines Polstermöbels verbirgt? Ein Gestell aus zusammengeklammerten Spanplatten oder aus verzapften Buchenhölzern? Eine Unterfederung oder nicht: Gurten, die bald durchhängen, Schlangenfedern, Federkern oder gar geschnürte Federn, die ihre Spannkraft noch nach 20 Jahren bewahren?*[3]

Mit BESESSEN. Die geheime Kunst des Polsterns gibt nun die aktuelle Ausstellung im GRASSI Museum für Angewandte Kunst Leipzig Antworten, wobei sich zeigt, wie nachhaltig die Arbeit jener ist, die heute noch handwerklich Polsterkonstruktionen herzustellen wissen. Insofern lässt sich diese Ausstellung auch als Plädoyer für ein Handwerk verstehen, das an Aktualität nicht verloren hat. Im Gegenteil: Es ist wichtiger denn je, wenn es gilt, gute Sitzmöbel zu bewahren, sie zu ertüchtigen und in aktiver Nutzung zu halten. Die virtuose Fingerfertigkeit der im Fachbereich der Raumausstatter aus der Fachgruppe Restauratoren im Handwerk e. V. organisierten Handwerker*innen fasziniert uns Betrachter*innen. Das Polsterhandwerk erweist sich als Beruf praktizierter Nachhaltigkeit, da dem Sitzmöbel neben Bequemlichkeit, ergonomischem Sitzkomfort und formaler Gültigkeit auch eine lange Lebenszeit gegeben wird und ökologisch unbedenkliche Materialien verwendet werden. Handwerk und Kunstfertigkeit zeigen sich dabei eng verbunden. So lüftet die Ausstellung einerseits das Geheimnis des Innenlebens ausdrucksstarker Sitzformen, während sie andererseits einen Beruf in den Fokus rückt, der Tradition mit Fortschritt und Zukunft verbindet.

Die Geschichte des gepolsterten Sitzmöbels reicht weit zurück. Vor diesem Hintergrund zeigen die folgenden Abschnitte chronologisch, wie der Komfort des Polsters aufgrund innovativer Ideen im Handwerk kontinuierlich gesteigert werden konnte. Die Konsequenzen der Einführung industrieller Fertigungsweisen im 19. Jahrhundert werden ebenso thematisiert wie der in immer kürzeren Zeiträumen sich wandelnde Geschmack der Konsumenten. Das gilt besonders für die Zeit nach dem Ersten Weltkrieg, als man angesichts einer massiv rückläufigen Bedarfslage über die zukünftige Bedeutung des Tapezier- und Polsterhandwerks als Produktionsgewerbe nachdachte. Eine 1935 der Rechts- und Staatswissenschaftlichen Fakultät der Martin-Luther Universität zu Halle-Wittenberg vorgelegte Dissertationsschrift *Über den Niedergang des Tapezier- und Polsterhandwerks als Produktionsgewerbe*[4] kam zu dem Schluss, dass das Handwerk mit seinen *durch individuelle Fertigung und durch ausgesprochene Persönlichkeitsentfaltung charakterisierten Herstellungsmethoden […] für die Schaffung von uniformierten Produkten nicht geeignet sei, und daher nicht mit der Serien- und Massenherstellung der Fabrikbetriebe mithalten könne.*[5] Dafür sei eine spürbare Bedarfsverschiebung verantwortlich, für die drei Faktoren ausschlaggebend seien:

– eine Geschmacksveränderung auf der Verbraucherseite, die durch Modeströmungen verursacht wird;
– der zunehmende Einsatz von Ersatzstoffen anstelle der eigentlichen Produkte;
– die in wirtschaftlicher Notzeit stark eingeschränkte Nachfrage nach bestimmten Produkten, besonders Qualitätsprodukten.[6]

about the quality of the materials? Who knows what is hidden underneath the oh so pretty, often thin dress of an upholstered piece of furniture? Is it a frame made of chipboard stapled together or of dovetailed beechwood? Are there springs or not: webbing that soon sags, zigzag springs, inner springs or even lashed springs that still retain their tension after 20 years?[3]

DEEP-SEATED: The Secret Art of Upholstery, the current exhibition at GRASSI Museum für Angewandte Kunst Leipzig, provides the answers, showing how enduring the work of those who still know how to craft upholstery constructions is today. In this respect, this exhibition can also be understood as making the case for a craft that has not lost any of its currency. On the contrary: it is more important than ever when it comes to preserving good pieces of seating furniture, making them fit for purpose and keeping them in use. The virtuoso dexterity of the craftsmen and -women organised in the specialist area of interior decorators of the Fachgruppe Restauratoren im Handwerk e.V. (RiH) is fascinating to watch. The craft of upholstery proves to be a profession of sustainability in practice, as the seating furniture is given a long life in addition to comfort, ergonomic seating comfort and formal significance, and ecologically safe materials are used. Craftsmanship and artistry are closely linked. Thus the exhibition, on the one hand, reveals the secret of the inner life of striking seating forms while, on the other hand, puts the focus on a profession that combines tradition with progress and the future.

Upholstered seating furniture has a long history. Against this background, the following sections show chronologically how the comfort of upholstery could be continuously increased due to innovative ideas in craftsmanship. The consequences of the introduction of industrial manufacturing methods in the nineteenth century are also discussed, as is the changing taste of consumers in ever shorter intervals. This is particularly true of the period after World War One, when, in the face of a massive decline in demand, the future of the wallpapering and upholstery trade as manufacturing industries was being considered. A dissertation on the industry's decline,[4] *Über den Niedergang des Tapezier- und Polsterhandwerks als Produktionsgewerbe*, submitted to the Faculty of Law and Political Science at the Martin Luther University in Halle-Wittenberg in 1935, came to the conclusion that the craft, *with its manufacturing methods characterised by individual production and marked personal development […] was not suitable for the creation of uniformed products and therefore could not keep up with the serial and mass production of the factories.*[5] According to the author, a noticeable shift in demand was responsible for this, for which he identified three decisive factors:

– a change in taste on the consumer side caused by fashion trends
– the increased use of substitutes in place of genuine products
– the greatly reduced demand for certain products, especially quality products, in times of economic hardship.[6]

Im Verlauf des 20. Jahrhunderts bestätigt sich dies immer wieder, denken wir nur an die grundsätzliche Ablehnung vieler Formen traditioneller Polstermöbel seitens führender Modernisten in den 1920er Jahren, an die Mangelzeiten nach zwei Weltkriegen und die Einführung verschiedener Kunststoffschäume, mit denen die Polsterfüllung durch einfachen Zuschnitt eines in vorgefertigten Blöcken zur Verfügung stehenden Materials leicht hergestellt werden kann. Doch besann man sich stets auch der Vorzüge handwerklich aufgebauter Polster. Die Geschichte des Polsterwesens verläuft daher trotz verschiedener, meist materialtechnisch oder gesellschaftlich begründeter Brüche kontinuierlich und erweist sich als vital, auch wenn nur wenige Nutzer*innen heute wissen, was sich tatsächlich unter Polsterbezügen verbirgt.

Vor diesem Hintergrund folgt der vorliegende Katalog der Ausstellungskonzeption und führt die Leser*innen chronologisch durch die Polsterwelten verschiedener Epochen, wobei konstruktiv-technische, materialspezifische und zeittypisch-soziologische Aspekte einbezogen werden. Daran schließt eine Betrachtung der textilen Bestandteile von Polsterungen an: Bezugsstoffe und Posamente, die im GRASSI Museum für Angewandte Kunst bewahrt werden. Nach Stichworten alphabetisch geordnet werden im Folgenden dann Begriffe zur Verarbeitungstechnologie, zu Arbeitsweisen, Material und Werkzeug erklärt sowie stilistische Besonderheiten ausgeführt. Exkurse widmen sich in diesem Abschnitt dem Aufbau der Arm- und Rückenlehnen und verschiedenen Kissenarten.
Ein umfangreicher Anhang nimmt schließlich die Objektbeschreibungen der in Ausstellung und Katalog gezeigten Sitzobjekte auf. Dort finden sich neben den Angaben zur Herkunft der Exponate, ihrer zeitlichen Zuordnung und den Maßen ergänzende Informationen zur Technologie, zum Polsteraufbau sowie Hinweise zu weiterführender Literatur.

Der Kompetenz in der Fachgruppe der Restauratoren im Handwerk e.V., Fachbereich Raumausstatter-Handwerk, Schloss Raesfeld, organisierten Handwerker*innen ist es zu verdanken, dass die bei dieser Ausstellung so wichtigen Technologiefragen beantwortet und in den Katalog integriert werden konnten.

Over the course of the twentieth century, this has been confirmed again and again, one need only consider the fundamental rejection of many forms of traditional upholstered furniture by leading modernists in the 1920s, the times of shortage after two world wars and the introduction of various polyurethane foams with which the upholstery filling can be easily produced by simply cutting a material available in prefabricated blocks. Nonetheless the advantages of handmade upholstery were never completely lost out of sight. Despite various disruptions, mostly due to material or social reasons, the history of upholstery is therefore continuous and proves to be vital, even if only a few users today know what is actually hidden under the upholstery covers.

Against this background, this catalogue follows the exhibition concept and leads the reader chronologically through the upholstered worlds of different periods, taking into account construction and technique as well as materiality and the prevailing sociological aspects of the time. This is followed by an examination of the textile components of upholstery: Upholstery fabrics and trimmings preserved in the GRASSI Museum für Angewandte Kunst. In alphabetical order by keyword, the following section explains terms relating to technical processes, working methods, materials and tools, as well as stylistic characteristics. Excursions in this section focus on the construction of armrests and backrests as well as different types of cushions.
Finally, an extensive appendix contains the object descriptions of the seating objects shown in the exhibition and catalogue. In addition to the origin of the exhibits, their dates and dimensions, there is supplementary information on the techniques, upholstery and references to further literature.

Thanks to the competence of the craftsmen and -women organised in the Fachgruppe der Restauratoren im Handwerk e.V., Fachbereich Raumausstatter-Handwerk, Schloss Raesfeld, it was possible to answer the technical questions that were so important for this exhibition and to incorporate them into the catalogue.

Renaissance – Barock – Rokoko
Thomas Schriefers

Bildnerische und plastische Darstellungen belegen, dass die ägyptischen Pharaonen bereits vor über 3.000 Jahren auf gepolsterten Stühlen saßen. So etwa der Vorsteher der Handwerker Amenemope mit seiner Frau Hathor, die auf einem thronähnlichen Stuhl sitzen.[7] Ein dem konkav geformten Sitz angepasstes Kissen (Ausschnitt, s. Abb. 6) sorgt für Komfort, auch wenn die Rückenlehne nicht gepolstert ist. Beispiele für den Einsatz von Sitzpolstern finden sich auch im antiken Griechenland, bei den Etruskern, im Römischen Reich, in frühchristlicher Zeit und im Mittelalter. Sie erscheinen auf Gefäßen, plastisch ausgebildet auf Sarkophagen, gemalt auf Wänden von Grabmälern und in illustrierten Handschriften. Sie zeigen nicht nur Formen, sondern vermitteln auch Eindrücke vom Umgang mit dem weichen, meist als Kissen ausgebildeten Sitzgrund, dessen Komfort lange Zeit vor allem besonderen Würdenträgern und dem Adel vorbehalten war.
Ein seit antiker Zeit verwendeter Sitztypus ist der Pliant, ein Klappstuhl mit x-förmig gekreuzten Beinen. Der Sitz selbst bestand aus einem textilen Material oder Leder, das sich leicht falten ließ. Darauf legte man Kissen, um den Sitzkomfort zu erhöhen. Im Mittelalter wurden neben Faltstühlen vor allem aber Pfosten- und Kastenstühle genutzt, auf die Gewebe und Kissen bzw. Polster meist aufgelegt wurden. Lose Flachpolster und Kissen dienten dann zunächst auch in der Renaissance noch als Auflagen für Stühle, doch zeigt ein Bild des italienischen Renaissancemalers Andrea Mantegna, auf dem die Familie und der Hofstaat Ludovicos III. Gonzaga zu sehen sind, dass Einzelstücke auch üppiger und bereits fest montiert gepolstert wurden. In dem Bild, zwischen 1465 und 1474 entstanden, stellt der Maler eine Szene aus dem Hofleben dar: Der Herzog sitzt auf einem Armlehnstuhl, der über ein üppiges Sitz- und Rückenpolster verfügt (Ausschnitt, s. Abb. 5). Bei genauem Hinsehen überzieht der Samtbrokat aber nicht nur die Polsterkissen, sondern auch die Holzbauteile des Stuhls, der zudem mit Fransen und Quasten versehen ist.[8]

Renaissance – Baroque – Rococo
Thomas Schriefers

Pictorial and sculptural representations prove that the Egyptian pharaohs were already sitting on upholstered chairs as early as over 3,000 years ago – for example, the official Amen-em-ope with his wife Hathor on a throne-like chair.[7] A cushion adapted to the concave shape of the seat (detail, fig. 6) provides comfort, even if the backrest is not upholstered. Examples of the use of seat cushions can also be found in Ancient Greece, among the Etruscans, during the Roman Empire, in early Christian times and in the Middle Ages. They appear on vessels, are sculpted on sarcophagi, painted on the walls of tombs and on the pages of illustrated manuscripts. They not only display formal qualities but also convey the approach to the soft seat base, usually in the form of a cushion, the comfort of which was for a long time reserved above all for special dignitaries and the nobility.
One type of seat used since ancient times is the *pliant*, a folding chair with X-shaped crossed legs. The seat itself was made of textile material or leather that could be easily folded, and cushions were placed on top to make the seat more comfortable. In the Middle Ages, however, in addition to folding chairs, mainly post chairs and box chairs were in use, on which textiles and cushions were usually placed.
Loose flat padding and cushions were still used as supports for chairs in the Renaissance. However, a painting by the Italian Renaissance painter Andrea Mantegna depicting the family and court of Ludovico III Gonzaga demonstrates that individual pieces were also upholstered more lavishly and already firmly mounted. In the picture, painted between 1465 and 1474, the painter depicts a scene from court life: the duke is sitting on an armchair with a sumptuously upholstered seat and backrest (detail, fig. 5). On closer inspection, however, the velvet brocade covers not only the upholstered cushions but also the wooden components of the chair, which is additionally adorned with fringes and tassels.[8]

Unsere Ausstellung zeigt fünf Beispiele für frühe Polstermöbel aus der Zeit vor dem Rokoko. Das früheste Exponat ist ein Renaissancestuhl aus den Beständen des GRASSI Museums für Angewandte Kunst, dessen mit Posamenten verzierte Flachpolsterung auf einem grob behauenen Brett aufgebracht und mit einer Doppelreihe großer Messingziernägel angeschlagen wurde (s. Abb. 9/10). Während hier Leder als Bezugsmaterial fungiert, ist der vom Lübecker St. Annen-Museum entliehene *Pfostenstuhl*[9] (s. Abb. 7/8) mit einem flachen Polster ausgestattet, das mit einem Seidenstoff bedeckt ist.

Wir haben das große Glück, einen Armlehnstuhl (s. Abb. 11/12) zeigen zu können, dessen Entstehung um 1620 datiert werden kann und der deutlich vermittelt, wie anspruchsvoll damals schon Polsterungen eingesetzt wurden. Der Stuhl befindet sich normalerweise im Germanischen Nationalmuseum Nürnberg und verfügt noch über sein ursprüngliches Hochpolster mit einer reichen Applikationsstickerei auf Sitz- und Armlehnen. 400 Jahre sind vergangen, ohne dass der Prachtstuhl, der auf seinem Samtbezug die beiden Wappen des *Heiligen Römischen Reichs (Deutscher Nation)* und der Stadt Ulm zeigt, seine repräsentative Ausdruckskraft eingebüßt hätte. Vielmehr vermittelt er einen Eindruck von der Meisterschaft des Polsterns im Frühbarock. Zwei weitere Barockstühle stammen aus den Beständen des GRASSI Museums für Angewandte Kunst: Bei dem einen handelt es sich um einen aus Birnholz geschnitzten Armlehnstuhl aus der Zeit um 1710 (s. Abb. 13/14), der mit Seidenstoff bezogen ist (eine Nachwebung, nicht mehr original) und über ein hohes und fest eingesetztes Polster mit einer darin verborgenen *Vorderkantenwulst* verfügt, während die Rücken- und Armlehnen aus einem Flachpolster bestehen. Der andere ist ein um 1750 entstandener Stuhl mit einem als Festpolster ausgebildeten Sitz und einer Gurtung aus handgewebtem Hanfmaterial (s. Abb. 15/16). Dabei handelt es sich um einen typisch sächsischen Barockstuhl, dessen Lederbezug per Handnaht aus verschiedenen Teilen zusammengefügt wurde.

Our exhibition presents five examples of early upholstered furniture from before the Rococo period. The earliest exhibit is a Renaissance chair from the collections of the GRASSI Museum für Angewandte Kunst, whose flat padding decorated with trimming was mounted on a roughly hewn board and struck with a double row of large brass decorative nails (figs. 9/10). While leather is the cover material here, the *post chair*[9] (figs. 7/8), on loan from St. Annen-Museum in Lübeck, has flat padding covered with a silk fabric.

We are fortunate to be able to show an armchair (figs. 11/12) whose origin can be dated to around 1620 and which clearly conveys how sophisticated upholstery was already used at that time. Usually preserved in the Germanisches Nationalmuseum in Nuremberg, this chair still has its original upholstery with rich appliqué embroidery on the seat and armrests. 400 years have passed without the magnificent chair, with its velvet upholstery depicting the two coats of arms of the Holy Roman Empire (German Nation) and the city of Ulm, losing its representative expressiveness. Instead, it conveys an impression of the mastery of upholstery during the early Baroque period. Two other Baroque chairs come from the holdings of the MAK Grassi: One is an armchair carved from pearwood, dating from around 1710 (figs. 13/14), covered with silk fabric (rewoven, no longer original) and features high and fixed upholstery with a *front edge roll* hidden inside, while the back- and armrests consist of flat padding. The other is a chair made around 1750 with a seat designed as a fixed upholstery and webbing made of hand-woven hemp (figs. 15/16). This is a typical Saxon Baroque chair, whose leather covering is hand-stitched together from various pieces.

5 (S. 16, p.16)
Stuhldetail aus einem Fresko von Andrea Mantegna, um 1465–1474
Chair detail from a fresco by Andrea Mantegna, around 1465–1474

6
Detail einer ägyptischen Statuette des Amen-em-ope und seiner Frau Hathor, Ägypten, 19. Dynastie (1292–1186 v. Chr.)
Detail of an Egyptian statuette of Amen-em-ope and his wife Hathor, Ägypten, 19th dynasty (1292–1186 BC)

7/8
Stuhl, um 1600 (die LÜBECKER MUSEEN –
St. Annen-Museum)

7/8
Chair, around 1600 (die LÜBECKER MUSEEN –
St. Annen-Museum)

9/10
Armlehnstuhl, um 1600/19. Jahrhundert
(GRASSI Museum für Angewandte Kunst Leipzig)

9/10
Armchair, around 1600/19th century
(GRASSI Museum für Angewandte Kunst Leipzig)

11/12
Armlehnstuhl, Ulm, um 1620
(Germanisches Nationalmuseum, Nürnberg)

11/12
Armchair, Ulm, around 1620
(Germanisches Nationalmuseum, Nuremberg)

13/14
Armlehnstuhl, um 1710/1720
(GRASSI Museum für Angewandte Kunst Leipzig)

13/14
Armchair, around 1710/1720
(GRASSI Museum für Angewandte Kunst Leipzig)

15/16
Stuhl, Sachsen, um 1750
(GRASSI Museum für Angewandte Kunst Leipzig)

15/16
Chair, Saxony, around 1750
(GRASSI Museum für Angewandte Kunst Leipzig)

17
Barockstuhl als Schichtmodell mit Festpolster,
um 1710 (Reinhardt Roßberg/Caroline Scarbata)

17
Baroque chair as a cutaway model with attached upholstery,
around 1710 (Reinhardt Roßberg/Caroline Scarbata)

Upholstery of a Baroque chair

The Baroque chair shown here, dated to around 1710 (fig. 17), had been left untouched until it was stripped – that is, until the time-worn components were taken off and safeguarded separately, so that its structure was in its original state. For example, the now cracked leather cover was fastened at the sides with galvanised decorative brass nails, which were underlaid with a leather strip. The front corners of the seat upholstery were not, as is often the case, laid in opposite directions as a box pleat but rather folded over towards the back, so that the position of the pleat could not be seen from the front. The stuffing found consisted of deer hair, a material typical of the Baroque period, which only served as a cover for the plant fibre stuffing underneath, a mixture of flax and grain stalks. The construction of the front edge made from a bundle of straw held together by three twines as an edge roll is particularly fascinating; here, it turns out that the twine was passed through the bottom linen layer in order to be nailed to the front rail. After removing the hand-woven hessian, webbing (= two stretched at seat depth and another one across) made of hand-woven hemp was finally revealed. Following this find, the wooden frame was restored before the upholstery could be rebuilt with the original materials found. The result (fig. 17), presented here with two cutaways, shows how the upholstery of a Baroque chair is usually constructed: The base is formed by the tightened webbing affixed to the chair frame with nails. On top of this is a layer of hessian, on the front edge of which sits the long-straw roll sewn to the base. Behind this is the filling made of plant fibre with a deer hair cover. A piece of calico pulled over it serves as a base for the leather cover, which has been reattached using the original leather border with largely original nails. A cutaway on the left side of the seat shows the layering of the seat cushion just described, which is higher than that of the backrest. Here, a material section shows that, comparable to the seat cushion stuffing, a mixture of flax stalks, cereal stalks and hay was placed on the base of hessian and in turn covered with deer hair. The usual calico cover was dispensed with, so that the leather cover, fastened to the frame with nails, could be affixed directly on top.[10]

Using the method described here, a second Baroque chair (figs. 223–225) from around 1700 was prepared for the exhibition's separate activity room. It is furnished with a corresponding upholstery so that visitors can try out for themselves how it feels to sit on a Baroque upholstered chair.[11]

During the Baroque period, the velvet and silk industry became increasingly important in Brandenburg-Prussia as a result of export-oriented trade policies. Silk, velvet and plush manufacturing boomed. Demand was great, as the padding was now higher and more voluminous, which greatly increased the comfort of the seating furniture. The bourgeoisie also began to imitate courtly furniture as a model for their own furnishings. The reason for this was the increasing economic power and the resulting desire to live comfortably. Walls were covered with textiles, rooms were carpeted and seating was softly upholstered.

komfortabel wohnen zu wollen. Wände wurden textil bespannt, Räume mit Teppichen ausgelegt und Sitzmöbel weich gepolstert.

In dem von König Ludwig XIV. regierten Frankreich organisierte damals der für die Wirtschaft zuständige und weitsichtige Finanzminister Jean-Baptiste Colbert das gesamte Manufakturwesen neu. Als Sohn eines Tuchhändlers kannte er das textilproduzierende Metier. So warb er Spezialisten für die Herstellung hochwertiger Textilien aus Flandern an und gründete 1663 die fortan unter staatlicher Aufsicht produzierende *Manufacture royale des tapisseries et des meubles de la Couronne*, die als Gobelin-Manufaktur bis heute besteht. Dadurch machte sich Frankreich von teuren Importen unabhängig und erhielt zudem die Möglichkeit, eigene Produkte zu exportieren. Im Zusammenwirken mit anderen nationalen Manufakturen entstand damals der *style Louis XIV*, der gezielt auch als Mittel politischer Propaganda eingesetzt wurde. So galt der Versailler Hof bald, weit über die Grenzen Frankreichs hinweg, als stilbildend und war Vorbild für gehobene Lebensart, Kunst und Geschmack.

Mit Luxus verband man besonders auch die immer komfortabler gepolsterten Sitzmöbel. So berichtete der Chevalier Lenormand de Beaumont (1728–1810) von farbig gefassten Stühlen, die mit schweren, mit Spitzenbesatz versehenen Stoffen bezogen waren. Wie man sich derartige Polsterstühle vorstellen darf, zeigt ein Stich, der eine besonders luxuriöse Variante darstellt (s. Abb. 18), die Ludwig XIV. selbst nutzte.[12] Zu sehen ist ein Armlehnstuhl mit Sitzpolsterung, auf der zusätzlich ein voluminöses Kissen lag. Dieses war mit Daunenfedern so üppig gefüllt, dass seine Oberfläche an die Oberkante der Armlehnen heranreichte. Fransen und Quasten vervollständigten den Eindruck opulenter Pracht. Ein derartiges Sitzmöbel war ein Gegenstand herrschaftlichen Prestiges. In seiner *Kunstgeschichte des Möbels* weist Adolf Feulner darauf hin, dass in der Üppigkeit solcher Objekte eine neue soziale Rangordnung ihren Ausdruck fand. Möbel dienten als Requisiten des höfischen Zeremoniells. Gemäß der geltenden Etikette wurden insbesondere Sitzmöbel in eine klar definierte *Skala der Würden*[13] eingeordnet. Feulner zitiert aus den

In the France of King Louis XIV, the far-sighted finance minister Jean-Baptiste Colbert reorganised the entire manufacturing sector. As the son of a cloth merchant, he was familiar with the textile-manufacturing trade. He recruited specialists for the production of high-quality textiles from Flanders and in 1663 founded the *Manufacture royale des tapisseries et des meubles de la Couronne*, which from then on produced under state supervision and still exists today as a tapestry manufactory. In this way, France became independent of expensive imports and was able to export its own products instead. In cooperation with other national manufactories, the *style Louis XIV* was created, which also served as a means of political propaganda. Soon, the Versailles Court was regarded as a trendsetter far beyond the borders of France and became a model for sophisticated savoir vivre, art and taste.

Luxury was also associated with increasingly comfortable upholstered seating. Lenormand de Beaumont (1728–1810), for example, reported on painted chairs upholstered in heavy, lace-trimmed fabrics. How such upholstered chairs might be imagined is shown in an engraving depicting a particularly luxurious example (fig. 18) used by Louis XIV himself.[12] It depicts an armchair with an upholstered seat on which an additional voluminous cushion lies. This was filled to the brim with down feathers so that its upper surface reaches the upper edge of the armrests. Fringes and tassels complete the opulent splendour, which is reinforced by the use of precious tapestry fabrics. Such a piece of seating furniture was an object of stately prestige. In his *Kunstgeschichte des Möbels*, Adolf Feulner points out that the opulence of such objects expressed a new social hierarchy. Furniture served as a prop for court ceremonial. In accordance with the prevailing etiquette, it was seating furniture in particular that was placed along a clearly defined *scale of dignity*.[13] Feulner quotes from the memoirs of the Duc de Saint-Simon,[14] who meticulously described life at the court of Louis XIV. The question of entitlement to certain seats played

Memoiren des Duc de Saint-Simon[14], der minutiös das Leben am Hof Ludwigs XIV. beschrieb. Die Frage nach dem Anrecht auf bestimmte Sitze spielt darin eine große Rolle. So war festgelegt, ob es Einzelnen erlaubt war, auf einem gepolsterten Armlehnstuhl *(fauteuil)*, einem Sessel *(chaise)*, dem Taburett *(placet)* oder Faltstuhl *(ployant)* Platz zu nehmen. So habe eine Herzogin, die bei einer Prinzessin zu Besuch war, sich ebenso wie ihre Gastgeberin auf einen bequemen Armlehnstuhl setzen dürfen. Mit dem Eintritt des Königs sei es beiden aber bewusst gewesen, dass sie auf Taburetts wechseln mussten, während für die Damen des Gefolges auf dem Boden liegende Kissen zur Verfügung standen.[15]
Diese Kissen nannte man ihrer quadratischen Form wegen auch *carreaux* und sie waren meist mit wertvollen Stoffen bezogen. Schon zu Zeiten König Johanns II. (1319–1364) wurden Kissen wegen ihrer Bequemlichkeit geschätzt, doch übertrafen die *carreaux*, welche für den Hof von Ludwig XIV. und seine Frau Marie-Thérèse angefertigt wurden, alles bis dahin Dagewesene. Während diese für zeremonielle Aufgaben vorgesehen waren, fanden einfachere Ausführungen ihren Einsatz bald auf verschiedensten Gebieten, etwa als weiche Auflager für das Knien in Kirchen. Auch im bürgerlichen Familienleben fanden die Carreaux ihren Platz. Henry Havard schreibt in seinem *Dictionnaire de l'Ameublement*, am Hofe Ludwig XIV. hätten sich derartige Polster als Kissenbegleiter für lange Nächte und als *Komplizen der Ruhe*[16] empfohlen. Diese Aufgabe sollte bald auch ein gepolstertes Möbel übernehmen, das wegen seiner an eine Liege erinnernden Form auch als langer Stuhl *(chaise longue)* bezeichnet wurde. Dabei galten die frühen Formen der *chaise longue* gerade bei den Männern als belastet, da sie wegen ihrer weichen Polsterung oft als Krankenliege genutzt worden war. So finden sich in den Memoiren des Duc de Saint-Simon Erinnerungen an seinen Besuch des an Gicht leidenden Prinzen de Conti, der, auf einer *chaise longue* ruhend, die Wärme des nahen Kaminfeuers genoss.

a major role. Whether individuals were allowed to sit on an upholstered armchair (*fauteuil*), an armchair (*chaise*), a tabouret (*placet*) or folding chair (*ployant*) was therefore predetermined. Therefore, a duchess visiting a princess was allowed to sit on a comfortable armchair, as was her hostess. With the entry of the king, however, both were aware that they had to change to *tabourets*, while cushions lying on the floor were available for the ladies of the entourage.[15] In reference to their square shape, such cushions were called *carreaux*, and they were covered in valuable fabrics. They had been appreciated for their comfort since the times of King Jean II (1319–1364), but the *carreaux* fabricated for the court of Louis XIV and his wife Marie-Thérèse surpassed even these. While they were intended to be used for ceremonial purposes, simpler versions soon were used in a variety of circumstances, including as a soft cushion when kneeling in church. These cushions also found a place in bourgeois family life. Henry Havard writes in his *Dictionnaire de l'ameublement* that at the court of Louis XIV, upholstery of this kind was recommended as a pillow companion for long nights and as an *accomplice to rest*.[16] This task was soon to be taken over by an upholstered piece of furniture, which was also called a long chair (*chaise longue*) because of its shape reminiscent of a lounger. The early forms of the *chaise longue* were fraught with ambiguous connotations, especially for men, since, due to their soft upholstery, they had been used as a couch for the sick. In the memoirs of the Duc de Saint-Simon, for example, we find recollections of his visit to the Prince de Conti, who was suffering from gout and who, resting on a *chaise longue*, enjoyed the warmth of the nearby fireplace. Elsewhere, Saint-Simon recounts a visit paid in 1710 by Louis XIV to his injured army commander

18
Darstellung der Kissen von Ludwig XIV. und Marie-Thérèse *(d'après une tapisserie de l'Histoire du Roy)*, aus dem Gobelin-Zyklus der Manufacture Royale des Gobelins (1665–1741)

18
Depiction of cushions by Louis XIV and Marie-Thérèse *(d'après une tapisserie de l'Histoire du Roy)*, from a Gobelin cycle by the Manufacture Royale des Gobelins (1665–1741)

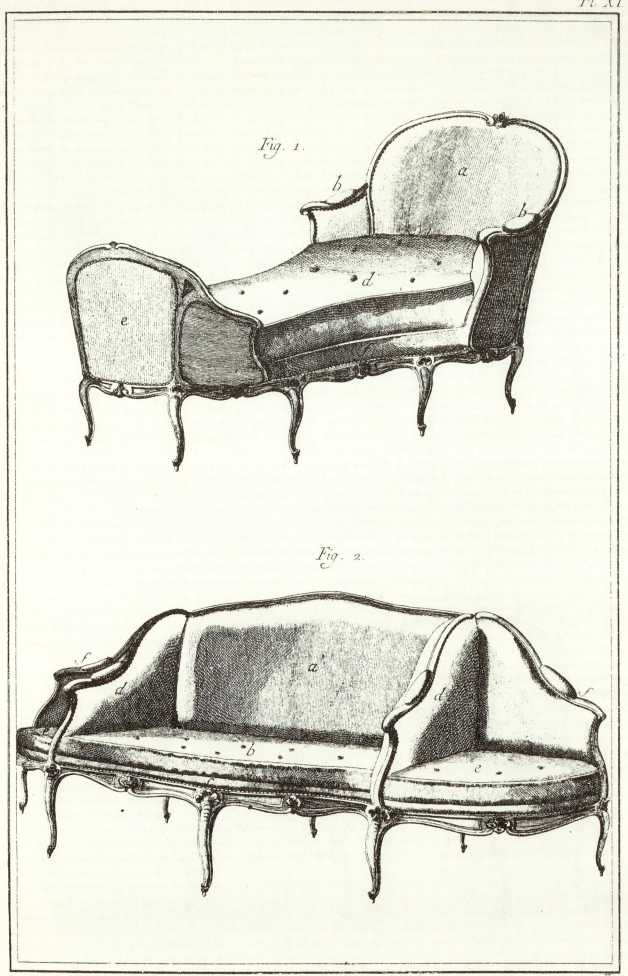

Tapissier, la Duchesse à Bateau et la Duchesse avec encogniure.

An anderer Stelle berichtet Saint-Simon von einem Besuch, den Ludwig XIV. 1710 seinem verletzten Heerführer Marschall de Villars abstattete – er empfing seinen König auf einer *chaise longue* ruhend.[17] Den Komfort eines weich gepolsterten, für das bequeme Lagern geeigneten Möbels wussten aber auch die französischen Prinzessinnen zu schätzen, die auf einem entsprechenden Polstermöbel drei Tage nach ihrer Entbindung die Glückwünsche von Gratulanten entgegennahmen. Damit dienten nun Polstermöbel neben dem bereits seit dem 16. Jahrhundert zeremoniell genutzten Paradebett repräsentativen Aufgaben. Aus der Krankenliege wurde ein bequemes Repräsentationsobjekt, dessen Formen sich immer verspielter präsentierten. Damals etablierte sich die *chaise longue* im feinen Salon z. B. der Madame Rose Bertin, die als Schneiderin, Hutmacherin und Modistin ein eigenes Geschäft unterhielt und die besondere Gunst von Marie Antoinette genoss. Wegen ihres Einflusses auf die Regentin sprachen Neider von ihr ironisch als einer *Mode-Ministerin*[18]. Madame Bertin wurde zu einer Stilikone des 18. Jahrhunderts, die, ähnlich unseren heutigen Influencer*innen, als Vorbild zitiert wurde. Es zeigte Wirkung, dass Madame Bertin selbst hochrangigste Gäste auf einer bequem gepolsterten *chaise longue* sitzend empfing. Hier zeigen sich die veränderten Konventionen einer Gesellschaft, die ihren Mittelpunkt nun verstärkt in eleganten Salons fand, wo man sich nach festgelegten Regeln über Mode und Welt austauschte.

In seiner Abhandlung *La toilette de Mme de Pompadour* gibt der französische Philosph und Schriftsteller Voltaire ein Gespräch zwischen der Marquise und Madame Tullia wieder, in dem die Einschätzung der Bequemlichkeit von Sitzmöbeln im Mittelpunkt steht. Dabei artikuliert sich der bereits angeführte Wandel der Umgangsformen, die zunehmend eine legerere Körperhaltung zuließen, was sich unmittelbar auch auf die Art der Möbel, zumal der Sitzmöbel, ihre Beschaffenheit und Nutzung auswirkte. So heißt es in dem kurzen von Henry Havard wiedergegebenen Dialog:

> Mme de Pompadour: *Madame, geben Sie mir die Ehre, dass Sie Platz nehmen. Ein Sessel für Madame Tullia.*
> Tullia: *Für mich, Madame? Aber soll ich auf diesem unbequemen kleinen Thron sitzen, von dem meine Beine auf den Boden hängen und ganz rot anlaufen?*
> Mme de Pompadour: *Worauf nehmen Sie denn normalerweise Platz, Madame?*
> Tullia: *Auf einer guten Liege, Madame.*
> Mme de Pompadour: *Ich verstehe, Sie sprechen von einem guten Canapé. Bitte, hier ist eines, auf dem Sie sich ganz bequem ausstrecken können.*[19]

Neben der augenscheinlichen Ähnlichkeit derartiger Sitzmöbel mit einer Liege verfügten die zweisitzigen *canapés* über ein Polster, das mit Seidengewebe bezogen wurde, oder, wie in weniger bemittelten Kreisen üblich, auch nur mit dem sogenannten *damas cafard* (falschem Damast) bedeckt war, der aus Mischgeweben aus verschiedenen Materialien mit glänzender, seidenartiger Oberflächenwirkung bestand und hochwertiger zu sein schien, als er tatsächlich war. Die Schwerfälligkeit des barocken Mobiliars wich nun spielerisch anmutenden und zierlich

Marshal de Villars, who received his king while, also, resting on a *chaise longue*.[17] Nonetheless, the comfort of a softly upholstered piece of furniture suitable for comfortable resting was also appreciated by the French princesses, who received congratulations from well-wishers on a piece of upholstered furniture for three days after giving birth. In this way upholstered furniture was increasingly used in representative contexts, next to the state bed, which had been in use since the sixteenth century. The hospital couch turned into a comfortable object of representation, the shapes of which became increasingly playful. At that time, the *chaise longue* established itself in the fine salon of, for example, Madame Rose Bertin, who ran her own business as a dressmaker and milliner and who enjoyed the special favour of Marie Antoinette. Because of her influence on the Regent, grudgers spoke of her ironically as a *Minister of Fashion*.[18] Madame Bertin became a style icon of the eighteenth century, cited as a role model, much like our influencers today. It made an impact that Madame Bertin received even the highest-ranking guests seated on a comfortably upholstered *chaise longue*. This demonstrates the changing conventions of a society that now increasingly found its focus in elegant salons, where people exchanged views on fashion and the world according to fixed rules.

In his treatise *La toilette de Mme de Pompadour*, the French philosopher and writer Voltaire reproduces a conversation between the Marquise and Madame Tullia which focuses on the assessment of the comfort of seating furniture. This articulated the aforementioned change in manners, which increasingly allowed for a more casual posture, which had a direct effect on the types of furniture, especially seating, its composition and use. Thus, the short dialogue reproduced by Henry Havard states:

> Mme de Pompadour: *Madame, give me the honour of your taking a seat. An armchair for Madame Tullia.*
> Tullia: *For me, Madame? But am I to sit on this uncomfortable little throne, from which my legs hang on the floor and turn all red?*
> Mme de Pompadour: *What do you usually sit on, Madame?*
> Tullia: *On a good chaise longue, Madame.*
> Mme de Pompadour: *I see, you are talking about a good canapé. Please, here is one on which you can stretch out comfortably.*[19]

In addition to the apparent similarity of such seating furniture to a couch, the two-seater *canapés* had an upholstery that was covered with silk fabrics, or, as was common in less well-off circles, the so-called *damas cafard* (false damask), which consisted of mixed fabrics with a shiny, silk-like appearance and seemed to be of higher quality than it was in reality. The gravity of Baroque furniture now gave way to seemingly playful and refined furnishings. The number of special types of seating furniture grew enormously, extended by the

---

19
La Duchesse à Bateau et la Duchesse avec encognure, aus: *Diderots Enzyklopädie. Die Bildtafeln* (1762–1777)

19
La Duchesse à Bateau et la Duchesse avec encognure, plate from: *Diderots Enzyklopädie: Die Bildtafeln* (1762–1777)

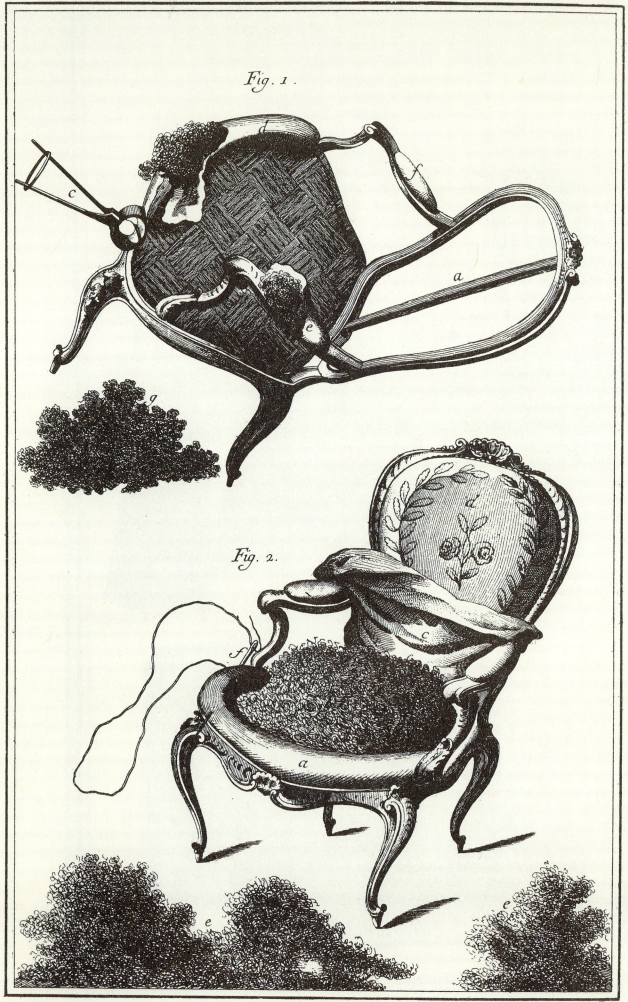

Tapissier, 1.ere et 2.me préparation de la façon de faire les Fauteuils.

verfeinerten Einrichtungsgegenständen. Die Zahl spezieller Sitzmöbel-Typen wuchs enorm an, erweitert durch das Angebot exzentrischer Luxusvarianten wie der *voyeuse* als Stuhl zum Rittlingssitzen oder der *duchesse* als ausladendem Ruhestuhl.[20] Dabei wurden immer mehr Teile der Holzkonstruktion mit Polstern überzogen. Gewirkte Bezüge bedeckten das Polster und verstärkten die Wirkung des Sitzmöbels. Auch die Canapés waren als Zweisitzer sehr begehrt. Der Enzyklopädist Antoine Furetière beschrieb entsprechende Modelle wegen ihrer üppigen Polsterung als eine Art Rucksack, in dem zwei Personen sehr bequem Platz finden konnten. Wie Furetières Ausführungen zu entnehmen ist, hatte die Bezeichnung anfänglich noch zur Verwirrung beigetragen, da man oft auch vom *sopha* sprach und nicht wenige Exemplare noch an profane Sitzbänke erinnerten. Doch konnte man sich auf das *canapé* legen und im weichen Polster bei Bedarf sogar gut schlafen. Henry Havard erinnert in diesem Zusammenhang an den französischen Autor Jean-François Regnard, der in seinem 1867 entstandenen Theaterstück *Le Distrait* (der Zerstreute)[21] einen Ritter bekunden ließ, er fühle sich von einem derartigen Fauteuil umarmt und ganz umfangen. Nirgends fühle er *sich so gut aufgehoben wie auf einem canapé*.[22]

Im 9. Band der berühmten, maßgeblich von Denis Diderot zwischen 1751 und 1780 zusammengestellten *Encyclopédie* finden sich nicht nur Darstellungen der Arbeit in einer Tapissier-Werkstatt, sondern auch Tafeln, auf denen verschiedene Polstermöbel der Zeit um 1771 zu sehen sind: u. a. *duchesse à bateau, duchesse avec encognure, bergère, chaise* und *ottomane*, wobei gerade der Name der letztgenannten auf die Sitzkissen-Tradition im Orient anspielt. Schließlich leitet sich die auch heute noch gebräuchliche Bezeichnung Sofa vom arabischen *suffa* ab, was ursprünglich ein mit Teppichen und Kissen belegtes Podest bezeichnete.

Die Bildtafeln in Diderots Enzyklopädie zeigen detailliert, wie kunstvoll Stühle im Frankreich des 18. Jahrhunderts gepolstert wurden. Zunächst nagelte man demnach auf der Oberseite des Sitzrahmens breite und lückenlos gelegte Hanfgurte im Kreuzverband auf. Im nächsten Schritt wurde die Vorderkante durch das Aufbringen einer mit Rosshaar gefüllten Leinwandwulst verstärkt. Die dabei entstehende Überformung des Rahmens bezeichnete man als *bourrelet*. Dazu nutzte man einige wenige bis heute eingesetzte Werkzeuge, u. a. die je nach Heftstich notwendige, sichelförmige oder gerade, Garniernadel, den Gurtspanner und Polsterhammer. Neben Rosshaar wurden diverse natürliche Füllmaterialien wie z. B. Stroh, Heu, Moos, See- und Alpengras eingesetzt. Die hier abgebildete Tafel VIII (s. Abb. 20) zeigt die Vorbereitung der Fasson-Arbeiten im Sitz und die Ausbildung der umlaufenden Kantenwulst, die, mit tierischen Haaren gefüllt, dem Polster Fülle gibt. Deutlich ist die angesetzte Zange zu sehen, mit der die Gurte gespannt werden, um sie mit Nägeln auf dem Holzgestell zu befestigen. In Fig. 2 (s. Abb. 20 unten) zeigt sich hinter der fertig ausgebildeten Kantenwulst die bereits mit tierischen Haaren ausgefüllte Sitzfläche, während das *bourrelet* noch mittels Nadel und Faden mit wenigen Stichen benäht wird, um die Kante zu verfestigen.

offer of eccentric luxury variants, such as the *voyeuse* as a chair for sitting astride on or the *duchesse*, a wide recliner.[20] More and more parts of the wooden construction were covered with upholstery, and the textiles intended for this were produced in special manufactories. Damask, brocade, silk, and also tapestry covers dressed the upholstery and enhanced the effect of the seating furniture. *Canapés* were also very much in demand as two-seaters. The encyclopaedist Antoine Furetière described the lush upholstery of such models as a kind of rucksack in which two people could sit very comfortably. As can be seen from Furetière's explanations, the designation had initially contributed to confusion, as people often also spoke of the *sopha* and quite a few examples were reminiscent of mundane benches. However, one could lay down on the *canapé* and even sleep well on the soft cushion if necessary. In this context, Henry Havard recalls the French author Jean-François Regnard, who in his 1867 play *Le Distrait* (The Dispersed)[21] had a knight declare that he felt embraced and completely enveloped by such a *fauteuil*. Nowhere would he feel as *at home as on a canapé*.[22]

In volume 9 of the famous *Encyclopédie*, largely written by Denis Diderot between 1751 and 1781, one can find not only depictions of the work process inside a *tapissier* workshop but also plates depicting different types of upholstered furniture from the period around 1771. These include a *duchesse à bateau, duchesse avec encognure, bergère*, a *chaise* and an *ottoman*; the name of the latter refers to the tradition of seating cushions in the orient. Afterall, the term *sofa*, which is still in use today, derives from the Arabic *suffa*, which originally described a platform covered with carpets and cushions.

The illustrations in Diderot's *Encyclopédie* depict in detail how elaborately chairs were upholstered in eighteenth-century France. First, wide hemp webbing was nailed to the top of the seat rail in a criss-cross pattern without any gaps. In the next step, the front edge was reinforced by forming a roll edge filled with horsehair. The resulting shape of the frame was called *bourrelet* in French. For this purpose, a few tools were used which are still in use today: among others, the, according to the task, crescent-shaped or straight needle, the web stretcher and the upholstery hammer. In addition to horsehair, various natural stuffing materials such as straw, hay, moss and sea or alpine grass were used. Plate VIII (fig. 20), illustrated here, shows the preparation of the tying, stuffing and stitching in the seat and the formation of the edge roll on all sides, which, once filled with animal hair, gives volume to the upholstery. One can clearly see the tongs that were used to stretch webbing in order to be affix them to the wooden rails using nails. In fig. 2 (fig. 20, below), behind the finished edge roll one can see the seat surface already filled, while the *bourrelet* is still being sewn with needle and thread with a few stitches to consolidate the edge.

20
Vorbereitung der Fassonarbeiten, aus: *Diderots Enzyklopädie: Die Bildtafeln* (1762–1777)

20
Preparation for stuffing and stitching the padding, plate from: *Diderots Enzyklopädie: Die Bildtafeln* (1762–1777)

Tapissier, Suite de la Façon d'un Fauteuil.

Werkzeug und Spiralfedern

Thomas Schriefers

Die in der Enzyklopädie von Denis Diderot abgebildeten Tapissier-Werkzeuge (s. Abb. 22) haben sich im Laufe der Jahrhunderte kaum verändert, da sich die wesentlichen Arbeiten der Herstellung eines Polsters bis heute gleichen. So bewährte sich der Tapezierhammer, der aus einem *flach gebogenen Hammerkopf und dem durch ein Stahlrohr (Feder) verstärkten Stiel aus Hartholz*[23] besteht: *Der eine Teil des Kopfes endigt in die runde Bahn, deren gebräuchliche Durchmesser 8, 9 und 10 mm betragen, der andere Teil in die Zange oder Klaue,* die zum Herausziehen kleinerer Stifte dient, für deren Entfernen keine Zange benötigt wird. Ein zweiter Hammer dient mit seinem kürzeren, stärkeren Kopf der Befestigung von Nägeln, die die Gurte fixieren. Die Beißzange eignet sich zum Herausziehen größerer Stifte und Nägel, während die mit einem scharfen Maul ausgestattete Zwickzange nur für das Abzwicken von Draht und dünnen Stiften verwendet wird.

Gurtenspanner und -zange erlauben, die unter dem Holzrahmen vorgesehenen Gurte so weit anzuziehen, dass sie, ohne an Zugkraft zu verlieren, im Holz befestigt werden können. Dabei besitzt der Spanner *an seiner unteren Kante einen Belag aus Stoff oder Leder zur Schonung empfindlicher Holzzargen.*[24] In seine Oberkante sind Metallspitzen eingelassen, die beim Vorgang des Gurtspannens in das verwendete Material eingreifen, um die Spannung der Bänder aufrechtzuhalten. Die bei Diderot bereits gezeigte Gurtenzange verfügt über zwei gezahnte Backen und einen klammerähnlichen Schieber, der entlang der Eisenarme verstellt werden kann, um sie bei Bedarf zu arretieren. Weitere Werkzeuge sind verschiedene Ahlen, mit denen beim Garnieren etwa das Füllmaterial gleichmäßig verteilt wird (Haarzieher) oder Löcher vorgeschlagen werden (Vorschlagahle), das Falzbein, das beim Umlegen der Kanten von Bezugsmaterialien hilfreich ist, das Locheisen, mit dem sauber umrissene Löcher aus Stoff oder Leder ausgestanzt werden und der Ritzer, der dem Anreißen der umzulegenden Lederkanten dient.

Bei Abschlagarbeiten, d. h. Tätigkeiten, die das Entkleiden des Stuhls bezwecken, wird das Losschlageisen verwendet. Es besteht traditionell aus einem Holzheft, in dem eine scharfe Stahlklinge steckt, die unten flach geschmiedet und abgekröpft ist. Diese eignet sich dafür, kräftige Nägel zu entfernen. Für das vorsichtige Ablösen wertvoller Ziernägel wird hingegen der Geißfuß, auch Nagelheber genannt, verwendet.

Tools and springs

Thomas Schriefers

The tapestry tools illustrated in Denis Diderot's encyclopaedia (fig. 22) have hardly changed over the centuries, as the essential work of making a piece of upholstery has remained the same to this day. Thus the claw hammer, which consists of a *flat curved hammer head and the hardwood handle reinforced by a steel tube (spring)*, proved its worth[23]: *One part of the head ends in the round track, the common diameters of which are 8, 9 and 10 mm, the other part in the claw*, which serves to pull out smaller pins, for the removal of which no tongs are needed. A second hammer, with its shorter, stronger head, is used to fasten the nails that fix the straps. The pliers are suitable for pulling out larger pins and nails, while the nippers, equipped with a sharp jaw, are only used for nipping wire and thin pins.

The web stretcher and tongs allow the webbing straps under the wooden frame to be tightened to such an extent that they can be fastened into the wood without losing tension. The lower edge of the stretcher is *covered with fabric or leather to protect sensitive wooden frames.*[24] Metal points are embedded in its upper edge, which engage with the material used during webbing in order to maintain the tension of the straps. The tongs, already shown in Diderot, have two serrated jaws and a clamp-like slide that can be adjusted along the iron arms to lock them in place when needed. Other tools include various awls for evenly distributing the filling material while stitching the edges (regulator) or for suggesting holes (bradawl); the folding tool, which is helpful when folding over the edges of cover materials; the punching iron, which is used to punch out neatly outlined holes in fabric or leather; and the cutter, which is used to scribe the leather edges to be folded over.

For ripping out and stripping the chair a chisel is used. Traditionally, it has a wooden handle with a sharp steel blade that is forged flat at the bottom and cranked. This is suitable for removing strong nails. For the careful removal of valuable ornamental nails, on the other hand, a tack lifter is used.

21
Fassonarbeiten, Bildtafel aus: *Diderots Enzyklopädie: Die Bildtafeln* (1762–1777)

21
Stuffing and stitching, plate from: *Diderots Enzyklopädie: Die Bildtafeln* (1762–1777)

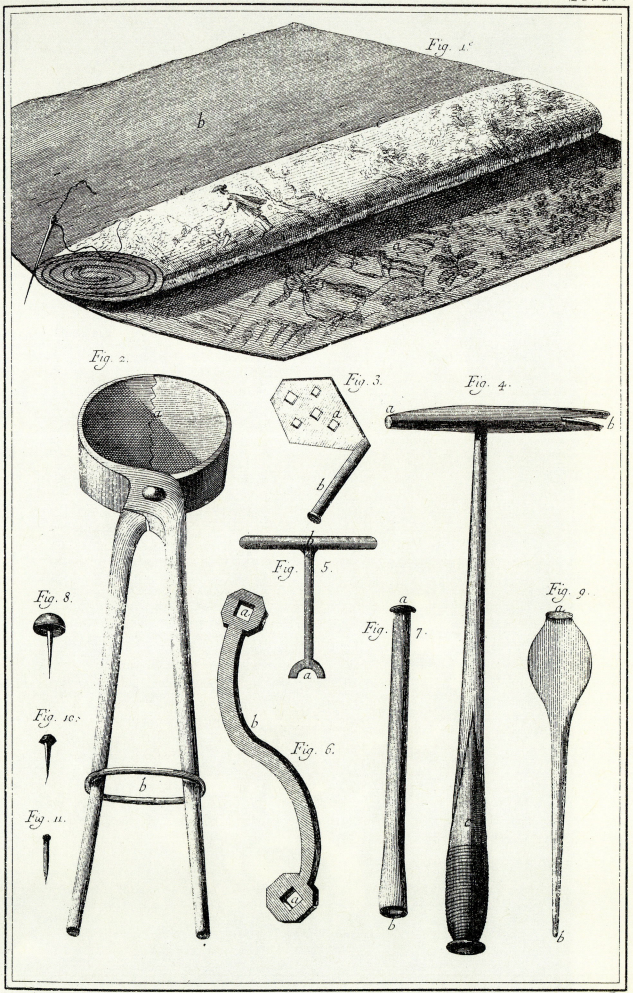

Tapissier, Façon du Point glacis, et Outils.

Auf der linken Seite ist eine Bildtafel aus Diderots Enzyklopädie zu sehen, die den Gebrauch einiger dieser Werkzeuge bereits im Rokoko nachweist (s. Abb. 22). Darauf fehlen, obwohl sie damals schon Verwendung fanden, die diversen Nadeln, mit denen Kantenwülste vernäht werden. Es ist das unentbehrliche Gerät zur Durchführung der präzisen Fasson-Arbeit. Eine Auswahl entsprechender Stichwerkzeuge zeigt das Foto vom Arbeitskissen eines heutigen Polsterers (s. Abb. 23): Markant sind die gebogenen Garniernadeln, die in verschiedenen Größen und Stärken ebenso im Gebrauch sind wie die geraden Arten. In dem 1953 verfassten *Lehrbuch zum Neuzeitlichen Polstern* erklären die Verfasser, ein guter Polsterer verfüge *mindestens über 6 in Größe und Stärke verschiedene Garniernadeln sowie über wenigstens 2 Nähnadeln für Nähte und Schnurarbeiten.*[25]

On the left is a plate from Diderot's *Encyclopédie* which demonstrates the use of some of these tools as early as the Rococo period (fig. 22). In it, although they were already in use at that time, the various needles used to sew edge rolls are missing. It is the indispensable tool for carrying out precise bridling and stitching. A selection of corresponding stitching tools is shown in the photo of the work cushion of a contemporary upholsterer (fig. 23): the curved needles, which are used in various sizes and thicknesses, as well as the straight types are striking. In the *Lehrbuch zum Neuzeitlichen Polstern*, written in 1953, the authors state that a good upholsterer has *at least 6 needles for bridling and stitching of different sizes and thicknesses as well as at least 2 needles for working seams and cord.*[25]

22
Werkzeuge des Tapissier, aus: *Diderots Enzyklopädie* (1762–1777)
Tools of a tapissier, in: *Diderots Enzyklopädie* (1762–1777)

23
Werkzeug des polsternden Raumausstatters heute
Tools of a modern upholsterer

Was Diderot nicht zeigt, ist die bald nach Erscheinen seiner Enzyklopädie am Ende des 18. Jahrhunderts auch im Polsterwesen aufkommende Sprungfeder, die die Arbeit des *Tapissiers* nachhaltig revolutionierte, insbesondere in Zeiten der Industrialisierung im 19. Jahrhundert, als neue maschinelle Verfahren immer leistungsfähigere Federn als Serienerzeugnisse herzustellen vermochten. Ihr Einsatz erhöhte die Flexibilität des Polsters enorm, benötigte nun allerdings auch mehr Raum und verlangte nach der besonderen Fähigkeit des Handwerkers, ihre Sprungkraft mittels Schnüren auf das gewollte Maß festzulegen. Zudem musste nun die Gurtung auf der Unterseite des Sitzrahmens befestigt werden, wodurch eine Mulde entstand, in der die Federn genügend Platz fanden, sodass sie wie gewünscht eingesetzt werden konnten. Dazu wurden sie in Gruppen angeordnet und untereinander verschnürt, damit der Druck der Körperlast sich gleichmäßig verteilen konnte.

Für die Polstermöbelfederung werden heute fast ausschließlich Taillenfedern aus industriell verarbeitetem Federstahldraht verwendet, während in früheren Zeiten unveredeltes Metall eingesetzt wurde, da es die gehärteten Materialien noch nicht gab. Bis heute werden Taillenfedern verkupfert, um sie vor Rost zu schützen. Im bereits zitierten Lehrbuch zum neuzeitlichen Polstern wird ausgeführt, dass die Enden der Federn heute fast durchweg eingeknotet sind (s. Abb. 24), während sie früher, als der Polsterer die Federn noch selbst herstellen musste, offen blieben oder mit Kapseln geschlossen wurden. Der verkupferte Draht war ursprünglich mit der Hand geformt worden. Mittels einer sogenannten *Federspindel* wurde er dann später über einem taillenförmigen Metallkern gedreht. So konnten mittels manueller Kraft Taillenfedern aus unterschiedlichen Drahtstärken und in verschiedenen Größen hergestellt werden.

Grundsätzlich richtet sich die Benennung der Federn nach Gangzahl und Drahtstärke, wobei man als Gang jeweils eine Wendung des Drahtes bezeichnet, sodass eine Taillenfeder mit vier Wendungen als 4-Gang-Feder bezeichnet wird. Im zweiten Katalogteil wird dieser Aspekt noch einmal detaillierter dargestellt und durch Angaben zum Einsatz der Möbelfedern ins Polster ergänzt. An dieser Stelle sei nur schon darauf hingewiesen, dass sich mit zunehmendem Einsatz der Sprungfedertechnik nicht nur die Arbeitsabläufe und der Polsteraufbau veränderten, sondern ein Mittel zur Verfügung stand, die unterschiedlichsten Grade von Festigkeit im Polster konstruktiv zu bestimmen.

Diderot does not show springs, which appeared in upholstery during the end of the eighteenth century, soon after the *Encyclopédie* had been published. These would revolutionise the *tapissier's* trade, especially during the industrialisation of the nineteenth century, when new machines made it possible to produce ever more efficient springs in serial production. Their use increased the flexibility of the cushion enormously but also required more space and demanded the special skill of the craftsman to regulate their bounce to the desired level by means of strings. In addition, the webbing now had to be attached to the underside of the seat rails, creating a hollow in which the springs had enough space to be used as desired. To do this, they were arranged in groups and tied together so that the pressure of the body weight could be evenly distributed.

Today, hourglass-shaped compression springs, or waisted springs, made of industrially processed sprung steel wire are used almost exclusively for upholstered furniture suspension, whereas in earlier times uncoated metal was used because the hardened materials did not yet exist. To this day, compression springs are copperplated to protect them from rust. The textbook on modern upholstery quoted above explains that today the ends of the springs are usually knotted (fig. 24), whereas in earlier times, when upholsterers still had to produce the springs themselves, they remained open or were closed with capsules. The copper-plated wire was originally formed by hand. By means of a so-called spring spindle, it was later twisted over a waist-shaped metal core. Thus, by means of manual force, waist springs could be made from wire of different thicknesses and in different sizes.

Springs are named according to the number of coils and the gauge of the wire. A coil is defined as one turn of the wire, so that a compression spring with four turns is called a 4-coil spring. In the second part of this catalogue, this aspect is described in more detail and supplemented by information on the use of springs in upholstery. At this point, it should be pointed out that with the increased use of spring technology, not only did the work processes and the padding construction change, but also a means was available to determine the varied degrees of firmness in the upholstery.

24
Taillenfeder mit Verknotung am obersten Gang

24
Waisted spring with knotting in the top gauge

The chamber horse – Sprung fitness equipment of the eighteenth century

Cordula Fink

You should be sure to take as much exercise every day as you can bear. I wish you would ask George Whitfield to send you the chamber-horse out of my dining room, which you should use half an hour at least daily.[26]

When John Wesley gave this advice to his niece Sarah in 1790, he was 87 years old, widely travelled and a dedicated church and life reformer, Methodist missionary and author living in London.[27] There, influential books on the subject of physical and mental training had been published for many years.[28] These were reviewed for a wide audience and their contents made available to a large readership, such as in 1704 a medical book by Francis Fuller (1670–1706), *Medicina Gymnastica: Or a Treatise Concerning the Power of Exercise [...]*.[29] It extolled the benefits of exercise, especially riding, as a form of exercise that challenged the whole body: *that the use of Exercise does conduce very much to the Preservation of Health, that it promotes the Digestions, raises the Spirits, refreshes the Mind, and that it strengthens and relieves the whole Man.*[30] In 1729, *Medicina Gymnastica* was already in its sixth edition. In an advertisement dated 15 March 1740, 36 years after its first publication, the book was advertised with the catchy short title *Fuller on Exercise*, well aware of the author's fame. 'A book worth Reading', wrote the reviewer in the subtitle.

Another doctor who preached vegetarianism and a healthy lifestyle based on exercise and enough sleep to the British aristocracy and the English trading elites was the Scott George Cheyne (1671–1743). Himself being extraordinarily overweight, he had undergone a successful vegetarian diet invented by himself and had been able to market it lucratively. In London as well as at the fashionable thermal springs at Bath, he was consulted by many prominent and wealthy patients. Among them were the Enlightenment thinker and writer Alexander Pope, the bestselling author Samuel Richardson as well as John Wesley mentioned earlier. In his 1724 *Essay of Health and Long Life*, Cheney advocated exercise, abstinence from meat while eating vegetables and milk and reducing the intake of alcoholic beverages. The book was reprinted six times during the first year after its publication and translated, among others, into French, Dutch, Latin and Italian. The companion was directed at the new group of those who did not move much due to their sedentary profession: *the Studious and the Contemplative [...] must make Exercise a Part of their Religion.*[31] Especially the use of a chamber horse was recommended as it was independent from available space or weather conditions. It comes as no surprise then that the chamber horse became a must-have for the upper classes, not just in Cheney's immediate environment. But what was a chamber horse? How was it made? What was its use?

British doctors had recommended the chamber horse, a spring construction covered in leather or fabric with

direkten Umfeld Cheneys das Chamber Horse zu einem Must-have der Oberschicht avancierte. Was aber verbarg sich hinter dem Begriff des Chamber Horse? Wie genau war es beschaffen? Wozu diente es?

Britische Ärzte empfahlen das Chamber Horse, eine von Leder oder Stoff mit seitlichen Lüftungsschlitzen umschlossene Federkonstruktion mit rundum sogfältig horizontal applizierten handgeschmiedeten Ziernägeln, fast 100 Jahre lang. Handgedrehte Federn, wie bei unserem Exemplar mit neun Gängen, lagen auf den vier gleich langen und breiten side vents and horizontally placed hand-crafted studs for almost a hundred years. Hand-turned springs, with nine coils, such as our example, were placed on four square boards. On these, 3 x 2 springs were arranged in parallel and screwed into the board for stabilization. The boards were connected at the lateral corners via a vertically running linen strap and fastened in this way. The upper end of the device, the fifth board, was used as a padded seat. It was often stuffed with horsehair since it was soft and fit for vigorous use.

25
Chamber Horse, England, 18. Jh. (Privatbesitz)

25
Chamber horse, England, 18th century (private collection)

Das Chamber Horse I The chamber horse

The trainees were advised to tense the muscles of the upper body by actively sitting or by a valiant up- and downward movement of their body in order to keep their balance on the accordion-like structure or to imitate the movement of trotting by placing the feet parallel with the upper body, knees and feet.[32]

Appearance and inner structure of the chamber horse can be seen in Thomas Sheraton's (1751–1806) book *Cabinet-Maker and Upholsterers Drawing Book* from 1793.[33] A kind of construction manual with texts and drawings, it renders a good impression of the construction. The inclusion of the chamber horse in Sheraton's influential style guide that also served as a kind of catalogue for his wealthy customers, demonstrates that chamber horses were still in demand at the end of the eighteenth century.

Regardless of their variety – different sizes existed as well as extravagantly decorated and more modest models – only a few makers of chamber horses are known by name. In the same 1740 edition of the *London Daily Post and General Advertiser* that had published the review of Fuller's *Medicina Gymnastica*, a certain Henry Marsh from the London city borough Clare Market was introduced as the inventor of a new fitness device advertised as the best on the market. Mr. Marsh, one reads, had already promising connections to the upper echelons of British society. The advertisement is directed at 'Ladies and Gentlemen' and thus addresses the intended target group of the gentry. The use was explicitly recommended for children.[34] Whether Henry Marsh may be considered the inventor of the chamber horse is open to doubt. In fact, the advertisement praises him as the inventor of the best model on the market. Another name has been passed down, since the children of King George III also played with a chamber horse. It was made by John Bradburn, the royal carpenter, in 1768. The expense is explicitly mentioned in the *Great Wardrobe Bill*.[35] For poorer classes a few chamber horses seem to have stood outside of apothecaries as exercise machines, for the payment of a fee of six cents an hour, as described in the weekly *The Cincinnati Lancet-Clinic* in 1894.[36] When this became customary remains unclear.

As a medical therapeutic aid, the chamber horse seems to be a uniquely British phenomenon during the eighteenth century. It was intended to ameliorate the effects of a change in lifestyles that was soon considered to be unhealthy caused by the rise of the British Empire and the beginning of industrialisation. In addition to the aristocracy and the wealthy classes, this also affected the growing middle class. They now increasingly led a sedentary life in administration, enjoyed, just as the gentry, several sumptuous meals a day and led a life devoted to socialising with plenty of alcohol, sweets, cakes and multi-course meat-heavy meals. As can be deducted from contemporary caricatures, this led to almost monstrous obesity and the rise of lifestyle diseases such as heart problems and strokes. The menus of Georg Friedrich Händel during his London years are an impressive example of such gluttony, as is the anecdote that a present by the British king to one of his court ladies was unsuccessful as the lady in question was too broad for a chamber horse.[37]

der Verwaltung aus, genoss wie der Adel mehrfach am Tag üppige Mahlzeiten und führte ein der Geselligkeit verpflichtetes Leben mit reichlich Alkohol, Süßigkeiten, Kuchen und mehrgängigen, fleischlastigen Mahlzeiten. Dies führte, in den Karikaturen der Zeit ablesbar, verbreitet zu fast monströser Fettleibigkeit und zu Zivilisationskrankheiten wie Herzbeschwerden oder Schlaganfällen. Die Angaben zu Georg Friedrich Händels Speiseplänen in seinen Londoner Jahren sind ein eindrucksvolles Beispiel dieser Völlerei wie auch die Überlieferung, dass ein Geschenk des britischen Königs für eine der Hofdamen sein Ziel verfehlte, da diese zu breit für das Chamber Horse gewesen sei.[37]

In Deutschland tauchen ähnliche Gefährte erst Ende des 19. Jahrhunderts, zu Zeiten der Industrialisierung Deutschlands auf, dann als *Reitapparat*[38] oder *Velotrab*[39] als *vollständiger Ersatz für das Reiten auf dem Pferde* und als *Spezialapparat für natürliche Entfettung* zum Weihnachtsfest angepriesen. 1907 wurde damit geworben, dass bereits *Tausende im Gebrauch* seien.[40] Das Marketing für Geräte, die die Exzesse der zu Wohlstand gekommenen Schichten ausgleichen sollen, ist grundsätzlich das gleiche wie zuvor in England, allerdings fokussierte man mit dem *Velotrab*, dessen Ausmaße sehr viel geringer waren, also weniger Platz in bürgerlichen Wohnstuben benötigten, eine Mittelschicht.

Moden wechseln, Bedürfnisse ändern sich und so landeten in Großbritannien viele Chamber Horses auf Speichern. Das Leder zerfiel, Mäuse und Motten nahmen sich ihrer an, sie wurden verschenkt, verkauft oder weitergegeben, so wie in Jane Austens Roman *Sanditon* von 1817, in dem sowohl der Gebrauch als auch der Verkauf eines Chamber Horse thematisiert werden.

Überlebt haben einige wenige Exemplare. Die meisten sind aus dem Umfeld des britischen Adels und der Oberschicht bekannt, sie befinden sich heute verstreut in Museen wie dem *Victoria and Albert Museum*, London, dem *Museum of Methodism and John Wesley's House*, London, dem *Science Museum*, London (dort wird ein spätes deutsches Modell aus Hildburghausen aufbewahrt, das zwischen 1870 und 1930 datiert ist), im *Georgian Museum* in Dublin, in einigen Häusern des National Trust, wie in *Belton House*, Lincolnshire, *Bolton Hall*, Bradford, *Chastelton House*, Oxfordshire. Die BBC hat in Kooperation mit dem British Museum, unterstützt von den beitragenden Museen, die Serie *A History of the World* aufgelegt. In ihr wurde auch das Chamber Horse als kulturelles Phänomen gewürdigt. Das in Leipzig ausgestellte Modell eines Chamber Horse (s. Abb. 25), dessen Provenienz auf mündliche Nachfrage nicht zu klären ist, wurde am 12.10.2018 vom Auktionshaus Duggleby & Stephenson of York[41] von einem schottischen Antiquitätenhändler ersteigert, bevor es im Jahr 2019 in eine Privatsammlung nach Köln verkauft wurde. Seine Maße betragen 83 x 73 x 52 cm. 2021/22 wurde es einer Restaurierung unterzogen, da der Bezugsstoff aus Rosshaar zerstört war, die innenliegenden Bretter und handgedrehten Taillenfedern aus Kupfer (s. Abb. 26) wurden wieder eingesetzt, viele der handgeschmiedeten Ziernägel und auch die gepolsterte Sitzfläche konnten weiterverwendet werden.

Similar devices appeared in Germany only during the late nineteenth century when the country was industrialised. At this time, they were referred to as a *Reitapparat* (riding apparatus)[38] or *Velotrab*[39] and marketed as a complete substitute for horseback riding and as 'a special device for natural slimming' during the Christmas period. In 1907 there were 'thousands in use', according to advertisements.[40] In terms of marketing, the device's intention to compensate the excesses of newly wealthy classes was largely the same as in England. However, the much smaller *Velotrab*, which took up much less space in bourgeois living rooms, targeted the middle class.

Fashions change, as do requirements, and so many chamber horses ended up in storage across Great Britain. The leather withered, mice and moths took over, they were gifted, sold or passed on. Such is the case in Jane Austen's 1817 novel *Sanditon*, in which both the use as well as the sale of a chamber horse are thematised.

A few specimens have survived. Most of them are known to have belonged to the British aristocracy and upper classes and are now scattered across museums such as the Victoria and Albert Museum, London; the Museum of Methodism & John Wesley's House, London; the Science Museum, London (where a late German model from Hildburghausen is kept, dated between 1870 and 1930); the Georgian Museum, Dublin and some National Trust houses such as Belton House, Lincolnshire; Bolton Hall, Bradford and Chastelton House, Oxfordshire. The BBC, in cooperation with the British Museum, supported by the contributing museums, has produced a series called *A History of the World*. There the chamber horse was honoured as a cultural phenomenon. The model of a chamber horse exhibited in Leipzig (fig. 25), whose provenance could not be clarified on enquiry, was bought at an auction from Duggleby Stephenson of York auction house[41] by a Scottish antiques dealer on 12 October 2018, before being sold to a private collection in Cologne in 2019. Its dimensions are 83 x 73 x 52 cm. In 2021–22 it underwent restoration, as the horsehair cover fabric had disintegrated; the interior boards and hand-turned copper waisted springs (fig. 26) were reinstated, many of the hand-forged decorative nails as well as the upholstered seat could be reused.

26
Blick in das geöffnete Chamber Horse, 18. Jh. (Privatbesitz)

26
View inside the opened chamber horse, 18th century (private collection)

Das Chamber Horse | The chamber horse

27/28
Armlehnstuhl, um 1765 (Stiftung Preußische Schlösser und Gärten Berlin-Brandenburg)
Armchair, around 1765 (Stiftung Preußische Schlösser und Gärten Berlin-Brandenburg)

29
Sofa, um 1780 (LÖFFLER COLLECTION, Reichenschwand)

29
Sofa, around 1780 (LÖFFLER COLLECTION, Reichenschwand)

30
Armlehnstuhl, um 1800 (Museum für Kunst und Kulturgeschichte Schloss Gottorf, Landesmuseen Schleswig-Holstein)

30
Armchair, around 1800 (Museum für Kunst und Kulturgeschichte Schloss Gottorf, Landesmuseen Schleswig-Holstein)

Spielarten des Klassizismus
Xenia Schürmann

In der zweiten Hälfte des 18. Jahrhunderts löste eine neue Formensprache die fließenden C-und S- Linien der Rokoko-Rocaillen ab. Inspiriert von den Zeugnissen der römischen Zivilisation, die Mitte des Jahrhunderts in Pompeji und Herkulaneum entdeckt und über Stichwerke verbreitet wurden sowie von den Erfahrungen der Künstler und Reisenden, die in Rom ihr Auge an den Überresten der Antike geschult hatten, begeisterte man sich zusehends für die Formen der Antike. Dabei schaute man nicht nur auf die römische Antike, auch Ägypten und Griechenland waren Quellen der Inspiration, die immer wieder zitiert wurden. Vergleicht man den Sessel (s. Abb. 27/28), ein *fauteil à la reine*, mit dem Sofa (s. Abb. 29) so fallen die Unterschiede der beiden in Frankreich gegen Mitte bzw. gegen Ende des 18. Jahrhunderts gefertigten Möbel sogleich ins Auge. Mit seiner breiten Sitzfläche, den gepolsterten Armlehnen und der vergleichsweise niedrigen Rückenlehne sowie den fließenden Kurven des Gestells erzählt der Sessel von der Entdeckung von *confort* und *commodité* als neuen Leitbegriffen eines Interieurs, mit denen sich der Adel vor allem in Paris von der barocken Strenge des Versailler Hofes abzusetzen versuchte. Während dieser Sessel vermutlich als Teil einer Garnitur als *meuble meublant* an einer Wand stand, auf deren Bespannung die Bezüge farblich abgestimmt waren, waren die *meubles courants* für die flexible Verteilung im Raum gedacht. Gerade hier findet sich eine große Bandbreite von Sonderformen, die den veränderten Ansprüchen in immer differenzierterer Weise entgegenkamen. So ermöglicht es die Voyeuse, deren Rückenpolster in eine breite Auflage übergeht, auf dieser die Hände bequem abzustützen. Die Duchesse wiederum, eine Art Liege, zeichnet sich durch viele Unterformen aus, die etwa das Auflegen der Füße oder das Sitzen mehrerer Personen ermöglichen. Sich elegant in diese Polster fallen zu lassen, sich auf ihnen in Anwesenheit anderer zu drapieren, setzte folglich eine genaue Kenntnis der Umgangsformen voraus, die sich nur durch das Verkehren in den richtigen Kreisen erlernen ließen.

Mit seinem klaren tektonischen Aufbau, der die einzelnen Elemente in Sockel, Gesimse und Friese gliedert, verrät das Sofa das Interesse an den Formen der antiken Architektur. Typisch sind das gefasste Holz sowie die Rückenlehne, die konisch zulaufenden kannelierten Beine sowie ein Dekor, das den Aufbau des Möbels betont, wie etwa das geschnitzte Flechtbandfries, das durch die Rosetten der Zargen unterbrochen wird. Für die Bezüge verwendete man nun häufig fein gemusterte Stoffe, hier etwa ein zartes Kettmuster. Der Stil des Frühklassizismus oder auch Louis-seize richtete sich gegen das nun veraltete Rokoko, wobei die geraden Formen durchaus auch als Ausdruck eines neuen rationaleren Zeitgeists interpretiert wurden.

Beiden Möbeln gemeinsam ist die Herstellung innerhalb der Schranken des Zunftwesens. Diese strengen Vorschriften regulierten die Pariser Handwerksbetriebe bis in das kleinste Detail. So mussten Möbel mit einem Firmenzeichen versehen werden, Gestell und Polster, aber auch Beschläge in verschiedenen Werkstätten produziert werden. Auch wenn zahlreiche Gerichtsakten belegen, dass immer wieder gegen die Zunftregeln verstoßen wurde, so brach erst die Einführung neuer Regeln 1791 mit dieser Tradition der handwerklichen Spezialisierung. Von nun an konnten Holz,

Variations of Classicism
Xenia Schürmann

During the second half of the eighteenth century, a new formal language replaced the sinuous S- and C-scrolls of the Rococo rocailles. Inspired by the remains of Roman civilisation which had been discovered in Pompeii and Herculaneum in the middle of the century and subsequently spread through engravings, as well as through the experiences of artists and tourists who had trained their eyes in Rome on the remains of the ancient world, the forms of antiquity were increasingly celebrated. Roman antiquity was not the only source of inspiration: Egypt and Greece were cited again and again.

Comparing the armchair (figs. 27/28), a *fauteuil à la reine*, to the sofa (fig. 29), the difference between the two pieces of furniture built in France during the middle and the end of the eighteenth century become apparent immediately. With its wide seat, upholstered armrests and comparatively low backrest, as well as the flowing curves of the frame, the armchair tells of the discovery of *confort* and *commodité* as new guiding concepts of an interior, with which the nobility, especially in Paris, tried to set itself apart from the Baroque austerity of the Versailles court. While this armchair probably stood against a wall as part of a set as a *meuble meublant* with colour-coordinated upholstery, the *meubles courants* were intended for flexible distribution in the room. Here in particular, a wide range of special forms can be found, which met the changing demands in manifold ways. For example, the *voyeuse*, whose back cushion merges into a wide support rest, makes it possible to rest one's hand comfortably on it. The *duchesse*, on the other hand, a kind of lounger, is distinguished by its many subforms, which allow, for example, to put one's feet up or to sit with several people. To let oneself fall elegantly into these cushions, to drape oneself on them in the presence of others, therefore required a precise knowledge of manners, which could only be learnt by circulating in the right circles.

With its clear tectonic constructions, that divides the single elements into plinths, cornices and friezes, the sofa tells of the interest in the forms of antique architecture. The painted wood, the backrest, the conical, tapered fluted legs as well as a decoration that emphasizes the construction of the piece, such as the carved interlace frieze interrupted by rosettes on the frame, are all typical features. Finely patterned textiles such as this delicate warp-patterned one were increasingly used for the upholstery. The neo-Classicism or Louis Seize style reacted against the now outdated Rococo. The straight lines were often interpreted as the expression of a new, more rational zeitgeist.

Both pieces were produced according to restrictions set by the guilds. These strict rules regulated Parisian workshops down to the smallest detail. All furniture had to be branded, frame and upholstery but also the fittings had to be produced in different workshops. Even though numerous court cases suggest that these guild rules were regularly broken, it was only the introduction of new regulations in 1791 that broke with this tradition of specialised craftsmanship. From then on wood, reliefs and gilded bronze ornament

VIII Cahier des Menuisiers. E.29.

DESSEINS à l'Usage des Artistes en Architecture en general et pour faire Sieges, chaises à bras, à dos, Canapes, Bois des Lits, Armoires et Bordures des Miroirs etc Specialement.

Inventées desinées et gravées par J.F. Hauer, rue S. Ursule à Paris.

Reliefs und Bronzevergoldungen in einer Werkstatt gefertigt werden.[42] Die Zeitenwende, die die Französische Revolution sowie im Jahr 1804 die Selbstkrönung Napoleon Bonapartes (1769–1840) zum Kaiser bedeuteten, spiegelte sich dabei weniger in den Personalien der Handwerksbetriebe, war doch die Großzahl der Betriebe bereits unter dem Ancien Régime tätig gewesen, sondern vor allem in den Formen eines weiteren klassizistischen Stils, des Empire (ca.1800–1814).

Für die Ausstattung der neuen Residenzen, die die neue gesellschaftliche Ordnung standesgemäß repräsentieren sollten, verließ sich der ehemalige General auf die Hilfe der Architekten Charles Percier (1764–1838) und Pierre François Léonard Fontaine (1762–1853). Deren Vorlagenwerk *Recueil de décorations intérieures* trug entscheidend zur Verbreitung des an der römischen Antike und Florentiner Renaissance angelehnten Stils bei. Ähnlich wie in der zeitgenössischen Bildenden Kunst waren hier die Interieurs, Möbelstücke und dekorativen Objekte als Umrisszeichnungen wiedergegeben. Dadurch ließen sich die auf die Grundideen reduzierten Entwürfe kostengünstig vervielfachen und gaben den ausführenden Handwerkern und potentiellen Auftraggebern dennoch genügend Gestaltungsfreiraum.[43]

Die Möbel des Empire sind noch architektonischer und geradliniger, Einlege- und filigrane Schnitzdekore, wie sie noch für den Klassizismus des Louis-seize typisch sind, verschwinden fast vollständig. Stattdessen begeisterte man sich für ungefasste Hölzer. Insbesondere das teure Mahagoni, das bereits Ende des 18. Jahrhunderts in England, wo man durch die Kolonien direkte Bezugsquellen hatte, massiv verarbeitet wurde, wurde zum Sinnbild dieses Stils. In Frankreich und dem Rest Europas wurde das Tropenholz jedoch fast ausschließlich als Furnier verwendet. Die Polster mit ihrer sogenannten Messerkante, die durch immer enger gesetzte Stichreihen zur Kante hin erreicht wurde, die fast parallel zum Gestell verlief, unterstützte die geraden Linien dieser Möbel visuell. Zusätzlich betont wurde diese Kante, aber auch der Abschluss zum Holz, durch das Anbringen von Kordeln und Ziernägeln.[44]

Die napoleonischen Feldzüge förderten die Verbreitung dieses Stils im restlichen Europa. So findet sich in Kassel, das von 1807 bis 1813 Residenzstadt des von Napoleon gegründeten Königreichs Westphalen war, über das sein jüngster Bruder Jérome Bonaparte (1784–1860) als König herrschte, ein Sessel *en gondole* mit vergoldeten Sphingen als Armlehnen (s. Abb. 32), dessen enge Gurtung auf eine französische Herkunft schließen lässt. Bei ihrer Ankunft in Kassel fanden Jérome und seine Gemahlin Katharina von Württemberg (1783–1835) ein fast kahles Schloss vor, hatte der Landgraf Wilhelm IX. (1743–1821) auf seiner Flucht doch die kostbaren Möbel und Wandbespannungen aus Lyoner Seide mitgenommen. Für die Befriedigung des immensen Bedarfs wurden aber auch lokale Werkstätten hinzugezogen, sodass der Stil auch nach der Niederlage Napoleons, vor allem in repräsentativen höfischen Kontexten, bis in die 1840er Jahre Verwendung fand.

Wie in Frankreich, so wurden die Möbelentwürfe auch in Deutschland meist von Architekten geliefert. So stammt der Armlehnsessel, dessen als vergoldete Greife gestaltete

31
Das Architekturmotiv im Möbelentwurf, Gravur Nummer VIII, Paris, Anfang 19. Jh. (GRASSI Museum für Angewandte Kunst Leipzig)

32
Armlehnsessel *en gondole*, Kassel, um 1800/1820
(Kassel, Museumslandschaft Hessen Kassel, Möbelsammlung)

32
Armchair *en gondole*, Kassel, around 1800/1820
(Kassel, Museumslandschaft Hessen Kassel, Möbelsammlung)

Armlehnen mit fast rechteckigen Polstern ausgestattet sind (s. Abb. 35/36), aus der Feder des Kasseler Hofarchitekten Johann Conrad Bromeis (1788–1855), der sie 1823 für das zweite Wohnzimmer des Corps de Logis von Schloss Wilhelmshöhe entwarf. Ausgeführt wurden sie von dem lokalen Schreinermeister Carl Christian Lauckhardt (1788–1867). Dabei kam der Seidendamast der Bezüge aus Lyon, die vergoldeten Bronzebeschläge aus Paris. Ebenfalls nicht unüblich für diese neue Generation von Gestaltern war, dass Bromeis, der bedingt durch die Kriegswirren nie die für seinen Berufsstand üblichen Studienreisen nach Paris und Rom unternommen hatte, sich eng an Vorlagenwerken orientierte. So war für Bromeis nicht nur der Recueil, sondern auch Pierre de La Mésangères (1761–1831) *Meubles et Objets de Goût* eine immer wieder zu Rate gezogene Inspirationsquelle. In Deutschland trugen ab Ende des 18. Jahrhunderts Zeitschriftenbeilagen, etwa *im Journal des Luxus und der Moden* oder dem *Magazin für Freunde des guten Geschmacks* entschieden dazu bei, dass diese Vorlagen nicht länger einem Fachpublikum vorbehalten waren, sondern auch an Laien und potentielle Auftraggeber verbreitet wurden.

Verbunden mit der Kontinentalsperre gegen England 1807 und dem damit einhergehenden Importembargo, begann man in Frankreich mit der Verwendung von „indigenen", also einheimischen, Hölzern als Furnier. Mit etwas Verzögerung wurde dies auch in Deutschland praktiziert. So geht der Stuhl mit einem Furnier aus Birkenwurzelholz (s. Abb. 33/34) ebenfalls auf den Entwurf von Bromeis von 1819 für das Mobiliar der Stuckgalerie des neuen Kasseler Residenzpalais zurück. Dass dieses Exemplar mit dem originalen Bezug aus gelbgrünem Seidendamast zu einem Paar gehört, das erst nachträglich, 1826, gefertigt wurde,[45] legt nahe, dass der Stil auch sieben Jahre später noch dem Repräsentationsbedürfnis entsprach.

Das Stuhlmodell eines weiteren Architekten, des preußischen Karl-Friedrich Schinkel (1781–1841), beweist, dass eine klare Trennung zwischen dem vermeintlich höfischen Klassizismus und dem gemütlichen Biedermeier des Bürgertums nicht immer möglich ist (s. Abb. 39/40). Während das Gestell an die x-förmigen Hocker der Antike angelehnt ist, verspricht das Polster mit der damals neumodischen Capitonéheftung einen Komfort, den man traditionellerweise eher den Ohrensesseln des Biedermeier zuschreibt. Unter dem violetten Velours verbirgt sich eine weitere Innovation der Zeit, eine geschnürte Springfeder, die erst Ende der 1820er Jahre weitere Verbreitung fand und in der zweiten Hälfte des Jahrhunderts nicht mehr wegzudenken war.[46]

rectangular padding (figs. 35/36) was designed by the Kassel court architect Johann Conrad Bromeis (1788–1855), who designed them for the second living room of the Corps de Logis at Schloss Wilhelmshöhe in 1823. They were executed by a local master carpenter, Carl Christian Lauckhardt (1788–1867). The silk damask used for the covers came from Lyon, the gilt bronze mounts from Paris. It was not unusual among this new generation of designers that Bromeis, who due to the turmoil of war had never undertaken the study trip to Rome and Paris customary for his profession, followed guidebooks closely. Thus, not only the *Recueil* but also Pierre de La Mésangère's (1761–1831) *Meubles et Objets de Goût* was a source of inspiration for Bromeis. In Germany, from the end of the eighteenth century, magazine supplements, for example in the *Journal des Luxus und der Moden* (Journal of Luxury and Fashion) or the *Magazin für Freunde des guten Geschmacks* (Magazine for Friends of Good Taste), contributed decisively to the fact that these models were no longer reserved for a specialist audience but were also disseminated to laypeople and potential clients.

In connection with the Continental Blockade against England in 1807 and the accompanying import embargo, France began to use 'indigenous' woods for veneer. With some delay, this was also practised in Germany. Thus, the chair with a veneer of birch root (figs. 33/34) also goes back to Bromeis' design of 1819 for the furniture of the stucco gallery of the new Residenzpalast in Kassel. The fact that this example featuring original upholstery of yellow-green silk damask belongs to a pair that was only made later, in 1826,[45] suggests that the style still met the need for representation seven years later.

The chair by another architect, the Prussian Karl-Friedrich Schinkel (1781–1841), proves that a clear distinction between a supposedly courtly Classicism and the homely Biedermeier of the bourgeoisie is not always possible. While the frame design is based on the X-shaped stools of antiquity, the upholstery with the then new deep buttoning promises a comfort traditionally attributed to Biedermeier wing chairs. Under the purple mohair velour hides another innovation of the time, a lashed spring, which only became more widespread at the end of the 1820s and was indispensable by the second half of the century.[46]

33/34
Stuhl, Kassel, 1826
(Kassel, Museumslandschaft Hessen Kassel, Möbelsammlung)

33/34
Chair, Kassel, 1826
(Kassel, Museumslandschaft Hessen Kassel, Möbelsammlung)

35/36
Armlehnsessel von Schloss Wilhelmshöhe, Johann Conrad Bromeis (Entwurf), Carl Christian Lauckhardt, Kassel (Herstellung), 1823 (Kassel, Museumslandschaft Hessen Kassel, Möbelsammlung)

35/36
Armchair from Schloss Wilhelmshöhe, Johann Conrad Bromeis (design), Carl Christian Lauckhardt, Kassel (execution), 1823 (Kassel, Museumslandschaft Hessen Kassel, Möbelsammlung)

Spielarten des Klassizismus l Variations of Classicism

37/38
Hocker, um 1830
(Kassel, Museumslandschaft Hessen Kassel, Möbelsammlung)

37/38
Stool, around 1830
(Kassel, Museumslandschaft Hessen Kassel, Möbelsammlung)

39/40
Armlehnsessel, Karl Friedrich Schinkel (Entwurf), um 1830
(LÖFFLER COLLECTION, Reichenschwand)

39/40
Armchair, Karl Friedrich Schinkel (design), around 1830
(LÖFFLER COLLECTION, Reichenschwand)

Spielarten des Klassizismus | Variations of Classicism 65

41/42 (S. 68/69)
Aufbau des Polsters eines klassizistischen Stuhls (Wolfgang Nerge, Doris Nolting, Obernkirchen/Löhne)

41/42 (p. 68/69)
Upholstery section of a Classicist chair (Wolfgang Nerge, Doris Nolting, Obernkirchen/Löhne)

Polsteraufbau eines klassizistischen Stuhls
Thomas Schriefers

Der hier abgebildete Stuhl (s. Abb. 41) wurde für die Ausstellung als Anschauungsmodell eines im Klassizismus üblichen Polsteraufbaus angefertigt. Der Buchenholzstuhl verfügt über eine zeittypische Rückenlehne in Medaillon-Form, kannelierte Balusterbeine mit Würfelabschluss und Blume sowie eine gestrichene Leinöl-Oberfläche in Cremeweiß. Damit die verschiedenen Schichten der Polsterung in Sitz und Rücken sichtbar werden, wurden entsprechende Schnitte vorgenommen, die den Blick hinein zulassen (s. Abb. 42). Den Polstergrund des Sitzes bildet eine Gurtung mit darüberliegender Leinenabdeckung, auf der das umlaufende und mit Brechflachs gefüllte *bourrelet* als Kantenwulst aufgesetzt wurde. Mit Leiter- und Vorderstich stabilisiert, bildet es den Rahmen für die entstehende Mulde, in die vier handgedrehte Taillenfedern eingesetzt und anschließend mit Stell- und Knotenfäden verschnürt wurden. Darauf ruht das wiederum mit Brechflachs ausgefüllte *Fassonpolster*, auf dem eine Pikierung aus Rosshaar mit Nessel- und Watteabdeckung schließlich den Untergrund für einen epochentypischen Seidenstoff mit Granatapfelmotiv darstellt.

Das Rückenpolster besitzt als Unterlage ein Leinengewebe, auf dem ein umlaufendes *bourrelet* mit Rosshaarfüllung sitzt. Dies bildet, mit drei Vorderstichen garniert, das Bett für den Einsatz von Rosshaar. Über einer Nesselschicht und der darauf liegenden Watteabdeckung wird auch hier dann der Seidenstoff aufgezogen.

Es zeigt sich der Wandel, der sich seit der Barockzeit vollzog. Er machte den Polsteraufbau komplexer und setzte den Einsatz von Sprungfedern voraus. Da deren Einsatz eine ausreichend tiefe Mulde im Sitz bedingt, wurde das *bourrelet* entsprechend hoch gebaut. Im Gegensatz zum zuvor dargestellten Aufbau des Barockpolsters wird hierbei der Sitz umlaufend mit einer Kantenwulst versehen, wodurch beim Einsatz der Federn ein Polstergewölbe entsteht, das, je nach Dimensionierung, die Innenkammer einer jeden geschnürten Federpolsterung kennzeichnet.[47]

Upholstery of a Classicist chair
Thomas Schriefers

The chair depicted here (fig. 41) was produced for the exhibition as a show model in order to demonstrate the typical upholstery of the Classicism period. The beechwood chair is fitted with a then typical backrest in medallion shape, fluted legs with corner blocks with paterae with flower motifs as well as a cream white surface painted with a linseed oil paint. In order to show the different steps undertaken to upholster the seat and backrest, corresponding cuts have been made to allow the view inside (fig. 42). The base is formed of a webbing with a cover of hessian cloth on which the stuffing for the flax edge roll, which runs all around, is attached. This is stabilised by blind stitching and top stitching and creates the frame for a recess into which four handmade coil springs are placed using slip knots, reef knots and French knots. On top sits another layer stuffed with flax, on which a layer of horsehair with covers of wadding and calico forms the base for a covering silk fabric with a pomegranate motif, typical for the period.

The backrest upholstery has a base of hessian with an all-around edge roll and horsehair stuffing. Held in place by blind stitching, it forms the base of further horsehair stuffing. Over a calico and a layer of wadding the silk fabric cover has been attached.

One can see the change from the Baroque period; the composition of upholstery was more complex and required the use of springs. Since this required a sufficiently deep recess, the edge role had to be correspondingly high. In contrast to the composition of Baroque upholstery depicted above, the seat has been fitted with an edge roll on all sides, creating a dome in the upholstery, which, depending on the dimensions, marks the interior of any lashed sprung upholstery.[47]

43
Blick auf den Leipziger Markt am Morgen, Aquarell wohl eines Leipziger Künstlers, um 1820 (GRASSI Museum für Angewandte Kunst Leipzig)

43
View of the Leipzig market in the morning, watercolour, presumably by a Leipzig-based artist, around 1820 (GRASSI Museum für Angewandte Kunst Leipzig)

Wohnformen im ersten Drittel des 19. Jahrhunderts

Thomas Rudi

Im Zusammenhang mit den Ideen der Aufklärung und der Rückbesinnung auf die Antike bahnte sich gegen Ende des 18. Jahrhunderts eine neue Ästhetik der Einfachheit an, die im Widerspruch zu dem luxuriösen Einrichtungsstil der vorherigen Jahrzehnte stand.[48] Dabei legte man gerade auf die Interieurgestaltung besonderen Wert. In der ersten Ausgabe des *Journals der Moden*[49], das von Friedrich Justin Bertuch 1786 in Weimar herausgegeben wurde, heißt es: *Kein Artikel des Luxus hat zu unserer Zeit mehr wesentliche Veränderungen und nützliche Verbesserungen erhalten, als das Ammeublement. Vordem trat Prunk dabey an die Stelle der wahren Reichheit, und kindische zweckwidrige Verzierungen hielt man oft für Schönheit und Geschmack. [...] Ein Meuble muß einfach und schön von Form, bequem und zweckmäßig zum Gebrauch, dauerhaft und sauber gearbeitet und gut von Material seyn, wenn man es für vollkommen erkennen soll.*[50] Der individuelle Wohnraum löste den bisher üblichen, von sozialen Rangordnungen bestimmten *Schauraum* ab.

Um 1810 war es üblich, sich in einem Zimmer um einen zentral platzierten runden Tisch zusammenzufinden, der in der Raummitte vor einem großen, meist repräsentativen Sofa platziert war und von Sesseln und Stühlen umringt wurde[51]. Auf schwere Möbel wurde verzichtet, die – wie noch wenige Jahre zuvor – entlang der Wände eines Raumes aufgereiht waren. Diese aufwendig eingerichteten und hauptsächlich der Repräsentation dienenden Salons und Paradezimmer wurden über geschlossene Läden und Vorhänge abgedunkelt und nur dann geöffnet, wenn Gäste erwartet wurden – beispielsweise sonntags nach dem Kirchgang oder an besonderen Festtagen. Oft blieb dann nicht mehr genügend Zeit, um den Raum zu beheizen, sodass er als *Kalte Pracht* verspottet wurde.[52]

Eine andere Neuerung war, dass das Holz der Möbel nicht mehr gefasst – also bemalt oder vergoldet – wurde, wie noch häufig zur Zeit des Barock und Rokoko, sondern dass stattdessen eher auf seine Qualität und die handwerkliche Verarbeitung Wert gelegt wurde.[53] Dabei spielten sowohl die Maserung als auch der Glanz und die Farbe des Furniers eine wichtige Rolle. Diese Faktoren bestimmten nun weitgehend die Optik der Möbel und machten ihre Qualität aus.

Die weiche, bequeme Polsterung der Sitzmöbel war bei dem Streben nach Behaglichkeit ein bedeutender Aspekt.[54] Allerdings konnte seit den 1820er Jahren vor allem bei Seitenrahmenstühlen[55] nach englischem Vorbild an die Stelle des Sitzflächenpolsters auch elastisches Stuhlgeflecht treten. Ebenso war die Rückenlehne oftmals ungepolstert – dies hing u. a. auch mit der damals üblichen steifen Sitzhaltung zusammen. Bei Stühlen erhob sich das Sitzpolster zunächst beträchtlich über den Zargenkranz, sodass sie relativ schwer wirkten. Um 1820 begann sich das nach englischem Vorbild herausnehmbare und dadurch auch besser zu reinigende Kissen durchzusetzen. Dadurch wirkten die Polster ähnlich flach wie diejenigen der Seitenrahmenstühle. Dagegen nahm das Volumen der Polsterung bei den Sofas, den Repräsentationsmöbeln der Zeit, ständig

Dwelling in the first third of the nineteenth century

Thomas Rudi

In the context of Enlightenment ideas and a return to antiquity, the late eighteenth century saw the rise of a new aesthetic of simplicity that stood in contrast to the luxurious style of furnishing of earlier decades.[48] At the same time, interior design played an important role. In the first volume of *Journal der Moden*,[49] published by Friedrich Justin Bertuch 1786 in Weimar, one finds, *No object of luxury has received more substantial change and useful amelioration than the ameublement. Before, luxury had taken the place of true richness, and childish un-useful decorations were too often mistaken for beauty and taste. [...] A piece of furniture must be simple and beautiful in form, comfortable und functional for use, durable and well-crafted and of good material if it is to be considered perfect.*[50] The individual *living room* replaced the until then usual *representational room* defined by social rank order.

Around 1810 it was customary to gather around a round table placed centrally in the room in front of a large, often representative sofa and surrounded by chairs and armchairs.[51] Heavy pieces of furniture that were lined up against the sides of the room – as had been customary just a few years earlier – were dispensed with. These carefully furnished salons and parade rooms, which served mostly representative purposes, were darkened by closed shutters and curtains and only opened when guest were expected, for example on Sundays after church or during special holidays. Often, there was little time to heat the room, so that it was derided as 'cold splendour' (*Kalte Pracht*).[52]

Another innovation was that the wood used to make furniture was no longer painted or gilded, as had been customary during the Baroque and Rococo. Instead, its quality and craftsmanship became more important.[53] Both the grain as well as the gloss and colour of the veneer played an important role. These factors largely determined the look of furniture pieces as well as their quality.

The soft, comfortable padding of seating furniture was an important aspect in the quest for comfort.[54] However, since the 1820s, especially for *Seitenrahmen* chairs[55] which were based on English drop-in seat models, a seat with woven canework has replaced the seat padding. Likewise, the backrest was often not upholstered; this was also due to the straight sitting position common at the time. For chairs, the seat upholstery often rose above the frame rails so that they became relatively heavy in appearance. Around 1820, the English custom of using cushions that could be taken out and were therefore easier to clean became more popular. Accordingly, the padding appeared as flat as those on *Seitenrahmen* chairs. Conversely, the volume of padding increased for sofas. The armrests became wider and were composed of, among others, cylindrical cushions filled almost entirely with horsehair. The wing chair (fig. 44) appeared as the embodiment of

44
Ohrensessel, um 1825 (LÖFFLER COLLECTION, Reichenschwand)

44
Wing chair, around 1825 (LÖFFLER COLLECTION, Reichenschwand)

zu. Die Armlehnen wurden immer breiter und setzten sich u. a. aus meist zylindrisch geformten Kissen zusammen, die fast ausschließlich mit Rosshaar gefüllt waren. Der Ohrensessel (s. Abb. 44) erscheint als die Verkörperung des Biedermeiermöbels schlechthin. In diesem Möbel, das meist mit Leder oder einem strapazierfähigen Stoff bezogen war, saß man bequem und konnte auch einmal ein *Nickerchen* machen, da der Kopf an die Backen des Sessels gelehnt werden konnte. Zum Arbeiten gab es häufig drehbare (s. Abb. 45/46) und mit kleinen Rollen versehene Schreibtischsessel (s. Abb. 43). Ihre Armlehnen waren oft etwas niedriger, damit sie nicht mit der Tischplatte kollidierten.

Bei den Farben der Polster herrschten häufig komplementäre Farbkontraste vor, die bereits im späten 18. Jahrhundert in Mode waren.[56] Dabei waren die Farben der Bezugsstoffe auch komplementär zu denjenigen der restlichen Textilien, die für die Raumausstattung Verwendung fanden.

Die meist einfarbigen Stoffbespannungen wurden von Borten und Schnüren in kontrastierenden Farben eingerahmt.[57] Aufgenähte Posamente betonten die Sitzkanten, die wiederum die einzelnen Polsterformen hervorhoben. Die Musterung der polychromen Möbelstoffe, aber auch der Wandbespannung und der Vorhänge, erfolgte in der Regel weniger in linearer, d. h. waagrechter, senkrechter oder diagonaler Ausrichtung, sondern verteilte sich gleichmäßig über die Fläche. Sie konnte relativ kleinteilig sein und dabei sogar ins Abstrakte gehen.

Die Qualität des Polsterstoffes variierte erheblich und richtete sich nach den finanziellen Möglichkeiten der Auftraggeber.[58] Neben einfarbigen oder bedruckten Baumwollgeweben wurden auch Seide oder gemusterter Samt verwendet. In Norddeutschland wurden Sitzmöbel vorzugsweise mit grünen gerippten Stoffen oder schwarzem Rosshaargewebe bezogen, einfache Stücke manchmal nur mit Wachstuch. Ebenso waren Bezüge mit Kanevas- und Petit-Point-Stickerei in Mode, die für Einzelstücke oder für ganze Garnituren im privaten Kreis entstanden. Gerne wurden die Polster mit Posamenten wie Schnüren, Kordeln, Quasten, Zierbändern oder Fransen verziert.

Die Kosten für qualitätvolle Bezugsstoffe waren hoch und übertrafen oft erheblich den Preis für das Gestell eines Sitzmöbels. Um die wertvollen Möbel vor Staub und dem Tageslicht zu schützen, wurden sie daher gerne mit Leinwandüberzügen, den Hussen, abgedeckt.[59]

Biedermeier furniture. These pieces of furniture, usually covered in leather or a durable fabric, allowed for comfortable seating and taking a nap, since one could rest one's head against the chair's wings. For working, office chairs which could often swivel (figs. 45–46) and had small castors were used (fig. 43). Their armrests were often lowered so that they did not collide with the tabletop.

The upholstery often featured complementary colour contrasts, that had already been fashionable during the late eighteenth century.[56] The colours of the covers matched those of the other textiles used for furnishing the room.

The usually monochrome covers were framed by borders and cords in contrasting colours.[57] Sewn-on trimmings highlighted the edges of the seat, which in turn highlighted the shapes of the padding. The patterns of polychrome textiles, as well as wall coverings and curtains, were usually not linear, i.e., horizontal, vertical or diagonal – but distributed evenly across the surface. At times they were relatively small, even bordering on abstract.

The quality of upholstery textiles varied considerably, according to the financial possibilities of the customer.[58] In addition to monochrome and printed cotton fabrics, silk or patterned velvet was used. In northern Germany, seating furniture was often covered in green ribbed textiles or black horsehair fabric, and simple pieces sometimes only with oilcloth. Covers with canvas or petit-point stitching were in fashion as well which were produced in private circles as single pieces or entire sets. The padding was often decorated with passementerie such as strings, cords, tassels, decorative ribbons or fringes.

The cost of quality cover textiles was high, often much higher than the price of the frame. In order to protect the valuable pieces of furniture against dust and daylight, they were often covered with canvas covers, the so-called slipcovers.[59]

45/46
Armlehndrehstuhl, um 1835 (LÖFFLER COLLECTION, Reichenschwand)

45/46
Swivel chair, around 1835 (LÖFFLER COLLECTION, Reichenschwand)

Wohnformen im ersten Drittel des 19. Jahrhunderts | Dwelling in the first third of the nineteenth century 75

Historismus und Jugendstil
Thomas Schriefers

Die Tatsache, dass den Nutzer*innen die kunstvoll verschnürten Sprungfedern im Inneren des Polsters verborgen waren, ließ das federnde Kissenwerk vielen geheimnisvoll erscheinen. Dabei erforderten Spiralfedern mehr Raum als eine Rosshaar- oder Federfüllung, weshalb dieses Polster von sich aus schon mehr Volumen besaß als frühere Sitzaufbauten. Eine Rosshaarschicht bildete oft die Unterlage für die textile Bespannung des Polsters. Das verhinderte aber nicht, dass das mit Sprungfedern ausgestattete Polster gerade im 19. Jahrhundert durch weitere Stofflagen bis zur Unkenntlichkeit verkleidet wurde. Einen Höhepunkt bildete um 1880 der sogenannte *comfortable chair*, der als eine auf seltsame Weise *zusammengehaltene Ansammlung von Kissen*[60] wahrgenommen wurde. Kunstvoll gefertigte Quasten vervollständigten die Gesamtwirkung, wobei die bis zum Boden hinabhängenden Schnürengebinde die Stuhlbeine verdeckten. Franz Sales Meyer merkt in seinem 1889 erschienenen *Handbuch der Ornamentik* an, hin und wieder würden nicht nur die Polster, sondern auch die Strukturteile mit Stoff überzogen[61]. Praktisch bedeutete dies, dass auch die Armlehnen komplett mit Polstern überzogen wurden. Hinzu kam der Einsatz von Quasten und Fransen, die schon in der Renaissance als Besatz von *Mobiliargegenständen*[62], insbesondere von Sitzmöbeln, Verwendung fanden. Polstersessel nahmen in dieser Zeit optisch an Schwere zu. Sigfried Giedion spricht kritisch von einem fast fleischigen Aussehen, das durch eine hügelförmig ausgebildete Oberfläche und eine kräftige *Capitonné*-Heftung verstärkt wurde. Gefüllt waren die rautenförmigen Polster mit Rosshaar oder den als Ersatzmaterial favorisierten Kokosfasern. Formal standen vor allem Vorbilder aus dem Rokoko Pate für verspielte Sitzkreationen wie den dreisitzigen *confident*, den gebläht wirkenden *Schmollstuhl*, das *fauteuil bébé*, die *borne*, die *petite boudeuse*, den *pouffe* und das zweisitzige *tête-à-tête* (s. Abb. 47/48), die sich nicht nur in Frankreich größter Beliebtheit erfreuten. Der im opulenten Gewand gebotene Komfort war schließlich Trumpf im Wettbewerb der Gastgeber, die um die Gunst prominenter Besucher*innen ihrer Salons buhlten.

Historicism and Jugendstil
Thomas Schriefers

Since the artfully lashed springs in the interior of the padding remained hidden from users, the springy cushions appeared mysterious to many. Since coil springs require more space than a filling made from horsehair or feather, they were more voluminous than earlier seats. A layer of horsehair was often used as a base for the textile cover of the upholstery. Nonetheless, this did not prevent that upholstery with springs were covered with further layers of fabric beyond recognition, especially during the nineteenth century. The high point was around 1880 with the so-called *comfortable chair*, perceived as a *collection of pillows stitched together*[60] in a rather curious way. Artfully crafted tassels completed the overall impression, while the cords hanging to the ground concealed the chair legs. Franz Sales Meyer mentions in his *Handbuch der Ornamentik*, published in 1889, that at times not only the upholstery but also the structural parts were covered in fabric.[61] This meant that the armrests were also entirely covered with padded textile. Additionally, tassels and fringes were used, which had already been in use during the Renaissance as adornment of 'furniture',[62] especially seating furniture. Over time upholstered armchairs became increasingly heavy in appearance. Sigfried Giedion critically mentions an almost fleshy appearance, reinforced by hill-shaped surfaces and deep buttoning. The diamond-shaped padding was filled with horsehair or coconut fibre, favoured as a substitute. In terms of form the Rococo period was a model for playful seat creations, such as the *confident* for three sitters, the seemingly distended *Schmollstuhl*, the *fauteuil bébé*, the *borne*, the *petite boudeuse*, the *pouffe* and the two-settee *tête-à-tête* (figs. 47/48), which were popular not just in France. Comfort in opulent dress was after all a trump card in the competition between hosts vying for the attention of prominent guests to their salons. Looking back, the author Hermann Missenharter tried

Rückblickend erklärt der Schriftsteller Hermann Missenharter den Erfolg entsprechender Polsterarrangements auch in Deutschland. Man habe endlich begonnen, sich ein wenig mehr um sein eigenes Wohlbehagen zu kümmern.[63] Damals schon seien auch hierzulande Salons eingerichtet worden, in denen ein Sofa mit etlichen dazugehörigen Fauteuils, die sogenannte Garnitur [...] *für den Empfang der Gäste bereitgestellt wurden: Man nannte dieses verkünstelte Möbel-Stillleben bescheiden auch die gute Stube, dieweil sie nicht nur viel vornehmer war als die übrigen Räume, in denen man tatsächlich wohnte, sondern auch immer aufgeräumt und sauber geputzt.*[64] Missenharter sah darin ein deutliches Indiz für die Neigung einer Generation, gesellschaftlich ein Doppelleben zu führen. So habe man sich tatsächlich voreinander geniert, dabei sehr höflich Distanz gewahrt, ohne zu merken, wie kränkend es für den Gast ist, wenn man ihm den Eintritt in das eigentliche Heim versperrt. Der Salon war demnach eine repräsentative Sonderzone, die so neutral und unpersönlich wie nur möglich ausgestattet wurde. Während Möbel wie das aus zwei einander zugewandten Sitzen bestehende *tête-á-tête* (s. Abb. 47/48) noch eine gewisse Intimität im Austausch zuließen, manifestierte das sogenannte *indiscret* (s. Abb. 230/231) als karussellartig angeordneter Dreisitzer die Neigung zum genierten Umgang miteinander, den Missenharter beschreibt. Schließlich war dort ein Sitzplatz für eine Anstandsdame bzw. eine dritte Person vorgesehen, was jede Intimität verhinderte.

Den Charakter des Salons bestimmte die meist teure Polstergarnitur. Ihr galt der Stolz der Wohnungsinhaber, *denen es saure Mühe war, vornehm zu tun und gute* to explain the success of such upholstery also in Germany. According to him, people had finally started to consider their own wellbeing.[63] Back then, salons were being furnished in this country, in which a sofa with several matching armchairs, the so-called set were provided for the reception of guests: *One called this artificial furniture still life modestly also the good room (Gute Stube), which was not only much more distinguished than the other rooms in which one actually lived but was also always tidy and clean.*[64] Missenharter saw this as a clear indication of the tendency of a generation to lead a double life socially. People were uneasy in front of each other but very politely kept their distance, without realising how offensive it was for the guest to be barred from entering the actual home. The salon was therefore a representative restricted zone, furnished as neutrally and impersonally as possible. While furniture such as the *tête-á-tête* (figs. 47/48), consisting of two seats facing each other, still allowed a certain intimacy in the exchange, the so-called *indiscret* (figs. 230/231), as a three-seater arranged in a carousel-like fashion, manifested the tendency towards the self-conscious communication that Missenharter describes. After all, a seat was provided for a chaperone or a third person, which prevented any intimacy.

The character of the salon was usually determined by an expensive upholstered furniture set. It was the object of pride of the apartment owner, *who took great pains to act distinguished and show good manners and who were always in fear of losing their dignified social standing if they appeared to make themselves too comfortable.*[65]

47/48
Zweisitziges Sofa *tête-à-tête*, Mainz, 1877
(LÖFFLER COLLECTION, Reichenschwand)
Two-sitter sofa *tête-à-tête*, Mainz, 1877
(LÖFFLER COLLECTION, Reichenschwand)

Manieren zu zeigen, und die dabei immer Furcht hatten, ihre würdige gesellschaftsfähige Haltung zu verlieren, wenn sie es sich behaglich[65] machten. Missenharter schrieb unnachsichtig, der Deutsche habe noch ziemlich weit ins neunzehnte Jahrhundert hinein überhaupt wenig Sinn für die Genüsse, die ein weich gepolsterter Sessel zu bieten hat, gehabt.[66]

Insgesamt wurde dieses Jahrhundert durch ein Wirrwarr gestalterischer Vorlieben in Architektur und Möbelbau bestimmt: Klassizismus, Empire, Biedermeier, Zweites Rokoko, Neogotik, Neurenaissance und Orient-Phantastereien bestanden zeitweilig nebeneinander, während die erste industrielle Revolution technische Bauformen hervorbrachte, die etwas ganz Neues ermöglichten. Die aus Glas und Eisen bestehenden Hüllen der Gewächshäuser, der Londoner Kristallpalast von 1851 und schließlich, als Krönung und Superlativ, der Pariser Eiffelturm von 1889 kündeten davon ebenso wie viele neue Metallgussbauteile, die in Neubauten integriert wurden. In den Industriebetrieben ersetzte Maschinentechnik zunehmend die Handarbeit und steigerte damit konstant den Takt der kraftverschlingenden Handarbeit. Vor diesem Hintergrund mutmaßte Fritz Spannagel 1937 in seiner Abhandlung über *Unsere Wohnmöbel* wohl zu Recht, die Sehnsucht nach vergangenen Zeiten sei eine Folge des Wunsches, sich von der neuen Zeit, deren Ausdruck in den Augen vieler immer hässlicher zu werden begann, abzuwenden.[67] Dabei hatte die rasant mechanisierte Welt im Transportwesen, in fast allen Bereichen der Produktion von Waren und längst auch im Haushalt Einzug gehalten. Selbst Staub musste man zuhause nicht mehr fürchten, seit 1859 erste Vakuum-Saugapparate für den privaten Hausbetrieb auf den Markt kamen.[68]

In Abkehr davon wandte man sich historischen Vorbildern zu, insbesondere den verspielten Rokoko-Formen aus der Zeit der Regentschaft von Ludwig XV. Das zeigt ein Blick z. B. in den *Guide du Fabricant de Meubles et du Décorateur*, der um 1860 als Verkaufskatalog die Stuhlmodelle der Firma M. Piaget bewarb (s. Abb. 49–54). Dort begegnen dem Betrachter die neu konfektionierten und gleichsam namentlich rückdatierten *fauteuils riches Louis XV*., eine *chaise longue Louis XV*., verschiedene *chauffeuses Louis XV*. und ein luxuriöser *pompadour confortable*, in Erinnerung an die berühmte Mätresse des Königs.

In Deutschland zitierte man vor allem Stilformen der Gotik und der Renaissance. Die im Folgenden abgebildeten Beispiele zeigen eine mit reichem Schnitzwerk ausgestattete *fumeuse* aus der Zeit um 1880 (s. Abb. 56–58), deren Sitz aus einem garnierten Fassonpolster besteht. Während hier als Bezug ein gemusterter Mohairvelours verwendet wurde, zeigt der von Georg Hulbe in seiner kunstgewerblichen Werkstatt in Hamburg um 1888 gebaute Stuhl (s. Abb. 59/60), wie kunstvoll auch geprägtes (punziertes und modelliertes) Leder als Bezugsmaterial eingesetzt wurde. Der Sitz dieses Stuhls ist als Flachpolster ausgeführt und nimmt eine Tendenz des Jugendstils vorweg, Sitzmöbel optisch zu verschlanken.

Dagegen vermitteln drei schwere Repräsentationssessel, wie aufwendig entsprechende Modelle (s. Abb. 61–63) mit hohen Sitz- und Rückenlehnenpolstern versehen waren. Durchweg handelt es sich dabei um geschnürte

Missenharter wrote rather harshly that, long into the nineteenth century, Germans found little sense in the pleasures offered by a softly upholstered armchair.[66]

Overall, this century was defined by a jumble of tastes in architecture and furniture design: Classicism, Empire, Biedermeier, Rococo Revival, Gothic Revival, neo-Renaissance and Orientalism existed temporarily side by side, while the Industrial Revolution developed technical forms of construction that made something entirely new possible. The glass and iron outer shells of the greenhouses, the 1851 London Crystal Palace and, finally, as crowning and superlative achievement, the Parisian Eiffel Tower from 1889 spoke of this, as did the new cast metal structures that were integrated into new buildings. In the industrial plants, machine technology increasingly replaced manual labour and thus constantly increased the pace of power-devouring manual labour. In this context, Fritz Spannagel probably rightly presumed in his essay *Unsere Wohnmöbel* that the desire for times gone by was a result of the wish to turn away from the new ages, that in the eyes of many appeared to be uglier and uglier.[67] Even so, mechanisation had entered the realm of transportation, almost all areas of the production of goods and into the household. Even dust no longer had to be feared at home, since the first vacuum cleaners for private use had been introduced in 1859.[68]

Turning away from all of this, one turned to historical models, especially the playful Rococo forms of the Louis XV regency. One can see this, for example, in the *Guide du Fabricant de Meubles et du Décorateur*, that advertised the chair models of the M. Piaget company (figs. 49–54) around 1860. Here, the reader could find the newly designed yet backdated names of pieces like *fauteuils riches Louis XV*, a *chaise longue Louis XV*, several *chauffeuses Louis XV* and a luxurious *pompadour confortable*, a nod to the famous mistress of the king.

In Germany, mostly Gothic and Renaissance styles were cited. The examples show a richly carved *fumeuse* from around 1880 (figs. 56–58) with an unsprung seat upholstery. While a patterned mohair velour covering fabric was used, the chair produced by Georg Hulbe in his arts and crafts workshop in Hamburg around 1888 (figs. 59/60) demonstrates how artfully embossed (tooled and shaped) leather was also used as a cover material. The seat of this chair was produced as a flat padding and anticipates the Jugendstil tendency to slim seating furniture in appearance.

In contrast, three heavy representative chairs convey how lavishly such models (figs. 61–63) with high seat and back rest padding were constructed. All of these are fitted with lashed spring constructions with an additional down cushion. This is true for the solid armchair from 1890 (fig. 61), which still has Historicist wood decoration, as well as for the armchair (fig. 62) offered by the Berlin furniture factory Hess & Rom, with its relief carving that already points towards the Jugendstil. While these two pieces have relatively static frames, another armchair with indicated wings (fig. 63) already has the curved form that is so typical for parts of Jugendstil furniture. Seat, back and armrests are equally luxuriously upholstered.

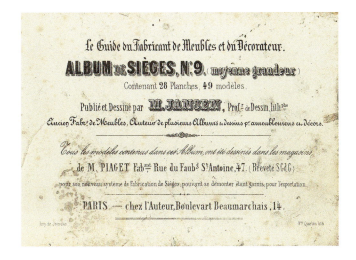

Federkonstruktionen, die oft zusätzlich über ein aufgelegtes Daunenkissen verfügen. Das gilt ebenso für den massiven, im Holzdekor noch dem Historismus zugewandten Armlehnstuhl von 1890 (s. Abb. 61) wie den 1899 von der Berliner Möbelfabrik Hess & Rom angebotenen Sessel (s. Abb. 62), der mit seiner üppigen Flachschnitzerei deutlich schon dem Jugendstil zuzurechnen ist. Während bei diesen beiden Stücken das Holzgestell noch relativ statisch wirkt, besitzt ein weiterer, mit angedeuteten Ohrenbacken versehener Armlehnstuhl (s. Abb. 63) bereits eine geschwungen-geschweifte Form, wie sie im Jugendstil für einen Teil des Mobiliars so typisch ist. Sitz, Rücken und Armlehnen verfügen hier gleichermaßen über eine luxuriöse Polsterung.

49–54
Titelblatt und fünf Seiten eines Kataloges für Stilmöbel aus dem *Guide du Fabricant de Meubles et du Décorateur* der Firma M. Piaget, Paris, um 1860 (GRASSI Museum für Angewandte Kunst Leipzig)
Cover and five pages of catalogue for period furniture from the *Guide du Fabricant de Meubles et du Décorateur* by the company M. Piaget, Paris, around 1860 (GRASSI Museum für Angewandte Kunst Leipzig)

55 (S. 80/81, p. 80/81)
Illustration von Émile Bayard zum Roman *Le Docteur Rameau* von Georges Ohnet, Paris 1889
Illustration by Émile Bayard for the novel *Le Docteur Rameau* by Georges Ohnet, Paris 1889

Historismus und Jugendstil | Historicism and Jugendstil   79

56–58
Stuhl *fumeuse* (Raucherstuhl), ca. 1870–1890
(LÖFFLER COLLECTION, Reichenschwand)

56–58
Chair *fumeuse* (smoker's chair), ca. 1870–1890
(LÖFFLER COLLECTION, Reichenschwand)

59/60
Stuhl, Georg Hulbe (Entwurf), Kunstgewerbliche Werkstatt Georg Hulbe, Hamburg (Herstellung), um 1888 (LÖFFLER COLLECTION, Reichenschwand)

59/60
Chair, Georg Hulbe (design), Kunstgewerbliche Werkstatt Georg Hulbe, Hamburg (production), around 1888 (LÖFFLER COLLECTION, Reichenschwand)

61
Armlehnstuhl, um 1890 (LÖFFLER COLLECTION, Reichenschwand)

61
Armchair, around 1890 (LÖFFLER COLLECTION, Reichenschwand)

84 Historismus und Jugendstil | Historicism and Jugendstil

62
Armlehnstuhl, Möbelfabrik Hess & Rom, Berlin (Entwurf und Herstellung), 1899 (LÖFFLER COLLECTION, Reichenschwand)

62
Armchair, Möbelfabrik Hess & Rom, Berlin (design and production), 1899 (LÖFFLER COLLECTION, Reichenschwand)

Historismus und Jugendstil l Historicism and Jugendstil **85**

63
Armlehnstuhl, um 1900 (LÖFFLER COLLECTION, Reichenschwand)

63
Armchair, around 1900 (LÖFFLER COLLECTION, Reichenschwand)

Der Philosoph und Kulturkritiker Walter Benjamin charakterisierte das 19. Jahrhundert als wohnsüchtig und traf damit den Kern der Befindlichkeiten einer Gesellschaft, die die Wohnung als Futteral begriff, *in das sich die Menschen mit allem Zubehör so tief einbetteten, dass man ans Innere eines Zirkelkastens denken könnte, wo das Instrument mit allen seinen Ersatzteilen in tiefe, meist violette Sammethöhlen gebettet, daliegt.*[69] Die dabei sich zuweilen ins Maßlose steigernde Kultivierung des Ausstattungskultes rief in den 1890er Jahren Kritiker wie den Architekten Adolf Loos auf den Plan, der dies als Ausdruck blinder Dekorationswut und stilistischer Beliebigkeit empfand. Von Werkstofffälschung, Surrogat und einer um sich greifenden Manie des Nachgemachten war die Rede. Loos sprach in diesem Zusammenhang sogar vom *Ornament als Verbrechen*[70]. Ein Gedanke, den man später gerne aufnahm, um die überbordende Wohnungseinrichtung der Gründerzeit insgesamt zu verurteilen.

In Belgien formierte sich in den 1890er Jahren der Widerstand gegen den Historismus und alle Formen rückwärtsgewandter Kunstproduktion. Dabei wurde die Zeitschrift *L'Art Moderne* zum Sprachrohr einer Bewegung, die jede stilistische Bevormundung ablehnte und zum künstlerischen Neudenken aufrief. Architekten wie Henry van de Velde, Victor Horta und Paul Hankar gaben dem später sogenannten Jugendstil ein unverwechselbares Gesicht und erregten mit ihren Entwürfen international großes Aufsehen. Als prominenter Kritiker des *Wiener Tageblatts* schrieb der Schriftsteller Ludwig Hevesi begeistert über ein Horta-Bauwerk, es weise nicht den leisesten Anklang an irgendeinen der historischen Stile auf, vielmehr sei es einfach, logisch und neu konzipiert.[71] In Wien fiel dies auf fruchtbaren Boden. Adolf Loos, Josef Hoffmann und Otto Wagner setzten dort unverwechselbare Zeichen für den Aufbruch. Konsequent schrieb Loos 1898 über Einrichtungsgegenstände und insbesondere Stühle, sie müssten vor allem praktisch sein.[72] Gegen jegliche Art historisierender Raumausstatter gerichtet, erklärte er, die Produktion praktischer Sessel würde den Menschen die Möglichkeit bieten, sich ohne Hilfe des Dekorateurs vollkommen einzurichten. Damit verband Loos den Wunsch, Tapezierer, Architekten, Maler, Bildhauer, Dekorateure und so weiter sollten sich, sobald es sich um Wohnräume und nicht um Prunkräume handelt, darauf beschränken, vollkommene, praktische Möbel in den Handel zu bringen.[73] Bislang sei man diesbezüglich ja auf den englischen Import angewiesen, ergänzt Loos mit Verweis auf die Möbel der *Arts-and-Crafts*-Bewegung, allen voran die von William Morris. Dieser war ein führender Vertreter der englischen Reformbewegung, die in der zweiten Hälfte des 19. Jahrhunderts angetreten war, das künstlerische Handwerk zu stärken.

Die Pariser Weltausstellung von 1900 gilt auch wegen ihrer umfangreichen Dokumentation als ein zuverlässiger Gradmesser für den damaligen Stand der Dinge auf fast allen Gebieten menschlichen Schaffens, so auch im Bereich der Innenraumgestaltung. Dabei zeigte sich die riesige Ausstellungsstadt, die im Zentrum der französischen Hauptstand entlang der Ufer viele Millionen Besucher*innen anzog, weitgehend historischen Bauformen verpflichtet. Neue Tendenzen fanden sich, neben wenigen eher privaten Präsentationen, eher in einzelnen Abteilungen nationaler Pavillons, etwa Deutschlands, wo u. a. auch die stilbildende Künstlerkolonie Mathildenhöhe Darmstadt Einrichtungsgegenstände präsentierte. Damit kündigte sich vorsichtig ein Wandel der Anschauungen an, der den Markt bald

The philosopher and cultural critic Walter Benjamin characterised the nineteenth century as addicted to dwelling and thus struck at the heart of the sensibilities of a society that understood their home as a receptacle *in which people with all their belongings could embed themselves so deeply that they resembled the interiors of a compass case, in which the instrument with all its accessories lies in deep, usually violet velvet hollows.*[69] The cultivation of an interior design obsession, which at times bordered on excess, alerted its critics in the 1890s, among them the architect Adolf Loos, who understood this as an expression of blind decorative mania and stylistic arbitrariness. There was talk of counterfeit materials, surrogates and a rampant mania for imitation. In this context, Loos even spoke of *Ornament as Crime*,[70] an idea that was later taken up to condemn the exuberant furnishings of the Wilhelminian period as a whole.

In the 1890s, resistance to Historicism and all other forms of backward-looking artistic production emerged in Belgium. The magazine *L'Art Moderne* became the mouthpiece of a movement that rejected any kind of stylistic paternalism and advocated artistic renewal. Architects such as Henry van de Velde, Victor Horta and Paul Hankar gave the distinctive appearance of the later so-called Jugendstil an unmistakable face and caused a great stir internationally with their designs. As a prominent critic of the *Wiener Tageblatt*, the writer Ludwig Hevesi wrote enthusiastically about a Horta building, stating that no historical stylistic references could be found; on the contrary, the building appeared to be simple, logical and newly conceived.[71] In Vienna, this fell on fertile ground, and Adolf Loos, Josef Hoffmann and Otto Wagner set the unmistakeable signs for a fresh start. In consequence, Loos wrote in 1898 that furnishing objects, especially chairs, had to be practical above all.[72] Writing against any kind of historicising interior designer, he declared that the production of practical armchairs would allow people to set up their spaces without any help from a decorator. Loos connected this to the wish that upholsterers, architects, painters, sculptors, decorators and so forth should limit themselves, as long as living rooms and not representative rooms were concerned, to producing perfect, practical pieces of furniture for the market.[73] For now, one had to make do with English imports, Loos added, in reference to the furniture of the *Arts and Crafts* movement, especially those by William Morris. He was a leading representative of the English reform movement that had emerged in the second half of the nineteenth century to strengthen artistic craftsmanship.

The Paris World's Exhibition from 1900 is considered to be, not least because of its extensive documentation, a reliable indicator of the state of affairs in almost all field of human endeavour at the time, including interior design. The gigantic exhibition city, which attracted millions of visitors to the borders of the river at the centre of the French capital, was largely dedicated to Historicising ways of building. New trends could rather be found, in addition to more private presentations, in several sections of the national pavilions, such as the German one, where the important artist colony Mathildenhöhe Darmstadt, among others, presented

64/65 (S. 90/91)
Sofa, um 1900 (Torsten Otto, Markkleeberg)

64/65 (p. 90/91)
Sofa, around 1900 (Torsten Otto, Markkleeberg)

nachhaltig verändern sollte. Das Beispiel der Firma Friedrich Otto Schmidt als einem bedeutenden Wiener Raumausstatter zeigt deutlich, wie ein Unternehmen, das mit großem Erfolg Einrichtungen im Stil des Historismus verkauft hatte, sich 1900 zu diversifizieren begann. In seinem Unternehmensporträt beschreibt Stefan Üner, wie sich die Firma einerseits auf die detailgetreue Wiedergabe alter Vorbilder konzentrierte, andererseits durch die Mitwirkung an den Reformideen des Museums für Kunst und Industrie und dem Einfluss von Adolf Loos und seinen Gestaltungskonzepten begann, die neuen Ideen zu verbreiten.[74] Historisierende Polstermöbel blieben zwar im Angebot, doch fanden sie sich nun verstärkt im Wettbewerb mit Gegenständen, die dem Anspruch folgten, in einer neuen Zeit adäquat neue Gegenstände auf den Markt zu bringen.

Unsere Ausstellung bildet den damals sich abzeichnenden Wandel formaler Vorlieben ab und macht deutlich, wie sich dabei der Aufbau hoher Festpolster durch neue Technologien veränderte bzw. eine Vorliebe für das elegant anmutende, leichtere Flachpolster entstand. Traditioneller zeigt sich hier noch ein Sofa der Zeit um 1900, das mit einem Mohairvelours bezogen und in Manier des Historismus noch mit Kordeln und Quasten ausgestattet ist (s. Abb. 64/65). An den Füßen integrierte Metallrollen erlauben es, das schwere, als geschnürte Federkonstruktion konzipierte Möbel zu versetzen, ohne es anheben zu müssen. Optisch erinnert das im Originalzustand sich präsentierende Exponat noch an die Gestaltwelt vor 1900, wobei die Ausbildung der gepolsterten Rückenlehne deutlich Jugendstilmerkmale trägt.

Den Bruch mit den von schweren Polstern überwölbten Sitzmöbeln des Historismus zeigen sehr deutlich die Stuhlmodelle von Henry van de Velde, Louis Majorelle, Georges de Feure und Josef Hoffmann. Im Vergleich zu früheren Modellen wirken sie filigran und schlank, nicht zuletzt auch wegen ihrer flachen Sitzpolster. Das gilt z. B. für den um 1902 von Henry van de Velde entworfenen Stuhl (s. Abb. 66), der ein Flachpolster besitzt, das nicht sichtbar ist, da es komplett zwischen den schlanken Zargen des Sitzrahmens verschwindet. Das Textile reduziert sich auf das verwendete Atlas-Gewebe, das, angeraut, den Eindruck vermittelt, als handele es sich um einen Velours. Man wird dadurch nicht von der im Entwurf angelegten Linie des Stuhls abgelenkt. Ähnlich flach zeigt sich das Polster bei dem von Georges de Feure 1900 gestalteten Mahagoni-Stuhl (s. Abb. 70/71), bei dem zusätzlich zwei flache Polstereinsätze als Spiegelflächen in die durch Schnitzwerk durchbrochene Rückenlehne eingepasst wurden. Der zart gemusterte Stoff korrespondiert hier mit den floralen Motiven des Holzrahmens und verschmilzt damit zu einer Einheit, die durch den Materialwechsel von Holz zu Textil in ihrer plastischen Wirkung noch verstärkt wird. Dagegen offenbart sich der um 1900 von Louis Majorelle in Nancy entworfene Hochlehner (s. Abb. 67–69) trotz seines optisch flachen Polsters bei genauerem Hinsehen als stärker gepolsterter Stuhl, was ein Blick unter den Sitz bestätigt. Der Wunsch nach Sitzkomfort führte hier zu einer Lösung, bei der der Polsteraufbau so flach wie möglich gehalten wurde, um formal dem Zeitgeschmack zu entsprechen. Gleichzeitig wird die künstlerische Marketeriearbeit in der Rückenlehne betont.

Einen Schritt weiter ging Josef Hoffmann, der seinen um 1906 bei Vienna Pancota in Rumänien produzierten Bugholzstuhl (s. Abb. 72–76) im Sitz mit einer geschnürten

interior design objects. These were the harbingers of a change of perception that would soon have a lasting impact on the market. The example of the Friedrich Otto Schmidt company, an important Viennese room decorator, exemplifies how a company that had achieved great success selling furniture in the Historicist style began to diversify around 1900. In a portrait of the company, Stefan Üner describes how, on the one hand, it concentrated on the faithful reproduction of old models and, on the other, started to spread the new ideas by taking part in the reform ideas of the Museum für Kunst und Industrie (Museum of Art and Industry) and under the influence of Adolf Loos and his design concepts.[74] Historicising upholstered furniture was still offered, but increasingly stood in competition with objects that followed the demand to adequately bring new objects to the market in a new era.

Our exhibition depicts the change in formal preferences that arose at that time and demonstrates how the construction of high upholstery changed through the use of new technology and how a tendency towards seemingly elegant, lighter flat cushioning emerged. A sofa from around 1900 presents itself more traditionally, with a mohair velour covering and fitted with cords and tassels in the Historicism style (fig 64/65). Metal castors integrated into the feet made it possible to move the heavy coil-sprung furniture around. Visually, the object, which is presented in its original state, is reminiscent of the design world before 1900, while the forms of the upholstered backrest clearly indicate Jugendstil characteristics.

The break with the Historicist seating furniture covered in heavy upholstery becomes very evident in the chair models by Henry van de Velde, Louis Majorelle, Georges de Feure and Josef Hoffmann. In comparison with earlier models, they seem delicate and slender, not least because of their flat seat upholstery. This is true, among others, for the chair (fig. 66) designed around 1902 by Henry van de Velde, with a flat upholstery that disappears between the slender edges of the seat frame. The fabric is reduced to an atlas textile, which, roughened, gives the impression of velour. This does not distract from the line of the chair design. Equally flat is the upholstery of a mahogany chair designed by Georges de Feure in 1900 (figs. 70/71) with two additional mirroring flat upholstery inserts fitted into the backrest and are broken up by the carving. Here, the finely patterned fabric corresponds with the floral motifs of the wooden frame and thus forms a unit that is reinforced in its sculptural effect by the material change from wood to textile. In contrast, the chair with a high backrest designed by Louis Majorelle around 1900 in Nancy (figs. 67–69), despite the flat appearance of its upholstery, reveals itself on closer inspection to be a more heavily upholstered chair, which is confirmed by taking a look underneath. The desire for seating comfort led to a solution in which the upholstery was kept as flat as possible in order to keep up with contemporary taste. At the same time, the artistic marquetry work of the backrest is emphasised.

Josef Hoffmann went even further when he fitted a bentwood chair (figs. 72–76), produced around 1906

Historismus und Jugendstil | Historicism and Jugendstil 91

Federkonstruktion versah, die er aber so flach zu halten verstand, dass sie hinter dem gebogenen Sitzrahmen verborgen bleibt. Erst der Blick von unten in die offene Konstruktion zeigt die von 3 x 3 Gurten gehaltene Taillenfederung, die zur leichten Wölbung der Sitzoberfläche beiträgt. In der Rückenlehne findet hingegen ein aufgelegtes und mit Werg gefülltes Flachpolster Anwendung. Insgesamt vermittelt Hoffmanns Armlehnstuhl das Bild eines leichten Sessels, der wegen seiner gebogenen Form und der durchlaufenden Arm- und Rückenlehne die Nutzer*innen umfängt, gleichsam das Sitzen abfedert und damit trotz der schlanken Erscheinung des Polsters mehr Sitzkomfort als erwartet bietet.

Dass auch im Jugendstil kräftige Hochpolster eingesetzt wurden, veranschaulichen hier stellvertretend drei Sessel, zwei von Richard Riemerschmid (s. Abb. 77/78 u. 79/80) und einer von Peter Behrens (s. Abb. 81/82). Die beiden erstgenannten Polstersessel wurden in den 1898 von Karl Schmidt gegründeten Dresdner Werkstätten für Handwerkskunst gefertigt. Sie zeigen zwei unterschiedliche Ansätze: Während Riemerschmid das um 1903 von ihm entworfene Modell (s. Abb. 77/78) fast komplett mit Bezugsstoff überzogen hatte, verzichtete er bei seinem Armlehnstuhl von 1904 (s. Abb. 79/80) darauf, um stattdessen den Schwung des Mahagoni-Holzrahmens auf die Ausformung des hohen Polsters zu übertragen. Auch technisch unterscheiden sich die beiden Modelle: Der kantigere Entwurf ist komplett, d. h. im Sitz, im Rücken und über die Armlehnen mit einer traditionell geschnürten Federkonstruktion ausgestattet. Zwar erweist sich der mit einer hohen Lehne ausgestattete Sessel von 1904 in Sitz- und Rückenlehne auch als geschnürte Federkonstruktion, doch finden sich im Sitz gekreuzte Stahlbänder (s. Abb. 79), die die bis dahin üblicherweise eingesetzten Leinengurte als Polstergrund ersetzen. Darin äußert sich die damals einsetzende Experimentierfreude der Entwerfer, aber auch der Anspruch, die Fertigung von Möbeln in Teilen auch maschinell durchführen zu können. Riemerschmid war einer der engagierten Befürworter einer anzustrebenden Maschinenfertigung, was sich u. a. in seinem Maschinenmöbel-Programm manifestieren sollte, das er 1906 auf der *3. Deutschen Kunstgewerbe-Ausstellung* in Dresden präsentierte. Entgegen der Tendenz formaler Vereinfachung und der damit einhergehenden Reduzierung von Schmuckformen entwarf Peter Behrens um 1904 einen luxuriösen Polstersessel (s. Abb. 81/82), dessen Form den Schwung einer stilisierten Lotusblüte aufnimmt. Mit dem dunkel gebeizten Äußeren des Mahagonigestells kontrastiert im Inneren eine flächendeckende Polsterung, die im Sitz- und Lehnenbereich über eine geschnürte Federkonstruktion verfügt. Ein zusätzlich aufgelegtes hohes Daunenkissen vervollständigt das Erscheinungsbild eines Polstersessels, in den man beim Platznehmen einsinkt, so wie es üblicherweise bei Klubsesseln erwartet wird. Die Opulenz des Gesamteindrucks wird dabei durch die starke Farbigkeit des verwendeten Bezugsstoffes verstärkt, in den zusätzlich echte Silberfäden eingewebt wurden.

Die damit verbundene Abkehr von traditionellen Formen forderte aber heftige Reaktionen der traditionellen Möbelindustrie heraus, deren Vertreter den von ihnen so bezeichneten *Hypermodernen*[75] vorwarfen, die bestätigte Vollkommenheit der Vorbilder früherer Stilepochen mutwillig auszuschließen. Entsprechend kampflustig editierte etwa die Erfurter Firma Ziegenhorn & Junker mehrere Bücher, in denen sie für selbst gefertigte historische Möbelformen

by Vienna Pancota in Romania, with a lashed spring construction which he kept so flat that it remained invisible behind the curved seat frame. By looking at the open construction from below, one can see the coil springs held in place by 3 x 3 strips of webbing, that add to the slightly domed seating surface. The backrest is made of an upholstery stuffed with tow. Overall, Hoffmann's armchair conveys the image of a lightweight chair which embraces the sitter with its curved shape and continuous arm- and backrest yet at the same time cushions the seat and, in this way, offers more seating comfort than expected, despite the upholstery's slender appearance.

Three armchairs, two by Richard Riemerschmid (figs. 77/78 and 79/80) and one by Peter Behrens (figs. 81/82), demonstrate that during Jugendstil sturdy upholstery was also in use. The two former upholstered armchairs were produced in the Dresden Werkstätten für Handwerkskunst, founded by Karl Schmidt in 1898. They show two entirely different approaches: while Riemerschmid covered his 1903 model (figs. 77/78) almost completely in fabric, he abandoned this approach in his 1904 model (figs. 79/80), instead transferring the curvature of the mahogany frame to the shape of the high upholstery. The two models also differ in technical terms: the more angular design is entirely – meaning seat, back and armrests – fitted with a traditional lashed spring construction. The 1904 chair with a high backrest is also fitted with lashed springs in the seat and backrest; however, crossed steel strips (fig. 79) have replaced the linen strips usually used for the webbing. This reflects the newly found enthusiasm for experimentation of the designers, as well as the requirement to be able to mechanically produce furniture parts. Riemerschmid was a committed advocate of mechanical production, which became evident, among others, in his machine furniture programme that he presented in 1906 at the *3. Deutsche Kunstgewerbe-Ausstellung* in Dresden. In contrast to the tendency towards formal simplification and the corresponding reduction of decorative forms, Peter Behrens designed a luxurious upholstered armchair (figs. 81/82) around 1904, whose shape takes up the curves of a stylised lotus blossom. The dark-stained mahogany frame of the outside contrasts with an entirely upholstered inside fitted with lashed springs in the seat and backrest areas. An additional high down pillow completes the appearance of an upholstered armchair into which one sinks when seated, as is usually expected of club chairs. The opulence of the overall impression is reinforced by the covering fabric, into which additional silver threads have been woven.

The corresponding departure from traditional forms also produced fierce reactions by the more traditionalist furniture industry, whose representatives accused those they referred to as *hypermoderns*[75] to intentionally excluding the confirmed perfection of models from earlier style epochs. Correspondingly combatively, the Erfurt-based Ziegenhorn & Junker company published several books in which they advertised their own historical furniture forms and advised that these would also fit perfectly into modern living spaces. The range includes, among others, a heavy upholstered armchair

warb und bekundete, diese würden auch in modernen Wohnräumen bestens zur Geltung kommen. Der Bogen spannt sich hier u. a. vom schweren Polstersessel im Stil Louis-quinze Nussbaum antikisiert, über ein Modell in *Prager Barock* bis zum Armlehnstuhl *im aparten Adam-Stil*.[76] Historischen Vorbildern nachempfundene Möbel fanden nach wie vor ihren Absatz, da sich mit ihnen Vorstellungen verbürgter Exklusivität und gediegene Wohnlichkeit verbanden. Zudem lieferten Firmen wie Ziegenhorn & Junker zum historischen Möbel auch die dazugehörige Geschichte, was sich schon damals als zugkräftige Werbemaßnahme erwies. Dass in diesem Marktsegment auch das traditionelle Polsterwesen weiter gepflegt wurde, liegt angesichts des Anspruchs zumindest jener Luxusmöbel-Anbieter auf der Hand.

in Louis XV antique-style walnut, a model in *Prague Baroque* and an armchair in *attractive Adam style*.[76] Furniture after historical models still found their market, since they were related to ideas of proven exclusivity and elegant homeliness. In addition, companies like Ziegenhorn & Junker provided their Historicising furniture with a corresponding narrative, which even back then proved to be an effective advertisement. That in this market segment traditional upholstery was still in fashion is evident in light of the aspirations of these luxury furniture suppliers.

66
Stuhl, Henry van de Velde (Entwurf), Hoftischlerei Fritz Scheidemantel, Weimar (Herstellung), 1903 (Dauerleihgabe für das GRASSI Museum für Angewandte Kunst Leipzig aus der Sammlung Pese, Nürnberg, seit 2020. Zur Schenkung vorgesehen.)

66
Chair, Henry van de Velde (design), Hoftischlerei Fritz Scheidemantel, Weimar (production), 1903 (On permanent loan to the GRASSI Museum für Angewandte Kunst Leipzig from the Pese Collection, Nuremberg, since 2020. Intended for donation.)

67–69
Stuhl, Louis Majorelle (Entwurf), Werkstatt Louis Majorelle, Nancy (Herstellung), um 1900 (LÖFFLER COLLECTION, Reichenschwand)

67–69
Chair, Louis Majorelle (design), workshop Louis Majorelle, Nancy (production), around 1900 (LÖFFLER COLLECTION, Reichenschwand)

70/71
Stuhl, Georges de Feure (Entwurf), um 1900 (LÖFFLER COLLECTION, Reichenschwand)

70/71
Chair, Georges de Feure (design), around 1900 (LÖFFLER COLLECTION, Reichenschwand)

Historismus und Jugendstil l Historicism and Jugendstil

72–76
Armlehnstuhl, Josef Hoffmann (Entwurf), Vienna Pancota, Pancota (Herstellung), um 1906 (LÖFFLER COLLECTION, Reichenschwand)

72–76
Armchair, Josef Hoffmann (design), Vienna Pancota, Pancota (production), around 1906 (LÖFFLER COLLECTION, Reichenschwand)

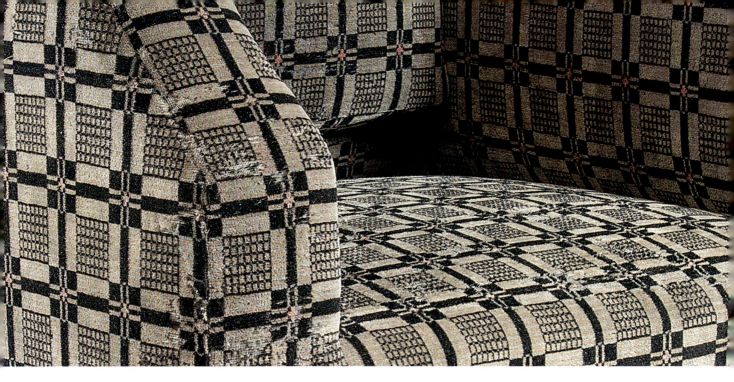

77/78
Armlehnsessel, Richard Riemerschmid (Entwurf), Dresdner
Werkstätten für Handwerkskunst (Herstellung), um 1903
(LÖFFLER COLLECTION, Reichenschwand)

77/78
Armchair, Richard Riemerschmid (design), Dresdner
Werkstätten für Handwerkskunst (production), around 1903
(LÖFFLER COLLECTION, Reichenschwand)

79/80
Armlehnsessel, Richard Riemerschmid (Entwurf), Dresdner Werkstätten für Handwerkskunst (Herstellung), 1904 (LÖFFLER COLLECTION, Reichenschwand)

79/80
Armchair, Richard Riemerschmid (design), Dresdner Werkstätten für Handwerkskunst (production), 1904 (LÖFFLER COLLECTION, Reichenschwand)

Historismus und Jugendstil | Historicism and Jugendstil

81/82
Armlehnsessel, Peter Behrens (Entwurf), vermutlich Keller & Reiner, Berlin (Herstellung), um 1910 (LÖFFLER COLLECTION, Reichenschwand)

81/82
Armchair, Peter Behrens (design), presumably Keller & Reiner, Berlin (production), around 1910 (LÖFFLER COLLECTION, Reichenschwand)

Historismus und Jugendstil | Historicism and Jugendstil

Andere Ansprüche – Neue Ideen
Thomas Schriefers

Während die eine Seite vehement für den Wert traditioneller Stilformen warb, wollte eine neue Generation von Architekten nach 1918 all das ersetzen, was sich in den vergangenen Jahrzehnten in den Wohnungen angesammelt hatte. Mit einem verächtlichen Blick zurück empfanden sie etwa eine neogotische Anrichte als Kitsch, dem entschieden der Kampf ansagt wurde. Jupp Ernst schrieb rückblickend mit bitterbösem Unterton, die ganze falsche Pracht (des Historismus) habe nur das Gute an sich gehabt, dass sie, um geschont zu werden, nicht benutzt werden durfte.[77] Der Feind sei *ein unsterblicher Ritter, dessen mittelalterlicher Geist allerorten herumspukt – ein richtiges Gespenst, das sich der Wohnungen bemächtigt hat*, schrieb Adolf Behne in seinem Buch *Neues Wohnen – Neues Bauen* (s. Abb. 85).[78] Im Kreis der Erneuerer war man sich jedenfalls einig, in Zeiten des technischen Fortschritts neue Standards durchsetzen zu wollen, die unter dem Postulat der Sachlichkeit alles Entbehrliche aus den Wohnungen verbannen sollten. In erster Linie handelte es sich dabei um die schweren Stoffe kunstvoll arrangierter *lambrequins* als Zierblenden für Fenster, dichte Samt-Vorhänge, dekorativ drapierte Raumteiler, entsprechende Auflagen auf Tischen und Polsterbezüge, kurz gesagt alles, was man mit dem Schlagwort Plüsch versehen konnte. Damit waren aus Sicht der Erneuerer natürlich auch die schweren mit Plüschstoffen bezogenen Polstersessel passé. Der überwiegende Teil der Menschen lebte in den 1920er Jahren aber nach wie vor im Mobiliar früherer Generationen, da, zumindest in Deutschland, im Ersten Weltkrieg kaum Schaden an Privateigentum entstanden war und neue Gegenstände für die meisten unerschwinglich waren. So waren Anschaffungskosten für neue Dinge vermeidbar. Diese wurden auch als unnötig erachtet, da man, gerade in Zeiten politischer und ökonomischer Unsicherheit, das ererbte Stück als Erinnerung schätzte. Genau das aber kritisierte der Architekt Bruno Taut, der in seiner Programmschritt über die neue Wohnung resigniert erklärte: *Solange die Menschen ihren Sinn auch innerhalb der bestehenden Wohnungen nicht ändern, wird das neue Bauen keinen Schritt weiter führen*.[79] Darauf bezog

Different demands – New ideas
Thomas Schriefers

While one side vehemently advocated the value of traditional styles, a new generation of architects set out after 1918 to replace everything that had accumulated inside apartments over the past decades. With a sneery look back they considered, among others, a Gothic Reviewal buffet to be kitsch that had to be fought by all means necessary. Jupp Ernst wrote full of scorn that the only good thing the entire false splendour (of Historicism) had brought was that it was never used in order to stay protected.[77] According to Adolf Behne in his book *Neues Wohnen – Neues Bauen* (fig. 85), the enemy was *an immortal knight, whose medieval ghost haunted everything – a real spectre that had taken over apartments*.[78] In the circle of reformers, one agreed that in times of technical advancements new standards had to be set which, under the postulate of objectivity, were to banish anything dispensable from the apartments. First and foremost, this meant the heavy fabrics of artfully arranged *lambrequins* as decorative screens for windows, dense velvet curtains, decoratively draped room dividers, corresponding table runners and upholstery covers – in short, everything that could be given the attribute 'plush'. From the point of view of the innovators, this of course also meant that heavy upholstered chairs covered with plush fabrics were a thing of the past.

During the 1920s, the majority of people continued to live with the furniture of older generations, since, at least in Germany, World War One had done little damage to private property and new items were unaffordable for most. In this way, costs for buying new things could be avoided. These were also considered unnecessary since, in times of political and economic uncertainty, heirlooms were valued as mementos. It was just this what architect Bruno Taut criticised when he declared gloomily in his treatise on

sich der Regierungsbaumeister a. D. Otto Schmidt in einem Wohnratgeber, der in Zeiten der Weltwirtschaftskrise 1930 für die entschiedene Erneuerung der heimischen Wohnwelten eintrat (s. Abb. 86).[80] Sein Titel war Programm: *Der alten Wohnung ein neues Gesicht geben*. Dies sollte Schule machen. Entsprechend anschaulich vermittelte der Autor, wie man es macht und was es kostet. Vorausgesetzt, der Leser war bereit, sich vom überkommenen Mobiliar zu trennen. Das zu erzielende Resultat vermittelte der erste Blick auf das Titelblatt des Buches (Ausschnitt, s. Abb. 83), auf dem zwei Wohnwelten einander gegenüberstanden: ein eher düster wirkender Salon auf der einen und ein farbiger, freundlich anmutender und lichter Raum auf der anderen Seite. Es gehe nicht darum, der Wohnung ein neues Gewand überzustreifen, sondern ihr ein neues Gesicht zu geben und sie neu zu denken.[81] Befreit von allen gesundheitsschädlichen Staubfängern und Bakterienbrutstätten[82] sollte sich das Zuhause in einen Ort der Gesundheit und des Wohlbefindens verwandeln. Den Weg dorthin beschrieb Schmidt in mehreren Schritten. Ersten Veränderungen sollten demnach weitergehende Eingriffe folgen, bevor die Wohnung schließlich als gesundete Umgebung des Menschen das Gefühl von Wohlbefinden verbreitet. Als entbehrlich galten, neben allein nur dekorativen Schaustücken, die Möbelgarnitur und vor allem das ausladende Polstersofa.[83] Diverse Ratgeber zeigten, wie man auch mit geringem Budget Hand anlegen konnte, um ein vorhandenes Möbelstück von allem zu befreien, was als Staubfänger dienen konnte. Das betraf vor allem die schweren Stoffe, ob sie den Tisch bekleideten, das Fenster einrahmten oder als Bezugsstoffe der Polstermöbel dienten.[84] Gleichzeitig forcierte man den Wechsel des Polsterinnenlebens: So warb die im thüringischen Ohrdruf angesiedelte Firma A. Knippenberg für ihre Patent-Draht-Polster, die als Ersatz für die alten Spiralfeder-Polster empfohlen wurden. In ihrer Annonce hieß es: *Greift nur hinein in Eure alten staubfangenden Polstermöbel und Gurtenmatratzen und sehet dagegen Knippenbergs*

new dwellings, *As long as people do not change their attitude inside existing homes, the new way of building will not lead one step ahead.*[79] The retired government architect Otto Schmidt referenced this in his guidebook on living, which during the Great Depression advocated for the decisive renewal of home living spaces (fig. 86).[80] The title was programme: *Der alten Wohnung ein neues Gesicht geben* (Giving the Old Apartment a New Face). This caught on. The author conveys vividly how to do just that and how much it would cost. On the condition that the reader was willing to part with their old furniture. The aim is illustrated on the title page (detail, fig. 83), where two living worlds stand in contrast: a rather gloomy salon on one side and another colourful, friendly and light room on the other. According to the brochure, the aim was not to simply hand the apartment metaphorical new clothes but to give it a new face and to rethink it.[81] Freed of any unhealthy dust catchers and bacteria hotbeds[82] the new home was to be transformed into a space of health and well-being. Schmidt describes the road ahead in several steps. First adjustments were to be followed by more far-reaching changes, until the flat had turned into a healthy environment and a source of well-being. Considered dispensable were, in addition to decorative show pieces, the furniture set and especially the large upholstered sofa.[83] Various guidebooks demonstrated how, even on a small budget, one could rid an existing piece of furniture of everything that could serve as a dust trap. This was the case for heavy fabrics, whether they clothed the table, framed the window, or were used as cover fabrics for upholstered furniture.[84] At the same time, a change of the upholstery interior was advocated:

83 (S. 102, p. 102)
Ausschnitt aus dem Titel des Buches von Otto Schmidt, *Der alten Wohnung ein neues Gesicht*, Stuttgart 1930
Detail of the cover of the book by Otto Schmidt, *Der alten Wohnung ein neues Gesicht*, Stuttgart 1930

84
Werbeanzeige der Firma von A. Knippenberg, Ohrdruf in Thüringen
Advertisement of the company by A. Knippenberg, Ohrdruf in Thuringia

Patent-Matratzen und Polster-Möbel mit Drahtpolster. Eine Illustration (s. Abb. 84) zeigt im Gegenüber das alte und das neue System: Wie das alte Polster nur unter starker Staubwolkenentwicklung zu reinigen ist, während sich das neue Gurtsystem scheinbar emissionslos säubern läßt.

Das moderne Haus solle das Leben erleichtern, forderte Sigfried Giedion in seiner 1929 erschienenen Programmschrift *Befreites Wohnen* (s. Abb. 87) und erklärte, dafür müsse man sich aber zunächst *vom Haus mit dem Ewigkeitswert … vom Haus mit den teuren Mieten, vom Haus mit den dicken Mauern … vom Haus, das uns durch seinen Unterhalt versklavt und vom Haus, das die Arbeitskraft der Frau verschlingt, trennen*.[85] Stattdessen sollte sich *das neue Haus mit Gebrauchswert […] in seiner ganzen Struktur im Gleichklang mit einem durch Sport, Gymnastik, sinngemäße Lebensweise befreiten Körpergefühl befinden: leicht, licht, beweglich*.[86] Folgt man dieser Forderung, dann verbieten sich schwer zu verrückende Möbelstücke, auch entsprechende Polstersessel. Hier greift die Reklame der Berliner Standard-Möbel-Produktion Lengyel & Co. (s. Abb. 88), die 1928 in einer Ausgabe der Zeitschrift *bauhaus*[87] für Breuer-Metallmöbel warb. Denn dort hieß es, die stoffbespannten Stahlrohrmöbel hätten die Bequemlichkeit von guten Polstermöbeln ohne aber deren Gewicht, Preis, Unhandlichkeit und unhygienische Beschaffenheit.[88]

Der Hersteller von Stahlrohr-Mobiliar argumentierte im Sinne der von progressiven Kreisen propagierten *Idee einer modernen hygienischen und sozialen Kultur*[89], für die auch auf großen Ausstellungen wie der 1926 in Düsseldorf veranstalteten *Ausstellung für Gesundheitspflege, soziale Fürsorge und Leibesübungen (GeSoLei)* geworben wurde. Eine hygienisch einwandfreie Umgebung sowohl im öffentlichen Bereich wie im privaten Zuhause, gesunde Ernährung und Sport galten als Grundvoraussetzung für ein zunehmend mobiles Leben. Hatte dort ein konventionelles Polstermöbel noch Platz? Puristen beantworteten diese Frage mit einem klaren Nein und erweiterten die Diskussion um das Für und Wider des Holzmöbels: *Möbel aus Holz oder Metall?*[90] titelte etwa Gustav Hassenpflugs Plädoyer für die Bevorzugung von Metallwerkstoffen. Dabei zeigt das Werk des Bauhaus-Absol-

the company A. Knippenberg, based in Ohrdruf, Thuringia, advertised their patented wire padding, which was recommended as a replacement for the old sprung furniture. The advertisement declared, *Just reach into your old dusty upholstered furniture and mattresses and take a look at Knippenberg's patented mattresses and upholstered furniture with wire upholstery*. An illustration (fig. 84) shows the new opposite the old system: while the old upholstery can only be cleaned by creating large dust clouds, the new webbing system can be cleaned apparently without creating any of these.

The new home was to make life easier, Sigfried Giedion demanded in his 1929 pamphlet *Befreites Wohnen* (Liberated Dwelling) (fig. 87), and explained that one had *to rid oneself of the house as eternal value – the house with high rents, the house with thick walls … the house that enslaves us through the costs of its upkeep and the house that devours female workforce*.[85] Instead, *the home with use value […] was to be in balance in its entire structure, with a body liberated by sports, gymnastics, a purposeful way of life: light, bright, mobile*.[86] If one followed these demands, furniture that could hardly be moved, including upholstered armchairs, was forbidden. This is taken up by the Berlin-based Standard-Möbel-Produktion Lengyel & Co. (fig. 88), that advertised Breuer metal furniture in a 1928 volume of Bauhaus magazine.[87] There, the fabric-covered tubular steel furniture was advertised as being as comfortable as good, upholstered furniture but without the weight, cost, unwieldiness and unhygienic nature.[88]

The producers of tubular steel furniture made their point according to the *idea of a modern hygienic and social culture*[89] advertised in progressive circles, which was also advertised through large exhibitions such as the *Ausstellung für Gesundheitspflege, soziale Fürsorge und Leibesübungen (GeSoLei)* in 1926 in Düsseldorf. A hygienic environment, both in the public sphere and in the private home, healthy nutrition and sport were taken as the basic conditions of an increasingly mobile lifestyle. Was there still a place for conventional upholstered furniture? Purists vehemently declined these questions and broadened the

BREUER-METALLMÖBEL

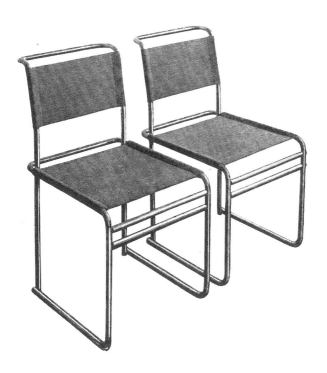

HOCKER, STÜHLE, DREHSTÜHLE, KLUBSESSEL, THEATERSESSEL, KLAPPSTÜHLE, TISCHE USW.

die stoffbespannten stahlrohrmöbel haben die **bequemlichkeit** von guten polstermöbeln, ohne deren gewicht, preis, unhandlichkeit und unhygienische beschaffenheit. je ein **typ** wurde für die notwendigen anwendungsarten ausgearbeitet und soweit verbessert, bis eine variation nicht mehr möglich war. hier ist zum ersten mal präzisionsstahlrohr zur konstruktion von sitzmöbeln verwendet worden. das stahlrohr ist in geringen querschnittdimensionen widerstandsfähiger als irgend ein anderes material, welches bisher für sitzmöbel angewandt wurde. es ergibt besondere **leichtigkeit** und auch eine besonders leichte erscheinung. sämtliche typen sind zerlegbar. die teile sind auswechselbar. beim transport spielt die leichtigkeit eine große rolle. ein stahlklubsessel z. b. wiegt ca. 6 kg (ein viertel bis ein sechstel eines gepolsterten klubsessels). in teile zerlegt lassen sich ca. 54 klubsessel oder ca. 100 rückenlehnstühle in 1 cbm verpacken. der preis eines klubsessels z. b. beträgt ca. 30 prozent von dem eines gepolsterten sessels. der eines theatersessels oder eines rückenlehnstuhles, beide mit stoffbespannung, beträgt ca. 75 prozent vom preise ähnlich flachgepolsterter holzmöbel. durch ihre haltbarkeit und hygienische beschaffenheit sind die **breuer-metallmöbel** im gebrauch ca. 200 proz. wirtschaftlicher als die üblichen sitzmöbel.

PRODUKTION UND VERTRIEB:

STANDARD-MÖBEL
LENGYEL & CO.
BERLIN W 62

Tel. Nollendorf 4009   BURGGRAFENSTRASSE 5

85/86/87 (S. 104, p.104)
Buchtitel von Adolf Behne, *Neues Wohnen – neues Bauen*, Leipzig 1930
Booktitle by Adolf Behne, *Neues Wohnen – neues Bauen*, Leipzig 1930
Buchtitel von Otto Schmidt, *Der alten Wohnung ein neues Gesicht*, Stuttgart 1930
Booktitle by Otto Schmidt, *Der alten Wohnung ein neues Gesicht*, Stuttgart 1930
Buchtitel von Sigfried Giedion, *Befreites Wohnen*, Zürich / Leipzig 1929
Booktitle by Sigfried Giedion, *Befreites Wohnen*, Zurich / Leipzig 1929

88
Werbeseite der Firma Standard-Möbel Lengyel & Co. Berlin, in: *bauhaus. Zeitschrift für Bau und Gestaltung*, Dessau, 2. Jg., Heft 1, 1928
Advertisement for the company Standard-Möbel Lengyel & Co. Berlin, in: *bauhaus: Zeitschrift für Bau und Gestaltung*, Dessau, vol. 2, no. 1, 1928

89–91
Sessel, sog. *Tugendhat-Sessel*, Modell „MR 70/9", Ludwig Mies van der Rohe (Entwurf), Berliner Metallgewerbe Josef Müller oder Bamberg Metallwerkstätten, Berlin-Neukölln (Herstellung), um 1930/1931 (LÖFFLER COLLECTION, Reichenschwand)

89–91
Armchair, so-called *Tugendhat Chair*, model "MR 70/9", Ludwig Mies van der Rohe (design), Berliner Metallgewerbe Josef Müller or Bamberg Metallwerkstätten, Berlin-Neukölln (production), around 1930/1931 (LÖFFLER COLLECTION, Reichenschwand)

venten Erich Dieckmann, dass man die neuen Ideen im Holzmöbelbau umsetzen konnte und dass nach wie vor Flach- und Hochpolster als geeignete Mittel der Förderung einer gesunden Sitzhaltung und der Gewährleistung bequemen Sitzens eingesetzt wurden.[91]

Dass Stahlrohrstühle durchaus auch als Polstermöbel entwickelt wurden, zeigten zudem Produzenten wie Thonet und Walter Knoll, die Anfang der 1930er Jahre entsprechende Polstermöbelserien auf den Markt brachten. Dabei wurden neuartige Systeme, wie die Verwendung von Zugfedern und Expandermaterial, erprobt, aber auch Sprungfedern eingesetzt. Diesem Aspekt folgt die Ausstellung in ihrer Auswahl verschiedener Metallstuhlmodelle, die auf den folgenden Seiten vorgestellt werden.

Am Anfang steht hier das Beispiel eines freischwingenden Lederpolstersessels, der als eine Ikone der Moderne verehrt wird. Es ist die einzigartige Kombination zweier Kissen mit einem Flachstahlgestell, das den Sitz des von Ludwig Mies van der Rohe um 1930/31 entworfenen Tugendhat-Sessels „MR 70/9" (s. Abb. 89–91) optisch fast schweben lässt. Von Schwere und Massivität keine Spur! Das liegt daran, dass die beiden s-förmig geschwungenen und durch Querstreben verbundenen Vorderbeine weit vorne angeordnet sind, wodurch der Sitz nach hinten weit auskragt (s. Abb. 90). Kräftige Lederbänder verbinden die Flachstahlträger (s. Abb. 89) und dienen als Auflager für zwei Kissen. Eine Besonderheit besteht darin, dass sich unter dem schwarzen Lederbezug der Sitz- und Rückenkissen jeweils 20 mit Werg bzw. Watte gefüllte und einzeln garnierte Kissen (als Weißpolster) befinden. Auch darin unterscheidet sich ein von den Firmen Berliner Metallgewerbe Josef Müller oder den Bamberg Metallwerkstätten, Berlin-Neukölln hergestelltes Original der beginnenden 1930er Jahre von späteren Nachbauten, in denen sich dann meist ein durchgängiges Daunenkissen oder sogar Schaumstoff findet, was nachvollziehbar ein völlig anderes und unvergleichbar schlechteres Sitzgefühl erzeugen musste. Da die händische Herstellung von 40 einzelnen kleinen Polsterkissen für nur einen Sessel entsprechend viel Zeit in Anspruch nahm und zudem enorme Meisterschaft im Handwerk voraussetzte, war der Tugendhat-Sessel „MR 70/9" immer schon ein teurer Luxusgegenstand.

discussion by adding questions regarding the use of wood furniture: *Furniture Made from Wood or from Metal?*[90] was thus the title of Gustav Hassenpflug's plaidoyer for metal materials. Nonetheless, projects by Bauhaus alumnus Erich Dieckmann demonstrate that the new ideas could be translated into wooden furniture and that flat and high upholstery was in use as a means to promote a healthy sitting position and comfortable seating.[91]

That tubular steel chairs could also be developed as upholstered furniture was demonstrated by producers such as Thonet and Walter Knoll, who brought such upholstered furniture series to the market in the early 1930s. New systems such as the use of tension springs and expander material were tested, as were coil springs. This is shown through several tubular steel chair models in the exhibition which will be introduced below.

The first is an example of a cantilevered leather cushioned chair that is hailed as an icon of modernity. The unique combination of two cushions with a steel frame lets the Tugendhat armchair "MR 70/9" (figs. 89–91) designed by Ludwig Mies van der Rohe almost float visually. Not a trace of weight and massiveness! This is due to the fact that the two S-curved front legs, connected by cross braces, are placed far in front so that the seat is cantilevered far to the back (fig. 90). Sturdy leather strips connect the steel frame (fig. 89) and serve as a base for two cushions. A special feature is the fact that under the seat and backrest's black leather cover 20 individually stitched cushions stuffed with tow and cotton are situated. This is one way in which an original produced in the early 1930s either by the Berliner Metallgewerbe Josef Müller company or the Bamberg Metallwerkstätten, Berlin-Neukölln, differs from later replicas. There, one usually finds a continuous down or even foam cushion, which was responsible for an entirely different and much worse seating experience, for the handmade production of 40 single small upholstered cushions for just one armchair took a corresponding amount of time and required a mastery of craftsmanship, which made the *Tugendhat* armchair "MR 70/9" an expensive luxury item from the start.

92/93 (S. 110/111)
Armlehnstuhl, Charles Siclis (Entwurf), Thonet Frères, Paris (Herstellung), 1934 (LÖFFLER COLLECTION, Reichenschwand)

92/93 (p. 110/111)
Armchair, Charles Siclis (design), Thonet Frères, Paris (production), 1934 (LÖFFLER COLLECTION, Reichenschwand)

Dagegen galten die in größeren Serien industriell produzierten Stahlrohrmöbel als vergleichsweise günstigere Variante. Sie seien *keine Einzelerzeugnisse kunstgewerblichen Könnens, sondern aus der Zweckbestimmung und aus dem Material heraus geformte, mit Maschinenleistung und Maschinenexaktheit[92] hergestellte, nach Erprobung genormte Serienstücke*, erklärte Hans Spiegel 1928, um zu ergänzen, Stahlrohr sei *formeigenwillig, ungeeignet für stilistische, dekorative Formspielerei[93]*. Das entsprach den Wünschen vieler Wohnreformer, die Metallmöbel folglich als Garanten einer zeitgemäß funktionalen Einrichtung schätzten. Und doch zeigt sich im Verlauf der 1930er Jahre, dass sich auch traditionelle Polstertypen wie der Ohrensessel durchaus mit Stahlrohr vereinen ließen. Dabei galt das Stahlrohrmöbel auch als Experimentalgegenstand, wenn neue Federungen erprobt wurden wie z. B. der Einsatz von Expander-Gummisträngen, die zwischen zwei parallel angeordneten Rohren gespannt wurden, um einen flexiblen Untergrund für die Aufnahme weicher Polsterkissen zu bilden. Dem entsprach etwa das von Anton Lorenz entworfene und 1932 vom Desta-Werk in Berlin hergestellte Fauteuil-Modell „KS 46" (s. Abb. 96–97), bei dem horizontal gespannte Gummistränge, die in Spiralen mit Haken auslaufen, als federnde Auflage für Kissen aus gummiertem Rosshaar dienten.[94] Der Einsatz von gummiummantelten Zugkabeln (s. Abb. 97) erwies sich als praktisch, weil dadurch auf die bei Metallfedern nötige Zwischenlage (Schonerdecke) zwischen Federung und Auflagekissen verzichtet werden konnte. Beim „KS 46" wurden durchgängige lose Kissen eingesetzt, die über einem Kern aus Gummikokos eine Kapokauflage besaßen. Bei einem zwei Jahre zuvor von Lorenz für Desta entworfenen Modell der Seriennummer „KS 42" (s. Abb. 98/99) lagen Sitz- und Rückenkissen noch auf Stahlrohrtraversen. Damit empfahl sich ein Kissenaufbau mit Endlosfederkern und Kantendraht sowie eine Federkernabdeckung mit Jutefederleinen. Das Polstermaterial bestand in diesem Fall aus einer Kokosfasermatte mit Watteabdeckung, Nessel und leichter Kantenabnähung. So lässt sich am Beispiel Desta zeigen, wie ein Unternehmen in einer Produktfamilie zeitnah verschiedene Möglichkeiten für Polster erprobte und im Markt einführte.

Bei der Sicherung eines von Charles Siclis 1934 für die französische Firma Thonet Frères entworfenen Stahlrohrstuhls mit Kupferbeschichtung (s. Abb. 92) und der dafür notwendigen Abnahme des noch originalen Lederbezugs kam eine frühe Form von Schaumstoff zum Vorschein (s. Abb. 93), ein Material, das bislang nicht zweifelsfrei identifiziert werden konnte. Es ist brüchig, weil verhärtet, doch stabil und überzieht ein geschlossenes Sitzpolster, das im Inneren eine geschnürte Federkonstruktion mit Afrik-Fasson aufweist. Darüber findet sich als Ersatz für die übliche Pickierung mit z. B. Rosshaar eben diese Schaumstoffdeckung. Die mit dem Sitz konstruktiv verbundene Rückenlehne zeigt denselben Aufbau. Das Polster ist im Gesamten durch einen Holzrahmen gefasst, der, komplett mit grünem Leder überzogen, in das Stahlrohrgestell eingesetzt wird. Darin ähnelt es dem formal ganz andersartigen Stahlrohr-Polsterstuhl (s. Abb. 100/101), bei dem ein konventioneller Polstersessel in den seitlich einen Dreiviertelkreis bildenden Stahlrohr-Rahmen eingesetzt wurde. Das komplett mit einem rot-weiß-schwarz gemusterten Wollstoff überzogene Sitzelement besteht im Polster aus einer geschnürten Federkonstruktion. Die Lehnenpolsterung ist aus garniertem Werg-Fasson. Im Gegensatz zu dem von Charles Siclis für Thonet Frères entworfenen

Tubular steel furniture that was industrially produced in larger numbers was considered to be a comparatively cheap variation. They *were not unique products of craftsmanship but serial pieces formed by their function and material, produced by machine force and exactitude[92] and normed through trial*, Hans Spiegel explained in 1928, added that tubular steel was *wilful in form and therefore* unsuitable *for any stylistic, decorative play of forms.*[93] This conformed to the wishes of many dwelling reformers, who valued metal furniture as a guarantor of contemporary functional design. Nevertheless, over the course of the 1930s it became evident that even traditional upholstery types, such as the wing chair, could be reconciled with tubular steel. Tubular steel furniture was also the object of experiments when new types of springs were tested, such as, for example, rubber expander strips, that were stretched between two parallel tubes in order to create a flexible base for soft upholstered cushions. In the same way, the armchair model "KS 46" (figs. 96/97), designed by Anton Lorenz and produced around 1932 by Desta in Berlin, is fitted with horizontal elastic bands with spiralised hooks at the ends, which serve as the base for cushions made from rubberised horsehair.[94] The use of rubber-coated push-pull cables (fig. 98) proved to be practical because it was now possible to forego the additional fabric layer between the springing and the cushion needed for metal springs. In the case of "KS 46", a loose pillow was used that had a rubberised coconut core with a covering of kapok. In a model with the serial number "KS 42", designed by Lorenz for Desta two years earlier (figs. 98/99), the seat and back cushions were still placed on tubular steel crossbars. This was paired with a cushion construction with open-spring core and edge wire as well as a hessian cover. The upholstery material in this case consisted of a coconut fibre mat with a wadding cover, calico and light edge stitching. In this way, the Desta example shows how a company in a short span of time was able to test different options for upholstery in a product family and introduce them to the market.

During the restoration of a tubular steel chair with copper plating designed by Charles Siclis in 1934 for the French company Thonet Frères (fig. 92) and the necessary removal of the still original leather covering, an early type of foam (fig. 93) was revealed, a material that has not yet been identified beyond doubt. It is brittle because it has hardened but is nonetheless stable and covers a closed seat cushion that has a lashed springing as well as palm fibre stuffing on the inside. The covering foam is a substitute for the horsehair stuffing usually used. The backrest, which is structurally connected to the seat, has the same composition. The upholstery is framed by a wooden frame, which is completely covered with green leather and dropped into the tubular steel frame. In this, it resembles the formally quite different tubular steel upholstered chair (figs. 100/101), in which a conventional upholstered armchair was inserted into the tubular steel frame forming a three-quarter circle at the side. The seat, completely covered with a red, white and black patterned woollen fabric, has lashed springing. The backrest padding is stuffed with bridled and stitched tow. In contrast to the tubular chair designed by Charles Siclis for Thonet Frères (fig. 92), it would also have been possible in terms of the design to provide legs made of

94 Werbeannonce für Epeda-Patent-Polster der Firma Ehlenbeck & Platte, Vohwinkel, 1930
Advertisement for patented Epeda upholstery by the company Ehlenbeck & Platte, Vohwinkel, 1930

95 Werbeannonce für die Schlaraffia-Federeinlage, Schlaraffia-Werke Hüser & Co., Barmen-Wichlinghausen, 1930
Advertisement for Schlaraffia spring inlays, Schlaraffia-Werke Hüser & Co., Barmen-Wichlinghausen, 1930

Rohrstuhl (s. Abb. 92) wäre es vom Entwurf her auch möglich gewesen, anstelle eines Stahlrohr-Gestells Beine aus Holz vorzusehen, doch entschied man sich für den Einbau in einen Metallrahmen, wohl um den Komfort des konventionellen Polstersessels mit dem modischen Chic der schlanken Stahlrohrformen zu verbinden. Dem entspricht der Ohrensessel (s. Abb. 103/104), der aus einem konventionellen Komfortpolsterelement und einer dieses umschließenden Rohrkonstruktion besteht. Hier schwingt der sonst so standfeste Ohrensessel, mit dem sich sprichwörtlich behagliche Ruhe und Zurückgezogenheit verbindet. Sowohl das Sitz- als auch das Rückenlehnenpolster bestehen aus einer geschnürten Federkonstruktion, versehen mit einer Fasson aus Werg und grauer Watte, wozu im Lehnenpolster noch Kokos hinzukommt.

Es besteht ein großer Unterschied zwischen dem beschriebenen Ohrenbackenschwinger und dem von Jindřich Halabala um 1930 für Spojené UP Závody in Brünn entworfenen Freischwinger des Modells „H91" (s. Abb. 102). Auf der einen Seite eine Stuhlmetamorphose im Sinne der konstruktiven Neuinterpretation eines traditionellen Ruhesessels und auf der anderen Seite ein weit auskragender Stahlrohrstuhl, in den eine dafür konzipierte Kissenkombination auf verspannten Eisengarnflächen lose eingelegt wird.

Die Kissen des „H91" bestehen aus einem Federkern der Schlaraffia-Werke Hüter & Co., welche mit der Markteinführung ihrer patentierten Metallrahmen-Federeinlage den Nerv der Zeit getroffen hatten. Deren Clou war laut einer Werbeannonce von 1930 (s. Abb. 95) ein fertig montierter Spiralfederaufbau, der so konstruiert war, das dessen metallenes Innenleben garantiert *undurchfühlbar* war. Ähnlich bewarb die im rheinischen Vohwinkel beheimatete Firma Ehlenbeck & Platte ihr Epeda-Patentpolster (s. Abb. 94), dessen Geflecht, ohne Knoten und ohne Drahtenden, versprach, immer weich zu bleiben und dauerhaft *absolut geräuschlos* zu funktionieren. Das Geheimnis des Komforts lüftete sich nur in Werbeanzeigen, die regelmäßig in führenden Fachzeitschriften wie der von Alexander Koch herausgegebenen *Innendekoration* erschienen.

Die vorgestellten Beispiele zeigen, dass der Einsatz traditioneller Polstertechniken bei Metallmöbeln durchaus keine Seltenheit war, wobei zuweilen überraschende Kreuzungen zwischen traditionellen und neuen Formen entstanden. Auf ein gut gefedertes Polster wollte man zuhause nicht verzichten, denn komfortables Sitzen war auch in Zeiten modernistischer Reformbewegungen gefragt. So ließ sich das u. a. von Hannes Meyer als Ideal geforderte *Wohnhaus als Wohnmaschinerie*[95] nicht durchsetzen. Das gilt insbesondere für den Bereich luxuriöser Wohnungen, für die weiterhin exklusive Polsterkreationen entstanden. Ein Beispiel ist der von Eileen Gray 1926 entworfene *Bibendum-Armchair*, der um 1930 in Paris u. a. in dem von Paul Ruaud für Madame Matthieu-Lévy gestalteten Glassalon (s. Abb. 110) seinen Platz fand. Dabei handelt es sich um einen schweren Klubsessel mit Polsterringen als einer kombinierten Arm-Rückenlehne. Der Name *Bibendum* nahm Bezug auf das Maskottchen der Michelin-Reifenwerke, die mit einem aus gestapelten Reifenringen zusammengesetzten Männchen Werbung machten. Der von Gray entworfene Sessel erinnert mit seinen drei Polsterlagen an entsprechende Reifenringe, wobei die weiche Lederpolsterung die Nutzer*innen komfortabel umfängt. Das Ganze ruht schließlich auf einem niedrigen Stahlrohrgestell, das wegen der Dominanz des Polsteraufbaus so weit zurücktritt, dass der Sessel fast zu schweben scheint.

wood instead of a tubular steel frame, but the decision was made to install it into a metal frame, probably in order to combine the comfort of the conventional upholstered armchair with the fashionable chic of the slender tubular steel forms. This is the case for the wing chair (figs. 103/104), which consists of a conventional upholstered element and a tubular construction enclosing it. Here, the otherwise so stable wing chair, combining proverbial cosy tranquillity and seclusion, swings. Both the seat and the backrest upholstery have lashed springing, fitted with a stuffing of tow and grey wadding, to which coconut fibre is added in the backrest upholstery.

There is a considerable difference between the winged swinger described above and the cantilever chair model "H91" designed by Jindřich Halabala around 1930 for Spojené UP Závody in Brno (fig. 102): on the one hand a chair metamorphosis in the sense of a constructive reinterpretation of a traditional recliner, on the other a wide cantilevered tubular steel chair on which a cushion combination designed for this purpose is loosely placed on braced iron thread surfaces.

The cushions of the "H91" consist of a spring core made by Schlaraffia-Werke Hüter & Co., who had struck a chord with the market launch of its patented metal frame spring insert. According to an advertisement from 1930 (fig. 95), the special feature of this product was a prefabricated spiral spring structure that was constructed in such a way that its metal interior was guaranteed to be *impalpable*. Similarly, the company Ehlenbeck & Platte, based in Vohwinkel in the Rhineland, advertised its Epeda patent cushion (fig. 94), whose weaving, without knots and without wire ends, promised to always remain soft and to function permanently and *with no noise whatsoever*. The secret of comfort was only revealed in advertisements that regularly appeared in leading trade magazines, such as *Innendekoration*, edited by Alexander Koch.

The examples presented demonstrate that the use of traditional upholstery techniques was by no means uncommon in metal furniture, with sometimes surprising crossovers between traditional and new forms. People did not want to do without a well-sprung upholstery at home, because comfortable seating was in demand even in times of modernist reform movements. Thus, the *Wohnhaus als Wohnmaschine* (Residential House as a Living Machine)[95] demanded as an ideal by Hannes Meyer, among others, could not be implemented. This was particularly true in the area of luxury flats, for which exclusive upholstered creations continued to be created. One example is the *Bibendum Armchair* designed by Eileen Gray in 1926, which found its place in Paris around 1930 in the glass salon designed by Paul Ruaud for Madame Matthieu-Lévy (fig. 110), among other places. It is a heavy club chair with upholstered rings serving as a combined arm- and backrest. The name *Bibendum* referred to the mascot of the Michelin tyre works, which advertised using a manikin composed of stacked tyre rings. With its three layers of upholstery, the armchair designed by Gray is reminiscent of corresponding tyre rings, while the soft leather upholstery comfortably embraces the user. The object rests on a low tubular steel frame, which, due to the dominance of the upholstery, recedes so far that the chair almost seems to float.

96/97
Armlehnsessel, Modell „KS 46", Anton Lorenz (Entwurf), DESTA, Berlin, ab 1933 Thonet Frankenberg (Herstellung), 1931 (LÖFFLER COLLECTION, Reichenschwand)

96/97
Armchair, model "KS 46", Anton Lorenz (design), DESTA, Berlin, from 1933 Thonet Frankenberg (production), 1931 (LÖFFLER COLLECTION, Reichenschwand)

98/99
Armlehnsessel, Modell „KS 42", Anton Lorenz (Entwurf), DESTA, Berlin (Herstellung), 1931 (GRASSI Museum für Angewandte Kunst Leipzig)

98/99
Armchair, model "KS 42", Anton Lorenz (design), DESTA, Berlin (production), 1931 (GRASSI Museum für Angewandte Kunst Leipzig)

100/101
Armlehnstuhl, 1928–1930 (LÖFFLER COLLECTION, Reichenschwand)

100/101
Armchair, 1928–1930 (LÖFFLER COLLECTION, Reichenschwand)

Andere Ansprüche – Neue Ideen | Different demands – New ideas **119**

102
Armlehnstuhl, Modell „H91", Jindřich Halabala (Entwurf),
Spojené UP Závody, Brünn, Tschechoslowakei (Herstellung),
um 1930 (LÖFFLER COLLECTION, Reichenschwand)

102
Armchair, model "H91", Jindřich Halabala (design), Spojené UP
Závody, Brno, former Czechoslovakia (production), around 1930
(LÖFFLER COLLECTION, Reichenschwand)

103/104 (S. 122/123)
Sessel, Kombination von Freischwinger und konventionellem Polstermöbel (LÖFFLER COLLECTION, Reichenschwand)

103/104 (p. 122/123)
Armchair, combination of a cantilevered chair and a traditionally upholstered piece of furniture (LÖFFLER COLLECTION, Reichenschwand)

105/106
Armlehnstuhl, 1920er/1930er Jahre (LÖFFLER COLLECTION, Reichenschwand)

105/106
Armchair, 1920s/1930s (LÖFFLER COLLECTION, Reichenschwand)

124 Andere Ansprüche – Neue Ideen l Different demands – New ideas

107–109
Armlehnstuhl, Heinz und Bodo Rasch (Entwurf), vermutlich L&C Arnold Schorndorf (Herstellung), um 1930 (LÖFFLER COLLECTION, Reichenschwand)

107–109
Armchair, Heinz and Bodo Rasch (design), presumably L&C Arnold Schorndorf (production), around 1930 (LÖFFLER COLLECTION, Reichenschwand)

110
Blick in den 1920 von Eileen Gray gestalteten Glas-Salon der Madame Mathieu-Lévy in der Rue de Lota, Paris, 1933 (in: *L'Illustration*, 1933)

110
View of the Glass Salon designed by Eileen Gray for Madame Mathieu-Lévy in rue de Lota, Paris, 1933 (in: *L'Illustration* 1933)

111 (links, left)
Werbung für Klubsessel (in: *L'Illustration*, 1933)
Advertisement for club chairs (in: *L'Illustration*, 1933)

112
Blick in einen Salon, der mit Klubsesseln ausgestattet ist (in: *L'Illustration*, 1933)
View of a room furnished with club chairs (in: *L'Illustration*, 1933)

113
Klubsessel, 1920er Jahre (LÖFFLER COLLECTION, Reichenschwand)

113
Club chair, 1920s (LÖFFLER COLLECTION, Reichenschwand)

Betrachtet man die Gestaltdiskussion der 1920er und beginnenden 1930er Jahre, dann kreist sie um die Frage nach dem, was unter moderner Wohnlichkeit zu verstehen ist. Als vorbildhaft galt schon Ende des 19. Jahrhunderts die angelsächsische Wohnwelt, an der sich reformorientierte Gestalter wie Adolf Loos und Josef Frank orientierten. Dazu gehörte ganz selbstverständlich auch das gepolsterte Fauteuil, auch wenn es nicht den Anspruch auf Leichtigkeit erfüllen konnte. Dass Frank entsprechendes Mobiliar in seinen Wohnräumen platzierte, erklärt Marlene Ott-Wodni mit der Haltung, dem Wunsch nach Bequemlichkeit den Vorrang gegenüber der Leichtigkeit zu einzuräumen.[96] Immerhin versah man die schweren Polstermöbel öfter mit Rollen, wodurch sie leichter ihren Standort wechseln konnten. Dass traditionelle Polstertechnologien selbst bei Metallmöbeln ihren Einsatz fanden, wurde bereits ausgeführt, weshalb sich im Folgenden der Blick auf Sitzmöbel mit Holzchassis und speziell jene Möbelformen richtet, die auf dem klassischen Klubsessel basieren.

Kommt zu federgepolsterten Sitz- und Rückenkissen noch die vollflächig gepolsterte Armlehne hinzu, so ergibt sich das volle Polstermöbel, z. B. der Klubsessel, den Gustav Adolf Platz 1933 als die bequemste Form des modernen Sessels ansah.[97] Dabei sei bei diesen Möbeln eine gewisse Massigkeit der Erscheinung nicht zu vermeiden, erklärte der Architekt einschränkend in Hinblick auf deren Einsatz in kleineren Wohnungen. Der Kunsthistoriker Kuno von Hardenberg hatte 1925 auch von *krötenbraunen Möbelsauriern*[98] gesprochen. Diese *hippopotamischen Gebilde aus Leder mit darunter verstecktem Knochenwerk* hätten ihm Ehrfurcht eingeflößt, wegen ihrer enormen Bequemlichkeit aber auch Bewunderung abgenötigt. Vor allem hätten derartige Sessel-Ungetüme dazu beigetragen, dass *Träume von bisher unbekannten Genüssen, von märchenhaften Siesten mit langen Zigarren, von der Zugehörigkeit zu einer bevorzugten, reichen und vornehmen Kaste, von Abenden mit Frack mit Gardenien im Knopfloch, von Whisky und großstädtischem Klubleben*[99] entstehen konnten. Mit dem Typus des Klubsessels (s. Abb. 111/112) verbanden sich so von Anfang an bestimmte Vorstellungen und Assoziationen, welche dem Käufer eines solchen Fauteuils das Bewusstsein gaben, allein schon dessen Besitz ermögliche die Verwirklichung all dieser Träume vom Leben der englischen Oberschicht. Dass entsprechende Sessel fast vollständig mit Leder überzogen waren, erklärt den Vergleich mit einem faltenwerfenden Dickhäuter. Doch lag das Erfolgsrezept im Aufbau der Polsterung begründet. So waren die Armlehnen bei aufwendigen Modellen nicht nur mit Füllstoffen gefüttert, sondern mit einer eigenen Federung versehen. Darauf geht der in Stuttgart an der Württembergischen Staatlichen Kunstgewerbeschule lehrende Architekt Adolf G. Schneck 1933 in seiner Abhandlung über *Das Polstermöbel*[100] detailliert ein. Darin zeigt er Fotos, Schnitte und Zeichnungen, die dem Betrachter die Vielfalt möglicher Handgriffe und deren Folgen für das sich einstellende Sitzgefühl vermitteln, etwa dann, wenn ein hochgepolsterter Sitz durch eine tiefere Schnürung der vorderen Federn den Nutzer*innen einen festeren Halt beim Sitzen garantiert, was gerade bei tiefer liegenden Sitzpolstern das Aufstehen erleichtert.[101]

Der abgebildete Klubsessel (s. Abb. 113) entspricht genau dem von Hardenberg beschriebenen Typus eines hippopotamischen Gebildes. Er ist schwer, mit braunem Leder bezogen, und vom Sitz her niedrig angelegt. Das Sitzpolster ist sehr hoch und verweist dadurch auf das Vorhandensein

Looking at the discussion around design of the 1920s and early 1930s, it revolves around the question of what is meant by modern living. Already at the end of the nineteenth century, the Anglo-Saxon world of dwelling was considered exemplary, and reform-oriented designers such as Adolf Loos and Josef Frank took their cue from it. This naturally included the upholstered armchair, even if it could not fulfil the demand for lightness. Marlene Ott-Wodni explains the fact that Frank placed corresponding furniture in his living rooms with the attitude of giving the desire for comfort precedence over lightness.[96] After all, the heavy upholstered furniture was often fitted with castors, which made it easier to change its location. The fact that traditional upholstery techniques were used even in metal furniture has already been explained, so in the following we will focus on seating furniture with wooden frames and especially those furniture forms based on the classic club chair.

If the fully upholstered armrest is added to the sprung seat and backrest cushioning, the result is a fully upholstered piece of furniture, for example the club chair, which Gustav Adolf Platz in 1933 considered to be the most comfortable form of the modern armchair.[97] However, a certain massiveness of appearance could not be avoided with this furniture, the architect explained with regard to its use in smaller apartments. In 1925, the art historian Kuno von Hardenberg had also spoken of *toad-brown furniture dinosaurs*.[98] These *hippopotamus-like structures made of leather with hidden bone work underneath* would have inspired in him not only respect but also admiration due to their enormous comfort. Above all, such seat monstrosities would have contributed to *dreams of hitherto unknown pleasures, of fairy-tale siestas with long cigars, of belonging to a privileged, rich and distinguished caste, of evenings in tails with gardenias in the buttonhole, of whisky and big-city club life*.[99] From the very beginning, the club chair type (figs. 111/112) was associated with certain ideas and associations which gave the buyer of such an armchair the idea that its possession alone would enable the realisation of all these dreams of an English upper-class lifestyle. The fact that such armchairs were almost completely covered with leather explains the comparison with a wrinkled pachyderm. But the recipe for success lay in the structure of the upholstery. For example, the armrests of more refined models were not only lined with filler but also fitted with their own springs. The architect Adolf G. Schneck, who taught at the *Württembergische Staatliche Kunstgewerbeschule* in Stuttgart, goes into this in detail in his 1933 treatise on upholstered furniture, *Das Polstermöbel*.[100] In the book he used photos, cross sections and drawings to show the reader the variety of possible manipulations and their consequences for the resulting seating experience, for example when a highly upholstered seat guarantees the user firmer support when sitting by depressing the front springs, which makes it easier to stand up, especially when the seat cushions are placed lower.[101]

The illustrated club chair (fig. 113) corresponds exactly to the hippopotamus type described by Hardenberg. It is heavy, covered with brown leather and has a low

einer im Sitz verborgenen Doppelfederung, die auch bei einem hohen Körpergewicht Bequemlichkeit versprach.[102]

Neben dem aus England importierten Klubsessel-Typus erfreute sich in den 1930er Jahren der Kanadier (s. Abb. 118–121) als in der Rückenlehne verstellbarer Ruhesessel großer Beliebtheit, wobei nicht wenige Modelle über lose eingelegte Kissenpolster verfügten. Entsprechende Polster waren oft mit handgewebten farbigen Stoffen bezogen und fügten sich so in den *Kanon einer Farbensymphonie des Wohnraumes* ein, was, so führt Hardenberg aus, der *Monotonie ewig brauner Lederhüllen erfreulicherweise* entgegenwirkte.[103] Die Redaktion der Zeitschrift *Die Form* sah in dem Umstand, dass handgewebte Stoffe in Zeiten vornehmlich industrieller Warenherstellung stark nachgefragt waren, ein Zeichen dafür, dass man das Eigene der handwerklichen Arbeit nicht in der individuellen Mustergestaltung, sondern in dem besonderen Charakter der handwerklichen Materialgestaltung suchte.[104]

Starke Impulse gaben die in klassischen Web- und Knüpftechniken entstandenen Textilien der Künstlerinnen am Bauhaus, z. B. Flachgewebe mit Leinwandbindung, für deren Herstellung die verschiedensten Materialien bis hin zu Kunstseiden und Metallfäden zur Anwendung kamen.[105] Michael Siebenbrodt betont in seiner Abhandlung zur Textilkollektion des Weimarer Bauhauses, durch unterschiedliche Zwirnung und verschiedene Materialstärken[106] seien interessante plastische Effekte erzielt worden. Die ästhetische Qualität von Stoffen mit Streifenstrukturen entstand etwa durch Kontraste matter und glänzender Garne[107] sowie eine wirkungsvolle Oberflächenplastizität, die geeignet war, dem Polster eine griffige Haptik zu verleihen.

Wie handwerkliche Polstertechnik in vereinfachter Form industriellen Fertigungsweisen angepasst wurde, zeigt der um 1935 von Alvar Aalto entworfene Schichtholz-Freischwinger der Modellnummer „400", kurz nur *Tank Chair* (s. Abb. 114/115) genannt. Auf der Weltausstellung in Brüssel 1935 und der Mailänder Triennale des Jahres 1936 hatte der von der finnischen ARTEK vertriebene Holzkufenstuhl großes Aufsehen erregt. Das in Leipzig ausgestellte Exemplar zeigt ihn mit dem originalen Bezug und einem schwarz-beige-orange gestreiften Stoff, der die Federhochpolster von Sitz und Rückenlehne bedeckt. Von der Polsterkonstruktion her weist der Stuhl die Merkmale einer klassisch geschnürten Sprungfedertechnik (s. Abb. 323) mit Afrik- und Rosshaardeckung auf. Aalto schätzte zwar die Hygiene und Leichtigkeit der Stahlrohrmöbel, doch kritisierte er die von ihm so empfundene optische, haptische und akustische Kälte derartiger Einrichtungsgegenstände.[108] Deshalb arbeitete er konsequent mit laminiertem Schichtholz, dessen federnde Eigenschaften Aalto bei der Gestaltung des *Tank Chairs* nutzte.

Die Ausstellung verdeutlicht anhand verschiedener Sitzmöbel der 1920er und 1930er Jahre, wie wirksam farbig gemusterte Bezugsstoffe eingesetzt wurden, um einen wichtigen Beitrag zur Wahrnehmung der Form des Polstermöbels zu leisten. Dabei zeigt sich, wie stark die Kenntnis der Gesetzmäßigkeiten bei der Flächenmusterung, etwa in Hinblick auf den Rhythmus, den ein Stoffdekor im Rapport abbildet, dazu beiträgt, die in der Stuhlform angelegte Struktur zu unterstreichen oder auch zu überspielen. Während ruhigere Punkt- und Linienmuster sich der Gesamtform eher unter-

seat. The seat upholstery is very high, indicating the presence of double springs hidden in the seat, which promised comfort even in the case of a high body weight.[102]

In addition to the club chair type imported from England, the so-called *Kanadier* armchair (figs. 118–121) also enjoyed great popularity in the 1930s, as a recliner with adjustable backrest, whereby quite a few models had loosely inserted cushion pads. The cushions were often upholstered in hand-woven colourful fabrics and thus blended into the *canon of a symphony of colours in living spaces*, which, as Hardenberg points out, was a welcome contrast to the *monotony of eternally brown leather covers*.[103] The editors of the magazine *Die Form* interpreted the fact that hand-woven fabrics were in great demand in times of primarily industrial production of goods as a sign that people were looking for the unique character of handicraft work not in the individual pattern design but in the special character of handcrafted materials.[104]

Strong impulses were given by the textiles created by the female artists at the Bauhaus. They employed classical weaving and knotting techniques, such as flat tabby weaves, for which a wide variety of materials were used, including artificial silks and metal threads.[105] In his treatise on the textile collection of the Weimar Bauhaus, Michael Siebenbrodt emphasises that interesting sculptural effects were achieved by using different twisting methods and material thicknesses.[106] The aesthetic quality of fabrics with striped structures was created, for example, by contrasts of matte and shiny yarns[107] as well as a striking surface plasticity that was suitable for giving the upholstery a non-slip feel.

The plywood cantilever chair model "400", short *Tank Chair* (figs. 114/115), designed by Alvar Aalto around 1935 shows how handcrafted upholstery technology was adapted in a simplified form to industrial production methods. At the World Exhibition in Brussels in 1935 and the Milan Triennale in 1936, the wooden sledge-foot chair distributed by the Finnish company ARTEK caused quite a stir. The object exhibited in Leipzig has its original upholstery and a black-beige-orange striped fabric covering the sprung high cushions of the seat and backrest. In terms of upholstery, the chair exhibits the characteristics of a classic lashed spring design (fig. 323) with palm fibre and horsehair stuffing. Although Aalto appreciated the hygiene and lightness of tubular steel furniture, he criticised what he perceived as the visual, tactile and acoustic coldness of such furnishings.[108] He therefore worked consistently with laminated plywood, the elastic properties of which Aalto used in the design of the *Tank Chair*.

Displaying a variety of seating furniture from the 1920s and 1930s, the exhibition illustrates how effectively colourful patterned upholstery fabrics were used to make an important contribution to the perception of the upholstered furniture form. It becomes clear to which degree the knowledge of the rules of surface pattern – for example with regard to the rhythm that a fabric pattern reproduces in its repeat – helps to emphasise or even mask the structure inherent in the shape of the chair. While calmer dot and line patterns

ordnen, entwickeln dynamisch-kontrastreich komponierte Dekors ggf. ein so starkes Eigenleben, dass sie von der Stuhlform ablenken. Dies geschieht z. B. bei dem dreibeinigen Armlehnstuhl: Er verfügt über eine markante Kopfstütze, die nach den Seiten Ohrenbacken ausbildet (s. Abb. 122/123). Polstertechnisch handelt es sich beim Sitzpolster um eine geschnürte Federkonstruktion, mit einer Fasson aus Afrik und Kokos, während sich in Armpolstern und Kopflehne garniertes Füllmaterial findet. Der Bezugsstoff zeigt geometrische Formen, welche an Pfeile erinnern und im Wechsel spannungsvoll gegeneinander gerichtet sind. So entsteht ein bewegtes Bild in Grün und Rosa, wobei schwarze Linien die Formen betonen und dem Ganzen zusätzlich Plastizität verleihen. Ein einfarbiger Stoff hätte das große Polster weitaus massiver wirken lassen, während das dynamische Stoffdekor optisch eher zur Entmaterialisierung des Volumens beiträgt. Vergleichbares gilt für den Art-déco-Kanadier (s. Abb. 119) als verstellbarem Ruhesessel, dessen Hochpolster mit einem Hoch-tief-Velours ausgestattet ist. Sein Charakter verstärkt das grafisch stark rhythmisierte Muster und erzeugt ein spektakuläres Bewegungsbild.

Derartige Polstermöbel initiieren ein optisches Erlebnis, das geeignet ist, auch schwerere Möbel grafisch zu verlebendigen. Das zeigen die auf den folgenden Seiten abgebildeten Stühle, die zumeist der Stilrichtung des Art-déco zuzuordnen sind (s. Abb. 128–135). Durchweg handelt es sich dabei um Hochpolsterstühle mit einer geschnürten Federkonstruktion, wobei bei vielen Modellen der Zeit auch Kissen eingesetzt werden, so z. B. bei dem Armlehnstuhl (s. Abb. 133/134), dessen Sitzpolsterung durch ein Federkernkissen mit Schlaraffia-Federkern erfolgt.

Zwei Beispiele verweisen auf die Tradition des *pouffe* als gepolstertem Hocker. Im Vorliegenden handelt es sich um mutmaßlich in Tschechien gefertigte Stücke, die in den 1930er Jahren entweder als garniertes Polster (s. Abb. 126/127) oder geschnürte Federkonstruktion mit einer Fasson aus Werg, Afrik, Kokos oder Rosshaar (s. Abb. 124/125) ausgerüstet wurden. In dem von Bücheler und Ulmschneider 1953 herausgegebenen *Lehrbuch für Neuzeitliches Polstern* heißt es zu den damals wertgeschätzten Sitzbegleitern, bei deren Aufpolstern sei darauf zu achten, die Federung nicht zu weich und zu hoch zu schnüren, *da sonst bei Benützung der Sitz schwimmt*[109], wodurch das Platznehmen unbequem und unsicher sei.

Neben dem Einsatz der geschnürten Federtechnik gibt die Ausstellung Beispiele für technische Neuerungen im Polsteraufbau, z. B. bei dem Armlehnstuhl (s. Abb. 137–139), den Paul Grießer für das von ihm 1929/30 konzipierte Möbelprogramm *WK 27 – Aufbauheim* vorsah.[110] Als Sitz dient hier ein Einlegekissen auf Federunterlage, während das Rückenpolster durch ein in Pfeifen angelegtes Kissen eingerichtet wurde. Das Sitzkissen ist mit einer Einlage aus Rosshaar oder Kokos versehen und sechsmal geheftet. Die Kissenhülle ist an den Nähten mit einer Kappnaht versehen und liegt auf doppelt gelegten Flachfedern (s. Abb. 139), die in den Seitenzargen des Holzrahmens mittels Spiralzugfedern eingehängt sind. Dagegen besteht die Lehne aus einem Kissen in drei Pfeifen, was bedeutet, dass es drei längliche, wulstartige Felder zeigt. Das Kissen ist an der Oberkante verdeckt angenagelt und an den unteren Ecken mit Druckknöpfen fixiert. Das Spannteil ist mit dem gleichen Stoff bezogen wie der Sitz, wobei es sich bei dem im Original erhaltenen Velours-Bezugsstoff um eine typische, flammenartige Musterung der Zeit handelt.

tend to subordinate themselves to the overall form, dynamically contrasting patterns can develop such a strong life of their own that they distract from the chair form. This is the case, for example, in the three-legged armchair, which has a distinctive headrest that forms wings at the sides (figs. 122/123). In terms of upholstery, the seat cushion is sprung, with a stuffing of palm fibre and coir, while in the arm cushions and headrest there is stitched and bridled stuffing. The cover fabric features geometric shapes, which are reminiscent of arrows set dynamically in alternate directions. This creates a moving image in green and pink, with black lines emphasising the shapes and lending the whole additional plasticity. A monochromatic fabric would have made the large upholstery appear far more solid, while the dynamic textile pattern visually contributes more to dematerialising the volume. A comparable example is the Art Deco *Kanadier* armchair (fig. 119), an adjustable recliner whose high cushion is equipped with a high-low velour. Its character reinforces the graphic, strongly rhythmic pattern and creates a spectacular image of movement. Upholstered furniture of this kind initiates a visual experience that is suitable for bringing even heavier objects to life graphically. This is illustrated by the chairs shown on the following pages, most of which are in Art Deco style (fig. 128–135). Throughout, these are chairs with lashed springing, although cushions are also used in many models of the period, such as the armchair (figs. 133/134) whose seat is upholstered with a sprung cushion with a Schlaraffia sprung core.

Two examples refer to the tradition of the *pouffe* as an upholstered stool. These are pieces presumably made in the Czech Republic in the 1930s which were worked as either stitched cushioning (figs. 126/127) or lashed springing with a stuffing of tow, palm fibre, coconut coir or horsehair (figs. 124/125). In the *Lehrbuch für Neuzeitliches Polstern*, published by Bücheler and Ulmschneider in 1953, it is stated with regard to the then valued seat companions that when upholstering them, care should be taken not to make the springing too soft and too high, as otherwise the seat *would float when in use*,[109] making sitting uncomfortable and unsafe.

In addition to the use of lashed spring technology, the exhibition provides examples of technical innovation in upholstery construction, such as the armchair (figs. 137–139) which Paul Grießer designed for the *WK 27 – Aufbauheim* furniture series he conceived in 1929–30.[110] The seat here is an inlaid cushion on a spring base, while the back cushion was furnished with a fluted cushion. The seat cushion has a stuffing of horsehair fibre or coconut coir and is secured six times. The cushion covering is cross stitched at the seams and rests on double laid flat springs (fig. 139), which are fitted into the side rails of the wooden frame by means of tension springs. The backrest consists of a cushion in three flutes, which means that it has three elongated, channel-like areas. The cushion is fixed to the upper edge using concealed nails and fixed at the lower corners with snap fasteners. It is upholstered in the same fabric as the seat, the velour covering fabric preserved in the original presents a flame-like pattern typical of the period.

114/115
Armlehnsessel, Modell „400", *Tank*, Alvar Aalto (Entwurf), Oy Huonekalu- ja Rakennustyötehdas, Turku (Herstellung), um 1935/1936 (LÖFFLER COLLECTION, Reichenschwand)

114/115
Armchair, model "400", *Tank*, Alvar Aalto (design), Oy Huonekalu- ja Rakennustyötehdas, Turku (production), around 1935/1936 (LÖFFLER COLLECTION, Reichenschwand)

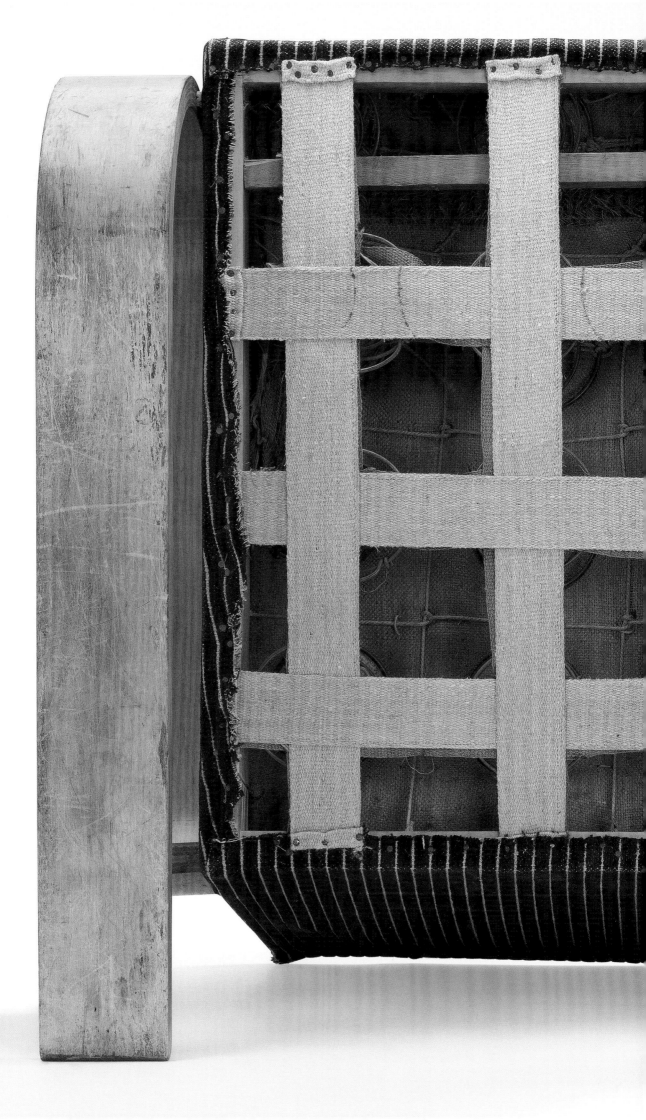

116/117
Armlehnstuhl, Erich Dieckmann (Entwurf), ehemalige Bauhochschule Weimar (Herstellung), vor 1928 (LÖFFLER COLLECTION, Reichenschwand)

116/117
Armchair, Erich Dieckmann (design), former Bauhochschule Weimar (production), before 1928 (LÖFFLER COLLECTION, Reichenschwand)

118–121
Sessel, sog. *Kanadier* mit einer Kettenzugmechanik, 1930er Jahre
(LÖFFLER COLLECTION, Reichenschwand)

118–121
Recliner, so-called *Kanadier*, with chain-hoist mechanism, 1930s
(LÖFFLER COLLECTION, Reichenschwand)

Andere Ansprüche – Neue Ideen | Different demands – New ideas **139**

122/123
Dreibeiniger Armlehnsessel, Otto Schulz (Entwurf zugeschrieben), Boet, Göteborg, Schweden, Jio Möbler (Herstellung), 1930er Jahre (LÖFFLER COLLECTION, Reichenschwand)

122/123
Three-legged armchair, Otto Schulz (design, attributed), Boet, Gothenburg, Sweden, Jio Möbler (production), 1930s (LÖFFLER COLLECTION, Reichenschwand)

124/125
Polsterhocker, sog. *pouffe*, um 1935 (LÖFFLER COLLECTION, Reichenschwand)

124/125
Upholstered stool, so-called *pouffe*, around 1935 (LÖFFLER COLLECTION, Reichenschwand)

126/127
Polsterhocker, sog. *pouffe*, um 1935 (LÖFFLER COLLECTION, Reichenschwand)

126/127
Upholstered stool, so-called *pouffe*, around 1935 (LÖFFLER COLLECTION, Reichenschwand)

Andere Ansprüche – Neue Ideen l Different demands – New ideas **143**

128–130
Armlehnstuhl für Kinder, um 1927 (LÖFFLER COLLECTION, Reichenschwand)

128–130
Children's armchair, around 1927 (LÖFFLER COLLECTION, Reichenschwand)

131/132
Armlehnstuhl, Emil Fahrenkamp (Entwurf?), um 1928
(LÖFFLER COLLECTION, Reichenschwand)

131/132
Armchair, Emil Fahrenkamp (design?), around 1928 (LÖFFLER COLLECTION, Reichenschwand)

133/134
Armlehnstuhl, Kem Weber (Entwurf zugeschrieben), um 1930 (LÖFFLER COLLECTION, Reichenschwand)

133/134
Armchair, Kem Weber (design, attributed), around 1930 (LÖFFLER COLLECTION, Reichenschwand)

135
Armlehnstuhl, um 1930 (LÖFFLER COLLECTION, Reichenschwand)

135
Armchair, around 1930 (LÖFFLER COLLECTION, Reichenschwand)

136 (S. 148/149, p. 148/149)
Einrichtung mit Polstermöbeln von Paul Griesser aus dem Programm *WK 27 – Aufbauheim* (in: Katalog *Warum WK-Möbel?*, Dresden 1930)
Interior with upholstered furniture by Paul Griesser from the programme *WK 27 – Aufbauheim* series (in: catalogue *Warum WK-Möbel?*, Dresden 1930)

137–139 (S. 152/153)
Armlehnsessel, aus dem Programm *WK 27 – Aufbauheim*, Paul Griesser (Entwurf), 1929/30 (GRASSI Museum für Angewandte Kunst Leipzig)

137–139 (p. 152/153)
Armchair, from the programme *WK 27 – Aufbauheim* series, Paul Griesser (design), 1929/30 (GRASSI Museum für Angewandte Kunst Leipzig)

140
Darstellung eines Wohnraums, Alfred Geißler (1904–1980),
Aquarell (Deutsches Stuhlbaumuseum Rabenau)
Depiction of a living space, Alfred Geißler (1904–1980),
watercolour (Deutsches Stuhlbaumuseum Rabenau)

141
Darstellung eines Wohnraums, Alfred Geißler (1904–1980),
Aquarell (Deutsches Stuhlbaumuseum Rabenau)
Depiction of a living space, Alfred Geißler (1904–1980),
watercolour (Deutsches Stuhlbaumuseum Rabenau)

Mit fulminanter Wirkung – Eine Sitzgruppe nach dem Entwurf von Ernst Max Jahn aus dem Jahr 1928

Thomas Andersch

Es wird immer etwas Besonderes und keinesfalls selbstverständlich sein, wenn sich ein Möbel trotz einer viele Jahre währenden Nutzung als Gebrauchsgegenstand in einem weitestgehend original erhaltenen Zustand überliefert hat und uns lediglich durch seine Alterungs- und Gebrauchsspuren die allgemeine Vergänglichkeit vor Augen geführt wird. Demgegenüber ist der Umgang mit stark überarbeiteten Möbeln, die nur noch wenig von ihrer ursprünglichen Entwurfsidee vermitteln, ungleich schwieriger. Hierbei wird letztlich nach einer individuellen Betrachtung und sorgfältigen Einzelfallprüfung nach einer Restaurierungskonzeption zu suchen sein, die zwischen konservierendem Bewahren und begründetem Erneuern entscheiden muss. Davon soll dieser Text erzählen.

Ab dem Jahr 1928 ließ sich der Leipziger Juwelier Ernst Treusch (1881–1968)[111] eine großzügige Etagenwohnung in der Ferdinand-Rohde-Straße 18 einrichten. Die Entwürfe lieferte der in Leipzig ansässige freie Architekt Ernst Max Jahn (1889–1979).[112] Die Männer waren sich freundschaftlich zugetan und fühlten sich durch ihre Mitgliedschaft im Deutschen Werkbund dessen Grundsätzen und Idealen verpflichtet.

Bei dem ausführenden Betrieb für den Innenausbau und die Anfertigung der Möbel handelte es sich um die renommierte Leipziger Tischlerei Carl Müller & Co. Alle Räume bildeten mit ihrer Ausstattung eine stilistische Einheit und können einer vornehm zurückhaltenden Moderne zugerechnet werden. Sämtliche Möbel, aber auch Beleuchtungskörper oder Bodenbeläge, waren individuell gefertigte Einzelstücke mit einer gediegenen handwerklichen Verarbeitung. Ein beredtes Zeugnis dieser gehobenen Wohnkultur stellt das Speisezimmer aus der Treusch-Wohnung dar, das 1994 in den Sammlungsbestand des GRASSI Museums für Angewandte Kunst übernommen werden konnte. Es wird gegenwärtig im dritten Teil der Ständigen Ausstellung des Museums präsentiert und zeigt sich ohne substantielle Eingriffe, würdevoll gealtert und in einem tadellos gepflegten Erhaltungszustand.[113]

Davon konnte bei der wenige Jahre später aus der Armin und Anneliese Treusch Stiftung übernommenen Sitzgruppe jedoch keine Rede sein, denn das Aussehen dieser Möbel hatte sich grundlegend gegenüber dem Originalzustand verändert. Dieses Ensemble war vormals ebenso Teil der Wohnungseinrichtung in der Ferdinand-Rohde-Straße und besteht im Einzelnen aus einem Sofa, einem Sessel (von ursprünglich zweien) und einem kleinen, runden Tisch. Die Überarbeitungen betrafen in erster Linie die erneuerten Bezüge der Polstermöbel und den veränderten Farbanstrich des Beistelltisches. Da sich diese verfälschenden Eingriffe als außerordentlich schwerwiegend und störend erwiesen, erschien eine Restaurierung der Oberflächen, d. h. der Bezugsstoffe und des Farbanstriches am Beistelltisch, in jedem Fall gerechtfertigt und angemessen. Die Bewahrung der recht gut erhaltenen Grundpolsterung an Sessel und Sofa hatte dabei oberste Priorität. Deren polstertechnische Aufarbeitung sollte unter konservatorischen Gesichtspunkten erfolgen.

With brilliant effect – A seating group designed by Ernst Max Jahn in 1928

Thomas Andersch

It will always be something special and by no means a given when a piece of furniture has survived in its largely original condition, despite many years of use as an object of utility, and we are only made aware of its general transience by its signs of aging and use. In contrast, it is much more difficult to deal with heavily reworked furniture that conveys only little of its original design idea. In this case, a restoration concept must ultimately be sought after individual consideration and careful case-by-case examination, which must decide between preservation and justified renewal. This is the subject of this text.

In 1928, the Leipzig jeweller and business owner Ernst Treusch (1881–1968)[111] had a spacious apartment built for him at Ferdinand-Rohde-Strasse 18. The designs were provided by the Leipzig-based freelance architect Ernst Max Jahn (1889–1979).[112] Both men were on friendly terms and, through their membership of the Deutscher Werkbund, felt committed to its principles and ideals.

The company responsible for the interior fittings and furniture was the renowned Leipzig carpenter workshop Carl Müller & Co. All rooms formed a stylistic unit with their furnishings and can be attributed to an elegantly restrained modernism. The entire furniture, as well as the lighting fixtures and floors, consisted of individually manufactured one-of-a-kind pieces of high-quality craftsmanship. The dining room in the Treusch apartment, which was added to the collection of the GRASSI Museum für Angewandte Kunst in 1994, is an eloquent testimony to this sophisticated living culture. It is currently presented in the third part of the museum's permanent exhibition and is presented without substantial interventions, gracefully aged and in an impeccably maintained state of preservation.[113]

However, this was not the case with the seating group taken over a few years later from the *Armin und Anneliese Treusch Stiftung*, as the appearance of this furniture had changed drastically from its original state. This ensemble was formerly also part of the apartment furnishings in Ferdinand-Rohde-Straße and consists of a sofa, an armchair (of originally two) and a small, round table. The revisions primarily concerned the renewed cover fabrics of the upholstered furniture and the altered colour scheme of the side table. Since these distorting interventions proved to be extraordinarily severe and disturbing, the restoration of the surfaces – that is, the cover fabrics and the paint on the side table – seemed justified and appropriate. The preservation of the quite well-preserved upholstery on the armchair and sofa were given top priority. Their refurbishment was to be carried out from a conservation point of view.

142
Armlehnsessel, Ernst Max Jahn (Entwurf), Carl Müller & Co., Leipzig (Herstellung), 1928 (GRASSI Museum für Angewandte Kunst Leipzig)

142
Armchair, Ernst Max Jahn (design), Carl Müller & Co., Leipzig (production), 1928 (GRASSI Museum für Angewandte Kunst Leipzig)

Nun war zwar der ursprüngliche Zustand der Möbel durch qualitätvolle Fotoaufnahmen (der Zeit geschuldet in Schwarz-Weiß) hervorragend dokumentiert, aber über die genaue Gewebestruktur und die Art der originalen Musterung des Bezuges oder dessen Farbigkeit herrschte zunächst völlige Unklarheit. Erst durch den glückhaften Fund zweier Fragmente des originalen Bezugsstoffes (s. Abb. 143) während der Überarbeitung der Polsterung am Armlehnsessel ergaben sich weiterführende Überlegungen zur Rekonstruktion. Denn wie sich zeigte, handelte es sich beim Originalbezug um ein Leinen mit aufgedrucktem Dekor in Siebdrucktechnik und nicht, wie zuerst vermutet, um ein gewebtes Muster. Zudem ließ sich durch intensive Recherche in den zeitgenössischen Zeitschriften zur Innenarchitektur als Entwerfer des Druckdekors Josef Hillerbrand (1892–1981)[114] und als Hersteller die Firma DeWeTex[115] ermitteln. Das 1923 als Deutsche Werkstätten-Textilgesellschaft m. b. H. gegründete Tochterunternehmen der Deutschen Werkstätten Hellerau produzierte eigenständig eine breite Palette von Heimtextilien, die vornehmlich nach Entwürfen gefertigt wurden, die von mit den Deutschen Werkstätten verbundenen Künstlern stammten. Auch Max Ernst Jahn war ab 1927 freier DW-Mitarbeiter und nutzte offenkundig seine Kontakte zum Dresdner Unternehmen für sein Leipziger Projekt. Betrachtet man alle überlieferten Fotos der Wohnetage der Familie Treusch, zeigt sich, dass auch für die Vorhänge der Fenster und für einen Türdurchgang DeWeTex-Druckstoffe Verwendung fanden. Da sich trotz aufwendiger Suche im umfangreichen Nachlass von Josef Hillerbrand keine Entwurfszeichnung unseres Dessins finden ließ, noch eine textile Musterprobe in den Spezialsammlungen anderer Museen aufzuspüren war[116], musste sich die Rekonstruktion auf die zwei gefundenen Fragmente des ursprünglichen Bezuges und auf die fotografische Dokumentation der Treusch-Wohnung stützen. Auch die anfängliche Idee, für den Nachdruck auf die originalgetreue Siebdrucktechnologie zurückzugreifen, stieß auf unüberwindliche Schwierigkeiten.[117] So blieb nichts anderes übrig, als die Zusammenarbeit mit einer auf den Digitaldruck textiler Flächen spezialisierten Werkstatt anzustreben.[118]

Als Erstes wurde durch eine digitale Bearbeitung der historischen Fotografien ein maßstabsgerechter Rapport des Druckmotives erstellt.[119] Daraus konnte dann die für das digitale Bedrucken erforderliche Druckdatei entwickelt werden. Darin eingeschlossen war das exakte Festlegen der Farbpalette, was die künstlerische Einfühlung in einen um etliche Farbtöne erweiterten „Farbklang" erforderlich machte, denn der diesbezügliche Aussagewert der beiden Bezugsstofffragmente war naturgemäß recht begrenzt. Zudem sind ganz bewusst gewisse Verschiebungen an den Konturen der Bildmotive einprogrammiert worden, um das meist unperfekte Druckbild der Siebdrucktechnik zu imitieren oder wenigstens anzudeuten.[120]

Nach der Konsolidierung der Polsterung an den Sitzmöbeln erfolgte das Beziehen mit der bedruckten Leinwand nach dem digital rekonstruierten Entwurf Hillerbrands. Anschließend wurden die Möbelkanten mit einer farblich passenden Kordel, der sogenannten Möbelschnur, abgedeckt.[121] An den Gestellen war einzig die Farbfassung an den Beinen zu reinigen und stellenweise zu retuschieren.

Die Restaurierung des runden Tisches war hingegen wesentlich aufwendiger. Da sich unter der dunkelbraunen

While the original state of the furniture was extraordinarily well documented through photographs (due to the time in black and white), the exact textile structure and original pattern of the cover as well as its colour was entirely unknown. It was only when, by chance, two fragments of the original cover fabric (fig. 143) were found when the armchair upholstery was refurbished that further considerations regarding the reconstruction could be made. It became clear that the original fabric was a linen with a screen-printed pattern and not, as originally presumed, a woven pattern. Through intensive research in contemporary interior design magazines, it was possible to identify Josef Hillerbrand (1892–1981)[114] as the designer of the pattern and the DeWeTex[115] company as the manufacturer. The subsidiary of the Deutsche Werkstätten Hellerau, which had been founded in 1923 as Deutsche Werkstätten-Textilgesellschaft m.b.H., produced independently a large range of home textiles, most of them after designs by artists connected to the Deutsche Werkstätten. Max Ernst Jahn, too, worked as a freelancer for DW and apparently used his contacts to the Dresden company for his project in Leipzig. When looking at the surviving photographs of the Treusch family apartment, it becomes evident that the curtains for the windows as well as one door frame are likewise made from DeWeTex fabrics. Despite elaborate research in the extensive estate of Josef Hillerbrand, no draft of our design could be found, nor could a textile sample be found in the special collections of other museums.[116] For this reason, the reconstruction had to be based on the two fragments of the original covering fabric found and on the photographic documentation of the Treusch apartment. Likewise, the initial idea of resorting to the original screen-printing technology for the reprint encountered insurmountable difficulties.[117] There was no option but to seek a collaboration with a workshop specialising in the digital printing of textiles.[118] The first step was to digitally process the historical photographs to create a scaled pattern repeat of the print motif.[119] From this, the print file required for digital printing could then be developed. This included the exact determination of the colour palette, which required artistic empathy for a 'colour tone' extended by several shades, because the information provided by the two cover fabric fragments in this respect was naturally quite limited. In addition, certain shifts in the contours of the image motifs were deliberately programmed to imitate or at least hint at the usually imperfect print result of the screen-printing technique.[120]

After the upholstery on the seating furniture was secured, it was covered with the printed linen fabric according to Hillerbrand's digitally reconstructed design. Subsequently, the borders of the furniture were covered with cord in a matching colour.[121] On the frame, only the colour on the legs needed to be cleaned and retouched in places.

The restoration of the round table, on the other hand, was much more complex. Since the original coloured lacquer had been almost completely preserved under the dark brown varnish overlay, its uncovering

Überfassung der originale Schleiflack nahezu komplett erhalten hatte, war dessen Freilegung dringend geboten und unumgänglich. Zu gewichtig ist der noble, graue Farbton, der das sehr durchdachte Farbkonzept der kleinen Möbelgruppe perfekt abrundet.

Die kraftvolle und in sich stimmige Ausstrahlung des rekonstruierten Druckstoffes, wie überhaupt der gesamten Möbelgruppe (s. Abb. 144), hat schließlich all unsere Erwartungen übertroffen. Eine schöne Bestätigung für die Richtigkeit des Entschlusses, sich in beschriebener Weise dieser nicht ganz einfachen Herausforderung gestellt zu haben.

was urgently required and unavoidable. Its noble grey colour, which perfectly rounds off the very well-thought-out colour concept of the small furniture group, is too significant.

The powerful and coherent appearance of the reconstructed printed fabric, as of the entire furniture group (fig. 144), finally exceeded all our expectations. A beautiful confirmation of having taken the right decision to take on this not entirely easy challenge in the manner described.

143
Fragment des originalen Bezugsstoffs, Josef Hillerbrand (Entwurf), Textil GmbH Dresden-Hellerau (DeWeTex) (Herstellung), 1928 (GRASSI Museum für Angewandte Kunst Leipzig)

143
Fragment of the original top cover fabric, Josef Hillerbrand (design), Textil GmbH Dresden-Hellerau (DeWeTex) (production), 1928 (GRASSI Museum für Angewandte Kunst Leipzig)

144
Möbelgruppe (Sessel, Sofa, Tisch), mit digital rekonstruiertem Stoff bezogen, Ernst Max Jahn (Entwurf), Carl Müller & Co., Leipzig (Herstellung), 1928 (GRASSI Museum für Angewandte Kunst Leipzig)

144
Furniture set (armchair, sofa, table), covered with digitally reconstructed fabric, Ernst Max Jahn (design), Carl Müller & Co., Leipzig (production), 1928 (GRASSI Museum für Angewandte Kunst Leipzig)

Mit fulminanter Wirkung | With brilliant effect **161**

Konventionen
Thomas Schriefers

Weitgehende Einigkeit besteht darin, dass Wohnformen immer eng mit gesellschaftlichen Konventionen verbunden sind. Gerade am Beispiel des Polstermöbels lassen sich Fragen nach zeitgemäßer Einrichtung erörtern. Das zeigt auch Heinrich Gerons Text *Moderne Wohnlichkeit*[122], in dem er bereits 1925 den neuzeitlichen Klubsessel als Repräsentanten einer neuen Geisteshaltung charakterisiert: *Ein guter, neuzeitlicher Klubsessel ist sachlich, ohne nüchtern zu sein, er ist bequem und doch nicht weichlingshaft, er ist wundervoll behaglich ohne trägemachende Behäbigkeit, er steht in unseren Heimen wie eine ständige Einladung, ungezwungen in ihm Platz zu nehmen und uns in seiner Wohnlichkeit geborgen zu fühlen.*[123]

Sich in Polstern zu räkeln oder auf dem Boden zu lagern, wurde zumindest in progressiven Kreisen akzeptiert, weshalb neue Sitzmöbeltypen entwickelt wurden. So kam in den frühen 1930er Jahren etwa das dem Liegestuhl entliehene Matratzenkissen dazu, das es erlaubte, sich auch ohne Gestell direkt auf dem Boden niederzulassen. Ob einzurollen, klappfähig oder modular in Einzelelementen konzipiert, stand das lose Kissen[124] zur beliebigen Verwendung und Zusammenstellung zur Verfügung, wie Adolf G. Schneck ausführt (s. Abb. 146–148). In seiner 1931 erschienenen Schrift *Zweckmäßiges Wohnen für jedes Einkommen* warb auch Werner Gräff für variabel einsetzbare Liegepolster.[125] Kubische Polster (s. Abb. 154) seien sehr einfach in der Form und Herstellung und könnten von jedem Dekorateur angefertigt werden, wobei sich deren Preis nach der Qualität des Bezugsstoffes und des Füllmaterials richte.[126] Auf die Wertarbeit

Conventions
Thomas Schriefers

It is generally agreed that forms of living are always closely linked to those of society and its conventions. The example of upholstered furniture in particular can be used to discuss issues of up-to-date interiors. Likewise, in his text *Moderne Wohnlichkeit* (Modern Living),[122] Heinrich Geron characterises the modern club chair as a representative of a new attitude as early as 1925: *A good, modern club chair is functional without being sober, it is comfortable without being all-too-soft, it is wonderfully comfortable without being sluggish, it stands in our homes like a constant invitation to take a seat in it without constraint and to feel secure in its homeliness.*[123]

Lolling in cushions or reclining on the floor became acceptable, at least in progressive circles, which gave rise to the development of new types of seating furniture. In the early 1930s, for example, came the mattress cushion, borrowed from the recliner, which made it possible to lie down directly on the floor without a frame. Whether rolled up, foldable or designed modularly in individual elements, the loose cushion[124] was available for any use and composition, as Adolf G. Schneck explains (figs. 146–148). In his 1931 text *Zweckmäßiges Wohnen für jedes Einkommen* (Practical Living for Every Income), Werner Gräff also promoted reclining cushions that could be used for a variety of purposes.[125] According to him, cubic cushions (fig. 154) were very simple in form and manufacture and could be made by any decorator, their price being determined by the quality of the top fabric and the stuffing material.[126] It was believed that the craftsmanship of a master upholsterer, who knew how to make complex

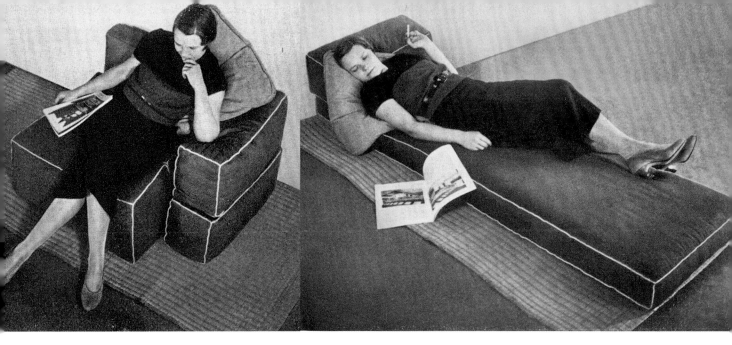

146–148
Sitzen auf losen Kissen zur beliebigen Verwendung und Zusammenstellung (in: Schneck 1933)

146–148
Sitting on a loose cushion for any desired use and arrangement (in: Schneck 1933)

eines auf komplexe Polsterei sich verstehenden Meisters glaubte man hier verzichten zu können. Doch ging es Gräff nicht darum, dem Handwerk Aufgaben zu entziehen. Vielmehr war er wie viele seiner progressiven Wohnberater-Kollegen davon überzeugt, dass die Kosten für Einrichtungsgegenstände reduziert und für kleinere Wohnungen vielseitiges Mobiliar angeboten werden müsse. So rückte das Typenmöbel in den Fokus der Entwerfer.

Dennoch verband sich auch weiterhin der Reiz des luxuriösen Komforts mit zum Teil schweren Polstermöbeln wie jenem, das Fritz August Breuhaus de Groot um 1934/1936 entworfen hatte (s. Abb. 149/150). Es besitzt ein hölzernes Untergestell aus massiver Buche im Sitz, in Rücken und auf den Armlehnen eine geschnürte Federkonstruktion mit freistehender vorderer Federreihe und englischer Kante, was bedeutet, dass die Polsterung vorne übersteht. Afrik und Rosshaar bedecken das garnierte Polster, auf dem ein weiches Daunenkissen zusätzlich aufgelegt ist. Der mit Blütenmotiven versehene Chinille-Bezug ist mit eingewebten Metallplätten versehen, die dazu beitragen, ein durch Lichtreflexionen erzeugtes Glitzern in das gewebte Blütenbild zu zaubern. Mit ähnlicher Wirkung werden Metallplätten üblicherweise um Seidenfäden gewickelt, bevor sie in Bezugsstoffen eingewebt werden, wie zum Beispiel beim bereits vorgestellten Fauteuil von Peter Behrens (s. Abb. 81). In dem hier verwendeten und von der Crimmitschauer Seidenmanufaktur Eschke nach originalen Bezugsresten rekonstruierten Material werden sie flächiger eingesetzt, sodass ihre Wirkung im Muster noch stärker zur Geltung kommt.

upholstery, could be dispensed with. But Gräff was not interested in taking tasks away from the craftsmen. Rather, like many of his progressive colleagues, he was convinced that the cost of furnishings had to be reduced and that versatile furniture had to be offered for smaller apartments. Thus, *Typenmöbel* (matching standardised furniture) moved into the focus of designers.

Nevertheless, the appeal of luxurious comfort continued to be associated with sometimes heavy upholstered furniture, such as that designed by Fritz August Breuhaus de Groot around 1934–36 (figs. 149/150). It has a wooden frame of solid beech and, in the seat, back and armrests, lashed springing, with a freestanding front row of springs and an English edge, which means that the upholstery protrudes in front. Palm fibre and horsehair cover the upholstery, on top of which a soft down pillow is additionally placed. The velour cover fabric with floral motif has metal platelets woven into it, which help to conjure up a glint in the woven floral image created by reflection of light. To similar effect, metal platelets are usually wrapped around silk threads before being woven into upholstery fabrics, as in the case of Peter Behrens's armchair presented above (fig. 81). In the material used here, which was reconstructed by the Eschke silk manufactory in Crimmitschau from original upholstery remnants, they are used more two-dimensional, so that their effect in the pattern is even more pronounced.

145 (S. 162 links, p.162 left)
Sitzen im Klubsessel (in: *Berliner Illustrierte Zeitung*, 1920er Jahre)
Sitting in a club chair (in: *Berliner Illustrierte Zeitung*, 1920s)

149/150
Armlehnsessel, Fritz August Breuhaus de Groot (Entwurf), um 1934/1936 (LÖFFLER COLLECTION, Reichenschwand)

149/150
Armchair, Fritz August Breuhaus de Groot (design), around 1934/1936 (LÖFFLER COLLECTION, Reichenschwand)

Konventionen | Conventions   165

Nach 1945
Thomas Schriefers

1948 erschien im Wiener Anton Schroll Verlag ein kleines Bändchen, in dem der Architekt Franz Schuster am Beispiel des Sessels fünf von ihm unterschiedene Stufen der Formentwicklung erläuterte: Urform, Grundform, Feinform und Zierform, wobei sich der letzteren noch die von Schuster so bezeichnete abwegige Trugform zugesellte.[127] Er wählte diese Reihung, um Kriterien für die Bewertung von Formlösungen festzulegen. Ziel war es, Antworten auf die Frage zu finden, wohin sich die Gestaltungsarbeit nach 1945 entwickeln würde.

Ein montiertes Foto (s. Abb. 151) zeigt eine Ansammlung von Armlehnstühlen, die, so Schuster, Versuche der Veränderung von Sesselformen durch konstruktive Neuerungen zeigen, welche er aber nicht bei allen Modellen im Zusammenbau und in der Formgebung als sinnvoll erachtete. Zu sehen sind gepolsterte Armlehnstühle mit verschiedenen Konstruktionsweisen, ergänzt durch einzelne Beispiele mit Tuch- bzw. Lederbespannung und Flechtwerk, denen Schuster polarisierend einen ungepolstert nackten Stahlblech-Stuhl gegenüberstellt. Er steht hier stellvertretend für *ein unvollkommenes und rohes Aussehen*, das nach Schusters Einschätzung jedes feinere Formempfinden beleidigt und die Hässlichkeit der Welt verursacht. Dabei sehen wir hier eine selbsttragende Schalenform, wie sie in der Folgezeit die Basis für viele Polstersessel bilden sollte. Diese erhielten mit Schaumstoff umkleidet erst ihren formalen Ausdruck. Auf diese Weise fasst das Sammelbild im subjektiven Überblick verschiedene Polsterkonzepte zusammen, die Anfang der 1950er Jahre nebeneinander weiterverfolgt wurden. Auch zeigen sie, was Schuster unter den Begriffen Fein- bzw. Zierform verstand: Formen, die dem Wunsch nach ästhetischer Vollendung entsprechen oder mehr dekorativen Gesichtspunkten folgen.

Fortan testete der Markt immer stärker die Grenzen des Käuferinteresses aus. Die Frage nach der marktrelevanten Akzeptanz neuer Formen erläuterte der Stardesigner Raymond Loewy in einem Bestseller, der in deutscher Übersetzung 1953 den Titel *Hässlichkeit verkauft sich schlecht*[128] erhielt. Darin spielt die von ihm als zukunftsweisend erachtete Stromlinienform eine zentrale Rolle. Beispiele für die Entwicklung der Silhouetten von Gewändern, Automobilen, Telefonapparaten und Möbeln wurden herangezogen, um die Entwicklung *zur beschleunigten Perspektive*[129] in Stromlinienform darzustellen. Züge und Schiffe erhielten nun ebenso ein schnittiges Äußeres wie Automobile und Toaster. Das Chassis eines Automobils, seinen technischen Aufbau und seine Verkleidung verglich Loewy mit dem menschlichen Körper, bei dem das Skelett den gleichen ästhetischen Bedingungen der Linienführung folge.[130] Der Designer sprach in diesem Zusammenhang auch von Tendenzen der Überfeinerung bzw. Überladung, mit der Konsequenz, dass eine Körperform als gefällig oder abstoßend empfunden werden könne. Dahinter verbarg sich das besondere Interesse an der Wechselwirkung vom Innenleben der Dinge und ihrer äußeren Form, die sich nach Loewys Auffassung so weit modischer Neuerung unterwerfen solle, wie sie *der Wunsch des Verbrauchers nach Neuartigkeit*[131] zulässt. Übertragen auf das Polstermöbel resultierte daraus ein fast grenzenloses Gestaltungsspektrum. In einem Beitrag

After 1945
Thomas Schriefers

In 1948, the Viennese Anton Schroll Verlag published a small volume in which the architect Franz Schuster used the armchair as an example to explain his five stages of form development: the original form, basic form, fine form and decorative form, the latter being joined by the so-called aberrant deceptive form.[127] He chose this order to define criteria for the evaluation of formal solutions. The goal was to answer the question of how design would develop after 1945.

A photo montage (fig. 151) shows an assemblage of armchairs which, according to Schuster, illustrates the attempts to change armchair forms through innovative construction, which he did not in all cases consider useful in terms of assembly and design. There are upholstered armchairs made using various methods, supplemented by examples with fabric or leather coverings and wickerwork, which Schuster contrasts with an un-upholstered, bare sheet steel chair. It represents an *imperfect and crude appearance* which, in Schuster's estimation, offends every finer sense of form and causes the ugliness of the world. We see here a self-supporting shell form, which was the basis for many upholstered chairs in the following period. Only when covered with foam material did they receive their formal expression. In this way, the image summarises, in a subjective overview, the various upholstery concepts that were pursued side by side in the early 1950s. They also show what Schuster understood by the terms fine or ornamental form: forms that correspond to the desire for aesthetic perfection or follow more decorative considerations.

From then on, the market increasingly tested the limits of buyer interest. The question of the relevant acceptance of new forms on the market was explained by the star designer Raymond Loewy in a bestseller, which was given the title *Ugliness Doesn't Sell*[128] and translated into German in 1953. In it, the streamlined shape, which he regarded as trendsetting, plays a central role. Examples of the development of silhouettes of garments, automobiles, telephones and furniture were used to illustrate the evolution to an *accelerated perspective*[129] in a streamlined form. Trains and ships were now given sleek exteriors, as were automobiles and toasters. Loewy compared the relationship between the chassis of an automobile, its technical structure and its cladding to the human body, in which the skeleton follows the same aesthetic conditions of line.[130] In this context, the designer also spoke of tendencies towards over-refinement or overloading, with the consequence that a body shape could be perceived as frivolous or repulsive. Behind this was a particular interest in the interaction between the inner life of things and their outer form, which, in *Loewy´s view, should be subject to fashionable innovation to the extent that the consumer's desire for novelty allowed*.[131] Applied to upholstered furniture, this resulted in an almost limitless range of designs. In an article for the weekly newspaper *Die Zeit*, Wolfgang Heyn stated in 1955 that upholstered furniture, following the new trend, should

151
Stuhlformen im Vergleich (in: Schuster 1948)

151
Chair shapes in comparison (in: Schuster 1948)

für die Wochenzeitung *Die Zeit* erklärte Wolfgang Heyn 1955 einschränkend, Polstermöbel sollten sich, dem neuen Trend folgend, von den Geraden und den ebenen Flächen anderer Holzmöbel abheben und organische Formen annehmen.[132] Damit verbinde sich die Abkehr von der Uniformität konfektionierter Herrlichkeit zugunsten individueller Lösungen.

Die im Westen Deutschlands in der sogenannten Wirschaftswunderzeit verbreitete Losung lautete: Schöner wohnen! Damit verband sich, was die Redaktion der Zeitschrift *Constanze* im gleichnamigen Sonderheft auf der ersten Seite als *Spaß am Wohnen und Bauen*[133] bewarb. Farbig sollten Wohnungen eingerichtet sein, praktisch und unkompliziert. Vor allem sollte der Käufer darauf achten, sich trendgerecht einzurichten, was bedeutete, immer öfter auch Möbel auszutauschen. Darin unterschied man sich deutlich vom Osten Deutschlands, wo man die mit den Moden assoziierte Kurzlebigkeit der Dinge und deren Verbrauch als unvereinbar mit den Zielen einer sozialistischen Gesellschaft verstand. Dabei verband beide Teile Deutschlands eine Auseinandersetzung mit dem Status Quo der Möbelproduktion. Der Bedarf war allgemein groß, da im Krieg vieles zerstört worden war, die neuen Wohnungen zudem kleiner und die Deckenhöhe geringer war. So galt es beiderseits der Zonengrenzen, geeignete Konzepte zu finden, den jeweiligen Aufbau zu forcieren. Im Osten standen sogar die Produkte der bedeutenden Deutschen Werkstätten Hellerau auf dem Prüfstand. Hermann Exner erklärte in seinem Beitrag eines Heftes der Zeitschrift *Bildende Kunst* 1956, Hellerau überwinde gerade den Bauhausstil.[134] Dabei wendete er sich gegen eine den Dingen anhaftende Kostbarkeit des Materials, der Form oder der Seltenheit und Kuriosität. Die Entstehung eines neuen Schönheitsgefühls hänge demnach eng mit der Ensemblefähigkeit des einzelnen Gegenstandes zusammen, die durch die Vereinfachung der Formen in greifbare Nähe rücke. Exner zitiert Adolf Behne aus dessen Schrift *Die Wohnung ohne Sorgen*, wenn er die Beziehungen der Dinge untereinander über die Einzigartigkeit des Einzelstücks hebt, die aus der kollektiven Erfahrung und dem meisterhaften Können der Hellerauer Fabrikarbeiter resultiere.[135]

Ein Beispiel dafür ist der Armlehnstuhl, den Selman Selmanagić um 1951 für die Deutschen Werkstätten Hellerau entwarf (s. Abb. 152/153). Auf bewährte Art ist der Sitz als Hochpolster mit traditioneller Federung auf einer 3×4-Gurtung aufgebaut und mit haltbaren verzinkten Federn ausgestattet. Ein zweifarbiges, grob gewebtes Gewebe, bildet den Bezug, der im Sitz durch eine an den Kanten angebrachte gelbe Kordel in seiner kräftigen Form betont wird. Die Ausformung der konkav gewölbten Rückenlehne vermittelt eine einladende Geste, verbunden mit sinnlicher Qualität, die durch die Materialität des griffigen Stoffes und die eingebrachte Knopfheftung verstärkt werden.

Einer der Leitsätze, die 1953 auf dem *Congrès International d'Esthétique Industrielle* in Paris von dem Designtheoretiker Jacques Viénot zusammengestellt wurden, lautete: *Der Ausdruck des Zwecks, der einem Gerät seine Schönheit gibt, sollte sich in der Art und Weise bemerkbar machen, wie er alle Sinne anspricht; nicht nur das Sehen, sondern auch das Hören, Fühlen und Bewegungsempfinden*.[136] Das gilt in besonderem Maße für Sitzmöbel und speziell für den gefederten

stand out from the straight lines and flat surfaces of other wooden furniture and take on organic forms.[132] According to him, this was a move away from the uniformity of ready-made splendour in favour of individual solutions.

The slogan spread throughout West Germany during the so-called economic miracle was *Live more beautifully!* This was associated with what the editors of the magazine *Constanze* advertised on the first page of the special issue of the same name as the *fun of living and building*.[133] Apartments had to be colourful, practical and uncomplicated. Above all, the buyer was to furnish fashionably, which meant replacing furniture more and more often. In this respect, there was a clear difference from East Germany, where the short life cycle of items and their consumption associated with fashion trends were seen as incompatible with the goals of a socialist society. At the same time, both parts of Germany were united by a dispute over the status quo of furniture production. The demand was great everywhere, since much had been destroyed during the war, and at the same time, the new apartments were smaller and built with lower ceilings. Thus, on both sides of the border, suitable concepts had to be found to drive the respective reconstruction. In the East, even the products of the important Deutsche Werkstätten Hellerau were put to the test. In his contribution to an issue of the magazine *Bildende Kunst* in 1956, Hermann Exner declared that Hellerau was in the process of overcoming the Bauhaus style.[134] In doing so, he turned against a preciousness of material, form, or rarity and curiosity inherent in objects. To him, the emergence of a new sense of beauty was closely related to the capacity of the individual object to fit into an ensemble, which was brought within reach by the simplification of forms. Exner quoted Adolf Behne from his book *Die Wohnung ohne Sorgen* (The Apartment without Worries) when he emphasised the relationships between objects over the uniqueness of the individual piece, which resulted from the collective experience and masterful skills of the Hellerau factory workers.[135]

An example of this is the armchair designed by Selman Selmanagić for the Deutsche Werkstätten Hellerau (figs. 152/153) in around 1951. In a proven way, the seat is constructed as a high cushion with traditional springing on a 3 x 4 webbing and equipped with durable galvanised springs. A bicoloured, coarsely woven fabric forms the top cover, which is accentuated in the seat by a yellow cord attached to the edges. The shaping of the concave curved backrest conveys an inviting gesture, combined with a sensual quality, which is enhanced by the materiality of the non-slip fabric and the deep buttoning.

One of the guiding principles that the design theoretician Jacques Viénot had put together on the occasion of the 1953 *Congrès International d'Esthétique Industrielle* in Paris was *the expression of utility, which lends beauty to a machine, should make itself evident in a way that speaks to all senses, not only sight but also hearing, touch and feeling of movement*.[136] This is especially true for seating furniture and especially

Sessel, da er, je nach Material und Polsterbeschaffenheit, auf die körperlichen Eigenheiten der Nutzer*innen reagiert und damit ihr Nervensystem unterschiedlich anspricht. Darauf bezog sich 1956 der Architekt Richard Neutra, der in seinem Buch *Gestaltete Umwelt*[137] die Bedeutung von taktilen Anreizen im Wohnumfeld betonte. Er sagte: *Wir dürfen nicht übersehen, dass Sitzen auf einem Polsterstuhl, Liegen auf einem Sofa mit Sprungfedermatratze, Treten auf einem dicken Teppich – oder, im Gegensatz dazu, auf eine Terrazzo-Treppe – bestimmte nervliche Reaktionen innerhalb der Muskeln selbst hervorruft.*[138] Neutra führte im Weiteren aus, dass in dem Moment, in dem wir unseren Körper in eine bestimmte Stellung bringen, unsere Muskeln sich durch äußeren physischen Kontakt deformieren, und zwar besonders an den Punkten, wo unser Körper gestützt wird.[139] Damit verbindet sich unser Empfinden von Komfort, das sich bei einer über einen längeren Zeitraum sitzenden Person im Ausmaß und in der Häufigkeit der Gewichtsverlagerung manifestiert.[140] Davon war auch der an der ETH Zürich lehrende Arzt und Forscher Étienne Grandjean überzeugt. Man betonte, eine zu starke Polsterung erhöhe den Druck zu sehr und führe zum Einschlafen der Gewebe.[141] Entsprechend bedeutsam sei die passgenaue Ausführung der Polsterarbeiten, bei der darauf geachtet werden müsse, dass die Beschaffenheit der federnden Volumen dazu beiträgt, Nutzer*innen das Gefühl einer wohltuenden Sitzhaltung zu vermitteln.

sprung chairs, since, depending on the material and make of the upholstery, they react to the physical characteristics of the user and address their nervous system in different ways. Richard Neutra referred to this in his 1946 book *Gestaltete Umwelt*,[137] when he emphasised the importance of tactile stimulation in the living environment. He said, *We should not overlook that sitting on an upholstered chair, laying on a sofa with a coil spring mattress, stepping on a thick carpet – or, on the contrary, a terrazzo staircase – provokes certain nervous reactions inside the muscles.*[138] Neutra went on to state that in the moment when we bring our body into a certain position, our muscles are deformed by exterior physical contact, especially in those areas where our body is supported.[139] This is connected to our feeling of comfort, that manifests itself in the amount a sitting person shifts their body weight over a longer period of time.[140] This was also the conviction of the doctor and researcher Etienne Grandjean, who taught at ETH Zurich. According to them, if the upholstery was too high this would raise the pressure too much and lead to stiff muscles[141] Correspondingly, a fit-to-measure construction of the upholstery was important, which ensured that the configuration of the sprung volumes provided sitters with a beneficial sitting posture.

152/153 (S. 170/171)
Armlehnstuhl, Selman Selmanagić (Entwurf), Deutsche Werkstätten Hellerau, Dresden (Herstellung), um 1951 (GRASSI Museum für Angewandte Kunst Leipzig)

152/153 (p. 170/171)
Armchair, Selman Selmanagić (design), Deutsche Werkstätten Hellerau, Dresden (production), around 1951 (GRASSI Museum für Angewandte Kunst Leipzig)

Als Wundermaterial galten in Ost und West neu entwickelte Schaumstoffe, die in den Fachschriften zum Polsterwesen schon in den 1930er Jahren als gut zu verarbeitende Schaumgummierzeugnisse Beachtung gefunden hatten. Dies waren Füllstoffe, die unter der Markenbezeichnung UVW als unverwüstliches Polster angepriesen wurden. Ein solches Produkt wurde etwa von der Hamburger Firma Emil Hauenschild hergestellt und bestand aus einer chemischen Gummimasse, in die Haare verschiedener Tiere eingebracht wurden. Fachleute wie Adolf G. Schneck beschieden dem Produkt eine außerordentliche Elastizität und Formbeständigkeit. Wegen der einfachen Art ihres Zuschnitts ließen sich zylindrische Hohlräume bilden, in die bei Bedarf geschnürte Spiralfedern eingesetzt werden konnten. Umschneider erklärte noch Anfang der 1950er Jahre euphorisch, die Vorteile dieses Polstermaterials seien so vielseitig, dass sich die einfach zuzuschneidenden Schaumstoffblocks, insbesondere in Amerika und in mehreren europäischen Ländern, sehr große Anwendungsbereiche erobert hätten.[142] Da sie hochelastisch sind, bleibe die Form auch nach vieltausendmaligem Be- und Entlasten erhalten. Zudem verteile sich die Last gleichmäßig über die ganze Berührungsfläche und dämpfe, wegen der porösen Beschaffenheit der Masse, Geräusche, die durch die Nutzung der Polster entstehen können. Auch erzeuge Schaumgummi keinen Staub, weil es durch seine unzähligen Luftkammern atme. Es sei deshalb auch gesund und hygienisch. Nicht zuletzt lasse sich der Werkstoff biegen, rollen, zusammenlegen, schneiden und kleben, um beliebige gewünschte Formen zu erzielen. Zwar könnten Kanten mit Schaumgummi nicht so hart und exakt herausgearbeitet werden, gab der Autor zu bedenken, um im gleichen Satz aber seiner Überzeugung Ausdruck zu verleihen, dass die neue Moderichtung darauf möglicherweise weniger Wert legt als auf den Vorzug einer komfortabel weichen Polsterung.
Im Düsseldorfer Econ-Verlag erschien 1952 ein Buch, welches das angebrochene *Jahrhundert der Kunststoffe in Wort und Bild* feierte.[143] Hansjürgen Saechtling schrieb im Vorwort begeistert, die Forderungen einer verfeinerten, alle Lebensbereiche durchdringenden Technik an ihre Werkstoffe habe nach Menge und Beschaffenheit in den letzten Jahrzehnten eine ganz außerordentliche Steigerung erfahren, deren Höhepunkt noch nicht erkennbar sei[144]: Kunststoffe galten als Baustoffe der Zukunft. Kritik kam aber früh schon von Architekten wie Hans Schwippert, der wegen der grenzenlosen Formbarkeit von Kunststoffen ein mögliches Ende der Werkgerechtigkeit als der schlüssigen Einheit von Material, Konstruktion und Verarbeitung befürchtete.[145] Hans Dieter Oestereich führte hingegen aus, der Kunststoff bleibe stets an die Maschine gebunden und sei dadurch formal auf deren technische Möglichkeiten angewiesen.[146] Ein aus ihm hergestelltes Einzelstück würde voraussichtlich immer zu den Ausnahmen zählen, doch überwog der Optimismus jener, die Produkte für einen rasant wachsenden Markt produzieren wollten. In seinem Text *Gediegen für Wenige – minder für Viele*[147] konstatiert Robert Maria Stieg in Hinblick auf Polstermöbel, dass damals die Rationalisierungsmaßnahmen der industriellen Produktion eben nicht nur mit einer neuen Bedarfsdeckungswelle, sondern auch mit einer neuen Mechanisierungswelle[148] zusammenfielen. Hinzu kam der Kostenfaktor. Die aufwendige Handarbeit des Meisters, der Fassonkissen individuell garniert, war teurer als der beherzte Zuschnitt eines Schaumstoffblocks, der letztlich auch vollautomatisiert vonstattengehen konnte.

The newly developed rubber foams were hailed as a miracle material in both East and West. Since the 1930s they had attracted the interest of specialist upholstery magazines as easy-to-process foam items. These were fillers that were advertised under the brand name UVW as indestructible upholstery. One such product was manufactured by the Hamburg company Emil Hauenschild and consisted of a chemical rubber mass into which the hairs of different animals had been worked. Experts such as Adolf G. Schneck attested to the product extraordinary elasticity and stability of form. Since they could be easily cut, they could be formed into cylindrical cavities into which lashed coil springs could be inserted. In the early 1950s Ulmschneider declared euphorically that the advantages of this upholstery material were so manifold that these easily cut foam blocks had conquered a wide scope of applications, especially in the US and several European countries.[142] Since they were elastic, they stayed true to form despite thousands of times of on and off loading. Furthermore, according to Ulmschneider, the load was spread evenly across the entire surface and, due to its porous qualities, muted sounds that occurred when using it. Moreover, the rubber foam did not create dust since it 'breathed' through its many air chambers. Because of this, it was healthy and hygienic. Finally, this material could be formed, rolled, folded, cut and glued in order to create any wanted shape. While it was not possible to create edges quite as sharp and precise, the author warned, in the same sentence that the new fashion possibly did not care too much about this in the face of comfortable, soft padding.

In 1952, the Düsseldorf Econ Verlag published a book which celebrated the dawn of the *Jahrhundert der Kunststoffe in Wort und Bild* (Century of Plastic in Word and Image).[143] Hansjürgen Saechtling wrote enthusiastically in the preface that the demands a refined technology encompassing all parts of life had for its materials in terms of quantity and quality had risen significantly, and without an end in sight[144]: rubber foams were considered to be the material of the future. Criticism was likewise raised early on by architects such as Hans Schwippert, who considered the endless formal possibilities of plastic to be a possible end to the coherent unit between material, construction and processing.[145] Hans Dieter Oestereich, on the contrary, remarked that plastics would always remain bound to the machine and was therefore limited by its technical capacities.[146] A unique piece made from it would presumably always remain an exception. Nevertheless, these were outweighed by the optimism of those who wanted to produce products for a rapidly growing market. In his text *Gediegen für Wenige – minder für Viele*[147] (Superior for the Few – Inferior for the Many), Robert Maria Stieg states with regard to upholstered furniture that the rationalisation of industrial production coincided not only with an increase in demand that had to be met but also with a new wave of mechanisation.[148] Another factor was cost. The elaborate handiwork of the master craftsman who had individually stitched cushions was more expensive than cutting a block of foam, which in the end could also be fully automated.

Sehr einfach in der Form und Herstellung sind kubische Polster (550:550:220 mm), die man einzeln oder in allerlei Kombinationen aneinandergerückt zum Sitzen oder Liegen benutzen kann.

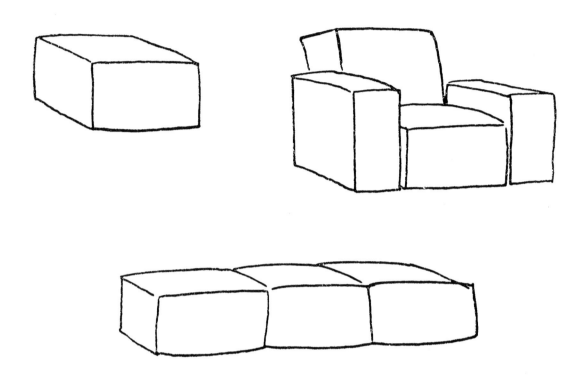

Jeder Dekorateur kann sie Ihnen anfertigen. Der Preis richtet sich nach der Qualität des Bezugsstoffes und des Füllmaterials.

In den 1960er Jahren veränderte die allgemein rasch anwachsende Zahl privater Fernseher und der damit verbundene *Flimmerbildkonsum*[149] die Gewohnheiten auch dahin, dass nicht mehr nur die Küche, sondern jetzt auch das Wohnzimmer bewohnt wurde.[150] Die nun weitgehend mit Schaumstoff gefüllten Polstergarnituren sollten der TV-konsumierenden Familie nicht nur ein bequemes, sondern auch entspanntes Sitzen ermöglichen. Denn wer mehrere Stunden auf einem Fleck ausharrt, sollte keine Rückenschmerzen bekommen und sich nicht über eingeschlafene Füße oder Beinkrämpfe beschweren müssen.[151] Hier drängt sich Christian Morgensterns Vierzeiler auf, der lautet:

Wenn ich sitze, will ich nicht
Sitzen, wie mein Sitzfleisch möchte,
Sondern wie mein Sitzgeist sich,
Säße er, den Stuhl sich flöchte.[152]

In diesem Fall hätte sich der Sitzgeist wohl mit dem Stumpfsinn regungsloser Fernsehlust abgefunden. Ganz anders deutete man aber Morgensterns Zeilen in der Zeitschrift *Kultur im Heim*, die in der DDR überaus populär war, indem der allgemeine Wandel der Ansprüche ins Feld geführt wurde. Demnach verknüpfte man nun selbstverständlich die ästhetischen Ansprüche des Sitzgeistes mit den anatomischen Wünschen des Sitzfleisches und der Konsequenz, dass der Erfolg wegen des Einsatzes neuer Kunststoffe ungleich größer wäre als zu Morgensterns Zeiten: *Denn dafür sorgen schon die neuzeitlichen Materialien, mit denen unsere Polstermöbelindustrie arbeitet, zum Beispiel die Betriebe in Waldheim und Oelsa-Rabenau.*[153]

Unter dem Titel *Sitzen – Sehen – Hören*[154] verwies Robert d'Hooghe 1957 im Mitteilungsblatt des Deutschen Werkbundes Werk und Zeit auf den Trend, dass in der Wohnung nun fast alle Sitzgelegenheiten als bequeme Sessel ausge-

During the 1960s, the rapidly growing number of privately owned television sets and the related consumption of flicker images[149] provoked a change in habits since it was no longer only the kitchen but also the living room that was inhabited.[150] The upholstered sets filled with foam were to enable a not only comfortable but also relaxed seating experience for the TV-watching family. After all, those who had remained in one spot were no longer to endure back pain or complain about aching feet or calves.[151] Christian Morgenstern's four-liner comes to mind:

Wenn ich sitze, will ich nicht
Sitzen, wie mein Sitzfleisch möchte,
Sondern wie mein Sitzgeist sich,
Säße er, den Stuhl sich flöchte.[152]

(When I sit, I do not want
To sit the way my sitting flesh wants to,
but how my sitting spirit,
If he were to sit, would weave the chair.)

In this case, the sitting spirit would probably have resigned itself to the stupor of motionless television pleasure. Morgenstern's lines were interpreted in a completely different way in the magazine *Kultur im Heim*, which was extremely popular in the GDR, by referring to the general change in demands. According to this, one now naturally linked the aesthetic demands of the sitting spirit with the anatomical desires of the sitting flesh and the consequence that success would be incomparably greater than during Morgenstern's times because of the use of new plastics: *For this is already ensured by the modern materials with which our upholstery industry works, for example the factories in Waldheim and Oelsa-Rabenau.*[153]

155
Detail aus Wohnraumbild, in: Hans Lewitzky, *Meine Wohnung*, Berlin 1962 (Archiv Thomas Schriefers)

155
Detail from Wohnraumbild, in Hans Lewitzky, *Meine Wohnung*, Berlin 1962 (Archive Thomas Schriefers)

formt würden. So entsprächen etwa die tief angelegten neuen Kaminstühle mit ihrer meist geschlossenen Polsterung dem für eine *damenhafte Konversation bestimmten Mulden-Sessel* und schließlich dem dick gepolsterten Lesesessel, der mit hohem Rücken, Kopfteil und hochgezogenen Seitenlehnen versehen ist. Das Volumen derartiger Sitzmöbel war zuweilen sehr groß und erlaubte den Gestaltern, bei ihren Entwürfen in expressiven Kurven zu schwelgen. Dass dies jedwede Übertreibung zuließ, zeigen entsprechende Polsterkreationen der 1950er Jahre. Doch sah man in der Wiederkehr des expressiv-skulpturalen Möbels auch eine Revision allzu grafischer Tendenzen in Architektur und Formgebung. Gustav Hassenpflug erinnerte diesbezüglich an die grafische Ausdeutung schwingender Stahlrohrstühle als Kurve im Raum und die daraus abgeleitete Kraft der Linie.[155] Dabei sei der Stuhl doch eine allseitig sichtbare Plastik, mit Rundungen, die nicht auf dem Reißbrett entstehe, davon zeigte man sich zumindest in modisch orientierten Gestalter- und Konsumentenkreisen überzeugt.

Erklärtes Ziel war es, gute Formen für alle anzubieten, und so einte Ost- und Westdeutschland das Interesse am Weg Skandinaviens, dessen Staaten sich schon in den 1930er Jahren als effektiv-moderne Staatswesen empfohlen hatten. Das Design Schwedens, Finnlands und Dänemarks galt gerade auf dem Gebiet des Möbelentwurfs international als vorbildlich. So pries man in beiden deutschen Staaten das Vorbild der Produkte etwa von Alvar Aalto, Hans J. Wegner und Arne Jacobsen und veranstaltete skandinavische Musterschauen.

Im Westen galt Arne Jacobsens opulenter *Egg-Chair* (s. Abb. 172) als Nonplusultra eleganten Polstersitzens, während das Augenmerk im Osten eher weniger extravaganten Modellformen galt. Dort konzentrierte sich das Kerninteresse vielmehr auf die Entwicklung geeigneter Sortimente und Produktgruppen, die aufgrund ihrer Systematik erlaubten,

In 1957, under the title *Sitzen – Sehen – Hören*[154] (Sitting – Seeing – Listening), Robert d'Hooge points in the pages of the Deutscher Werkbund newspaper *Werk und Zeit* to the trend that almost all seating furniture was now designed as comfortable armchairs. For example, the low-slung new fireside armchairs with their mostly closed upholstery would correspond to the *easy armchair intended for ladylike conversation* and, finally, to the heavily upholstered reading armchair with a high back, headrest and raised side rests. The volume of such seating was sometimes very large and allowed the designers to indulge in expressive curves in their designs. That this left room for all kinds of exaggerations can be seen from the upholstery creations of the 1950s. At the same time, the return of expressive, sculptural furniture was also considered to be a revision of all-too-graphic tendencies in architecture and design. In this context, Gustav Hassenpflug recalls the graphic interpretation of swinging tubular steel chairs as a curve in space and the power of the line derived from this.[155] That the chair was instead a three-dimensional sculpture the shapes of which did not emerge on the drafting table, was instead the conviction, at least in fashionable circles of designers and consumers.

The declared aim was to offer good forms to everyone, in this way East and West Germany were united in their interest in Scandinavia, whose countries had made a positive impression of an effective, modern government as early as the 1930s. Swedish, Finnish and Danish design was an international role model of furniture design. In the German states the products of Alvar Aalto, Hans J. Wegner and Arne Jacobsen were considered exemplary and exhibitions of Scandinavian design were staged.

156
Detail aus Titel der Zeitschrift *Kultur im Heim*, Heft 1/63 (Archiv Thomas Schriefers)

156
Detail of magazin cover *Kultur im Heim*, no. 1/63 (Archive Thomas Schriefers)

Standards immer wieder nachzujustieren, damit sie sich langfristig bewähren konnten. Dabei richtete sich der Blick auf Fragen der Materialökonomie und den Anspruch nach Beständigkeit, denn die verwendeten Werkstoffe waren teilweise rar und teuer. Verschwendung galt als unerwünscht. Hier artikuliert sich ein grundlegender Unterschied zu Westdeutschland, wo die Entwicklung von Produkten nicht primär als gesellschaftliche Aufgabe verstanden wurde. Folgen wir den Gedanken von Jürgen Klepka, dann analysierte man im Osten bedacht *die Beziehungen zwischen funktionaler Komplexität und gestalterischer Qualität in ihrem Rang für die Planung und Bewertung der Qualität* gerade auch von Polstermöbeln.[156] Als idealer Partner bot sich in der DDR die 1954 gegründete *Arbeitgemeinschaft industrieller Forschungsvereinigungen „Otto von Guericke" e.V. (AiF)* an, die eingerichtet worden war, um an der Schnittstelle zwischen Wirtschaft, Wissenschaft und Staat insbesondere mittelständischen Unternehmen immer neue Impulse für innovative Verfahren, Produkte und Dienstleistungen zu geben. Rückblickend würdigte Jürgen Klepka die Leistungsfähigkeit des AiF gerade auch im Bereich der Möbelproduktion als Teil einer abgestimmten Staatspolitik auf dem Gebiet der Formgestaltung.[157] Ziel war es demnach, Qualität planbar zu machen. Eberhard Geißler konkretisierte dies für Polstermöbel, als er 1977 in der Zeitschrift *form + zweck* eine anschauliche Tabelle veröffentlichte, in der funktionelle, konstruktive und formale Aspekte der Polstermöbel zueinander in Bezug gesetzt wurden.[158] Neben der Nutzer- und Raumbeziehung, der Gestellbeschaffenheit und Polsterfüllung wurden darin Volumen und Einsinktiefe bestimmten Produkten idealtypisch zugeordnet.
Für Modernität stand international ein einfacher, mit Schaumstoff gefüllter Sesseltyp, der sich in vielen Eingangs- und Wartezonen fand. In seinem Film *Playtime*[159] setzte der französische Filmemacher Jacques Tati diesem speziellen Typus 1967 ein cineastisches Denkmal. Dafür schickte Tati

In the West Arne Jacobsen's opulent *Egg Chair* (fig. 172) was considered to be the ultimate in elegant upholstered seating, while in the East the focus was on less extravagant furniture forms. There, one was more interested in the development of suitable series and products groups with systems that made it possible to readjust standards so that they could be used for a long time. Material economy was in the focus as was the demand for wear resistance as some of the used materials were rare and expensive. Squander was not welcome. This is a fundamental difference to West Germany, where the development of products was not primarily considered to be an undertaking with societal implications. According to Jürgen Klepka, in the East one analysed *the relationships between functional complexity and design quality in their importance for planning and evaluation of quality*, especially also for upholstered furniture.[156] An ideal partner in the GDR was the *Arbeitsgemeinschaft industrieller Forschungsvereinigungen 'Otto von Guericke' e.V. (AiF)*, founded in 1954 as an interface between business, science and the state in order to provide especially mid-size companies with new impulses for innovative productions, products and services. Looking back, Jürgen Klepka credits the achievements of the AiF, particularly in regard to furniture production as part of a planned state policy in the area of design.[157] The aim was to make quality plannable. Eberhard Geißler made this more concrete for upholstered furniture when, in 1977, he published a table in the magazine *form + zweck* which related functional, constructive and formal aspects of upholstered furniture.[158] In addition to the user and space relationship, the make of the frame and the stuffing, it was the volume and the depth to which one could sink into certain products that were ordered in ideal-typical form.

157
Die Erkundungen eines Polsterstuhls durch Monsieur Hulot im Film *Playtime*, Ablauf zeichnerisch dargestellt von Thomas Schriefers

157
Exploration of an upholstered chair by Monsieur Hulot in the movie *Playtime*, sequence drawn by Thomas Schriefers

seinen Filmhelden *Monsieur Hulot* in einer modernen Konzernzentrale in einen fast komplett verglasten und an ein Aquarium erinnernden Warteraum. Ein spiegelglatter Boden, eloxiertes Aluminium und Glas umgaben den staunend Wartenden, dessen Blick zwangsläufig auf die einzige Möblierung im Raum fallen musste. Dies waren kurzbeinige, schwarz bezogene Sessel streng kubischer Form, die nur aus einem Vierkantgestell mit angeschraubten Sitz- und Rückenpolstern bestanden. Die vom Filmregisseur auf die Spitze getriebene Attraktion des mit Kunstleder bezogenen Polstermöbels war aber dessen Geräuscherzeugung, wenn man darauf Platz nahm: So entstand ein intensiver Ton in dem Moment, in dem sich beim Platznehmen durch das Körpergewicht die Sitzform eindellte, gefolgt von einem anschwellenden Ton mit abschließendem „Plopp", wenn man sich wieder erhob. Unwiderstehlich ist die Szene (s. Abb. 157), in der Hulot das Rückenkissen mit einem beherzten Handrücken-Schlag eindrückt, um dann aufmerksam zu beobachten, wie sich das Material nach einem kurzen Moment langsam wieder in die ursprüngliche Form zurückversetzt, bis ein finales „Plopp" die vollständige Wiederherstellung vermeldet. François Ede und Stephane Goudet bringen es in ihrer Würdigung des filmischen Werks von Jacques Tati auf den Punkt, wenn sie von den *fauteuils pouffent*[160] sprechen. Dabei klingen hier nicht die Stühle, sondern ihre Polster, auch wenn sich nicht endültig klären lässt, ob sie stöhnen, sprechen oder kichern.

Loungen

Unkompliziert, doch nicht profan soll er sein, attraktiv, haptisch reizvoll und einladend. Die Rede ist vom Lounge-Sessel, der verspricht, *dem müden Erfolgsmenschen die Rolle des energiegeladenen Gespanntseins*[161] für eine Weile abzunehmen. Im weich gepolsterten Komfortsessel soll die Bewegungsfreiheit nicht eingeschränkt werden und sich dennoch das Gefühl der Behaglichkeit einstellen. Dabei gilt, was Charles Eames zum Charakter des von ihm entworfenen Lounge-Chair sagte: Er solle die Fähigkeit zur Anpassung

Internationally, a foam-filled chair of the kind found in many entrance and waiting areas was emblematic of modernity. In his movie *Playtime*,[159] the French filmmaker Jacques Tati created a cinematic monument to this special chair type. For this, Tati sent his film hero *Monsieur Hulot* to a modern corporate headquarters in an almost completely glazed waiting room reminiscent of an aquarium. A mirror-smooth floor, anodised aluminium and glass surround the astonished person waiting, whose gaze is inevitably drawn to the only furniture in the room. These are short-legged armchairs covered in black fabric of strictly cubic form, consisting only of a square frame with bolted-on seat and back cushions. But the attraction of the upholstered furniture covered in fake leather, taken to the extreme by the film director, was the sounds it made when one sat down: an intense sound was produced at the moment when one's body weight caused the seat to buckle, followed by a swelling sound with a final 'plop' when one stood up again. The scene (fig. 157) in which Hulot presses the back cushion in with a spirited backhand blow, only to observe attentively how the material slowly returns to its original shape after a brief moment, before a final 'plop' announced that the shape had been completely restored, is charming. François Ede and Stephane Goudet put it in a nutshell in their appreciation of Jacques Tati's cinematic work when they speak of *fauteuils pouffent*.[160] It is not the chairs that sound here, but their cushions, even if it cannot be definitively clarified as to whether they moan, speak or giggle.

Lounging

It should be uncomplicated but not mundane, attractive, haptically delightful and welcoming. We are speaking of the lounge chair and its promise to relieve *tired successful people from energetic excitement*[161] for a while. In the softly upholstered comfort armchair,

Nach 1945 | After 1945   **177**

haben, wie ein permanent genutzter Fanghandschuh eines Baseballspielers, der mit der Zeit zur zweiten Haut seines Nutzers wird und individuelle Züge annimmt. Eine Werbeannonce der Herman Miller Collection, die damals den Lounge-Chair produzierte, zeigt 1960 das Foto eines in die Lektüre seiner Zeitung vertieften Mannes, dessen Konturen sich im gedämpften Licht der Szene mit dem Sessel zu vereinen scheinen. Dazu heißt es in fetten Lettern: *Bitte nicht stören!* Ergänzt von dem Hinweis, dass er sich aber auch nicht stören ließe, denn dazu fühle er sich in seinem Lounge-Chair *viel zu wohl, zu behaglich, zu bequem*.[162] Vergessen war der ironisch in Szene gesetzte Schaukampf, den der italienische Künstler Bruno Munari 1944 mit einem massiv anmutenden Polstersessel ausgefochten hatte: die anstrengende Erkundung diverser Positionen auf der Suche nach Komfort und Ruhe, die sich in der Folge von 14 Aufnahmen als zum Teil gewagt-akrobatischer und durchweg verkrampfter Akt darstellt (s. Abb. 158).

Dass der Anspruch einer komfortablen Polsterung in den 1950er Jahren zur Entwicklung außergewöhnlicher Polstermöbel führte, zeigt in unserer Ausstellung eine Auswahl von acht Lounge-Sesseln, von denen die Mehrzahl mit Schaumstoffprodukten ausgepolstert sind. Darin äußert sich zum einen die Begeisterung für das Neue, zum anderen die unkomplizierte Verarbeitung und die damit verbundene Zeitersparnis, welche die Arbeit mit dem flexiblen Füllmaterial mit sich brachte. Hinzu kamen neue Konstruktionsweisen der Stühle, etwa der Einsatz von Metall- oder Kunststoffschalen, die nur noch ummantelt werden mussten, wodurch die für Federschnürungen bedeutsamen Sitzmulden entfielen. Ein entsprechendes Statement ist der 1948 von Eero Saarinen mit dem dazugehörigen Fußhocker entworfene *Womb Chair* (s. Abb. 159): Hier ruht auf einem Stahlgestell eine Fiberglasschale, auf der Latexschaum aufgebracht ist. Die zusätzlich lose aufgelegten Sitz- und Rückenpolster sind hingegen mit Daunen gefüllt.

Trotz der Neuerungseuphorie wusste man aber nach wie vor bewährte Polsteraufbauten zu schätzen. Das zeigt der Armlehnstuhl (s. Abb. 160–162), den der Architekt und Möbelbauer Karl Nothhelfer Anfang der 1950er Jahre für die in Stuttgart-Bad Cannstatt beheimatete Firma Schörle & Gölz entwarf. Noch während des Krieges war 1942 Nothelfers *Fachbuch für Polsterer, Stuhlbauer, Entwerfende und Schulen* erschienen, in dem er Erfahrungen gesammelt, aufbereitet und systematisiert hatte. Dem entsprach der von ihm entworfene Ohrensessel, dessen Sitzpolsterung aus einem Federkissen besteht. Dieses wiederum liegt auf Federblech-Bandfedern auf, die mit dem Holzrahmen des Sitzes verschraubt sind. Im flacheren Rückenpolster wurden hingegen Wellenfedern eingesetzt. So erprobte man Kombinationen. Das gilt gleichermaßen für die Arbeit des dänischen Designers Hans J. Wegner, von dem wir den 1951 präsentierten Armlehnsessel *Papa Bear* (s. Abb. 169/170) ausstellen. Dessen Sitzpolster bildete Wegner als ein auf einem Gurtgrund ruhendes Latex-Kissen aus, während im Rücken ein Taschenfederkern und eine Fasson aus Feinwerg für Komfort sorgen.

Die als Halbzeuge angebotenen Federkernpolster erwiesen sich als praktisch, da sich ihr Einsatz mit traditionellen Polsterarbeiten kombinieren ließ. Das gilt auch für den von Dietrich Hinz für Carl Sasse in Lauenau gestalteten Armlehnstuhl *Casala 788* (s. Abb. 165/166), bei dem das Polster auf

freedom of movement should not be restricted, but at the same time a feeling of comfort should emerge. What Charles Eames said about the *Lounge Chair* he designed applies: it should have the ability to adapt like a permanently used baseball player's glove, which over time becomes the user's second skin and takes on individual characteristics. A 1960 advertisement by the Herman Miller Collection, who used to produce the armchair, shows a man absorbed by his newspaper, whose outlines seem to blend with the armchair in the low light. Bold letters read: 'Please do not disturb!', supplemented by the remark that he would not be interrupted anyway, as this lounge chair was much too comfortable, too cosy.[162] Forgotten was the ironic show fight that the Italian artist Bruno Murani had fought in 1941 with a massive, upholstered armchair: the exhausting search for comfort and peace through various positions, depicted in fourteen images as an at times acrobatic and thoroughly tense act (fig. 158).

That the demand for comfortable upholstery led to the development of extraordinary upholstered furniture during the 1950s is demonstrated in our exhibition by eight examples of lounge chairs, the majority of which are upholstered using foam material. This is an expression, on the one hand, of the enthusiasm for new things and, on the other, its uncomplicated processing and related time savings which came with using this flexible filling material. New were also the construction methods for chairs, for example using metal and plastic shells, which only needed covering, making the recesses for springing unnecessary. One such statement is the *Womb Chair* (fig. 159), designed in 1948 by Eero Saarinen with a matching footstool: a fibreglass shell covered in latex foam sits on top of a steel frame. The additional loose back and seat cushion are filled with down.

Despite the euphoria for new things, trusted upholstery was still in favour. This is evident in an armchair (figs. 160–162) which the architect and craftsman Karl Nothhelfer designed for the Stuttgart-Bad Cannstatt-based company Schörle & Gölz in the early 1950s. In his *Fachbuch für Polsterer, Stuhlbauer, Entwerfende und Schulen*, published during the war, in 1942, he had collected, reworked and systematised know-how. This corresponded with the wing chair designed by him with a sprung seat. The sprung cushion is attached to spring steel sheet flat spiral springs which are in turn screwed to the seat's wooden frame. For the flatter backrest, zigzag springs were used. This is how combinations were tested. This is also true for the 1951 armchair *Papa Bear* (figs. 169/170) by the Danish designer Hans J. Wegner. The upholstery is made from a latex cushion placed on webbing, while in the back, pocket springs and a fine tow filling provide comfort.

The pocket spring core upholstery offered as a semi-finished product proved to be practical, as its use could be combined with traditional upholstery. This also applies to the *Casala 788* armchair (figs. 165/166), designed by Dietrich Hinz for Carl Sasse in Lauenau, in which the cushioning rests on spring bands, with

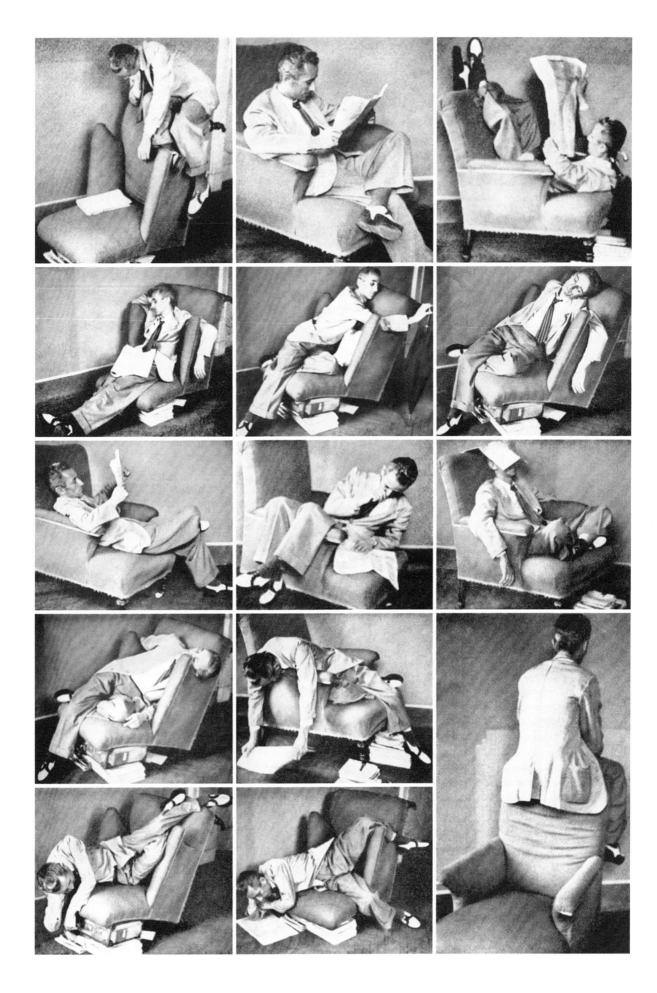

158
Bruno Munari, *Ich suche Komfort in einem Sessel*, 1944 (Corraini Edizioni 2013)

158
Bruno Munari, *Seeking Comfort in an Uncomfortable Chair*, 1944 (Corraini Edizioni 2013)

Federbändern aufliegt, wobei für den Rücken ein Fassonpolster eingesetzt wurde. Wegen der geringeren Dimensionierung der Polsterstärken beließ man es bei der Ausbildung eines stilistisch vergleichbaren Kindersesselchens (s. Abb. 167/168) bei einer Bedeckung der Bandfederung durch Kokos und graue Watte.

Einen ganz anderen Polsteraufbau besitzt der 1956 von Osvaldo Borsani als Dreh- und Kippsessel konzipierte *Poltrona girevole P 32* (s. Abb. 171), in dessen Innerem neben Mechanik eine Metallschale als formgebende Basis für eine kombinierte Rücken- und Armlehnenpolsterung aus Latexformschaum dient. Miteinander verspannte Gummigurte bilden dabei das Gerüst für die Ausformung des Stuhls, der mit einem blauen Jerseystoff in zeittypischem Baumwoll-Synthetik-Mix bezogen ist. Während sich der Polsteraufbau des P 32 als komplex erweist, bestand der berühmte von Arne Jacobsen entworfene *Egg Chair* (s. Abb. 172) in seiner Ausführung von 1958 aus einem verstärkten Styropor-Korpus, den ein Latexformpolster vollflächig bedeckt.

Die Verwendung überaus frei formbarer Kunsttoffe machte es möglich, entsprechende Sitzformen zu gestalten, dabei ersetzten diese das traditionell geschnürte Federpolster zunehmend auch bei weniger futuristischen Sitzmöbeln wie z. B. dem 1961 von Johannes Spalt für die Franz Wittmann Möbelwerkstätten entworfenen Sessel *Constanze* aus der Elementgruppe *C, E12* (s. Abb. 173/174). Der mit einem hellbraunen Rindsleder bezogene Sessel hätte wegen seiner großen Polsterhöhe auch mit einer Federkonstruktion versehen sein können, doch besteht der Sitz aus einem Latexschaumkissen, das auf einem Wellenfedergrund ruht.

a stitched upholstered cushion used for the back. Because of the smaller thickness, a stylistically comparable children's chair (figs. 167/168) was kept with the flat spiral springs covered with coconut fibre and grey cotton wadding.

The upholstered armchair *Poltrona girevole P 32* (s. fig. 171), designed in 1956 by Osvaldo Borsani, is a swinging swivel chair with an entirely different construction. In addition to mechanical parts, the interior is made from a metal shell that forms the basis for a combined back- and armrest made of latex foam padding. Stretched rubber straps are the base for the chair form, which is covered in a blue jersey, a cotton-synthetic mix typical of the period. While the P 32 has complex upholstery, in its 1958 version the famous *Egg Chair* (fig. 172) by Arne Jacobsen was made from a reinforced polystyrene frame and full-surface latex padding.

The use of freely formable foam material made it possible to create any suitable seat shape and increasingly replaced traditional sprung upholstery, also in the case of less futuristic seating such as, for example, the armchair *Constanze* from the group C, E12 (figs. 173/174), designed in 1961 by Johannes Spalt for the Franz Wittmann Möbelwerkstätten. The armchair, covered in light-brown cow leather could have been fitted with springs due to its seat height, but instead is made from latex cushions on a zigzag spring base.

159
Sitzkombination, Armlehnstuhl mit Fußhocker *Womb Chair*, Eero Saarinen (Entwurf), Knoll Associates, New York (Herstellung), 1948 (LÖFFLER COLLECTION, Reichenschwand)
Seating combination, *Womb Chair* armchair with stool, Eero Saarinen (design), Knoll Associates, New York (production), 1948 (LÖFFLER COLLECTION, Reichenschwand)

160–162
Armlehnstuhl mit Federkissen als Sitz auf Federblech-Bandfedern, Karl Nothhelfer (Entwurf), Schörle & Gölz, Stuttgart-Cannstatt (Herstellung), 1950er Jahre (LÖFFLER COLLECTION, Reichenschwand)

160–162
Armchair with sprung cushion as a seat with spring-sheet flat spiral springs, Karl Nothhelfer (design), Schörle & Gölz, Stuttgart-Cannstatt (production), 1950s (LÖFFLER COLLECTION, Reichenschwand)

Nach 1945 | After 1945

163/164
Stuhl, Werner Stachelroth (Entwurf), 1951/1952 (GRASSI Museum für Angewandte Kunst Leipzig)

163/164
Chair, Werner Stachelroth (design), 1951/1952 (GRASSI Museum für Angewandte Kunst Leipzig)

165/166
Armlehnstuhl *Casala 788*, Dietrich Hinz (Entwurf), Carl Sasse, Lauenau, Deister (Herstellung), 1953–1958 (LÖFFLER COLLECTION, Reichenschwand)

165/166
Armchair *Casala 788*, Dietrich Hinz (design), Carl Sasse, Lauenau, Deister (production), 1953–1958 (LÖFFLER COLLECTION, Reichenschwand)

167/168
Armlehnstuhl für Kinder, um 1955 (LÖFFLER COLLECTION, Reichenschwand)

167/168
Children's armchair, around 1955 (LÖFFLER COLLECTION, Reichenschwand)

169/170
Armlehnstuhl *Papa Bear*, Hans J. Wegner (Entwurf), AP. Stolen, Kopenhagen (LÖFFLER COLLECTION, Reichenschwand)

169/170
Armchair *Papa Bear*, Hans J. Wegner (design), AP. Stolen, Copenhagen (LÖFFLER COLLECTION, Reichenschwand)

171
Armlehnstuhl *Poltrona girevole P 32*, Osvaldo Borsani (Entwurf), Tecno S.p.A., Mailand (Herstellung), 1956 (LÖFFLER COLLECTION, Reichenschwand)

171
Armchair *Poltrona girevole P 32*, Osvaldo Borsani (design), Tecno S.p.A., Milan (production), 1956 (LÖFFLER COLLECTION, Reichenschwand)

172
Schalensessel *Egg Chair*, Arne Jacobsen (Entwurf), Fritz Hansen A/S, Kopenhagen (Herstellung), 1958 (GRASSI Museum für Angewandte Kunst Leipzig)

172
Shell chair *Egg Chair*, Arne Jacobsen (design), Fritz Hansen A/S, Kopenhagen (production), 1958 (GRASSI Museum für Angewandte Kunst Leipzig)

173/174
Sessel *Constanze*, Elementgruppe *C, E12*, Johannes Spalt (Entwurf), Franz Wittmann Möbelwerkstätten, Etsdorf am Kamp, Österreich (Herstellung), 1961 (LÖFFLER COLLECTION, Reichenschwand)

173/174
Armchair *Constanze*, element group *C, E12*, Johannes Spalt (design), Franz Wittmann Möbelwerkstätten, Etsdorf am Kamp, Austria (production), 1961 (LÖFFLER COLLECTION, Reichenschwand)

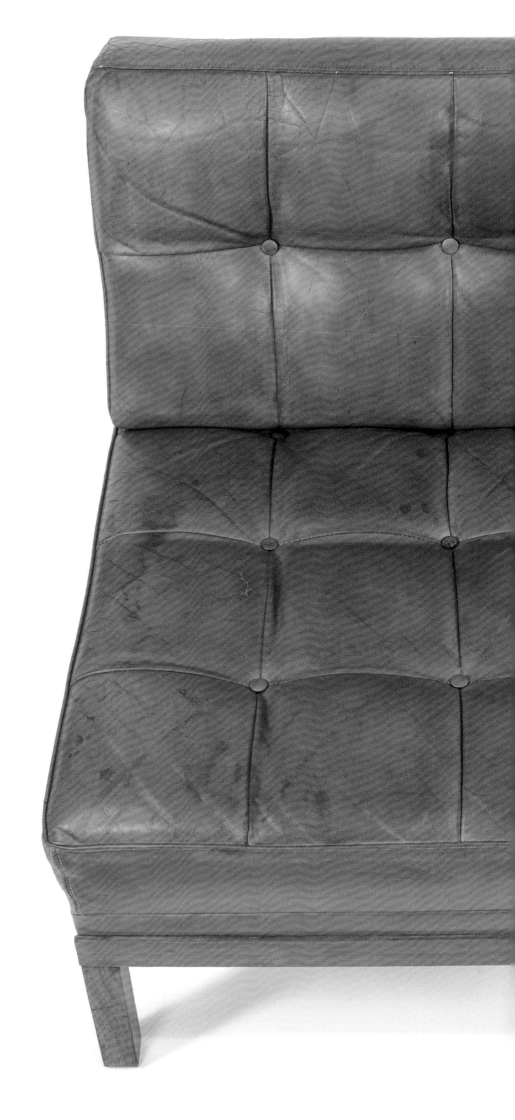

175/176
Sitzobjekt *Joe*, Gionatan de Pas, Donato D'Urbino und Paolo Lomazzi (Entwurf), Poltronova, Florenz (Herstellung), 1970
(LÖFFLER COLLECTION, Reichenschwand)

175/176
Seat object *Joe*, Gionatan de Pas, Donato D'Urbino and Paolo Lomazzi (design), Poltronova, Florence (production), 1970
(LÖFFLER COLLECTION, Reichenschwand)

Es war wohl die Selbstverständlichkeit einer engen Verbindung zwischen den zweckgebundenen und den zweckfreien Künsten, die wesentlichen Anteil daran hatte, dass sich in Italien nach 1945 eine besondere Tradition schöpferischer Umweltgestaltung entwickeln konnte. Das gilt in besonderem Maße für die visionären Formexperimente der 1960er und 1970er Jahre. Sie verliehen einer Welt Form und Substanz, die frei von den Zwängen eines Systems[163] ergründete, was denkbar und möglich sei. Das zeigen etwa die italienischen Entwürfe der späten 1960er Jahre. Es sind Sitzobjekte, die absichtsvoll zum Spiel auffordern: z. B. die von Gionatan De Pas, Donato D'Urbino und Paolo Lomazzi vorgestellte Sitz-Liege-Insel *Joe* (s. Abb. 175/176). Der Name bezog sich auf die Baseball-Legende Joe DiMaggio, weshalb die wahlweise mit Leder oder Jeansstoff bezogene Sitzinsel die Gestalt eines riesigen Fanghandschuhs annahm. In seiner überdimensionalen Größe wirkte der mit Polyurethanschaum gefüllte Polster-Joe wie ein Pop-Art-Objekt. Sich darin niederzulassen hieß, sich ganz selbstverständlich unorthodox zu lagern, zu spielen, Spaß zu haben oder einfach nur bequem zu ruhen.

Während *Joe* wegen seiner enormen Dimensionierung und seines hohen Gewichtes von mehr als 50 kg eher unbeweglich ist, ist der Sitzsack *Sacco* (s. Abb. 177/178), den Piero Gatti, Cesare Paolini und Franco Teodoro 1968 präsentierten, mobil. Hunderte aufgeschäumter Polystyrol-Kugeln füllen den Ledersack, der sich der jeweiligen Haltung seiner Nutzer*innen anpasst. Das italienische Wort *sacco* bedeutet in deutscher Übersetzung Sack und bezeichnet punktgenau, was das gleichnamige Sitzobjekt verspricht: Sitzen auf einer losen Füllung, die in ihrer flexiblen Hülle genügend Raum hat, sich neu zu konfigurieren, um immer wieder neue Sitzformen auszubilden. So steht der *Sacco* für ein erklärtermaßen unangepasstes Wohnverhalten, das festgelegte Sitzarrangements nicht mehr zwingend vorsieht und den Nutzer*innen gleichzeitig einen gewissen Spieltrieb abverlangt.

Für Freizeit- und Wasservergnügungen entwarfen Gionatan De Pas, Donato D'Urbino, Paolo Lomazzi und Carla Scolari 1967 den schwimmfähigen, nur aus einer verschweißten PVC-Hülle mit Ventil bestehenden *Blow Chair* (s. Abb. 181/182).

It was probably the naturally close connection between the applied and fine arts, that made it possible for a specific design tradition to emerge in Italy after 1945. This is especially true for the visionary formal experiments of the 1960s and 1970s. They gave shape and substance to a world that explored what was conceivable and possible, free from the constraints of a system.[163] This is evident, for example, in the Italian designs of the late 1960s. These are seating objects that intentionally invite people to play, for example, the seat-recliner Joe presented by Gionatan De Pas, Donato D'Urbino and Paolo Lomazzi (figs. 175/176). The name referred to baseball legend Joe DiMaggio, which is why the armchair, either covered in leather or denim, took on the shape of a giant catcher's glove. In its oversized form, the polyurethane-foam-filled *Joe* looked like a Pop Art object. To sit down on it was to lie down, play, have fun or simply rest comfortably in an unorthodox way as a matter of course.

While Joe, with its enormous size and heavy weight of over 50 kilograms, is rather inflexible, the bean bag Sacco (figs. 177/178, 219) presented by Piero Gatti, Cesare Paolini and Franco Teodor in 1968 is mobile. Hundreds of polystyrene balls fill the leather bag that adjusts to each user's posture. The Italian word *sacco* translates as sack and describes precisely what the seating object of the same name promises: sitting on a loose filling, which has enough space in its envelope to reconfigure itself in order to create new seat shapes again and again. Thus, *Sacco* stands for a decidedly non-conformist dwelling behaviour that no longer requires fixed seating arrangements and at the same time demands a certain playfulness from its users.

For leisure and activities in the water, Gionatan De Pas, Donato D'Urbino, Paolo Lomazzi and Carla Scolari designed the floatable *Blow Chair* (figs. 181/182) in 1967, made only from heat-sealed PVC with ventil. Imagined as an inflatable padding, *Blow* stunned the public. The plastic armchair made of air chambers was delivered folded in small packets and could be put to

177/178
Sitzsack *Sacco*, Piero Gatti, Cesare Paolini und Franco Teodoro (Entwurf), Zanotta S.p.A., Mailand (Herstellung), 1968 (LÖFFLER COLLECTION, Reichenschwand)

177/178
Beanbag *Sacco*, Piero Gatti, Cesare Paolini and Franco Teodoro (design), Zanotta S.p.A., Milan (production), 1968 (LÖFFLER COLLECTION, Reichenschwand)

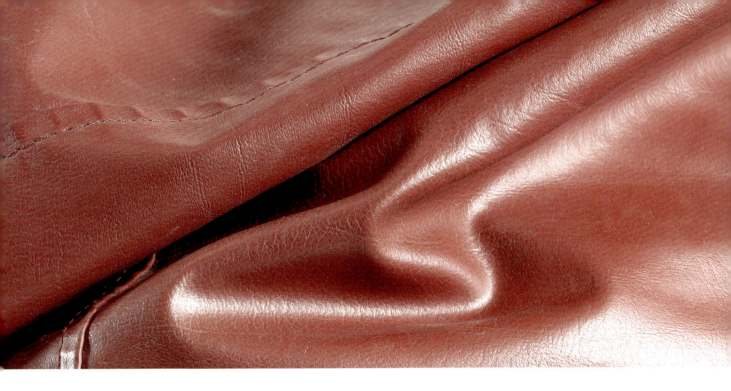

Als aufblasbares Sitzpolster konzipiert, verblüffte *Blow* die staunende Öffentlichkeit. Der mit Luftkammern versehene Kunststoffsessel wurde, dünn zusammengefaltet, im kleinen Päckchen geliefert und war sofort bereit, durch Ansetzen einer Luftpumpe seine nutzbare Form anzunehmen. Bezogen auf die traditionelle Kunst des Polsterns könnte man den *Blow* auch als Anti-Polster bezeichnen, da hier keinerlei handwerklichen Kenntnisse nötig waren, um in kürzester Zeit selbst einen federnden Sitzbegleiter zu erschaffen. Wenn wir in unserer Ausstellung das Geheimnis des Polsterns ein Stück weit lüften wollen, dann erweist sich die durchsichtige Kunststoffmembran zwar als hilfreich, um hineinzuschauen, gleichzeitig aber auch als enttäuschend, da wir nichts darin sehen als nur Luft! Ob die italienischen Designer bei ihrer Kreation vielleicht auch augenzwinkernd an den damals von Michelangelo Antonioni in Italien gedrehten und im selben Jahr 1967 in Cannes preisgekrönten Film *Blow-Up* anspielen, ist nicht verbürgt. Doch nutzen sie die Mehrdeutigkeit des Verbs *to blow* ähnlich wie Antonioni im Film, indem sie neben dem Aufblasen als Vergrößern auch Deutungen wie Wegwehen, Verschwinden und Verblassen in Kauf nehmen. Neben dem Wunsch nach Mobilität wurde in den 1960er Jahren aber auch der Traum vom entrückten Ruhen in wohliger Abgeschiedenheit auf die Spitze getrieben, da Entwerfer Sitzobjekte als Einhausungen vorsahen, die spätere *Cocooning*-Konzepte vorwegnahmen. Dem entspricht der 1963 von Eero Aarnio für Asko gestaltete *Ball Chair* (s. Abb. 179/180). Laut Werbung war es ein perfektes Sitznest zum Chillen, Träumen und Sich-Anschmiegen. Dabei war die harte Außenschale im Inneren nur mit einem Wattepolster und einem wattierten Schaumstoffkissen für den Sitz mit Cordstoffbezug ausgestattet.

In Zeiten der Pop-Kultur wurde die Polsterwelt immer starkfarbiger. Zudem konnotierten Designer und Künstler das Sitz- und insbesondere das Polstermöbel verstärkt ironisch, indem sie ihm eine semantische Bedeutung gaben und seine Erscheinung ins Absurde steigerten. Schaumstoffe machten es möglich, so plakative Sitzgebilde wie den vom chilenischen Architekten, Bildhauer und Maler Roberto Antonio Sebastián Matta 1970 geschaffenen *MAgriTTA* (s. Abb. 185/186) oder

use immediately with the help of an air pump. In relation to the traditional craft of upholstery, one could describe *Blow* as an anti-upholstery, since no craftsmanship was necessary in order to create a bouncy seating companion in short time. If in this exhibition our aim is to unveil the secrets of upholstery, the see-through plastic membrane is useful to get a look inside but at the same time disappointing, as there is nothing to see but air! Whether the Italian designers were perhaps also alluding tongue in cheek to the film *Blow-Up*, made in Italy at the time by Michelangelo Antonioni and won an award at Cannes in the same year, 1967, is not known. But they make use of the ambiguity of the verb *to blow* in a similar way to Antonioni in the film, accepting interpretations such as blowing away, disappearing, and fading away in addition to blowing up as in enlarging.

In addition to the desire for mobility, the 1960s also saw the dream of faraway rest in comfortable seclusion rising, as designers created seating objects as capsules that anticipated later concepts of cocooning. This is true for the *Ball Chair* (figs. 179/180), created by Eero Aarnio for Asko in 1963. According to the advertisement, it was the perfect seat nest for chilling, dreaming and cuddling. In fact, the hard outer shell was only fitted with only cotton padding inside as well as a padded foam cushion for the seat with corduroy cover.

In the times of Pop culture, the world of upholstery became ever more colourful. In addition, designers and artists increasingly connoted seating and, in particular, upholstered furniture ironically, lending it semantic meaning and elevating its appearance to the absurd. Plastic foams made it possible to form such striking seating structures as *MAgriTTA* (figs. 185/186), created by Chilean architect, sculptor and painter Roberto Antonio Sebastián Matta in 1970, or the red-lipped Bocca sofa (figs. 191/192) designed by Studio 65 (Piero Gatti, Cesare Paolini, Franco Teodoro) in 1971. However, while the sight of these upholstered individuals still conveyed a sense of cuddly materiality,

Nach 1945 | After 1945 **197**

179/180
Schalensessel *Ball*, Eero Aarnio (Entwurf), Asko, Lahti (Herstellung), 1963 (LÖFFLER COLLECTION, Reichenschwand)

179/180
Shell chair *Ball*, Eero Aarnio (design), Asko, Lahti (production), 1963 (LÖFFLER COLLECTION, Reichenschwand)

das von Studio 65 (Piero Gatti, Cesare Paolini, Franco Teodoro) 1971 entworfene, rote Lippen zeigende, Sofa *Bocca* (s. Abb. 191/192) auszubilden. Während sich beim Anblick dieser Polsterindividualitäten aber noch ein Gefühl anschmiegsamer Materialität vermittelte, lässt der Blick auf das vom gleichen Team ebenfalls 1971 vorgestellte *Capitello* (s. Abb. 189/190) nur den Schluss zu, dass es sich bei diesem Objekt um einen massiven Steinkoloss handeln muss. Dabei überraschte die tatsächlich als Sitzmöbel konzipierte Kippvariante einer ionischen Säule samt Kapitell jene, die wagten, darauf Platz zu nehmen, da sie feststellten, dass die Masse aus Polyurethanschaum nachgab. Ein derartiges Polstermöbel mutet alles andere als bequem an und spielt mit der irreführenden Anmutung eines harten Steins, der es nicht ist. Die Gruppe ikonischer Polsterobjekte ergänzt hier das 1973 von Eero Aarnio entworfene *Pony* (s. Abb. 187/188), das als Sitzmöbel die stilisierte Form eines kleinen Pferdes wiedergibt. Um darauf Platz zu nehmen, bedarf es eines gewissen Elans, sich auf den Rücken des Polstertieres zu schwingen, worauf man dann rittlings sitzt. Das Innere besteht aus einem mit Polyurethan geschäumten Metallgestell, das die Form des Sitzobjektes vorgibt. Brauner Veloursstoff bekleidet schließlich das Pony, das sich als wenig komfortables Polstermöbel erweist.

Komplett mit Vinyl-Kunstleder überzogen zeigen sich das formgeschäumte Sitzobjekt des 1966 von Liisi Beckmann unter der Modellnummer „870" entworfenen Sessels *Karelia* (s. Abb. 193/194) und die Tagesliege *Superonda* (s. Abb. 195/196), die 1967 von der Architektengruppe Archizoom (Andrea Branzi, Gilberto Corretti, Paolo Deganello, Massimo Morozzi) entworfen wurde. Derartige Sitzobjekte waren nutzbare Skulpturen, die befühlt werden wollten, wie der von Gaetano Pesce entworfene *Up 5 Chair* von 1969 mit kugelförmigem Fußteil (s. Abb. 197/198) oder Nanna Ditzels *Polyester Chair* (s. Abb. 199/200) von 1965, der den Hinweis auf seine Polsterbeschaffenheit schon im Namen trägt.

Dass die Basis des *Polyester Chair* eine geschwärzte Sperrholzplatte mit drehbaren Rollen bildet, auf der ein zugeschnittener Vollschaumkörper aufgebracht und mit einem angerauten atlasbindigen Flachgewebe angetackert wurde, zeigt, dass das Polsterobjekt eher als formales Experiment und modisch temporäres Sitzerlebnis denn als alterungsbeständig vererbbare Anlage empfunden wurde. Die Idee und deren Umsetzung stand im Vordergrund, weshalb in diesen Entwürfen die Lust der Gestalter:innen am formal-konstruktiven Ausloten von Möglichkeiten spürber wird.

Das vermittelt auch der *Tube Chair* (s. Abb. 183/184), den Joe Colombo 1969 aus vier liegenden, walzenähnlichen Zylindern entwarf, die durch Stahlklammern miteinander verbunden waren. Die Polsterung bestand einzig aus einem relativ flachen Kissen aus Polyurethanschaum, auf das ein blaues Vinylkunstleder aufgezogen ist. Bequem war ein solches Möbel nicht, dafür war es interessant und außergewöhnlich. Nicht zuletzt gilt das auch für die 1970 von Titti Saracino und Giovanni de Lucchi entworfene Liege *Diapason* (s. Abb. 201). Sie verfügt über eine viergeteilte mit Polyesterwatte gefüllte Kissenauflage mit Velourslederbezug, die auf einer Edelstahlplatte aufliegt. Ist deren Materialanmutung bereits wenig sinnlich und eher kalt, so verstärkt der als Betonblock ausgebildete Fuß der Liege diesen Eindruck. Federung versprechen allein die weitgehend frei schwebende Metallplatte und das aufliegende Kissen. Der Polsteraufbau ist maximal reduziert und pur, weshalb dieses Polstermöbel wenig Geheimnisvolles verbirgt, dafür aber eine eindrucksvolle Funktionsplastik darstellt.

a glance at *Capitello* (figs. 189/190), presented by the same team in 1971, can only lead to the conclusion that this object must be a solid stone colossus.

In fact, this toppled variation of an Ionic column and capital was in fact made for sitting and surprised all those who dared to take a seat when they discovered that the polyurethane foam mass caved when sat on. Such a piece of upholstered furniture appears to be anything but comfortable and plays on the false appearance of hard stone, which it is not. To this group of iconic seating furniture one can add *Pony* (figs. 187/188), designed by Eero Aarnio in 1973 in the stylised shape of a pony. To take a seat on it requires a certain elan to swing onto the back of the upholstered animal, on which one sits astride. The interior consists of a metal frame foamed with polyurethane, which gives the seat object its shape. Finally, brown velour fabric covers the pony, which turns out to be not very comfortable upholstered furniture.

The foamed seat object of the armchair *Karelia* (figs. 193/194), designed in 1966 by Liisi Beckmann under the model number "870" and of the day bed *Superonda* (figs. 195/196), designed in 1967 by the architecture group Archizoom (Andrea Branzi, Gilberto Corretti, Paolo Deganello, Massimo Morozzi), are covered entirely in vinyl leatherette. Such seating objects were usable sculptures that could be touched, such as the *Up 5 Chair* with a spherical footrest (figs. 197/198), designed by Gaetano Pesce in 1969, or Nanna Ditzel's 1965 *Polyester Chair* (figs. 199/200), which carries its materiality in its title.

That the base of *Polyester Chair* was a blackened plywood plate with castors, onto which a cut full foam body on which a roughened atlas-bonded flat weave has been tacked, demonstrates that the upholstery object was considered to be a formal experiment and a fashionable temporary seating experience rather than an investment resistant to ageing which could be passed down. The emphasis was placed on the idea and its execution, which is why these objects tell of the designers' joy to test the boundaries of what was possible in terms of form and construction.

This becomes evident in the *Tube Chair* (figs. 183/184) as well, which Joe Colombo constructed from four barrel-like tubes held together by steel brackets. The padding was made from relatively flat polyurethane foam with a blue vinyl cover. While not comfortable, such a piece of furniture was interesting and extraordinary.

Finally, the same is true for the chaise lounge *Diapason* (fig. 201), designed by Titti Saracino and Giovanni de Lucchi in 1970. It is made of a four-part cushion filled with polyester wadding with a velour leather cover, which rests on a stainless-steel plate. While the materials already appear to be little sensual and cold, this is reinforced by the concrete block that makes up the lounger's foot. Springing is only provided by the mostly free-floating metal plate and the cushion. The upholstery is maximally reduced and pure, which is why this upholstered furniture hides few secrets but is nonetheless an impressive functional sculpture.

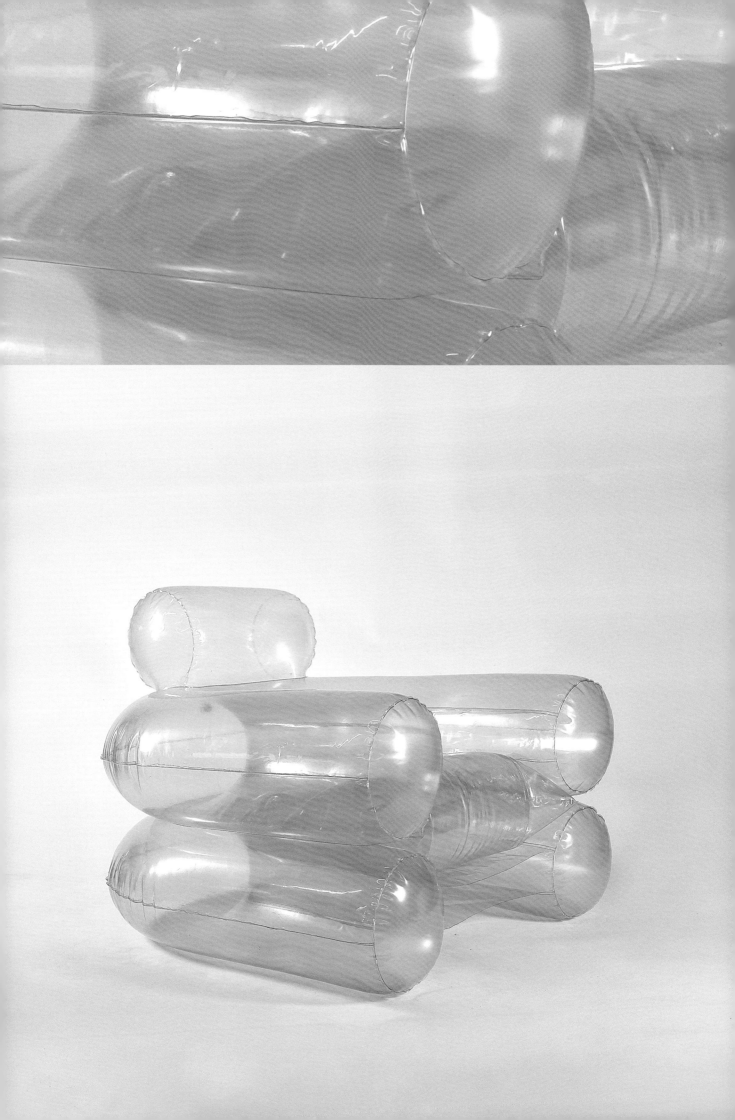

181/182 (S. 200, p. 200)
Sitzobjekt *Blow*, Gionatan de Pas, Donato D'Urbino, Paolo Lomazzi und Carla Scolari (Entwurf), Zanotta S.p.A., Mailand (Herstellung), 1967 (LÖFFLER COLLECTION, Reichenschwand)
Seat object *Blow*, Gionatan de Pas, Donato D'Urbino, Paolo Lomazzi and Carla Scolari (design), Zanotta S.p.A., Milan (production), 1967 (LÖFFLER COLLECTION, Reichenschwand)

183/184
Sitzobjekt *Tube Chair*, Joe Colombo (Entwurf), Flexform, Mailand (Herstellung), 1969 (LÖFFLER COLLECTION, Reichenschwand)
Seat object *Tube Chair*, Joe Colombo (design), Flexform, Milan (production), 1969 (LÖFFLER COLLECTION, Reichenschwand)

185/186
Sitzobjekt *MAgriTTA*, Roberto Sebastián Matta (Entwurf), Simon International für Gavina, Bologna (Herstellung), 1970 (LÖFFLER COLLECTION, Reichenschwand)

185/186
Seat object *MAgriTTA*, Roberto Sebastián Matta (design), Simon International for Gavina, Bologna (production), 1970 (LÖFFLER COLLECTION, Reichenschwand)

187/188
Sitzobjekt *Pony*, Eero Aarnio (Entwurf), Stendig, New York (Herstellung), 1973 (LÖFFLER COLLECTION, Reichenschwand)

187/188
Seat object *Pony*, Eero Aarnio (design), Stendig, New York (production), 1973 (LÖFFLER COLLECTION, Reichenschwand)

189/190
Sitzobjekt *Capitello*, Studio 65 – Piero Gatti, Cesare Paolini und Franco Teodoro (Entwurf), Gufram, Balangero, Turin (Herstellung), 1971 (LÖFFLER COLLECTION, Reichenschwand)

189/190
Seat object *Capitello*, Studio 65 – Piero Gatti, Cesare Paolini and Franco Teodoro (design), Gufram, Balangero, Turin (production), 1971 (LÖFFLER COLLECTION, Reichenschwand)

191/192
Sofa *Bocca/Marilyn*, Studio 65 – Piero Gatti, Cesare Paolini und Franco Teodoro (Entwurf), Gufram, Balangero, Turin (Herstellung), 1971 (LÖFFLER COLLECTION, Reichenschwand)

191/192
Sofa *Bocca/Marilyn*, Studio 65 – Piero Gatti, Cesare Paolini and Franco Teodoro (design), Gufram, Balangero, Turin (production), 1971 (LÖFFLER COLLECTION, Reichenschwand)

193/194
Sessel *Karelia*, Modell „870", Liisi Beckmann (Entwurf), Zanotta S.p.A., Mailand (Herstellung), 1966 (LÖFFLER COLLECTION, Reichenschwand)

193/194
Armchair *Karelia*, model "870", Liisi Beckmann (design), Zanotta S.p.A., Milan (production), 1966 (LÖFFLER COLLECTION, Reichenschwand)

195/196
Tagesliege *Superonda*, Archizoom Associati – Andrea Branzi, Gilberto Coretti, Paolo Deganello und Massimo Morozzi (Entwurf), Poltronova, Florenz (Herstellung), 1966 (LÖFFLER COLLECTION, Reichenschwand)

195/196
Day lounger *Superonda*, Archizoom Associati – Andrea Branzi, Gilberto Coretti, Paolo Deganello and Massimo Morozzi (design), Poltronova, Florence (production), 1966 (LÖFFLER COLLECTION, Reichenschwand)

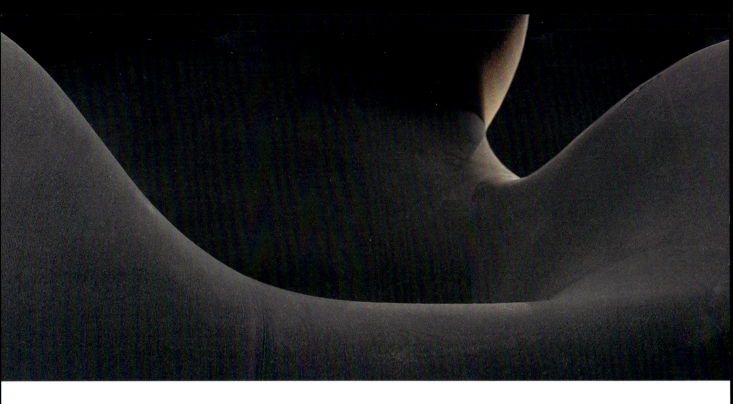

197/198
Sitzobjekt *Up 5* mit Fußteil, Gaetano Pesce (Entwurf), C & B (daraus wurde B & B), Novedrate, Como (Herstellung), 1969 (LÖFFLER COLLECTION, Reichenschwand)

197/198
Seat object *Up 5* with stool, Gaetano Pesce (design), C & B (later B & B), Novedrate, Como (production), 1969 (LÖFFLER COLLECTION, Reichenschwand)

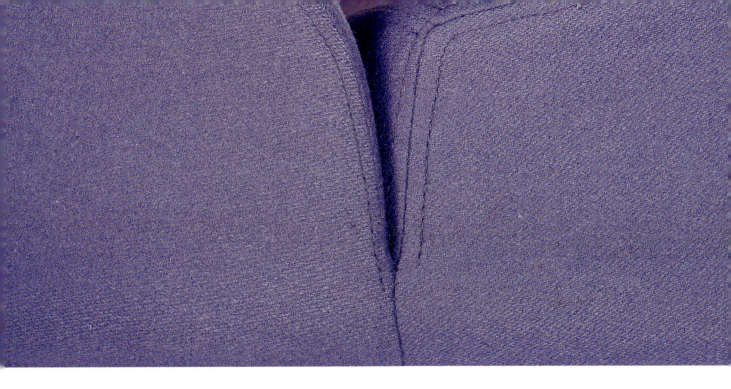

199/200
Sitzobjekt *Polyester Chair*, Nanna Ditzel (Entwurf), Polyether Industri (Herstellung), 1965 (GRASSI Museum für Angewandte Kunst Leipzig)

199/200
Seat object *Polyester Chair*, Nanna Ditzel (design), Polyether Industri (production), 1965 (GRASSI Museum für Angewandte Kunst Leipzig)

201
Liege *Diapason*, Titti Saracino und Giovanni de Lucchi (Entwurf), Elleduemilla, Cormano, Lombardei (Herstellung), 1970 (LÖFFLER COLLECTION, Reichenschwand)

201
Lounger *Diapason*, Titti Saracino und Giovanni de Lucchi (design), Elleduemilla, Cormano, Lombardy (production), 1970 (LÖFFLER COLLECTION, Reichenschwand)

Nach 1945 | After 1945 **211**

Polster für Kinder

Kindermobiliar gab es immer schon. Bereits in den Grabstätten ägyptischer Pharaonen fanden sich entsprechende Stühle. Im ausgehenden 19. Jahrhundert erkannten dann Firmen wie z. B. Thonet schnell einen lukrativen Markt und boten bald ein breites Spektrum ihrer Modelle auch als Kinderversionen an. Dabei wurden die Formen der Erwachsenenmöbel sorgfältig auf Kindermaße übertragen. Das gilt später gleichermaßen für Modelle heute gefeierter Designer, etwa Alvar Aalto, Gerrit Rietveld und Marcel Breuer, die ihre Stühle selbstverständlich auch für die „kleinen Erwachsenen" modifizierten. Zwar avancierte das Kind dadurch *zum gleichberechtigten Mitbewohner*[164], wie es Franz Schuster 1927 formulierte, doch kann man die Frage stellen, wo hier der kindliche Spieltrieb angeregt wurde. Zwar entstanden auch in Wechselwirkung mit der reformorientierten Montessori-Bewegung Konzepte, die genau das zu leisten suchten, doch blieb es lange bei der Praxis, Kinderstühle denen der Erwachsenen nachzuempfinden. Das zeigen, bezogen auf Polstermöbel, in unserer Ausstellung zwei Beispiele: zum einen das mit einer geschnürten Federkonstruktion und Afrikfasson gepolsterte Art-déco Sesselchen (s. Abb. 128–130) und zum anderen das die Formen der späten 1960er Jahre aufnehmende Kindersesselchen mit baumwollgefüllten Kisseneinlagen (s. Abb. 210–212). Sie korrespondieren mit drei Spielsitzen, denen man gleich ansieht, dass hier keine Vorbilder aus der Erwachsenenwelt bemüht wurden. Das gilt insbesondere für den mit Fahrwerk und Rädern ausgestatteten Marienkäfer der Marke Steiff (s. Abb. 204–206), der in den 1950er Jahren den Erfolg der Plüschtiere von Margarete Steiff auf ein bewegliches Spielpolster übertrug. Im Inneren des mit Gummifühlern ausgestatteten Marienkäfers dient Holzwolle als Füllmaterial. Damit gleicht dessen Polsterung der eines anderen Klassikers, dem von Renate Müller 1969 als therapeutisches Spielobjekt entworfenen Rupfentier-Nilpferd *Mocky* (s. Abb. 202/203), das allerdings nicht mit einem Kräuselvelours wie der Maikäfer bezogen ist, sondern mit kräftigem Juteleinen, das punktuell durch Lederapplikationen verstärkt wird. Das von der H. Josef Leven KG in Sonneberg produzierte Nilpferd-Objekt gilt heute als Ikone des DDR-Designs.

Neben diesen für Kinder entworfenen und mit natürlichen Materialien gefüllten Polstersitzen zeigen wir einen Hocker, dessen Holzgestell mit Polyurethan umschäumt wurde. Er stellt eine Phantasiefigur mit Fischschuppenoberfläche dar, mit großen Augen und einem kräftigen, freundlich ausgeformten Mund (s. Abb. 207–209). Damit die reliefierte Oberfläche beim Spielen nicht unangenehm reibt, besteht der starkfarbige, 1980 von Sophie Roberty und Christophe Beauséjour entworfene Hocker aus einem gummiartigen Material, das aus Gründen der Haltbarkeit behautet wurde, d. h. einen entsprechenden Überzug erhielt, der Abrieb verhindert. Das Polster ist ein gegossener Korpus ohne Bezugsstoff. So ist der Hocker robust, in seiner Nutzung überaus einfach, kantenlos und weich. Wegen der rundum geschlossenen Oberfläche schützt das Polster zudem vor möglichen Verletzungen eines erkundungsfreudigen Kleinkindes, das mit dem Hocker spielt.

Upholstery for children

Furniture for children has always existed. Even in tombs of Egyptian pharaohs such chairs have been found. In the late nineteenth century, companies such as Thonet recognised a lucrative market and offered a wide range of their products in children's versions. In this case, the shapes of adult furniture were carefully converted to child size. This is also true for the models of today's celebrated designers such as Alvar Aalto, Gerrit Rietveld and Marcel Breuer, who naturally modified their chairs for 'little adults'. While the child was turned into an *equal co-inhabitant*,[164] as Franz Schuster put it in 1927, the question to which degree the child's playfulness was encouraged remains. While concepts that tried to accomplish this were developed, for example in conjunction with the Montessori reform movement, for long, chairs for children followed those for adults. This becomes evident in two chairs in our exhibition: on the one hand, the Art Deco armchair (figs. 128–130) upholstered with lashed springs and palm fibre stuffing and, on the other hand, an armchair with cotton-filled cushions (figs. 210–212) that takes up the forms of the late 1960s. They correspond with three play seats, which immediately make evident that no model from the adult world was used. This is especially true for the ladybird fitted with chassis and castors from the Steiff brand (figs. 204–206), which in the 1950s translated the success of Margarete Steiff's stuffed animals to a mobile upholstered play object. In the interior of the ladybird, with rubber antennae, wood excelsior has been used as a stuffing. The upholstery is similar to that of another classic, the burlap hippo *Mocky* (figs. 202/203), designed by Renate Müller in 1969 as a therapeutic plaything, which in contrast to the ladybird is not covered with a curly velour but with crash as well as leather applications. The hippo object, produced by H. Josef Leven KG in Sonneberg, is today considered an icon of GDR design.

In addition to these upholstered seats designed for children and upholstered using natural materials, we display a stool with a polyurethane foamed wooden frame. It is a phantastical figure with a surface of fish scales, big eyes and a pronounced friendly mouth (figs. 207–209). To prevent the relief surface from rubbing uncomfortably during play, the vibrantly coloured stool, designed in 1980 by Sophie Roberty and Christophe Beauséjour, is made of a rubber-like material that has been laminated for durability – that is, given an appropriate coating to prevent abrasion. The cushion is a moulded body without covering fabric. Thus, the stool is robust, exceedingly simple in its use, edgeless and soft. Because of the all-round closed surface, the cushion also protects against possible injury to an exploratory toddler playing with the stool.

202/203
Spielobjekt/Rupfentier Nilpferd *Mocky*, Renate Müller (Entwurf), H. Josef Leven KG, Sonneberg, DDR (Herstellung), 1969 (LÖFFLER COLLECTION, Reichenschwand)

202/203
Play object/jute animal hippopotamus *Mocky*, Renate Müller (design), H. Josef Leven KG, Sonneberg, GDR (production), 1969 (LÖFFLER COLLECTION, Reichenschwand)

Nach 1945 I After 1945 **213**

204–206
Kinderfahrzeug *Marienkäfer* mit Rollen, Margarete Steiff (Entwurf), Steiff, Deutschland (Herstellung), 1950er Jahre (LÖFFLER COLLECTION, Reichenschwand)

204–206
Children vehicle *Marienkäfer* with castors, Margarete Steiff (design), Steiff, Deutschland (production), 1950s (LÖFFLER COLLECTION, Reichenschwand)

207–209
Kinderhocker, Sophie Roberty und Christophe Beauséjour (Entwurf), Paris (Herstellung), um 1980 (LÖFFLER COLLECTION, Reichenschwand)

207–209
Children's stool, Sophie Roberty and Christophe Beauséjour (design), Paris (production), around 1980 (LÖFFLER COLLECTION, Reichenschwand)

Nach 1945 | After 1945 **215**

210–212
Armlehnstuhl für Kinder, 1960er/1970er Jahre (LÖFFLER COLLECTION, Reichenschwand)

210–212
Children's armchair, 1960s/1970s (LÖFFLER COLLECTION, Reichenschwand)

Kommunikation, Spiel und Provokation

Von der Sperrmüllmatratze zur Récamière im Blümchen-Look ist ein Text des Architektur- und Designkritikers Volker Fischer überschrieben, der 1987 zurückblickt, um an eine allgemeine Zeit des Protestes und *auf Gruppenerfahrung rekurrierende Wohnsituationen*[165] der 1970er Jahre zu erinnern. Damals suchten viele den kollektiven Konventionsbruch. Das gerade Sitzen auf Stühlen galt manchem als spießig. Daher übertrug ein Teil der jungen Generation das auf Demonstrationen erprobte *sit-in* auch in den Wohnbereich, wo das Liegen und Lümmeln auf Matratzen oder *das Ruhen auf alternativen Sitzmöbeln*[166] als adäquate Form des Sich-Niederlassens empfunden wurde. Der Kulturhistoriker Hajo Eickhoff erklärt, die Jugend habe in den 1960er Jahren die Stühle verlassen, um sich in vielfacher Hinsicht zu bewegen: *Der Mensch soll gehen, laufen, stehen oder bodennah lagern. Soll nomadisch leben*[167], erläutert er die Haltung jener, die auf die Straße gingen, um gegen die allgemeinen Verhältnisse zu demonstrieren. Künstlerisch überhöht, folgt dieser Devise das *Reifensofa*, das die Arbeitsgruppe *Des-In* 1975 präsentierte. Die aus sechs Studenten und einem Dozenten der Hochschule für Gestaltung Offenbach bestehende Initiative befasste sich mit Recycling-Design und der Wiederverwendung gebrauchter Dinge. In diesem Fall reaktivierten sie abgefahrene Autoreifen, aus denen sie das Chassis eines Sofas stapelten. Die Polsterung bestand aus einem passgenau geschneiderten Kissen, das in den nur bedingt federnden Gummirahmen eingelegt wurde.

Der Do-it-yourself-Charakter derartiger Design-Experimente entsprach dem Trend, abgelegten Dingen ein zweites Leben zu geben. Da kam es gerade recht, dass damals viele begannen, die ererbten Möbel abzustoßen. In dieser Zeit versammelte sich an Straßenrändern als Sperrmüll, was heute teilweise auch im Museum zu finden sein könnte. Zu den begehrten Entdeckungen gehörten alte Matratzen, die dann meist mit Cord, Jute, Leinen oder Jeans bezogen wurden.[168] Fischer schreibt, dem Sitzbedürfnis wurde so auf billige Weise Genüge getan, da solche Matratzen zudem als antikapitalistisch und, da durch ihre Einzelform nicht präjudiziert, als offen und demokratisch angesehen wurden. Der Autor sah hier ein Indiz für eine Haltung zum Wohnen, die gleichermassen Ausdruck ökonomischer Not wie ästhetischen Protestes gegen das normierte Kaufhaus- und Schöner-Wohnen-Mobiliar war. Das gefederte Spielpolster wurde ebenso Symbol variabler Beziehungen wie Ausdruck eines erklärten Kommunikationswillens. Dabei wollte man sich von dem Korsett der Sitzkonventionen früherer Generationen befreien. Dieser Tendenz folgend, hatte die Möbelindustrie längst das Thema der Wohnlandschaft aufgenommen und zahlreiche Polstermodulserien auf den Markt gebracht, die vielfältigste Nutzungsmöglichkeiten anboten. Klaus-Dieter Mädzulat bringt es in in der Zeitschrift *form + zweck* nicht nur für den Osten Deutschlands auf den Punkt, wenn er das Merkmal kombinierter Sitz-Liege-Möbel als gruppenbildend und verhaltensbestimmend charakterisiert.[169]

Volker Fischer zitierte in seinem bereits erwähnten Text zum Polstervergnügen der 1970er Jahre aus einem Werbetext, den das Einrichtungshaus Musterring 1972 in einem seiner Produktkataloge veröffentlichte. Zu dem aus Polsterbausteinen bestehenden Programm *MR 333* hieß es da unter der

Communication, play and provocation

Von der Sperrmüllmatratze zu Récamière im Blümchen-Look (From Streetside Mattress to Récamière in Floral Look) is the title of a text by architecture and design critic Volker Fischer, who in 1987 looked back to reflect on the time of protest and the *living situations made for collective experience*[165] of the 1970s. At the time, many sought to collectively break with conventions. Sitting up straight on a chair was considered bourgeois by some. The young generation took the sit-in practiced during demonstrations to the living space, where lying and lounging on mattresses or *resting on alternative seating furniture*[166] was perceived as an appropriate form of settling down. The cultural historian Hajo Eichoff explains that during the 1960s young people had left their chairs in order to move in many ways: *Man was supposed to walk, run, stand or lounge near the floor. He was to live nomadically*,[167] he explains the attitude of those who took to the streets to demonstrate against the state of things. Artistically exaggerated, the *Reifensofa* by the collective *Des-In* from 1975 confirms this slogan. The initiative, made up of six students and their tutor from the Hochschule für Gestaltung Offenbach, took up recycling design and the reuse of second-hand objects. In this way, they reactivated worn tyres from which they assembled the sofa frame. The padding was made from made-to-measure cushions that were inserted into the only partly sprung rubber frame.

The do-it-yourself character of such design experiments corresponded with the trend to give unused objects a second life. It was timely that many had begun to sell off their inherited furniture. At the time, one could find objects gathered on roadside collections as bulky waste, some of which could today be found in the museum. Among the coveted discoveries were old mattresses, which were subsequently usually covered with corduroy, jute, linen or denim.[168] Fischer writes that the need for seating was thus satisfied in a cheap way, since such mattresses were also seen as anti-capitalist and, since not prejudiced by their individual form, as open and democratic. The author saw here an indication of an attitude to living that was equally an expression of economic need and aesthetic protest against the standardised department store and *Schöner Wohnen* (Beautiful Living [Magazine title]) furniture. The sprung play cushion became as much a symbol of changing relationships as an expression of a declared will to communicate. The aim was to free oneself from the corset of seating conventions of earlier generations. Following this tendency, the furniture industry had taken up the topic of living landscapes and brought various modular upholstered series to the market which could be used in a variety of ways. Klaus-Dieter Mädzulat put it in a nutshell in the magazine *form + zweck*, not only for the East of Germany, when he characterised the feature of combined seat-reclining furniture as conducive to forming groups and determining behaviour.[169]

In his text on upholstered pleasures of the 1970s mentioned above, Volker Fischer quotes the advertisement published by the furniture store Musterring in its 1972 product catalogue. As a description of its series

Überschrift *Sitzvergnügen bis zum Liegen*[170]: *Mobil heißt das Spiel! Die althergebrachte ‚Sitzordnung' ist passé. Bei uns erwartet Sie eine ganz neue Wohnwelt mit Polstermöbeln und rundum weichen Polsterelementen zum Variieren, Kombinieren, Experimentieren. Damit Sie es sich bequem machen können nach Lust und Laune – heute so, morgen so und übermorgen anders. Die Musterring-Designer haben Ihnen fürs Wohnzimmer das Bett gemacht. Lassen Sie sich überraschen*.[171] Dieser verdeckt erotische Hinweis war ebenso Teil der Werbestrategien verschiedener Hersteller wie das klare Bekenntnis zur fast grenzenlosen Flexibilität raffiniert konzipierter Polsterbausteine, die ein Höchstmaß an Anpassungsfähigkeit bei unterschiedlichster Beanspruchung garantierten.

So warb das *VEB Werk Reform* 1973 für das von Roland Kretschmann entworfene *Polstermöbel-System 74* mit der flexiblen Addierbarkeit der Grundkörper, mittels derer es möglich war, die Liegelänge bzw. die Sitzbreite von 1.000 mm an aufwärts in Sprüngen von jeweils 100 mm (Rastermaß) zu vergrößern. Damit konnte das Maß dem individuellen Bedürfnis angeglichen werden.[172] Modulare Polsterelemente sah man auch mit Blick auf den modebewussten Konsumenten als ideal an, um Bezüge öfter einmal auszutauschen.[173] Damit unterschied sich das Konzept *Reform 74* von anderen Polstermöbel-Sortimenten, deren Sessel oft schon nach relativ kurzer Zeit als altmodisch empfunden wurden. Werner Ehrhardt erklärte, modular konfigurierte Sitzmöbel folgten hingegen notwendigen Prämissen wie Langlebigkeit, Neutralität und Universalität[174].

Vor allem legte man im Osten Deutschlands Wert auf Variabilität, Material- und Raumökonomie: Sitzen sollte weich und wohlig sein und unkonventionelle Lösungen erlauben. Das von Jürgen Klepka in *form + zweck* beworbene *Programm Stralsund* verband dementsprechend den Vorteil eines Elementarprogramms (Variabilität) mit der Leichtigkeit fußbodenfreier Gestaltungen. Verschiedene Sitz- und Liegekombinationen wurden durch Reihung ermöglicht und gestatteten die rationale Ausnutzung der Stellfläche.[175] Dabei vollzog sich, was Hans Lewitzky schon 1961 in seinem Ratgeber *Meine Wohnung*[176] in Abkehr vom Garnitur-Möbel gefordert hatte: Das repräsentative Polster-Schaustück wurde endlich durch eine spezielle Form der Anbaumöbel ersetzt, die handlich waren, die Einrichtung eines Raumes jederzeit leicht verändern ließen und auch bei der Veränderung der Wohnungsgröße keine Schwierigkeiten verursachten.[177]

Dass man im Osten Deutschlands den teilweise kurios anmutenden Sitzformen mancher Designer im Westen kritisch gegenüberstand, vermittelt eine Glosse, in der Klaus-Dieter Mädzulat 1973 von einer Zumutung spricht, sich *auf Polsterschlangen und Schutthaufen von Schaumballen oder Schnipseln zu lümmeln*.[178] Ob er dabei an die provokanten Sitzmodelle italienischer Designer dachte, ist nicht gesichert. Doch lässt sich annehmen, dass er wohl auch die extraganten Modelle etwa der italienischen Gruppe Archizoom vor Augen gehabt haben mag.

MR 333 made from upholstered elements one reads the following under the caption *Sitzvergnügen bis zum Liegen (Sitting pleasure until lying down)*[170]: *Mobile is the name of the game! The traditional "seating arrangement" is passé. A whole new world of living awaits you, with upholstered furniture and soft upholstered elements to vary, combine and experiment with. So that you can make yourself comfortable according to your mood – today like this, tomorrow like that and the day after tomorrow differently. The Musterring designers have made the bed for your living room. Let yourself be surprised*.[171] This covertly erotic reference was just as much a part of the advertising strategies of various manufacturers as the clear commitment to the almost limitless flexibility of cleverly designed upholstered modules, which guaranteed maximum adaptability to a wide variety of demands.

In this way *VEB Werk Reform* 1973 advertised the *Polstermöbel System 74*, designed by Roland Kretschmann with flexible add-on basic forms, which made it possible to increase the chaise lounge length or seat width of 1,000 mm in 100 mm steps (grid dimension). In doing this, the measurements could be made to suit individual requirements.[172] Modular upholstered elements were also ideal for fashionable customers who were able to change covers frequently.[173] This differentiated the concept *Reform 74* from other series whose armchairs were considered outdated after a relatively short while. Werner Ehrhardt declared that modular seating furniture followed instead necessary premises such as longevity, neutrality and universality.[174]

Especially in eastern Germany emphasis was placed on variability and the economic use of material and space. Seating had to be soft and comfortable and allow for unconventional solutions. The *Programm Stralsund* advertised by Jürgen Klepka in *form + zweck* correspondingly combined the advantages of a modular system (variability) with the ease of designs that freed up floor space. Different seating and lying combinations were made possible by placing them in line and, thus enabling a rational use of space.[175] The departure from furniture sets that Hans Lewitzky had already demanded in 1961 in his guide *Meine Wohnung*[176] became a reality: the representative upholstered show piece was replaced by a specific form of modular furniture that were handy, made it possible to change the room set-up anytime and was unproblematic if the apartment size changed.[177]

That in eastern Germany, the partially curious seat forms of some Western designers were met with scepticism becomes evident in a 1973 essay, in which Klaus-Dieter Mädzulat speaks of the imposition of lounging on *snakes of upholstery and piles of rubble from foam bales or snippets*.[178] Whether he was thinking of the provocative seating models of Italian designers is not certain. But it can be assumed that he probably also had the extravagant models of the Italian group Archizoom in mind.

213
Polstersessel, VEB Möbelkombinat Berlin, DDR (Herstellung), 1975
(GRASSI Museum für Angewandte Kunst Leipzig)

213
Upholstered armchair, VEB Möbelkombinat Berlin, GDR (production), 1975 (GRASSI Museum für Angewandte Kunst Leipzig)

214
Oświęcim, 28.11.2006, aus der Serie *Zufällige Begegnungen* von Stefan Kraus

214
Oświęcim, 28.11.2006, from the photography series *Zufällige Begegnungen* by Stefan Kraus

Rethinking
Thomas Schriefers

A photo gets to the heart of it: placed next to a rubbish container, the upholstered armchair (fig. 214)[179] is the sad echo of a formerly proudly presented status symbol, that has been discarded as it no longer fits the taste of the time. Since the 1970s, this tendency has rapidly increased as objects lost their formal validity in ever shorter periods of time. In this way, what had been fashionable today, could already been outdated tomorrow.

This unsustainable fact inspired the organisers of the exhibition *Vorsicht: Polstermöbel!* in Vienna in 1990 to find answers to the question of how this disastrous circle could be broken. The focus was the consequences of a development in which the increased production of furniture sets relates to faster consumption, material degradation and the problem of disintegrating foam material. The catalogue displayed sections of popular products of different manufacturers that demonstrated that the usual sandwich construction of pieced-together foam materials had nothing in common with the masterly craftsmanship behind the padding of earlier times. Research showed that only a few very expensive models had, at least partially, been crafted according to the art of the trade. Instead, most upholstered seats were assembled from different solid foam volumes that had been placed next to and on top of each other like bricks. Here, the organisers came in to question the use of such products. In exchange, the demand for justness in work and sustainability became louder. In eastern Germany, *form + zweck* magazine took up the critical issue and reviewed the Viennese exhibition thoroughly. It was there that a product aesthetic in the service of an ever more rapid consumption was revealed, whose harmful superficiality could only be met be boycotting products and producers.[180] As the initiator of the exhibition, Robert Maria Stieg bellicosely referred to the exhibition as a means to create *an ideal front against any kind of surrogate culture and low-quality industrial production*.[181] The cut-open sections of furniture ultimately revealed what could be considered *the result of structural omissions, the use of lesser materials and conscious breaches of the rules of craftsmanship*.[182]

In his book *Möbel des 20. Jahrhunderts*,[183] published in 1980, Philippe Garner connected an introduction to 1980sthe design of the 1980s with a short review of the recently by-gone decade, to which he attested the designers' interest in the industrial as the most important tendency.[184] Products that had originally been developed for technical tasks were increasingly used for the construction of buildings and furnishings. The high-tech euphoria of the 1980s was already well underway and would be articulated in manifold ways. An early example is the *Rover Seat Chair* (figs. 215–217), designed by Ron Arad in 1981, for which an automobile seat originally produced for a Rover car was fastened to a tubular frame as used for scaffolding. The *fauteuil*, realised by One Off Ltd in London, is upholstered with

215–217
Sessel *Rover Seat Chair*, Ron Arad (Entwurf), One Off Ltd., London (Herstellung), 1981 (LÖFFLER COLLECTION, Reichenschwand)

215–217
Armchair *Rover Seat Chair*, Ron Arad (design), One Off Ltd., London (production), 1981 (LÖFFLER COLLECTION, Reichenschwand)

fabrizierter, Automobilsitz auf einen dem Gerüstbau entlehnten, Rahmen aus Rundrohr aufgesetzt wurde. Das bei One Off Ltd. in London realisierte Fauteuil besitzt ein Polster, bei dem über einem Federkern Gummikokos und graue Watte die Unterlage für den gehefteten Lederbezug bilden. Dagegen wirkt das Sitzobjekt *Embryo* (s. Abb. 218), das Marc Newson 1988 konzipierte, formal eher wie eine phantasievoll-ironische Interpretation des Sitzmöbels als keimendes Gebilde, analog zu einem Lebewesen in der frühen Form seiner Entwicklung. Neopren, ein im Automobilbau und für Sportbekleidung eingesetzter Synthesekautschuk, bedeckt das schwellende Polstervolumen, das herausfordernd orange leuchtet.

Dass man sich intensiv mit Füllungen oder Nichtfüllungen der Polster beschäftigte, zeigen auch zwei weitere Beispiele. So das Sitzkissen *Memo* (s. Abb. 221/222), welches Ron Arad 1999 für die Londoner Inflate Studios entwarf. Auf den ersten Blick erinnert es an den *Sacco* der 1960er Jahre (s. Abb. 178 u. 219), doch unterscheidet es sich davon durch die Art der Polsterfüllung. Zwar finden sich in dessen Innerem auch Polystyrolkugeln, doch dient hier ein Ventil dem Absaugen der im Sack befindlichen Luft, wodurch darin ein Vakuum entsteht, das dazu beiträgt, dass das Kissen seine gegebene Form behält. Die Ausbildung der Polsterform geschieht hier auf außergewöhnliche Weise unter Berücksichtigung physikalischer Gesetzmäßigkeiten. Ganz anders gingen 2007 Riccardo Blumer und Matteo Borghi beim Entwurf ihres Hightech-generierten *Entronauta Chair* (s. Abb. 220) vor, für den ein beflockter PVC-Bezug mit Polyurethan gefüllt wird, um anschließend in einer Tiefziehform zu erstarren. Dabei verfestigt sich das Material und ist tatsächlich weniger weich im Sitz als es das hier zu sehende Modell mit lockerem Faltenwurf uns vormacht. Hier zeigt sich, dass ein Polster nicht immer hält, was es äußerlich verspricht.

Heute boomt der Markt der Polstermöbel, wobei Kriterien wie ökologische Nachhaltigkeit und Materialunbedenklichkeit den Kauf eines entsprechenden Gegenstandes zunehmend beeinflussen. Dennoch gelten nach wie vor oft noch

a sprung core covered with rubberised coconut fibre and grey cotton padding, on top of which the leather covers have been tacked. In contrast, the seating object *Embryo* (fig. 218), designed by Marc Newson in 1988, appears in the shape of a phantastic-ironic interpretation of seating furniture as a germinating structure, an analogy to a being in the first phases of its development. Neoprene, a synthetic India rubber used for automobile fabrication and sportswear, covers the padded volume, which shines in provocative orange.

That one was intensely occupied with the stuffing or non-stuffing of upholstery becomes evident in two further examples. For example, the bean bag *Memo* (figs. 220/221), designed by Ron Arad for the London-based Inflate Studios in 1999. While at first sight it seems to resemble *Sacco* from the 1960s (figs. 178, 219), it differs in terms of filling. While one can find polystyrene balls in the inside, a ventil for extracting air has been fitted, which creates a vacuum, allowing the cushion to maintain its form. Here, the formation of the upholstery form occurs in an extraordinary way, taking into account the laws of physics. Riccardo Blumer and Matteo Borghi took a completely different approach in 2007 when they designed their high-tech *Entronauta Chair* (fig. 222), for which a flocked PVC cover was filled with polyurethane and then set in a thermoforming mould. During the process, the material solidifies and is actually less soft to the touch than the loosely draped model seen here would have us believe. This shows that a cushion does not always deliver what it promises on the outside.

Today, the market for upholstered furniture is booming, while criteria such as ecological sustainability and material safety increasingly influence the purchase decision. Nevertheless, considerations such as cosiness and comfort are still the most important argument when buying upholstered furniture, such as the slim two-sitter *Loveseat*, which became a bestseller on the

Umdenken | Rethinking **223**

218
Sitzobjekt *Embryo*, Marc Newson (Entwurf), Ideé, Japan (Herstellung), 1988 (LÖFFLER COLLECTION, Reichenschwand)
Seat object *Embryo*, Marc Newson (design), Ideé, Japan (production), 1988 (LÖFFLER COLLECTION, Reichenschwand)

219
Sitzsack *Sacco*, 1968 (LÖFFLER COLLECTION, Reichenschwand)
Beanbag *Sacco*, 1968 (LÖFFLER COLLECTION, Reichenschwand)

220
Stuhl *Entronauta*, Riccardo Blumer und Matteo Borghi (Entwurf), Desalto, Cantù, Como (Herstellung), 2007 (LÖFFLER COLLECTION, Reichenschwand)
Chair *Entronauta*, Riccardo Blumer and Matteo Borghi (design), Desalto, Cantù, Como (production), 2007 (LÖFFLER COLLECTION, Reichenschwand)

221/222
Sitzkissen *Memo*, Ron Arad (Entwurf), Inflate Studios, London (Herstellung), 1999 (LÖFFLER COLLECTION, Reichenschwand)
Seat cushion *Memo*, Ron Arad (design), Inflate Studios, London (production), 1999 (LÖFFLER COLLECTION, Reichenschwand)

Umdenken | Rethinking **225**

Bequemlichkeit und Komfort als vorrangige Argumente für die Anschaffung eines Polstermöbels, z. B. eines doppelsitzigen, schlanken *Loveseat*, der 2019 auf der britischen Verkaufsplattform Swoon zum Bestseller avancierte.[185] Gründe dafür waren kleine, aber teure Wohnungen, veränderte Familienstrukturen und der Wunsch nach Mobilität. Es hieß, zwar sei die heilige Zweisamkeit von Sofa und Fernseher längst zerbröckelt, doch suche man einen Platz, an dem in Ruhe die Phones und Pads betrachtet werden können. Unabhängig davon erweist sich das gepolsterte Sofa heute durchaus als geschätzter Teil der Wohnung, als Lebensinsel, Objekt der Identifikation und Aktionsbühne: etwa in der seit 30 Jahren im Fernsehen ausgestrahlten Kult-Zeichentrickserie *The Simpsons*, in der die Familiencouch eine zentrale Rolle spielt. Sie ist das Zentrum familiären Zusammenlebens und zugleich noch viel mehr. Und zwar dann, wenn das Polstermöbel ein Eigenleben entwickelt, in einer Szene etwa anfängt, die Familie wie ein Rodeo-Pferd anzuspringen oder ein anderes Mal zum Schleudersitz mutiert.[186] Die Quintessenz lautet: Das Polstermöbel lebt und erweist sich, nicht nur im Trickfilm, als Elaborat einer narrativen Idee, die Emotionen weckt.[187]

Doch auch im realen Leben bewährt sich das Polstermöbel im Single-Haushalt, in der Familienwohnung und in der WG. Das in vielen Netzwerken propagierte *Couchsurfing*, bei dem sich Menschen gegenseitig Schlafgelegenheiten in verschiedenen Städten offerieren, wäre ohne das gut gepolsterte Möbel gar nicht möglich.[188] Dabei leistet das Polstermöbel viel mehr, erklärte 2008 die Journalistin Annabel Wahba im *Zeit-Magazin*, nachdem sie die Sitzplätze ihrer Vergangenheit[189] besucht hatte. Sie erinnerte sich, für sie als Heranwachsende seien die Sessel der Erwachsenen viel spannender gewesen als die sogenannten kindgerechten Möbel. Der weinrote Samtbezug des Familiensofas sei sehr weich gewesen, schreibt Wahba, die als Kind Spaß daran hatte, darauf zu liegen und an den daran hängenden Quasten und Fransen zu ziehen. Hinzu kam die Geschichte der 2008 immer noch an Ort und Stelle stehenden Polstermöbel, denn sie waren Erbstücke der geliebten Großmutter; Möbel, die um 1880 angeschafft worden waren und immer noch in Gebrauch sind.

Folgt man den Betrachtungen des Industriedesigners Ed van Hinte, dann erzählen uns Polstermöbel Geschichten aller Art, die unter ihrer Haut abgelagert wurden.[190] Ihr nicht sichtbares Innenleben unterstützt diese Vermutung und erzeugt Neugier für das, was sich unter möglicherweise auch faltigen Bezugsstoffen verbirgt. Der amerikanische Künstler Saul Steinberg vermittelt dies in der eingangs abgebildeten Zeichnung (s. Abb. 3), die einen Mann zeigt, der den Flachkopf eines Stethoskops an das Rückenpolster hält, dort, wo man bei einem Menschen das Herz vermuten würde.[191] Offensichtlich ist der Dargestellte bemüht, Töne aus dem Inneren des Sitzmöbels abzuhören, das, so muss man schlussfolgern, lebt.

Der Polstersessel als Persönlichkeit oder sogar als Alter Ego? Jedenfalls bekundet die Zeichnung ein besonderes Interesse am Innleben des voluminösen Wohnbegleiters und bringt auf den Punkt, was die Ausstellung *BESESSEN. Die geheime Kunst des Polsterns* bezweckt: Im ersten Schritt außergewöhnliche Meisterwerke des Polsterns aus 400 Jahren zu zeigen, um parallel zu vermitteln, wie sich der Aufbau der Polster aufgrund konstruktiver Neuerungen, neuer Materialien und steigender Ansprüche veränderte.

British trading platform Swoon in 2019.[185] Explanations could be found in small but expensive apartments, changed family structures and the desire for mobility. While the quiet togetherness of sofa and television set was now a thing of the past, the search was on for a place where mobile phones and tablets could be looked at in peace.

Irrespective of this, the upholstered sofa today proves to be a valued part of the home, an island of life, an object of identification and a stage for action, for example in the cult animated series *The Simpsons*, which has been broadcast on television for 30 years, in which the family couch plays a central role. It is the centre of family life and, at the same time, much more. This is when the upholstered furniture develops a life of its own, for example when it starts jumping at the family like a rodeo horse in one scene or mutates into an ejector seat in another.[186] The bottom line is: upholstered furniture is alive and proves to be an elaboration of a narrative idea that arouses emotions, and not just in animated films.[187]

In real life, too, upholstered furniture proves itself, be it in the single household, family apartment or shared accommodation. Couchsurfing, advertised across many networks, where people offer sleeping places to one another, would not be possible without well-padded furniture.[188] But upholstered furniture is so much more, declared the journalist Annabel Wahba in 2008 in *Zeit-Magazin* after she had revisited the seats of her past.[189] She remembered that, growing up, the adult armchairs had been much more interesting than the so-called child-appropriate furniture. The wine-red velvet cover of the family couch was very soft, Wahba writes, who, as a child, took pleasure in lying on it and pulling at the tassels and fringes. In addition came the history behind the upholstered furniture pieces that still stood at the same place in 2008, as they had been heirlooms from her beloved grandmother, furniture that had been acquired in 1880 and was still in use.

Following the considerations of industrial designer Ed van Hinte, upholstered furniture tells all sort of tales that have been embedded underneath their skins.[190] Their invisible interior supports this assumption and fosters curiosity about what lays underneath the at times wrinkled covers. The American artist Saul Steinberg conveys this in the drawing illustrated at the beginning of the book (fig. 3), in which a man points the head of a stethoscope against a backrest pad, where one would presume the location of a person's heart.[191] Apparently, the man depicted is trying to hear sounds from the interior of the seat, which, one has to conclude, is alive.

The upholstered armchair as a personality or even as alter ego? In any case, the drawing testifies to a specific interest in the interior of the voluminous living companion and puts the aim of the exhibition *DEEP-SEATED: The Secret Art of Upholstery* in a nutshell: firstly, to show extraordinary masterpieces of upholstery from over 400 years in order to also convey how its construction has changed according to structural innovations, new materials and increased demands.

Hören, Schauen, Fühlen, Sitzen
Thomas Schriefers

Eigens für unsere Ausstellung angefertigte Modelle zeigen, was wir normalerweise nur vermuten können. Es ist die handgefertigte Undercoverwelt gepolsterter Sitzmöbel, die im Museum aufs Podest gestellt werden, was bedeutet, sie von Nutz- in Schauobjekte umzuwidmen. Da man sich nun nicht mehr daraufsetzen kann, verlieren sie ihre ursprüngliche Bestimmung als benutzbares Sitzmöbel, die vom Betrachter aber grundsätzlich mitgedacht wird. Da historische Sitzmöbel aufgrund ihres Alters sehr empfindlich sind und schon bei geringster Beanspruchung beschädigt werden könnten, werden sie im Museum zu unberührbaren Exponaten. Das fragile Erbe wird geschützt, um ein museales Weiterleben zu gewährleisten.

Weil sich mit Polstersesseln immer aber auch sinnliche Aspekte verbinden, ist in unserer Ausstellung ein separater Bereich eingerichtet, wo sich Hören, Schauen, Fühlen und auch Sitzendürfen vereinen. Man erreicht diesen von den Schauräumen abgetrennten Saal durch einen abgedunkelten Klangtunnel, der gewissermaßen als Schleuse fungiert und, auf dem Weg hindurch, dazu einlädt, einer Symphonie von Arbeits- und Nutzgeräuschen zu lauschen, wie sie in Polsterwerkstätten entstehen. Handwerkliches Schaffen wird dort in seiner Komplexität sinnlich erlebbar. Der Weg führt dann in den großen Aktionsraum, wo neben der Lust am Schauen, Hören und Sich-Informieren, vierzehn zeittypisch gepolsterte Stühle praktisch ausprobiert werden können: Hier ist Fühlen, Tasten und Sitzen nicht nur erlaubt, sondern erwünscht!

Wie sitzt man auf einem flachen Polster, gefedert oder ungefedert? Wie auf Schaumstoff im niedrigen Cocktailsessel oder im ausladenden Salonmöbel? Der Sitzkomfort lässt sich sinnlich erfahren, vergleichen und begründen, da die von den beteiligten Restauratoren zur Verfügung gestellten Sitzmöbel ergänzend in ihrem Aufbau erläutert werden. Doch steht hier das persönliche Empfinden im Vordergrund. Dieses bildet schließlich die Grundlage für ein eigenes Statement, das im Aktionsraum direkt auf einer langen Wand schriftlich festgehalten werden kann.

Austausch und Kommunikation finden auch in Sonderveranstaltungen statt, bei denen zu bestimmten Terminen Handwerksmeister*innen Interessierte in ihre *geheime Kunst* des Polsterns einweihen und Arbeitsweisen vorführen. Dieser Bereich ist zwischen den beiden Schausälen der Ausstellung lokalisiert und bildet auf diese Weise eine Art Marktplatz, auf dem persönliche Ansprüche ermittelt, kommuniziert und diskutiert werden. Dabei werden die Besucher*innen für den dritten Teil der Ausstellung sensibilisiert. Hier gilt allerdings wieder, dass die empfindlichen Exponate nur betrachtet und nicht berührt werden dürfen. Dafür entschädigt das eindrucksvolle Bild eines Dialogs von 40 chronologisch in Gruppen zueinander gestellten Polstermöbeln aus der Zeit von 1900 bis 2008 aus der LÖFFLER-COLLECTION, die in der Orangerie des GRASSI Museums für Angewandte Kunst Leipzig versammelt sind.

Listening, seeing, touching, sitting
Thomas Schriefers

The models made especially for our exhibition show what we can normally only assume. It is the handmade undercover world of upholstered seating furniture that is placed on a pedestal in the museum, which means transforming it from a useful object into a display object. Since one can no longer sit on it, it loses its original purpose as usable seating furniture, which is, however, reimagined by the viewer. Since pieces of historical seating furniture are very sensitive due to their age and could be damaged by even the slightest wear, they become untouchable exhibits in the museum; the fragile heritage is protected to ensure that they may live on in the museum.

Since upholstered furniture is always connected to the sensual, a separate area in our exhibition has been set apart where seeing, looking, feeling and being allowed to sit are combined. The area, which is separated from the showrooms, can be reached through a darkened sound tunnel that functions as a kind of portal and, on the way through, invites visitors to listen to a symphony of working and usage sounds as they are produced in upholstery workshops. There, the complexity of craftsmanship can be experienced with all the senses. The path then leads to the large activity room, where, in addition to the pleasure of looking, listening and informing oneself, fourteen upholstered period chairs can be tried out: here, feeling, touching and sitting not only are allowed, but desired!

How does one sit on a flat cushion, sprung or unsprung? How on foam in the low cocktail chair or in the cantilevered salon furniture? Seating comfort can be experienced, compared and justified through the senses, as the seating furniture provided by the participating restorers is additionally explained in its construction. Nevertheless, the focus here is on personal perception. It forms the basis for a personal statement that can be written down directly on a long wall in the activity room.

Exchange and communication also take place in special events during which, on certain dates, master craftsmen and -women initiate interested visitors into their secret art of upholstery and demonstrate working methods. This area is located between the two showrooms of the exhibition and thus forms a kind of marketplace where personal demands are identified, communicated and discussed. In the process, visitors are prepared for the third part of the exhibition. Here, however, the delicate exhibits again may only be looked at and not touched. This is compensated for by the impressive image of a dialogue of 40 pieces of upholstered furniture chronologically arranged in groups from the period 1900 to 2008 from the Löffler Collection, which are gathered in the Orangerie of the GRASSI Museum für Angewandte Kunst Leipzig.

Die im Aktionsbereich nutzbaren Polstermöbel wurden von den an der Ausstellung beteiligten Restaurator*innen zur Verfügung gestellt, gereinigt und im Polster neu aufgebaut, sodass sie von den Besucher*innen besessen werden können. Dabei wurde darauf geachtet, dass Polstertechniken Verwendung fanden, die in der Epoche, in die die Sitzgegenstände stilistisch einzuordnen sind, tatsächlich eingesetzt wurden. So sitzt man bei zwei Biedermeierstühlen (s. Abb. 226 u. 227) auf einer Federpolsterung und spürt im dreisitzigen *indiscret* (s. Abb. 230/231), wie es sich anfühlt, auf einem capitonnégehefteten Polster Platz zu nehmen. Die dem Jugendstil zuzuordnende Bank (s. Abb. 234) verfügt über ein Flachpolster, das kaum Volumen besitzt, während die *bergère confessionnal* (s. Abb. 228/229) eine hohe Federpolsterung auszeichnet. Auf einem Barockstuhl der Zeit um 1700 (s. Abb. 223–225) erfährt man, wie es sich anfühlt, auf einem Polster zu sitzen, das im Inneren mit Naturmaterialien ausgefüllt und mit einer Langstroh-Vorderkante ausgestattet ist. Andere Sitzerfahrungen machen die Besucher*innen im Ohrensessel des Biedermeier (s. Abb. 237), im Klub- oder Cocktailsessel (s. Abb. 236, 238, 240). Neben der Art des Polsterns unterscheiden sie sich durch die Formen, die Stoffbezüge, die Sitzhöhe und Einsinktiefe, was mit dem Härtegrad der meist geschnürten Federpolsterung zusammenhängt.

Wie sitzt man im üppigen Polstersessel des Historismus, wie im thronähnlichen Jugendstilfauteuil (Abb. 232) oder auf einem niedrigen Hocker (s. Abb. 239)? Wer auf diese Fragen Antworten sucht, kann sie in diesem Bereich, der zum Vergleich durch Sitzwechsel auffordert, finden. Dabei ist beabsichtigt, die Besucher*innen auch zum Gespräch

The upholstered furniture that can be used in the activity area was made available by the conservators involved in the exhibition, who cleaned and rebuilt the upholstery so that visitors can sit on it. Care was taken to ensure that upholstery techniques were used that were actually employed in the period to which the seating objects belong stylistically. Thus, in the case of the two Biedermeier chairs (figs. 226, 227), one sits on sprung upholstery, and in the three-seater *Indiscret* (figs. 230/231), one can experience what it feels like to sit on deep-buttoned upholstery. The bench belonging to the Jugendstil period (fig. 234) has flat padding with hardly any volume, while the *bergère en confessionnal* (figs. 228/229) is characterised by high sprung upholstery. On a Baroque chair from around 1700 (figs. 223–225), visitors experience what it feels like to sit on an upholstery that is filled with natural materials on the inside and features a long-straw front edge. Visitors will have another sitting experience on the Biedermeier wingback chair (fig. 237), or in the club or cocktail chair (figs. 236, 238, 240). In addition to the type of upholstery, they differ in terms of shape, fabric covering, seat height and depth of yield, which is related to the degree of hardness of the mostly lashed sprung upholstery.

How does one sit in the opulent upholstered armchair of Historicism, how in the throne-like Jugendstil *fauteuil* (fig. 232) or on a low stool (fig. 239)? Those seeking answers to these questions can find them in this area, which invites comparison by means of changing seats. The intention is also to encourage visitors to talk

223–225
Barockstuhl, mit Langstroh-Vorderkante und Lehne mit Flachpolster, um 1700 (Reinhardt Roßberg, Markkleeberg)

223–225
Baroque chair, with long-straw edge roll and backrest with flat padding, around 1700 (Reinhardt Roßberg, Markkleeberg)

untereinander zu animieren, wenn etwa Erfahrungen und Einschätzungen ausgetauscht werden.

Zusätzliche Informationen vermitteln sich auf den Wandflächen, wo auf historische Zusammenhänge, stilistische Unterschiede, technische Fragen, zeittypische Konventionen und Materialbesonderheiten eingegangen wird.

Auf die hier versammelten Sitzbegleiter beziehen sich ganz konkret auch die Arbeitsberichte der Restaurator*innen, die ihre Stücke eigens für den Aktionsbereich der Ausstellung *BESESSEN. Die geheime Kunst des Polsterns* zur Verfügung gestellt und aufbereitet haben. Sie sind Mitglieder der Fachgruppe der Restauratoren im Handwerk e.V. des Fachbereichs der Raumausstatter und des Bundesverbandes der Restauratoren im Raumausstatterhandwerk e.V. Mit ihrer Expertise waren sie prädestiniert, ganz praktisch anschauliche Modelle zur Erläuterung verschiedener Arbeitstechniken zu erstellen. Es entstanden Arbeitsberichte und Dokumentationen, die in der Ausstellung zu sehen sind und im Aktionsbereich die sinnlichen Erfahrungen durch technische Erklärungen ergänzen.

Ein wichtiger Baustein der Zusammenarbeit waren mehrere Arbeitstreffen in verschiedenen Werkstätten und das gemeinsame Schaffen in den Räumen der Akademie des Handwerks Schloss Raesfeld. Dort trafen sich die aus ganz Deutschland angereisten Mitwirkenden, die ihre Arbeitsmittelpunkte in Hersbruck, Kleinmachnow, Löhne, Ludwigsburg, Lübeck, Markkleeberg, Obernkirchen (Vehlen), Osnabrück, Potsdam, Schalksmühle, Steinheim und Waabs haben. Alphabetisch geordnet sind dies Astrid Boeck, Maximilian Busch, Volker Engels, Edmund Graf, Alexander Hahlbeck, Rolf Hegenbart, Bernd Lehmkuhl, Wolfgang

to each other, for example by exchanging experiences and assessments.

Additional information is provided by the wall texts, in which historical connections, stylistic differences, technological issues, conventions typical of the period, and material characteristics are discussed.

The seats on display are subject of the work reports by the conservators who made their pieces available and prepared them especially for the activity area of the exhibition *DEEP-SEATED: The Secret Art of Upholstery*. They are members of the Fachgruppe der Restauratoren im Handwerk e.V. of the Fachbereich der Raumausstatter and the Bundesverband der Restauratoren im Raumausstatterhandwerk e.V. With their expertise, they were predestined to create very practical illustrative models to explain various working techniques. Work reports and documentations were created, which can be viewed in the exhibition and complement the sensual experiences with technical explanations in the activity area.

An important component of the collaboration were several work meetings in different workshops and the joint work in the rooms of the Akademie des Handwerks Schloss Raesfeld. The participants meeting there had travelled from all over Germany and had their workspaces in Hersbruck, Kleinmachnow, Löhne, Ludwigsburg, Lübeck, Markkleeberg, Obernkirchen (Vehlen), Osnabrück, Potsdam, Schalksmühle, Steinheim and Waabs. In alphabetical order, these are Astrid Boeck, Maximilian Busch, Volker Engels, Edmund Graf, Alexander Hahlbeck, Rolf Hegenbart, Bernd Lehmkuhl,

226
Biedermeierstuhl, Hochpolster mit Federung in Randformpolster, um 1810 (Reinhardt Roßberg, Markkleeberg)
Biedermeier chair, high, sprung upholstery with edge roll, around 1810 (Reinhardt Roßberg, Markkleeberg)

227
Biedermeierstuhl, Festpolstersitz mit stark garnierter Kante, um 2000, Nachbau nach Wiener Vorbild (Reinhardt Roßberg, Markkleeberg)
Biedermeier chair, attached upholstered seat with firmly stitched-up edge, around 2000, reproduction after Viennese model (Reinhardt Roßberg, Markkleeberg)

228/229
Bergère Confessionnal Chipier Style Louis XV. (Porterchair), geschnürte Federkonstruktion, Nayar France (Entwurf und Herstellung, im Stil Louis XV.), 2021/2022 (Privatbesitz)

228/229
Bergère Confessionnal Chipier Style Louis XV. (porter chair), lashed sprung construction, Nayar France (design and production, in the style Louis XV), 2021/2022 (private collection)

Nerge, Doris Nolting, Stefan Oswald, Torsten Otto, Reinhardt Roßberg, Karin Semkowicz und Bernhard Ziegler, denen zu verdanken ist, dass die Besucher*innen im Aktionsraum fühlen können, welche Bedeutung eine individuell gefertigte Polsterung für das Empfinden von Bequemlichkeit hat. Damit verbindet sich zum Einen ein Plädoyer für ein Handwerk, das mit seiner langen Tradition gerade heute zeigt, wie zeitgemäß es ist, da die Arbeit der polsternden Raumausstatter*innen sich als nachhaltig erweist und dazu beiträgt, dass qualitätvolle Sitzgegenstände funktionsfähig erhalten werden können. Zum Anderen zeigt die Ausstellung, wie feinsinnig gearbeitet wird, wenn etwa das Innenleben der Polstermöbel gebaut wird. Kleine Filme demonstrieren an verschiedenen Stellen, wie die komplexesten Bindungen von Meisterhand virtuos hergestellt werden. Dass jedes Polster immer wieder neuer Lösungen bedarf, verdeutlicht, dass die technisch versierte Arbeit es erfordert, schöpferisch zu gestalten, um passgenau umzusetzen, was einer bestimmten Sitzmöbelidentität entspricht. Das Geheimnis des Polsterns liegt daher nicht zuletzt auch in der besonderen Fähigkeit der Restaurator*innen, die es verstehen, in großer Zugewandtheit und mit viel Sensibilität die ihnen anvertrauten Möbel zu bearbeiten.

Wolfgang Nerge, Doris Nolting, Stefan Oswald, Torsten Otto, Reinhardt Roßberg, Karin Semkowicz and Bernhard Ziegler, who are to thank for the fact that visitors to the activity space can feel the significance of individually crafted upholstery for a sense of comfort. On the one hand, this is a plea for a craft that, with its long tradition, shows how contemporary it is today, since the work of the upholstering interior decorators proves to be sustainable and contributes to the fact that quality seating objects can be kept functional. On the other hand, the exhibition shows how sophisticated the work is when, for example, the interior of the upholstered seat is built. Short films demonstrate at various points how the most complex weaves are made with virtuosity by master craftsmen. The fact that each piece of upholstery requires ever new solutions makes it clear that the technically skilled work requires creative design thinking in order to implement precisely what corresponds to a certain seating furniture identity. The secret of upholstery therefore lies not least in the special skills of the restorers, who know how to work on the furniture entrusted to them with great dedication and sensitivity.

230/231 (S. 232/233)
Indiscret, geschnürte Federkonstruktion mit Capitonné-Heftung, um 1880 (Karin Semkowicz, Steinheim-Bergheim)

230/231 (p. 232/233)
Indiscret, lashed sprung construction with deep-buttoning, around 1880 (Karin Semkowicz, Steinheim-Bergheim)

Hören, Schauen, Fühlen, Sitzen | Listening, seeing, touching, sitting 233

232/233
Armlehnstuhl, geschnürte Federkonstruktion, um 1900
(Astrid Boeck, Waabs)

232/233
Armchair, lashed sprung construction, around 1900
(Astrid Boeck, Waabs)

234 Hören, Schauen, Fühlen, Sitzen | Listening, seeing, touching, sitting

234
Sofa, Flachpolsterung, 20. Jh. (Privatbesitz)

234
Sofa, flat padding, 20th century (private collection)

235/236
Armlehnsessel, ca. 1915–1925 (Stefan Oswald, Hersbruck)

235/236
Armchair, ca. 1915–1925 (Stefan Oswald, Hersbruck)

237
Ohrensessel, um 1900 (Rolf Hegenbart, Kleinmachnow)

237
Wing chair, around 1900 (Rolf Hegenbart, Kleinmachnow)

238
Cocktailsessel, 1950er Jahre (Volker Engels, Schalksmühle)

238
Cocktail chair, 1950s (Volker Engels, Schalksmühle)

238 Hören, Schauen, Fühlen, Sitzen | Listening, seeing, touching, sitting

239
Hocker mit Capitonné-Heftung, 21. Jh. (Bernhard Ziegler, Gundelsheim)
Stool with deep-buttoning, 21st century (Bernhard Ziegler, Gundelsheim)

240
Klubsessel, Hochpolster, ca. 1925 (Reinhardt Roßberg, Markkleeberg)
Club chair, high padding, ca. 1925 (Reinhardt Roßberg, Markkleeberg)

241 (S. 240/241, p. 240/241)
Dekorationsstoff, Weberhof Lübz, Gottfried Hensen und Gretel Schmitz (Entwurf und Herstellung), 1967 (GRASSI Museum für Angewandte Kunst Leipzig)
Decorative fabric, Weberhof Lübz, Gottfried Hensen and Gretel Schmitz (design and production), 1967 (GRASSI Museum für Angewandte Kunst Leipzig)

500 Jahre Textilien für Polstermöbel

Ein Überblick anhand von Beispielen aus der Sammlung des GRASSI Museums für Angewandte Kunst Leipzig

Stefanie Seeberg

Textilien sind zentraler Bestandteil von Polstermöbeln. Der Bezug des Polsters bestimmt mit Farbigkeit, Musterung, Material und Struktur auf einer großen Fläche entscheidend das Erscheinungsbild eines Möbels ebenso wie das Sitzgefühl, das es bietet. Bezeichnenderweise wurde der Begriff *meuble* im 17. und 18. Jahrhundert oft auch nur für den Dekorationsstoff verwendet, der häufig nicht nur Bezugsstoff des Polstermöbels war, sondern auch für Wandbespannungen und Vorhänge eingesetzt wurde. So sind auch die meisten der im Folgenden vorgestellten Gewebe keine expliziten Bezugsstoffe, sondern Ausstattungstextilien, die als Bezüge eingesetzt werden konnten.[192] Borten, Quasten und Fransen, sogenannte Posamente, vollenden das Polstereiwerk (s. folgendes Kap.). Vor allem in vorindustrieller Zeit waren Bezugstextilien und Posamente in Material und Herstellung äußerst kostspielig. Entsprechend lagen die Kosten für die Textilien eines Polstermöbels oft weit über der für die Tischlerarbeit, die heute gerade bei historischen Möbeln als das wichtigere Element erscheint.[193] Dies liegt zum einen an der unter dem Eindruck maschinell gefertigter Massenware verlorengegangenen Wertschätzung textiler Materialien und Fertigungstechniken. Ein weiterer Grund ist die Überlieferungssituation. Die empfindlichen Textilien sind meist nicht mehr im Original erhalten und wurden erneuert, während das Gestell die Zeit in der Regel besser überstanden hat. Auch unter den in Ausstellung und Katalog gezeigten Exponaten weisen viele einen neuen Bezug auf. Die für heutige Bezugsstoffe geltenden Kriterien von Lichtbeständigkeit und Abriebfestigkeit mit Kategorisierungen nach Scheuertouren lassen sich selbstverständlich nicht auf historische Bezugsstoffe übertragen.

Einen Einblick in die lange Geschichte der Bezugsstoffe europäischer Polstermöbel geben in Ausstellung und Katalog, neben den auf einzelnen Möbeln erhaltenen historischen Bezügen, ausgewählte Beispiele aus der Textilsammlung des GRASSI Museums für Angewandte Kunst. Die Sammlung enthält eine Fülle herausragender Stücke von frühen italienischen Textilien des 16. Jahrhunderts bis zu Geweben der Gegenwart. Die historischen Muster wurden zu entscheidenden Teilen in den ersten Jahrzehnten des 1874 eröffneten Museums überwiegend aus dem Kunsthandel zusammengetragen. Ziel war es damals, ein möglichst breites Spektrum vielfältiger Beispiele und Vorbilder aus unterschiedlichen Regionen und Epochen für Kunstschaffende zusammenzustellen. Gleichzeitig spiegelt der Sammlungsbestand auch die für das Museum große Bedeutung seines Entstehungsortes Leipzig als Handels- und Messestadt. Von Anfang an, und verstärkt mit Etablierung der Grassimessen in den 1920er Jahren, wurde auch aktuelles Design gesammelt.[194] Ausgewählte Stücke aus diesem reichen Sammlungsbestand können im Rahmen dieser Ausstellung erstmals publiziert werden.[195] Der Fokus der Objektauswahl liegt auf Geweben. Gestickte und gewirkte Möbelbezüge, die aus Platzgründen ausgeklammert werden mussten, seien hier zumindest erwähnt,

500 years of furnishing textiles for upholstered furniture

An overview using examples from the collection of the GRASSI Museum für Angewandte Kunst Leipzig

Stefanie Seeberg

Textiles and trimmings make up a key component of upholstered furniture. With its colour, pattern, material and structure across a large surface, the top cover is a decisive factor in how a piece of furniture is perceived and what kind of sitting experience it offers. Tellingly, during the seventeenth and eighteenth century the word *meuble* was often used to refer to the decorative textiles, which usually were not only utilized as cover fabrics of upholstered furniture but also as wallcoverings and curtains.[192] For this reason, most of the textiles presented below are not explicitly cover fabrics but furnishing textiles, that could be used as covers. Braids, tassels and fringes, so called trimmings, complete the upholstery (see following chapter). Especially during the pre-industrial area, the material and production of upholstery fabric and trimmings were extremely costly. Correspondingly, the cost for textiles for an upholstered piece was usually far greater than those for the carpentry, which today, especially in the case of historical furniture, appears to be the more important element.[193] This is due to a lost appreciation for textile materials and manufacturing techniques as a result of the impact of machine-produced mass goods. Another reason is the state of conservation. The fragile textiles are often not conserved in their original form and were renewed, while the frame usually stood the passage of times. Among the objects in the exhibition and the catalogue, many have been covered in a new fabric. The criteria of lightfastness and abrasion-resistance with categorisations according to abrasion cycles that apply to today's upholstery fabrics cannot, of course, be transferred to historical upholstery fabrics.

In addition to the historical fabrics that have survived on individual pieces of furniture, selected examples from the Textile Collection of the GRASSI Museum für Angewandte Kunst provide an insight in the exhibition as well as the catalogue into the long history of furnishing textiles in Europe. The collection holds an abundance of extraordinary pieces from early Italian textiles of the sixteenth century to contemporary weaves. The historical samples were for the most part assembled through acquisitions from the art market during the early decades of the museum, which opened in 1874. At the time, the aim was to put together a wide variety of various examples and models from different regions and epochs for artists and craftsmen. Simultaneously, the holdings also reflect its location Leipzig, as a trading and fair town, which is of great importance to the museum. From the beginning, and increasingly after the Grassi Fairs had been established in the 1920s, contemporary design was also collected.[194] Selected pieces from this rich collection are published for the first time in the context of this exhibition.[195] The focus of the objects selected is fabrics. Embroidered and warp-knitted furniture covers, which have been

242/243
Brokatell, Bezug einer Stuhllehne, Italien, 17. Jh.
(GRASSI Museum für Angewandte Kunst Leipzig)

242/243
Brocatelle, cover of a chair backrest, Italy, 17th century
(GRASSI Museum für Angewandte Kunst Leipzig)

500 Jahre Textilien für Polstermöbel | 500 years of furnishing textiles for upholstered furniture 243

denn gerade ihnen kam über die Jahrhunderte eine besondere Rolle zu: Einerseits ist gerade Stickerei die ideale Technik, mit der sich Bilder und Zeichen auf die Bezüge bringen lassen. Andererseits bietet sie die Möglichkeit, mit relativ einfachen Mitteln diese selbst zu gestalten und mit einer persönlichen Note zu versehen. So waren schon im Mittelalter gestickte Kissen Träger für Bilder, Wappen und Texte. Spätestens seit dem 16. Jahrhundert findet sich auf und in Mustertüchern und -büchern eine Vielzahl von Flächenmustern, die sich für Kissen- und Polsterbezüge eigneten.[196] Bis zu Beginn des 20. Jahrhunderts spielte die Stickerei eine wichtige Rolle für die Gestaltung von Möbelbezügen (Abb. 27).[197]

Wie im Einführungskapitel (S. 13) dargelegt, reicht die Geschichte des gepolsterten bzw. mit weichen Auflagen komfortabel gestalteten Sitzmöbels in die antiken Kulturen zurück. Detailreiche Darstellungen von Sitz- und Liegemöbeln auf Gefäßen und Grabmonumenten vorchristlicher Zeit lassen erahnen, welche Rolle den Textilien zukam.[198] Wenn auch nicht als dokumentarische Quellen zu werten, vermitteln sie doch einen Eindruck, wie Textilien unter Berücksichtigung von Farbgebung, Musterung und Material für Komfort und Erscheinungsbild der Möbel genutzt wurden. Ähnliches gilt für das Mittelalter. Obwohl die Überlieferungslage textiler Objekte etwas günstiger ist, sind es immer noch vor allem Bildzeugnisse, die uns heute eine Vorstellung von Textilien und Polstern auf Möbeln geben. Noch im

left aside due to space issues, are briefly mentioned here, as they took on a special role over the centuries: on the one hand, embroidery is the perfect technique with which to apply images and symbols to covers; on the other hand, it provides the possibility to create them oneself with relatively simple means and to lend them a personal note. As early as the Middle Ages, embroidered cushions were the support for images, coats of arms and texts. At the very least since the sixteenth century, a multitude of patterns can be found in samplers and pattern books suitable for cushions and upholstery covers.[196] Until the early twentieth century, embroidery played an important role in the design of furniture cover textiles (fig. 27).[197]

As explained in the introductory chapter (p. 16), the history of upholstered or softly cushioned seating furniture goes back to the cultures of antiquity. Detailed depictions of seating and lounging furniture on vessels and funeral monuments of the pre-Christian period let us divine the importance placed on textiles.[198] While they cannot be counted as a document source, they nonetheless convey an impression of how textiles were used for the comfort and appearance of furniture, following considerations regarding colour, pattern and material. Something similar applies to the Middle Ages. Although more textile objects have stood the test of time, it is predominantly pictorial sources that give us an idea

244/245
Brokatell, Italien, 16. Jh. (GRASSI Museum für Angewandte Kunst Leipzig)

244/245
Brocatelle, Italy, 16th century (GRASSI Museum für Angewandte Kunst Leipzig)

15. Jahrhundert bleiben bewegliche Auflagen wie Kissen und Banklaken beliebt. Die Möglichkeiten der textilen Techniken wurden vielfältig genutzt: Die Beispiele sind gewebt, gewirkt oder gestickt und in verschiedenen Materialien wie Wolle, Seide, Leinen und Metallfäden ausgeführt.

**Möbelbezüge in der frühen Neuzeit –
Trendsetter Italien**

Seit dem 16. Jahrhundert beginnen sich fest montierte Möbelbezüge zu etablieren, wie zahlreiche Bilddarstellungen, vor allem Porträts, dokumentieren (Abb. 5) und wie sie ab 1600 auch zunehmend in erhaltenen Beispielen überliefert sind. Dennoch behielt man sich die Möglichkeit vor, den Bezugsstoff zu wechseln. So gab es Sommer- und Winterbezüge oder besonders kostbare Textilien, die nur für hohen Besuch aufgezogen wurden bzw. für die sonstige Nutzung mit einfacheren Bezügen geschützt wurden.[199]

Unbestritten war Italien bei den Bezugsstoffen im 16. und 17. Jahrhundert führend. Die Geschichte der europäischen Möbeltextilien ist über gut drei Jahrhunderte eng mit der Geschichte der Seidenweberei verknüpft. Nachdem Seide in Europa lange kostbare Exportware aus dem Osten war, hatten sich in Italien und Spanien ab dem 13. Jahrhundert führende Zentren der Seidenproduktion entwickelt.[200] Die für die europäischen Herrscherhäuser und sozialen Eliten so begehrten Gewebe kamen nun aus Städten wie Venedig, Florenz, Genua oder Valencia. Genua spezialisierte sich auf Ausstattungstextilien und besaß Mitte des 16. Jahrhunderts eine blühende Textilproduktion von internationalem Ruf, den es bis ins 18. Jahrhundert behaupten konnte.[201] In der reichen Stadtrepublik mit ihren berühmten Palästen wurde für den eigenen Bedarf und den Export gearbeitet. Die Gestaltung der Muster wurde auch durch die Funktion der Gewebe beeinflusst: Im Unterschied zu den meist kleineren Designs für Kleiderstoffe zeigen Ausstattungstextilien gerne auch größere Musterrapporte.[202] Zum Bestand des GRASSI Museums gehören herausragende Beispiele solcher italienischer Seiden- und Samtgewebe. Das Halbseidengewebe mit Löwen wurde in den 1890er Jahren als Beispiel eines Genueser Stoffes erworben (Abb. 244/245). Ursprünglich für eine repräsentative Raumausstattung um 1600 entstanden, gehört es zu den Höhepunkten der Sammlung. Nur wenige Jahre nach dem Ankauf des hier gezeigten Fragments konnte aus der Sammlung Wilhelm Bodes ein zweites noch größeres Stück des gleichen Gewebes erworben werden.[203] Ein weiteres Beispiel ist das Brokatellgewebe mit roter Musterung auf goldgelbem Grund (Abb. 242/243). Dank der an Ober- und Unterkante noch vorhandenen Borten mit langen Goldfransen lässt sich noch gut seine ursprüngliche Montage als Bezug einer Stuhllehne erahnen. Bei beiden Beispielen handelt es sich um für Ausstattungstextilien gerne verwendete sogenannte Brokatelle, Halbseidengewebe, bei denen der Grundschuss aus Leinen im Muster mit Seidenfäden im Lancierschuss kombiniert wurde.[204]

of textiles and cushions on furniture. As late as the fifteenth century, loose padding such as cushions and bench covers were popular. The possibilities of textile technologies were used in a variety of ways: for example, woven, warp-knitted, embroidered, and executed in different materials such as wool, silk, linen and metal threads.

**Furnishing textiles of the early modern period –
Italy as a trendsetter**

From the sixteenth century onwards, permanently mounted furniture covers began to be established, as documented by numerous pictorial representations, especially portraits (fig. 5), and increasingly preserved in surviving examples from 1600 on. Nevertheless, the possibility to change the cover fabric was upkept. There were summer and winter covers or particularly precious textiles that were only mounted for high-ranking visitors or protected with simpler covers for other uses.[199]

Without competition, Italy was a leader in cover fabrics during the sixteenth and seventeenth century. The history of European furnishing textiles is closely connected to the history of silk weaving over the course of almost three hundred years. After silk had long been a precious export from the East, Italy and Spain developed into leading centres of silk production from the thirteenth century onwards.[200] The fabrics, so coveted by the European ruling houses and social elites, now came from cities such as Venice, Florence, Genoa or Valencia. Genoa specialised in textiles for furnishings and in the mid sixteenth century had thriving textile manufactories of international reputation, which it was able to maintain into the eighteenth century.[201] In the rich city republic with its famous palaces, goods were produced for local demand as well as for the export market. The pattern design was also influenced by the intended function of the textile: in contrast to the usually smaller patterns for sartorial textiles, furnishing textiles usually had larger pattern repeats.[202] In the collection of GRASSI Museum are excellent examples of such Italian silk and velvet fabrics. The semi-silk fabric featuring lions (figs. 244/245) was acquired in the 1890s as an example of Genovese fabric. Originally manufactured for a representative room furnishing around 1600, it is now one of the highlights of the collection. Just a few years after the purchase of the fragment on display, a second, even larger piece of the same fabric could be purchased from the Wilhelm Bode collection.[203] Another example is the brocatelle fabric with a red pattern on a golden yellow ground (figs. 242/243). Thanks to the trimmings with long fringes that have been preserved on the upper and lower edges, the original use as a backrest cover is still perceptible. Both examples are made from a fabric, that was favoured for furnishing textiles, the so-called brocatelle, a semi-silk fabric comprising a silk pattern weft on a coarse linen ground.[204]

246
Ziselierter Samt, Italien, um 1600 (?) (GRASSI Museum für Angewandte Kunst Leipzig)
Chiselled velvet, Italy, around 1600 (?) (GRASSI Museum für Angewandte Kunst Leipzig)

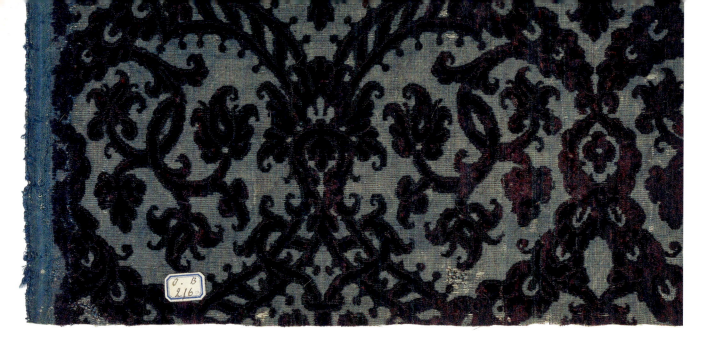

Besonders beliebt und exklusiv, gerade auch für Ausstattungstextilien, waren seit dem 15. Jahrhundert Samtgewebe. Wegen des erhöhten Materialbedarfs – der charakteristische Flor wurde durch zusätzliche, über Ruten in Schlingen gelegte Kettfäden gebildet, die je nach gewünschter Oberflächenstruktur geschnitten oder gepresst wurden – war Samt sehr teuer und nur für eine kleine wohlhabende Gesellschaftsgruppe erschwinglich.[205] Günstigere Gewebe mit samtartigem Flor, als Mokett oder Plüsch bezeichnet, wurden ab dem 17. Jahrhundert in der gleichen Technik auch aus anderen Materialien, vor allem aus Wolle, dem steigenden Absatz folgend in zunehmenden Mengen in Flandern, England, Nordfrankreich und auch in Deutschland produziert.[206] Exemplarisch stehen hier die beiden Seidensamtgewebe aus dem 17. Jahrhundert mit zeittypischer, relativ kleine Musterung (Abb. 246, 247).
Eine andere für die Innenraumdekoration beliebte Technik wurde für den um 1620 entstandenen noch in situ erhaltenen Bezug auf dem Stuhl aus dem Rathaus zu Ulm gewählt (Abb. 11/12). Auf der bezogenen Sitzfläche und den Armlehnen wurden die Ornamentmotive in gelber Seide als Applikationsstickerei auf schwarzem Samt aufgenäht.
In dieser Technik sind auch zwei hier gezeigte Beispiele aus der Sammlung des GRASSI Museums für Angewandte Kunst gefertigt. Die beiden reich mit Pflanzenmotiven und Ranken verzierten Bahnen entstanden um 1600 in Italien und Spanien. Sie sind als Dekorationsstoffe von Paradebetten, zentrale repräsentative Möbel des 16. und 17. Jahrhunderts, vorstellbar. An beiden sind die originalen Fransenborten erhalten (Abb. 249, 251).

Since the fifteenth century, velvet fabrics were particularly popular and exclusive textiles, especially for furnishing. Due to the increase in material required – the characteristic pile was formed by introducing rods to an additional pile warp to create raised loops, which could be cut or pressed, depending on the desired surface structure – velvet was very expensive and only accessible to a small wealthy social group.[205] Cheaper fabrics with velvet-like pile, called moquette or plush, were produced from the seventeenth century onwards using the same technique in other materials, especially wool, in increasing quantities in Flanders, England, Northern France and also Germany.[206] Examples of velvet are the two silk textiles from the mid seventeenth century with a relatively small pattern typical of the time (figs. 246, 247). Another popular technique used in interior decoration was employed for the chair from Ulm Town Hall with its 1620 cover still in place (figs. 11/12). On the covered seat and the armrests, the ornamental motifs in yellow silk were embroidered appliqués stitched to the black velvet. Two of the examples from the collection of the GRASSI Museum für Angewandte Kunst on display here are made with this technique. The two strips, richly decorated with plant motifs and twines were produced around 1600 in Italy and Spain. They may have been used as furnishing fabrics for parade beds, a central piece of representative furniture in the sixteenth and seventeenth centuries. Both have been preserved with their original fringes (figs. 249, 251).

247
Ziselierter Samt, Venedig (?), 17. Jh. (GRASSI Museum für Angewandte Kunst Leipzig)
Chiselled velvet, Venice (?), 17th century (GRASSI Museum für Angewandte Kunst Leipzig)

248
Seidengewebe, Atlas liseré, Italien, Mitte 17. Jh. (GRASSI Museum für Angewandte Kunst Leipzig)
Silk weave, atlas liseré, Italy, mid 17th century (GRASSI Museum für Angewandte Kunst Leipzig)

Barock – Frankreichs Führungsrolle

Im 17. Jahrhundert zeigten sich Veränderungen in der Mode der Bezugsstoffe ebenso wie in der Produktion der Seidengewebe. Zwar waren italienische Gewebe international weiterhin an erster Stelle gefragt, sodass etwa in Frankreich *à la façon de Genes* (in Genueser Art) gefertigt wurde, englische Entwürfe schickte man zur Umsetzung nach Venedig und berühmte Genueser Muster wie das Dreiblütenmuster *(tre fiori)* (Abb. 248) oder das *della palma*-Motiv wurden auch in anderen europäischen

Baroque – France's pole position

The seventeenth century saw changes in the fashion for furnishing textiles as well as in the production of silks. Italian fabrics continued to be in first place internationally, so that in France, for example, pieces were being produced *à la façon de Genes* (in the Genoese style), English designs were sent to Venice for execution and famous Genoese patterns such as the three-flower pattern *(tre fiori)* pattern (fig. 248) or the *della palma* motif were also woven in other European countries.[207] Nonetheless, France was able to

249
Applikationsstickerei (Fragment), Italien (Genua?), 17. Jh. (GRASSI Museum für Angewandte Kunst Leipzig)
Appliqué embroidery (fragment), Italy (Genoa?), 17th century (GRASSI Museum für Angewandte Kunst Leipzig)

250
Borte, Italien, 17. Jh. (GRASSI Museum für Angewandte Kunst Leipzig)
Border, Italy, 17th century (GRASSI Museum für Angewandte Kunst Leipzig)

251 (S. 251, p.251)
Applikationsstickerei, Italien oder Spanien, Anfang 17. Jh. (GRASSI Museum für Angewandte Kunst Leipzig)
Appliqué embroidery, Italy or Spain, early 17th century (GRASSI Museum für Angewandte Kunst Leipzig)

500 Jahre Textilien für Polstermöbel | 500 years of furnishing textiles for upholstered furniture

Ländern gewebt.²⁰⁷ Andererseits konnte Frankreich ab der zweiten Hälfte des 17. Jahrhunderts seinen Einfluss in Produktion und Handel im Textilbereich deutlich ausbauen. Lyon hatte sich seit dem 16. Jahrhundert zu einem Zentrum der Seidenweberei entwickelt, das entscheidend an Zugkraft gewann, u. a. durch das 1667 durch Jean-Baptiste Colbert unter Ludwig XIV. erlassene Reglement.²⁰⁸ Zu Beginn des 18. Jahrhunderts waren Lyoneser Seiden weltberühmt. Besonders Entwürfe der Künstler Jean Revel (1684–1751) und Philippe de Lasalle (1723–1804) waren international gefragt.²⁰⁹ Webtechnische Neuerungen wie der *point rentré* ermöglichten feine Farbübergänge, die den Mustern, bevorzugt naturalistische Blumenmotive, mehr Plastizität und naturnahe Kolorierung verliehen.²¹⁰ Neben nach wie vor beliebten monochromen Seidendamasten (Abb. 254) entstanden Gewebe mit komplexen, farbigen Mustern.²¹¹ Ein Beispiel mit nuancierter Zeichnung naturnaher Blüten auf braunem Grund aus der Zeit um 1735 ist im Bestand des Museums vorhanden (Abb. 252/253). Gegenüber den bisher bevorzugten kräftigen Farben werden ab den 1770er Jahren helle Pastelltöne beliebter.²¹²

Auch in England und Deutschland wurden ab dem 17. Jahrhundert eigene Seidenmanufakturen aufgebaut. Beide Länder profitierten dabei vom Wissenstransfer durch hugenottische Flüchtlinge aus Frankreich.²¹³ Zudem wurden Zeichner aus Frankreich für Muster der Seidengewebe nach Berlin geholt.²¹⁴ In ihrer Blütezeit produzierten die Berliner Manufakturen für die Ausstattung des neuen Palais ab 1740 bis zur Fertigstellung 1768 hochwertige Seidengewebe.²¹⁵ Auch Leipzig spielte eine wichtige Rolle. Hier eröffnete Johann Daniel Crafft (1624–1697) mit Unterstützung des sächsischen Kurfürsten Johann Georg II. 1674 die erste Seidenmanufaktur Deutschlands.²¹⁶ Andreas Dietrich Apel (1662–1718), der zunächst im Seidenhandel tätig war, gelang es ab 1700, eine große Seidenmanufaktur aufzubauen.²¹⁷ Nachweislich wurde exklusive Ware, wie die Apelschen Banden, auch für die Schlossausstattungen nach Berlin und Dresden geliefert.²¹⁸

Nicht zu unterschätzen ist seit dem 15. Jahrhundert der hohe Anteil importierter Seidengewebe, darunter besonders osmanischer und chinesischer Textilien. In manchen Fällen lässt sich aufgrund des regen wechselseitigen Austausches nicht eindeutig feststellen, welche Muster beispielsweise in China unter europäischem Einfluss oder in Europa durch asiatische Vorbilder entstanden.²¹⁹ Aus heutiger Sicht erstaunlich ist das schon in der Vergangenheit herrschende Diktat schnelllebiger Mode und der auf den Manufakturen lastende hohe Druck stets neue, absatzfähige Muster für die Gewebe zu entwerfen. Wegen des hohen Bedarfs an immer neuen Entwürfen wurden zuerst in Lyon, dann auch in anderen Zentren Zeichenschulen gegründet.²²⁰ Anregungen und Vorlagen für die sich schnell ändernden Mustermotive verbreiteten sich unter anderem über die Druckgrafik.²²¹ Insgesamt waren die Mustermoden für Ausstattungsstoffe etwas langlebiger als für Bekleidung, für die Mitte des 18. Jahrhunderts in Frankreich saisonal neue Entwürfe erschienen.²²² So lag der Copyright-Schutz für Kleiderstoffe bei sechs Jahren, für Möbelstoffe dagegen bei 25 Jahren.²²³ Bei der Konzeption und Wirkung historischer Polsterbezüge spielte immer auch das Ensemble der Raumausstattung eine entscheidende Rolle. Bereits für Spätmittelalter und Frühe Neuzeit bezeugen Rechnungsbücher und Inventare von Residenzausstattungen sorgfältig aufeinander abgestimmte Textilien der Innenraumausstattungen. In den 1540er Jahren wurden für die Jagdschlösser des Kurfürsten Moritz von

significantly expand its influence in production and trade in the textile sector from the second half of the seventeenth century. Since the sixteenth century, Lyon had developed into a centre of silk weaving, which gained decisive traction, among other things through the regulations issued in 1667 by Jean-Baptiste Colbert under Louis XIV.²⁰⁸ At the beginning of the eighteenth century, Lyon silks were world-famous. Designs by the artists Jean Revel (1684–1751) and Philippe de Lasalle (1723–1804) in particular were in international demand.²⁰⁹ Weaving innovations such as the *point rentré* made fine colour transitions possible, which gave the patterns, preferably naturalistic floral motifs, more plasticity and near-natural colouring.²¹⁰ In addition to the still popular monochrome silk damasks (fig. 254), fabrics with complex, coloured patterns were created.²¹¹ An example with a nuanced drawing of near-natural blossoms on a brown ground from around 1735 can be found in the museum's collection (figs. 252/253). In contrast to the previously preferred strong colours, light pastel shades became more popular from the 1770s onwards.²¹²

From the seventeenth century onwards, silk manufactories were also built in England and Germany. Both countries profited from the knowledge transfer through the French Huguenot refugees.²¹³ In addition, draughtsmen were recruited from France for Berlin-based manufactories.²¹⁴ In their heyday, the Berlin manufactories produced quality silk fabrics for the furnishing of the new Palais from 1740 until its completion in 1768.²¹⁵ Leipzig equally played an important role. Here, Johann Daniel Crafft (1624–1697) opened the first German silk manufactory with the support of the Saxon elector Johann Georg II.²¹⁶ Andreas Dietrich Apel (1662–1718), formerly active in the silk trade, succeeded in 1700 in setting up a large silk manufactory.²¹⁷ It has been proven that exclusive wares, such as the *Apelsche Bande*, were delivered to furnish palaces in Berlin and Dresden.²¹⁸

Not to be underestimated is the high proportion of imported silk fabrics since the fifteenth century, including, in particular, Ottoman and Chinese textiles. In some cases, due to the lively mutual exchange, it is not possible to clearly determine which patterns originated, for example, in China under European influence or in Europe through Asian models.²¹⁹ From today's point of view, the dictates of fast-moving fashions and the high pressure on manufacturers to constantly design new, marketable patterns for fabrics are astonishing. Because of the high demand for ever new designs, drawing schools were founded first in Lyon, then in other places.²²⁰ Inspirations and templates for the rapidly changing pattern motifs spread through graphic prints, among other channels.²²¹ On the whole, the pattern fashions for furnishing fabrics were somewhat more long-lived than those for clothing, for which in the middle of the eighteenth century new designs were published each season in France.²²² The copyright for clothing textiles was six years, but 25 years for furniture textiles.²²³

The ensemble of room furnishings has always played a decisive role in the conception and effect of historical upholstery. Inventories and account books of residential furnishings attest to carefully coordinated textiles used in interior furnishings as early as the late medieval and early modern period. In the 1540s, wall coverings, upholstered seat covers, tablecloths and bed curtains for the hunting lodges of Elector Moritz of Saxony were all

252/253
Seidengewebe, Frankreich (?), 1735–1750 (GRASSI Museum für Angewandte Kunst Leipzig)

252/253
Silk weave, France (?), 1735–1750 (GRASSI Museum für Angewandte Kunst Leipzig)

Sachsen Wandbespannung, Bezüge der gepolsterten Sitzmöbel, Tischdecken und Bettvorhänge aus dem gleichen Gewebe gefertigt.[224] Im 18. Jahrhundert ist dieses *en suite* genannte Ausstattungskonzept die Regel wie Darstellungen, Inventare und einige noch in Schlössern und Familiensitzen erhaltene Beispiele zeigen.[225]
Sowohl für Wandbespannungen als auch für Möbelbezüge waren über die Jahrhunderte monochrome Seidendamaste beliebt.[226] Faszinierend ist die starke Reliefstruktur dieser auf dem Handwebstuhl gefertigten Gewebe mit ihren über Kett- und Schussfadensysteme erzeugten einfarbigen Mustern. Diese Reliefstruktur zusammen mit dem je nach Richtung der Fäden unterschiedlich reflektierenden Licht erzeugt die deutliche Lesbarkeit dieser einfarbigen Muster und ist charakteristisch für historische Gewebe. Dies sind Eigenschaften, die bei Neubezügen zu beachten sind. Für den Neubezug des um 1700 entstandenen Polstersessels aus den Beständen des GRASSI (Abb. 13/14) wurde ein nachgewebter monochrom roter Seidendamast mit Blatt- und Blütenmotiven der sächsischen Firma Eschke gewählt. Vom Originalbezug waren nur kleine Fragmente erhalten, anhand derer das ursprüngliche Webmuster nicht rekonstruierbar war. Bei dem bereits im 19. Jahrhundert erfolgten Neubezug hatte man sich für ein Halbseidengewebe nach Art der gezeigten im 17. Jahrhundert beliebten Brokatelle entschieden.[227] Dieses Beispiel zeigt anschaulich, wie sehr die Entscheidung für den Bezug eines historischen Polstermöbels auch die Deutung und Erscheinung des Möbels beeinflusst.

made of the same fabric.[224] In the eighteenth century, this furnishing concept, called *en suite*, was the rule, as depictions, inventories and a few examples still preserved in castles and family residences demonstrate.[225]

Monochromatic silk damasks have been popular over the centuries both for wall coverings as well as for furniture cover fabrics.[226] The strong relief structure of these handloom-woven fabrics with their monochrome patterns produced by the creative use of warp and weft is fascinating. The relief structure in combination with the light reflections that change according to the direction of the threads makes this monochrome pattern clearly legible and is characteristic of historical fabrics. These are qualities one has to considered when reupholstering. For the new cover of the upholstered armchair from around 1700 in the GRASSI Collection (figs. 13/14), a rewoven monochrome red silk damask with leaf and floral motifs by the Saxon company Eschke was selected. Only small fragments of the original cover had been preserved, which could not be used to reconstruct the original weaving pattern. When the object had been reupholstered in the nineteenth century, a semi-silk fabric was chosen in the style of the brocatelle shown here, popular during the seventeenth century.[227] This example demonstrates how the decision on a cover fabric for historical upholstered furniture influences the interpretation and viewing of the furniture piece.

254
Seidendamast, Frankreich, 18. Jh. (GRASSI Museum für Angewandte Kunst Leipzig)

254
Silk damask, France, 18th century (GRASSI Museum für Angewandte Kunst Leipzig)

255
Seidendamast, Frankreich, 18. Jh. (GRASSI Museum für Angewandte Kunst Leipzig)
Silk damask, France, 18th century (GRASSI Museum für Angewandte Kunst Leipzig)

256/257
Rosshaargewebe, Italien, 18. Jh. (GRASSI Museum für Angewandte Kunst Leipzig)
Horsehair weave, Italy, 18th century (GRASSI Museum für Angewandte Kunst Leipzig)

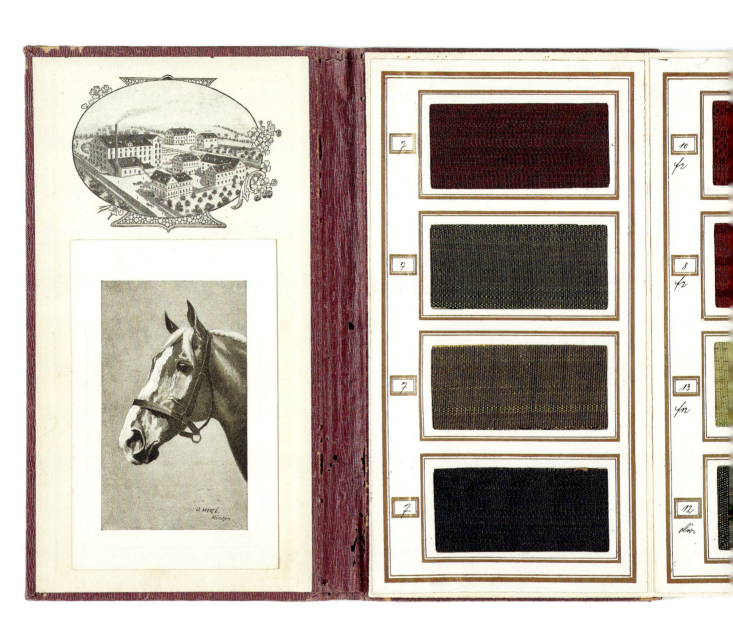

258
Musterbuch Rosshaargewebe, Firma Mechanische Rosshaarweberei Lengenfeld Lenk und Co. GmbH, 1910er Jahre (GRASSI Museum für Angewandte Kunst Leipzig)

258
Sample book of horsehair weaves, Mechanische Rosshaarweberei Lengenfeld Lenk und Co. GmbH, 1910s (GRASSI Museum für Angewandte Kunst Leipzig)

500 Jahre Textilien für Polstermöbel | 500 years of furnishing textiles for upholstered furniture

Technische Innovationen – neue Moden

Mit grundlegenden gesellschaftlichen und politischen Umbrüchen, neuen Vorstellungen und Ideen in der Zeit der Aufklärung und der Französischen Revolution gingen Ende des 18. Jahrhunderts zwingend Veränderungen in Geschmack und Mode auch in der Raumausstattung einher, die von der Neubewertung der Antike und einer Ästhetik der Einfachheit geprägt waren. In Klassizismus und Biedermeier bevorzugte man sich voneinander absetzende Farben, gerne in komplementären Gegenüberstellungen[228] (vgl. Beitrag T. Rudi, S. 70). Revolutionär wirkten sich nun aber auch technische Erfindungen aus. Besonders die Textilherstellung war stark durch die Industrialisierung geprägt bzw. war umgekehrt treibende Kraft für diese. Um 1805 hatte Joseph-Marie Jacquard in Lyon die Musterwebmaschine erfunden.[229] Die maschinelle Fertigung von Textilien der verschiedenen Techniken, nicht nur Gewebe, sondern auch Stickerei und Textildruck, löste zunehmend herkömmliche Handarbeit ab. Dies zog neue Herausforderungen und Aufgaben für Ausführung und Gestaltung nach sich. Ebenso änderten sich der Absatzmarkt und die Ansprüche der Verbraucher. Polstermöbel wurden Bestandteil der gehobenen bürgerlichen Einrichtung. Als Reaktion auf die zunehmende Mechanisierung entstanden verschiedene Gegenbewegungen, darunter als einflussreichste ab Mitte des 19. Jahrhunderts die englische Arts and Crafts-Bewegung, die eine Neubewertung handgefertigter Textilien mit sich brachten.[230] „Naturnahe" florale Motive bestimmen die Designs von William Morris. Der hier gezeigte Handdruck auf Samt wurde 1887 von John Henry Dearle (1859–1932) entworfen, der ab 1890 maßgebender Textilentwerfer bei Morris & Co. war und nach dem Tod von William Morris 1896 die künstlerische Leitung der Firma übernahm. Das Muster wurde unter dem Namen *Cherwell* in verschiedenen Farbstellungen aufgelegt[231] (Abb. 259). Florale Motive bestimmen auch den Dekorationsstoff mit Päonien, den Georges de Feure (1868–1943) um 1899 entwarf (Abb. 260). Er entstand sowohl als Wandbespannung als auch als Bezugsstoff der Möbel für die Ausstattung des Salons im Pavillon Art Nouveau von Siegfried Bing auf der Weltausstellung Paris 1900 und wurde von der Firma Deuss & Oetker in Krefeld ausgeführt.[232] Der Entwurf spiegelt die in Europa um 1900 starken Einflüsse ostasiatischer Kunst, die u. a. durch den Kunsthandel Siegfried Bings gefördert wurden.[233]

In Deutschland schlossen sich als Reaktion auf die Industrialisierung Künstler, Architekten und Kunsthandwerker in dem 1907 gegründeten Deutschen Werkbund zusammen. In der Textilfirma der Deutschen Werkstätten Hellerau entstanden unter dem Namen DeWeTex (Deutsche Werkstätten, Textil GmbH) vor allem Dekorationsstoffe, darunter Möbeltextilien, besonders Gewebe und Druckstoffe.[234] Druckstoffe aus Baumwolle, zunächst im Holzdruckverfahren gefertigt, waren schon im 18. Jahrhundert für Dekorationsstoffe, darunter auch für Möbelbezüge, beliebt.[235] Die Mechanisierung der Baumwolldruckerei mit Erfindung der Walzendruckmaschine 1783 trieb die Verbreitung weiter voran.[236] Im Zuge der Reformbewegung wurde der Hand-

259
Druckstoff, Handdruck auf Samt, Morris & Co. (Entwurf und Herstellung), um 1885 (GRASSI Museum für Angewandte Kunst Leipzig)

druck wiederentdeckt (Abb. 259). Mit der Erfindung neuer farbkräftiger und lichtechter Textilfarben bekamen ab den 1910er Jahren Druckstoffe als Bezugsstoffe neue Bedeutung. Josef Hillerbrand (1892–1981) entwarf für die DeTeKu (Deutsche Textile Kunst) in den 1920er Jahren farbkräftige Muster (vgl. Beitrag T. Andersch, S. 156–159). Zum Bestand des GRASSI Museums für Angewandte Kunst gehört ein großes Konvolut an Mustern der DeTeKu. Die bereits 1904 in Leipzig gegründete Firma hatte sich auf Gewebe und handbedruckte Stoffe für Möbel-, Dekorationsstoffe und Teppiche spezialisiert und sich dem deutschen Werkbund angeschlossen. Die meisten Entwürfe stammen von Erich Kleinhempel (1874–1947), dem künstlerischen Leiter der Firma, der Textildesignerin Herta Michel-Koch (1881–1960), Gründungsmitglied der Darmstädter Sezession, und dem Architekten und Designer Albin Müller (1871–1941).[237] (Abb. 261–264)

Wichtige Kriterien für Möbelstoffe waren und sind bis heute Haltbarkeit und Strapazierfähigkeit. Neben der Kombination verschiedener Materialien wie Leinen und Seide (vgl. Abb. 242–245) wurde vor allem mit Rosshaar experimentiert. Das gezeigte Beispiel aus dem 18. Jahrhundert entstand in Italien (Abb. 256/257). Zu Beginn des 20. Jahrhunderts wurde in Sachsen die Produktion ausgebaut (Abb. 258): 1908 wurde die Rosshaarweberei Schriever & Co. Dresden in Coswig gegründet, 1914 meldete die mechanische Rosshaarstoffweberei Lengenfeld ein Patent für einen Spezialwebstuhl an.[238] In beiden Firmen wurden in den 1930er Jahren in Zusammenarbeit mit dem Bauhaus neue Gewebe angefertigt. Die für Weberei und Textildesign am Bauhaus einflussreiche Textilkünstlerin Otti Berger (1898–1944 in Auschwitz) ersetzte Rosshaar durch stabilen Endlosfaden. Für ihr Möbelstoff-Doppelgewebe aus Kunstfaser erhielt sie 1934 das deutsche Reichspatent. Hergestellt und vertrieben wurde das Gewebe über die Rosshaarweberei Schriever & Co. Dresden.[239] Ein Muster eines solchen Gewebes von Otti Berger wurde 2021 für einen Bezug eines Stahlrohrsessels von Anton Lorenz im Bestand des GRASSI Museums in einer Interpretation von Katharina Jebsen nachgewebt[240] (Abb. 98, 99).

Die Möbeltextilien der zweiten Hälfte des 20. Jahrhunderts spiegeln die Aufbruchsstimmung der Zeit nach dem Zweiten Weltkrieg. In den 1950er und 1960er Jahren entstanden Stoffe in kräftigen Farben. Traditionelle Materialien und Techniken wurden in neuen Anwendungen erprobt und man experimentierte international mit neuen Materialien wie Viskose und Kunststoffoberflächen. In der Sammlung des GRASSI Museums finden sich repräsentative Beispiele für Ausstattungstextilien der DDR. Exemplarisch für das Design der 1960er Jahre sind Wollgewebe aus einem Konvolut, das 1967 vom Weberhof Lübz, einem wichtigen Produktionsort für handgewebte, moderne Gewebe der DDR, angekauft wurde (Abb. 241, 269, 270). Die Suche nach zeitgemäßen Bezugsstoffen setzt sich auch heute fort. In Textildesign und Materialforschung wird mit neuen Möglichkeiten experimentiert. Themen wie Dauerhaftigkeit, Nachhaltigkeit und intelligente Reaktivität der *smart materials* stehen im Vordergrund.[241] Nachdem in den vergangenen Jahrzehnten neue Materialien bevorzugt wurden, ist derzeit eine Rückkehr zu natürlichen, ökologisch gut vertretbaren Materialien festzustellen. Möbelbezüge, darunter auch Sitzbezüge für hochwertige Flugzeuge, werden bevorzugt wieder mit Wolle gefertigt.[242]

rediscovered (fig. 249). With the invention of new colourful and non-fading textile inks, printed fabrics gained new importance from the 1910s onwards. Josef Hillerbrand (1892–1981) designed colourful patterns for DeTeKu (Deutsche Textile Kunst) in the 1920s (see article by T. Andersch, pp. 156–159). The holdings of the GRASSI Museum für Angewandte Kunst include a large collection of DeTeKu patterns. The company, founded in Leipzig as early as 1904, specialised in woven and hand-printed fabrics for upholstery, furnishing fabrics and carpets and joined the German Werkbund. Most of the designs were created by Erich Kleinhempel (1874–1947), the artistic director of the company, the textile designer Herta Michel-Koch (1881–1960), a founding member of the Darmstadt Secession, and the architect and designer Albin Müller (1871–1941)[237] (figs. 261–264).

Durability and resistance were and are to this day important criteria for upholstery fabrics. In addition of combinations of different materials such as linen and silk (see figs. 242–245), experiments with horsehair also took place. In the early twentieth century, production was increased in Saxony (fig. 258): in 1908, the horsehair weaving mill Schriever & Co. Dresden was established in Coswig, and in 1914 the mechanical horsehair weaving mill Lengenfeld applied for a patent for a special loom.[238] In the 1930s, both companies cooperated with the Bauhaus to produce new textiles. The influential textile artist for weaving and textile design Otti Berger (1898–1944) replaced horsehair with continuous filament. For her upholstery fabric double weave made from synthetic fibre she was awarded the German Reich patent in 1934. The fabric was manufactured and distributed by Rosshaarweberei Schriever & Co. Dresden.[239] A sample of such a fabric by Otti Berger was rewoven for the upholstery fabric of a tubular steel chair in the GRASSI Museum Collection in an interpretation by Katharina Jebsen[240] (figs. 98, 99).

The furniture textiles of the second half of the twentieth century reflect the spirit of optimism after World War Two. In the 1950s and 1960s, fabrics in bold colours were produced. Traditional materials and techniques were employed in new applications, and experiments with new materials such as viscose and synthetic surfaces were taking place internationally. In the collection of GRASSI Museum one can find representative examples of furniture fabrics from the GDR. Exemplary of the design of the 1960s are woollen fabrics from a batch that was acquired in 1967 from Weberhof Lütz, an important production site of hand-woven, modern weaves in the GDR (figs. 241, 269, 270).

The search for modern upholstery fabrics continues today. In textile design and material research, experimentation with new possibilities is underway. Topics such as durability, sustainability and the intelligent response of smart materials are at the forefront of these.[241] After the turn towards new synthetic materials in the last decades, one can now witness a return to natural, ecological materials. Furniture fabrics, including those for seating in high-end aeroplanes, are increasingly made from wool again.[242]

260
Dekorationsstoff mit Päonien, Georges de Feure (Entwurf), Deuss & Oetker, Krefeld (Herstellung), um 1899 (GRASSI Museum für Angewandte Kunst Leipzig)

261
Muster Möbelbezug, Albin Müller (Entwurf), Deutsche Textile Kunst / DeTeKu Rudolf Hiemann (Herstellung), 1920er Jahre (GRASSI Museum für Angewandte Kunst Leipzig)
Sample furniture cover fabric, Albin Müller (design), Deutsche Textile Kunst / DeTeKu Rudolf Hiemann (production), 1920s (GRASSI Museum für Angewandte Kunst Leipzig)

262
Muster Möbelbezug, Wilhelm Poetter (Entwurf), Deutsche Textile Kunst / DeTeKu Rudolf Hiemann (Herstellung), 1920er Jahre (GRASSI Museum für Angewandte Kunst Leipzig)
Sample furniture cover fabric, Wilhelm Poetter (design), Deutsche Textile Kunst / DeTeKu Rudolf Hiemann (production), 1920s (GRASSI Museum für Angewandte Kunst Leipzig)

263
Muster Möbelbezug, Erich Kleinhempel (Entwurf), Deutsche Textile Kunst / DeTeKu Rudolf Hiemann (Herstellung), 1920er Jahre (GRASSI Museum für Angewandte Kunst Leipzig)
Sample furniture cover fabric, Erich Kleinhempel (design), Deutsche Textile Kunst / DeTeKu Rudolf Hiemann (production), 1920s (GRASSI Museum für Angewandte Kunst Leipzig)

264
Muster Möbelbezug, Herta Koch (Entwurf), Deutsche Textile Kunst / DeTeKu Rudolf Hiemann (Herstellung), 1920er Jahre (GRASSI Museum für Angewandte Kunst Leipzig)
Sample furniture cover fabric, Herta Koch (design), Deutsche Textile Kunst / DeTeKu Rudolf Hiemann (production), 1920s (GRASSI Museum für Angewandte Kunst Leipzig)

265
Musterkarte mit Möbelstoff, D. M. W. Mitglied der Deutschen Werkstätten, 1920er Jahre (GRASSI Museum für Angewandte Kunst Leipzig)

265
Sample card with furniture fabric, D. M. W. Mitglied der Deutschen Werkstätten, 1920s (GRASSI Museum für Angewandte Kunst Leipzig)

266
Stoffmustermappe, Deutsche Textile Kunst / DeTeKu Rudolf Hiemann, 1920er Jahre (GRASSI Museum für Angewandte Kunst Leipzig)

266
Fabric sample folder, Deutsche Textile Kunst / DeTeKu Rudolf Hiemann, 1920s (GRASSI Museum für Angewandte Kunst Leipzig)

267/268
Möbelstoff, Sigmund von Weech (Entwurf), Handweberei
Sigmund von Weech, Schaftlach (Herstellung), um 1925–1929
(GRASSI Museum für Angewandte Kunst Leipzig)

267/268
Furniture cover fabric, Sigmund von Weech (design), Handweberei
Sigmund von Weech, Schaftlach (production), around 1925–1929
(GRASSI Museum für Angewandte Kunst Leipzig)

269
Dekorationsstoff, Weberhof Lübz, Gottfried Hensen und Gretel Schmitz (Entwurf und Herstellung), 1967 (GRASSI Museum für Angewandte Kunst Leipzig)

269
Decorative fabric, Weberhof Lübz, Gottfried Hensen and Gretel Schmitz (design and production), 1967 (GRASSI Museum für Angewandte Kunst Leipzig)

270
Dekorationsstoff, Weberhof Lübz, Gottfried Hensen und Gretel Schmitz (Entwurf und Herstellung), 1967 (GRASSI Museum für Angewandte Kunst Leipzig)

270
Decorative fabric, Weberhof Lübz, Gottfried Hensen and Gretel Schmitz (design und production), 1967 (GRASSI Museum für Angewandte Kunst Leipzig)

271
Detail einer Quaste,
Italien, 17. Jh. (GRASSI
Museum für Angewandte
Kunst Leipzig)
Detail of a tassel, Italy,
17th century (GRASSI
Museum für Angewandte
Kunst Leipzig)

Filigrane Kunstwerke: Borten und Quasten
Stefanie Seeberg

Der Abschluss der Polsterarbeit an einem Möbel ist das Aufbringen der Posamente. Borten, Fransen und Quasten aus kostbaren Materialien wie Seide und Gold sind Zierelemente, die entscheidend zum Erscheinungsbild und Wert historischer Möbel beitrugen. Borten verdeckten die Polsternägel und bildeten den Übergang zwischen der meist hölzernen Konstruktion und der textilen Oberfläche, dem Bezugsstoff des Polsteraufbaus. Vor allem aber setzten Posamente in Farbigkeit und Material einen entscheidenden Akzent in der Gesamtgestaltung des Möbels. In der Posamenterie entstanden kostbare, filigrane Kunstwerke, deren Bedeutung und Faszination heute weitgehend in Vergessenheit geraten ist, für die jedoch in der Vergangenheit immense finanzielle Mittel und Arbeitszeit investiert wurden. Anschaulich wird dies in den überlieferten Rechnungen für den Krönungsstuhl von Charles II. 1661: Während für die Fertigung des Stuhls 9 £ berechnet wurden, kosteten die Posamente aus Gold und Silber 29 £.[243] Die Bezeichnung *Posamente* leitet sich vom französischen *passementerie* (passement) ab und benennt laufende (passer) und aufgesetzte Zierelemente.[244] Posamente sind oft Kompositwerke aus unterschiedlichen Techniken und Materialien. Sie werden und wurden gewebt, in Flecht- und Knoten- bzw. Knüpftechniken gearbeitet und können Elemente in Klöppelspitze oder Makramee umfassen. Meist sind sie aus Seide und Edelmetallen gefertigt, aber auch Leinen, Holz und Papier konnten eingesetzt werden.

Im 19. Jahrhundert waren Posamente als kleinformatige, aufwendig gearbeitete und kostbare Werke angewandter Kunst international begehrte Objekte für die entstehenden Museumssammlungen.[245] Das GRASSI Museum für Angewandte Kunst Leipzig besitzt eine herausragende Sammlung von Quasten und Borten mit Beispielen ab ca. 1600 aus verschiedenen Ländern und Regionen. Die meisten Stücke wurden in den 1890er Jahren in der Aufbauphase des Museums erworben. Kostbare Beispiele wurden von namhaften Kenner*innen und Kunsthändler*innen wie Julius Böhler und Stefan Zatelli in München oder Franz Bock in Aachen erworben. Bereits 1892 wurden ausgewählte Stücke der inzwischen renommierten Sammlung im ersten Katalog zu dieser Objektgruppe von Emil Kumsch publiziert.[246] 1911 zeigte und publizierte Marie Schuette in der Spitzenausstellung eine Auswahl weißer Leinenquasten.[247] Danach gerieten die Posamente allgemein weitgehend in Vergessenheit. Eine neue Wertschätzung historischer Posamente wurde durch Restaurator*innen in den 1970er Jahren angestoßen.[248] Erst in jüngster Vergangenheit erfolgten, vor allem im Kontext größerer Restaurierungsprojekte, erste grundlegende Untersuchungen von kunst- und kulturhistorischer Seite.[249] Die Objekte im GRASSI Museum warten noch auf ihr wissenschaftliche Erfassung. Eine Auswahl kann nun im Rahmen dieser Ausstellung Öffentlichkeit und Forschung zugänglich gemacht werden.[250]

Polster und Kissen mit Borten, Fransen und Quasten zu verzieren, hat eine lange Tradition. Da meist aus empfindlichen Materialien wie Wolle, Seide und Metalllahn gefertigt und zudem an exponierten Stellen wie Kanten und Ecken angebracht, haben sich aus weiter zurückliegenden Zeiten kaum Beispiele dieser kunstvollen Schmuckelemente erhalten. Aus dem 14. Jahrhundert sind Exemplare an Taschen und Kleidungsstücken überliefert.[251] Vor allem zeugen

Delicate artworks: Braids and tassels
Stefanie Seeberg

The final touch of upholstering a piece of furniture is the application of passementerie. Braids, fringes and tassels made from costly materials such as silk and gold are decorative elements which had a decisive impact on the appearance and value of historical furniture. Braids conceal the nails and create a transition between the usually wooden frame and the textile surface – that is, the cover fabric of the upholstery. Finally, passementerie impacts the overall appearance of a piece of furniture in its colour and materiality. Costly, delicate artworks were created in passementerie, the importance and fascination of which today have largely been forgotten but in which in the past considerable financial means and working hours were invested. This becomes evident in the invoices for the coronation seat of Charles II. From 1661: While for the construction of the chair £ 9 were charged, the passementerie made from gold and silver cost £ 29.[243] The term passementerie goes back to the French *passement* and refers to continuing (*passer*) and applied decorative elements.[244] Passementerie items are often composite structures made using different techniques and materials. They are and have been woven, worked in braiding, knotting or tying techniques and can include elements of bobbin lace and macramé.

During the nineteenth century, passementerie was in demand internationally as small-scale, intricately crafted and valuable objects of decorative art for the emerging museum collections.[245] The GRASSI Museum für Angewandte Kunst Leipzig holds an excellent collection of tassels and braids from around 1600 onwards, with examples from different countries and regions. Most pieces were acquired during the 1890s, during the development phase of the museum. Valuable examples were acquired from well-known experts and art dealers, such as Julius Böhler and Stefan Zatelli in Munich and Franz Bock in Aachen. As early as 1892, selected pieces from the by now renowned collection were published in the first catalogue on such objects by Emil Kumsch.[246] In 1911, Marie Schuette displayed and published a selection of white linen tassels in an exhibition on lace.[247] After that, passementerie fell into oblivion. A re-evaluation of historical passementerie by conservators took place in the 1970s.[248] It was only recently, especially in the context of larger conservation projects, that basic research was undertaken by art historians and cultural historians.[249] However, the objects at GRASSI Museum are still waiting to be scientifically recorded. A selection can now be presented to the public and researchers within the context of this exhibition.[250]

Adorning upholstery and cushions with braids, fringes and tassels has a long tradition. Since they were usually made from delicate materials such as wool, silk and metal lamella and applied to exposed areas such as the edges and corners, few examples have been preserved from more distant times. From the fourteenth century, examples mainly from bags and clothing have been preserved.[251] Pictorial sources in particular testify the spread and importance of passementerie. Few of the various cushions depicted on funerary monuments with reclining figures lack tassels at the corner as well

272
Borte mit Fransen, Spanien, 17. Jh. (GRASSI Museum für Angewandte Kunst Leipzig)

272
Border with fringe, Spain, 17th century (GRASSI Museum für Angewandte Kunst Leipzig)

273
Borte mit Fransen, Italien oder Spanien, 17. Jh. (GRASSI Museum für Angewandte Kunst Leipzig)

273
Border with fringe, Italy or Spain, 17th century (GRASSI Museum für Angewandte Kunst Leipzig)

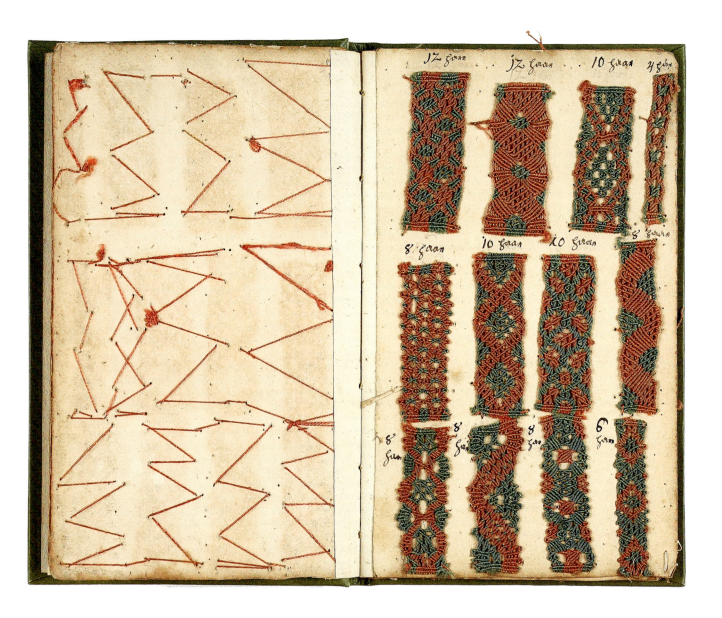

jedoch bildliche Darstellungen von der Verbreitung und Bedeutung der Posamente. An kaum einem der zahlreichen Kissen, die an Grabdenkmälern mit Liegefiguren dargestellt sind, fehlen Quasten an den Ecken sowie Schmuckborten und -kordeln entlang der Kanten. Borten mit langen Fransen, von denen Beispiele aus der Zeit nach 1600 in Ausstellung und Katalog gezeigt werden (Abb. 272, 273), sind seit dem Spätmittelalter in Bilddarstellungen sowie in Innenraumgestaltungen auf Wandmalereien oder Bauskulpturen zu entdecken.

Die ab dem 16. Jahrhundert u. a. durch die vermögende Oberschicht der reichen Handelsstädte wachsende Nachfrage, Produktion und damit auch Überlieferung der Posamente lässt sich entsprechend der Verbreitung der Polstermöbel nachvollziehen. Parallel zu den Bezugsstoffen kommen in ganz Europa begehrte Quasten und Borten im 16. und 17. Jahrhundert vor allem aus Italien, wohingegen

as decorative braids and cords along the edges. Braids with long fringes, examples of which from the time after 1600 are displayed in the exhibition and the catalogue (fig. 272, 273), have been discovered in pictorial depictions as well as in interiors on wall paintings or architectural sculptures since the late Middle Ages.

The increase in demand, production and correspondingly the amount of surviving passementerie can be traced to the spread of upholstered furniture due, among other things, to the wealthy elites of rich trading towns since the sixteenth century. In parallel with the upholstery fabric, tassels and braids were sought-after throughout Europe during the sixteenth and seventeenth centuries, especially those from Italy, while in the eighteenth century France was the most influential. Since the fashion for braids and tassels

274
Muster von Makrameeborten, Deutschland, 17. Jh.
(GRASSI Museum für Angewandte Kunst Leipzig)

274
Sample of macramé borders, Germany, 17th century (GRASSI Museum für Angewandte Kunst Leipzig)

im 18. Jahrhundert Frankreich den Stil der Posamenterie bestimmt. Wegen der gesamteuropäischen Verbreitung der Mode für Borten und Quasten ist es jedoch oft nicht eindeutig zu bestimmen, ob eine Quaste oder Borte in Frankreich, Italien oder England gefertigt wurde. Dennoch gab es nationale oder regionale Ausprägungen und Vorlieben. Auch in Deutschland, etwa in Sachsen und Preußen, wurden Posamente gefertigt.[252] So entwickelte sich im 17. und 18. Jahrhundert mit dem vorhandenen Know-how in der Kunst der Klöppelspitze u. a. Annaberg zu einem wichtigen Zentrum der Posamentenherstellung.[253] Eine eingehende Untersuchung der Geschichte der Posamenterie steht noch aus. Vergleichbar anderen Werkgruppen wurden auch Posamente in den Werkstätten von Frauen und Männern gefertigt.[254]

Technische Neuerungen und die Verfügbarkeit von Materialien hatten Einfluss auf Gestaltung und Kosten der Posamente. Eine wichtige Rolle spielte die Herstellung von Metalllahn (Abb. 271, 283). Neben reinem Gold- und Silberdraht wurden dafür auch kostengünstigere leonische Drähte, versilberte oder vergoldete Kupferdrähte und Bänder verwendet. Diese Metalldrähte mussten bis ins 17. Jahrhundert aufwendig mit der Hand gezogen werden.[255] 1681 entstand in Leipzig die erste deutsche Manufaktur für die Herstellung von Golddrähten.[256] Für den steigenden Bedarf der höfischen Ausstattung nach französischem Vorbild am Hofe Ludwigs XIV. (1638–1715) wurden Gold- und Silbermanufakturen gegründet, so 1693 in Berlin.[257]

In Leipzig wurden Goldposamente, Borten wie Quasten in der Silber- und Goldmanufaktur von Andreas Dietrich Apel (1662–1718) gefertigt. Die Apelschen Manufakturen, in denen, wie im vorhergehenden Kapitel erwähnt, auch kostbare Seidengewebe produziert wurden, waren für Möbel und Posamente Hauptlieferant für den sächsischen Hof unter August dem Starken. Einige Beispiele dieser Leipziger Goldposamente lassen sich noch heute im Dresdner Schloss bewundern.[258]

Insgesamt aber veränderten sich Technik und Material der Posamentenherstellung über die Jahrhunderte kaum.[259] Modelle und Muster wurden von den Posamentenwerkstätten auch über Modeströmungen hinweg weiterverwendet. So lassen sich Quasten und Borten oft nicht eindeutig datieren und lokalisieren.[260]

Borten

Borten bilden den größten Anteil der Posamente für Möbel. Die zeitaufwendige Fertigung dieser bis in das 19. Jahrhundert hinein überwiegend handgefertigten Objekte ist heute kaum mehr vorstellbar. Borten wurden aus Seide, Leinen und Metallfäden gewebt, geknüpft, geknotet oder geklöppelt. Am häufigsten und bis heute in der Polsterarbeit verbreitet sind gewebte Borten. Diese wurden in der Vergangenheit auf Handwebstühlen gefertigt. Exemplarisch für die große Vielfalt gewebter Borten zeigen wir in Ausstellung und Katalog eine kleine Auswahl an Stücken aus dem 17. bis 19. Jahrhundert. (Abb. 281, 282) In der Sammlung des Museums ist zudem ein großer Bestand geknoteter Borten in Makrameetechnik aus dem 16. bis 18. Jahrhundert erhalten. Diese 1 bis 3,5 cm breiten und etwa 6 cm langen Musterabschnitte wurden in einer kaum fassbaren Vielzahl unterschiedlicher Knotenarten und Mustervariationen in verschiedenen Farbkombinationen in feinen Seidenfäden handgefertigt (Abb. 274). Borten mit langen Fransen waren

spread throughout Europe, it is often not possible to determine definitely whether a tassel or braid was manufactured in France, Italy or England. Nevertheless, there were national and regional variations and preferences. In Germany, too, passementerie was produced, for example in Saxony and Prussia.[252] Thus, during the seventeenth and eighteenth centuries, places such as Annaberg became important centres of passementerie production due to the already existing know-how in bobbin lace production.[253] A history of passementerie is still to be written. Comparable to other object groups, passementerie was produced in workshops by both men and women.[254]

Technical innovations and the availability of materials influenced the design and costs of passementerie. Metal lamella likewise played an important role (fig. 271, 283). In addition to wire made from pure gold and silver, cheaper alternatives such as leonic wire or silver- or gold-plated copper wire and trimmings were used.[255] In 1681, the first German manufactory for the production of gold wires was established in Leipzig.[256] In order to meet the increased demand for courtly furnishings after the French model of the court of Louis XIV (1638–1715), gold and silver manufactories were founded, among others in Berlin in 1693.[257] In Leipzig, gold passementerie, braids as well as tassels, were produced in the silver and gold manufactory of Andreas Dietrich Apel (1662–1718). The Apelsche Manufakturen, which, as mentioned in the previous chapter, also produced valuable silk fabrics and were the main supplier of the Saxon court of August the Strong. A few examples of these Leipzig gold passementerie items can still be admired in the Dresden castle.[258]

Overall, little has changed over the centuries in the production of passementerie in terms of technique and material.[259] Models and patterns were used by workshops regardless of fashions. As a result, tassels and braids can often not be unequivocally dated and localized.[260]

Braids

Most passementerie for furniture consists of braids. The time-intensive production of these objects, which were mostly handcrafted until the nineteenth century, is hard to imagine. Braids were woven from silk, linen and metal threads, as well as knotted, tied, and tatted. Most common in upholstery until this day are woven braids. In the past, these were produced using hand loom weaving. As an example of the wide variety of woven braids, we present in the exhibition and the catalogue a small selection of pieces from the seventeenth until nineteenth century (fig 281, 282). Furthermore, the museum collection holds many knotted braids made with macramé techniques from the sixteenth and seventeenth century. These samples, with a width of 1–3.5 cm and a length of about 6 cm, were handcrafted using fine silk threads in different colour combinations with an incredible variety of different knots and pattern variations (fig. 274). Braids with long fringes were already popular in the Middle Ages and the Early Modern period and are documented in many pictorial depictions of the time on the edges of beds, armchairs, furnishing fabrics and tapestries in both sacral and

bereits im Mittelalter und in der Frühen Neuzeit beliebt und sind in zahlreichen Bilddarstellungen aus diesen Epochen an Kanten von Betten, Sesseln, Möbel- und Wandbehängen im weltlichen wie im sakralen Bereich dokumentiert. Die langen Seidenfransen konnten einfarbig gehalten sein, beliebt waren aber auch Wechsel von bis zu vier Farben[261] (Abb. 272). Wie hier die Wahl der Farben auf den zugehörigen Stoff abgestimmt war, zeigen Fransenborten, die noch original an zwei Applikationsstickereien montiert sind. Diese waren ursprünglich Teil einer Raumausstattung, etwa einer Wandverkleidung oder Bestandteil eines Paradebetts (Abb. 249, 250). Je nach Kontext wurden Fransen auch in Metallfäden mit Gold, Silber oder leonischem Metall gefertigt. An dem gezeigten Bezugsstoff einer Stuhllehne ist noch die Borte mit Goldfransen vorhanden, die hier sehr exklusiv mit rot-gelbem Brokatellgewebe kombiniert wurde (Abb. 242/243). Gefragt waren aber auch Kombinationen von Seiden- und Metallfransen (Abb. 273).

Ende des 17. Jahrhunderts kommen Borten mit Pompons und mit in kleinen Quästchen endenden Fransen in Mode. Sie wurden vor allem in Italien, aber auch in anderen Ländern gefertigt[262] (Abb. 275–278). Beliebt waren Borten mit gebogten Unterkanten. Ein aufwendig gestaltetes Beispiel ist das Fragment einer italienischen Borte aus dem 17. Jahrhundert (Abb. 275). Anfang des 18. Jahrhunderts werden Gestaltung und Farbigkeit solcher Borten mit langen Fransen und Gehängen leichter und verspielter. Typisch sind eingefügte Gehänge, die aus geknüpften Elementen, Balletten (mit Seide und Metalllahn umsponnene Pergamentstreifen), Schleifen oder mit Seidenfäden überspannten Holzformen gestaltet wurden[263] Die gleichen Elemente finden sich auch an Quasten dieser Zeit (Abb. 292). Nach 1800 finden Gehänge mit überspannten Holzformen, u. a. mit spiralförmig gedrehten Körpern international großen Anklang (Abb. 279, 280).

Schon erwähnt wurde die seit dem 17. Jahrhundert vor allem in der höfischen Raumausstattung zunehmende Bedeutung von Gold- bzw. Metallborten. Auf Möbeln und in Darstellungen auf Gemälden sind um die Mitte des 18. Jahrhunderts Silber- und Goldborten überliefert.[264] Der Bestand des GRASSI Museums für Angewandte Kunst umfasst eine große Anzahl solcher Metallborten, von denen hier eine kleine Auswahl gezeigt wird (Abb. 283).

mundane contexts. The long silk fringes could be monochrome, but up to four colours used interchangeably was also popular[261] (fig. 272). The way in which the selection of colours was made according to the matching fabric can be seen in fringes that have been preserved on two pieces of appliqué embroidery. They were originally part of a room furnishing, such as a tapestry or a state bed (fig. 249, 250). Depending on the context, fringes were made from metal threads in gold, silver or leonic metal. The upholstery fabric of a chair backrest, shown here, still has its original braid with a gold hanging fringed edge which was combined with an exclusive red-yellow brocatelle weave (fig. 242/243). Combinations of silk and metal fringes were also in demand (fig. 273).

At the end of the seventeenth century, braids with pompons and fringes ending in small tassels became fashionable (figs. 275–278). They were mainly produced in Italy, but also other countries[262] Braids with scalloped lower edges were also popular. One elaborately designed example is a fragment of an Italian braid from the seventeenth century (fig. 275). In the early eighteenth century, the design and colour of such braids with long fringes and pendants became lighter and more playful. Inserted pendants such as knotted elements, ballets (parchment strips covered in silk or metal lamella), bows or wooden forms covered with silk threads are typical.[263] The same elements can also be found on tassels of the period (fig. 292). After 1800, pedants with covered wooden forms, including bodies twisted in a spiral, became very popular internationally (figs. 279, 280).

The increasing importance of gold or metallic braid since the seventeenth century, especially in courtly interior decoration, has already been mentioned. Around the middle of the eighteenth century, silver and gold laces were found on furniture and in their depictions in paintings.[264] The holdings of the GRASSI Museum für Angewandte Kunst include a large number of such metallic borders, a small selection of which is shown here (fig. 283).

275 Borte mit Fransen und Quasten, Italien, 17. Jh. (GRASSI Museum für Angewandte Kunst Leipzig)

275 Border with fringe and tassels, Italy, 17th century (GRASSI Museum für Angewandte Kunst Leipzig)

276
Borte mit Makramee und Fransen, Italien (?), 17. Jh. (?)
(GRASSI Museum für Angewandte Kunst Leipzig)

276
Border with macramé and tassels, Italy (?), 17th century (?)
(GRASSI Museum für Angewandte Kunst Leipzig)

277
Borte, Italien (?), 17. Jh. (?)
(GRASSI Museum für Angewandte Kunst Leipzig)

277
Border, Italy (?), 17th century (?)
(GRASSI Museum für Angewandte Kunst Leipzig)

278
Borte, Italien (?), Ende 17. Jh.
(GRASSI Museum für Angewandte Kunst Leipzig)

278
Border, Italy (?), late 17th century
(GRASSI Museum für Angewandte Kunst Leipzig)

Filigrane Kunstwerke: Borten und Quasten | Delicate artworks: Braids and tassels

279
Borte mit Gehänge, 19. Jh. (GRASSI Museum für Angewandte Kunst Leipzig)

280
Borte mit Gehänge, 19. Jh. (GRASSI Museum für Angewandte Kunst Leipzig)

279
Border with pendants, 19th century (GRASSI Museum für Angewandte Kunst Leipzig)

280
Border with pendants, 19th century (GRASSI Museum für Angewandte Kunst Leipzig)

281
Drei gewebte Borten, Italien, 17.–19. Jh. (GRASSI Museum für Angewandte Kunst Leipzig)

281
Three woven borders, Italy, 17th–19th century (GRASSI Museum für Angewandte Kunst Leipzig)

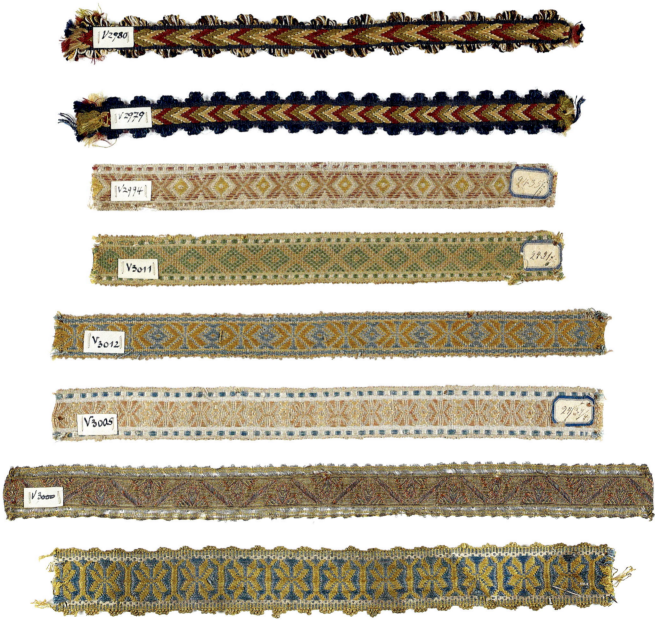

282
Acht Borten, Italien, 17.–18. Jh. (GRASSI Museum für Angewandte Kunst Leipzig)

282
Eight borders, Italy, 17th–18th century (GRASSI Museum für Angewandte Kunst Leipzig)

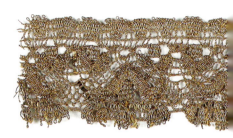

283
Acht Metallborten, 17.–19. Jh. (GRASSI Museum für Angewandte Kunst Leipzig)

283
Eight metal borders, 17th–19th century (GRASSI Museum für Angewandte Kunst Leipzig)

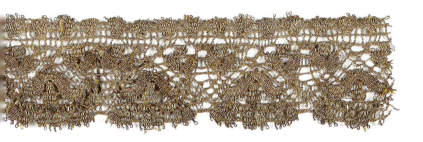

Filigrane Kunstwerke: Borten und Quasten | Delicate artworks: Braids and tassels **281**

Quasten

Eine besondere Gruppe unter den Posamenten bilden die Quasten. Meist aus Seide und Metalllahn, häufig auf Holzkörpern gearbeitet, finden sich Elemente in verschiedenen Knüpf- und Flechttechniken, in Makramee und Spitze. An Möbeln und in der Innenraumausstattung, aber auch an Kleidung, Accessoires und Waffen waren Quasten Schmuckelemente, die Bedeutung, Reichtum und Stand von Objekt und Person betonten. So findet man sie auf frühen Darstellungen repräsentativer Armlehnstühle wie in dem im Einführungskapitel genannten Fresko Mantegnas (Abb. 5). Besonders offensichtlich wird ihre repräsentative Bedeutung auf dem berühmten Doppelportrait *Die Gesandten* von Hans Holbein d. J. von 1533: An der in kostbarer Metallarbeit gefertigten Dolchscheide in der Hand Jean de Dintevilles hängt eine große, aufwendig in schwarzen Seiden- und Goldfäden gearbeitete Quaste.[265] Solch kostbare Exemplare wurden vor Licht, Staub und mechanischer Beschädigung in eigens dafür gefertigten Schutzüberzügen aufbewahrt.[266]

Die ältesten Quasten im Bestand des GRASSI Museums für Angewandte Kunst entstanden im 17. Jahrhundert überwiegend in Italien und zeigen die vielfältigen Gestaltungsmöglichkeiten in hoher Qualität. Die überflochtenen Köpfe zeigen unterschiedliche Farbkombinationen und Musterstrukturen. Durch Elemente in Samtoptik mit geschnittenem langem Flor wurden Akzente gesetzt[267] (Abb. 289). Entsprechend der Gestaltung der Fransenborten wurden auch bei den Quasten Seiden- und Metallfäden kombiniert. Besonders exklusiv waren Quasten, die mit einem hohen Anteil an Edelmetall gefertigt wurden (Abb. 290).
Im 18. Jahrhundert werden entsprechend den Borten auch Quasten verspielter und leichter. Dies zeigt sich sowohl in der Vorliebe für hellere Farbtöne als auch im eingesetzten Material und der Formensprache. Beliebte Gestaltungselemente sind nun Schleifen, Balletten und Crepinengehänge, die aus mit feinen Seidenfäden umsponnenen Papierstreifen und zarten Gewebebändern gebildet werden (Abb. 291–295). Eine sächsische Variante der zweiten Hälfte des 17. Jahrhunderts sind Quasten mit kleinen Figuren, von denen einzelne Beispiele in verschiedenen Sammlungen, so auch im GRASSI Museum erhalten sind (Abb. 287/288).[268] Noch in reicher Farbigkeit und mit verspielten Schmuckelementen zeigt das Quastenpaar mit langen Fransen in der schmalen gestreckten Form schon Vorlieben des Klassizismus (Abb. 296, 297). Im 19. Jahrhundert sind Quasten in vielfältigen Formvarianten reich überliefert.
Heute gibt es nur noch wenige Werkstätten, die die Techniken der Posamenterie beherrschen. Der Fortbestand dieser Kunsttechniken, die u. a. für Restaurierung und Erhalt historischer Möbel und Raumausstattungen essentiell sind, ist inzwischen gefährdet. Derzeit werden die kleinen handgefertigten Kunstwerke – meist in einfacheren technischen Ausführungen und erschwinglichen Materialien – in der DIY-Bewegung wiederentdeckt. Quasten finden sich in diesem Jahr als selbstgefertigte Extras an Taschen, Kleidung oder in der Raumdekoration.

Tassels

Tassels are a special group of passementerie. Similarly made from silk and metal lamella, often worked over wooden forms, they are elements constructed from different knotting or braiding techniques, in macramé or lace. Found on furniture as well as in the interior, but also on clothing, accessories and weapons, tassels were decorative elements that emphasized the importance, wealth and standing of an object or a person. Thus, they can be found on early depictions of representative armchairs, such as the fresco by Mantegna mentioned in the introduction (fig. 5). Their representative meaning is particularly apparent in the famous double portrait *The Ambassadors* by Hans Holbein the Younger from 1533: a large tassel, elaborately worked in black silk and gold threads, hangs from the scabbard made of precious metalwork in the hand of Jean de Dintevilles.[265] Such valuable examples were protected against light, dust and mechanical damage by keeping them in specifically made protective covers.[266]

The oldest tassels in the holdings of GRASSI Museum für Angewandte Kunst were produced in Italy during the seventeenth century and reflect a variety of design possibilities of high quality. The braided forms show different colour combinations and pattern structures. Accents were set by elements in velvet look with a cut long pile[267] (fig. 289). In keeping with the design of the fringes, silk and metal threads were also combined in the tassels, and those made with a high proportion of precious metal were particularly exclusive (fig. 290).
In the eighteenth century, tassels also became more playful and lighter, in line with the braids. This can be seen in the preference for lighter shades as well as in the material used and the formal language. Popular design elements were now bows, ballets and crepine pendants, which are made of paper strips covered with fine silk threads and delicate fabric ribbons (figs. 291–295). A Saxon variant from the second half of the seventeenth century are tassels with small figurines, individual examples of which are preserved in various collections, including the GRASSI Museum (figs. 287/288).[268] Still richly coloured and with playful ornamental elements, a pair of tassels with long elongated fringes already displays the tastes of Classicism (figs. 296/297). For the nineteenth century, many tassels have been preserved in a variety of forms.
Today, few workshops master the techniques of passementerie. The survival of these artistic techniques, which are essential for the restoration and conservation of historical furniture and room furnishings, among other things, is now endangered. At the moment, these small hand-crafted works of art are re-discovered in the DIY movement, often in more simply crafted models and affordable materials. This year, tassels can be found as homemade additions to bags and clothing or in interior decoration.

284/285
Quaste, Italien, 17. Jh./18. Jh. (GRASSI Museum für Angewandte Kunst Leipzig)

284/285
Tassel, Italy, 17th/18th century (GRASSI Museum für Angewandte Kunst Leipzig)

Filigrane Kunstwerke: Borten und Quasten | Delicate artworks: Braids and tassels **283**

286
Quaste, Frankreich, 17. Jh. (GRASSI Museum für Angewandte Kunst Leipzig)
Tassel, France, 17th century (GRASSI Museum für Angewandte Kunst Leipzig)

287/288
Quaste, Sachsen, 17. Jh. (GRASSI Museum für Angewandte Kunst Leipzig)
Tassel, Saxony, 17th century (GRASSI Museum für Angewandte Kunst Leipzig)

289
Quaste, Italien, 17. Jh. (GRASSI Museum für Angewandte Kunst Leipzig)

289
Tassel, Italy, 17th century (GRASSI Museum für Angewandte Kunst Leipzig)

290
Quaste, Italien oder Spanien, 17. Jh. (GRASSI Museum für Angewandte Kunst Leipzig)

290
Tassel, Italy or Spain, 17th century (GRASSI Museum für Angewandte Kunst Leipzig)

291/292
Quaste, Italien, 18. Jh. (?) (GRASSI Museum für Angewandte Kunst Leipzig)

291/292
Tassel, Italy, 18th century (?) (GRASSI Museum für Angewandte Kunst Leipzig)

293
Quaste, Deutschland (?), 18. Jh. (GRASSI Museum für Angewandte Kunst Leipzig)

293
Tassel, Germany (?), 18th century (GRASSI Museum für Angewandte Kunst Leipzig)

294
Quaste, 18. Jh. (GRASSI Museum für Angewandte Kunst Leipzig)
Tassel, 18th century (GRASSI Museum für Angewandte Kunst Leipzig)

295
Quaste mit Ballettengehängen, 18. Jh. (GRASSI Museum für Angewandte Kunst Leipzig)
Tassel with ballets pendants, 18th century (GRASSI Museum für Angewandte Kunst Leipzig)

296
Quaste, Frankreich (?), Ende 18. Jh. (GRASSI Museum für Angewandte Kunst Leipzig)
Tassel, France (?), late 18th century (GRASSI Museum für Angewandte Kunst Leipzig)

297
Quaste, Frankreich (?), Ende 18. Jh. (GRASSI Museum für Angewandte Kunst Leipzig)
Tassel, France (?), late 18th century (GRASSI Museum für Angewandte Kunst Leipzig)

Filigrane Kunstwerke: Borten und Quasten | Delicate artworks: Braids and tassels **291**

Armlehn- und Rückenlehnpolster

Maximilian Busch

Die eigenständige formsprachliche Entwicklung der Arm- und Rückenlehne macht es notwendig, diesen, gesondert vom Sitz, Aufmerksamkeit zu schenken. Sitzpolsterungen spiegeln in der Regel den Verlauf der Zarge wider. Mit fortschreitender polstertechnischer Entwicklung bilden Rücken- und Armlehnen eine eigene Stilistik aus. Beginnend in Frankreich ab der Regierungszeit Ludwig XVI. entwickeln sich in relativ kurzer Zeit die unterschiedlichsten Formen. Sie entwickeln im ausgehenden 18. Jahrhundert ihre eigene Formensprache und haben eine eigenständige Betrachtung verdient.

Seinen Anfang nahm wohl alles mit einem stärker werdenden Bedürfnis nach Bequemlichkeit und sich ständig ändernden ästhetischen Ansprüchen der gehobenen Gesellschaftsschichten. Während in der Gotik noch buchstäblich auf Holz gesessen wurde und die höchste Bequemlichkeit ein aufgelegtes Kissen bot, wurden in der Renaissance am gesamten Möbel schon rudimentäre Polster- und Bezugsarbeiten ausgeführt. Beispielsweise ist auf einem Gemälde von Anthonis Mor aus dem Jahr 1554 Queen Mary auf einem komplett mit Stoff bezogenen Sessel sitzend abgebildet.

Trotz der extrem dünnen Beweislage mangels fehlender Originale können die zahlreichen Abbildungen sitzender Menschen auf den verschiedensten Möbeln als Beweis für die Entwicklung fest mit Stoff bezogener Möbel gelten. Zumindest in Großbritannien und auch Deutschland waren damals bei einigen Möbeln schon nicht nur die Sitzfläche, sondern ebenso die Armlehnen sowie die Rückenlehne mit Stoff bezogen. Folglich dürften sich zeitgleich auch die ersten einfachen Polster entwickelt haben. Ein Stoffbezug auf blankem Holz bietet nur eine geringe zu erwartende Lebensdauer. Im Zusammenhang mit dem hohen wirtschaftlichen Aufwand der vorindustriellen Gewebeproduktion und den daraus resultierenden Preisen kann zumindest eine einfache Unterpolsterung der Gewebe als sicher gelten.

Füllstoffe hierfür kamen vermutlich aus der lokalen Vegetation, auch das Haar vom Reh oder anderen Wildtieren wurde genutzt. Als pflanzliche Füllstoffe haben dabei zum Beispiel je nach Gegend Gras, Seegras oder auch Moos ebenso wie Flachsreste aus der Leinenproduktion gedient. Gegen Ende des Barock werden Polsterungen im Sitzbereich langsam plastischer. Sie nehmen eine eindeutige, der Formensprache des Möbels folgende Gestalt an. Im Rokoko verstetigt sich der Prozess und gipfelt in einem enormen Entwicklungsschub.

Im Besitz der Stiftung Preußische Schlösser und Gärten befindet sich eine große Sammlung friderizianischer Rokokomöbel. Einige wenige weisen noch die ursprünglichen Polsterungen auf. An diesen Möbeln lassen sich Bourrelets auf den Vorderzargen des Sitzes und vereinzelt im Rückenlehnbereich nachweisen. Befunde dieser Art konnten bisher nur über haptische Proben erlangt werden. Um an sichere Informationen zum genauen Aufbau der Rückenlehnpolster aus dieser Zeit zu gelangen, müssen die Polster auseinandergenommen werden. Tatsache ist, dass die erfühlten Kantenwülste nur im Kopfbereich vorgefunden wurden und weder im Sitz noch in der Rückenlehne umlaufend ausgeführt wurden. Weiter befindet sich in der Sammlung eine Reihe zusammengehöriger Armlehnstühle

298
Armlehnstuhl mit freigelegtem Rückenpolster, Potsdam, um 1765
(Stiftung Preußische Schlösser und Gärten Berlin-Brandenburg)

Upholstering arm- and backrests

Maximilian Busch

The independent design development of arm- and backrests makes it necessary to pay them special attention, in isolation from the seat. Seat upholstery usually follows the shape of the frame. With the development of upholstery techniques arm- and backrests developed an individual style. Beginning in France with the reign of Louis XVI, a variety of forms developed in a relatively short span of time. In the late eighteenth century they developed a specific formal language and are worthy of independent consideration.

In the beginning there was presumably an increased demand for comfort and the changing aesthetic requirements of the elites. While in the Gothic period, one literally sat on wood, with nothing but a cushion to provide any comfort, during the Renaissance basic upholstery and fabric coverings were already made for all parts of the furniture piece. This can be seen in a 1554 painting by Anthonis Mor depicting Queen Mary in an armchair that is entirely covered in fabric.

Despite the lack of evidence due to a lack of original pieces, various depictions of people seated on a variety of furniture can be taken as evidence of the development of furniture with fixed fabric coverings. At least in the case of Great Britain and also Germany, some of these objects were not only covered in fabric on the seat but also the arm- and backrests. The first basic upholstery was thus probably developed at the same time. A fabric cover on bare wood only has a short expected lifespan. In the context of the high economic expenditure of pre-industrial fabric production and the resulting prices, at least a basic padding can be presumed.

Fillings probably derived from local vegetation, but also the hair of deer and other wildlife. As plant-based stuffing, there was, for example, grass, seagrass or moss as well as flax rests from linen production, depending on the region. At the end of the Baroque period, seat upholstery became more plastic. They take on a specific shape which followed the formal language of the furniture. During the Rococo period, this process became more established and culminated in an enormous surge in development.

A large collection of Frederician Rococo furniture can be found in the possession of the Stiftung Preußische Schlösser und Gärten. A few pieces are preserved with their original upholstery. There, one can find edge rolls on the front of the frame as well as occasionally in the backrest.

Until now, such findings could only be obtained by examining samples through touch. In order to obtain more reliable information on the construction of backrest upholstery from this period, it has to be disassembled. It becomes clear that the edge rolls that were felt could only be found in the head area and did not run around the seat or the backrest. Furthermore, the collection includes a set of armchairs from around 1765 (fig. 27/28). These chairs likewise have the earliest

298
Armchair with exposed backrest, Potsdam, around 1765
(Stiftung Preußische Schlösser und Gärten Berlin-Brandenburg)

299
Schichtmodell einer Armlehnpolsterung aus dem Klassizismus
(Maximilian Busch RiH, 2021)

299
Cutaway model of armrest padding from the Classicism period
(Maximilian Busch RiH, 2021)

aus den Jahren um 1765 (s. Abb. 27/28). Auch diese Stühle weisen noch die erste Polsterung auf. Hier findet sich neben einem garnierten Bourrelet auf der Vorderzarge im Sitz eine vollflächige Fasson in der Rückenlehne, die an drei Seiten garniert ist. Dies ist der bislang älteste Fund einer Polsterung in dieser Technik. Depeschen aus Bayreuth zeigen, dass im Jahr 1763 zwei französische Tapissiers aus Paris am Hof des Preußenkönigs Anstellung fanden. Mit großer Wahrscheinlichkeit sind ebendiese Handwerker für die Polsterung der genannten Stuhlreihe verantwortlich. Es kann davon ausgegangen werden, dass sie diese Technik aus ihrer Heimat mitbrachten. Der relativ komplexe Aufbau des Fassonpolsters legt den Schluss nahe, dass diese Technik im Herkunftsland der beiden Tapissiers schon länger praktiziert wurde.

Die Armlehnpolsterungen sind hier immer noch reine Flachpolster. Ein neues Material erlaubte es aber den Tapezierer*innen des 18. Jahrhunderts, immer formstabilere und langlebigere Polsterungen aufzubauen: das Rosshaar. Unter Zuhilfenahme von Druck, Feuchtigkeit und Hitze wurden die Haare in Zöpfe gedreht. Durch diese Behandlung bekam es eine dauerhafte Kräuselung, wodurch es zu einem vorzüglichen Polstermaterial wurde. Vor allem an höfischen Möbeln, in Kutschen und an sonstigen Dingen, die einer bequemen Polsterung bedurften, wurde das neue Material massenhaft verwendet. Erste Nachweise für die Nutzung des Rosshaars finden sich in der Enzyklopädie Diderots und d'Alemberts, erschienen 1751. Die Annahme, dass diese Technik schon länger existiert, liegt nahe.

Mit der Inthronisierung Ludwig XVI. im Jahre 1774 wurde von Frankreich ausgehend eine neue Formensprache entwickelt. Weg von runden, teils schwülstigen Formen hin zu einer neuen Geradlinigkeit. Damit einhergehend wurden neue Anforderungen an die auszuführenden Polsterarbeiten gestellt. Die zuvor runden Polsterausformungen passten nicht mehr zum Grundgedanken des neuen Architekturstils. Es entstand die Notwendigkeit zur Weiterentwicklung der bis dato bewährten Techniken. Bis dahin rund ausgearbeitete Kanten wurden immer eckiger und exakter. Armlehnstühle Marie-Antoinettes im Petit Trianon in Versailles, die sich heute noch im ursprünglichen Zustand befinden sollen, zeigen nun auch eigenständig ausgearbeitete Armlehnen.

Hier haben die Polsterungen der Armlehnen keinen ablesbaren, direkten Bezug zum Gestell, sondern sind eigenständige Elemente mit eigener Aussage, die sich in den formsprachlichen Kontext des Möbels klar einbeziehen lässt. Das Ausarbeiten dieser trapezförmigen Armlehnen (s. Abb. 299) setzt ein hohes Maß an Verständnis für verschiedene Materialien und deren Einsatzbereiche sowie ein genaues Wissen um verschiedene Garniertechniken voraus. Während sich in der Rückenlehne mehrere immer wiederkehrende Formvarianten ausfindig machen lassen, bleiben die trapezförmige und die rechteckige Armlehne vorerst die vorherrschenden.

Trotz der gesellschaftlichen Unruhen während und nach der Revolution ging die Entwicklung der Möbelarchitektur stetig voran – weg von royalen, reich geschmückten, in Gold gefassten Möbeln hin zu schlichteren, eher bürgerlich anmutenden. In der Zeit des Directoire finden sich vermehrt konkave, trapezförmige Rückenlehnen, bei denen die Polsterungen nach unten hin auslaufen. Die bis dahin bekannten Formen werden zu dieser Zeit keinesfalls verdrängt.

Mutmaßlich in der kurzen Periode des Consulat wird der Grundstein für eine Technik gelegt, die die Polsterkunst zu ihrer Formvollendung führen sollte. Eine neue Ausprägung der Armlehne wird entwickelt. Dem Geschmack der Zeit ist es wohl geschuldet, dass viele Armlehnen nicht mehr in eckig

kind of upholstery. In addition to the stitched and bridled front roll in the seat frame, there is full-surface padding in the backrest, which has been stitched on three sides. To date, this is the oldest example of an upholstery executed in this technique. Dispatches sent from Bayreuth show that two French *tapissiers* from Paris were employed at the court of the Prussian king in 1763. Most likely it was these craftsmen who were responsible for the upholstery of the chair set mentioned above. It can be assumed that they brought the technique with them from their home country. The relatively complex construction of the upholstery leads to the conclusion that this technique had already been practiced for some time in the two upholsterers' country of origin.

Armrest upholstery was still made with thin padding at this point. A new material made it possible for *tapissiers* of the eighteenth century to create ever more stable and long-lasting upholstery: horsehair. Using pressure, moisture and heat, the hair was twisted into braids. By using this treatment they became permanently curled and an excellent stuffing material. The new material was used en mass, especially in the context of court furniture, carriages as well as other objects that needed comfortable padding. The first evidence for the use of horsehair can be found in the encyclopaedia by Diderot and d'Alembert published in 1751. It can be assumed that the technique had been in use for some time.

With the coronation of Louis XVI, in 1774, a new formal language developed in France: away with the rounded, at times overblown shapes, and towards a new rectilinearity – and, with this, new demands were raised for upholstery. The round upholstery shapes of earlier forms no longer suited the ideas behind the new architectural style. Therefore, the techniques used thus far had to be developed further. Previously round edges became increasingly sharp and exact. Armchairs belonging to Marie-Antoinette at the Petit Trianon in Versailles, which are said to be in their original state, also exhibit individually upholstered armrests.

Here, the paddings of the armrest have no direct relationship to the frame but are autonomous elements with a distinct message that can be integrated clearly into the formal language of the furniture. The making of these trapezoid armrests (fig. 299) depends on a great understanding of different materials and their usage as well as an exact knowledge of different stitching and upholstery techniques. While for the backrest several recurring shape variations can be identified, trapezoid and rectangular armrests remained at the fore.

Despite social unrest during and after the Revolution, the development of furniture design progressed – away from royal, richly adorned gilded furniture, towards more simple, rather bourgeois pieces. During the Directoire era, concave, trapezoid backrests with padding that becomes flatter at the bottom appeared. The shapes that had been popular until then, however, still prevailed.

Presumably during the short Consulat period, the foundation stone was laid for a technique which would lead the art of upholstery to its formal perfection. A new form of armrest was developed. It is probably due to the taste of the time that many armrests no longer ended in angular hand knobs, but tended more and more towards rounded shapes. These new shapes required new upholstery techniques to emerge.

300/301
Modell einer Tonnenarmlehne aus dem Klassizismus (Maximilian Busch RiH, 2021)

300/301
Model of a bolster armrest padding from the Classicism period (Maximilian Busch RiH, 2021)

ausgearbeiteten Handknäufen enden, sondern mehr und mehr zu abgerundeten Formen tendieren. Diese neuen Formen bedürfen neuer Polstertechniken zur Herausbildung. Wie immer in der Polsterei muss sich die Formensprache des Gestells in der des Möbels wiederfinden lassen. Es kann davon ausgegangen werden, dass der Ausarbeitung der Rundung verschiedene Entwicklungsstadien vorangingen. Perfektion erreichte sie dann im Empire mit der tonnenförmigen Ausführung (s. Abb. 300/301).

Die technischen Anforderungen an Polsterer sind hoch. Die Armlehne besteht aus mehreren Einzelteilen, die genau aneinander gearbeitet werden müssen. Fehler in der Fasson sind, einmal aufgetreten, nicht mehr zu korrigieren. Mit dem Ende des Empire geht auch die Epoche der exakten Linienführung langsam ihrem Ende entgegen. Trotz einiger Nachwehen des Empire in der Möbelkunst bahnt sich der Historismus langsam seinen Weg ins Zentrum der Aufmerksamkeit der Polstereien. Das fördert immer runder werdende und bald gänzlich mit Stoff bezogene Möbel. Wo bis zum Empire klar ablesbar blieb, welches Glied des Möbels betrachtet wird und eine eigenständige Betrachtung ganz praktisch möglich war, flossen nun die Übergänge vom Rücken zu den Armlehnen stärker ineinander. Vorher bloß im Sitz verarbeitete Metallfedern kamen nun auch in Rückenlehnen erstmalig zum Einsatz. Einen definitiven Nachweis über Federn in der Rückenlehne finden sich in einem Stuhl des Möbelkünstlers August Stühler um 1830 (Bothe/Rietz 2019, S. 74)

Im Verlauf des 19. Jahrhunderts bahnte sich die Metallfeder ihren Weg in die Polsterei, und natürlich auch in die Rückenlehnen. Dies dürfte wohl vor allem an dem immer besser werdenden Federstahl gelegen haben. Während Federstahl im Verlauf des 18. Jahrhunderts noch deutlich weicher ist, wird wahrscheinlich ausgehend von Großbritannien und dem dortigen industriellen Vorschub der Metallindustrie die Qualität des Stahls immer besser, bis dann im späteren 19. Jahrhundert Metallfedern in den unterschiedlichsten Höhen und Stärken produziert werden können.

Die klare Linienführung des Polsters wird im Vergleich zur Zeit des Empire immer undefinierter, wohl durch eine Wiederbelebung der runden Formen des Rokoko und Barock. Dafür werden die Bezugsarbeiten immer raffinierter. Rückenlehnen werden vermehrt in Rautenheftungen gearbeitet, die in den Armlehnen weitergeführt werden und ineinander verschwimmen. Um die Heftungen werden teilweise Spiegel gefertigt, teils mit separaten kleinen Heftungen, glatt, oder auch in exakte Falten gelegt. Möbelschnüre umspielen die Rundungen der Arm- und Rückenlehne, verdecken Handnähte oder werden als optische Trennlinien in Vertiefungen eingenäht.

Es ist eine Zeit, in der die Arbeit der Möbelbauenden immer weiter in den Hintergrund rückt, weil das gesamte Möbel mit Stoff überzogen ist – manche nennen es die Hochzeit der Tapezierer*innen. Holzoberflächen sind immer weniger präsent, dafür prächtige Stoffe. Mittlerweile ist es unmöglich, die Rücken- oder Armlehne jeweils gesondert zu betrachten, da die Elemente ineinander übergehen.

Dieser Trend konnte sich halten, bis Designer des Art déco wie Jacques-Emile Ruhlmann wieder Arm- und Rückenlehnen als definierte Bauteile des Möbels in Erscheinung treten ließen. Mit dem ausgehenden 19. Jahrhundert entwickelte sich eine neue Art von Möbel. Dies waren schwere, große, komplett bepolsterte und oft mit Leder bezogene Sessel und Sofas, die sich durch die Verarbeitung von Metallfedern in allen Bauteilen auszeichneten. Spätestens hier kann man Möbel nicht mehr in Bauteile unterteilen und diese losgelöst voneinander betrachten. Eine ganzheitliche Betrachtung ist hier unumgänglich.

As always with upholstery, the formal language of the frame must be reflected in that of the furniture. It can be assumed that the development of the curvature was preceded by various stages of development. It reached its perfection in the Empire period with the barrel-shape (figs. 300/301).

The technical requirements for upholsterers are high. The armrest is made from different individual pieces that have to be worked together precisely. A mistake made during stitching cannot be corrected. With the end of the Empire period, the era of exact lines slowly also came to an end. Despite a few Empire echoes, the art of furniture saw Historicism slowly shift into the centre of attention. Furniture became even more round and, in the end, was entirely covered in fabric. While during the Empire the individual elements of the furniture could be contemplated and looked at, now the transition from back- to armrest became increasingly fluid. Metal springs, which until then had only been used for the seat, were now being used in the back for the first time. Definitive proof of a sprung backrest can be found in the chair by the furniture artist August Stühler from around 1830 (Bothe/Rietz 2019, p. 74).

Over the course of the nineteenth century, the metal spring made its way into upholstery, and of course also into backrests. This was probably mainly due to the ever-improving quality of spring steel. While spring steel was still much softer during the eighteenth century, the quality of the steel improved, probably due to the industrial advances of the metal industry in Great Britain, to an extent that in the late nineteenth century metal springs could be produced in the most varied heights and thicknesses.

The clear lines of upholstery became increasingly less defined compared to the Empire period, presumably also due to a revival of the rounded shapes of the Rococo and Baroque styles. In contrast, the fabric coverings became progressively more refined. Diamond-shaped deep buttoning was increasingly found on backrests which is continued onto the armrests and blurs into one another. Mirror discs were sometimes made around the stitching, sometimes with separate small stitches, smooth, or laid in precise folds. Cords accentuated the curvature of arm- and backrest, covered hand-sewn seams and were stitched into recesses as visual dividing lines.

It is a period in which the craft of the furniture maker slides into the background, since the entire object is covered in fabric – some refer to it as the heyday of the *tapissiers*. Wooden surfaces become less present while splendid fabrics do. It became impossible to consider back- and armrests separately since these elements merged into one another.

This trend remained fashionable until Art Deco designers such as Jacques-Emile Ruhlmann resurfaced armrests and backrests as defined elements of the furniture once more. During the late nineteenth century, a new kind of furniture emerged. These were heavy, large, fully upholstered armchairs and sofas, often covered in leather, which were defined by the use of metal springs in all elements. From this point onwards, it is no longer possible to divide furniture into components and consider them separately from each other. A holistic consideration is unavoidable here.

302
Lehnendetail, Armlehnsessel mit Capitonné-Heftung, Karl Friedrich Schinkel (Entwurf), um 1830 (LÖFFLER COLLECTION, Reichenschwand)

302
Detail of a backrest, armchair with deep-buttoning, Karl Friedrich Schinkel (design), around 1830 (LÖFFLER COLLECTION, Reichenschwand)

303
Lederkissen mit Feder-/ Daunenfüllung, Frankreich, 1805–1810
(Privatbesitz)

303
Leather cushion with feather/down stuffing, France, 1805–1810
(private collection)

304/305
Carreau Piqué Kissen (Maximilian Busch RiH, 2021)

304/305
Carreau piqué cushion (Maximilian Busch RiH, 2021)

Kissen

Maximilian Busch

Die Geschichte des Kissens ist eine noch recht unerforschte. Kissen als Zeitzeugen des Bedürfnisses nach Bequemlichkeit sind in ihrer Zahl sehr gering. Hier zeigt sich ein generelles Problem – dass Materialien der Polsterer sehr vergänglich sind. Wo Steinmetze auf teilweise jahrtausendealte Zeugnisse ihrer Kunst blicken können, haben Polsterer es schwerer, historische Originale zu finden. Das Material, sprich Textilien und Füllmaterialien, ist stark von Alterung und auch Schädlingen bedroht. Somit bleibt uns also, wenn es um Objekte vor der Renaissance geht, nichts weiter übrig, als Zeichnungen, wenn vorhanden, historische Rechnungen, Wandmalereien oder ähnliche Quellen zu studieren, um Schlüsse daraus ziehen zu können.

Jedoch sind hier gute Quellen vorhanden. So lassen sich zum Beispiel in zahlreichen ägyptischen Wandmalereien Kissen nachweisen. Teilweise scheint es, dass diese Kissen exakt der Form des Sitzmöbels entsprechen. Jedoch dürften die Künstler hier ihre eigene Interpretation des Gesehenen festgehalten haben. Es ist doch eher schwer vorstellbar, dass Handwerker*innen des alten Ägypten Wissen um Techniken hatten, die bei uns in der Exaktheit der Ausarbeitung erst im französischen Empire des beginnenden 19. Jahrhunderts praktiziert wurden. Fest steht jedoch, dass es Kissen gab. Deren Füllung dürfte ein Spiegel der heimischen Vegetation sein, ebenso sind Federn und Tierhaare denkbar. Ob damals auch Matratzen genutzt wurden, bleibt Spekulation. In ägyptischen Grabkammern fanden sich zwar mit Geflecht bespannte Liegen, ob darauf aber jemals Matratzen lagen, lässt sich nicht mehr klären.

Das Auftreten von Sitzkissen zieht sich durch die Geschichte. Sie sind auf antiken griechischen Vasen, römischen Wandmalereien und später im Mittelalter auf sakralen Zeichnungen in Büchern auf Pergament zu sehen.

Die Füllung der Kissen dürfte ebenso pflanzlicher oder tierischer Herkunft gewesen sein. Federn haben zwar einen hohen Isolationswert und sind im Ansitz weich, müssen jedoch nach jeder Nutzung aufgeschüttelt werden. Die Inlays waren bis in 19. Jahrhundert hinein mutmaßlich weitestgehend aus Leder, wegen deren Weichheit vorrangig wohl aus Ziegen- oder Schafsleder (s. Abb. 303). Die ersten textilen Inlays mit Kammerunterteilung lassen sich erst im 19. Jahrhundert nachweisen. Pflanzliche und vorranging tierische Füllungen waren für Sitz- und Rückenlehnkissen eher gängig. Diese Art Kissen bedürfen jedoch einer weiteren Behandlung vor dem Bezug. Sie müssen abgeheftet werden. Wann Kissen das erste Mal abgeheftet wurden, lässt sich aber nicht klären. Allerdings findet sich ein abgeheftetes Kissen auf einem Stuhl Queen Marys von ca. 1550 in der Winchester Cathedral, das vermutlich die ursprüngliche Polsterung darstellt. Dieses „Abheften" erfüllt einen einfachen Zweck. Es verhindert eine ungewollte Materialverschiebung. Es ist denkbar, dass dies auch schon bei antiken Vorgängern praktiziert wurde.

Durch das enge Abheften von Kissen, lassen sich auch dauerhafte Formen erarbeiten. Wohl ab dem Rokoko entwickelte sich eine für die damaligen Tapezierer*innen innovative Technik, die es ihnen erlaubte, Kissen zu fertigen, die nicht nur permanent formstabil waren, sondern gleichzeitig auch der Formensprache des jeweiligen Möbels

Cushions

Maximilian Busch

The history of cushions is still very much unexplored. Contemporary witnesses to the desire for comfort, cushions are very few in number. This is due to a general problem: upholsterer's materials are highly perishable. Whereas stonemasons can look back on in some cases thousands of years of testimonies to their art, upholsterers have difficulties in finding historical originals. The materials, textiles and stuffing, are endangered by ageing and pests. In this way, when we consider objects from before the Renaissance period, we have no other option than to study drawings, if available, historical invoices, frescoes and similar sources. Nonetheless, good sources are available. For example, there are many Egyptian murals that depict cushions. It seems, in some instances, that these cushions exactly fitted the form of the seating furniture. However, the artists probably captured their own interpretation of what they saw. It seems little likely that craftsmen from Ancient Egypt knew about techniques that were not executed with such exactitude until the French Empire style of the early nineteenth century. What is clear, however, is that cushions existed. Their stuffing was most likely a reflection of local vegetation, presumably also feathers and animal hair. Whether mattresses were being used at the time remains subject of speculation. Although daybeds covered with wickerwork have been found in Egyptian burial chambers, it cannot be clarified whether mattresses were placed on them.

The appearance of seat cushions runs throughout history. They can be seen on ancient Greek vases, Roman wall paintings and later in the Middle Ages on sacred drawings on parchment in books.

The stuffing of the pillows is equally likely to have been of plant or animal origin. Although feathers are valued for their high insulation and are soft when sat upon, they have to be fluffed up after each use. Until the nineteenth century, the inlays were presumably made of leather, mainly goatskin or sheepskin because of its softness (fig. 303). The first textile inlays that were subdivided into chambers cannot be traced until the nineteenth century. Vegetal and primarily animal hair fibre stuffings were more common for seat and back cushions. However, these types of cushions require further treatment before being covered. Bridle ties have to be sewn in. It is not possible to determine when this first happened. However, there is a cushion with bridle ties on a Queen Mary chair from around 1550 in Winchester Cathedral, which probably constitutes the original upholstery. Bridle ties serve a simple purpose. They prevent the unwanted shifting of material. It is conceivable that this was also practised on antique precursors. By using narrow bridling, durable cushion forms can be created. Probably from the Rococo period on, a, for the *tapissiers* of the time, innovative technique developed which made it possible to produce cushions that not only kept their shape but followed the formal language of each piece of furniture. In the depot of the Stiftung Preußische Schlösser und Gärten

306/307
Schichtmodell eines Carreau Piqué-Kissens aus dem Klassizismus (Maximilian Busch RiH, 2021)

306/307
Layer model of a carreau piqué cushion from the Classicism period (Maximilian Busch RiH, 2021)

entsprachen. Im Depot der Stiftung Preußische Schlösser und Gärten finden sich beispielsweise zu Tafelstühlen des Rokoko gehörige Kissen in ebendieser Ausführung. In der Fachsprache nennt sich diese Art Carreau Piqué. Ein Carreau Piqué (s. Abb. 304/305) ist durch seine spezielle Verarbeitung extrem fest und über viele Jahre formstabil. Während frühe Carreaus noch, ganz der Formensprache des Rokoko entsprechend, eher rund und flach waren, wurden die klassizistischen Verwandten immer geradliniger und zum Teil auch höher. Anzutreffen ist diese Art der Polsterauflage aber eigentlich nur bei höfischen oder aus gutsituierten Kontexten stammenden Möbeln.

Die Fertigung eines Carreau ist sehr zeitaufwendig und wird damit schon immer kostspielig gewesen sein. Dabei ist die Füllung für die Kosten, aber natürlich auch für das spätere Aussehen, mitverantwortlich. Ein Carreau mit einer Rosshaarfüllung lässt sich immer exakter ausarbeiten als eines mit rein pflanzlichen Materialien. Gleichzeitig war Rosshaar für Polsterungen aber schon immer ein aufwendiger zu produzierender Rohstoff als eine „gemähte Wiesenfüllung": Stroh, Moos oder was sonst noch an regional auffindbaren pflanzlichen Rohstoffen für Polsterungen zur Verfügung stand. Zur Perfektion gelangte das Carreau Piqué dann im französischen Empire mit Bodenhöhen von zwölf und mehr Zentimetern (s. Abb. 306/307). Das Fertigen eines solchen Kissens ist nicht nur zeitintensiv, sondern erfordert auch viel Wissen um Materialien und deren Wechselwirkungen. Jedes Kissen, selbst bei einem Ensemble, ist eine Einzelanfertigung, da in Zeiten ohne maschinelle Unterstützung natürlich auch jedes Stuhlgestell im Detail anders war. Verdrängt hat das Carreau seinen Verwandten, das mit Federn gefüllte Kissen, jedoch nie. Vielmehr geht es hier um unterschiedliche Möbeltypen mit unterschiedlichen Anforderungen und Ansprüchen. Ein bauschiges Daunenkissen (s. Abb. 303) hat einen höheren Komfort als feste Carreaus und eben deshalb auch andere Anwendungsbereiche, weshalb sehr wahrscheinlich in einem zum bequemen Verweilen gefertigten Sessel auch eher ein Kissen mit Daunen und kein Carreau zu finden war.

Gleichzeitig mit dem Carreau zeigte sich noch ein weiterer Kissentyp in Möbeln: der wie eine Matratze gearbeitete. Dieser wird, ebenso wie das Carreau, flächig abgeheftet und hat ebenso eine Kantenausbildung. Jedoch bei weitem nicht in dem Maße wie das Carreau, sondern eben wie die einer Matratze. Auch ist die Füllung hier weniger stramm. Man könnte dies sozusagen als Zwischenform zwischen Daunenkissen und Carreau betrachten. Markant sind dort die sichtbaren Abheftpunkte auf der Kissenfläche, die mit sogenannten Abheftpuscheln verziert werden. Frühe Beispiele hierfür lassen sich etwa in der Villa Hamilton in Wörlitz finden.

we can find Rococo dining chairs with cushions made in precisely this way. In professional jargon this type is called a *carreau piqué* cushion. A *carreau piqué* (figs. 304/305) is extremely firm due to its fabrication and retains its shape over many years. While early *carreaux* in the formal language of the Rococo era were rather round and flat, their Classicist relatives became ever more linear and at times higher. This kind of upholstery, however, can only be found on furniture from courtly or well-off contexts.

The fabrication of these *carreau* is very time-consuming and must therefore always have been accordingly expensive. The stuffing plays a role not only in the costs but also, of course, in the later appearance. A *carreau* with horsehair fibre stuffing can be shaped more precisely than one made from vegetal material. At the same time, horsehair has always been much more labour-intensive in its production than 'mown meadow filling': straw, moss or whatever else was available for upholstery in terms of regional vegetal raw materials. The *carreau piqué* had its heyday during the French Empire style with feather edges of up to twelve centimetres or more (figs. 306/307). The production of such a cushion is not only time-consuming but also requires a lot of knowledge about materials and their reciprocal effects. Each cushion, even in a set, is a unique piece, since in an era without machine support, each chair frame differed in its detail. The *carreau*, however, never managed to replaced its relative, the down cushion. Rather, different types of furniture had different requirements and demands. A bulgy down cushion (fig. 303) is more comfortable than a firm *carreau* and therefore can be used in different contexts. For this reason, an armchair made for relaxation would have been more likely fitted with a down pillow than a *carreau*.

At the same time as the *carreau*, another type of cushion appeared on furniture: the mattress-like cushion. Just like the *carreau*, this cushion is stitched and bridled all-over and also has a formed edge, however not nearly to the same extent as the *carreau* but rather like that of a mattress. The filling is also less firm. One could regard this as an intermediate form between a down cushion and a *carreau*. What is striking here is the visible bridling points on the cushion's surface, which are finished with shallow buttoning. Early examples of this can be found, for example, in the Villa Hamilton in Wörlitz.

Glossar: Fachbegriffe, Materialien, Arbeitstechniken

Dieser Abschnitt ist alphabetisch geordnet. Die Auswahl der Begriffe folgt dem Inhalt dieses Buches und bezieht sich auf die Exponate der Ausstellung *BESESSEN. Die geheime Kunst des Polsterns*. Eine fachliche Zuarbeit erfolgte durch Stefan Oswald, Rheinhardt Roßberg und Max Busch. Grundlage der textilen Fachbegriffe ist das Vokabular des Fachverbandes CIETA (Online-Wörterbuch des Centre International d'Etude des Textiles Anciens: Vocabulaire – Le vocabulaire du CIETA (17.06.2022), für Posamente zudem: Glossar, in: Evers 2014.).

Abschlagen bezeichnet den Vorgang, bei dem das vorhandene Polstermaterial eines Stuhls gelöst wird, bevor das Gestell gereinigt und die neue Polsterung aufgebaut wird.

Armchair (engl.) Armlehnstuhl, Sessel, Fauteuil (franz.).

Balletten sind Schmuckelemente der Posamente: Streifen, meist aus Pergament manchmal auch aus Papier oder Metall, werden mit Seiden- oder Metallfäden umsponnen und zu Zierformen, meist Blüten gebogen.

Bergère (frz.) ist ein niedriger Fauteuil mit größerer Sitztiefe und kompletter Auspolsterung der Rücken- und Seitenlehnen (s. Abb. 289).

Bergère en confessionnal (frz.) leitet sich vom Beichtstuhl ab, umschließt die Sitzenden und besitzt ein loses Sitzkissen. Ein entsprechendes Exponat findet sich im Aktionsbereich der Ausstellung (s. Abb. 229/230).

Bezugsstoffe sind nach heutigen Kriterien polstergeeignete Textilien, die scheuerbeständig und lichtecht sein sollten. Auf historische Bezugsstoffe lassen sich diese Maßstäbe nicht anwenden. Für einen Überblick über 500 Jahre Bezugsstoffe für Polstermöbel siehe in diesem Buch S. 240–269.

Borne (frz.) nennt sich ein kreisförmiges Polstermöbel, dessen mittig angebrachte Rückenlehne die Form eines Kegelstumpfs besitzt, auf dem üblicherweise Pflanzen, Statuen oder Lampen positioniert wurden. Man könnte hier auch von einem runden Sofa sprechen, das für den Mittelpunkt eines Salons konzipiert war.

Boudeuse (frz.) bezeichnet ein üppig gepolstertes Sitzmöbel, das aus zwei voneinander abgewandten Sitzen besteht, die eine gemeinsame Rückenlehne haben. Wegen der wenig kommunikativen Ausrichtung der beiden Sitze bürgerte sich in den 1870er Jahren auch der Name *Schmollstuhl* ein.

Bourrelet: Dem Französischen entlehnt, bezeichnet das Bourrelet eine Kantenwulst, die mit Polstermaterialien gefüllt wird. Sie bildet den Rahmen für eine Mulde unter der Sitzfläche, in die Materialien (vgl. Füllmaterialien) eingearbeitet werden. Im Barock wurde das Bourrelet als Wulst an der Vorderkante ohne Garnierung ausgebildet, später dann umlaufend und mit ein bis zwei Stichen benäht, um die Kante zu verfestigen.

Canapé (frz.) heißt ein breiter Rückensessel, auf dem mindestens zwei Personen bequem Platz nehmen können, weshalb es in der Literatur zuweilen auch als *Plaudersofa* bezeichnet wird.

Cantille: sehr feine, aus Draht gedrehte Spirale.

Carreau und **Carreau Piqué** (frz.) bezeichnet Kissen, die in Sessel eingelegt werden (vgl. dazu den Text zu Kissen von Maximilian Busch, S. 300–303).

Glossary: Technical terms, materials, techniques

This section is ordered alphabetically and is supplemented by texts on, among other things, armrest and backrest upholstery and cushioning. The selection of terms follows the content of this book and relates to the exhibits in the exhibition *DEEP-SEATED. The Secret Art of Upholstery*. Technical assistance was provided by Stefan Oswald, Reinhardt Roßberg and Max Busch. The technical textile terms are based on the vocabulary of the professional association CIETA (online dictionary of the Centre International d'Etude des Textiles Anciens: Vocabulaire – Le vocabulaire du CIETA (17 June 2022); for passementerie, see also the Glossary in Evers 2014.).

Armchair, also *fauteuil* (French) or *Sessel* (German), a chair with arms.

Ballets belong to the group of passementerie: strips, mostly from parchment, at times paper or metal, which are covered with silk or metal threads and bent into decorative shapes, often flower blossoms.

Bergère (French), a low armchair with a wider seat, fully upholstered back- and armrests (fig. 228/229).

Bergère en confessionnal (French) refers to a confessional, it encloses the sitter and has a loose seat cushion. A corresponding exhibit can be found in the activity area of the exhibition (fig. 228/229).

Borne (French) is a circular piece of upholstered furniture with a central backrest in the shape of a truncated cone on which usually plants, statues or lamps were placed. One could also refer to it as a round sofa, intended for the centre of a salon.

Boudeuse (French) is a voluptuously upholstered piece of furniture, made from two seats facing away from each other with a single backrest. Because of the non-communicative direction of the seats, it was referred to as a *Schmollstuhl* (sulking chair) in German during the 1870s.

Bourrelet (French), a roll edge filled with padding. It creates a depression below the seat into which materials (see Stuffings) can be placed. During the Baroque period the *bourrelet* was used on the front edge without stitching; later it was stitched all the way round using one or two rows of blind stitching in order to firm the edge. The term is not common in English.

Bridling is a large running stitch which penetrates and determines the depth of stuffing, used to hold down and stabilise (scrim) coverings. Another expression is sewing bridle ties.

Calico is a fabric, often white cotton, used to cover the second stuffing before the cover fabric.

Canapé (French) is the name of a wide-back chair on which at least two people can sit comfortably, which is why it is sometimes referred to in (German) literature as a *Plaudersofa* (chatting sofa).

Cantille is an extremely fine spiral made of wire.

Canvas serves as the preferred base layer for lashing. Thus, springs are usually sewn to this tear-resistant hessian. Sturdy, closely woven and sometimes double-

309
Holzkiste mit Werkzeug für Polsterarbeiten

309
Wooden box with tools for upholstery

Chamber Horse nennt man ein mechanisches Sitzgerät mit Federn und Polsterung zur Imitation des Reitens in Innenräumen. Siehe Beitrag auf S. 42-45.

Corelle: Schmuckelement am Übergang zwischen Schnur und Quastenkörper oder Quastenkopf und Fransen.

Crépines sind aus gebogenen und/oder geflochtenen Gimpen gebildete Zierborten (Posamente).

Damast ist eine Gewebeart, vgl. Gewebe (-bindungen).

Damas cafard (frz.) täuscht den echten aus Seidenfäden bestehenden und glänzenden Damast vor, wird aber aus Kostengründen durch Verarbeitung von Baum- und Schafwolle sowie Leinengarn hergestellt.

Duchesse bezeichnet im Französischen eine Herzogin, beschreibt aber auch ein textiles Gewebe mit hoher Fadendichte und Glanzwirkung. Im Sitzmöbelbereich bezeichnet die *duchesse* eine spezielle Art langer Liege.

Durchnähen bedeutet, dass ein Polster in gleichmäßigen Abständen durch Abwärtsziehen der Nadel mit einem gut gewachsten Garnierfaden durchstoßen wird, um die Abdeckung mit den Federn zu verbinden und gleichzeitig zu fixieren. Damit wird verhindert, dass bei der Benutzung des Polsters das aufgebrachte Material seitlich wegdriftet.

Faden: Der Faden ist ein fortlaufendes, durch Spinnen, Verdrehen oder andere Verfahren aus unterschiedlichen Rohstoffen gewonnenes Material. Beim Polstern unterscheiden sich Fäden gemäß ihrem Einsatz und fungieren als dicke, meist dreifach gedrehte, Schnürfäden zum Schnüren von Metallfedern im Sitz sowie als zweifach gedrehte auch in Rücken- und Armlehnpolsterungen. Der Aufnähfaden ist hingegen mitteldick, meist zweifach gedreht und dient u. a. zur Fixierung von Federn. Der Garnierfaden wird zum Garnieren der Fasson und der Handnähfaden für das Fertigen von Handnähten eingesetzt. Sie alle bestehen aus Hanf- oder Leinenfasern, in der modernen Polsterei auch aus Polyester oder Baumwolle.

Fasson: Der Begriff ist dem Französischen entlehnt und heißt übersetzt: richtige, übliche Form, Machart, Art und Weise. Fassonieren bedeutet also, die Polsterauflagen und das verwendete Material in die der Funktion entsprechende Form zu bringen. Die Fasson-Arbeit am Polster bezeichnet das Auflegen des zunächst losen, durch Einlasieren verdichteten Materials, dann dessen Formung und Stabilisierung zum Zwecke der nachhaltigen Sicherung der Form.
Nachdem das die Federschnürung abdeckende Federleinen darauf befestigt wurde, wird dieses am stabilisierenden Kantendraht (oder an der Kantenschnur) angenäht. Anschließend erfolgt das Einziehen der Lasierstiche in die Federleinwand und das Einschlagen der Nägel zum Einhängen der Fassonleinwand. Daraufhin wird das Polstermaterial, Rosshaar oder Palmfaser, in die Lasierfäden eingedreht oder eingeschoben und gut verzupft. Dabei ist darauf zu achten, dass die Kante beim Einarbeiten gut und sorgfältig gefüllt wird, damit kein Nachfüllen erforderlich wird. Beim Aufbringen des Füllmaterials beginnt man in der Mitte, um es dann zum Rand hin zu verteilen. Dann folgt der Vorgang des Garnierens, bei dem aus dem breiten Sortiment der verschiedenen Nadeltypen des Polsterhandwerks die dem jeweiligen Polster angemessene ausgewählt wird, um es damit dann in Form zu vernähen.

Federhochpolster bestehen aus einem Aufbau mit hohen Federn, die sieben bis zehn Windungen bzw. Gänge aufweisen. Dazu wird an der Schnürung der Federn ein der Form des vorgesehenen Sitzes angepasster Kantendraht angebunden. Über dem aufgelegten Federleinen wird dann die Fasson aufgebaut und am Kantendraht angenäht.

woven linen is used for this. In preindustrial times, hemp and later jute threads were used, sometimes also paper and in GDR times white synthetic fibres. In addition to the hessian or burlap is the more pliable scrim and the medium-dense woven linen (for covering the parts of furniture to be upholstered, for example on the rear of the backrest) used to cover the stuffing.

Carreau and **carreau piqué** (French) are cushions placed on armchairs (see the text on cushions by Maximilian Busch, pp. 300–303).

Chamber horse is the name given to an indoor mechanical seating device with springs and padding to imitate riding. Cordula Fink has contributed a detailed article on its cultural and historical significance (pp. 42–45).

Core thread is the inside thread around which a second thread is spun.

Corelle describes decorative elements placed on the transition between a cord and a tassel body, or the tassel head and the fringes.

Crépines are trimmings made from scalloped and braided gimps (passementerie).

Damask is a type of fabric, see Woven textiles.

Damas cafard (French) is an imitation of the genuine, shiny damask made of silk threads, but to reduce costs it is made by processing cotton, sheep's wool and linen yarn.

Duchesse (French), French for 'duchess', is a textile with a high thread count and shiny appearance. In seating furniture *duchesse* describes a specific type of long lounger.

Fasson is the first padding. The German word *Fasson* is borrowed from French and translates as the 'correct', 'usual form', 'manner of making', or 'way'. The verb *fassonieren* therefore means forming the overlay and the stuffing material so that it corresponds to the desired function. Creating a *Fasson* on the upholstery means laying on the material, which is initially loose and compacted by bridling, then tufting it for the purpose of securing the shape long term.
After the hessian covering of the springs has been attached, it is sewn to the stabilising edge wire (or edge cord). Then the bridle ties are stitched to the hessian, and the nails are hammered in to attach the scrim. Then the stuffing, horsehair or palm fibre is twisted or pushed under the bridle ties and plucked well. Care must be taken to fill the edge well when working it in, so that no refilling is necessary. The application of the stuffing starts in the centre and then spreads it towards the edges. This is followed by the process of stitching, where the appropriate needle for the particular upholstery is selected from the wide range of different types and then sewn into shape.

Fixed seat is an upholstered seat which cannot be taken out of the frame.

Flat padding usually forgoes the height of a sprung construction. This is exemplified by the model illustrated (figs. 310/311), which Reinhardt Roßberg prepared using original materials from the 1920s. It is a leather-covered flat cushion on an insert frame, where the 2 x 2 jute webbing is covered with jute canvas. On top of this is the padding made of wood wool with a fine tow cover.

310/311
Flachpolster auf Einlegerahmen, Anfang 1920er Jahre
(Privatbesitz)

310/311
Flat padding on a drop-in seat frame, early 1920s
(private collection)

Federkissen bestehen aus vorfabrizierten Zylinder-, Bonnell- und Taschenfederkernen, die in eine Hülle aus Spannleinen oder Vliesstoff eingenäht werden.

Federspindel ist die Bezeichnung für ein Werkzeug, mit dem auf einer entsprechend ausgeformten Metallform Drähte mittels händischer Drehung einer Kurbel so gedreht wurden, dass Taillenfedern mit unterschiedlicher Höhe hergestellt werden konnten.

Festpolster nennt man ein Polster, das nicht aus dem Rahmen herausgenommen werden kann.

Flachfedern bestehen *aus einem schlingen- oder zickzackförmig gebogenen Stahldraht, der im ruhenden Zustand fast einen geschlossenen Kreis bildet.* Das erklärt Walter Naumann in seinem Fachbuch für Tapezierer und führt weiter aus, dass sie bei der Verarbeitung auseinandergezogen werden, bevor die Enden in vorher auf den Rahmen befestigte Scharniere eingehängt werden, *die dann mit Gurtnägeln geschlossen werden* (Naumann 1958, S. 91).

Flachpolster verzichten meist auf den hohen Aufbau einer Federkonstruktion. Das zeigt exemplarisch das abgebildete Anschauungsmodell (s. Abb. 310/311), das Reinhard Roßberg mit Originalmaterialien der 1920er Jahre aufbereitet hat. Dabei handelt es sich um ein lederbezogenes Flachpolster auf Einlegerahmen, bei dem die 2 x 2-Jutegurtbespannung mit einem Jutefederleinen bedeckt wird. Darüber liegt eine Polsterung aus Holzwolle mit Feinwerg-Abdeckung. Der Bezug ist ein handgewichstes, braunes Polsterleder. Auch wenn es sich hierbei um einen typischen Flachpolstereinlegesitz handelt, zeigt dieses Beispiel eine Besonderheit, da die Polsterung als Folge der Materialknappheit im Ersten Weltkrieg in Holzwolle (anstelle von Werg, Afrik oder Rosshaar) ausgeführt wurde.

Flor wird aus senkrecht, dicht von einem Grundgewebe abstehenden Fäden gebildet. Bei Samtgeweben werden diese aus geschnittenen oder geschlossenen Schlingen gebildet.

Fransen: *Wenn am Ende eines Stoffes die diesem Ende parallelen Fäden ausgezogen werden, so bilden die quer laufenden, stehen bleibenden Fäden die denkbar einfachste Franse. Werden die Fäden derselben, … büschelweise unter sich verknüpft und verknotet, so entsteht die gewöhnliche Franse* (Meyer 1889, S. 210). Fransen an Quasten und Fransenborten sind wichtige Zierelemente an Möbeln und in der Raumausstattung. Sie werden oft aus kostbaren Materialien wie Seiden- und Goldfäden und mit kunstvollen Gehängen aus Balletten gebildet. Die Drellier- bzw. Stengelfranse besteht aus gedrehten Fäden oder Kordeln.

Füllmaterialien bilden neben den Sprungfedern das Volumen des Polsters. Sie helfen, Unebenheiten auszugleichen, geben dem Polster sein Volumen und Komfort. Die Vielfalt geeigneter Materialien ist groß. In den Kolonialzeiten im 18. und 19. Jahrhundert hatte sich das Angebot noch einmal erweitert, sodass zu den in Europa verwendeten Materialien weitere hinzukamen. Im Folgenden werden die meistverwendeten Füllmaterialen aufgeführt:
– Afrik, auch Crin d'Afrique oder Palmfaser genannt, bezeichnet fächerförmige Blätter der in Marokko und Algerien wild wachsenden Zwergpalme. Diese werden zerfasert und in Stränge gedreht. Sie sind sehr biegsam und federnd und sind gelbgrün. Afrik soll als Schiffsballast und Kolonialware nach Europa gekommen sein. Mit der Verwendung ist wohl im letzten Viertel des 19. Jahrhunderts begonnen worden. Es setzte sich als billiges, aber recht haltbares Polstermaterial durch.
– Alpengras wurde vor allem im Süden Deutschlands verwendet und bestand aus abgemähten und getrockneten Wiesenhalmen, während in Küstenregionen Norddeutschland eher getrocknetes Seegras verwendet wurde.

The cover is a brown hand-rubbed antiqued leather. Even though this is a typical flat sprung drop-in seat, this example has a special feature, as the cushioning was made of wood wool (instead of tow, palm fibre or horsehair) as a result of the shortage of materials during the First World War.

Foam cushions are made in a sandwich construction from two foam pieces of complementary density and compression featuring a harder core and a soft surface. Sometimes latex foam is also used to cover the pillow's core. Due to the many possible combinations using different densities and compression firmness as well as the use of latex foam, very different cushioning effects can be achieved.

Fringe: *If at the end of a fabric the threads parallel to this end are pulled out, then the crosswise running threads that remain standing form the simplest fringe imaginable. If the same threads … are knotted together in bunches, the usual fringe is formed* (Meyer 1889, p. 210). Fringes on tassels and fringed borders are important decorative elements on furniture and in interior decoration. They are often made of precious materials such as silk and gold threads and with elaborate pendants of ballets. The buillon fringe consists of twisted threads or cords.

Gimp is a wrapped thread consists of a core thread around which further thread, ribbon, parchment or a metal strip is spun. A common element of eighteenth- and nineteenth-century trimmings used on upholstery; gimp here refers to a flat braid incorporating gimp thread.

High sprung pads are made from a construction of high springs comprising seven to ten coils. At the point where the springs are lashed, a wire in the shape of the seat is placed. The *Fasson* is then placed on top of the hessian and is attached to the edge wire.

Indiscret (figs. 230/231) is the name of a piece of seating furniture consisting of three or four armchairs arranged in a circle. It was designed for the Parisian salons at the end of the nineteenth century and was used for conversation; however, a discreet dialogue was not possible, as the third seat was usually occupied by another person listening in.

Lace is made from braided and interlaced yarns or from fabrics that are open-worked or embroidered/sewn by pulling through threads. According to the different techniques, a distinction is made between bobbin lace (crossed and braided threads) and needle lace with stretched, embroidered threads. The term may also refer to braids.

Lambrequins (French, *lambeau* = scrap) are pelmets or draperies on window and door openings. They were used as ornaments on bed canopies, throne canopies and furniture.

Lamella, see Metal threads.

Lashing (fig. 311) comprises two-ply or three-ply twine used to tie down the waisted springs. There is plain and star lashing, and, if the springs are very high, one can also add centre lashing. The lashing is made using the following knots: loop or sling, clove hitch knot or slip knot. Over several work steps, waisted springs (more rarely also conical springs) are fixed to the webbing with a strong twine, sewn to the webbing with several stitches and

312
Schichtmodell eines Kapok-Kissens (Privatbesitz)

312
Cutaway model of a kapok cushion (private collection)

- Baumwolle ist eine Samenfaser, die von strauchartigen Sumpfpflanzen stammt. Diese wachsen in feuchtwarmen Regionen bis zu einer Höhe von 1,70 Metern und kommen in z. B. Ägypten Nord- und Südamerika, Ostindien, Zentralasien und China vor. Schon in altägyptischer Zeit ist die Baumwolle eine begehrte Textilfaser, da es sich dabei um fast reine Zellulose handelt, die eine gute Spinnfähigkeit besitzt. Dafür werden die geöffneten Samenkapseln gepflückt und die flaumartigen Fasern davon abgetrennt. Im Polsterwesen werden diese Baumwollfasern (Linters) als Watte verarbeitet.
- Holzfasern wurden zu Beginn des 20. Jahrhunderts als preiswertes Material eingesetzt, wegen ihrer Kurzlebigkeit aber nicht geschätzt.
- Jute ist eine einjährige Pflanze in Strauchform, deren Stängel eine Länge von drei bis vier Metern erreichen kann. Jute wird vor allem in Indien, China und Nordafrika (Algerien) angebaut und bedarf eines feuchten subtropischen Klimas. Nachdem die geernteten Fasern geröstet wurden, werden sie von Hand ausgelöst und anschließend gesponnen. Als Naturfaser ist die Jute vollständig biologisch abbaubar, sie besitzt ein hohes Wasseraufnahmevermögen und eine hohe Dehnfestigkeit, was sie beim Polstern u. a. für die Verarbeitung in Gurten und Spannleinen empfiehlt.
- Kapok wird vom gleichnamigen Baum gewonnen, der in Java, Ceylon, Sumatra, Indien vorkommt, weshalb das Material im Wesentlichen auch von dort eingeführt wird. Der Kapokbaum besitzt schotenähnliche Fruchtkapseln, in denen die Samenkörner – jedes für sich – in seidenweichen Fasern eingebettet liegen. Der Vorzug dieses Materials ist seine Eigenschaft, so gut wie keine Feuchtigkeit aufzunehmen. Daher eignet es sich besonders auch für eine Verwendung in feuchten Räumen. Das Material wurde auch für die Anfertigung von Kissen eingesetzt, die in den 1930er Jahren bei Stahlrohrstühlen Verwendung fanden. Ein solches Kissen fertigte Bernd Lehmkuhl als Anschauungsmodell (s. Abb. 312) für unsere Ausstellung an. Es zeigt im Kern eine Gummikokosmatte, die mit Kapokfasern umpolstert ist. Die Kanten des mit Leinen bezogenen Kissens sind mit einem Vorderstich (ca. 2 cm Stichlänge) garniert, um die Form zu fixieren. Die Fläche ist in einem Raster von ca. 8 x 8 cm durchgeheftet, um ein Verrutschen des Kapokmaterials zu verhindern. Die Stiche wurden schließlich mit Baumwollfasern abgedeckt.
- Kokosfasern werden aus den Früchten der Kokospalme gewonnen. Dafür werden Kokosnüsse gespalten, in heißem Wasser eingeweicht, gequetscht und die Faser von der Schale getrennt. Kokosfasern sind äußerst haltbar und werden in der Polsterei als Pikiermaterial verwendet. Die veredelte und oftmals eingefärbte Kokosfaser nennt man Elancrin (besteht manchmal auch aus Palmfasern). Es wurde um 1920 eingeführt und dient in der Regel beim Pikieren als Rosshaarersatz.
- Moose sind in der Natur immergrüne, polsterbildende Pflanzen, die hauptsächlich an feuchten, schattigen Stellen den Boden, Baumstämme, Steine oder Ähnliches überziehen. Sie besitzen die Fähigkeit, große Mengen an Wasser zu speichern. Dass sie auch als Polsterfüllung eingesetzt wurden, zeigt folgendes Beispiel: Das abgebildete, mehrfach garnierte Moospolster (s. Abb. 305/306) stammt aus der Zeit um 1820, ist unrestauriert, im Originalzustand und zeigt das verwendete Füllmaterial in noch erkennbaren Ballen; das Fassonleinen ist grob handgewebt und dicht; einige handgeschmiedete Nägel befinden sich noch im Leinen. Es besitzt eine separat gearbeitete Vorderkante, die in den Sitz integriert ist; die Kanten sind zweimal mit einfachem Matratzenstich garniert. Auch zeigt der Befund noch Fragmente von Lasierfäden, die für das Pikieren vorgesehen sind.
- Rosshaar gilt als traditionell wichtigstes und zugleich edelstes Fasson- und Formmaterial, da es, aus dem Schweif oder der Mähne des Pferdes (zuweilen auch dem Schweif des Rindes) gewonnen, natürlich und zudem sehr elastisch ist. Das gekräuselte Rosshaar besitzt als Füllmaterial eine

then, using various techniques, joined with cords and attached to the chair rails.
- French lashing, also called right-angled lashing, is where the top of the spring is tied four times. So that the intermediate threads do not catch the knots of these spring rings, they must already be aligned at an angle of 45 degrees when the springs are sewn onto the webbing. This lashing is mainly used for seating surfaces that will have a slope, such as armchairs and sofa seats.
- German lashing, also called diagonal lashing, is where the top of the springs is tied eight times. The knots of the upper spring rings must be aligned at an angle of about 22.5 degrees. This type of lashing creates a firmer spring because there are more lashing threads attached to the upper spring. It is used for smooth seating surfaces such as chairs, armchairs with cushions on, stools, furniture for resting on and mattresses.

Macramé (Arabic *migramah*) is a knotting technique introduced to Europe from the Middle East in the Middle Ages which is also used to make passementerie. In the sixteenth and seventeenth centuries, very fine pieces were made from silk and metal threads (fig. 274).

Metal threads
- Lamella (silver/gold): narrow metal thread of flat or rolled metal wire.
- Leonic wire: substitute for gold or silver threads, for example silver- or gold-plated copper wire.
- Single: thread made from lamella wound around a core thread.

Moulded tassels is the result of a familiar techniques in which the head (= mould) of the tassel is wrapped in braided threads. In some variations this is done with a basketweave pattern (Paul Dornbrach, Posamentier-Kunstgewerbe 1894, pp. 55–56).

Passementerie, or trimmings, derived from the French word *passement*, refers to plaited, knotted or woven decorative elements such as braids, fringes, cords, tassels, lace and flounces. For an overview of historical trimmings using examples from the Grassi MAK Collection, see pp. 270–291 in this book.

Pattern repeat is the smallest unit of a repeating design on a textile.

Pickierung (German) is the second stuffing, a process in which the first layer of padding, in German *Fasson*, is covered with an additional layer of stuffing, such as horsehair, in order to cushion the seams, which can otherwise be felt. This in turn is covered with wadding and calico.

Pile is formed by dense threads which project upwards from a ground fabric. In the case of velvet, it is made from cut or closed loops.

Pouffe (French) is the name given to a softly upholstered stool which in the nineteenth century was fitted with fringes that reached down to the floor. On the *pouffe*, which was intended to be positioned in the centre of the room, the sitters would involuntarily adopt a crouching, changing posture, wrote Sigfried Giedion, who in this context also mentions the *fauteuil bébé* as a *pouffe* with the *rudiment of a backrest* (Giedion 1987, p. 413).

Reel is a device onto which metal wire is wound by hand in order to create a hourglass-shaped cone shaped or, also, waisted spring.

313/314
Mooskissen, um 1820 (Privatbesitz)

313/314
Moose cushion, around 1820 (private collection)

lange Lebensdauer. In seinem Lehrbuch zum Polstermöbel weist Adolf G. Schneck aber darauf hin, dass Rosshaar nie mit der Maschine in kurze Einzelteile zerrissen wird, sondern immer nur mit der Hand gezupft wird. Das strapazierfähige Rosshaar ist zudem beliebtes Material für Bezugsstoffe (vgl. Abb. 256–258, Text S. 260)
- Stroh wurde schon sehr früh als einfaches Füllmaterial genutzt, ebenso wie Werg, das bei der Produktion von Leinenstoffen anfällt und in verschiedenen Qualitäten erhältlich ist.

Garnierung bezeichnet die Technik, mit der die Polsterkanten benäht werden, um sie zu verfestigen und die gewünschte Form zu verwirklichen. Dafür bedient man sich verschiedener Nadeln, mit denen unterschiedliche Stichtechniken ausgeführt werden. Vorderstich, Hinterstich und der ab Mitte des 19. Jahrhunderts bevorzugt eingesetzte Leiterstich sind mögliche Nähtechniken, die geeignet sind, den Kanten die angestrebte Form dauerhaft zu geben.

Gewebe(-bindungen)
Die drei Grundbindearten für Kett- und Schussfäden von Geweben sind Leinwand-, Köper- und Atlasbindungen. Sie sind Basis bzw. Komponenten komplexer Gewebebindungen.
- Atlasbindung: Die Bindungspunkte von Atlasgeweben berühren sich nicht und werden zudem oft von flottierenden Kettfäden verdeckt. Die Gewebeoberfläche erscheint so sehr glatt und glänzend.
- Brokatell: aus der Gruppe der Lampasgewebe. Charakteristisch sind die reliefartig erhöhten Musterpartien, die durch die Kombination des atlasbindigen Seidengewebes mit einem Grundschuss aus Leinen entsteht.
- Broschiert ist ein Gewebe, bei dem der durch einen Schusseintrag gebildete Mustereffekt nicht über die ganze Webbreite läuft, sondern nur auf das Motiv beschränkt ist.
- Damast: Gewebe mit einem Kett- und Schusssystem, bei dem sich Hintergrund und Muster durch den Wechsel von Kett- und Schussbindung unterscheiden.
- Gros de Tours: Gewebe mit abgeleiteter Leinwandbindung, in der der Schuss aus je zwei Fäden gebildet wird.

Gewebe für Polsteraufbauten werden als Auflagen oder Bezüge (vgl. Kapitel 500 Jahre Bezugsstoffe, S. 240–269) genutzt und besitzen in ihrer Beschaffenheit größte Bedeutung für die Stabilität des Polsters. Häufig eingesetzte Gewebe sind:
- Jutegewebe, je nach Arbeitszweck als Fasson-, Spann- oder Federleinen, wird in unterschiedlichen Dichten und Gewichten aus den Jutefasern hergestellt, die an anderer Stelle auch lose als Füllmaterial Verwendung finden.
- Molton oder Kalmuk sind Leinwandbindungen in Köper oder Baumwolle, die beidseitig aufgeraut als Weißpolster, d. h. als Untergrund des Bezugs, genutzt werden, damit sich die Fasern der Pikierung aus Kokos oder Rosshaar nicht durch den Bezugsstoff hindurch abzeichnen.
- Nesseltuch oder auch Baumwollnessel in Leinwandbindung, der heute aus Baumwolle hergestellt wird, während in früherer Zeit Brennnesselfasern Verwendung fanden. Im Handel findet sich der Baumwollnessel üblicherweise als ungebleichter und ungefärbter Rohnessel.

Gimpe ist ein Garn, das aus einem Kernfaden (Seele) besteht, um den ein Faden, Bändchen, Pergament- oder Metallstreifen gesponnen ist. Häufiges Element von Posamenten/Möbelbesätzen des 18. und 19. Jahrhunderts sind aus diesem zusammengesetzten Garn gebildete Gimpenborten.

Gurtung: Gurte bilden den Grund bzw. die Basis des Polsteraufbaus. Sie werden mit dem Stuhlgerüst so verbunden, dass sie der Belastung durch den menschlichen Körper standhalten. Es wird zwischen Längs- und Quergurten unterschieden, was deren Positionierung über Kreuz entspricht. Damit sie vor der Befestigung ausreichend gespannt werden können, wird der Gurtspanner eingesetzt, der hilft, sie unter Spannung zu

Restaurator*in im Raumausstatterhandwerk, short RiH, is a protected designation that leads to the title of conservator in the trade after passing an examination following further specialist training. Training is provided in a total of nineteen trades, including interior decorating.

Rolled edge provides stability to the upholstery and shapes the front edge of, for example, a Baroque chair (fig. 17).

Schlaraffia upholstery (fig. 95) are loose cushions of increased stability that maintain a high level of flexibility. They are fitted with special spring inlays and are offered under the patented name Schlaraffia.

Springs give bounce to the upholstery. The first springs were still hand-turned, with the wire ends open. Subsequent models were then encased at the ends with sheet metal loops before today's spring emerged as a model with knotted wire ends. The advantage of the most commonly used waisted (double-coned) springs is their great elasticity, which allows them to be tied by lashing them at a certain height, tension and position so that they can only move down and up when loaded or unloaded and cannot move to the side. This type of upholstery is very time-consuming and therefore more expensive than the foam filling often used today, but it is considered an elementary technique of the interior decorator. Because of its great resistance to ageing, it stands for quality and sustainability.

Sprung cushions are made of a prefabricated core with cylindrical, double-cone or pocket springs, which are inserted into pockets of calico or fleece.

Stripping refers to the act of removing the old coverings, fillings and springing of a chair before the frame can be cleaned and reupholstered.

Stitching serves to additionally stabilise the upholstery surface and to graphically structure it, for example into regular diamond-shaped pattern repeats, diamonds with pipes, half-diamonds with pipes, squares and rectangles. Deep-buttoning (figs. 317/318) is especially well known. See also Tufting.

Stitching through means piercing padding at even intervals by pulling the needle downwards using a well-waxed thread to join the cover to the springs and fix it at the same time. This prevents the material from shifting when the upholstery is used. See also Tufting and Bridling.

Stuffing creates the padding's volume in addition to the springs. It helps to compensate for unevenness and gives the cushion its volume and comfort. The variety of suitable materials is large. In the colonial times of the eighteenth and nineteenth centuries, the range had expanded even further, so that more materials were added to those used in Europe. The most commonly used stuffing materials are listed below:
- Palm fibre, also Afrik or *crin d'afrique*: refers to the fan-shaped leaves of the dwarf palm tree that grows wild in Morocco and Algeria. These are frayed and twisted into strands. They are very flexible, springy and are yellow-green in colour. Palm fibre is said to have come to Europe as ship ballast and colonial goods. Its use probably began in the last quarter of the nineteenth century. It became accepted as a cheap but quite durable upholstery material.
- Quaking sedge: primarily used in southern Germany and made from mowed and dried meadow stalks, while

315
Blick unter einen Klubsessel, Hochpolster, ca. 1925 (Privatbesitz)

316
Blick unter einen Armlehnstuhl, Erich Dieckmann (Entwurf), ehemalige Bauhochschule Weimar (Ausführung), vor 1928 (LÖFFLER COLLECTION, Reichenschwand)

315
View underneath a club chair, high padding, ca. 1925 (private collection)

316
View underneath an armchair, Erich Dieckmann (design), former Bauhochschule Weimar (execution), before 1928 (LÖFFLER COLLECTION, Reichenschwand)

halten, während mit dem Gurthammer Nägel durch das Gewebe in die Stuhlzargen getrieben werden. Als Polstergrund dient der durch Überkreuzlegen entstandene Verband z. B. dem Setzen der Federn und dem weiteren Aufbau des Polsters. Dabei werden unterschieden:
- Die Weitgurtung, bei der die Gurte mit Abstand zueinander als erste Trägerschicht des Polsters auf oder unter die Zargen des Stuhls genagelt werden. Bei einer geschnürten Federkonstruktion stehen die Federn meist auf den Gurtkreuzen der von unten gegen die Zarge genagelten Gurten.
- Die Enggurtung, bei der die Gurte ohne Zwischenraum nebeneinander befestigt werden. Falls keine Federn eingesetzt werden, so wie im Barock, wird das Polstermaterial meistens direkt aufgebracht, wenn nicht zuvor ein dichtes Leinengewebe als Zwischenschicht aufgelegt wurde.

Heftungen dienen der zusätzlichen Stabilisierung der Polsterfläche und deren grafischer Gliederung etwa in regelmäßige und in Rapporten wiederholte Rauten, Rauten mit Pfeifen, halbe Rauten mit Pfeifen, Quadrate und Rechtecke. Berühmt ist die tief in das Polster eingreifende Capitonné-Heftung (s. Abb. 317/318).

Indiscret (s. Abb. 230/231) nennt sich ein Sitzmöbel, das aus drei oder vier im Kreis angeordneten Sesseln besteht. Es wurde im ausgehenden 19. Jahrhundert für die Pariser Salons konzipiert und diente dem Gespräch, das allerdings nicht im diskreten Zwiegespräch möglich war, da auf dem dritten Platz meist eine weitere Person als Zuhörer*in Platz nahm.

Kantenwulst: Sie gibt dem Polster Stabilität und der Vorderkante etwa eines Barockstuhls seine Form (s. Abb. 17).

Lambrequins (französ. lambeau = der Lappen) sind Querbehänge bzw. Verblendungen an Fenster- und Türöffnungen. Sie wurden als Verzierungen an Betthimmeln, Thronbaldachinen und Möbeln verwendet.

Lahn: siehe Metallfaden.

Leinwand dient als bevorzugte Abdeckschicht für die Schnürung. So werden Federn meist am reißfesten Federleinen festgenäht. Dafür wird stabiles, eng gewebtes und zuweilen auch doppelbödig gewebtes Leinen eingesetzt. Vorindustriell wurden Hanf-, später Jutefäden verwendet, teilweise auch Papier und zu DDR-Zeiten weiße Synthetikfasern. Neben dem Federleinen wird das geschmeidigere Fassonleinen, das mitteldicht gewebte Spannleinen (zum Abspannen von im fertig bezogenen Zustand zu verdeckenden Möbelteilen z. B. auf der Rückseite der Rückenlehne) und das Schechterleinen als Umhüllung der Fasson verwendet.

Makramee (vom arabischen migramah) ist eine im Mittelalter aus dem Nahen Osten nach Europa eingeführte Knüpftechnik, die auch zur Herstellung von Posamenten eingesetzt wird. Im 16. und 17. Jahrhundert entstanden sehr feine Arbeiten aus Seiden- und Metallfäden (Beispiel Abb. 274).

Metallfaden
- Lahn (Silber/Gold): flacher Metallfaden aus geschlagenem bzw. gewalztem Metalldraht
- Leonische Metallfäden: Ersatz für Gold- und Silberfäden, z. B. versilberte oder vergoldete Kupferdrähte
- Gespinst: Faden mit einem um einen Seelenfaden gesponnenen Metalllahn.

Musterrapport: kleinste Einheit der sich im Gewebe wiederholenden Musterzeichnung.

Pickierung gilt als Vorgang, bei dem die auf der Fasson liegende Polsterschicht zum Ausgleichen der sonst spürbaren Nähstiche mit feinen Polstermaterialien wie z. B. Rosshaar

in coastal regions of northern Germany dried seagrass was more commonly used.
- Cotton: a seed fibre that comes from shrub-like marsh plants. These grow in warm, humid regions up to a height of 1.7 metres and are found, for example, in Egypt, North and South America, the East Indies, Central Asia and China. Cotton has been a sought-after fibre since Ancient Egyptian times, as it is almost pure cellulose with good spinning properties. For this, the opened bolls are picked and the downy fibres are separated from them. In upholstery, these cotton fibres (linters) are processed as wadding.
- Wood fibres: used as a cheap material at the beginning of the twentieth century but were not appreciated because of their short life.
- Jute: an annual shrub whose stem can reach a length of three to four metres. Jute is mainly cultivated in India, China and North Africa (Algeria) and requires a humid subtropical climate. After the harvested fibres have been roasted, they are podded by hand and then spun. As a natural fibre, jute is completely biodegradable, has a high capacity for absorbing water and does not break when stretched, which is why it is recommended it for upholstery, among other things, in processing webbing strips and hessian.
- Kapok: obtained from the tree of the same name, which is found in Java, Ceylon, Sumatra and India, from where most of the material is also imported. The kapok tree has pod-like fruit capsules in which each of the seeds are embedded separately in silky-soft fibres. The advantage of this material is its ability to absorb almost no moisture. This makes it particularly suitable for use in damp rooms. The material was also used to make cushions for tubular steel chairs in the 1930s. Bernd Lehmkuhl made such a cushion as an illustrative model (fig. 312) for our exhibition. The core of the cushion is rubberised coconut fibre matting upholstered with kapok fibres. The edges of the linen-covered cushion were fastened with a blind stitch (approx. 2 cm in stitch length) to form the shape. The surface was bridled in a grid of approx. 8 x 8 cm to prevent the kapok material from slipping. Finally, the stitches were covered with cotton fibre.
- Coconut fibre, also coir: obtained from the fruit of the coconut palm. For this, coconuts are split, soaked in hot water, crushed and the fibre is then separated from the husk. Coconut fibre is extremely durable and used in upholstery as a material for the (second) stuffing. The refined and often dyed coconut fibre is called elancrin (sometimes consisting of palm fibre). It was introduced around 1920 and is usually used as a substitute for horsehair stuffing.
- Mosses: in nature these are evergreen, cushion-forming plants that mainly cover the ground, tree trunks, stones or similar in damp, shady places. They have the ability to store large amounts of water. That they were also used as upholstery filling is shown by the following example: the moss upholstery illustrated featuring multiple edge stitchings (figs. 306/307) dates from around 1820, is unrestored, in its original condition and shows the filling material used in recognisable bales; the hessian is coarsely hand-woven and dense; some hand-forged nails can still be seen in the linen. It has a separately worked front edge integrated in the seat, and the edges are blind stitched twice. The finding also shows fragments of threads intended for sewing.
- Horsehair: traditionally considered the most important and at the same time noblest material for shaping and filling, as it is obtained from the tail or mane of the horse (sometimes also from the tail of the cow), is natural and is also very elastic. The crimped horsehair has a long life as a filling material. In his *Textbuch zum*

317/318
Schichtmodell eines Hocker-Kissens (Privatbesitz)

317/318
Cutaway model of a stool cushion (private collection)

überdeckt wird, die wiederum eine Abdeckung aus Watte oder Molton erhält.

Posament bezeichnet, vom französischen Wort passement abgeleitet, geflochtene, geknüpfte oder gewebete Zierelemente wie Borten, Fransen, Kordeln, Litzen, Quasten, Spitzen und Volants. Zu einem Überblick über historischer Posamente an Beispielen aus dem Bestand des GRASSI Museums für Angewandte Kunst vgl. in diesem Buch S. 270–291.

Pouffe (frz.) wird ein weich gepolsterter Hocker genannt, der im 19. Jahrhundert mit Fransen versehen wurde, die bis zum Boden reichten. Auf dem für Positionen in der Raummitte vorgesehenen *pouffe* nehmen die Sitzenden unwillkürlich eine kauernde, wechselnde Haltung ein, schrieb Siegfried Giedion, der in diesem Zusammenhang auch das *fauteuil bébé* als *pouffe* mit dem *Rudiment einer Lehne* erwähnt (Giedion 1987, S. 413).

Quasten (oder Troddeln) bestehen aus einem Kopf (meist aus einer mit Fäden belegten Holzform) und Fransen. Beispiele finden sich schon bei den Assyrern, später in der Renaissance und im Barock und schließlich im 19. Jahrhundert, als sich Quasten an Polstermöbeln größter Beliebtheit erfreuten. So nahm Franz Sales Meyer entsprechende Muster (s. Abb. 315) in sein systematisch geordnetes *Handbuch der Ornamentik* auf, das 1889 im Verlag von E. A. Seemann in Leipzig erschienen ist. Darin heißt es: *Die Quaste oder Troddel bildet sich dadurch, dass aus einem kugeligen, konischen, cylindrischen oder auch reicher profilierten Ansatze, der seine Verzierung durch Umspinnen und Umflechten erhält, ein Büschel von Fäden oder Schnüren gerade abfällt. Als Vorbild kann die Schnur mit einfachem Knoten gelten, wobei das Aufdrehen oder Auflösen der Schnur durch den Knoten verhindert wird* (Meyer 1889, S. 208–210). Vgl. zu Quasten in diesem Katalog auch S. 282–291.

Randformpolster ungarniert (s. Abb. 319/320): Der hier gezeigte, um 1810 datierte, Biedermeierstuhl besitzt ein für die Zeit typisches Randformpolster, in das vier handgedrehte Taillenfedern eingesetzt sind. Er gilt als Lehrbeispiel für eine frühe Federpolsterung mit einer an drei Seiten umlaufenden Kantenwulst. Bevor der Stuhl restauriert wurde, zeigte er das Bild eines stark nach oben gewölbten Polsters, das fast gebläht wirkte. Der damit verbundene Verlust der ursprünglichen Form resultierte aus dem schlechten Zustand der Federschnürung, die an vielen Stellen Risse aufwies, weswegen sie dem Druck der Federkraft kaum mehr etwas entgegenzusetzen hatte. So waren die ursprünglich gebändigten Federn emporgeschnellt, allein noch gebremst durch die darüberliegende Leinenabdeckung und den Lederbezug, der in seinem altersbedingt brüchigen Zustand dann allerdings auch Schaden genommen hatte. Die vorsichtige Abpolsterung des Stuhls bis auf den Gurtgrund offenbarte dessen Aufbau. Demnach ruht das Polster auf einer 2 x 2-Gurtung, d. h. 2 x 2 sich kreuzenden Hanfgurten, auf denen ein Leinengewebe die Basis für die Ausbildung der Kantenwülste und der Positionierung der Sprungfedern bildet. Die zwischen den Polsterklötzen der Vorderbeine und den Hinterstollen aufgesetzten Kantenwülste waren typischerweise mit Langstroh gefüllt. Hinsichtlich der Beschaffenheit der handgedrehten Federn konnte festgestellt werden, dass bei ihnen die Ober- und Unterringe nicht, wie sonst, mit dem nächsten Ring zusammengebunden, sondern offen sind. Die brüchige, diagonal angelegte Schürfung wurde dann originalgetreu rekonstruiert, bevor darüber ein adäquat altes Leinen aufgebracht wurde, um im nächsten Schritt an den Federn sowie an der nachgarnierten und somit gerichteten Polsterwulstkante angenäht zu werden. Dabei wurde das leicht aufgearbeitete Bestandspolstermaterial wieder aufgebracht, durchgenäht, angenagelt und mit einem Kantenstich versehen. Eine Kombination von Ross- und Rehhaar wurde gemäß des Befundes als Ausgleichsfläche aufgebracht und mit einem Nesselbezug bedeckt, wie ein Anschauungsmodell zeigt (s. Abb. 227). Da es sich um ein Paar Biedermeierstühle

Polstermöbel, however, Adolf G. Schneck points out that horsehair is never torn into short individual pieces by machine but always plucked by hand. The hard-wearing horsehair is also a popular material for cover fabrics (figs. 256–258, text p. 260).

– Straw: used very early on as a simple stuffing material, as was tow, which is a by-product of linen fabric production and available in various qualities.

– Edge stitching refers to the technique used to strengthen the upholstery at the seams and achieve the desired shape. Various needles are used for this purpose, each used with a different stitch. Blind stitch, top stitch and blanket stitch, which was preferred from the middle of the nineteenth century, are possible techniques suitable for giving the edges their lasting and desired form.

Tapissier, or upholsterer, from the French word *tapissier*, is the job title for craftspeople who were primarily responsible for upholstering seating furniture and covering walls and window openings. In Germany, unlike in Austria, this term has now been replaced by Raumausstatter*in.

Tassels consist of a head (usually a wooden form covered with thread) and fringing. Examples can be found as early as the Assyrians, later in the Renaissance and Baroque and finally in the nineteenth century, when they enjoyed great popularity on upholstered furniture. Franz Sales Meyer included corresponding patterns (fig. 315) in his systematically arranged *Handbuch der Ornamentik*, which was published by E. A. Seemann in Leipzig in 1889. He explains, *The tassel is formed by a tuft of threads or cords falling straight from a spherical, conical, cylindrical or more richly profiled base, which is decorated by spinning and braiding around it. The cord with a simple knot can be regarded as a model, in which the untwisting or unravelling of the cord is prevented by the knot* (Meyer 1889, pp. 208–210). See on tassels also pp. 282–291 in this catalogue.

Tête-à-tête (figs. 47/48) refers to a piece of seating furniture with two seats facing each other that allows for a confidential private conversation as well as an intimate rendezvous. In contrast to the *Indiscret*, there is no room for listeners: you are left well alone.

Top covers are, according to contemporary standards, fabrics suitable for upholstery which should be abrasion-resistant and lightfast. These standards cannot be applied to historical upholstery fabrics. For an overview of 500 years of upholstery fabrics, see in this book, pp. 240–269.

Tufting is the technique of bridling and compressing stuffed parts of chairs, cushions and mattresses in order to hold the filling in place and to ensure the seat's depth and firmness.

Upholstered edge (figs. 319/320): The Biedermeier chair shown here, dated around 1810, has an edge roll typical of the period, in which four hand-turned waisted springs are inserted. It is considered an example of early sprung upholstery with an edge roll running around three sides. Before the chair was restored, the upholstery appeared as a strong dome that looked almost distended. The associated loss of the original shape resulted from the poor condition of the spring lashing, which was torn in many places, so that it could hardly withstand the spring's pressure. Thus, the originally tamed springs had shot upwards, slowed down only by the overlying linen cover and the leather cover, which in its age-related brittle state had also suffered damage. Carefully stripping the

319/320
Schichtmodell eines Randformpolsters, ungarniert (Fragment), um 1800 (Privatbesitz)

319/320
Cutaway model of an edge roll cushion, unstitched (fragment), around 1800 (private collection)

handelt, die für die Ausstellung untersucht und aufgearbeitet wurden, war es möglich, ein Exemplar für dessen Einsatz im separaten Aktionsraum bereitzustellen. Die Ausführung übernahm Torsten Otto, während Reinhardt Roßberg den Arbeitsbericht verfasste, in dem die gewonnenen Erkenntnisse festgehalten wurden und der auch diesem Abschnitt über das Randformpolster zugrunde liegt.

Raumausstatter*in ist in Deutschland seit der 1965 erfolgten Reformierung der Handwerksordnung die offizielle Berufsbezeichnung für Handwerker*innen auf dem breiten Gebiet der Innenraumgestaltung, wozu neben dem Polstern und Bespannen von Möbeln auch das Verlegen von Bodenbelägen, der Entwurf und die Realisation von textilen Wandbehängen, die Anbringung von Wandbespannungen und Tapeten und die Herstellung von Sonnenschutzvorrichtungen gehören. Vor 1965 gab es die Berufsbezeichnung Tapezierer, siehe → Tapissier.

Restaurator*in im Raumausstatterhandwerk ist eine geschützte Bezeichnung, die aufgrund der bestandenen Prüfung nach einer fachlichen Weiterbildung zur Bezeichnung Restaurator*in im Handwerk führt. Insgesamt wird in 19 Gewerken ausgebildet, wozu auch das Raumausstatterhandwerk zählt.

Samt: Gewebe mit Flor, der aus Florketten über Ruten gebildet wird; die dabei entstehenden Schlingen werden nach dem Webvorgang mit einer durch die Nut der Rute geführten Klinge aufgeschnitten. Beim ziselierten Samt wird das Muster durch aufgeschnittenen und unaufgeschnittenen Flor gebildet, wobei die unaufgeschnittenen Stellen höher sind als die ungeschnittenen.

Schaumstoffkissen werden in Sandwichbauweise aus zwei Schaumstoffen mit aufeinander abgestimmten Raumgewichten und Stauchhärten mit einem härteren Kern und einer weichen Oberfläche hergestellt. Mitunter wird zur Abdeckung des Kissenkerns auch Latexschaum verwendet. Aufgrund der vielen Kombinationsmöglichkeiten mit verschiedenen Raumgewichten und Stauchhärten sowie durch die Verwendung von Latexschaum lassen sich sehr unterschiedliche Polstereffekte erzielen.

Schlaraffia-Polster (s. Abb. 95) sind lose Einlegekissen mit besonderer Stabilität bei gleichzeitig hoher Elastizität. Sie beinhalten spezielle Federeinlagen, die unter dem patentierten Namen Schlaraffia auf dem Markt angeboten werden.

Schnürung (s. Abb. 323): Zum Schnüren der Taillenfedern verwendet man dreifache und zweifache Schnürfäden. Das Schnürungssystem besteht aus Stell-, Knoten- und Retourschnur. Bei Federhochpolstern kommt noch eine zusätzliche Herzschnur hinzu. Die Schnürung wird mit folgenden Befestigungsarten ausgeführt: Schlaufe oder Schlinge, Bohne oder Schleifknoten, Knoten oder Überknoten, Doppelbohne oder Kreuzknoten. Zu kurze Schnüre werden mit Verbindungsknoten oder Weberknoten angesetzt. In mehreren Arbeitsschritten werden Taillenfedern (seltener auch Kegelfedern) mit einem kräftigen Bindfaden auf der Gurtung fixiert, mit mehreren Stichen an der Gurtung festgenäht und anschließend in verschiedenen Techniken mit Schüren verbunden und an den Stuhlzargen angeschlagen:
– Die französische Schnürung, auch rechtwinklige Schnürung genannt, fasst die oberen Federringe viermal. Damit die Zwischenfäden die Knoten dieser Federringe nicht erfassen, müssen sie schon beim Aufnähen der Federn auf den Gurten in einem Winkel von 45 Grad ausgerichtet werden. Diese Schnürung wird vor allem für Sitzflächen, die ein Gefälle aufweisen sollen, wie Sessel und Sofasitze, verwendet.
– Die deutsche Schnürung, auch diagonale Schnürung genannt, fasst die oberen Federringe achtmal. Die Knoten der oberen Federringe müssen etwa im Winkel von 22,5 Grad ausgerichtet sein. Diese Art der Schnürung ergibt eine

chair down to the webbing revealed its structure. According to this, the upholstery rests on 2 x 2 webbing, meaning 2 x 2 intersecting hemp straps on which a linen fabric forms the basis for the formation of the edge rolls and the positioning of the springs. The edge rolls placed between the cushioning pads of the front and rear legs were typically filled with long straw. The upper and lower rings of the hand-turned springs are not tied to the next ring, as is usually the case, but are open. The brittle, diagonally applied lashing was then reconstructed true to the original before an adequately old linen was placed over it to be sewn to the springs as well as to the re-stitched upholstered edge roll, which was now straightened in the next step. During the process, the lightly refurbished existing stuffing material was reapplied, attached with bridle ties, nailed on and given an edge stitch. A combination of horsehair and deer hair was applied to balance out the surface according to the findings and was covered with a nettle cover, as an illustrative model shows (fig. 227). As this is a pair of Biedermeier chairs that were examined and refurbished for the exhibition, it was possible to provide a specimen for use in the separate activity room. Torsten Otto was responsible for the execution, while Reinhardt Roßberg wrote the work report in which the findings were recorded and which also forms the basis of this section on rolled edge upholstery.

Raumaustatter*in is the gender-sensitive term used since the reform of the Crafts Code in 1965 and the official occupational title in Germany for craftspeople in the broad field of interior design, which, in addition to upholstering and covering furniture, also includes laying floor coverings, designing and realising textile wall hangings, applying wall coverings and wallpapers and producing sun protection devices. Before 1965, the occupational title of upholsterer was used; see Tapissier.

Velvet consists of a pile warp, which, by inserting rods during the weaving process, produces above a base weave raised loops, which are subsequently cut. Ciselé velvet is a figured velvet, whose pattern is formed by cut and uncut pile, which results in the uncut areas being higher than the cut ones.

Voyeuse (French), or *prie-dieu* chair, refers to a piece of salon furniture popular since the middle of the eighteenth century as a conversation chair: *voyeuse* can be translated from French as *spectator* and describes the use of the upholstered chair from which card players could be comfortably watched. People sat astride it, facing the back of the chair, so that their elbows could rest in comfort on the upholstered backrest. Some models had an integrated box in the wide backrest in which games or smoking utensils could be stored. These variants are called *ponteuse* or *fumeuse*, depending on their use (figs. 56–58). As it was uncomfortable for ladies to sit with their legs wide apart due to their overhanging dresses and it was also considered unseemly, the upholstered seat was positioned low, allowing one to also kneel on it.

Weaves
The three basic weaves for warp and weft threads are tabby, twill and atlas. They are the base or the elements of more complex weaves.
– Atlas: a weave where the binding points do not touch and are often covered by a warp float. The textile's surface is very smooth and shiny.
– Brocatelle: a lampas-woven fabric characterised by high relief patterns created from combining silk with a coarse linen weft. Brocaded describes a pattern formed by a weft whose use is confined to the width of the

321/322
Stuhl, um 1810 (Reinhardt Roßberg, Markkleeberg)

321/322
Chair, around 1810 (Reinhardt Roßberg, Markkleeberg)

härtere Federung, da die oberen Federringe öfter von Schnürfäden erfasst werden. Sie wird verwendet für glatte Sitzflächen wie Stühle, Sessel mit aufgelegtem Kissen, Hocker, Ruhemöbel und Matratzen.

Seele wird der innere Faden genannt, um den ein anderer Faden oder Metallahn gesponnen wird.

Spikat oder Fassonspikat ist eine häufig angewandte Technik, mit der der Holzkörper (= Fasson) von Quasten überflochten wird. Die Bezeichnung Würfelspikat bezieht sich auf das geflochtene Muster (Paul Dornbrach, Posamentier-Kunstgewerbe 1894, S. 55f.).

Spitze wird aus geflochtenen und verschlungenen Garnen oder aus durch Ausziehen von Fäden durchbrochenen oder bestickten bzw. benähten Geweben gebildet. Entsprechend der verschiedenen Techniken wird u. a. zwischen Klöppelspitze (verkreuzte und geflochtene Fäden) und Nadelspitzen mit aufgespannten, umstickten Fäden unterschieden.

Sprungfedern verleihen der Polsterung Elastizität. Die ersten Federn waren noch handgedreht, wobei die Drahtenden offen waren. Folgemodelle waren dann an ihren Enden mit Blechschlaufen gekapselt, bis die heutige Sprungfeder als Modell mit verknoteten Drahtenden entstanden ist. Der Vorteil der meist verwendeten taillierten (mittig verschlankten) Federn ist deren große Elastizität, die es erlaubt, sie durch Schnürung in einer bestimmten Höhe, Spannung und Stellung so zu binden, dass sie sich bei einer Be- und Entlastung nur ab- und aufwärts bewegen und nicht zur Seite ausweichen können. Diese Art des Polsterns ist sehr zeitaufwendig und dadurch teurer als die heute oft verwendete Schaumstofffüllung, doch gilt sie als elementare Technik des Raumausstatters. Wegen ihrer großen Alterungsbeständigkeit steht sie für Qualität und Nachhaltigkeit.

Tapissier oder Tapezierer leitet sich vom französischen Wort tapissier ab und ist die Berufsbezeichnung für Handwerker, die vor allem für die Polsterung von Sitzmöbeln und die Verkleidung von Wänden und Fensteröffnungen verantwortlich waren, wobei diese Bezeichnung in Deutschland, anders als in Österreich, heute durch Raumausstatter*in ersetzt wurde.

Tête-à-tête (s. Abb. 47/48) bezeichnet ein Sitzmöbel mit zwei einander zugewandten Sitzen, das ein vertrauliches Gespräch unter vier Augen sowie ein intimes Stelldichein erlaubt. Im Gegensatz zum *Indiscret* ist hier kein Platz für Zuhörer vorgesehen. Man bleibt unter sich.

Tressen: gewebte Borten aus Metallfäden.

Voyeuse (frz.) bezeichnet ein seit Mitte des 18. Jahrhunderts beliebtes Salonmöbel als Konversationsstuhl: *voyeuse* lässt sich aus dem Französischen mit *Zuschauerin* übersetzen und beschreibt die Nutzung des Polsterstuhls, von dem aus Kartenspielern bequem zugeschaut werden kann. Dabei saß man darauf, dem Stuhlrücken zugewandt, rittlings, sodass sich die Ellbogen auf der gepolsterten Rückenlehne bequem aufstützen ließen. Manche Modelle besaßen in der breiten Rückenlehne ein integriertes Kästchen, in dem Spiel- oder auch Rauchutensilien untergebracht werden konnten. Diese Varianten heißen, je nach Nutzung *ponteuse* oder *fumeuse* (s. Abb. 56–58). Da für Damen das breitbeinige Sitzen wegen ihrer ausladenden Kleider unbequem war und zudem als unschicklich galt, wurde der gepolsterte Sitz so tief positioniert, dass man darauf auch knien konnte.

Weißbezug ist der Vorbezug zumeist aus weißem Nesselgewebe vor dem Aufbringen der sichtbaren Polsterabdeckung.

motif and does not run across the whole weave.
– Damask: textile whose pattern and base is formed by contrasting the weft and warp directions.
– Gros de Tours: Weave with a weft rib with two picks in each shed.

Fabrics for upholstery are used for top covers and loose covers (see chapter '500 years of furnishing textiles', pp. 240–269), and their composition is of great importance for the stability of the padding. Frequently used textiles include
– Jute cloth: serves different purposes, such as covering the springs or holding stuffing in place, is produced in different weaves and weights from jute fibre, which may also be used as either a non-woven or loose stuffing in other places. Other terms are hessian, scrim or tarp.
– Molleton or calico: tabby weaves made from twill or cotton and used to cover the coir or horsehair stuffing, so that the fibres do not show through.
– Nettle, or also cotton nettle: a tabby weave today made from cotton but in the past was made of nettle fibre. Usually sold as unbleached, undyed cloth.

Webbing consists of strips that form the base or foundation of upholstery. They are attached to the chair rails so that they withstand the weight of the human body. A web stretcher is used so that the webbing is sufficiently tight, while a hammer is used to insert the tacks flat through the fabric into the rail. The basketweave pattern is the foundation on which, for example, the springs can be lashed. A distinction is made between
– Wide webbing: where the straps are nailed at a distance from each other as the first support layer of the upholstery on or underneath the rails of the chair. With lashed springing, the springs are usually positioned at the point where the straps interweave the webbing nailed to the rail from below.
– Tight webbing: where the straps are fastened side by side with no space between them. If no springs are used, as in the Baroque period, the upholstery material is usually applied directly on top, unless a dense linen fabric has been laid down beforehand as an intermediate layer.

Yarn is a continuous material made by the spinning, twisting or processing by other means of different raw materials. In upholstery, yarns are differentiated according to their purpose and are used as either thick, usually three-ply, thread in order to lash the metal springs to the frame or as two-ply thread for back- and armrests. A medium, two-ply basting thread is used for fixing the springs. The edging thread is used for stitching the stuffing and hessian as well as the seams. They are all made from hemp or linen fibre, and in modern upholstery also from polyester or cotton.

Zigzag springs are made from *wire in a sinuous or zigzag shape that is initially rolled up*, as Walter Naumann explains in his *Fachbuch für Tapezierer*; he goes on to explain that they are unrolled and attached to the rails of the chair *with a clip which is nailed down* (Naumann 1958, p. 91). Another term is sinuous spring.

323
Modell einer geschnürten Federung (Privatbesitz)

323
Model of lashed springing (private collection)

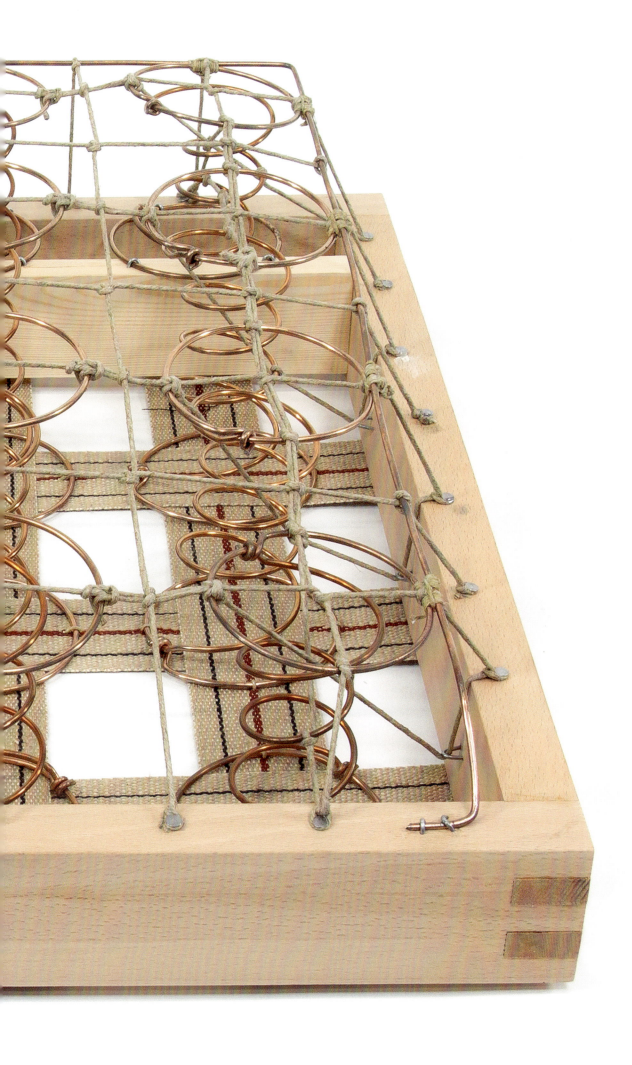

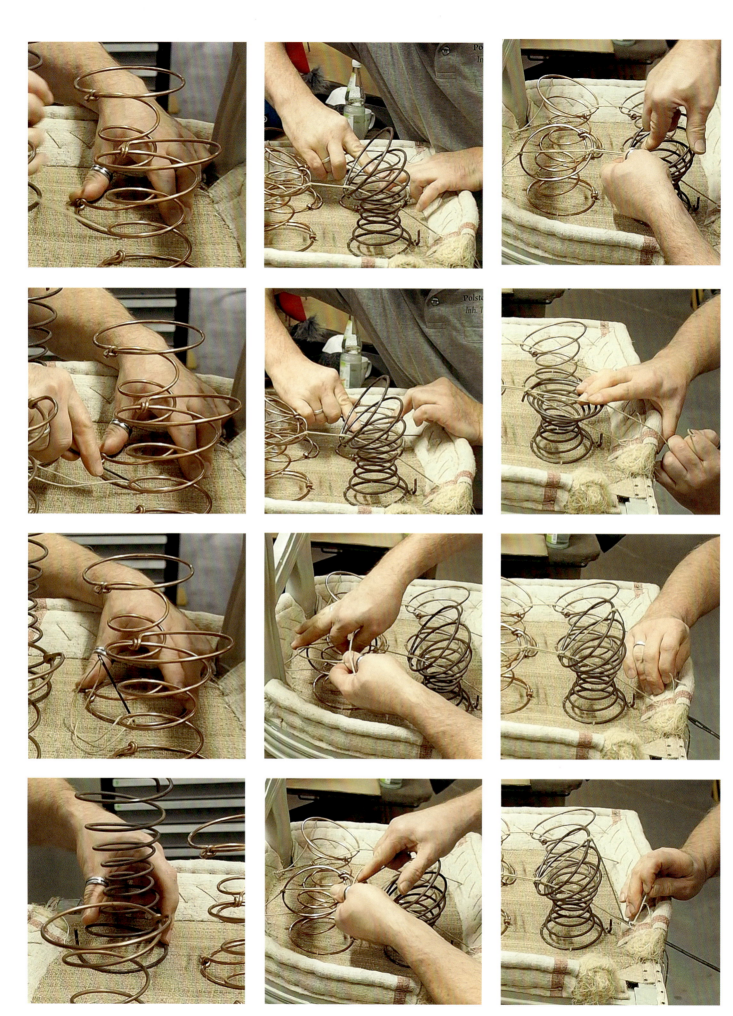

324–347
Filmstills zur geschnürten Federung

324–347
Stil frame showing lashed springing

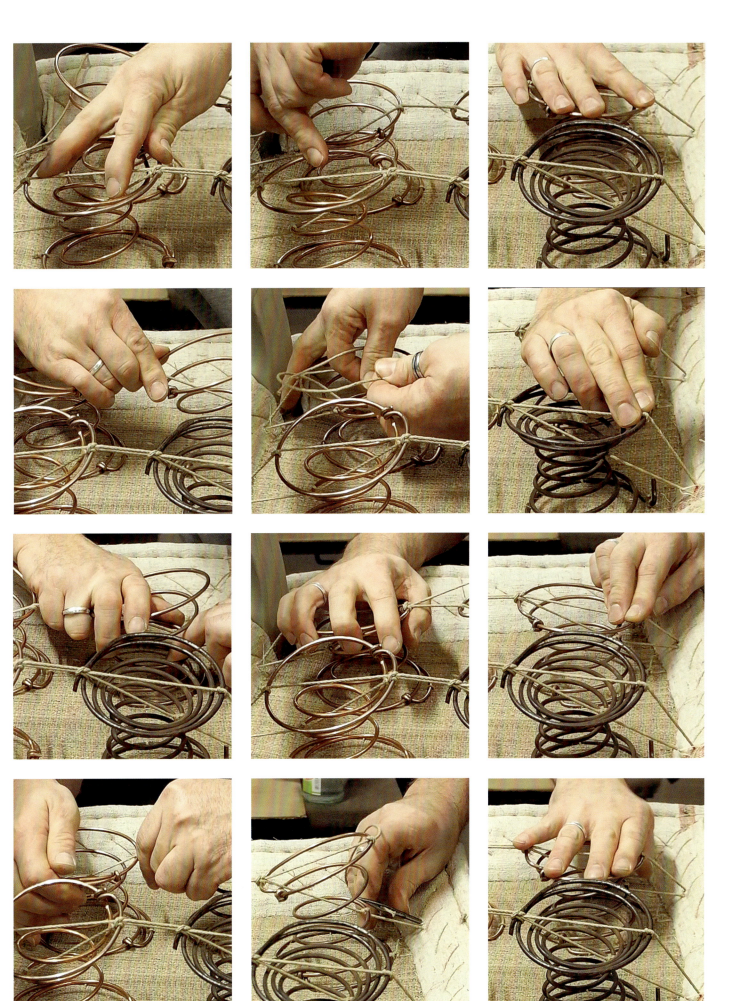

Objekt und Bild

Im Folgenden werden alle im Katalog abgebildeten Exponate und Illustrationen in der Reihenfolge ihres Erscheinens katalogisiert. Dies umfasst die Bezeichnung des Objektes, dessen Provenienz bzw. den Hinweis auf die Eigentümer*innen, zu Entwurfsverfasser*innen, Angaben zu Herstellung, Datierung, Material, Technologie, Polsteraufbau, zum Bezugsstoff und die Objektmaße. Fachliche Anmerkungen werden durch Hinweise auf Objektbefunde, die Restaurierung und die daran Beteiligten sowie Sponsoren, mögliche Literaturverweise und einen Fotonachweis ergänzt.
Für die Objektmaße gilt, wenn nicht anders angegeben: Höhe x Breite x Tiefe.
Abkürzungen: H = Höhe, B = Breite, T = Tiefe, D = Durchmesser

1
Blick in das Innenleben eines Polstersofas – **Fotografie**: Juliane Rückriem, Köln, 2012.

2
Konzeptzeichnung von Thomas Schriefers.

3
Illustration von Saul Steinberg, aus: *The Art of Living*. New York 1949, Archiv Thomas Schriefers.

4
Vom Innenleben der Polster, Zeichnungen von Thomas Schriefers.

5
Stuhldetail aus einem Fresko von Andrea Mantegna, das die Familie und den Hofstaat von Ludovico III. Gonzaga darstellt, aus: Campbell 2018, S. 208.

6
Detail einer ägyptischen Statuette des Amen-em-ope und seiner Frau Hathor, aus: Köppen 1904, S. 73.

7/8
Stuhl – **Eigentum**: die LÜBECKER MUSEEN – St. Annen-Museum, Lübeck – **Entwurf**: unbekannt – **Herstellung**: z. Zt. unbekannt – **Datierung**: um 1600 – **Technologie**: Gestell aus Buchenholz (Ergänzung am Stuhlbein: Eiche) – **Bezug**: Seide – **Maße**: 108 x 42 x 38 cm – **Anmerkung**: Ankauf von Witte & Co., Hamburg – **Fotografie**: Michael Haydn, Lübeck.

9/10
Armlehnstuhl – **Eigentum**: GRASSI Museum für Angewandte Kunst Leipzig – **Inventarnummer**: 1943.30 – **Provenienz**: Stiftung Fritz von Harck, ehemals im Blauen Zimmer der Villa Harck, Leipzig, 1943 – **Entwurf**: unbekannt – **Herstellung**: unbekannt – **Datierung**: Italien, um 1600/19. Jahrhundert – **Technologie**: Gestell aus Nussbaumholz, lederbezogener Polstersitz, Polster der Rückenlehne vermutlich lederbezogene Pappe – **Polsteraufbau**: der konstruktive Sitzuntergrund ist ein behauenes Brett, das mit Leder bezogen und mit einer Doppelreihe großer Messingziernägel angeschlagen ist; die untere Ziernagelreihe fixiert eine hellblaue Fransenborte mit Bindequasten und gebogter Unterkante; die Lehne scheint überarbeitet mit auf einem Brett oder Pappe aufgezogenem Leder, auch mit einer Doppelreihe Ziernägel angeschlagen, diese aber offensichtlich jüngeren Datums; den unteren Lehnenabschluss bildet ebenfalls eine Fransenborte mit Bindequasten – **Bezug**: Leder – **Objektmaße**: 122 x 62 x 55 cm, Sitzhöhe: 59 cm – **Anmerkung**: Sitz vermutlich mit originalem Lederbezug – **Literatur**: *Mitteilungen des städtischen Museums für Kunsthandwerk zu Leipzig / Grassimuseum und seines Freundes- und Förderkreises e. V.*, Sonderheft:

Objects and images

In the following, all exhibits and illustrations shown in the catalogue are catalogued in the order of their appearance. This includes the name of the object, its provenance or reference to the owner, the designer, information on the origin, date, material, technique, upholstery and cover fabric, and the object's dimensions. Technical notes are supplemented by references to the condition of the object, its conservation and those involved in it, as well as sponsors, possible literature references and a photo reference. Unless otherwise stated, the following applies to the object dimensions: height x width x depth.
Abbreviations: H = height, W = width, D = depth, Dia. = diameter, L = length

1
View into the interior of an upholstered sofa – **Photo**: Juliane Rückriem, Cologne, 2012.

2
Conceptual drawing by Thomas Schriefers.

3
Illustration by Saul Steinberg, in *The Art of Living*, New York 1949, Archive Thomas Schriefers.

4
Vom Innenleben der Polster [On the Interior Life of Upholstery], illustrations by Thomas Schriefers.

5
Chair detail from a fresco by Andrea Mantegna depicting the family and court of Ludovico III. Gonzaga, in Campbell 2018, p. 208.

6
Detail of an Egyptian sculpture of Amen-em-ope and his wife Hathor, in Köppen 1904, p. 73.

7/8
Chair – **Property**: die LÜBECKER MUSEEN – St. Annen-Museum, Lübeck – **Design**: unknown – **Origin**: at present unknown – **Date**: around 1600 – **Technique**: beechwood frame (addition on the chair leg: oak) – **Object measurements**: 108 x 42 x 38 cm – **Notes**: acquired from Witte & Co., Hamburg – **Photo**: Michael Haydn, Lübeck.

9/10
Armchair – **Property**: GRASSI Museum für Angewandte Kunst Leipzig – **Inventory number**: 1943.30 – **Provenance**: Stiftung Fritz von Harck, formerly in the Blue Room of Villa Harck, Leipzig, 1943 – **Design**: unknown – **Origin**: unknown – **Date**: Italy, around 1600/19th century – **Technique**: walnut frame, leather-covered upholstered seat, backrest upholstery presumably leather-covered board – **Upholstery**: the structural base of the seat is a hewn board covered with leather and fastened with a double row of large decorative brass nails; the lower row of decorative nails is held in place by a light-blue fringed border with tassels and a scalloped lower edge; the backrest appears to have been reworked with leather mounted on board or card-board, also fastened with a double row of decorative nails, but these are obviously of a more recent date; the lower end of the backrest is also fastened with a fringed border with tassels – **Cover**: leather – **Object measurements**: 122 x 62 x 55 cm, seat H: 59 cm – **Notes**: seat presumably with original leather cover – **Literature**: *Mitteilungen des städtischen Museum für Kunsthandwerk zu Leipzig/Grassimuseum und seines*

Die Stiftung Fritz von Hark, Heft 6, Leipzig 1997, S. 696; Vergleichsbeispiele in: Feulner 1927, S. 157ff.; Richard Graul: *Schöne Möbel aus 5 Jahrhunderten*, S. 47; Herbert Hoffmann: *Sitzmöbel aus 6 Jahrhunderten*. Stuttgart 1938, S. 36 u. 39. – **Restaurierung:** Thomas Andersch Dipl. Rest. – **Fotografie:** Esther Hoyer/GRASSI Museum für Angewandte Kunst Leipzig.

11/12
Armlehnstuhl – **Eigentum:** Germanisches Nationalmuseum, Nürnberg – **Inventarnummer:** HG6468 – **Entwurf:** unbekannt – **Herstellung:** Ulm – **Datierung:** um 1620 – **Technologie:** Der große Stuhl besteht aus geschnitztem Nussbaumholz auf vier geraden, mit Krallen ausgehenden Füßen. Die beiden Armlehnen enden je in einer in Blattwerk auslaufenden weiblichen Halbfigur mit teilweiser Vergoldung; ebenso die beiden Enden der Rückenlehne. Die Füße sind durch geschnitzte und vergoldete Zwischenbretter (je mit dem Kopf in der Mitte) verbunden, Bezug: Der gepolsterte Sitz und die Armlehnen sind mit reicher Applikationsstickerei versehen (gelbe Seide auf schwarzem Samt), ebenso das frei hängende Rückenstück, das mittig die Wappen des Reiches und der Stadt Ulm zeigt – **Objektmaße:** 142 x 72 cm – **Literatur:** Hans Stegmann: *Katalog der Gewebesammlung des Germanischen Nationalmuseums, 2. Teil: Stickereien, Spitzen und Posamentierarbeiten*. Nürnberg 1901, S. 25; Hans Stegmann: Die Holzmöbel des Germanischen Museums, in: *Mitteilungen des Germanischen Nationalmuseums Nürnberg*, 1903, S. 90, Tafel 4; Meister-Jedding: *Das schöne Möbel*, 1958, Abb. 262; Kreisel-Himmelheber: *Die Kunst des dt. Möbels*, Bd.1. München 1968, S. 285, Abb. 657 – **Fotografie:** Germanisches Nationalmuseum Nürnberg (Foto: Monika Runge).

13/14
Armlehnstuhl – **Eigentum:** GRASSI Museum für Angewandte Kunst Leipzig – **Inventarnummer:** V4156 a – **Provenienz:** Alter Bestand – **Entwurf:** unbekannt – **Herstellung:** Italien – **Datierung:** um 1710/20 – **Technologie:** Das Gestell ist aus Birnbaumholz geschnitzt, der Sitz besteht aus einem hohen Festpolster mit Vorderkantenwulst, die Lehne aus einem Flachpolster auf Spannleinen – **Polsteraufbau:** Das hohe Festpolster besteht aus Brechflachs (analog dem Befund der Lehne) auf Spannleinen mit Vorderkantenwulst aus Rehhaaren, darüber ein Leinenunterbezug und ein Seidenbezug (moderne Nachwebung) mit Handnähten und modern ergänzten Posamenten; die Lehne besteht aus einem Flachpolster auf Spannleinen mit Leinennesselbezug – **Bezug:** Seidenbezug (moderne Nachwebung) mit Handnähten und modern ergänzten Borten mit Bindequasten an der Unterkante – **Objektmaße:** 118 x 67 x 48 cm, Sitzhöhe 51 cm – **Anmerkung:** Die ursprüngliche Technologie konnte nicht mit Sicherheit belegt werden. Sie wurde aufgrund der Befunde und Vergleichsbefunde mit analogen Materialien rekonstruiert – **Literatur:** Vergleichsbeispiel in: Peter Hughes: *The Wallace Collection, Catalogue of Furniture*. Bd. 1. London 1996, S. 266 u. 267; – **Restaurierung:** Thomas Andersch Dipl. Rest. (Holzarbeiten) und Reinhardt Roßberg RiH (Polsterung) – **Fotografie:** Esther Hoyer/GRASSI Museum für Angewandte Kunst Leipzig.

15/16
Stuhl – **Eigentum:** GRASSI Museum für Angewandte Kunst Leipzig – **Inventarnummer:** V5460 – **Provenienz:** Alter Bestand – **Entwurf:** unbekannt – **Herstellung:** Sachsen – **Datierung:** um 1750 – **Technologie:** Holzkonstruktion mit Sitz als Festpolster auf Gurtung mit Lederbezug; das Gestell besteht aus dunkelbraun gebeiztem und lackiertem Rotbuchenholz – **Polsteraufbau:** Der Sitz verfügt über eine 2x2-Gurtung mit handgewebten Hanfgurten; handgewebtes Federleinen; die untere Polsterung besteht aus Stroh, die Abdeckung ist unklar – **Bezug:** Erstbezug: monochromes braunes Seidengewebe (Gros de Tours liseré) mit floraler Musterung; Zweitbezug: Leder mit kassettierter Pressung – **Objektmaße:** 100 x 44 x 52 cm,

Freundes- and Förderkreises e.V., special issue: *Die Stiftung Fritz von Hark*, no. 6, Leipzig 1997, p. 696; comparative examples in Feulner 1927, p. 157ff.; Richard Graul, *Schöne Möbel aus 5 Jahrhunderten*, p. 47; Herbert Hoffmann, *Sitzmöbel aus 6 Jahrhunderten*, Stuttgart 1938, pp. 36, 39 – **Conservation:** Thomas Andersch Dipl. Rest. – **Photo:** Esther Hoyer/GRASSI Museum für Angewandte Kunst Leipzig.

11/12
Armchair – **Property:** Germanisches Nationalmuseum, Nuremberg – **Inventory number:** HG6468 – **Design:** unknown – **Origin:** Ulm – **Date:** around 1620 – **Technique:** the large chair is made from carved walnut on four straight clawed feet. The armrests both end in a partially gilded female half-length figure, as do the ends of the backrests. The feet are connected by carved and gilded aprons (each with a central head). The upholstered seat and the armrests are richly decorated with embroidery (yellow silk on black velvet) as is the detached backrest with the central crests of the Reich and the city of Ulm – **Object measurements:** 142 x 72 cm – **Literature:** P. Hans Stegmann, *Katalog der Gewebesammlung des Germanischen Nationalmuseums*, 2. Teil: Stickereien, Spitzen und Posamentierarbeiten, Nürnberg 1901, p. 25; Hans Stegmann, 'Die Holzmöbel des Germanischen Museums', in *Mitteilungen des Germanischen Nationalmuseums*, Nuremberg 1903, p. 90, plate 4; Peter Wilhelm Meister and Hermann Jedding, *Das schöne Möbel*, Heidelberg 1958, fig. 262; Heinrich Kreisel and Georg Himmelheber, *Die Kunst des dt. Möbels*, vol. 1, Munich 1968, p. 285, fig. 657 – **Photo:** Germanisches Nationalmuseum, Nuremberg (Monika Runge).

13/14
Armchair – **Property:** GRASSI Museum für Angewandte Kunst Leipzig – **Inventory number:** V4156 a – **Provenance:** old inventory – **Design:** unknown – **Origin:** Italy – **Date:** around 1710/1720 – **Technique:** carved beech frame, seat with high upholstery with edge roll, backrest with flat padding on hessian – **Upholstery:** the high attached sprung upholstery is made from flax (as is the backrest) on hessian with an edge roll made from deer hair, with a covering of scrim as well as a silk top fabric (modern re-weave) with hand-sewn seams and added passementerie; the backrest is a flat pad on hessian with calico cover – **Cover:** silk cover (modern re-weave) hand-sewn and modern added borders with tassels on the lower rail – **Object measurements:** 118 x 67 x 48 cm, seat H: 51 cm – **Notes:** the original upholstery could not be verified entirely. It was reconstructed on the basis of the findings and comparative findings using analogous materials – **Literature:** comparative example in Peter Hughes, *The Wallace Collection, Catalogue of Furniture*, vol. 1, London 1996, pp. 266, 267 – **Conservation:** Thomas Andersch Dipl. Rest. (woodwork) and Reinhardt Roßberg RiH (upholstery) – **Photo:** Esther Hoyer/GRASSI Museum für Angewandte Kunst Leipzig.

15/16
Chair – **Property:** GRASSI Museum für Angewandte Kunst Leipzig – **Inventory number:** V5460 – **Provenance:** old inventory – **Design:** unknown – **Origin:** Saxony – **Date:** around 1750 – **Technique:** wooden construction with attached seat on webbing with leather cover; frame made from dark-brown stained and lacquered common beech – **Upholstery:** seat with 2 x 2 webbing with hand-woven hemp strips; hand-woven hessian; lower stuffing with straw, cover material not clear – **Cover:** first cover: monochrome brown silk weave (Gros de Tours liseré) with floral pattern; second cover: leather with coffered pressing – **Object measurements:** 100 x 44 x 52 cm, seat

Sitzhöhe 48 cm – **Literatur:** Vergleichsbeispiel in: Rudolf von Arps-Aubert: *Sächsische Barockmöbel 1700–1770*. Berlin 1939, Tafel 24. – **Restaurierung:** Stäbchenergänzung am linken Fuß durch Andreas Schwabe Dipl. Rest.; Rückbau zweier nicht originaler Stege zwischen Vorder- und Hinterbeinen, Oberflächenreinigung und Retusche von Thomas Andersch Dipl.-Rest. – **Fotografie:** Esther Hoyer/GRASSI Museum für Angewandte Kunst Leipzig.

17
Stuhl als Schnittmodell – **Eigentum:** Caroline Scarbata – **Entwurf:** unbekannt – **Herstellung:** unbekannt – **Datierung:** um 1710 (?) – **Technologie:** Buche, farbig gefasst; der Sitz besteht aus einem Festpolster mit Vorderkantenwulst auf Gurtung und Leinen, die Lehne aus einem Flachpolster auf Spannleinen – **Polsteraufbau:** Der Sitz verfügt über eine Gurtung 2x1 handgewebter Hanfgurte; Federleinen: handgewebtes Leinen grob; an der Vorderkante Langstrohbündel, dahinter besteht das hohe Festpolster aus verschiedenen Gräsern mit Rehhaardeckung, Unterbezug gestreiftes Leinen; die Lehne ist ein Flachpolster aus Gräsern mit Rehhaar (wie Sitz) auf gespanntem Leinen (Bezug wie Sitz) – **Bezug:** gefärbtes Maroquinleder mit Ziernägeln auf Lederband – **Objektmaße:** 116 x 52,5 x 61 cm, Sitzhöhe 51,5 cm – **Anmerkung:** Im Originalzustand überkommen ohne Überarbeitungen, handgewebte Hanfgurte, feuervergoldete, gegossene Messingziernägel, handgeschmiedete Nägel für Gurte, Unterleinen, Unterbezug und Bezugsleder, Polstermaterial: Rehhaare und Langstroh – **Fördernde:** Reinhardt Roßberg RiH (Arbeitsleistung) – **Restaurierung:** Holzarbeiten und Oberfläche von Thomas Andersch Dipl. Rest., Rekonstruktion Mittelsteg von Arnd Müller, Drechslermeister, Polsteraufbau von Reinhardt Roßberg RiH – **Fotografie:** LÖFFLER COLLECTION, Reichenschwand.

18
Kissen von Ludwig XIV. und Marie-Thérèse (*d'après une tapisserie de l'Histoire du Roy*), aus: Havard 1894, Bd. 1, S. 567, Archiv Thomas Schriefers.

19
La Duchesse à Bateau et la Duchesse avec encognure, aus: *Diderots Enzyklopädie. Die Bildtafeln (1762–1777)*, Archiv Thomas Schriefers.

20
Der erste und der zweite Schritt der Vorbereitung eines Fassonpolsters, aus: *Diderots Enzyklopädie. Die Bildtafeln 1762–1777*, 3. Bd. Augsburg 1995, S. 2256, Archiv Thomas Schriefers.

21
Fassonarbeiten, Bildtafel zur Arbeit des Tapissier in Diderots Enzyklopädie, aus: *Diderots Enzyklopädie. Die Bildtafeln 1762–1777*, 3. Bd. Augsburg 1995, S. 2257, Archiv Thomas Schriefers.

22
Verschiedene Werkzeuge des Tapissier, aus: *Diderots Enzyklopädie. Die Bildtafeln 1762–1777*, 3. Bd. Augsburg 1995, S. 2246, Archiv Thomas Schriefers.

23
Werkzeug des polsternden Raumausstatters heute – **Fotografie:** Cordula Fink, 2021.

24
Taillenfeder mit Verknotung am obersten Gang – **Fotografie:** Cordula Fink, 2021.

25
Chamber Horse – **Eigentum:** Cordula Fink – **Entwurf:** z. Zt.

H: 48 cm – **Literature:** comparative example in Rudolf von Arps-Aubert, *Sächsische Barockmöbel 1700–1770*, Berlin 1939, plate 24 – **Conservation:** Andreas Schwabe Dipl. Rest. (added rod on the left foot), Thomas Andersch Dipl.-Rest. (reconstruction of two non-original stretchers between front and back legs, surface cleaning and retouching) – **Photo:** Esther Hoyer/GRASSI Museum für Angewandte Kunst Leipzig.

17
Chair as cutaway model – **Property:** Caroline Scarbata – **Design:** unknown – **Origin:** unknown – **Date:** around 1710? – **Technique:** beech, painted; seat with attached padding with an edge roll on webbing and hessian base; backrest with flat padding on scrim – **Upholstery:** seat with 2 x 1 webbing with hand-woven hemp strips; hessian; hand-woven coarse linen, on the front edge long straw bundle, the high attached upholstery behind made from different grasses with deer hair covering, undercover of striped linen; backrest is flat padding with grasses and deer hair (same as seat) on stretched linen (undercover same as seat) – **Cover:** dyed Morocco leather with decorative nails on leather border – **Object measurements:** 116 x 52.5 x 61 cm, seat H: 51.5 cm – **Notes:** in original state without modifications, hand-woven hemp webbing, fire-gilded, decorative cast-brass nails, hand-forged nails for webbing, hessian, padding and leather cover, upholstery material: deer hair and long straw – **Sponsors:** Reinhardt Roßberg RiH (work) – **Conservation:** Andersch Dipl. Rest. (woodwork and surface), woodturning master Arnd Müller (surface, re-construction stretcher, Reinhardt Roßberg RiH (upholstery) – **Photo:** LÖFFLER COLLECTION, Reichenschwand.

18
Cushions of Louis XIV and Marie-Thérèse (*d'après une tapisserie de l'Histoire du Roy*), in Havard 1894, vol. 1, p. 567, Archive Thomas Schriefers.

19
La Duchesse à Bateau et la Duchesse avec encognure, plate from: *Diderots Enzyklopädie: Die Bildtafeln (1762–1777)*, Archive Thomas Schriefers.

20
The first and second step in the preparation of the upholstery, in *Diderots Enzyklopädie: Die Bildtafeln 1762–1777*, vol. 3, Augsburg 1995, p. 2256, Archive Thomas Schriefers.

21
Working the padding, picture plate on the work of the tapissier in Diderot's encyclopaedia, in *Diderots Enzyklopädie: Die Bildtafeln 1762–1777*, vol. 3, Augsburg 1995, p. 2257, Archive Thomas Schriefers.

22
Different tools of the tapissier, in *Diderots Enzyklopädie: Die Bildtafeln 1762–1777*, vol. 3, Augsburg 1995, p. 2246, Archive Thomas Schriefers.

23
Tools of a modern upholsterer – **Photo:** Cordula Fink, 2021.

24
Waisted spring with connecting knots in the top gauge – **Photo:** Cordula Fink, 2021.

25
Chamber horse – **Property:** Cordula Fink – **Design:** at

unbekannt – **Herstellung:** z. Zt. unbekannt – **Datierung:** England, 18. Jh. – **Technologie:** Gestell aus Mahagoniholz. Die Unterkonstruktion des Polsters besteht aus Nadelholz, versehen mit handgedrehten Stahlfedern und Rosshaarbedeckung – **Bezug:** Rosshaar – **Objektmaße:** 83 x 73 x 52 cm – **Restaurierung:** Elisabeth Riß, Raumausstattermeisterin und Stefan Oswald RiH – **Fotografie:** LÖFFLER COLLECTION, Reichenschwand.

26
Blick in das geöffnete Chamber Horse – **Fotografie:** Cordula Fink, 2021.

27
Armlehnstuhl – **Eigentum:** Stiftung Preußische Schlösser und Gärten Berlin-Brandenburg – **Inventarnummer:** IV 67 – **Entwurf:** z. Zt. unbekannt – **Herstellung:** z. Zt. unbekannt – **Datierung:** um 1765 – **Technologie:** Das Buchenholzgestell ist in geschweifter Sitzform gestaltet und beige lackiert, die Rückenlehne im Hochoval, von Holzleisten umrahmt – **Polsteraufbau:** Auf einer französischen Enggurtung liegt ein garniertes Bourrelet in Rosshaar. Der Spiegel ist ebenso in Rosshaar ausgebildet und bis auf den Gurtgrund durchgenäht. Die Rückenlehne besitzt eine hybride Fasson mit drei garnierten Seiten ohne flächige Durchnähung, mit einer Füllung aus Rosshaar – **Bezug:** Kanevasstickerei im Perlstich aus Seide und Wolle – **Objektmaße:** 112,5 x 85,5 x 77 cm – **Anmerkung:** Die Polsterung befindet sich im unberührten Originalzustand – **Restaurierung:** Der Bezug ist nicht ursprünglich, um 1840. – **Fotografie:** Stiftung Preußische Schlösser und Gärten Berlin-Brandenburg.

28
Armlehnstuhl, wie Position 27, doch im geöffneten Zustand – **Fotografie:** Stiftung Preußische Schlösser und Gärten Berlin-Brandenburg.

29
Sofa – **Eigentum:** LÖFFLER COLLECTION, Reichenschwand – **Inventarnummer:** 02626 – **Entwurf:** z. Zt. unbekannt – **Herstellung:** z. Zt. unbekannt – **Datierung:** Louis Seize, um 1780 – **Technologie:** Holz massiv, geschnitzt, deckend in beige/grauer Farbe gefasst; Sitz: ovale Form mit 5 Füssen (konisch, säulenartig gedrechselt); Lehne: ovale Form – **Polsteraufbau:** der Sitz weist eine geschnürte Feder mit Fasson aus Werg und Rosshaar auf, während das Rückenlehnen-Medaillon und Armlehnen aus Rosshaar garniert ist – **Bezug:** kettgemustert, Seide, nach Original nachgewebt – **Objektmaße:** 96 x 161 x 80 cm; Sitzhöhe: 47 x 132 x 60 cm – **Anmerkung:** Die Polsterung zeigt den unberührten Originalzustand, Bezugsstoff und Postament wurden nach Befund rekonstruiert.

30
Armlehnstuhl – **Eigentum:** Museum für Kunst und Kulturgeschichte Schloss Gottorf, Landesmuseen Schleswig-Holstein – **Zugangsnummer:** 1976/318a – **Entwerfer:** z. Zt. unbekannt – **Hersteller:** z. Zt. unbekannt – **Datierung:** um 1800 – **Technologie:** Tiefer, nach hinten ausschwingender Armlehnsessel mit schmalen Seitenwangen, die innen und außen flach gepolstert sind. Die Rückenlehne ist durchbrochen und trägt in der Mitte ein Gitterwek. Alle Außenkanten sind mit geriefeltem Messingblech beschlagen – **Bezug:** schwarzgold gestreifter Rosshaarbezug – **Objektmaße:** 92 x 66 x 84 cm – **Restaurierung:** Astrid Boeck RiH – **Fotografie:** Museum für Kunst und Kulturgeschichte Schloss Gottorf, Landesmuseen Schleswig-Holstein.

31
Das Architekturmotiv im Möbelentwurf: Gravur Nummer VIII (Paris, Anfang 19. Jh.) mit Zeichnungen von Möbeln aus

present unknown – **Origin:** at present unknown – **Date:** England, 18th century – **Technique:** mahogany frame, the under-construction is made of softwood, fitted with hand-turned steel springs and horsehair cover – **Cover:** horsehair – **Object measurements:** 83 x 73 x 52 cm – **Conservation:** Raumausstattermeisterin Elisabeth Riß and Stefan Oswald RiH – **Photo:** LÖFFLER COLLECTION, Reichenschwand.

26
View inside the opened chamber horse – **Photo:** Cordula Fink, 2021.

27
Armchair – **Property:** Stiftung Preußische Schlösser and Gärten Berlin-Brandenburg – **Inventory number:** IV 67 – **Design:** at present unknown – **Origin:** at present unknown – **Date:** around 1765 – **Technique:** beechwood frame with curved seat and beige lacquer, oval backrest framed by wooden rails all around – **Upholstery:** French narrow webbing with stitched edge roll filled with horsehair. Horsehair stuffing, bridle tied to the webbing. Backrest with hybrid form, stitched up on three edges without extensive stitching and with horsehair stuffing – **Cover:** hand-sewn silk cover with passementerie on lower rail – **Object measurements:** 112.5 x 85.5 x 77 cm – **Notes:** upholstery in original state – **Conservation:** cover fabric is not original. Embroidery probably from the first half of the 19th century – **Photo:** Stiftung Preußische Schlösser and Gärten Berlin-Brandenburg.

28
Armchair, same as no. 27, but opened – **Photo:** Stiftung Preußische Schlösser and Gärten Berlin-Brandenburg.

29
Sofa – **Property:** LÖFFLER COLLECTION, Reichenschwand – **Inventory number:** 02626 – **Design:** at present unknown – **Origin:** at present unknown – **Date:** Louis XVI, around 1780 – **Technique:** solid wood, carved, opaque paint in beige/grey; seat: oval shape with five feet (conic, tapered); backrest: oval shape – **Upholstery:** lashed, sprung seat with stuffing of tow and horsehair; backrest medallion and armrests upholstered with horsehair – **Cover:** warp pattern, silk, re-weave after original – **Object measurements:** 96 x 161 x 80 cm, seat: 47 x 132 x 60 cm – **Notes:** upholstery in original state, cover fabric and passementerie reconstructed according to findings.

30
Armchair – **Property:** Museum für Kunst and Kulturgeschichte Schloss Gottorf, Landesmuseen Schleswig-Holstein – **Accession number:** 1976/318a – **Design:** at present unknown – **Producer:** at present unknown – **Date:** around 1800 – **Technique:** Low, backward-curved armchair with narrow side panels, which are upholstered flat on the inside and outside. The backrest is openwork and has latticework in the middle. All outer edges are covered with ribbed brass plate – **Cover:** haircloth with black and golden stripes – **Object measurements:** 92 x 66 x 84 cm – **Conservation:** Astrid Boeck RiH – **Photo:** Museum für Kunst und Kulturgeschichte Schloss Gottorf, Landesmuseen Schleswig-Holstein.

31
The architectural motif in furniture design, engraving number VIII (Paris, early 19th century) with drawings of furniture from the graphic series *Cahier des Menuisiers*, GRASSI Museum für Angewandte Kunst Leipzig – **Inventory number:** 1919.

Objekt und Bild | Objects and images **329**

der grafischen Reihe: *Cahier des Menuisiers*, Sammlung GRASSI Museum für Angewandte Kunst Leipzig – **Inventarnummer:** 1919.

32
Armlehnsessel *en gondole* – **Eigentum:** Kassel, Museumslandschaft Hessen Kassel – **Inventarnummer:** SM 2.1.2107 – **Entwerfer:** z. Zt. unbekannt – **Hersteller:** z. Zt. unbekannt – **Datierung:** 1800/1820 – **Technologie:** Gestell aus Mahagoniholz massiv und auf Buchenholz furniert. Vorderbeine und Armlehnen sind in Lindenholz geschnitzt, kreidegrundiert und auf gelbem und rotem Poliment im Wechsel Glanz- und Mattvergoldung ausgeführt. Der Sessel besitzt geschnitzte und goldgefasste Vorderbeine mit Armlehnstützen in Gestalt einer Sphinx auf Klauenfuß. Die Armlehnen sind aus nach hinten geschwungenen und vergoldeten Flügeln gebildet, die oben gepolstert und mit grüner Seide bezogen sind – **Bezug:** Seidenbezug in Grün, Dunkelgrün und Ocker. Reliefsamt mit Schattiermanier. Versilberte Metallfäden mit Baumwollseele. Kordel. Ein kleines gefundenes Stofffragment zeigt hellblaue Seidencannellé als vermutlichen Erstbezug – Auf dem Polstersitz zeigt sich das Bild einer großen Rosette mit Rankenwerk, auf der Rückenlehne sind zwei hochgestellte und weinlaubumrankte Fackeln zu sehen, die den Rahmen für eine Vase mit Lorbeergirlanden bilden – **Objektmaße:** 83 x 71 x 66 cm – **Fotografie:** Museumslandschaft Hessen Kassel, Möbelsammlung (Foto: Katrin Venhorst).

33/34
Stuhl – **Eigentum:** Kassel, Museumslandschaft Hessen Kassel – **Inventarnummer:** SM 2.1.1579 – **Entwerfer:** z. Zt. unbekannt – **Hersteller:** z. Zt. unbekannt – **Datierung:** 1826 – **Technologie:** Das Gestell besteht aus Buchenholz, mit einem Furnier aus Birkenwurzelholz, Mahagoni – **Bezug:** Seidendamast: grün, gelb, hellbraun und ockerfarben als Atlasbindung – **Objektmaße:** 91,5 x 49 x 53,5 cm, Sitzhöhe: 47 cm – **Fotografie:** Museumslandschaft Hessen Kassel, Möbelsammlung (Foto: Katrin Venhorst).

35/36
Armlehnsessel – **Eigentum:** Kassel, Museumslandschaft Hessen Kassel – **Inventarnummer:** SM 2.1.2463 – **Entwerfer:** Johann Conrad Bromeis – **Ausführung:** Carl Christian Lauckhardt – **Datierung:** 1823 – **Technologie:** Gestell in Mahagoniholz, furniert, Blindholz Rotbuche (?), Eichenholz, Holz geschnitzt, Bronze, vergoldet – Vierkantbeine, etwas ausgestellt und leicht konisch auslaufend, die Hinterbeine direkt in die Holme der Rückenlehne übergehend. Auf die glatten Zargen sind Bronzebeschläge aufgebracht. Auf der Zargenfront zeigt sich mittig eine Rosette mit seitlichen Blattstäben, die in Zapfen enden. Die Stützen der Armlehnen sind als vollplastische und vergoldete Greifen ausgebildet, deren Vorderbeine auf einem zylindrischen, blattverzierten Podest aufsetzen und deren Flügel die Armlehnen tragen. Der Hinterleib der Greifen geht in eine geschwungene, mit Akanthusblatt belegte Zierform über – **Bezug:** purpurrote Seide, auf der Sitzfläche versehen mit einem Rosettenmotiv, von eingerollten Akanthusblättern umrahmt. Das Rückenpolster ziert ein Blumenmotiv mit Lorbeerzweigen. Bordüren unterschiedlicher Größe zeigen Füllhörner im Rapport. Gelb-rot gestreifte Kordeln vervollständigen die Polsterung – **Objektmaße:** 100 x 68 x 63 cm – **Provenienz:** Auf der Innenseite der Zarge steht in Blei geschrieben: Carl Lauckhardt Bro.7 zweites Wohnzimmer – **Anmerkung:** Der Stuhl stand ab 1823 im Mittelbau von Schloss Wilhelmshöhe, Beletage, im roten Wohnzimmer. Nach Auftrag von Kurfürst Wilhelm II. lieferte Johan Bromeis den Entwurf, die Ausführung erfolgte durch den Kasseler Schreinermeister Carl Lauckhardt. Der Seidendamast kam aus Lyon und die vergoldeten Bronzen aus Paris – **Fotografie:** Museumslandschaft Hessen Kassel, Möbelsammlung (Foto: Katrin Venhorst).

32
Armchair *en gondole* – **Property:** Kassel, Museumslandschaft Hessen Kassel – **Inventory number:** SM 2.1.2107 – **Design:** at present unknown – **Producer:** at present unknown – **Date:** 1800/1820 – **Technique:** mahogany frame and beech veneer. Front legs and armrests are carved in lime wood, with chalk base and alternating bright and matt gilding on yellow and red chalk. The armchair has carved and gilded front legs with sphinxes as armrests that rest on claw feet. The armrests are made from gilded, backward-curved wings and are upholstered on top with a green silk cover – **Cover:** silk cover in green, dark green and ochre. Hatched pile-on-pile velvet; silver-plated metal threads with cotton thread core; cord; a found small, light-blue fabric fragment presumably the first cover – On the seat a large rosette with scrollwork, on the back two torches entwined with vine that frame a vase with laurel festoon – **Object measurements:** 83 x 71 x 66 cm – **Photo:** Museumslandschaft Hessen Kassel (Katrin Venhorst).

33/34
Chair – **Property:** Kassel, Museumslandschaft Hessen Kassel – **Inventory number:** SM 2.1.1579 – **Design:** at present unknown – **Producer:** at present unknown – **Date:** 1826 – **Technique:** beech frame with birch burr wooden veneer, mahogany – **Cover:** silk damask: green, yellow, light brown and ochre as satin weave – **Object measurements:** 91.5 x 49 x 53.5 cm, seat H: 47 cm – **Photo:** Museumslandschaft Hessen Kassel (Photo: Katrin Venhorst).

35/36
Armchair – **Property:** Kassel, Museumslandschaft Hessen Kassel – **Inventory number:** SM 2.1.2463 – **Design:** Johann Conrad Bromeis – **Execution:** Carl Christian Lauckhardt – **Date:** 1823 – **Technique:** mahogany frame, veneered (common) beech frame?, oak, carved, bronze, gilded. Square legs, flared and slightly tapered, the back legs merging directly into the spars of the backrest. Bronze mounts on all smooth rails. The front rails with a central rosette with lateral leaf bars ending in tenons. The supports of the armrests are fully sculpted with gilded griffins whose front legs rest on a cylindrical, leaf-decorated pedestal and whose wings support the armrests. The abdomen of the griffins merges into a curved decorative form covered with acanthus leaves – **Cover:** crimson silk, on the seat with rosette motif surrounded by scrolled acanthus leaves. Backrest with floral motif and laurel branches, borders of different sizes with cornucopias as repeat pattern. Yellow-red cords – **Object measurements:** 100 x 68 x 63 cm – **Provenance:** on the inside rail written in graphite: 'Carl Lauckhardt Bro.7 zweites Wohnzimmer' – **Notes:** from 1823, the chair stood in the middle building of Wilhelmshöhe Palace, piano nobile, in the red living room. The design was commissioned by Elector Wilhelm II from Johann Conrad Bromeis and executed by the master carpenter Carl Lauckhardt from Kassel. The silk damask came from Lyon and the gilded bronze mounts from Paris – **Photo:** Museumslandschaft Hessen Kassel (Katrin Venhorst).

37/38
Stool – **Property:** Kassel, Museumslandschaft Hessen Kassel – **Inventory number:** SM 2.1.289 – **Design:** at present unknown – **Execution:** at present unknown – **Date:** around 1830 – **Technique:** beech frame, partially black lacquer, legs in bronze shoes, upholstered seat with tassels on all four sides – **Cover:** yellow silk – **Object measurements:** 56.5 x 67 x 51 cm – **Photo:** Museumslandschaft Hessen Kassel (Katrin Venhorst).

37/38
Hocker – **Eigentum:** Kassel, Museumslandschaft Hessen Kassel – **Inventarnummer:** SM 2.1.289 – **Entwerfer:** z. Zt. unbekannt – **Hersteller:** z. Zt. unbekannt – **Datierung:** um 1830 – **Technologie:** Buchenholzgestell, teils schwarz lackiert. Die Beine stecken in Bronzeschuhen. Die Sitzfläche ist gepolstert und an allen vier Seiten mit Gehänge versehen – **Bezug:** gelbe Seide – **Objektmaße:** 56,5 x 67 x 51 cm – **Fotografie:** Museumslandschaft Hessen Kassel, Möbelsammlung (Foto: Katrin Venhorst).

39/40
Armlehnsessel – **Eigentum:** LÖFFLER COLLECTION, Reichenschwand – **Inventarnummer:** 02662 – **Entwurf:** Karl Friedrich Schinkel – **Herstellung:** z. Zt. unbekannt – **Datierung:** um 1830 – **Technologie:** Das Gestell ist aus Eichen- und Kiefernholz massiv, dünn lackiert, mit Federkernpolsterung, der Sitz ruht auf Kufenfüßen mit geschnitzten Schmuckelementen, dazwischen zwei gedrechselte Streben, Armlehnen schneckenartig gebogen; die Lehne ist leicht geschwungen – **Polsteraufbau:** Sitz und Rückenlehne verfügen beide über eine geschnürte Federkonstruktion, versehen mit Fasson aus Werg und Capitonné-Heftung – **Bezug:** perkin-violetter Mohairvelours in Capitonné-Heftung – **Objektmaße:** 112,5 x 68 x 90 cm, Sitzhöhe: 47,5 cm – **Literatur:** *Die Kunstwelt*, Heft 1, 1912–1913, S. 439; Karl Friedrich Schinkel: *Architektur, Malerei, Kunstgewerbe*. Berlin 1981, S. 298f. – **Restaurierung:** Bei der original erhaltenen Polsterung wurde lediglich die Capitonné-Heftung mit neuem Rosshaar ergänzt, während Bezug und Posamente neu aufgebracht wurden. Die Porzellannägel stammen aus der Zeit – **Restaurierung:** Stefan Oswald RiH, Posamente: Posamenten Müller – **Fotografie:** LÖFFLER COLLECTION, Reichenschwand.

41/42
Stuhl (Schnittmodell) – **Eigentum:** Wolfgang Nerge, Doris Nolting – **Datierung:** 19. und 21. Jahrhundert – **Technologie:** Buchenholzgestell mit Rückenmedaillon, kannelierte Balusterbeine mit Würfelabschluss, gestrichene Leinöloberfläche in Cremeweiß – **Polsteraufbau:** Gurtung mit Leinengurten, Leinenabdeckung, umlaufendes Hoch-Bourlet aus Brechflachs garniert mit Leiter- und einem Vorderstich; Schnürung aus vier handgedrehten Federn mit Stell- und Knotfaden; Fassonpolster aus Brechflachs, einfach durchgenäht, Pikierung aus Rosshaar, Nessel- und Watteabdeckung; Rückenpolsteraufbau: mit Leinen bezogene Pappe, umlaufendes Bourlet aus Rosshaar, mit drei Vorderstichen garniert, Rosshaarfüllung, Nessel- und Watteabdeckung – **Bezug:** Seide mit Granatapfelmotiv – **Objektmaße:** 96 x 51 cm x 47,5 cm – **Fördernde:** Stoff: Dedar, Posamente: Doris Nolting RiH, Wolfgang Nerge RiH, Arbeitsleistung: Stefan Kloss RiH (Oberfläche), Torsten Otto RiH (Polsterung Sitz) und Stefan Oswald RiH (Polsterung Lehne, Bezug) – **Fotografie:** LÖFFLER COLLECTION, Reichenschwand.

43
Aquarell – **Eigentum:** GRASSI Museum für Angewandte Kunst Leipzig – **Inventarnummer:** B.2020.77 – **Provenienz:** Erworben mit Unterstützung von Reinhardt Roßberg, Markkleeberg, 2020 – **Entwurf:** unbekannter, wohl Leipziger Künstler, Blick auf den Leipziger Markt am Morgen. Bleistift, Feder in Schwarz, Gouache, weiß gehöht. Um 1820 – **Objektmaße:** 42,3 x 33 cm auf 50 x 38,5 cm.

44
Ohrensessel – **Eigentum:** LÖFFLER COLLECTION, Reichenschwand – **Inventarnummer:** 01883 – **Entwurf:** z. Zt. unbekannt – **Herstellung:** z. Zt. unbekannt – **Datierung:** um 1825 – **Technologie:** Die Bauteile der Konstruktion bestehen aus europäischen Laub- und Nadelhölzern. Der runde Sitz ist drehbar gehalten und ruht auf vier Säbelbeinen, ist mit Kirsche furniert und auf der Oberfläche dünn lackiert; Kirschfurnier überzieht auch den geschweiften Holzrahmen der

39/40
Armchair – **Property:** LÖFFLER COLLECTION, Reichenschwand – **Inventory number:** 02662 – **Design:** Karl Friedrich Schinkel – **Origin:** at present unknown – **Date:** around 1830 – **Technique:** solid oak and pine frame, thin lacquer with spring-core upholstery, on X-frame feet (with carved decoration); stretchers, armrests curved, curved backrest – **Upholstery:** seat and backrest with a lashed sprung construction, tow stuffing and deep-buttoned – **Object measurements:** 112.5 x 68 x 90 cm, seat H: 47.5 cm – **Literature:** *Die Kunstwelt*, no. 1, 1912–13, p. 439; Karl Friedrich Schinkel, *Architektur, Malerei, Kunstgewerbe*, Berlin 1981, pp. 298–298 – **Conservation:** original upholstery, only horsehair added to the deep-buttoning, while cover and passementerie were recovered. Porcelain nails from the period – **Conservation:** Stefan Oswald RiH; passementerie: Posamenten Müller – **Photo:** LÖFFLER COLLECTION, Reichenschwand.

41/42
Chair (sectional model) – **Property:** Wolfgang Nerge, Doris Nolting – **Date:** 19th and 21st century – **Technique:** beech frame with back medallion, fluted baluster legs with cubic end piece, surface painted with linseed oil in cream-white – **Upholstery:** webbing with linen straps, stitched-up flax edge roll on all sides with blind and top stitch, lashing with four hand-turned springs; flax-fibre stuffing, stitched, second stuffing with horsehair, wadding and calico cover; back upholstery: linen-covered board, edge roll on all sides with three blind stitches, horsehair stuffing, wadding and calico cover – **Cover:** silk with pomegranate motif – **Object measurements:** 96 x 51 cm x 47.5 cm – **Sponsors:** Dedar (fabric), Doris Nolting RiH (passementerie), Wolfgang Nerge RiH, Stefan Kloss RiH (work, surface), Torsten Otto RiH (seat upholstery), Stefan Oswald RiH (backrest, cover upholstery) – **Photo:** LÖFFLER COLLECTION, Reichenschwand.

43
Watercolour – **Property:** GRASSI Museum für Angewandte Kunst Leipzig – **Inventory number:** B.2020.77 – **Provenance:** Acquired with the support of Reinhardt Roßberg, Markkleeberg, 2020– **Design:** unknown, presumably Leipzig-based artist, view of the Leipzig market in the morning. Graphite, black pen, gouache, heightened with white; around 1820 – **Object measurements:** 42,3 x 33 cm on 50 x 38,5 cm.

44
Wing chair – **Property:** LÖFFLER COLLECTION, Reichenschwand – **Inventory number:** 01883 – **Design:** at present unknown – **Origin:** at present unknown – **Date:** around 1825 – **Technique:** construction made from European deciduous and coniferous wood – the round seat can turn and rests on four bow legs, veneered with cherrywood and thinly lacquered; the curved wooden frame of the high, winged back is veneered in the same way – **Upholstery:** lashed, sprung construction with tow stuffing and horsehair cover while back and armrests are stuffed with horsehair – **Cover:** patterned mohair velour; restored using historical fabric – **Object measurements:** 127.5 x 69 x 75 cm, seat H: 51 x 50 x 50 cm – **Conservation:** fabric and passementerie from the period, upholstery reconstructed using materials from the period, Stefan Oswald RiH – **Photo:** LÖFFLER COLLECTION, Reichenschwand.

45/46
Swivel armchair – **Property:** LÖFFLER COLLECTION, Reichenschwand – **Inventory number:** 01148 – **Design:** at present unknown – **Origin:** at present unknown – **Date:** around 1835 – **Technique:** different solid woods, round,

hohen Rückenlehne mit Ohrenbacken – **Polsteraufbau:** Der Sitz verfügt über eine geschnürte Federkonstruktion mit Wergfasson und Rosshaardeckung, während die Rückenpolsterung und die Armlehnen mit einer garnierten Rosshaarfasson ausgestattet sind – **Bezug:** gemusterter Mohairvelours, restauriert unter Verwendung eines historischen Gewebes – **Objektmaße:** 127,5 x 69 x 75 cm, Sitzhöhe: 51 x 50 x 50 cm – **Restaurierung:** Stoff und Posamente stammen aus der Zeit, die Polsterung wurde unter Verwendung von Materialien aus der Zeit rekonstruiert, Stefan Oswald RiH – **Fotografie:** LÖFFLER COLLECTION, Reichenschwand.

45/46
Armlehndrehstuhl – **Eigentum:** LÖFFLER COLLECTION, Reichenschwand – **Inventarnummer:** 01148 – **Entwurf:** z. Zt. unbekannt – **Herstellung:** z. Zt. unbekannt – **Datierung:** um 1835 – **Technologie:** Verschiedene Massivhölzer, der Sitz hat eine runde Form, ist drehbar gelagert und ruht auf vier geschweiften Beinen aus massivem Kirschbaumholz versehen mit Zargen aus Kirschfurnier, die Oberfläche besitzt eine dünne Lackschicht; die ebenfalls geschweifte Lehne besteht aus teilweise massiven und furnierten Bauteilen – **Polsteraufbau:** Der Sitz basiert auf einer geschnürten Federkonstruktion mit Wergfasson und Rosshaardeckung, während die ungeöffnete Rückenpolsterung und die Armlehnen vermutlich über eine Rosshaarfasson verfügen – **Bezug:** gemusterter Velours, Flor stellenweise abgerieben – **Objektmaße:** 82,5 x 57,5 x 63 cm, Sitzhöhe: 51 x 50 x 50 cm – **Restaurierung:** Die Oberfläche wurde gereinigt, sonst befindet sich der Stuhl im unberührten Originalzustand – **Fotografie:** LÖFFLER COLLECTION, Reichenschwand.

47/48
Zweisitziges Sofa *tête-à-tête* – **Eigentum:** LÖFFLER COLLECTION, Reichenschwand – **Inventarnummer:** 03202 – **Entwurf:** z. Zt. unbekannt – **Herstellung:** Mainz – **Datierung:** 1877 – **Technologie:** Polstergestell aus Buchen- oder Lindenholz, mit gedrechselten Füßen, die über Hirschhornrollen verfügen, wodurch sich das Möbel leichter versetzen lässt – **Polsteraufbau:** Der Sitz verfügt über eine geschnürte Federkonstruktion mit Afrikfasson und Rosshaar, die Lehne über eine Capitonné-Heftung (Rosshaar und Afrik) – **Bezug:** Rekonstruktion nach Befund des originalen Gewebes (Cammann Gobelinmanufaktur) – **Objektmaße:** 70 x 140 x 74 cm – **Restaurierung:** Originale Polsterung restauriert von Elisabeth Riß Raumausstattermeisterin, Julia Szentesi, Stefan Oswald RiH; Posamente rekonstruiert und restauriert von Simone Howe – **Fotografie:** LÖFFLER COLLECTION, Reichenschwand.

49–54
Titelblatt und fünf Seiten eines Kataloges für Stilmöbel aus dem *Guide du Fabricant de Meubles et du Décorateur*, der um 1860 als Verkaufskatalog die Stuhlmodelle der Firma M. Piaget bewarb, Originalkatalog im Archiv Thomas Schriefers.

55
Illustration von Émile Bayard zum Roman *Le Docteur Rameau* von Georges Ohnet, aus: *L'Illustration*, Nr. 2394 vom 12.1.1889, S. 41, Originalzeitschrift im Archiv Thomas Schriefers.

56–58
Stuhl *fumeuse* – **Eigentum:** LÖFFLER COLLECTION, Reichenschwand – **Inventarnummer:** 02986 – **Entwurf:** z. Zt. unbekannt – **Herstellung:** z. Zt. unbekannt – **Datierung:** ca. 1870–1890 – **Technologie:** Der Sitz hat eine ovale Form mit gerader Hinterkante, gerade verlaufende Zargen, profiliert, vier gedrechselte Beine in Säulenform, Vollholz, dunkel lackiert: Die Lehne ist komplett geschnitzt, teils durchbrochen und besitzt einen profiliert-rechteckigen Rahmenaufsatz mit Polsterdeckung – **Polsteraufbau:** Im Sitz findet sich ein garniertes Fassonpolster auf Gurtgrund, Werg und Rosshaar, auf der

swivel seat on four sabre legs made from solid cherrywood. Thin lacquer surface, the equally curved back from solid and veneered elements – **Upholstery:** seat with lashed sprung upholstery with tow stuffing and horsehair cover, the unopened upholstery of backrest and armrests presumably stuffed with horsehair – **Cover:** patterned velour, pile partially rubbed away – **Object measurements:** 82.5 x 57.5 x 63 cm, seat: 51 x 50 x 50 cm – **Conservation:** surface was cleaned, otherwise the chair is in untouched original state – **Photo:** LÖFFLER COLLECTION, Reichenschwand.

47/48
Two-sitter sofa *tête-à-tête* – **Property:** LÖFFLER COLLECTION, Reichenschwand – **Inventory number:** 03202 – **Design:** at present unknown – **Origin:** Mainz – **Date:** 1877 – **Technique:** beech and limewood frame with turned feed with staghorn casters so that the object can be easily moved – **Upholstery:** seat with lashed sprung construction with palm fibre and horsehair stuffing, deep-buttoned backrest (horsehair and palm fibre) – **Cover:** reconstruction after fragments of original fabric (Cammann Gobelinmanufaktur) – **Object measurements:** 70 x 140 x 74 cm – **Conservation:** Raumausstattermeisterin Elisabeth Riß (restoration of original upholstery), Julia Szentesi, Stefan Oswald RiH, Simone Howe (reconstruction and restoration of passementerie) – **Photo:** LÖFFLER COLLECTION, Reichenschwand.

49–54
Cover and five pages from a catalogue of period furniture, *Guide du Fabricant de Meubles et du Décorateur*, which was used as a sales catalogue to advertise the chair models of the M. Piaget company around 1860; original catalogue at Archive Thomas Schriefers.

55
Illustration by Émile Bayard from the novel *Le Docteur Rameau* by Georges Ohnet in *L'Illustration*, no. 2394, 12 January 1889, p. 41; original newspaper at Archive Thomas Schriefers.

56–58
Chair *fumeuse* – **Property:** LÖFFLER COLLECTION, Reichenschwand – **Inventory number:** 02986 – **Design:** at present unknown – **Origin:** at present unknown – **Date:** ca. 1870–90 – **Technique:** oval seat with straight back edge, straight rails, carved, four turned column legs, solid wood, dark lacquer: carved, pierced backrest with sloping rectangular shelf with padding – **Upholstery:** seat with tow and horsehair stuffing on webbing, on the shelf horsehair cushion – **Cover:** patterned mohair velour, presumably printed – **Object measurements:** 82.5 x 46 x 68 cm, seat: 44 x 45 x 45 cm – **Notes:** 'Fumeuse' used as a smoker's chair, a variation of the voyeuse with a compartment for smoking utensils and pipes – **Conservation:** surfaces cleaned, otherwise in untouched original state – **Photo:** LÖFFLER COLLECTION, Reichenschwand.

59/60
Chair – **Property:** LÖFFLER COLLECTION, Reichenschwand – **Inventory number:** 02785 – **Design:** Georg Hulbe – **Origin:** Kunstgewerbliche Werkstatt Georg Hulbe, Hamburg – **Date:** around 1888 – **Technique:** solid nutwood frame; transparent lacquer; seat tapered to the back, rails with chip carving, four turned baluster legs – **Upholstery:** seat with flat fine tow stuffing, backrest without stuffing – **Cover:** (punched and modelled) leather – **Object measurements:** 86.5 x 45.5 x 49 cm, seat: 44.5 x 45.5 x 38 cm – **Literature:** Paul von Salvisberg, *Chronik der deutsch-nationalen Kunstgewerbe-Ausstellung in Munich 1888*, Munich 1888, p. 228 – **Conservation:** saddler Birgit Baer – **Photo:** LÖFFLER COLLECTION, Reichenschwand.

Lehne ein aufgelegtes Rosshaarpolster – **Bezug:** gemusterter Mohairvelours, wohl bedruckt – **Objektmaße:** 82,5 x 46 x 68 cm; Sitzhöhe: 44 x 45 x 45 cm – **Anmerkung:** *fumeuse* gebräuchlich als Raucherstuhl in Abwandlung einer Voyeuse mit einem Fach für Rauchutensilien und Pfeifen – **Restaurierung:** Oberflächen gereinigt, ansonsten unberührter Originalzustand – **Fotografie:** LÖFFLER COLLECTION, Reichenschwand.

59/60
Stuhl – **Eigentum:** LÖFFLER COLLECTION, Reichenschwand – Inventarnummer: 02785 – **Entwurf:** Georg Hulbe – **Herstellung:** Kunstgewerbliche Werkstatt Georg Hulbe, Hamburg – **Datierung:** um 1888 – **Technologie:** Gestellkonstruktion in Nussholz massiv, transparent lackiert; der Sitz ist nach hinten konisch verlaufend, die Zargen mit Kerbschnitzerei versehen und die vier Beine balusterförmig gedrechselt – **Polsteraufbau:** Der Sitz ist als Feinwergflachpolster ausgeführt, die Lehne besitzt keine Unterfütterung – **Bezug:** punziertes und modelliertes Leder – **Objektmaße:** 86,5 x 45,5 x 49 cm; Sitzhöhe: 44,5 x 45,5 x 38 cm – **Literatur:** Paul von Salvisberg: *Chronik der deutsch-nationalen Kunstgewerbe-Ausstellung in München 1888*, S. 228 – **Restaurierung:** Birgit Baer, Sattlerin – **Fotografie:** LÖFFLER COLLECTION, Reichenschwand.

61
Armlehnstuhl – **Eigentum:** LÖFFLER COLLECTION, Reichenschwand – **Inventarnummer:** 03117 – **Entwurf:** z. Zt. unbekannt – **Herstellung:** z. Zt. unbekannt – **Datierung:** um 1890 – **Technologie:** Das Gestell besteht aus Eichenholz massiv, ist schwarz gebeizt und lackiert und mit einer Flachschnitzerei versehen – **Polsteraufbau:** Das Sitz- und Rückenlehnenpolster besteht aus einer geschnürten Federkonstruktion, mit einer Fasson aus Werg und Rosshaar, wobei auf dem Sitz zusätzlich ein Daunenkissen aufgelegt ist; auf den Armlehnen wurde ein garniertes Flachpolster aufgebracht – **Bezug:** gemusterter Mohairvelours aus der Zeit – **Objektmaße:** 148 x 69 x 70 cm; Sitzhöhe: 52 x 54 x 50 cm – **Restaurierung:** Polsterung restauriert und teilrekonstruiert unter Verwendung originalen Materials, Elisabeth Riß, Raumausstattermeisterin – **Fotografie:** LÖFFLER COLLECTION, Reichenschwand.

62
Armlehnstuhl – **Eigentum:** LÖFFLER COLLECTION, Reichenschwand – **Inventarnummer:** 02591 – **Entwurf und Herstellung:** Möbelfabrik Hess & Rom, Berlin – **Datierung:** 1899 – **Technologie:** Gestell Eiche massiv, transparent lackiert; die Rahmen und Zargen sind aus Buchenholz gefertigt, die Zargen besitzen zusätzlich Anleimer aus massivem und profiliertem Eichenholz; die Rückenlehne ist mit reicher Flachschnitzerei und Durchbrüchen versehen – **Polsteraufbau:** Der geschnürte Sitz hat eine Fasson aus Werg und Rosshaar, zusätzlich ist ein Rosshaarkissen aufgelegt – **Bezug:** gemusterter Mohairvelours, restauriert unter Verwendung eines historischen Gewebes – **Objektmaße:** 139 x 73 x 70 cm; Sitzhöhe: 55 x 60 x 55 cm – **Literatur:** *Moderne Kunst. Illustrierte Zeitschrift*, Heft 14/1900, S. 164 – **Restaurierung:** Die Polsterung wurde rekonstruiert und teilrestauriert, Stoff und Posamente aus der Zeit, Elisabeth Riß, Raumausstattermeisterin – **Fotografie:** LÖFFLER COLLECTION, Reichenschwand.

63
Armlehnstuhl – **Eigentum:** LÖFFLER COLLECTION, Reichenschwand – **Inventarnummer:** 02014 – **Entwurf:** z. Zt. unbekannt – **Herstellung:** z. Zt. unbekannt – **Datierung:** um 1900 – **Technologie:** Das Gestell besteht aus massivem Eichenholz, ist schwarz/leicht grünlich gebeizt und lackiert, mit einer geschwungen-geschweiften Form; die Seiten der hohen Rückenlehne erinnern an Ohrenbacken – **Polsteraufbau:** Das Sitzpolster besteht aus einer geschnürten Federkonstruktion, mit einer Fasson aus Werg und Rosshaar; darauf aufgelegt ein mit Rosshaar gefülltes Kissen; die Armlehnen sind garniert und

61
Armchair – **Property:** LÖFFLER COLLECTION, Reichenschwand – **Inventory number:** 03117 – **Design:** at present unknown – **Origin:** at present unknown – **Date:** around 1890 – **Technique:** solid oakwood frame, stained black and lacquered, with flat carving – **Upholstery:** seat and back upholstery with lashed sprung construction, tow and horsehair padding, seat with additional down squab; armrests with flat padding – **Cover:** patterned mohair velour of the period – **Object measurements:** 148 x 69 x 70 cm, seat: 52 x 54 x 50 cm – **Conservation:** Raumausstattermeisterin Elisabeth Riß (upholstery restoration and partial reconstruction using original materials) – **Photo:** LÖFFLER COLLECTION, Reichenschwand.

62
Armchair – **Property:** LÖFFLER COLLECTION, Reichenschwand – **Inventory number:** 02591 – **Design/Origin:** Möbelfabrik Hess & Rom, Berlin – **Date:** 1899 – **Technique:** solid oakwood frame, transparent lacquer; beech frame and rails, additional elements on rails with solid and profiled oakwood,; backrest with rich flat carving and openwork – **Upholstery:** the lashed seat with tow and horsehair stuffing, additional horsehair cushion – **Cover:** patterned mohair velour, restored using historical fabric – **Object measurements:** 139 x 73 x 70 cm, seat: 55 x 60 x 55 cm – **Literature:** *Moderne Kunst: Illustrierte Zeitschrift*, no. 14, 1900, p. 164 – **Conservation:** Raumausstattermeisterin Elisabeth Riß (upholstery reconstruction and partial restoration, fabrics and passementerie from the period) – **Photo:** LÖFFLER COLLECTION, Reichenschwand.

63
Armchair – **Property:** LÖFFLER COLLECTION, Reichenschwand – **Inventory number:** 02014 – **Design:** at present unknown – **Origin:** at present unknown – **Date:** around 1900 – **Technique:** solid oakwood frame, stained and lacquered black, slightly green with curved shape; sides of the high backrest resemble wings – **Upholstery:** seat upholstery from lashed sprung construction, tow and horsehair stuffing, horsehair-stuffed squab; upholstered armrests with tow and horsehair stuffing; backrest with horsehair and tow stuffing – **Cover:** patterned mohair velour, restored using historical fabric of the period – **Object measurements:** 137 cm x 87.5 x 74.5 cm, seat: 52 x 66 x 48 cm – **Conservation:** Raumausstattermeisterin Elisabeth Riß (upholstery reconstruction) – **Photo:** LÖFFLER COLLECTION, Reichenschwand.

64/65
Sofa – **Property:** Torsten Otto, Markkleeberg – **Designer:** at present unknown – **Producer:** at present unknown – **Date:** around 1900 – **Technique:** beech frame, two sabre back legs and two turned front legs on metal casters – **Upholstery:** jute webbing, waisted springs, hessian, natural fibre stuffing – **Cover:** mohair velour with cords and tasselled fringe – **Object measurements:** 100 x 136 x 65.5 cm, seat: 52.5 x 136 x 60 cm – **Notes:** sofa in original state – **Photo:** LÖFFLER COLLECTION, Reichenschwand.

66
Chair – **Property:** On permanent loan to the GRASSI Museum für Angewandte Kunst Leipzig from the Pese Collection, Nuremberg, since 2020. Intended for donation. – **Design:** Henry van de Velde – **Origin:** Court carpenter Fritz Scheidemantel, Weimar – **Date:** 1903 – **Technique:** European beech frame and coniferous wood, lacquered; seat is traditional flat upholstery, backrest is flat upholstery with braids – **Upholstery:** seat on 2 x 3 webbing (renewed), lightweight canvas cover;

Objekt und Bild I Objects and images **333**

verfügen über eine Fasson aus Werg und Rosshaar; die Rückenlehne ist als garniertes Rosshaarpolster ausgebildet, ebenfalls mit einer Fasson aus Werg und Rosshaar versehen – **Bezug:** gemusterter Mohairvelours, restauriert unter Verwendung eines historischen Gewebes aus der Zeit – **Objektmaße:** 137 cm x 87,5 x 74,5 cm, Sitzhöhe: 52 x 66 x 48 cm – **Restaurierung:** Die Polsterung wurde rekonstruiert, Elisabeth Riß Raumausstattermeisterin – **Fotografie:** LÖFFLER COLLECTION, Reichenschwand.

64/65
Sofa – **Eigentum:** Torsten Otto, Markkleeberg – **Entwerfer:** z. Zt. unbekannt – **Hersteller:** z. Zt. unbekannt – **Datierung:** um 1900 – **Technologie:** Das Gestell ist aus Buchenholz gefertigt, die zwei hinteren Beine besitzen eine leicht geschweifte Form, wohingegen die zwei vorderen Beine gedrechselt sind und auf Metallrollen stehen – **Polsteraufbau:** Jutegurte, Taillenfedern, Jutefederleinen, Naturpolstermaterialien – **Bezug:** Mohairvelours mit Kordeln und Quastenfranse – **Objektmaße:** 100 x 136 x 65,5 cm, Sitzhöhe: 52,5 x 136 x 60 cm – **Anmerkung:** Das Sofa befindet sich im Originalzustand – **Fotografie:** LÖFFLER COLLECTION, Reichenschwand.

66
Stuhl – **Eigentum:** Dauerleihgabe für das GRASSI Museum für Angewandte Kunst Leipzig aus der Sammlung Pese, Nürnberg, seit 2020. Zur Schenkung vorgesehen. – **Entwurf:** Henry van de Velde – **Herstellung:** Hoftischlerei Fritz Scheidemantel, Weimar – **Datierung:** 1903 – **Technologie:** Gestell aus Rotbuchenholz und Nadelholz, lackiert; der Sitz ist als traditionelles Flachpolster und die Lehne als Flachpolster mit Borte ausgeführt – **Polsteraufbau:** Das Sitzpolster ruht auf einer 2 x 3-Gurtung (erneuert), darüber ein leichtes Jutefederleinen; darüber ein flaches Polster; die Lehne ist ein Flachpolster auf Pappgrund mit Bortenabdeckung – **Bezug:** ein Atlasgewebe, welches angeraut erscheint, um Velourscharakter vorzutäuschen – **Objektmaße:** 95 x 45,5 x 48 cm; Sitzhöhe: 47 cm – **Anmerkung:** Der Stuhl wurde wahrscheinlich für das Nietzsche-Archiv in Weimar gefertigt. Bezugsstoff und Borte wahrscheinlich noch original, ursprünglich grün, inzwischen ausgeblichen – **Restaurierung:** bis auf Neugurtung im Originalzustand – **Literatur:** Vergleichsbeispiele in: Wolf D. Pecher, *Henry van de Velde. Das Gesamtwerk. Gestaltung*, Bd. 1, München 1981, S. 272, 273, Nr. 1137, Abb. S. 241; Klaus-Jürgen Sembach, Birgit Schulte (Hg.): *Henry van der Velde, Ein europäischer Künstler seiner Zeit*. Köln 1992, S. 262; Gerhard Bott: *Endlich ein Umschwung. Design 1900*. Kataloge des Museums- und Kulturvereins Schloss Albeck, 1996, S. 132, Abb. 71 – **Fotografie:** Esther Hoyer/GRASSI Museum für Angewandte Kunst Leipzig.

67–69
Stuhl – **Eigentum:** LÖFFLER COLLECTION, Reichenschwand – **Inventarnummer:** 03359 – **Entwurf:** Louis Majorelle – **Herstellung:** Werkstatt Louis Majorelle, Nancy, Frankreich – **Datierung:** um 1900 – **Technologie:** Holzgestell mit geschweifter Sitzform und hoher Rückenlehne; der Sitz besteht aus gebogenen bzw. geschwungenen Zargen, vier Beine konisch nach unten zulaufend, Vorderbeine kanneliert, Gestell Teak massiv (?), ursprünglich lackiert (Lackreste, eingefärbter Lack, möglicherweise dunkler Schellack); die Lehne besteht aus einem mit div. Laubhölzern (Platane, Buche, Wenge?) marketierten Lehnenbrett, und zwei profilierten Stäben, Rückseite und Seiten furniert (Teak ?) – **Polsteraufbau:** Der Sitz ist eine geschnürte Federkonstruktion auf Leinwandgrund, Fasson aus Werg oder Rosshaar – **Bezug:** geprägtes Leder – **Objektmaße:** 99 x 43 x 49,5 cm; Sitzhöhe: 48 x 42 x 36 cm – **Anmerkung:** Das Sitzpolster wirkt wie ein Flachpolster, ist tatsächlich aber ein Feder-Hochpolster – **Literatur:** Alastair Duncan: *Louis Majorelle. Meister des Art Nouveau Design*. München, 1991, S. 101 – **Restaurierung:** Originalzustand, Oberflächen gereinigt, Leder restauriert: Birgit Baer, Sattlerin – **Fotografie:** LÖFFLER COLLECTION, Reichenschwand.

flat padding; backrest with flat padding on board base with borders – **Cover:** atlas weave, apparently roughened in order to feign velour – **Object measurements:** 95 x 45.5 x 48 cm, seat H: 47 cm – **Notes:** the chair was probably produced for the Nietzsche Archive in Weimar. Cover fabric and border are presumably original, originally green now faded – **Conservation:** original state, apart from the new webbing – **Literature:** comparative examples in Wolf D. Pecher, *Henry van de Velde: Das Gesamtwerk: Gestaltung*, vol. 1, Munich 1981, pp. 272, 273, no. 1137, fig. p. 241; Klaus-Jürgen Sembach and Birgit Schulte (eds), *Henry van der Velde: Ein europäischer Künstler seiner Zeit*, Cologne 1992, p. 262; Gerhard Bott, *Endlich ein Umschwung: Design 1900*, exh. cat. Museums- and Kulturvereins Schloss Albeck, 1996, p. 132, fig. 71 – **Photo:** Esther Hoyer/GRASSI Museum für Angewandte Kunst Leipzig.

67–69
Chair – **Property:** LÖFFLER COLLECTION, Reichenschwand – **Inventory number:** 03359 – **Design:** Louis Majorelle – **Origin:** Louis Majorelle workshop, Nancy, France – **Date:** around 1900 – **Technique:** wooden frame with curved seat and high backrest; seat with curved rails, four tapered legs, fluted front legs, solid? teak frame, originally lacquered (lack paint remnants, coloured lacquer, probably dark shellac); back splat is veneered (marquetery) with different coniferous wood (plantain, beech, wenge?), two profiled back top and veneered sides (teak?) – **Upholstery:** seat with lashed sprung construction on webbing, tow and horsehair stuffing – **Cover:** embossed leather – **Object measurements:** 99 x 43 x 49.5 cm, seat: 48 x 42 x 36 cm – **Notes:** the seat padding seems to be flat padding but is in fact a high sprung padding – **Literature:** Alastair Duncan, *Louis Majorelle: Meister des Art Nouveau Design*, Munich 1991, p. 101 – **Conservation:** original state, surface cleaned, saddler Birgit Baer (leather restoration) – **Photo:** LÖFFLER COLLECTION, Reichenschwand.

70/71
Chair – **Property:** LÖFFLER COLLECTION, Reichenschwand – **Inventory number:** 03074 – **Design:** Georges de Feure – **Origin:** at present unknown – **Date:** around 1900 – **Technique:** beech seat frame, solid mahogany frame, transparent lacquer, carved; openwork carved back – **Upholstery:** flat padding with horsehair stuffing, seat on webbing – **Cover:** patterned wool fabric, decorative border – **Object measurements:** 88 x 43 x 51.5 cm, seat: 44 x 38 x 39 cm – **Literature:** Gabriel P. Weisberg, *Art Nouveau Bing: Paris Style 1900*, New York 1986, p. 184; Roberta Waddell, *The Art Nouveau Style in Jewelry, Metalwork, Glass, Ceramics, Textiles, Architecture and Furniture*, New York 1977, p. 255; Charlotte Fiell and Peter Fiell, *1000 Chairs*, Cologne 2005, p. 40 – **Conservation:** original state, surface cleaned, upholstery and top cover untouched – **Photo:** LÖFFLER COLLECTION, Reichenschwand.

72–76
Armchair – **Property:** LÖFFLER COLLECTION, Reichenschwand – **Inventory number:** 02829 – **Design:** Josef Hoffmann – **Origin:** Vienna Pancota, Pancota, Romania (brand stamp) – **Date:** around 1906 – **Technique:** solid beech frame; thinly lacquered; slightly curved rails, oval plywood, stained black, as armrest ornament; four turned stiles standing on flat, round feet, U-shaped flat rails (three connected with form spring); curved backrest joins the armrests – **Upholstery:** seat with lashed sprung construction, tow stuffing, upholstery of the backrest is a tow cushion – **Cover:** original mohair velour, originally turquoise-black; yellow geometric pattern, today turned beige-green, original decorative border – **Object meas-

70/71
Stuhl – **Eigentum:** LÖFFLER COLLECTION, Reichenschwand – **Inventarnummer:** 03074 – **Entwurf:** Georges de Feure – **Herstellung:** z. Zt. unbekannt – **Datierung:** um 1900 – **Technologie:** Der Sitzrahmen besteht aus Buchenholz, das Gestell ist Mahagoniholz massiv, transparent lackiert, beschnitzt; die Lehne ist durchbrochen geschnitzt – **Polsteraufbau:** Rosshaarflachpolster, Sitzfläche auf Gurtgrund – **Bezug:** gemusterter Wollstoff, Zierborte – **Objektmaße:** 88 x 43 x 51,5 cm; Sitzhöhe: 44 x 38 x 39 cm – **Literatur:** Gabriel P. Weisberg: *Art Nouveau Bing: Paris Style 1900*. New York 1986, S. 184; Roberta Waddell: *The Art Nouveau Style in Jewelery, Metalwork, Glass, Ceramics, Textiles, Architecture and Furniture*. New York 1977, S. 255; Charlotte & Peter Fiell: *1000 Chairs*. Köln 2005, S. 40 – **Restaurierung:** Originalzustand, Oberflächen gereinigt, Polster und Bezug unberührt – **Fotografie:** LÖFFLER COLLECTION, Reichenschwand.

72–76
Armlehnstuhl – **Eigentum:** LÖFFLER COLLECTION, Reichenschwand – **Inventarnummer:** 02829 – **Entwurf:** Josef Hoffmann – **Herstellung:** Vienna Pancota, Pancota, Rumänien (Brandstempel) – **Datierung:** um 1906 – **Technologie:** Gestellkonstruktion aus Buchenholz massiv, braun gebeizt und dünn lackiert, leicht gebogen verlaufende Zargen, oval geformtes Bugholz, schwarz gebeizt, als Armlehnen-Ornament; vier gedrechselte Rundstäbe stehen auf flachen runden Füßchen, U-förmige flache Leisten (drei Stück mit Formfeder verbunden); die Lehne hat eine gebogene Form und geht in die Armlehnen über – **Polsteraufbau:** Der Sitz verfügt über eine geschnürte Federkonstruktion, mit einer Fasson aus Werg, während das Polster der Rückenlehne aus einem aufgelegten Flachpolster aus Werg besteht – **Bezug:** originaler Mohairvelours, ursprünglich türkis-schwarz-gelb geometrisch gemustert, heute beige grünlich verbräunt, Zierborte original – **Objektmaße:** 76 x 55,5 x 55,5 cm; Sitzhöhe: 48 x 47 x 48 cm – **Restaurierung:** originale Polsterung und originaler Bezug, beides restauriert, Elisabeth Riß, Raumausstattermeisterin – **Literatur:** Simon Yates: *Illustrierte Geschichte der Möbel. Stühle*. Köln 1996, S. 92f. – **Fotografie:** LÖFFLER COLLECTION, Reichenschwand.

77/78
Armlehnsessel – **Eigentum:** LÖFFLER COLLECTION, Reichenschwand – **Inventarnummer:** 01728 – **Entwurf:** Richard Riemerschmid – **Herstellung:** Dresdner Werkstätten für Handwerkskunst – **Datierung:** um 1903 – **Technologie:** Nussholz massiv, transparent lackiert – **Polsteraufbau:** Sitz, Rücken und Armlehnen weisen eine geschnürte Federkonstruktion auf, im Sitz mit Afrikafasson und Rosshaar, in den Rücken- und Armlehnen mit Wergfasson und Rosshaar – **Bezug:** Mohairvelours mit geometrischer Ornamentik (bedruckt?), restauriert unter Verwendung eines historischen Gewebes [2] – **Objektmaße:** 105,5 x 85 x 74 cm; Sitzhöhe: 46 x 56 x 50 cm – **Restaurierung:** Arm- und Sitzpolster wurden unter Verwendung originaler Materialien restauriert – **Anmerkung:** Bezug und Rückenlehne im Originalzustand – **Literatur:** Winfried Nerdinger: *Richard Riemerschmid: Vom Jugendstil zum Werkbund*. München 1982, S. 174f. – **Fotografie:** LÖFFLER COLLECTION, Reichenschwand.

79/80
Armlehnsessel – **Eigentum:** LÖFFLER COLLECTION, Reichenschwand – **Inventarnummer:** 02315 – **Entwurf:** Richard Riemerschmid – **Herstellung:** Dresdner Werkstätten für Handwerkskunst – **Datierung:** 1904 – **Technologie:** Gestell aus Mahagoniholz, dünn lackiert, an den Füßen versehen mit Rollen aus Messing und Horn; vier nach hinten konisch verjüngte Füße, gerade Zargen, wobei die Vorderzarge geschweift ist – **Polsteraufbau:** Sitz und Rückenlehne weisen eine geschnürte Federkonstruktion auf, im Sitz auf Stahlbändern mit einer Fasson aus Werg, in der Lehne mit einer Fasson urements: 76 x 55.5 x 55.5 cm, seat: 48 x 47 x 48 cm – **Conservation:** Raumausstattermeisterin Elisabeth Riß restoration of original upholstery and cover) – **Literature:** Simon Yates, *Illustrierte Geschichte der Möbel: Stühle*, Cologne 1996, pp. 92–93 – **Photo:** LÖFFLER COLLECTION, Reichenschwand.

77/78
Armchair – **Property:** LÖFFLER COLLECTION, Reichenschwand – **Inventory number:** 01728 – **Design:** Richard Riemerschmid – **Origin:** Dresdner Werkstätten für Handwerkskunst – **Date:** around 1903 – **Technique:** solid nut-wood, transparent lacquer – **Upholstery:** seat, back and armrests with lashed sprung construction, seat stuffed with palm fibre and horsehair, back and armrests with tow and horsehair – **Cover:** mohair velour with geometric ornament (printed?), restored using historical fabric – **Object measurements:** 105.5 x 85 x 74 cm, seat: 46 x 56 x 50 cm – **Conservation:** arm and seat upholstery restored using original materials – **Notes:** top cover and backrest in original state – **Literature:** Winfried Nerdinger, *Richard Riemerschmid: Vom Jugendstil zum Werkband*, Munich 1982, pp. 174–175 – **Photo:** LÖFFLER COLLECTION, Reichenschwand.

79/80
Armchair – **Property:** LÖFFLER COLLECTION, Reichenschwand – **Inventory number:** 02315 – **Design:** Richard Riemerschmid – **Origin:** Dresdner Werkstätten für Handwerkskunst – **Date:** 1904 – **Technique:** mahogany frame, thinly lacquered, feed with metal and horn casters; four tapered feet, straight rails, curved front rail – **Upholstery:** seat and back with lashed sprung construction, with steel webbing in the seat and tow stuffing, tow stuffing in back – **Cover:** wool fabric, reconstructed after original findings in geometric pattern (design Richard Riemerschmid?), on backrest in original, rest reconstructed – **Object measurements:** 109 x 68 x 83 cm, seat: 48 x 57 x 55 cm – **Conservation:** upholstery original and restored – **Literature:** Winfried Nerdinger, *Richard Riemerschmid: Vom Jugendstil zum Werkband*, Munich 1982, pp. 159–160, 176 – **Photo:** LÖFFLER COLLECTION, Reichenschwand.

81/82
Armchair – **Property:** LÖFFLER COLLECTION, Reichenschwand – **Inventory number:** 03066 – **Design:** Peter Behrens – **Origin:** presumably Keller & Reiner, Berlin – **Date:** around 1910 – **Technique:** solid mahogany frame, stained dark and lacquered, with lashed sprung construction, stuffing of tow and horsehair with an additional down cushion in the seat – **Cover:** reconstructed patterned silk with silk thread after original findings (design Peter Behrens?) – **Object measurements:** 79.5 x 82 x 71 cm, seat: 50 x 52 x 52 cm – **Literature:** *Innendekoration*, no. 21, 1910, pp. 130–131 – **Conservation:** Raumausstattermeisterin Elisabeth Riß (reconstruction and restoration of original upholstery and down cushion after findings); Simone Howe (reconstruction of passementerie), Taucha; cover: reweave by Eschke Seidenmanufaktur, Crimmitschau – **Photo:** LÖFFLER COLLECTION, Reichenschwand.

83
Detail of the cover of the book cover by Otto Schmidt, *Der alten Wohnung ein neues Gesicht*, Stuttgart 1930. Schmidt 1930, Archive Thomas Schriefers.

84
Detail from an advertisement by the company A. Knippenberg, Ohrdruf in Thuringia, Archive Thomas Schriefers.

aus Werg – **Bezug:** nach Originalbefund rekonstruiertes Wollgewebe mit geometrischem Muster (Entwurf Richard Riemerschmid?), an der Rückenlehne original, übriger Bezug rekonstruiert – **Objektmaße:** 109 x 68 x 83 cm; Sitzhöhe: 48 x 57 x 55 cm – **Restaurierung:** Polsterung original und restauriert – **Literatur:** Winfried Nerdinger: *Richard Riemerschmid. Vom Jugendstil zum Werkbund*. München 1982, S. 159f. u. 176 – **Fotografie:** LÖFFLER COLLECTION, Reichenschwand.

81/82
Armlehnsessel – **Eigentum:** LÖFFLER COLLECTION, Reichenschwand – **Inventarnummer:** 03066 – **Entwurf:** Peter Behrens – **Herstellung:** vermutlich Keller & Reiner, Berlin – **Datierung:** um 1910 – **Technologie:** Gestell aus Mahagoniholz massiv, dunkel gebeizt und lackiert, versehen mit verleimten Leisten – **Polsteraufbau:** Sitz- und Lehnenpolster bestehen aus einer geschnürten Federkonstruktion, mit einer Fasson aus Werg und Rosshaar, wobei auf das Sitzpolster zusätzlich ein Daunenkissen aufgelegt ist – **Bezug:** nach Originalbefund rekonstruierte gemusterte Seide mit Silberfaden (Entwurf Peter Behrens?) – **Objektmaße:** 79,5 x 82 x 71 cm; Sitzhöhe: 50 x 52 x 52 cm – **Literatur:** *Innedekoration*, Heft 21/1910, S. 130f. – **Restaurierung:** Originale Polsterung restauriert und Daunenkissen nach Befund rekonstruiert von Elisabeth Riß, Raumausstattermeisterin; Posamente rekonstruiert von Simone Howe, Taucha; Bezug: Nachwebung von Eschke Seidenmanufaktur, Crimmitschau – **Fotografie:** LÖFFLER COLLECTION, Reichenschwand.

83
Ausschnitt aus dem Titel des Buches von Otto Schmidt: *Der alten Wohnung ein neues Gesicht*. Stuttgart 1930. Schmidt 1930, Archiv Thomas Schriefers.

84
Ausschnitt aus einer Werbeanzeige der Firma von A. Knippenberg, Ohrdruf in Thüringen, Archiv Thomas Schriefers.

85
Titel des Buches von Adolf Behne: *Neues Wohnen – neues Bauen*. Leipzig 1930, Archiv Thomas Schriefers.

86
Titel des Buches von Otto Schmidt: *Der alten Wohnung ein neues Gesicht*. Stuttgart 1930, Archiv Thomas Schriefers.

87
Titel des Buches von Sigfried Giedion: *Befreites Wohnen*. Zürich / Leipzig 1929, Archiv Thomas Schriefers.

88
Werbeseite der Firma Standard-Möbel Lengyel & Co. Berlin, in: *bauhaus. Zeitschrift für Bau und Gestaltung*. Dessau, 2. Jg., Heft 1/1928, S. 17, Archiv Thomas Schriefers.

89–91
Sessel, sog. *Tugendhat-Sessel*, Modell „MR 70/9" – **Eigentum:** LÖFFLER COLLECTION, Reichenschwand – **Inventarnummer:** 01640 – **Entwurf:** Ludwig Mies van der Rohe – **Herstellung:** Berliner Metallgewerbe Josef Müller oder Bamberg Metallwerkstätten, Berlin-Neukölln, – **Datierung:** um 1930/31 – **Technologie:** Das Sitzkissen lagert auf zwei S-förmig geschwungenen und durch Querstreben verbundenen Vorderbeinen, die in verchromtem Flachstahl ausgebildet sind; darauf sitzt der rechtwinklige Flachstahlrahmen, der, nach hinten auskragend, das Rückenkissen hält – **Polsteraufbau:** Sitz und Lehne sind jeweils als einzelne garnierte Kissen aus Werg mit Watte (als Weißpolster) ausgebildet (je Quadrat ein Kissen) – **Bezug:** originales schwarzes Schweinsleder – **Objektmaße:** 83 x 76,5 x 76 cm; Sitzhöhe: 42,5 x 74 x 52 cm – **Literatur:** *Mies van der Rohe. Möbel und Bauten in Stuttgart, Barcelona, Brno*. Weil am Rhein 1998, S. 97ff.; Klaus-Jürgen Sembach: *Contem-*

85
Coverof the book by Adolf Behne, *Neues Wohnen – neues Bauen*, Leipzig 1930, Archive Thomas Schriefers.

86
Cover of the book by Otto Schmidt, *Der alten Wohnung ein neues Gesicht*, Stuttgart 1930, Archive Thomas Schriefers.

87
Cover of the book by Sigfried Giedion, *Befreites Wohnen*, Zurich/Leipzig 1929, Archive Thomas Schriefers.

88
Full-site advertisement of the company Standard-Möbel Lengyel & Co. Berlin, in *bauhaus. Zeitschrift für Bau and Gestaltung*, Dessau, vol. 2, no. 1, 1928, p. 17, Archive Thomas Schriefers.

89–91
Armchair, so-called *Tugendhat Chair*, model "MR 70/9" – **Property:** LÖFFLER COLLECTION, Reichenschwand – **Inventory number:** 01640 – **Design:** Ludwig Mies van der Rohe – **Origin:** Berliner Metallgewerbe Josef Müller or Bamberg Metallwerkstätten, Berlin-Neukölln – **Date:** caaround 1930–31 – **Technique:** seat cushion placed on two S-curved front legs connected through cross braces, formed in chromed flat steel; rectangular flat-steel that holds the cantilevered back cushion – **Upholstery:** seat and backrest with individually worked cushions, stuffed with tow and covered with padding (one cushion per square) – **Cover:** original black pig leather – **Object measurements:** 83 x 76.5 x 76 cm, seat: 42.5 x 74 x 52 cm – **Literatura:** *Mies van der Rohe: Möbel and Bauten in Stuttgart, Barcelona, Brno*, Weil am Rhein 1998, p. 97ff.; Klaus-Jürgen Sembach, *Contemporary Furniture: An International Review of Modern Furniture 1950 to the Present*, Stuttgart 1982, p. 21 – **Conservation:** untouched original state – **Photo:** LÖFFLER COLLECTION, Reichenschwand.

92/93
Armchair – **Property:** LÖFFLER COLLECTION, Reichenschwand – **Inventory number:** 01770 – **Design:** Charles Siclis – **Origin:** Thonet Frères, Paris – **Date:** 1934 – **Technique:** tubular steel frame, copper-plated, four R-shaped legs turn into armrests; two stretchers provide stability for the wooden seat block – **Upholstery:** seat with lashed sprung construction with palm fibre and foam, the seat rests attached to the tubular steel frame are wooden forms covered in green leather; backrest with palm fibre stuffing and foam – **Cover:** green leather – **Object measurements:** 87 x 61 x 58 cm, seat: 46.5 x 48 x 40 cm – **Notes:** an early foam was used, the material has not yet been identified – **Literature:** *Mobilier et Décoration*, no. 1, 1935, p. 22ff. – **Conservation:** restored leather cover, cleaned tubular steel, original upholstery – **Photo:** LÖFFLER COLLECTION, Reichenschwand.

94
Advertisement for patented Epeda upholstery by Firma Ehlenbeck & Platte, Vohwinkel, published, among other medias, in the advertisement section of the magazine *Innen-Dekoration*, vol. 41, no. 9, 1930, n.p., Archive Thomas Schriefers.

95
Advertisement for Schlaraffia spring inlay, published, among other media, in the advertisement section of the magazine *Innen-Dekoration*, vol. 41, no. 9, 1930, n.p., Archive Thomas Schriefers.

porary Furniture. An International Review of Modern Furniture 1950 to the Present. Stuttgart 1982, S. 21 – **Restaurierung:** unberührter Originalzustand – **Fotografie:** LÖFFLER COLLECTION, Reichenschwand.

92/93
Armlehnstuhl – **Eigentum:** LÖFFLER COLLECTION, Reichenschwand – **Inventarnummer:** 01770 – **Entwurf:** Charles Siclis – **Herstellung:** Thonet Frères, Paris – **Datierung:** 1934 – **Technologie:** Stahlrohrgestell mit Kupferbeschichtung (kupferplatiniert), vier Beine verlaufen R-förmig in Armlehnen; zwei Querstreben geben dem hölzernen Sitzrahmen Halt – **Polsteraufbau:** Das Sitzpolster besteht aus einer geschnürten Federkonstruktion mit Afrikfasson, Pikierung und Schaumstoff; die auf den Stahlrohrrahmen aufgesetzten Armlehnen bestehen aus einem mit grünem Leder überzogenen Holzformteil; die Rückenlehne besteht aus einer garnierten Afrikfasson, Pikierung und Schaumstoff – **Bezug:** grünes Leder – **Objektmaße:** 87 x 61 x 58 cm; Sitzhöhe: 46,5 x 48 x 40 cm – **Anmerkung:** Hier wurde ein früher Schaumstoff verwendet, ein Material, das bislang nicht ermittelt werden konnte – **Literatur:** *Mobilier et Décoration*, Heft 1/1935, S. 22ff. – **Restaurierung:** Lederbezug restauriert, Stahlrohr gereinigt, Polsterung original – **Fotografie:** LÖFFLER COLLECTION, Reichenschwand.

94
Werbeannonce für Epeda-Patent-Polster der Firma Ehlenbeck & Platte, Vohwinkel, veröffentlicht u. a. im Anzeigenteil der Zeitschrift *Innendekoration*, 41. Jg, Heft 9/1930, ohne Paginierung, Archiv Thomas Schriefers.

95
Werbeannonce für die Schlaraffia-Federeinlage, veröffentlicht u. a. im Anzeigenteil der Zeitschrift *Innendekoration*, 41. Jg, Heft 9/1930, ohne Paginierung, Archiv Thomas Schriefers.

96–97
Armlehnsessel, Modell „KS 46" – **Eigentum:** LÖFFLER COLLECTION, Reichenschwand – **Inventarnummer:** 01750 – **Entwurf:** Anton Lorenz – **Herstellung:** DESTA, Berlin, ab 1933 Thonet Frankenberg – **Datierung:** 1931 – Technologie: Das verchromte Stahlrohrgestell bildet einen Rahmen, dessen gebogene Form es erlaubt, dass Sitz, Rücken und Armlehne ineinander verlaufen, die auf das Rohr aufgeschraubten Armlehnen bestehen aus schwarz lackiertem Holz; als Auflage für die Polsterkissen dienen zwischen den Rohren gespannte, parallel angeordnete und mit Haken befestigte Expander-Gummistränge – **Polsteraufbau:** Es handelt sich um ein durchgängiges loses Kissen, das über einen Kern aus Gummikokos und eine Kapokauflage verfügt – **Bezug:** beigefarbenes, gemustertes Viskose-Mischgewebe aus den 1930er Jahren für Restaurierung verwendet – **Objektmaße:** 90 x 62,5 x 90,5 cm; Sitzhöhe: 45,5 x 53 x 50 cm – **Literatur:** *Innendekoration*, Heft 52/1941, S. 295; *2100 metal tubular chairs. A typology by Otakar Máčel*. Rotterdam 2006, S. 163 – Restaurierung: Kissen rekonstruiert – **Fotografie:** LÖFFLER COLLECTION, Reichenschwand.

98/99
Armlehnsessel, Modell „KS 42" – **Eigentum:** GRASSI Museum für Angewandte Kunst Leipzig – **Inventarnummer:** 2019.589 a-c – **Provenienz:** Schenkung Hermann Naumann, Dittersbach – **Entwurf:** Anton Lorenz – **Herstellung:** DESTA, Berlin – **Datierung:** 1931 – **Technologie:** Verchromtes Stahlrohrgestell mit Armlehnauflagen aus Kunststoff – **Polsteraufbau:** Die Kissen von Sitz und Lehne besitzen einen Endlosfederkern mit Kantendraht (Prinzip Schlaraffia) und eine Federkernabdeckung mit Jutefederleinen; das Polstermaterial besteht aus einer Kokosfasermatte mit Watteabdeckung, Nesselbezug und leichter Kantenabnähung – **Bezug:** rekonstruiertes Schriever-Doppelgewebe mit künstlichem Rosshaar, mit Kantenbiesen – **Anmerkung:** Die Rekonstruktion erfolgte nach einem

96–97
Armchair, model "KS 46" – **Property:** LÖFFLER COLLECTION, Reichenschwand – **Inventory number:** 01750 – **Design:** Anton Lorenz – **Producers:** DESTA, Berlin, from 1933 Thonet Frankenberg – **Date:** 1931 – **Technique:** Chrome-plated tubular steel frame that blends seat, backrest and armrests, the screwed-in armrests are made from black lacquered wood; the base for the padded cushions is made from stretched, parallel expander elastic bands with spiralised hooks at the ends – **Upholstery:** squab with coir core and kapok cover – **Cover:** beige patterned viscose mix from the 1930s used for restoration – **Object measurements:** 90 x 62.5 x 90.5 cm, seat: 45.5 x 53 x 50 cm – **Literature:** *Innendekoration*, no.52, 1941, p. 295; Otakar Macel, *2100 Metal Tubular Chairs*, Rotterdam 2006, p. 163 – **Conservation:** cushion reconstructed – **Photo:** LÖFFLER COLLECTION, Reichenschwand.

98/99
Armchair, model "KS 42" – **Property:** GRASSI Museum für Angewandte Kunst Leipzig – **Inventory number:** 2019.589 a–c – **Provenance:** donation by Hermann Naumann, Dittersbach – **Design:** Anton Lorenz – **Origin:** DESTA, Berlin – **Date:** 1931 – **Technique:** Chrome-plated tubular steel frame with foam armrest pads – **Upholstery:** seat and backrest cushion with open spring cushion and edging wire (Schlaraffia principle) and a spring core covered with hessian; stuffing of coir mat with wadding, calico and slightly stitched edges – **Cover:** reconstructed Schriever double-weave with artificial horsehair border tuck – **Notes:** reconstruction after a weave sample from the period of origin by Otti Berger (1898–1944) – **Object measurements:** 78 x 60.5 x 80.5 cm, seat H: 43 cm – **Literature:** *Moderne Bauform*, vol. 32, 1933, p. 195; Alexander von Vegesack, *Deutsche Stahlrohrmöbel*, Munich 1986, pp. 50, 51; Otakar Macel, *2100 Metal Tubular Chairs*, Rotterdam 2006, p. 158; DESTA Stahlmöbel catalogue and price list, no. 301, Berlin 1930–/31; Heckhoff / Jebsen 2021 – **Conservation:** Reinhardt Roßberg, RiH (reconstruction of seat and backrest cushion), Katharina Jebsen (reconstruction of the cover textile), supported by Sächsisches Staatsministerium für Regionalentwicklung and the Kulturstiftung des Freistaates Sachsen. Co-financed by tax funds contingent on the 2021 budget passed by the Saxon state parliament. – **Photo:** Esther Hoyer/GRASSI Museum für Angewandte Kunst Leipzig.

100/101
Armchair – **Property:** LÖFFLER COLLECTION, Reichenschwand – **Inventory number:** 02119 – **Design:** at present unknown – **Origin:** at present unknown – **Date:** 1928–30 – **Technique:** tubular steel frame with inserted upholstered armchair with solid beech frame rails, cantilevered – **Upholstery:** seat with lashed sprung construction and tow stuffing, backrest with tow stuffing – **Cover:** original wool fabric with red-white-black pattern – **Object measurements:** 80 x 67 x 80 cm, seat: 43.5 x 47 x 50 cm – **Conservation:** Raumausstattermeisterin Elisabeth Riß (restoration of original fabric and upholstery) – **Photo:** LÖFFLER COLLECTION, Reichenschwand.

102
Armchair, model "H91" – **Property:** LÖFFLER COLLECTION, Reichenschwand – **Inventory number:** 00515 – **Design:** Jindřich Halabala – **Origin:** Spojené UP Závody, Brno, former Czechoslovakia – **Date:** around 1930 – **Technique:** chrome-plated tubular steel frame; U-shaped feet/sledge feet; backrest transforms into seat, armrests in solid nut-wood, screwed on – **Upholstery:** seat and backrest upholstery as cushion made from Schlaraffia core spring with coir stuffing; on steel yarn – **Cover:** original multi-

Objekt und Bild | Objects and images **337**

Webmuster aus der Entstehungszeit von Otti Berger (1898–1944). – **Objektmaße:** 78 x 60,5 x 80,5 cm; Sitzhöhe: 43 cm – **Literatur:** Vgl.: *Moderne Baumform*, 32. Jg., 1933, S. 195; Alexander von Vegesack: *Deutsche Stahlrohrmöbel*. München 1986, S. 50 u. 51; *2100 metal tubular chairs. A typology by Otakar Máčel*. Rotterdam 2006, S. 158; Katalog und Preisliste NR. 301 Desta Stahlmöbel, Berlin 1930/31; Heckhoff / Jebsen 2021 – **Restaurierung:** Rekonstruktion von Sitz- und Lehnenkissen von Reinhardt Roßberg, RiH; Rekonstruktion des Bezugsstoffes durch Katharina Jebsen, gefördert durch das Sächsische Staatsministerium für Regionalentwicklung und die Kulturstiftung des Freistaates Sachsen. Diese Maßnahme wurde mitfinanziert durch Steuermittel auf der Grundlage des vom Sächsischen Landtag beschlossenen Haushaltes, 2021. – **Fotografie:** Esther Hoyer/GRASSI Museum für Angewandte Kunst Leipzig.

100/101
Armlehnstuhl – **Eigentum:** LÖFFLER COLLECTION, Reichenschwand – **Inventarnummer:** 02119 – **Entwurf:** z. Zt. unbekannt – **Herstellung:** z. Zt. unbekannt – **Datierung:** 1928–1930 – **Technologie:** Stahlrohrgestell mit eingesetztem Polstersessel-Korpus, dessen Zargen aus Buchenholz massiv bestehen und das nach dem Prinzip des Freischwingers funktioniert – **Polsteraufbau:** Das Sitzpolster ist eine geschnürte Federkonstruktion mit einer Fasson aus Werg, die Lehnenpolster bestehen aus garnierter Wergfasson – **Bezug:** originaler rot weiß schwarz gemusterter Wollstoff – **Objektmaße:** 80 x 67 x 80 cm; Sitzhöhe: 43,5 x 47 x 50 cm – **Restaurierung:** Stoff und Polster original und restauriert Elisabeth Riß, Raumausstattermeisterin – **Fotografie:** LÖFFLER COLLECTION, Reichenschwand.

102
Armlehnstuhl, Modell „H91" – **Eigentum:** LÖFFLER COLLECTION, Reichenschwand – **Inventarnummer:** 00515 – **Entwurf:** Jindřich Halabala – **Herstellung:** Spojené UP Závody, Brünn, Tschechoslowakei – **Datierung:** um 1930 – **Technologie:** Verchromtes Stahlrohrgestell; U-förmiges Fußgestell/Kufengestell, Lehne geht in Sitz über, Armauflagen aus Nussholz massiv, lackiert, angeschraubt – **Polsteraufbau:** Sitz- und Rückenlehnenpolster in Kissenform bestehen aus einem Schlaraffia-Federkern mit Kokosfasson; sie liegen auf Eisengarnflächen auf – **Bezug:** originales mehrfarbig kleingemustertes Mischgewebe in Grau-Blau-Gelb-Tönen – **Objektmaße:** 80 x 59 x 94 cm; Sitzhöhe: 44 x 50 x 56 cm – **Literatur:** *Jindřich Halabala a Spojené uměleckoprůmyslové v Brně*. Brünn 2003, S. 37, 84, 90, 105 – **Restaurierung:** Originalzustand – **Fotografie:** LÖFFLER COLLECTION, Reichenschwand.

103/104
Sessel – **Eigentum:** LÖFFLER COLLECTION, Reichenschwand – **Inventarnummer:** 03203 – **Entwurf:** z. Zt. unbekannt – **Herstellung:** z. Zt. unbekannt – **Datierung:** um 1930 – **Technologie:** Stahlgestell, verchromt; die sichtbaren Korpusteile des Sitzpolsterkastens bestehen aus Nussholz massiv, die nicht sichtbare, eigentliche Polster-Unterkonstruktion aus Buchenholz massiv, die vordere Zarge zeigt Nussfurnier. Es ist eine Kombination von Freischwinger und konventionellem Polstermöbel mit Holzgestell – **Polsteraufbau:** Sitz- und Rückenlehnenpolster bestehen aus einer geschnürten Federkonstruktion mit einer Fasson aus Werg und Watte, wobei im Lehnenpolster noch Kokos hinzukommt; die Armlehnenpolster sind garniert unter Verwendung von Werg und Kokos – **Bezug:** weiß-rot gemusterter Wollstoff, restauriert unter Verwendung eines historischen Gewebes – **Objektmaße:** 100 x 80 x 90 cm, Sitzhöhe: 45 x 68 x 53 cm – **Restaurierung:** Polsterung im Originalbestand restauriert, Bezug aus der Zeit – **Fotografie:** LÖFFLER COLLECTION, Reichenschwand.

coloured small pattern on mixed fabric in shades of grey, blue and yellow – **Object measurements:** 80 x 59 x 94 cm, seat: 44 x 50 x 56 cm – **Literature:** *Jindřich Halabala a Spojené uměleckoprůmyslové v Brně*, Brno 2003, pp. 37, 84, 90, 105 – **Conservation:** original – **Photo:** LÖFFLER COLLECTION, Reichenschwand.

103/104
Armchair – **Property:** LÖFFLER COLLECTION, Reichenschwand – **Inventory number:** 03203 – **Design:** at present unknown – **Origin:** at present unknown – **Date:** around 1930 – **Technique:** chromed-steel frame; the visible elements of the drop-in seat solid nut-wood, the invisible actual upholstery base in solid beech, nut-wood veneer on front rail. A combination of cantilevered chair and conventional upholstered furniture with wooden frame – **Upholstery:** seat and backrest upholstery with lashed sprung construction, tow stuffing, backrest additionally with coconut fibre; armrests stuffed with tow and coconut fibre – **Cover:** wool fabric with white-red pattern, restored using historical fabric – **Object measurements:** 100 x 80 x 90 cm, seat: 45 x 68 x 53 cm – **Conservation:** upholstery restored to original state, top cover from the period – **Photo:** LÖFFLER COLLECTION, Reichenschwand.

105/106
Armchair – **Property:** LÖFFLER COLLECTION, Reichenschwand – **Inventory number:** 02121 – **Design:** at present unknown – **Origin:** at present unknown – **Date:** 1920s/1930s – **Technique:** chrome-plated tubular steel frame – **Upholstery:** seat with lashed sprung construction with tow stuffing; armrests stuffed with tow and coconut fibre; backrest with lashed sprung construction with tow stuffing – **Cover:** restored using historical weave – **Object measurements:** 90 x 68 x 100 cm, seat: 38 x 57 x 62 cm – **Conservation:** seat and backrest reconstructed using original elements, armrests original – **Photo:** LÖFFLER COLLECTION, Reichenschwand.

107–109
Armchair – **Property:** LÖFFLER COLLECTION, Reichenschwand – **Inventory number:** 01342 – **Design:** Heinz and Bodo Rasch – **Origin:** probably L&C Arnold Schorndorf – **Date:** around 1930 – **Technique:** tubular steel frame, chrome-plated – **Upholstery:** seat upholstery stuffed with palm and coconut fibre, the backrest upholstery with coconut fibre – **Cover:** black-red-yellow striped wool fabric, restored using historical fabric – **Object measurements:** 73.5 x 52 x 60 cm, seat H: 49.5 cm, Dia.: 46 cm – **Conservation:** Backrest original, seat restored using original material, restored using historical fabric, Stefan Oswald RiH – **Photo:** LÖFFLER COLLECTION, Reichenschwand.

110
Photograph. View of the glass salon of Madame Mathieu-Lévy in rue de Lota, Paris, designed in 1920 by Eileen Gray. Visible are the famous upholstered armchairs designed by Eileen Gray: *Serpent Armchair* and *Bibendum Chair*, in *L'Illustration*, special issue: *Intérieurs modernes*, 27 May 1933, Archive Thomas Schriefers.

111
Advertisement for club chairs, in *L'Illustration*, special issue: *Intérieurs modernes*, 27 May 1933, Archive Thomas Schriefers.

112
View of a room furnished with club chairs, in *L'Illustration*, special issue: *Intérieurs modernes*, 27 May 1933, Archive Thomas Schriefers.

105/106
Armlehnstuhl – **Eigentum:** LÖFFLER COLLECTION, Reichenschwand – **Inventarnummer:** 02121 – **Entwurf:** z. Zt. unbekannt – **Herstellung:** z. Zt. unbekannt – **Datierung:** 1920er/30er Jahre – **Technologie:** Stahlrohrgestell, verchromt – **Polsteraufbau:** Das Sitzpolster besteht aus einer geschnürten Federkonstruktion, mit einer Fasson aus Werg; die Armlehnenpolsterung aus garniertem Werg mit Kokos, die Rückenpolsterung aus einer garnierten Federkonstruktion mit einer Fasson aus Werg – **Bezug:** Restauriert unter Verwendung eines historischen Gewebes – **Objektmaße:** 90 x 68 x 100 cm; Sitzhöhe: 38 x 57 x 62 cm – **Restaurierung:** Sitz und Rücken rekonstruiert unter Verwendung originaler Teile, Armlehnen original – **Fotografie:** LÖFFLER COLLECTION, Reichenschwand.

107–109
Armlehnstuhl – **Eigentum:** LÖFFLER COLLECTION, Reichenschwand – **Inventarnummer:** 01342 – **Entwurf:** Heinz und Bodo Rasch – **Herstellung:** vermutlich L&C Arnold Schorndorf – **Datierung:** um 1930 – **Technologie:** Stahlrohrgestell, verchromt – **Polsteraufbau:** Das Sitzpolster besteht aus Afrik- und Kokosfasson, das Rückenpolster aus Kokosfasson – **Bezug:** schwarz-rot-gelb-weiß gestreifter Wollstoff, restauriert unter Verwendung eines historischen Gewebes – **Objektmaße:** 73,5 x 52 x 60 cm; Sitzhöhe: 49,5 cm, D: 46 cm – **Restaurierung:** Rücken unberührtes Original, Sitz unter Verwendung originalen Materials restauriert, restauriert mit Gewebe aus der Zeit, Stefan Oswald RiH – **Fotografie:** LÖFFLER COLLECTION, Reichenschwand.

110
Fotografie. Blick in den 1920 von Eileen Gray gestalteten Glas-Salon der Madame Mathieu-Lévy in der Rue de Lota, Paris. Zu sehen sind darin die berühmten von Eileen Gray entworfenen Polstersessel: der *Serpent Armchair* und der *Bibendum Chair*, aus: *L'Illustration*, Sonderausgabe: *Intérieurs modernes*, 27. Mai 1933, Archiv Thomas Schriefers.

111
Annonce, Werbung für Klubsessel, aus: *L'Illustration*, Sonderausgabe: *Intérieurs modernes*, 27. Mai 1933, Archiv Thomas Schriefers.

112
Blick in einen Salon, der mit Klubsesseln ausgestattet ist, aus: *L'Illustration*, Sonderausgabe: *Intérieurs modernes*, 27. Mai 1933, Archiv Thomas Schriefers.

113
Klubsessel – **Eigentum:** LÖFFLER COLLECTION, Reichenschwand – **Inventarnummer:** 01562 – **Entwurf:** z. Zt. unbekannt – **Herstellung:** z. Zt. unbekannt – **Datierung:** 1920er Jahre – **Technologie:** Gepolstertes und mit Leder überzogenes Holzgestell mit Kugelfüßen aus Eichenholz, gebeizt und dünn lackiert – **Polsteraufbau:** Das Sitzpolster weist eine doppelte Federung auf (Schnürung), auch die Armlehnen sind gefedert; die Rückenlehne verfügt über eine geschnürte Federkonstruktion, mit einer Fasson aus Werg und Rosshaar – **Bezug:** dunkelbraunes Leder – **Objektmaße:** 78 x 87 x 87 cm; Sitzhöhe: 46 x 50 x 50 cm – **Restaurierung:** originaler Zustand, gereinigt und partiell am Leder restauriert – **Fotografie:** LÖFFLER COLLECTION, Reichenschwand.

114/115
Armlehnsessel, Modell „400", *Tank* – **Eigentum:** LÖFFLER COLLECTION, Reichenschwand – **Inventarnummer:** 00586 – **Entwurf:** Alvar Aalto – **Herstellung:** Oy Huonekalu- ja Rakennustyöehdas Ab, Turku, Finnland – **Datierung:** um 1935/36 – **Technologie:** Gestellkonstruktion aus gebogenem Birkenschichtholz, transparent lackiert, wobei die Armlehnen C-förmig in die Kufenfüße verlaufen; die Rückenlehne

113
Club chair – **Property:** LÖFFLER COLLECTION, Reichenschwand – **Inventory number:** 01562 – **Design:** at present unknown – **Origin:** at present unknown – **Date:** 1920s – **Technique:** upholstered leather-covered wooden frame with oakwood ball feet, stained and thinly lacquered – **Upholstery:** double-sprung seat, lashed, armrests are equally sprung; backrest upholstered with tow and horsehair stuffing – **Cover:** dark-brown leather – **Object measurements:** 78 x 87 x 87 cm, seat: 46 x 50 x 50 cm – **Conservation:** original, cleaned, leather partially restored – **Photo:** LÖFFLER COLLECTION, Reichenschwand.

114/115
Armchair, model "400", *Tank* – **Property:** LÖFFLER COLLECTION, Reichenschwand – **Inventory number:** 00586 – **Design:** Alvar Aalto – **Origin:** Oy Huonekalu- ja Rakennustyöehdas Ab, Turku, Finland – **Date:** around 1935–36 – **Technique:** frame with bent birch plywood, transparent lacquer, C-shaped armrests turn into sledge feet; cantilevered backrest – **Upholstery:** seat and backrest with lashed sprung construction with palm fibre stuffing and horsehair cover – **Cover:** original black-beige striped fabric of linen and wool – **Design:** Kitty Fisher, attributed – **Object measurements:** 72 x 77 x 78 cm, seat: 39 x 54 x 57 cm – **Literature:** *Alvar Aalto: Architecture and Furniture*, exh. cat. Museum of Modern Art, New York 1938; Eva B. Ottillinger, *Alvar Aalto Möbel: Die Sammlung Kossdorff*, Vienna 2002, p. 50 – **Conservation:** original condition – **Photo:** LÖFFLER COLLECTION, Reichenschwand.

116/117
Armchair – **Property:** LÖFFLER COLLECTION, Reichenschwand – **Inventory number:** 03354 – **Design:** Erich Dieckmann – **Origin:** execution by the former Bauhochschule Weimar (brand stamp Bauhochschule Weimar & Signatur ED) – **Date:** before 1928 – **Technique:** solid beech and alder construction; bog oak frame, transparent lacquer, partial lipping – **Upholstery:** seat and backrest with lashed sprung construction, both with tow and horsehair stuffing – **Cover:** original red small-patterned flat weave with cream-coloured dots (linen?) – **Object measurements:** 72 x 62.5 x 81 cm, seat: 41 x 48.5 x 56 cm – **Literature:** *Möbel der Staatlichen Bauhochschule Weimar*, Weimar (around 1925?), pp. 8, 12, 28; Erich Dieckmann, *Möbelbau in Holz, Rohr and Stahl*, Stuttgart 1931, pp. 34, 48–49 – **Conservation:** original upholstery, surfaces cleaned – **Photo:** LÖFFLER COLLECTION, Reichenschwand.

118–121
Recliner, so-called *Kanadier* – **Property:** LÖFFLER COLLECTION, Reichenschwand – **Inventory number:** 03199 – **Design:** at present unknown – **Origin:** at present unknown – **Date:** 1930s – **Technique:** solid beech frame, stained and thinly lacquered; reclining backrest – **Upholstery:** seat and backrest with lashed sprung construction, each with tow or palm fibre stuffing with coconut fibre – **Cover:** original blue-beige patterned velour – **Object measurements:** 87 x 67 x 87 cm, seat: 42 x 48 x 60 cm – **Notes:** armchair uses chain-hoist mechanism to recline seat and backrest – **Conservation:** original upholstery and cover fabric, surfaces cleaned – **Photo:** LÖFFLER COLLECTION, Reichenschwand.

122/123
Armchair – **Property:** LÖFFLER COLLECTION, Reichenschwand – **Inventory number:** 01530 – **Design:** Otto Schulz, attributed – **Origin:** Boet, Gothenburg, Sweden, Jio Möbler – **Date:** 1930s – **Technique:** three-legged nutwood frame, transparent lacquer – **Upholstery:** seat with lashed sprung upholstery construction, stuffing

schwingt frei – **Polsteraufbau:** Sowohl Sitz- als auch Rückenpolster verfügen über eine geschnürte Federkonstruktion mit Afrikfasson und Rosshaardeckung – **Bezug:** originaler schwarz-beige-oranger Streifenstoff aus Leinen und Wolle, Entwurf: Kitty Fisher zugeschrieben – **Objektmaße:** 72 x 77 x 78 cm; Sitzhöhe: 39 x 54 x 57 cm – **Literatur:** *Exhibition „Alvar Aalto: Architecture and Furniture"*, The Museum of Modern Art. New York 1938; Eva B. Ottillinger: *Alvar Aalto Möbel. Die Sammlung Kossdorff.* Wien 2002, S. 50 – **Restaurierung:** Originalzustand – **Fotografie:** LÖFFLER COLLECTION, Reichenschwand.

116/117
Armlehnstuhl – **Eigentum:** LÖFFLER COLLECTION, Reichenschwand – **Inventarnummer:** 03354 – **Entwurf:** Erich Dieckmann – **Herstellung:** Ausführung durch die ehemalige Bauhochschule Weimar (Brandstempel Bauhochschule Weimar & Signatur ED) – **Datierung:** vor 1928 – **Technologie:** Konstruktionshölzer aus Buchen- und Erlenholz massiv; Gestell aus Mooreiche, transparent lackiert, z. T. Anleimer – **Polsteraufbau:** Sowohl das Sitzpolster wie auch das Rückenlehnenpolster sind als geschnürte Federkonstruktion ausgeführt, jeweils mit einer Fasson aus Werg und Rosshaar – **Bezug:** originales kleingemustertes rotes Flachgewebe mit cremefarbenen Tupfen (Leinen?) – **Objektmaße:** 72 x 62,5 x 81 cm; Sitzhöhe: 41 x 48,5 x 56 cm – **Literatur:** *Möbel der Staatlichen Bauhochschule Weimar*, o. J. (um 1925?), S. 8, 12, 28; Erich Dieckmann: *Möbelbau in Holz, Rohr und Stahl.* Stuttgart 1931, S. 34, 48, 49 – **Restaurierung:** Polsterung original, Oberflächen gereinigt – **Fotografie:** LÖFFLER COLLECTION, Reichenschwand.

118–121
Sessel, sog. *Kanadier* – **Eigentum:** LÖFFLER COLLECTION, Reichenschwand – **Inventarnummer:** 03199 – **Entwurf:** z. Zt. unbekannt – **Herstellung:** z. Zt. unbekannt – **Datierung:** 1930er Jahre – **Technologie:** Gestell aus Buchenholz massiv, gebeizt und dünn lackiert; die Lehne ist in ihrer Neigung verstellbar – **Polsteraufbau:** Sitz- und Rückenlehnenpolster bestehen aus einer geschnürten Federkonstruktion, jeweils mit einer Fasson aus Werg oder Afrik mit Kokos ausgestattet – **Bezug:** originaler blau-beige gemusterter Velours – **Objektmaße:** 87 x 67 x 87 cm; Sitzhöhe: 42 x 48 x 60 cm – **Anmerkung:** Der Kanadier besitzt zur Verstellung von Sitz und Rückenlehne eine Kettenzugmechanik – **Restaurierung:** Originalbestand bei Polsterung und Stoff, Oberfläche gereinigt – **Fotografie:** LÖFFLER COLLECTION, Reichenschwand.

122/123
Armlehnsessel – **Eigentum:** LÖFFLER COLLECTION, Reichenschwand – **Inventarnummer:** 01530 – **Entwurf:** Otto Schulz zugeschrieben – **Herstellung:** Boet, Göteborg, Schweden, Jio Möbler – **Datierung:** 1930er Jahre – **Technologie:** Dreibeiniges Gestell aus Nussholz, transparent lackiert – **Polsteraufbau:** Das Sitzpolster ist eine geschnürte Federkonstruktion mit einer Fasson aus Afrik und Kokos, während die Armpolster und die Kopflehne mit Ohrenbacken mit garniertem Afrik und Kokos gepolstert sind – **Bezug:** Restauriert unter Verwendung eines historischen geometrisch grün-schwarz-rosa gemusterten Gewebes aus der Zeit – **Objektmaße:** 96 x 73 x 84 cm; Sitzhöhe: 46 x 53 x 60 cm – **Restaurierung:** Arm- und Rückenpolster original; der Sitz wurde nach Befund mit historischen Materialien rekonstruiert – **Fotografie:** LÖFFLER COLLECTION, Reichenschwand.

124/125
Polsterhocker, sog. *pouffe* – **Eigentum:** LÖFFLER COLLECTION, Reichenschwand – **Inventarnummer:** 01105 – **Entwurf:** z. Zt. unbekannt – **Herstellung:** z. Zt. unbekannt – **Datierung:** um 1935 – **Technologie:** Stahlrohrgestell, vernickelt/verchromt? – **Polsteraufbau:** Das Sitzpolster besteht aus einer geschnürten Federkonstruktion mit einer Fasson aus Werg oder Afrik mit

with palm and coconut fibre, armrests and the winged headrest upholstered with a palm fibre and coconut fibre stuffing – **Cover:** restored using historical geometric green-black-pink patterned fabric from the period – **Object measurements:** 96 x 73 x 84 cm, seat: 46 x 53 x 60 cm – **Conservation:** arm- and backrest original; seat reconstructed after findings using historical materials – **Photo:** LÖFFLER COLLECTION, Reichenschwand.

124/125
Upholstered stool, a so-called *pouffe* – **Property:** LÖFFLER COLLECTION, Reichenschwand – **Inventory number:** 01105 – **Design:** at present unknown – **Origin:** at present unknown – **Date:** around 1935 – **Technique:** tubular steel frame, chrome-/nickel-plated? – **Upholstery:** seat with lashed sprung construction with stuffing of tow or palm fibre with coconut fibre or horsehair – **Cover:** original red-beige velour (synthetic?) – **Object measurements:** 43 x 54 x 49.5 cm, seat: 43 x 44 x 46 cm – **Conservation:** original – **Photo:** LÖFFLER COLLECTION, Reichenschwand.

126/127
Upholstered stool, so-called *pouffe* – **Property:** LÖFFLER COLLECTION, Reichenschwand – **Inventory number:** 01106 – **Design:** at present unknown – **Origin:** at present unknown, presumably former Czechoslovakia – **Date:** around 1935 – **Technique:** seat base made from round wooden board with four flat, rectangular feet, stained black and thinly lacquered – **Upholstery:** with tow and horsehair – **Cover:** green and red wool pinglé – **Object measurements:** H: 42 cm, D: 42 cm – **Literature:** Robert Bücheler and Otto Ulmschneider, *Neuzeitliches Polstern*, Munich 1953 – **Conservation:** original – **Photo:** LÖFFLER COLLECTION, Reichenschwand.

128–130
Children's armchair – **Property:** LÖFFLER COLLECTION, Reichenschwand – **Inventory number:** 00880 – **Design:** at present unknown – **Origin:** at present unknown – **Date:** around 1927 – **Technique:** solid hardwood frame, stained dark and thinly lacquered – **Upholstery:** seat with lashed sprung upholstery and palm fibre stuffing, back and armrest upholstery with palm fibre stuffing – **Cover:** original, patterned velours – **Object measurements:** 64 x 43 x 43 cm, seat: 37 x 27 x 30 cm – **Conservation:** original – **Photo:** LÖFFLER COLLECTION, Reichenschwand.

131/132
Armchair – **Property:** LÖFFLER COLLECTION, Reichenschwand – **Inventory number:** 01889 – **Design:** Emil Fahrenkamp? – **Origin:** at present unknown – **Date:** ca. 1928 – **Technique:** solid cherrywood frame; transparent lacquer, inside of rails stained dark, straight front legs and sabre back legs – **Upholstery:** seat padding from rubberised coconut fibre cushion with kapok cover on webbing, backrest is a stitched horsehair cushion – **Cover:** restored using historical fabric – **Object measurements:** 77 x 59.5 x 63 cm, seat: 49 x 49 x 41 cm – **Conservation:** top cover fabric from the period, Stefan Oswald RiH (reconstruction of upholstery) – **Photo:** LÖFFLER COLLECTION, Reichenschwand.

133/134
Armchair – **Property:** LÖFFLER COLLECTION, Reichenschwand – **Inventory number:** 01566 – **Design:** Kem Weber, attributed – **Origin:** at present unknown – **Date:** around 1930 – **Technique:** solid cherrywood frame, transparent lacquer, seat probably made from plywood – **Upholstery:** seat with sprung core cushion with a Schlaraffia spring core, coconut fibre stuffing on covered

Kokos oder Rosshaar – **Bezug:** originaler rot-beiger Velours (Synthetik?) – **Objektmaße:** 43 x 54 x 49,5 cm; Sitzhöhe: 43 x 44 x 46 cm – Restaurierung: Originalzustand – **Fotografie:** LÖFFLER COLLECTION, Reichenschwand.

126/127
Polsterhocker, sog. *pouffe* – **Eigentum:** LÖFFLER COLLECTION, Reichenschwand – **Inventarnummer:** 01106 – **Entwurf:** z. Zt. unbekannt – **Herstellung:** z. Zt. unbekannt, vermutlich Tschechoslowakei – **Datierung:** um 1935 – **Technologie:** Der Sitzboden besteht aus einer runden Holzplatte mit vier flachen, rechteckigen Füßen, die schwarz gebeizt und dünn lackiert sind – **Polsteraufbau:** es handelt sich um ein garniertes Polster, vermutlich aus Werg und Rosshaar – **Bezug:** originaler grüner und roter Wollepinglé – **Objektmaße:** H: 42 cm, D: 42 cm – **Literatur:** Bücheler und Ulmschneider: *Neuzeitliches Polstern*, 1953 – **Restaurierung:** unberührter Originalzustand – **Fotografie:** LÖFFLER COLLECTION, Reichenschwand.

128–130
Armlehnstuhl für Kinder – **Eigentum:** LÖFFLER COLLECTION, Reichenschwand – **Inventarnummer:** 00880 – **Entwurf:** z. Zt. unbekannt – **Herstellung:** z. Zt. unbekannt – **Datierung:** um 1927 – **Technologie:** Gestell aus Laubholz massiv, dunkel gebeizt und dünn lackiert – **Polsteraufbau:** Das Sitzpolster besitzt eine geschnürte Federkonstruktion mit Afrikfasson, während die Rücken- und Armlehnenpolsterung über eine garnierte Afrikfasson verfügen – **Bezug:** originaler gemusterter Velours – **Objektmaße:** 64 x 43 x 43 cm; Sitzhöhe: 37 x 27 x 30 cm – **Restaurierung:** unberührter Originalzustand – **Fotografie:** LÖFFLER COLLECTION, Reichenschwand.

131/132
Armlehnstuhl – **Eigentum:** LÖFFLER COLLECTION, Reichenschwand – **Inventarnummer:** 01889 – **Entwurf:** Emil Fahrenkamp (?) – **Herstellung:** z. Zt. unbekannt – **Datierung:** um 1928 – **Technologie:** Das Gestell ist aus Kirsche massiv, transparent lackiert, die Zargeninnenseiten sind dunkel gebeizt, hinten mit geschwungenen und vorne mit geraden Beinen ausgestattet – **Polsteraufbau:** Als Sitzpolster dient ein Gummikokoskissen mit Kapokauflage auf Gurtgrund, als rückwärtiges Lehnenpolster ein garniertes Rosshaarkissen – **Bezug:** Restauriert unter Verwendung eines historischen Gewebes – **Objektmaße:** 77 x 59,5 x 63 cm; Sitzhöhe: 49 x 49 x 41 cm – **Restaurierung:** Stoff aus der Zeit, Polsterung rekonstruiert Stefan Oswald RiH – **Fotografie:** LÖFFLER COLLECTION, Reichenschwand.

133/134
Armlehnstuhl – **Eigentum:** LÖFFLER COLLECTION, Reichenschwand – **Inventarnummer:** 01566 – **Entwurf:** Kem Weber zugeschrieben – **Herstellung:** z. Zt. unbekannt – **Datierung:** um 1930 – **Technologie:** Das Gestell ist aus Kirschholz massiv, transparent lackiert, die Sitzfläche vermutlich Sperrholz – **Polsteraufbau:** Die Sitzpolsterung erfolgt durch ein Federkernkissen mit Schlaraffia-Federkern, mit Fasson aus Kokos auf bezogenem Brettgrund, die Lehnenpolsterung durch ein garniertes Kissen aus Kokos – **Bezug:** originaler ripsbindiger geometrisch gemusterter Stoff in Braun-Rot – **Objektmaße:** 96 x 63 x 66,5 cm; Sitzhöhe: 49 x 53 x 44 cm – Restaurierung: Oberflächen gereinigt, Polsterung original – **Fotografie:** LÖFFLER COLLECTION, Reichenschwand.

135
Armlehnstuhl – **Eigentum:** LÖFFLER COLLECTION, Reichenschwand – **Inventarnummer:** 01852 – **Entwurf:** z. Zt. unbekannt – **Herstellung:** z. Zt. unbekannt – **Datierung:** um 1930 – **Technologie:** Das Gestell ist aus Ulmenholz, transparent lackiert, Konstruktionsholz Pappel, die Zargen Ulme furniert; die Armlehnen gehen gedreht in die Vorderbeine board base; backrest upholstered with coconut fibre filling – **Cover:** original rib-weave fabric in brown-red with geometric pattern – **Object measurements:** 96 x 63 x 66.5 cm, seat: 49 x 53 x 44 cm – **Conservation:** surfaces cleaned, original upholstery – **Photo:** LÖFFLER COLLECTION, Reichenschwand.

135
Armchair – **Property:** LÖFFLER COLLECTION, Reichenschwand – **Inventory number:** 01852 – **Design:** at present unknown – **Origin:** at present unknown – **Date:** around 1930 – **Technique:** elmwood frame, transparent lacquer, construction timber poplar, the frame rails veneered with elm, turned armrests that blend into the front legs – **Upholstery:** seat and back upholstery with lashed sprung drop-in frame, stuffing with tow or palm fibre – **Cover:** original patterned mohair moquette – **Object measurements:** 107.5 x 64 x 100 cm, seat: 40.5 x 48 x 57 cm – **Conservation:** surfaces cleaned, upholstery cleaned, original state – **Photo:** LÖFFLER COLLECTION, Reichenschwand.

136
Photograph, example of interior with upholstered furniture by Paul Griesser from the *WK 27 – Aufbauheim* series. The picture was printed in the catalogue *Warum WK-Möbel?* (Dresden 1930) and depicts a sitting-lounging corner from the *WK 27 – Aufbauheim* programme, among others, with the GRASSI armchair, republished in Hans Wichmann, *Aufbruch zum Neuen Wohnen: Deutsche Werkstätten und WK-Verband 1898–1970*, Basel/Stuttgart 1978, p. 293, Archive Thomas Schriefers.

137–139
Armchair, from the *WK 27 – Aufbauheim* series – **Property:** GRASSI Museum für Angewandte Kunst Leipzig – **Inventory number:** 2020.431 – **Provenance:** donation from Sammlung Sadowski – **Design:** Paul Griesser – **Origin:** unknown – **Date:** 1929–30 – **Technique:** wooden frame with cushion inlay (seat) on springing with fluted cushion (backrest) – **Upholstery:** the seat cushion has an insert of horsehair or coconut fibre and is stitched six times; the cushion cover has a cut seam at the edges; the cushion rests on covered special springing, double flat springs attached to the sides with coil springs, between the upper and lower springs a sprung steel ring with an internal coil spring; the backrest consists of a cushion in three flutes, probably filled with simple upholstery wadding; the cushion is nailed on at the upper edge and fixed at the lower corners with press studs; the clamping is covered with fabric – **Cover:** original velour cover fabric with a horizontal flame like pattern typical of the period – **Notes:** original state; of formerly nine tufts, two buttons have remained, which appear horn-like and might be early synthetic products – **Object measurements:** 79 x 64.5 x 84 cm, seat H: 39 cm – **Literature:** Hans Wichmann, *Deutsche Werkstätten and WK-Verband 1898–1990, Aufbruch zum neuen Wohnen*, Munich 1992, p. 275 – **Conservation:** missing buttons replaced – **Photo:** Esther Hoyer/GRASSI Museum für Angewandte Kunst Leipzig.

140
Watercolour depicting a living space, draft – **Property:** Deutsches Stuhlbaumuseum Rabenau – **Inventory number:** 1242_9 – Design and artistic execution: Alfred Geißler (1904–1980) – **Technique:** brush with watercolour over graphite – **Measurements:** 19.7 x 26.6 cm – **Photo:** Deutsches Stuhlbaumuseum Rabenau.

über – **Polsteraufbau:** Sitz- und Lehnenpolster sind in geschnürter Federkonstruktion auf Einlegerahmen ausgeführt, die Fasson vermutlich mit Werg oder Afrik – **Bezug:** originaler gemusterter Mohairmokett – **Objektmaße:** 107,5 x 64 x 100 cm; Sitzhöhe: 40,5 x 48 x 57 cm – **Restaurierung:** Oberflächen gereinigt, Polster gereinigt, Originalzustand – **Fotografie:** LÖFFLER COLLECTION, Reichenschwand.

136
Fotografie, Beispiel für die Einrichtung mit Polstermöbeln von Paul Griesser aus dem Programm *WK 27 – Aufbauheim*. Das Bild war im Katalog *Warum WK-Möbel?* (Dresden 1930) abgebildet und zeigt eine Sitz-Liege-Ecke des Programms *WK 27 – Aufbauheim*, u.a. mit dem GRASSI-Sessel, wiederveröffentlicht in: Hans Wichmann: *Aufbruch zum Neuen Wohnen. Deutsche Werkstätten und WK-Verband 1898–1970.* Basel und Stuttgart 1978, S. 293, Archiv Thomas Schriefers.

137–139
Armlehnsessel, aus dem Programm *WK 27 – Aufbauheim* – **Eigentum:** GRASSI Museum für Angewandte Kunst Leipzig – **Inventarnummer:** 2020.431 – **Provenienz:** Schenkung aus der Sammlung Sadowski – **Entwurf:** Paul Griesser – **Herstellung:** unbekannt – **Datierung:** 1929/30 – **Technologie:** Holzgestell mit Einlegekissen auf Federunterlage (Sitz) und in Pfeifen befestigtem Kissen (Lehne) – **Polsteraufbau:** Das Sitzkissen ist mit einer Einlage aus Rosshaar oder Kokoshaar versehen und sechsmal abgeheftet; die Kissenhülle ist an den Nähten mit einer Kappnaht versehen; das Kissen liegt auf einer abgedeckten Federung aus Spezialfedern, doppelt gelegte Flachfedern seitlich mit Spiralfedern angehängt, zwischen oberer und unterer Feder ein Federstahlring mit innenliegender Spiralfeder; die Lehne besteht aus einem Kissen in drei Pfeifen, das wahrscheinlich mit einfacher Polsterwatte gefüllt ist; das Kissen ist an der Oberkante verdeckt angenagelt und an den unteren Ecken mit Druckknöpfen fixiert; das Spannteil ist mit Stoff bezogen – **Bezug:** der noch im Original erhaltene Velours-Bezugsstoff weist eine typische querliegende, flammenartige Musterung dieser Zeit auf – **Anmerkung:** offensichtlich Originalzustand; von den ursprünglich neun Anheftpunkten sind bei noch zweien die Knöpfe erhalten, die hornartig anmuten und frühe Kunststoffprodukte sein könnten – **Objektmaße:** 79 x 64,5 x 84 cm; Sitzhöhe: 39 cm – **Literatur:** Vgl.: Hans Wichmann: *Deutsche Werkstätten und WK-Verband 1898–1990, Aufbruch zum neuen Wohnen*. München 1992, S. 275. – **Restaurierung:** fehlende Knöpfe ergänzt – **Fotografie:** Esther Hoyer/GRASSI Museum für Angewandte Kunst Leipzig.

140
Aquarell mit Darstellung eines Wohnraums, Entwurf – **Eigentum:** Bestand Deutsches Stuhlbaumuseum Rabenau – **Inventarnummer:** 1242_9 – **Entwurf und künstlerische Ausführung:** Alfred Geißler (1904–1980) – **Technik:** Pinsel mit Wasserfarbe über Bleistift – **Maße:** 19,7 x 26,6 cm – **Fotografie:** Deutsches Stuhlbaumuseum Rabenau.

141
Aquarell mit Darstellung eines Wohnraums, Entwurf – **Eigentum:** Bestand Deutsches Stuhlbaumuseum Rabenau – **Inventarnummer:** 1242_8 – **Entwurf und künstlerische Ausführung:** Alfred Geißler (1904–1980) – **Technik:** Pinsel mit Wasserfarbe über Bleistift – **Maße:** 16 x 22,5 cm – **Fotografie:** Deutsches Stuhlbaumuseum Rabenau.

142
Armlehnsessel (siehe Abb. 144).

143
Fragment des originalen Bezugsstoffs im Bestand des GRASSI Museum für Angewandte Kunst Leipzig.

141
Watercolour depicting a living space, draft – **Property:** Deutsches Stuhlbaumuseum Rabenau – **Inventory number:** 1242_8 – **Design and artistic execution:** Alfred Geißler (1904–1980) – **Technique:** brush with watercolour over graphite – **Measurements:** 16 x 22.5 cm – **Photo:** Deutsches Stuhlbaumuseum Rabenau.

142
Armchair (see fig. 144).

143
Fragment of the original cover fabric from the collection of GRASSI Museum für Angewandte Kunst Leipzig.

144
Furniture set – **Property:** GRASSI Museum für Angewandte Kunst Leipzig – **Inventory number:** 2015.229 (armchair), 2015.230 (sofa), 1995.92 (table) – **Provenance:** Armin and Anneliese Treusch Stiftung, Leipzig, 1995 and 2015 – **Design:** Ernst Max Jahn (furniture), Josef Hillerbrand (cover) – **Producer:** furniture: Carl Müller & Co., Leipzig, cover fabric: reconstruction after the original by Deutsche Werkstätten, Textil GmbH Dresden – Hellerau (DeWeTex) – **Date:** 1928 – **Technique:** the seat is a high cushion with stitched and covered stuffing, traditionally with waisted springs (sofa 7 x 4/armchair 3 x 4); the backrest is equally fitted with a high cushion, lightweight stuffing and stitching as well as waisted springs; the armrests are flat padding on hessian – **Upholstery:** wide webbing with waisted springs placed on intersections; hessian; broken flax stuffing, stitched edges; palm fibre stuffing and white wadding; cover with borders and cords; backrest with row of springs at height of lower back on jute hessian; light padding; second stuffing with calico (stitched through); armrests with light padding; on jute hessian and calico (stitched through) – **Cover:** screen-printed fabric after a design by Josef Hillerbrand/DeWeTex, digitally reconstructed after a textile fragment – **Object measurements:** sofa: 74 x 144.5 x 74.5 cm, armchair: 71 x 63 x 68 cm, table: H: 69.5 cm, D: 78 cm – **Notes:** behind armrests the original fabric was found, analysed and reconstructed; the original webbing of the sofa could be exposed and reinforced, the seat was fitted with additional jute straps – **Literature:** *Moderne Bauformen, Monatshefte Julius Hoffmann*, Stuttgart, no. XXXI, 1932 – **Conservation:** Die Stoffdruck Manufaktur Emmedingen (fabric reconstruction), Reinhardt Roßberg RiH (upholstery) – **Photo:** Esther Hoyer/GRASSI Museum für Angewandte Kunst Leipzig.

145
Sitting in a club chair, photograph from a newspaper, 1920s, Archive Thomas Schriefers.

146–148
Sitting on loose cushion for any desired use and arrangement, in Adolf G. Schneck, *Das Polstermöbel*, published on behalf of Württembergisches Landesgewerbeamtes, Stuttgart 1933, p. 7, Archive Thomas Schriefers.

149/150
Armchair – **Property:** LÖFFLER COLLECTION, Reichenschwand – **Inventory number:** 03214 – **Design:** Fritz August Breuhaus de Groot – **Origin:** at present unknown – **Date:** around 1934–36 – **Technique:** solid beech frame, four dark-brown stained and lacquered feet – **Upholstery:** seat, armrests and back with lashed sprung construction with loose front spring row and English edge, with palm fibre and horsehair stuffing, as well as a down squab, the backrest tufted with horsehair – **Cover:** patterned chenille

144
Möbelgruppe – **Eigentum:** GRASSI Museum für Angewandte Kunst Leipzig – **Inventarnummer:** 2015.229 (Sessel), 2015.230 (Sofa), 1995.92 (Tisch) – **Provenienz:** Armin und Anneliese Treusch Stiftung, Leipzig, 1995 und 2015 – **Entwurf:** Möbel: Ernst Max Jahn – **Bezug:** Josef Hillerbrand – **Herstellung:** Möbel: Carl Müller & Co, Leipzig, Bezugsstoff: Rekonstruktion nach Original der Deutschen Werkstätten, Textil GmbH Dresden – Hellerau (DeWeTex) – **Datierung:** 1928 – **Technologie:** Der Sitz ist als Hochpolster mit Fasson und Pikier traditionell mit Taillenfedern (Sofa 7x4/Sessel 3x4) ausgestattet; auch die Rückenlehne ist als Hochpolster ausgeführt, allerdings mit leichter Fasson und Pikier und mit einer Taillenfederreihe; die Armlehnen sind Flachpolster auf Spannleinen – **Polsteraufbau:** Weitgurtung mit Taillenfedern auf Gurtkreuz; Jutefederleinen; Fasson aus Brechflachs, garnierte Kanten; Pikier aus Afrik mit Watteabdeckung in Weiß; Bezug mit Boden und Kordel; die Lehne verfügt über eine Federreihe im Lendenbereich auf Spannleinen (Jute); leichte Fasson; Pikier mit Nesselbezug (leicht durchgenäht); Armlehnen mit leichter Fasson auf Jutespannleinen mit Nesselbezug (leicht durchgenäht) – **Bezug:** im Siebdruckverfahren bedruckter Stoff nach einem Entwurf von Josef Hillerbrand/DeWeTex, nach Textilfragment digital rekonstruiert – **Objektmaße:** Sofa: 74 x 144,5 x 74,5 cm, Armlehnstuhl: 71 x 63 x 68 cm, Tisch: H 69,5 cm, D 78 cm – **Anmerkung:** Hinter zwei Armlehnstollen konnte Originalstoff geborgen, analysiert und rekonstruiert werden; beim Sofa wurde die Originalgurtung wieder freigelegt und gefestigt, beim Sessel wurden Ersatzgurte aus Jute eingebracht – **Literatur:** *Moderne Bauformen, Monatshefte Julius Hoffmann.* Stuttgart XXXI. Jahrgang 1932 – **Restaurierung:** Stoffrekonstruktion: Die Stoffdruck Manufaktur Emmedingen, Polsterarbeiten: Reinhardt Roßberg RiH – **Fotografie:** Esther Hoyer/GRASSI Museum für Angewandte Kunst Leipzig.

145
Sitzen im Klubsessel. Fotografie aus einer Zeitung, 1920er Jahre, Archiv Thomas Schriefers.

146–148
Sitzen auf losen Kissen zur beliebigen Verwendung und Zusammenstellung, aus: Adolf G. Schneck: *Das Polstermöbel*, hrsg. im Auftrag des Württembergischen Landesgewerbeamtes. Stuttgart 1933, S. 7, Archiv Thomas Schriefers.

149/150
Armlehnsessel – **Eigentum:** LÖFFLER COLLECTION, Reichenschwand – **Inventarnummer:** 03214 – **Entwurf:** Fritz August Breuhaus de Groot – **Herstellung:** z. Zt. unbekannt – **Datierung:** um 1934/1936 – **Technologie:** Untergestell in Buchenholz massiv, vier Füße dunkelbraun gebeizt und lackiert – **Polsteraufbau:** Der Sitz, die Armlehnen und der Rücken verfügen über eine geschnürte Federkonstruktion mit freistehender vorderer Federreihe und englischer Kante, mit Afrikfasson und Rosshaar, ergänzt durch ein lose aufgelegtes Daunenkissen, das Rückenpolster mit Rosshaarheftung – **Bezug:** gemusterter, mit Metallfäden durchwirkte Chenille – **Objektmaße:** 73,5 x 92 x 110 cm; Sitzhöhe: 29 x 63,5 x 102,5 cm – **Literatur:** *Innendekoration*, Heft 47/1936, S. 90, 100 – **Restaurierung:** Polsterung original, restauriert, Elisabeth Riß, Raumausstattermeisterin, Stoff rekonstruiert durch Eschke Seidenmanufaktur, Crimmitschau – **Fotografie:** LÖFFLER COLLECTION, Reichenschwand.

151
Stuhlformen, aus: Franz Schuster: *Der Stil unserer Zeit. Die fünf Formen des Gestaltens der äußeren Welt des Menschen. Ein Beitrag zum kulturellen Wiederaufbau.* Wien 1948, Archiv Thomas Schriefers.

with metal threads – **Object measurements:** 73.5 x 92 x 110 cm, seat: 29 x 63.5 x 102.5 cm – **Literature:** *Innendekoration*, no. 47, 1936, pp. 90, 100 – **Conservation:** original upholstery, Raumausstattermeisterin Elisabeth Riß (restoration), Eschke Seidenmanufaktur, Crimmitschau (fabric reconstruction) – **Photo:** LÖFFLER COLLECTION, Reichenschwand.

151
Chair shapes, in Franz Schuster, *Der Stil unserer Zeit: Die fünf Formen des Gestaltens der äußeren Welt des Menschen: Ein Beitrag zum kulturellen Wiederaufbau*, Vienna 1948, Archive Thomas Schriefers.

152/153
Armchair – **Property:** GRASSI Museum für Angewandte Kunst Leipzig – **Inventory number:** 2005.234 – **Provenance:** donation from Sammlung Höhne, Berlin, 2005 – **Design:** Selman Selmanagić – **Origin:** Deutsche Werkstätten, Dresden – Hellerau – **Date:** around 1951 – **Technique:** wooden frame with seat in traditional upholstery technique with springing and backrest as tufted cushion – **Upholstery:** high-padded seat with traditional upholstery on 3 x 4 webbing (double-webbing in middle); galvanized springs 2/3/3 sewn on four times (not knotted); coarse hessian; French lashing according to the position of the springs – **Cover:** two-tone red-yellow small-patterned fabric, seat with border and (yellow) cords; backrest with simple cover; buttoned with five covered buttons due to the concave curvature – **Object measurements:** 75.5 x 68 x 75 cm, seat H: 43 cm – **Literature:** comparative examples in Hans Lewitzky, *Wohnraumgestaltung*, Berlin 1957, pp. 142, 143; Aida Abadzic Hodic, *Selman Selmanagić und Bauhaus*, Berlin 2018, p. 227 – **Conservation:** original condition – **Photo:** Esther Hoyer/GRASSI Museum für Angewandte Kunst Leipzig.

154
Depiction of simple cushion furniture, in Werner Gräff, *Zweckmässiges Wohnen für jedes Einkommen*, Potsdam 1931, Archive Thomas Schriefers.

155
Detail of interior photography, in Hans Lewitzky, *Meine Wohnung*, Berlin 1962, Archive Thomas Schriefers.

156
Detail of the cover of the magazine *Kultur im Heim*, no. 1, 1963, Archive Thomas Schriefers.

157
Exploration of an upholstered chair by Monsieur Hulot in the movie *Playtime*, sequence drawn by Thomas Schriefers.

158
Bruno Munari, *Seeking Comfort in an Uncomfortable Chair*, photograph (Corraini Edizioni 2013).

159
Seating combination, *Womb Chair* armchair with footstool – **Property:** LÖFFLER COLLECTION, Reichenschwand – **Inventory numbers:** 00250 and 01855 – **Design:** Eero Saarinen – **Origin:** Knoll Associates, New York, USA – **Date:** 1948 – **Technique:** steel frame with fibreglass shell – **Upholstery:** latex foam, loose seat and back down cushions (also produced with latex stuffing) – **Cover:** original grey-on-grey fabric, Kvadrat Hallingdal fabric – **Object measurements:** armchair: 90 x 97 x 90 cm, seat: 44 x 50 x 45 cm, footstool: 43 x 69 x 49 cm – **Literature:** Klaus-Jürgen Sembach, *Contemporary Furniture: An Inter-*

152/153
Armlehnstuhl – **Eigentum:** GRASSI Museum für Angewandte Kunst Leipzig – **Inventarnummer:** 2005.234 – **Provenienz:** Schenkung aus der Sammlung Höhne, Berlin, 2005 – **Entwurf:** Selman Selmanagić – **Herstellung:** Deutsche Werkstätten Hellerau, Dresden – **Datierung:** um 1951 – **Technologie:** Holzgestell mit Sitz in traditioneller Polstertechnik mit Federung und Lehne als Festpolsterung mit Abheftung – **Polsteraufbau:** Der Sitz ist als Hochpolster mit traditioneller Federung auf 3x4-Gurtung (Mitte Doppelgurt) aufgebaut; verzinkte Federn 2/3/3 vierfach angenäht (nicht verknotet); Federleinen grob; französische Schnürung der Federlage angepasst – **Bezug:** zweifarbiges, rot-gelbes, kleinbemustertes Gewebe, Sitz mit Boden und Kordel (gelb) gearbeitet; die Lehne ist einfach bezogen, aufgrund der konkaven Wölbung mit fünf bezogenen Knöpfen abgeheftet – **Objektmaße:** 75,5 x 68 x 75 cm, Sitzhöhe 43 cm – **Literatur:** Vergleichsbeispiele: Hans Lewitzky: *Wohnraumgestaltung*. Berlin 1957, S. 142 u. 143; Aida Abadzic Hodic: *Selman Selmanagic und das Bauhaus*. Berlin 2018, S. 227 – **Restaurierung:** Originalzustand – **Fotografie:** Esther Hoyer/ GRASSI Museum für Angewandte Kunst Leipzig.

154
Darstellung von einfachen Kissenmöbeln, aus: Werner Gräff: *Zweckmässiges Wohnen für jedes Einkommen*. Potsdam 1931, Archiv Thomas Schriefers.

155
Detail aus Wohnraumbild, aus: Hans Lewitzky: *Meine Wohnung*. Berlin 1962, Archiv Thomas Schriefers.

156
Detail aus Titel der Zeitschrift *Kultur im Heim*, Heft 1/63, Archiv Thomas Schriefers.

157
Die Erkundungen eines Polsterstuhls durch *Monsieur Hulot* im Film *Playtime*, Ablauf zeichnerisch dargestellt von Thomas Schriefers.

158
Bruno Munari: *Seeking Comfort in an Uncomfortable Chair*, Fotografie (Corraini Edizioni 2013).

159
Sitzkombination, Armlehnstuhl mit Fußhocker *Womb Chair* – **Eigentum:** LÖFFLER COLLECTION, Reichenschwand – **Inventarnummern:** 00250 und 01855 – **Entwurf:** Eero Saarinen – **Herstellung:** Knoll Associates, New York, USA – **Datierung:** 1948 – **Technologie:** Stahlgestell mit Fiberglasschale – **Polsteraufbau:** Latexschaum, lose Sitz- und Rückenkissen mit Daunenfüllung (auch mit Latexfüllung ausgeführt) – **Bezug:** originaler Stoff grau in grau, Kvadrat Hallingdal– **Objektmaße:** Armlehnstuhl: 90 x 97 x 90 cm; Sitzhöhe: 44 x 50 x 45 cm; Fußhocker: 43 x 69 x 49 cm; Sitzhöhe: 43 x 55 x 49 cm – **Literatur:** Klaus-Jürgen Sembach: *Contemporary Furniture. An International Review of Modern Furniture 1950 to the Present*. Stuttgart 1982, S. 102; Charlotte u. Peter Fiell: *1000 chairs*. Köln 2005, S. 229 – **Restaurierung:** Schaumstoff erneuert, originaler Bezug gereinigt – **Fotografie:** LÖFFLER COLLECTION, Reichenschwand.

160–162
Armlehnstuhl – **Eigentum:** LÖFFLER COLLECTION, Reichenschwand – **Inventarnummer:** 02845 – **Entwurf:** Karl Nothhelfer – **Herstellung:** Schörle & Gölz, Stuttgart-Cannstatt – **Datierung:** 1950er Jahre – **Technologie:** Das Gestell besteht aus Buche, Kirsche, Ahorn massiv, ist lackiert und an den Kanten gerundet; vier Beine sind konisch ausgebildet und bodennah gebogen; die Armlehnen sind ebenfalls gebogen; die Rückenlehne verfügt über Ohrenbacken – **Polsteraufbau:** Das Sitz-

national Review of Modern Furniture 1950 to the Present, Stuttgart 1982, p. 102; Charlotte and Peter Fiell, *1000 Chairs*, Cologne 2005, p. 229 – **Conservation:** foam renewed, original cover fabric cleaned – **Photo:** LÖFFLER COLLECTION, Reichenschwand.

160–162
Armchair – **Property:** LÖFFLER COLLECTION, Reichenschwand – **Inventory number:** 02845 – **Design:** Karl Nothhelfer – **Origin:** Schörle & Gölz, Stuttgart-Cannstatt – **Date:** 1950s – **Technique:** frame from solid beech, cherrywood and maple; lacquered with rounded edges; four conical legs, curved towards the end; armrests likewise curved; winged backrest – **Upholstery:** seat upholstery is a sprung cushion with coconut fibre stuffing. It is placed on spring-sheet flat fibre springs, which are attached to the frame; back upholstery with zigzag springs, coconut fibre upholstery and grey wadding; original lime green bouclé – **Object measurements:** 100 x 72 x 87 cm, seat: 41 x 55 x 47 cm – **Literatur:** *Bauen + Wohnen*, no. 6, 1952, pp. 264, 282 – **Conservation:** original – **Photo:** LÖFFLER COLLECTION, Reichenschwand.

163/164
Chair – **Property:** GRASSI Museum für Angewandte Kunst Leipzig – **Inventory number:** 2014.523 – **Provenance:** private donation, 2014 – **Design:** Werner Stachelroth – **Date:** 1951–52 – **Technique:** drop-frame with traditional flat padding on flat fibre springs – **Upholstery:** later upholstery with plastic foam and Selfa-springs was removed; new construction according to findings; three opposing flat springs; jute hessian; one layer of cloth wadding; calico; cotton top cover – **Cover:** new cover with a 1950s-inspired plain weave; warp: black cotton wool, weft: black cotton wool/grey wool – **Object measurements:** 80.5 x 47 x 55 cm – **Notes:** reconstructed according to findings with original springs of the period and suitable conservation status – **Literature:** comparative examples in Werner Stachelroth, 'Der Stuhlbau steht zur Diskussion', *Holz and Wohnraum*, vol. 1, no. 7, 1953, pp. 217, 218 – **Conservation:** Thomas Andersch (wooden surface) and Reinhardt Roßberg RiH (upholstery) – **Photo:** Esther Hoyer/GRASSI Museum für Angewandte Kunst Leipzig.

165/166
Armchair *Casala 788* – **Property:** LÖFFLER COLLECTION, Reichenschwand – **Inventory number:** 01153 – **Design:** Dietrich Hinz – **Origin:** Carl Sasse, Lauenau, Deister, Germany – **Date:** 1953–58 – **Technique:** solid beech frame, cherry-maple veneer; solid legs and armrests; round tapered front legs, the backrests are conical with a rail. Upholstery: seat with high spring core padding on sprung steel base, backrest upholstery with coconut fibre and grey wadding, with feathers used in the lower back area – **Cover:** original black-yellow striped wool fabric – **Object measurements:** 113 x 75.5 x 79 cm, seat: 43 x 58 x 50 cm – **Literature:** *Katalog Casala Polstermöbel*, 1953; Richard Bermpohl and Hans Winkelmann, *Das Möbelbuch*, Gütersloh 1958, p. 63 – **Conservation:** original – **Photo:** LÖFFLER COLLECTION, Reichenschwand.

167/168
Children's armchair – **Property:** LÖFFLER COLLECTION, Reichenschwand – **Inventory number:** 01082 – **Design:** at present unknown – **Origin:** at present unknown – **Date:** around 1955 – **Technique:** solid beech frame; stained dark and lacquered, tipping backwards with four tapered legs – **Upholstery:** seat upholstery coil springs with coconut fibre stuffing and grey wadding, backrest in coconut fibre and grey wadding – **Cover:** original patterned velour

polster ist ein Federkissen mit Kokosfasson. Es liegt auf Federblech-Bandfedern, die mit dem Gestell verschraubt sind; das Rückenpolster besteht aus Wellenfedern, Kokosfasson und grauer Watte – **Bezug:** originaler lindgrün-brauner Bouclé – **Objektmaße:** 100 x 72 x 87 cm; Sitzhöhe: 41 x 55 x 47 cm – **Literatur:** *Bauen + Wohnen*, Heft 6/1952, S. 264 und 282 – **Restaurierung:** unberührter Originalzustand – **Fotografie:** LÖFFLER COLLECTION, Reichenschwand.

163/164
Stuhl – **Eigentum:** GRASSI Museum für Angewandte Kunst Leipzig – **Inventarnummer:** 2014.523 – **Provenienz:** Schenkung aus Privatbesitz, 2014 – **Entwurf:** Werner Stachelroth – **Datierung:** 1951/52 – **Technologie:** Einlegerahmen mit traditionellem Flachpolster auf Flachfedern – **Polsteraufbau:** neuere Polsterung mit Schaumstoff und Selfa-Federn wurde entfernt; Neuaufbau nach Befundlage: drei gegenläufige Flachfedern; Juteleinen; als Polstermaterial Lumpenwatte einfach aufgelegt; Nesselbezug Baumwolle – **Bezug:** Neubezug mit Gewebe aus den 50er Jahren in abgeleiteter Leinwandbindung, Kette: schwarze Baumwolle, Schuss: schwarze Baumwolle/graue Wolle – **Objektmaße:** 80,5 x 47 x 55 cm – **Anmerkung:** Nach Befund mit geborgenen Originalfedern der Entstehungszeit und adäquatem Ersatzmaterial rekonstruiert; Restauriert mit Originalgewebe aus der Entstehungszeit – **Literatur:** Vergleichsbeispiele: Werner Stachelroth: Der Stuhlbau steht zur Diskussion, in: *Holz und Wohnraum*, 1. Jg., Heft 7, 1953, S. 217 u. 218. – **Restaurierung:** Thomas Andersch (Holzoberfläche) und Reinhardt Roßberg RiH (Polsterung) – **Fotografie:** Esther Hoyer/GRASSI Museum für Angewandte Kunst Leipzig.

165/166
Armlehnstuhl *Casala 788* – **Eigentum:** LÖFFLER COLLECTION, Reichenschwand – **Inventarnummer:** 01153 – **Entwurf:** Dietrich Hinz – **Herstellung:** Carl Sasse, Lauenau, Deister, Deutschland – **Datierung:** 1953–1958 – **Technologie:** Das Gestell besteht aus Buchenholz massiv, belegt mit einem Kirsche-Ahorn-Furnier; Beine und Armlehnen sind massiv, die Vorderbeine kegelförmig verjüngt, die Hinterbeine konisch eckig mit Querstrebe – **Polsteraufbau:** der Sitz besteht aus einem hohen Federkernpolster, das auf einem Federbandgrund aufliegt; die Rückenlehne bildet ein Fassonpolster aus Kokos und grauer Watte mit dem Einsatz von Federn im Lendenbereich – **Bezug:** originaler schwarz-gelb gestreifter Wollstoff – **Objektmaße:** 113 x 75,5 x 79 cm; Sitzhöhe: 43 x 58 x 50 cm – **Literatur:** *Katalog Casala Polstermöbel* 1953; R. Bermphol u. H. Winkelmann: *Das Möbelbuch*. Gütersloh 1958, S. 63 – **Restaurierung:** unberührter Originalzustand – **Fotografie:** LÖFFLER COLLECTION, Reichenschwand.

167/168
Armlehnstuhl für Kinder – **Eigentum:** LÖFFLER COLLECTION, Reichenschwand – **Inventarnummer:** 01082 – **Entwurf:** z. Zt. unbekannt – **Herstellung:** z. Zt. unbekannt – **Datierung:** um 1955 – **Technologie:** Das Gestell besteht aus Buchenholz massiv, dunkel gebeizt und lackiert, formal ist es nach hinten kippend und mit vier konisch nach unten verjüngten Beinen versehen – **Polsteraufbau:** Das Sitzpolster besteht aus Federbändern mit Kokosfasson und grauer Watte, das Rückenpolster aus Kokosfasson und grauer Watte – **Bezug:** originaler gemusterter Kräuselvelours in Rot-Braun – **Objektmaße:** 55 x 42,5 x 54 cm; Sitzhöhe: 28 x 34 x 34 cm – **Restaurierung:** unberührter Originalzustand – **Fotografie:** LÖFFLER COLLECTION, Reichenschwand.

169/170
Armlehnstuhl *Papa Bear* – **Eigentum:** LÖFFLER COLLECTION, Reichenschwand – **Inventarnummer:** 00560 – **Entwurf:** Hans J. Wegner – **Herstellung:** AP. Stolen, Kopenhagen, Dänemark – **Datierung:** 1951 – **Technologie:** Untergestell Buche massiv, vier Beine konisch zulaufend in Eichen- bzw. Eschenholz (?) massiv, criselé in red-brown – **Object measurements:** 55 x 42.5 x 54 cm, seat: 28 x 34 x 34 cm – **Conservation:** unaltered original condition – **Photo:** LÖFFLER COLLECTION, Reichenschwand.

169/170
Armchair *Papa Bear* – **Property:** LÖFFLER COLLECTION, Reichenschwand – **Inventory number:** 00560 – **Design:** Hans J. Wegner – **Origin:** AP. Stolen, Copenhagen, Denmark – **Date:** 1951 – **Technique:** solid beech frame, four tapered legs in solid oak or ash?, transparent lacquer (glued across several elements) – **Upholstery:** latex seat cushion on webbing, backrest with pocket spring core and fine tow stuffing – **Cover:** original black-beige wool flat weave – **Object measurements:** 99.5 x 91 x 93 cm, seat: 38 x 57 x 51 cm – **Literature:** Christian Holmsted Olesen, Wegner: *Just One Good Chair*, Ostfildern 2014, pp. 208–209; Charlotte and Peter Fiell, Chairs: *1000 Masterpieces of Modern Design, 1800 to the Present Day*, London 2012, p. 290 – **Conservation:** fabric and upholstery original, reconstructed (uniting fragments of two chairs into one) – **Photo:** LÖFFLER COLLECTION, Reichenschwand.

171
Armchair *Poltrona girevole P 32* – **Property:** LÖFFLER COLLECTION, Reichenschwand – **Inventory number:** 01083 – **Design:** Osvaldo Borsani – **Origin:** Tecno P.p.A., Milan, Italy – **Date:** 1956 – **Technique:** swivelling and tiltable seat on a foot made of a black lacquered iron frame with four round brass surfaces that enable it to stand well – **Upholstery:** the seat and combined backrest and armrest upholstery from latex foam, applied to the iron frame, a metal shell and rubber webbing – **Cover:** original blue jersey in a cotton- synthetic mix – **Object measurements:** 85 x 85 x 75 cm, seat: 40 x 54 x 50 cm – **Conservation:** reconstructed plastic foam in PUR plastic foam, the construction, mechanism and cover fabric are original – **Photo:** LÖFFLER COLLECTION, Reichenschwand.

172
Shell chair *Egg Chair* – **Property:** GRASSI Museum für Angewandte Kunst Leipzig – **Inventory number:** 2018.265 – **Provenance:** donation by Friedhelm Wachs, 2018 – **Design:** Arne Jacobsen – **Origin:** Fritz Hansen A/S, Copenhagen, Denmark – **Date:** 1958 – **Technique:** the seat body is made from fibre-reinforced plastic with foam padding and leather cover (in 1958 the Egg Chair was made from polystyrene, reinforced with hessian soaked in artificial resin and upholstered with latex cushions). Seat cushion also made from latex. Only the modern armchair was made from fibre-reinforced plastic, the seat made from a plastic-foam cushion with leather cover, the turnable feet from chrome-plated steel – **Upholstery:** seat cushion: plastic-foam piece with leather cover, fabric base (fragments), zipper, piped edge; the plastic body is upholstered synthetic foam, the seat bottom has been separately inserted in the size of the seating cushion and highlighted by a double fell seam – **Cover:** red leather glued to plastic foam, leather clamping has been attached using piping and hand stitching – **Object measurements:** 107 x 80 x 60 cm – **Literature:** Charlotte and Peter Fiell, *1000 Chairs*, Cologne 2007; GRASSI Museum für Angewandte Kunst (ed.), *Made in Denmark: Formgestaltung seit 1900*, Stuttgart 2018, p. 149 – **Conservation:** original condition – **Photo:** Esther Hoyer/GRASSI Museum für Angewandte Kunst Leipzig.

173/174
Armchair *Constanze*, element group *C, E12* – **Property:** LÖFFLER COLLECTION, Reichenschwand – **Inventory**

dunkelbraun gebeizt und lackiert; Armlehnen in Teak massiv, transparent lackiert (aus mehreren Teilen verleimt) – **Polsteraufbau:** Das Sitzpolster ist ein Latexkissen auf Gurtgrund, während die Lehne einen Taschenfederkern und eine Fasson aus Feinwerg aufweist – **Bezug:** originales schwarz-beige gemustertes Wollflachgewebe – **Objektmaße:** 99,5 x 91 x 93 cm; Sitzhöhe: 38 x 57 x 51 cm – **Literatur:** Christian Holmsted Olesen: *Wegner. Just one good Chair*. Ostfildern 2014, S. 208f.; Charlotte u. Peter Fiell: *Chairs. 1000 Masterpieces of Modern Design, 1800 to the Present Day*. London 2012, S. 290 – **Restaurierung:** Stoff und Polsterung original rekonstruiert (Fragmente von zwei Stühlen zu einem vereint) – **Fotografie:** LÖFFLER COLLECTION, Reichenschwand.

171
Armlehnstuhl *Poltrona girevole P 32* – **Eigentum:** LÖFFLER COLLECTION, Reichenschwand – **Inventarnummer:** 01083 – **Entwurf:** Osvaldo Borsani – **Herstellung:** Tecno S.p.A., Mailand, Italien – **Datierung:** 1956 – **Technologie:** Der dreh- und kippbare Sitz lagert auf einer Fußkonstruktion als schwarz lackiertes Eisengestell mit vier runden Messingflächen, die einen guten Stand gewährleisten – **Polsteraufbau:** Die Sitz- und die kombinierte Rücken-/Armlehnenpolsterung besteht aus Latexformschaum, der auf einem Eisengestell, einer Metallschale und einem Gummigurtverband aufgebracht wurde – **Bezug:** originaler blauer Jersey in Baumwoll-Synthetik-Mix – **Objektmaße:** 85 x 85 x 75 cm; Sitzhöhe: 40 x 54 x 50 cm – **Restaurierung:** Schaumstoff rekonstruiert in PUR-Schaum, die Konstruktion, Mechanik sowie der Bezug sind original – **Fotografie:** LÖFFLER COLLECTION, Reichenschwand.

172
Schalensessel *Egg Chair* – **Eigentum:** GRASSI Museum für Angewandte Kunst Leipzig – **Inventarnummer:** 2018.265 – **Provenienz:** Schenkung Friedhelm Wachs, 2018 – **Entwurf:** Arne Jacobsen – **Herstellung:** Fritz Hansen A/S, Kopenhagen, Dänemark – **Datierung:** 1958 – **Technologie:** Der Sesselkorpus besteht aus fiberglasverstärktem Kunststoff mit Schaumstoffpolsterung und Lederbezug (1958 besteht der *Egg Chair* aus Styropor, das mit Kunstharzgetränkten Federleinenbinden verstärkt ist und mit einem Latexformpolster gepolstert ist). Auch das Sitzkissen besteht aus einem Latexformpolster. Erst die modernen Sessel werden aus fiberglasverstärktem Kunststoff gefertigt, das Sitzpolster besteht aus einem Schaumstoffkissen mit Lederbezug; das drehbare Fußgestell aus verchromtem Stahl – **Polsteraufbau:** Sitzkissen: Schaumstoffformteil mit Lederbezug, Stoffboden (Fragmente), Reißverschluss, Randkeder; der Kunststoffkorpus ist mit Schaumstoff gepolstert; der Sitzboden ist in Größe des Sitzkissens separat eingesetzt und mit einer Doppelkappnaht abgesetzt – **Bezug:** auf den Schaumstoff aufgeklebtes rotes Leder; das Lederspannteil ist mit einem Keder und per Handnaht angebracht – **Objektmaße:** 107 x 80 x 60 cm – **Literatur:** Charlotte u. Peter Fiell: *1000 chairs*. Köln, 2007; GRASSI Museum für Angewandte Kunst (Hg.): *Made in Denmark, Formgestaltung seit 1900*. Stuttgart 2018, S. 149 – **Restaurierung:** Originalzustand – **Fotografie:** Esther Hoyer/GRASSI Museum für Angewandte Kunst Leipzig.

173/174
Sessel *Constanze*, Elementgruppe C, E12 – **Eigentum:** LÖFFLER COLLECTION, Reichenschwand – **Inventarnummer:** 03014 – **Entwurf:** Johannes Spalt – **Herstellung:** Franz Wittmann Möbelwerkstätten, Etsdorf/Kamp, Österreich – **Datierung:** 1961 – **Technologie:** Das Gestell besteht aus Buchenholz (Zargen) und Nuss- bzw. Teakholz massiv (Füße) – **Polsteraufbau:** Der Sitz weist eine Latexschaumpolsterung auf Wellenfedergrund auf – **Bezug:** originales hellbraunes Reinanilin-Rindsleder – **Maße:** 71 x 71 x 72 cm; Sitzhöhe: 40 x 71 x 53 cm – **Restaurierung:** unberührter Originalzustand, Oberflächen gereinigt, Leder restauriert, Birgit Baer, Sattlerin – **Fotografie:** LÖFFLER COLLECTION, Reichenschwand.

number: 03014 – **Design:** Johannes Spalt – **Origin:** Franz Wittmann Möbelwerkstätten, Etsdorf/Kamp, Austria – **Date:** 1961 – **Technique:** beech frame (rails) and solid nut-wood or teak (feet) – **Upholstery:** seat with latex foam upholstery on zigzag spring base – **Cover:** original light-brown aniline cow leather – **Object measurements:** 71 x 71 x 72 cm, seat: 40 x 71 x 53 cm – **Conservation:** original condition, surfaces cleaned, leather restored, saddler Birgit Baer – **Photo:** LÖFFLER COLLECTION, Reichenschwand.

175/176
Seat object *Joe* – **Property:** LÖFFLER COLLECTION, Reichenschwand – **Inventory number:** 00256 – **Design:** Gionatan de Pas, Donato D'Urbino, Paolo Lomazzi – **Origin:** Poltronova, Florence, Italy – **Date:** 1970 – **Technique:** metal frame with wooden board on coasters as upholstery base – **Upholstery:** padding made from polyurethane foam – **Cover:** original denim-blue linen fabric – **Object measurements:** 96 x 175 x 110 cm, seat: 41 x 70 x 55 cm – **Literature:** *Design Furniture from Italy: Design, Object, Image: Culture and Technology of the Italian Furniture 1950–1980*, Rome 1980, p. 177; Miriam Stimpson, *Modern Furniture Classics*, New York 1987, p. 156; Charlotte and Peter Fiell, *1000 Chairs*, Cologne 2005, p. 422 – **Conservation:** original – **Photo:** LÖFFLER COLLECTION, Reichenschwand.

177/178/219
Beanbag *Sacco* – **Property:** LÖFFLER COLLECTION, Reichenschwand – **Inventory number:** 00152 – **Design:** Piero Gatti, Cesare Paolini and Franco Teodoro – **Origin:** Zanotta P.p.A., Milan, Italy – **Date:** 1968 – **Technique/Upholstery:** beanbag filled with foamed polyurethane balls – **Cover:** wine-red vinyl – **Object measurements:** 90 x 70 x 76 cm – **Literature:** Philippe Garner, *Möbel des 20. Jahrhunderts*. London 1980, p. 197; *Design Furniture from Italy: Design, Object, Image: Culture and Technology of the Italian Furniture 1950–1980*, Rome 1980, p. 169; Klaus-Jürgen Sembach, *Contemporary Furniture: An International Review of Modern Furniture 1950 to the Present*, Stuttgart 1982, p. 124; Charlotte and Peter Fiell, *1000 Chairs*, Cologne 2005, pp. 410–411 – **Conservation:** original condition – **Photo:** LÖFFLER COLLECTION, Reichenschwand.

179/180
Shell chair *Ball* – **Property:** LÖFFLER COLLECTION, Reichenschwand – **Inventory number:** 00221 – **Design:** Eero Aarnio – **Origin:** Asko, Lahti, Finland – **Date:** 1963 – **Technique:** fibreglass shell, cast aluminium foot, lacquered white, interior fitted with cord-covered plastic foam – **Upholstery:** seat is a loose, wadded foam cushion; back and side upholstery is a loose cushion stuffed with wadding – **Cover:** original red cotton cord fabric – **Object measurements:** 120 x 110 x 95 cm, seat: 44 x 57 x 50 cm – **Literature:** Gerd Hatje and Elke Kaspar, *New Furniture: Neue Möbel*, 9, Stuttgart 1966, p. 45; Charlotte and Peter Fiell, *1000 Chairs*, Cologne 2005, p. 369 – **Conservation:** original condition – **Photo:** LÖFFLER COLLECTION, Reichenschwand.

181/182
Seat object *Blow* – **Property:** LÖFFLER COLLECTION, Reichenschwand – **Inventory number:** 00154 – **Design:** Gionatan de Pas, Donato D'Urbino, Paolo Lomazzi and Carla Scolari – **Origin:** Zanotta S.p.A., Milan, Italy – **Date:** 1967 – **Technique:** inflatable armchair – **Upholstery:** welded plastic pockets – **Cover:** PVC? – **Object measurements:** 72 x 110 x 90 cm, seat: 38 x 47 x 53 cm – **Literature:** *Design Furniture from Italy: Design, Object, Image:*

175/176
Sitzobjekt *Joe* – **Eigentum:** LÖFFLER COLLECTION, Reichenschwand – **Inventarnummer:** 00256 – **Entwurf:** Gionatan de Pas, Donato D'Urbino, Paolo Lomazzi – **Herstellung:** Poltronova, Florenz, Italien – **Datierung:** 1970 – **Technologie:** Die Polsterbasis bildet ein Metallrahmen auf Holzplatte mit Rollen – **Polsteraufbau:** Das Polster besteht aus Polyurethanschaum – **Bezug:** originaler jeansblauer Leinenstoff – **Objektmaße:** 96 x 175 x 110 cm; Sitzhöhe: 41 x 70 x 55 cm – **Literatur:** *Design Furniture from Italy. Design, object, image. Culture and Technology of the Italian Furniture 1950–1980*. Rom 1980, S. 177; Miriam Stimpson: *Modern Furniture Classics*. New York 1987, S. 156; Charlotte u. Peter Fiell: *1000 chairs*. Köln 2005, S. 422 – **Restaurierung:** unberührter Originalzustand – **Fotografie:** LÖFFLER COLLECTION, Reichenschwand.

177/178/219
Sitzsack *Sacco* – **Eigentum:** LÖFFLER COLLECTION, Reichenschwand – **Inventarnummer:** 00152 – **Entwurf:** Piero Gatti, Cesare Paolini u. Franco Teodoro – **Herstellung:** Zanotta S.p.A., Mailand, Italien – **Datierung:** 1968 – **Technologie/Polsterung:** Sitzsack, gefüllt mit aufgeschäumten Polystyrolkugeln – **Bezug:** weinrotes Vinyl – **Objektmaße:** 90 x 70 x 76 cm – **Literatur:** Philippe Garner: *Möbel des 20. Jahrhunderts*. London 1980, S. 197; *Design Furniture from Italy. Design, object, image. Culture and Technology of the Italian Furniture 1950–1980*. Rom 1980, S. 169; Klaus-Jürgen Sembach: *Contemporary Furniture. An International Review of Modern Furniture 1950 to the Present*. Stuttgart 1982, S. 124; Charlotte u. Peter Fiell: *1000 chairs*. Köln 2005, S. 410f. – **Restaurierung:** unberührter Originalzustand – **Fotografie:** LÖFFLER COLLECTION, Reichenschwand.

179/180
Schalensessel *Ball* – **Eigentum:** LÖFFLER COLLECTION, Reichenschwand – **Inventarnummer:** 00221 – **Entwurf:** Eero Aarnio – **Herstellung:** Asko, Lahti, Finnland – **Datierung:** 1963 – **Technologie:** Fiberglasschale, Fuß aus Aluminiumguss, weiß lackiert, Innenraum mit einem cordbezogenen Schaumstoff ausgekleidet – **Polsteraufbau:** Das Sitzpolster ist ein loses, wattiertes Schaumstoffkissen; das Rücken- und Seitenpolster ist ein loses, mit Watte gefülltes Kissen – **Bezug:** originaler roter Baumwollcordstoff – **Objektmaße:** 120 x 110 x 95 cm; Sitzhöhe: 44 x 57 x 50 cm – **Literatur:** Gerd Hatje, Elke Kaspar: *New Furniture. Neue Möbel*, Nr. 9. Stuttgart 1966, S. 45; Charlotte u. Peter Fiell: *1000 chairs*. Köln 2005, S. 369 – **Restaurierung:** unberührter Originalzustand – **Fotografie:** LÖFFLER COLLECTION, Reichenschwand.

181/182
Sitzobjekt *Blow* – **Eigentum:** LÖFFLER COLLECTION, Reichenschwand – **Inventarnummer:** 00154 – **Entwurf:** Gionatan de Pas, Donato D'Urbino, Paolo Lomazzi u. Carla Scolari – **Herstellung:** Zanotta S.p.A., Mailand, Italien – **Datierung:** 1967 – **Technologie:** Mit Luft gefüllter, aufblasbarer Armlehnsessel – **Polsteraufbau:** Kunststoffkammern, verschweißt – **Bezug** = Hülle, PVC (?) – **Objektmaße:** 72 x 110 x 90 cm; Sitzhöhe: 38 x 47 x 53 cm – **Literatur:** *Design Furniture from Italy. Design, object, image. Culture and Technology of the Italian Furniture 1950–1980*. Rom 1980, S. 141; Klaus-Jürgen Sembach: *Contemporary Furniture. An International Review of Modern Furniture 1950 to the Present*. Stuttgart 1982, S. 124; Charlotte u. Peter Fiell: *Chairs. 1000 Masterpieces of Modern Design, 1800 to the Present Day*. London 2012, S. 438; Charlotte u. Peter Fiell: *1000 chairs*. Köln 2005, S. 413 – **Restaurierung:** unberührter Originalzustand – **Fotografie:** LÖFFLER COLLECTION, Reichenschwand.

183/184
Sitzobjekt *Tube Chair* – **Eigentum:** LÖFFLER COLLECTION, Reichenschwand – **Inventarnummer:** 00509 – **Entwurf:** Joe *Culture and Technology of the Italian Furniture 1950–1980*, Rome 1980, p. 141; Klaus-Jürgen Sembach, *Contemporary Furniture: An International Review of Modern Furniture 1950 to the Present*, Stuttgart 1982, p. 124; Charlotte and Peter Fiell, *Chairs: 1000 Masterpieces of Modern Design, 1800 to the Present Day*, London 2012, p. 438; Charlotte and Peter Fiell, *1000 Chairs*, Cologne 2005, p. 413 – **Conservation:** original condition – **Photo:** LÖFFLER COLLECTION, Reichenschwand.

183/184
Seat object *Tube Chair* – **Property:** LÖFFLER COLLECTION, Reichenschwand – **Inventory number:** 00509 – **Design:** Joe Colombo – **Origin:** Flexform, Milan, Italy – **Date:** 1969 – **Technique:** four cylinders covered with polyurethane foam and blue vinyl synthetic leather, the horizontal cylinders (castors) are held together by steel brackets – **Upholstery:** seat padding made from PUR foam – **Cover:** vinyl synthetic leather – **Object measurements:** 57 x 61 x 105 cm, seat: 28 x 24 x 59 cm – **Literature:** Ignazia Favata, *Joe Colombo and Italian Design of the Sixties*, Milan 1988, pp. 82–83; Vittorio Fagone and Ignazia Favata, *Joe Colombo*, Pero/Milan 2011, pp. 82–83; Philippe Garner, *Sixties Design*, Cologne 2008, p. 165; Charlotte and Peter Fiell, *1000 Chairs*, Cologne 2005, p. 360 – **Conservation:** original condition, surfaces cleaned – **Photo:** LÖFFLER COLLECTION, Reichenschwand.

185/186
Seat object *MAgriTTA* – **Property:** LÖFFLER COLLECTION, Reichenschwand – **Inventory number:** 01141 – **Design:** Roberto Sebastián Matta – **Origin:** Simon International for Gavina, Bologna, Italy – **Date:** 1970 – **Technique:** fibreglass-reinforced seat as base for upholstery – **Upholstery:** PUR foam cushion, foam-moulded – **Cover:** original black and green jersey, a cotton synthetic – **Object measurements:** 59 x 84 x 92 cm – **Literature:** Sébastien Faucon et al., *Collector – œuvres du Centre national des arts plastiques*, Paris 2011, pp. 60–61; Charlotte and Peter Fiell, *1000 Chairs*, Cologne 2005, p. 420 – **Conservation:** original – **Photo:** LÖFFLER COLLECTION, Reichenschwand.

187/188
Seat object *Pony* – **Property:** LÖFFLER COLLECTION, Reichenschwand – **Inventory number:** 00432 – **Design:** Eero Aarnio – **Origin:** Stendig, New York, USA – **Date:** 1973 – **Technique/Upholstery:** metal frame with foam-moulded PUR plastic foam – **Cover:** original brown velour – **Object measurements:** 89 x 65 x 110 cm, seat: 55 x 40 x 55 cm – **Literature:** Charlotte Fiell, *Scandinavian Design*, Cologne 2002, p. 88ff.; Charlotte and Peter Fiell, *1000 Chairs*, Cologne 2005, p. 471 – **Conservation:** original condition – **Photo:** LÖFFLER COLLECTION, Reichenschwand.

189/190
Seat object *Capitello* – **Property:** LÖFFLER COLLECTION, Reichenschwand – **Inventory number:** 00251 – **Design:** Studio 65 (Piero Gatti, Cesare Paolini, Franco Teodoro) – **Origin:** Gufram, Balangero, Turin, Italy – **Date:** 1971 – **Technique/Upholstery:** polyurethane plastic foam, form-moulded and laminated – **Cover:** none – **Object measurements:** 82 x 114 x 111 cm, seat: 42 x 97 x 40 cm – **Literature:** Klaus-Jürgen Sembach et al., *Möbeldesign des 20. Jahrhunderts*, Cologne 1993, p. 206; Miriam Stimpson, *Modern Furniture Classics*, New York 1987, p. 156; Charlotte and Peter Fiell, *1000 Chairs*, Cologne 2005, p. 431 – **Conservation:** original condition – **Photo:** LÖFFLER COLLECTION, Reichenschwand.

Colombo – **Herstellung:** Flexform, Mailand, Italien – **Datierung:** 1969 – **Technologie:** Vier mit Polyurethanschaumstoff belegte Zylinder mit blauem Vinylkunstlederbezug; die liegenden Zylinder(Rollen) werden durch Stahlklammern zusammengehalten – **Polsteraufbau:** Sitzpolster aus PUR-Schaum – **Bezug:** Vinylkunstleder – **Objektmaße:** 57 x 61 x 105 cm; Sitzhöhe: 28 x 24 x 59 cm – **Literatur:** Ignazia Favata: *Joe Colombo and Italian Design of the Sixties.* Mailand 1988, S. 82f.; Vittorio Fagone, Ignazia Favata: *Joe Colombo.* Pero/Mailand 2011, S. 82f.; Philippe Garner: *Sixties Design.* Köln 2008, S. 165; Charlotte u. Peter Fiell: *1000 chairs.* Köln 2005, S. 360 – **Restaurierung:** Originalzustand, Oberflächen gereinigt – **Fotografie:** LÖFFLER COLLECTION, Reichenschwand.

185/186
Sitzobjekt *MAgriTTA* – **Eigentum:** LÖFFLER COLLECTION, Reichenschwand – **Inventarnummer:** 01141 – **Entwurf:** Roberto Sebastián Matta – **Herstellung:** Simon International für Gavina, Bologna, Italien – **Datierung:** 1970 – **Technologie:** Glasfaserverstärkte Sitzschale als Basis für die Polsterung – **Polsteraufbau:** PUR-Schaumstoffkissen, formgeschäumt – **Bezug:** originaler schwarzer und grüner Jersey in Baumwoll-Synthetik-Mix – **Objektmaße:** 59 x 84 x 92 cm – **Literatur:** Sébastien Faucon u. a.: Collector – œuvres du Centre national des arts plastiques. Paris 2011, S. 60f.; Charlotte u. Peter Fiell: 1000 chairs. Köln 2005, S. 420 – **Restaurierung:** unberührter Originalzustand – **Fotografie:** LÖFFLER COLLECTION, Reichenschwand.

187/188
Sitzobjekt *Pony* – **Eigentum:** LÖFFLER COLLECTION, Reichenschwand – **Inventarnummer:** 00432 – **Entwurf:** Eero Aarnio – **Herstellung:** Stendig, New York, USA – **Datierung:** 1973 – **Technologie/Polsterung:** Metallgestell mit formgeschäumtem PUR-Schaumstoff – **Bezug:** originaler brauner Veloursstoff – **Objektmaße:** 89 x 65 x 110 cm; Sitzhöhe: 55 x 40 x 55 cm – **Literatur:** Charlotte Fiell: *Scandinavian design.* Köln 2002, S. 88ff.; Charlotte u. Peter Fiell: *1000 chairs.* Köln 2005, S. 471 – **Restaurierung:** unberührter Originalzustand – **Fotografie:** LÖFFLER COLLECTION, Reichenschwand.

189/190
Sitzobjekt *Capitello* – **Eigentum:** LÖFFLER COLLECTION, Reichenschwand – **Inventarnummer:** 00251 – **Entwurf:** Studio 65 (Piero Gatti, Cesare Paolini, Franco Teodoro) – **Herstellung:** Gufram, Balangero, Turin, Italien – **Datierung:** 1971 – **Technologie/Polsterung:** Polyurethanschaumstoff, formgeschäumt und „behautet" – ohne Bezug – **Objektmaße:** 82 x 114 x 111 cm; Sitzhöhe: 42 x 97 x 40 cm – **Literatur:** Klaus-Jürgen Sembach u. a.: *Möbeldesign des 20. Jahrhunderts.* Köln 1993, S. 206; Miriam Stimpson: *Modern Furniture Classics.* New York 1987, S. 156; Charlotte u. Peter Fiell: *1000 chairs.* Köln 2005, S. 431 – **Restaurierung:** unberührter Originalzustand – **Fotografie:** LÖFFLER COLLECTION, Reichenschwand.

191/192
Sofa *Bocca/Marilyn* – **Eigentum:** LÖFFLER COLLECTION, Reichenschwand – **Inventarnummer:** 00418 – **Entwurf:** Studio 65 (Piero Gatti, Cesare Paolini, Franco Teodoro) – **Herstellung:** Gufram, Balangero, Turin, Italien – **Datierung:** 1971 – **Technologie/Polsterung:** Polyurethanschaumstoff formgeschäumt – **Bezug:** Polyurethan – **Objektmaße:** 83 x 210 x 78 cm – **Literatur:** Klaus-Jürgen Sembach u. a.: *Möbeldesign des 20. Jahrhunderts.* Köln 1993, S. 205; Charlotte u. Peter Fiell: *Modern Furniture Classics. Postwar to post-modernism.* London 2001, S. 127, 140; Charlotte u. Peter Fiell: *1000 chairs.* Köln 2005, S. 433 – **Restaurierung:** unberührter Originalzustand – **Fotografie:** LÖFFLER COLLECTION, Reichenschwand.

193/194
Sessel *Karelia* Modell „870" – **Eigentum:** LÖFFLER COLLECTION, Reichenschwand – Inventarnummer: 00408 – **Entwurf:** Liisi

191/192
Sofa *Bocca/Marilyn* – **Property:** LÖFFLER COLLECTION, Reichenschwand – **Inventory number:** 00418 – **Design:** Studio 65 (Piero Gatti, Cesare Paolini, Franco Teodoro) – **Origin:** Gufram, Balangero, Turin, Italy – **Date:** 1971 – **Technique/Upholstery:** polyurethane foam, foam-moulded – **Cover:** polyurethane – **Object measurements:** 83 x 210 x 78 cm – **Literature:** Klaus-Jürgen Sembach et al., *Möbeldesign des 20. Jahrhunderts*, Cologne 1993, p. 205; Charlotte and Peter Fiell, *Modern Furniture Classics: Postwar to Post-Modernism*, London 2001, pp. 127, 140; Charlotte and Peter Fiell, *1000 Chairs*, Cologne 2005, p. 433 – **Conservation:** original condition – **Photo:** LÖFFLER COLLECTION, Reichenschwand.

193/194
Armchair *Karelia*, model "870" – **Property:** LÖFFLER COLLECTION, Reichenschwand – **Inventory number:** 00408 – **Design:** Liisi Beckmann – **Origin:** Zanotta S.p.A., Milan, Italy – **Date:** 1966 – **Technique/Upholstery:** volume made from foam-moulded polyurethane foam – **Cover:** black vinyl, detachable – **Object measurements:** 60 x 75 x 82 cm, seat: 33 x 75 cm x 57 cm – **Literature:** Giuliana Gramigna, *Repertorio del Design Italiano 1950–2000*, vol. 2, Turin 2011, p. 123; *Modern Furniture: 150 Years of Design*, Königswinter 2009, p. 398; Sarah Colombo, *The Chair: An Appreciation*, San Diego 1997, p. 21; Charlotte and Peter Fiell, *Chairs: 1000 Masterpieces of Modern Design*, 1800 to the Present Day, London 2012, p. 473 – **Conservation:** original condition – **Photo:** LÖFFLER COLLECTION, Reichenschwand.

195/196
Daybed *Superonda* – **Property:** LÖFFLER COLLECTION, Reichenschwand – **Inventory number:** 01028 – **Design:** Archizoom Associati (Andrea Branzi, Gilberto Coretti, Paolo Deganello, Massimo Morozzi) – **Origin:** Poltronova, Florence, Italy – **Date:** 1966 – **Technique:** covered foam cushion – **Upholstery:** polyurethane foam – **Cover:** white vinyl – **Object measurements:** 35 x 235 x 100 cm – **Literature:** Pier Carlo Santini, *Facendo mobili*, Florence 1977, p. 17; Charlotte and Peter Fiell, *1000 Chairs*, Cologne 2005, pp. 408–409; https://www.poltronova.it/superonda/; https://www.poltronova.it/1967/10/16/superonda/ – **Conservation:** original condition, surfaces cleaned – **Photo:** LÖFFLER COLLECTION, Reichenschwand.

197/198
Seat object *Up* with footrest – **Property:** LÖFFLER COLLECTION, Reichenschwand – **Inventory numbers:** 00427 and 02590 – **Design:** Gaetano Pesce – **Origin:** C & B (later B & B), Novedrate, Como, Italy – **Date:** 1969 – **Technique/Upholstery:** foam-moulded PUR plastic foam – **Cover:** original black jersey cotton-synthetic mix – **Object measurements:** seat: 105 x 110 x 122 cm, seat: 43 x 55 x 49 cm, footrest: Dia.: 57 cm – **Literature:** Gerd Hatje and Elke Kaspar, *New Furniture: Neue Möbel, 10*, Stuttgart 1971, p. 48; *md: Moebel Interior Design*, no. 12, 1969, p. 86; Philippe Garner: Sixties Design, Cologne 2008, pp. 160–161; Charlotte and Peter Fiell, *Chairs: 1000 Masterpieces of Modern Design, 1800 to the Present Day*, London 2012, p. 506; Charlotte and Peter Fiell, *1000 Chairs*, Cologne 2005, pp. 400–401 – **Conservation:** original – **Photo:** LÖFFLER COLLECTION, Reichenschwand.

199/200
Seat object *Polyester Chair* – **Property:** GRASSI Museum für Angewandte Kunst Leipzig – **Inventory number:** 2018.131 – **Provenance:** donation by Friedhelm Wachs, 2018 – **Design:** Nanna Ditzel – **Origin:** Dansk Polyether

Beckmann – **Herstellung:** Zanotta S.p.A., Mailand, IT – **Datierung:** 1966 – **Technologie/Polsteraufbau:** Das Volumen besteht aus formgeschäumtem Polyurethanschaum – **Bezug:** schwarzes Vinyl, abnehmbar – **Objektmaße:** 60 x 75 x 82 cm; Sitzhöhe: 33 x 75 cm x 57 cm – **Literatur:** Giuliana Gramigna: *Repertorio del Design Italiano 1950–2000*, Bd. 2. Turin 2011, S. 123; *Modern Furniture. 150 Years of Design.* Königswinter 2009, S. 398; Sarah Colombo: *The Chair. An Appreciation.* San Diego 1997, S. 21; Charlotte u. Peter Fiell: *Chairs. 1000 Masterpieces of Modern Design, 1800 to the Present Day.* London 2012, S. 473 – **Restaurierung:** unberührter Originalzustand – **Fotografie:** LÖFFLER COLLECTION, Reichenschwand.

195/196
Tagesliege *Superonda* – **Eigentum:** LÖFFLER COLLECTION, Reichenschwand – **Inventarnummer:** 01028 – **Entwurf:** Archizoom Associati (Andrea Branzi, Gilberto Coretti, Paolo Deganello, Massimo Morozzi) – **Herstellung:** Poltronova, Florenz, Italien – **Datierung:** 1966 – **Technologie:** Bezogene Schaumstoffkissen – **Polsteraufbau:** Polyurethanschaum – **Bezug:** weißes Vinyl – **Objektmaße:** 35 x 235 x 100 cm – **Literatur:** Pier Carlo Santini: *Facendo mobili.* Florenz 1977, S. 17.; Charlotte u. Peter Fiell: *1000 chairs.* Köln 2005, S. 408 f.; https://www.poltronova.it/superonda/ und https://www.poltronova.it/1967/10/16/superonda/ – **Restaurierung:** Originalzustand, Oberflächen gereinigt – **Fotografie:** LÖFFLER COLLECTION, Reichenschwand.

197/198
Sitzobjekt *Up 5 mit Fußteil* – **Eigentum:** LÖFFLER COLLECTION, Reichenschwand – **Inventarnummern:** 00427 und 02590 – **Entwurf:** Gaetano Pesce – **Herstellung:** C & B (daraus wurde B & B), Novedrate, Como, Italien – **Datierung:** 1969 – **Technologie/Polsterung:** Formgeschäumter PUR-Schaumstoff – **Bezug:** originaler schwarzer Jersey Baumwoll-Synthetik-Mix – **Objektmaße:** Sessel: 105 x 110 x 122 cm; Sitzhöhe: 43 x 55 x 49 cm; Fußteil: D 57 cm – **Literatur:** Gerd Hatje, Elke Kaspar: *New Furniture. Neue Möbel*, Nr. 10. Stuttgart 1971, S. 48; *md. Moebel Interior Design.* 12/1969, S. 86; Philippe Garner: *Sixties Design.* Köln 2008, S. 160f.; Charlotte u. Peter Fiell: *Chairs. 1000 Masterpieces of Modern Design, 1800 to the Present Day.* London 2012, S. 506; Charlotte u. Peter Fiell: *1000 chairs.* Köln 2005, S. 400f. – **Restaurierung:** unberührter Originalzustand – **Fotografie:** LÖFFLER COLLECTION, Reichenschwand.

199/200
Sitzobjekt *Polyester Chair* – **Eigentum:** GRASSI Museum für Angewandte Kunst Leipzig – **Inventarnummer:** 2018.131 – **Provenienz:** Schenkung Friedhelm Wachs, 2018 – **Entwurf:** Nanna Ditzel – **Herstellung:** Dansk Polyether Industri – **Datierung:** 1965 – **Technologie:** Vollschaumstoff bezogen – **Polsteraufbau:** Auf eine geschwärzte Sperrholzplatte mit drehbaren Rollen ist ein zweiteiliger Vollschaumkörper (formgeschäumt, gefräst oder geschnitten) aufgebracht und mit einem angerauten atlasbindigen, violetten Wollgewebe bezogen – **Bezug:** Gewebeteile mit Doppelkappnähten zusammengefügt – **Objektmaße:** 57 x 67 x 90 cm – **Literatur:** GRASSI Museum für Angewandte Kunst (Hg.): *Made in Denmark, Formgestaltung seit 1900.* Stuttgart 2018, S. 220 – **Restaurierung:** Originalzustand – **Fotografie:** Esther Hoyer/GRASSI Museum für Angewandte Kunst Leipzig.

201
Liege *Diapason* – **Eigentum:** LÖFFLER COLLECTION, Reichenschwand – **Inventarnummer:** 00818 – **Entwurf:** Titti Saracino & Giovanni de Lucchi – **Herstellung:** Elleduemilla, Cormano, Lombardei, Italien – **Datierung:** 1970 – **Technologie:** Standsicherheit gibt ein Zementblock, auf dem eine gefalzte Edelstahlplatte die Unterlage für die Polsterauflage bildet – **Polsteraufbau:** Kissen als viergeteilte Polsterauflage mit Polyesterwattefüllung – **Bezug:** Veloursleder – **Objektmaße:** 56,5 x 60 x 173 cm; Sitzhöhe: 30 x 50 x 130 cm – **Restaurierung:** unberührter

Industri – **Date:** 1965 – **Technique:** foam covered – **Upholstery:** on a blackened plywood board with castors, a two-part foam body (fully foam-moulded, milled or cut) is attached and covered with a roughened satin weave, violet wool fabric – **Cover:** fabric elements attached with double-edge seam – **Object measurements:** 57 x 67 x 90 cm – **Literature:** GRASSI Museum für Angewandte Kunst (ed.): *Made in Denmark, Formgestaltung seit 1900*, Stuttgart 2018, p. 220 – **Conservation:** original – **Photo:** Esther Hoyer/GRASSI Museum für Angewandte Kunst Leipzig.

201
Lounger *Diapason* – **Property:** LÖFFLER COLLECTION, Reichenschwand – **Inventory number:** 00818 – **Design:** Titti Saracino & Giovanni de Lucchi – **Origin:** Elleduemilla, Cormano, Lombardy, Italy – **Date:** 1970 – **Technique:** structural stability is provided by a concrete block on which a folded stainless-steel plate forms the base for the upholstery – **Upholstery:** cushion with four compartments with polyester wadding stuffing – **Cover:** velour leather – **Object measurements:** 56.5 x 60 x 173 cm, seat: 30 x 50 x 130 cm – **Conservation:** original condition – **Photo:** LÖFFLER COLLECTION, Reichenschwand.

202/203
Play object/jute animal hippopotamus *Mocky* – **Property:** LÖFFLER COLLECTION, Reichenschwand – **Inventory number:** 01861 – **Design:** Renate Müller – **Origin:** H. Josef Leven KG, Sonneberg – **Date:** 1969 – **Technique/Upholstery:** jute animal stuffed with wood fibre on a metal frame – **Cover:** original burlap and leather painted red and blue – **Object measurements:** 37 x 33 x 77 cm – **Literature:** Kimberly Birks, *Design for Children*, London 2018, n.p. (no. 85) – **Conservation:** original condition – **Photo:** LÖFFLER COLLECTION, Reichenschwand.

204–206
Children's vehicle *Marienkäfer* with castors – **Property:** LÖFFLER COLLECTION, Reichenschwand – **Inventory number:** 02582 – **Design:** Margarete Steiff – **Origin:** Steiff, Deutschland – **Date:** 1950s – **Technique:** ladybird body with black lacquered tubular steel frame and rubber antlers and wheels – **Upholstery:** wood wool stuffing – **Cover:** original red ruffled velour – **Object measurements:** 33 x 28 x 55 cm – **Conservation:** original condition – **Photo:** LÖFFLER COLLECTION, Reichenschwand.

207–209
Children's stool – **Property:** LÖFFLER COLLECTION, Reichenschwand – **Inventory number:** 00944 – **Design:** Sophie Roberty and Christophe Beauséjour – **Origin:** Pylones, Paris, France – **Date:** around 1980 – **Technique/Upholstery:** wooden frame, PUR foam-moulded, laminated and painted in various colours – **Cover:** none – **Object measurements:** 37.5 x 33 x 39 cm – **Conservation:** original – **Photo:** LÖFFLER COLLECTION, Reichenschwand.

210 212
Children's armchair – **Property:** LÖFFLER COLLECTION, Reichenschwand – **Inventory number:** 00904 – **Design:** at present unknown – **Origin:** at present unknown – **Date:** 1960s/1970s – **Technique:** plywood frame, lacquered in beige/grey – **Upholstery:** tacked down seat and back cushion, stuffing of cotton wadding – **Cover:** original multicoloured jacquard flat weave in grey and beige tones – **Object measurements:** 45 x 54 x 49 cm, seat: 23 x 32 x 32 cm – **Conservation:** original – **Photo:** LÖFFLER COLLECTION, Reichenschwand.

Originalzustand – **Fotografie:** LÖFFLER COLLECTION, Reichenschwand.

202/203
Spielobjekt/Rupfentier Nilpferd *Mocky* – **Eigentümer:** LÖFFLER COLLECTION, Reichenschwand – **Inventarnummer:** 01861 – **Entwurf:** Renate Müller – **Herstellung:** H. Josef Leven KG, Sonneberg – **Datierung:** 1969 – **Technologie/Polsterung:** Mit Holzwolle gefülltes Rupfentier auf einem Metallgestell – **Bezug:** originales Juteleinen und deckfarbezugerichtetes Leder in Rot und Blau – **Objektmaße:** 37 x 33 x 77 cm – **Literatur:** Kimberly Birks: *Design for Children*. London, 2018, o. S. (Nr. 85) – **Restaurierung:** unberührter Originalzustand – **Fotografie:** LÖFFLER COLLECTION, Reichenschwand.

204–206
Kinderfahrzeug *Marienkäfer* mit Rollen – **Eigentum:** LÖFFLER COLLECTION, Reichenschwand – **Inventarnummer:** 02582 – **Entwurf:** Margarete Steiff – **Herstellung:** Steiff, Deutschland – **Datierung:** 1950er Jahre – **Technologie:** Marienkäferkorpus auf schwarz lackiertem Rundstahl-Gestell, mit Gummifühlern- und -rädern – **Polsteraufbau:** Holzwolle – **Bezug:** originaler roter Kräuselvelours – **Objektmaße:** 33 x 28 x 55 cm – **Restaurierung:** unberührter Originalzustand – **Fotografie:** LÖFFLER COLLECTION, Reichenschwand.

207–209
Kinderhocker – **Eigentum:** LÖFFLER COLLECTION, Reichenschwand – **Inventarnummer:** 00944 – **Entwurf:** Sophie Roberty und Christophe Beauséjour – **Herstellung:** Pylones, Paris, Frankreich – **Datierung:** um 1980 – **Technologie/Polsterung:** Mit PUR umschäumtes (formgeschäumtes) Holzgestell, behautet und farbig gefasst – ohne Bezug – **Objektmaße:** 37,5 x 33 x 39 cm – **Restaurierung:** unberührter Originalzustand – **Fotografie:** LÖFFLER COLLECTION, Reichenschwand.

210–212
Armlehnstuhl für Kinder – **Eigentum:** LÖFFLER COLLECTION, Reichenschwand – **Inventarnummer:** 00904 – **Entwurf:** z. Zt. unbekannt – **Herstellung:** z. Zt. unbekannt – **Datierung:** 1960er/1970er Jahre – **Technologie:** Gestell aus Sperrholz, deckend farbig lackiert (beige/grau) – **Polsteraufbau:** festgesteckter Sitz und Rückenkissen, Füllung vermutlich Baumwolle – **Bezug:** originales mehrfarbiges Jacquard-Flachgewebe in Grau- und Beigetönen – **Objektmaße:** 45 x 54 x 49 cm; Sitzhöhe: 23 x 32 x 32 cm – **Restaurierung:** unberührter Originalzustand – **Fotografie:** LÖFFLER COLLECTION, Reichenschwand.

213
Polstersessel – **Eigentum:** GRASSI Museum für Angewandte Kunst Leipzig – **Inventarnummer:** 2000.504 – **Provenienz:** Schenkung Thomas Andersch, Ragewitz, 2000 – **Entwerfer:** z. Zt. unbekannt – **Hersteller:** VEB Möbelkombinat Berlin – Datierung: um 1975 – **Technologie:** Hartschaum-Korpus mit eingelegten Polsterkissen und zwei seitlich angesetzten Armlehnen-Elementen; Sitz und Lehne als bezogene Vollschaumkissen mit Abheftung, Armlehnen mit gepolstertem Unterbau und Bezug – **Polsteraufbau:** Sitz- und Rückenlehnenkissen sind Vollschaumkissen (wahrscheinlich formgeschäumt); eine Fixierung in Form einer Abnähung ist eingearbeitet, um einen exakten Bezug der gewölbten Polsterform zu erreichen; die Schaumstoff-gefüllten Armlehnen sind unifarben bezogen – **Bezug:** gestreifter Malimostoff (in 1949 in der DDR patentiertem Nähwirkverfahren) – **Objektmaße:** 69 x 82 x 76 cm; Sitzhöhe: 42 cm – **Anmerkung:** Die Polsterkissen von Sitz und Lehne sind miteinander verbunden und die Armlehnen mit Flügelschrauben am Korpus befestigt; es besteht die Möglichkeit, mehrere Sitzelemente miteinander zu verbinden, um dadurch einen 2- bzw. 3-Sitzer zu bilden; der Hartschaum des Korpus ist weiß lackiert; der Bezugsstoff zeigt eine zeittypische Kombination von abgepasst gestreiftem Stoff und unifarbenem Stoff – **Restaurierung:**

213
Upholstered armchair – **Property:** GRASSI Museum für Angewandte Kunst Leipzig – **Inventory number:** 2000.504 – **Provenance:** donation by Thomas Andersch, Ragewitz, 2000 – **Designer:** at present unknown – **Producer:** VEB Möbelkombinat Berlin – **Date:** around 1975 – **Technique:** rigid foam body with padding inlay and two armrest elements at the sides; seat and backrest as covered foam cushions with stitching, armrests with upholstery and cover fabric – **Upholstery:** seat and backrest with foam cushions (probably foam-moulded); stitching used to fix in order to fit cover precisely into the curved padded form; foam-filled armrests with monochrome cover – **Cover:** striped malimo fabric (stitch-bonding technique patented in the GDR in 1949) – **Object measurements:** 69 x 82 x 76 cm, seat H: 42 cm – **Notes:** upholstered cushions of seat and backrests are connected and the armrests fitted to the body using wing screws; it is possible to connect several seat elements, creating a 2- or 3-seater in the process; the rigid foam of the body is lacquered white; cover fabric with combination of striped and monochrome fabrics typical of the period – **Conservation:** original – **Literature:** comparative example in *Möbel and Wohnaum*, vol. 30, no. 1, 1977, p. 24; Katja Böhme and Andreas Ludwig (eds), *Alles aus Plaste: Versprechen and Gebrauch in der DDR*, Vienna/Cologne/Weimar 2012, pp. 180–184 – **Photo:** Esther Hoyer/GRASSI Museum für Angewandte Kunst Leipzig.

214
Oświęcim, 28.11.2006, photo by Stefan Kraus from his photo series *Zufällige Begegnungen*, 2006–2017, © Stefan Kraus, Cologne.

215–217
Armchair *Rover Seat Chair* – **Property:** LÖFFLER COLLECTION, Reichenschwand – **Inventory number:** 00156 – **Design:** Ron Arad – **Origin:** One Off Ltd., London, Great Britain – **Date:** 1981 – **Technique:** original Rover seat with metal tubular steel frame – **Upholstery:** sheet metal frame with spring core, rubberized coir, grey wadding – **Cover:** black leather – **Object measurements:** 75 x 69 x 92 cm, seat: 37 x 50 x 49 cm – **Literature:** Ron Arad, *No Discipline*, Paris 2008, p. 72; Charlotte and Peter Fiell, *1000 Chairs*, Cologne 2005, p. 502 – **Conservation:** original – **Photo:** LÖFFLER COLLECTION, Reichenschwand.

218
Seat object *Embryo* – **Property:** LÖFFLER COLLECTION, Reichenschwand – **Inventory number:** 00628 – **Design:** Marc Newson – **Origin:** Idée, Japan – **Date:** 1988 – **Technique:** PUR foam-moulded form on three stainless-steel legs – **Upholstery:** wire frame, PUR foam-moulded – **Cover:** orange neoprene – **Object measurements:** 80 x 81 x 84 cm, seat: 43 x 50 x 45 cm – **Literature:** Alice Rawsthron, Marc Newson, London 1999, p. 26ff.; Modern Furniture: 150 Years of Design, Königswinter 2009, p. 232; Charlotte and Peter Fiell, *Chairs: 1000 Masterpieces of Modern Design, 1800 to the Present Day*, London 2012, p. 619 – **Conservation:** unaltered original condition – **Photo:** LÖFFLER COLLECTION, Reichenschwand.

219
See beanbag *Sacco* 177/178.

Originalzustand – **Literatur:** Vergleichsbeispiel in: *Möbel und Wohnraum*, 30. Jg., Heft 1, 1977, s. 24; Katja Böhme, Andreas Ludwig (Hg.): *Alles aus Plaste, Versprechen und Gebrauch in der DDR*. Wien/Köln/Weimar 2012, S. 180–184. – **Fotografie:** Esther Hoyer/GRASSI Museum für Angewandte Kunst Leipzig.

214
Oświęcim, 28.11.2006, Fotografie von Stefan Kraus aus seiner Fotoreihe *Zufällige Begegnungen*, 2006–2017, © Stefan Kraus, Köln.

215–217
Sessel *Rover Seat Chair* – **Eigentum:** LÖFFLER COLLECTION, Reichenschwand – **Inventarnummer:** 00156 – **Entwurf:** Ron Arad – **Herstellung:** One Off Ltd., London, GB – **Datierung:** 1981 – **Technologie:** Originaler Roversitz auf metallenem Rundrohr-Gestell – **Polsteraufbau:** Blechrahmen mit Federkern, Gummikokos, grauer Watte – **Bezug:** schwarzes Leder – **Objektmaße:** 75 x 69 x 92 cm; Sitzhöhe: 37 x 50 x 49 cm – **Literatur:** Ron Arad: *No Discipline*. Paris 2008, S. 72; Charlotte u. Peter Fiell: *1000 chairs*. Köln 2005, S. 502 – **Restaurierung:** unberührter Originalzustand – **Fotografie:** LÖFFLER COLLECTION, Reichenschwand.

218
Sitzobjekt *Embryo* – **Eigentum:** LÖFFLER COLLECTION, Reichenschwand – **Inventarnummer:** 00628 – **Entwurf:** Marc Newson – **Herstellung:** Idée, Japan – **Datierung:** 1988 – **Technologie:** PUR-formgeschäumte Form auf drei Edelstahlbeinen – **Polsteraufbau:** Drahtgestell in PUR formgeschäumt – **Bezug:** orangefarbenes Neopren – **Objektmaße:** 80 x 81 x 84 cm; Sitzhöhe: 43 x 50 x 45 cm – **Literatur:** Alice Rawsthron: *Marc Newson*. London 1999, S. 26ff.; *Modern Furniture. 150 Years of Design*. Königswinter 2009, S. 232; Charlotte u. Peter Fiell: *Chairs. 1000 Masterpieces of Modern Design, 1800 to the Present Day*. London 2012, S. 619 – **Restaurierung:** unberührter Originalzustand – **Fotografie:** LÖFFLER COLLECTION, Reichenschwand.

219
Siehe Sitzsack *Sacco* 177/178.

220
Stuhl *Entronauta* – **Eigentum:** LÖFFLER COLLECTION, Reichenschwand – **Inventarnummer:** 00659 – **Entwurf:** Riccardo Blumer u. Matteo Borghi – **Herstellung:** Desalto, Cantù Provinz Como, Italien – **Datierung:** 2007 – **Technologie/Polsterung:** Der beflockte PVC-Bezug wird mit PUR gefüllt, das in einer Tiefziehform erstarrt (nicht geschäumt) – **Objektmaße:** 81 x 60 x 61 cm; Sitzhöhe: 43,5 x 43 x 42 cm – **Literatur:** https://www.moma.org/collection/works/129213 und https://www.desalto.it/en-us/company/designers/blumer-borghi – **Restaurierung:** unberührter Originalzustand – **Fotografie:** LÖFFLER COLLECTION, Reichenschwand.

221/222
Sitzkissen *Memo* – **Eigentum:** LÖFFLER COLLECTION, Reichenschwand – **Inventarnummer:** 00441 – **Entwurf:** Ron Arad – **Herstellung:** Inflate Studios, London, GB – **Datierung:** 1999 – **Technologie/Polster/Bezug:** Geschweißter PVC-Bezug (Hülle), gefüllt mit aufgeschäumten Polystyrolkugeln; ein Ventil dient dem Absaugen der im Sack befindlichen Luft; so entsteht ein Vakuum, das dazu beiträgt, dass das Kissen seine Form behält – **Objektmaße:** H: 50 cm, D: 80 cm – **Restaurierung:** unberührter Originalzustand – **Fotografie:** LÖFFLER COLLECTION, Reichenschwand.

223–225
Barockstuhl – **Eigentum:** Reinhardt Roßberg – **Entwurf:** unbekannt – **Herstellung:** unbekannt – **Datierung:** um 1700 (Polsterung nach barockem Vorbild) – **Technologie:** Holzgestell mit

220
Chair *Entronauta* – **Property:** LÖFFLER COLLECTION, Reichenschwand – **Inventory number:** 00659 – **Design:** Riccardo Blumer and Matteo Borghi – **Origin:** Desalto, Cantù Province, Como, Italy – **Date:** 2007 – **Technique/Upholstery:** flocked PVC cover filled with PUR foam, which hardens in a deep-drawing mould (foam not used) – **Object measurements:** 81 x 60 x 61 cm, seat: 43.5 x 43 x 42 cm – **Literature:** https://www.moma.org/collection/works/129213; https://www.desalto.it/en-us/company/designers/blumer-borghi – **Conservation:** unaltered original condition – **Photo:** LÖFFLER COLLECTION, Reichenschwand.

221/222
Seat cushion *Memo* – **Property:** LÖFFLER COLLECTION, Reichenschwand – **Inventory number:** 00441 – **Design:** Ron Arad – **Origin:** Inflate Studios, London, Great Britain – **Date:** 1999 – **Technique/Upholstery/Cover:** welded PVS cover, filled with foamed polystyrene balls; valve to extract air, resulting in a vacuum that lets the pillow retain its form – **Object measurements:** H: 50 cm, Dia.: 80 cm – **Conservation:** unaltered original condition – **Photo:** LÖFFLER COLLECTION, Reichenschwand.

223–225
Baroque chair – **Property:** Reinhardt Roßberg – **Design:** unknown – **Origin:** unknown – **Date:** around 1700 (upholstery after a Baroque model) – **Technique:** wooden frame with upholstered seat and backrest, seat: long-straw edge roll and backrest as flat padding typical of the period – **Upholstery:** seat as higher flat padding with separate long-straw edge roll on hessian over hand-woven hemp strip webbing; stuffing of flax fibre and deer hair; calico; backrest as flat padding with flax fibre stuffing on scrim with calico cover – **Notes:** reconstruction of historical upholstery using corresponding materials (such as handwoven hemp webbing, long straw, deer hair etc.); edge pleat located in top cover and close nailing typical of the period; back covered with plain fabric (typical of baroque wall furniture) – **Literature:** *Diderots Enzyklopädie: Die Bildplaten 1762–1777*, vol. 3, Augsburg 1995 – **Sponsors:** LÖFFLER COLLECTION, Reichenschwand (fabric), Torsten Otto (decorative nails, webbing material) – **Conservation:** Volker Bielitz (woodwork, surfaces), Alexander Hahlbek RiH (upholstery reconstruction) – **Photo:** LÖFFLER COLLECTION, Reichenschwand.

226
Biedermeier chair – **Property:** Reinhardt Roßberg – **Design:** unknown – **Origin:** unknown – **Date:** around 1810 (upholstery after historical model) – **Technique:** seat with a high padding with sprung upholstery with edge rolls all around – **Upholstery:** on a 2 x 2 webbing of hand-woven hemp strips with stitched-up edge roll all round, four hand-drawn waisted springs are positioned and knotted; on top a cover of stitched and stuffed upholstery as well as a second stuffing, covered with leather top cover with leather attached by hand-sewing and piping; attached with porcelain decorative nails – **Notes:** original porcelain-head decorative nails – **Object measurements:** 87 x 45 x 47 cm, seat: 48.5 x 45 x 41 cm – **Sponsors:** Torsten Otto RiH (work), Stefan Oswald RiH (leather top cover), furniture conservator Reinhardt Reichardt RiH (added wooden elements) – **Conservation:** Torsten Otto RiH (examination, reconstruction), Thomas Andersch Dipl. conservator (seat surface) – **Photo:** LÖFFLER COLLECTION, Reichenschwand.

gepolstertem Sitz und Lehne, Sitz: epochentypisch mit Langstroh-Vorderkante und Lehne mit Flachpolster – **Polsteraufbau:** Als Sitz fungiert ein erhöhtes Flachpolster mit separater Vorderkantenwulst aus Langstroh auf Leinen über Gurtung aus handgewebten Hanfgurten (geborgen); Brechflachs mit Rehhaar als Polstermaterial; Leinennesselunterbezug; die Lehne ist als Flachpolster aus Brechflachs auf Spannleinen mit Leinennesselabdeckung ausgebildet – **Bezug:** Seide mit Messingziernägeln – **Anmerkung:** Es handelt sich hier um die Rekonstruktion eines historischen Polsteraufbaus mit entsprechenden Materialien (z. B. handgewebte Hanfgurte, Langstroh, Rehhaare etc.); Lage der Eckfalte im Bezug sowie Perlstabnagelung zeittypisch; Spannteil mit Blindstoff bezogen (kennzeichnend für barocke Wandmöbel) – **Literatur:** *Diderots Enzyklopädie. Die Bildtafeln 1762–1777*, 3. Bd. Augsburg 1995 – **Fördernde:** LÖFFLER COLLECTION, Reichenschwand (Stoff), Torsten Otto (Ziernägel, Grundmaterial) – **Restaurierung:** Volker Bielitz (Holzarbeiten, Oberfläche), Alexander Hahlbek RiH (Polsterrekonstruktion) – **Fotografie:** LÖFFLER COLLECTION, Reichenschwand.

226
Biedermeierstuhl – **Eigentum:** Reinhardt Roßberg – **Entwurf:** unbekannt – **Herstellung:** unbekannt – **Datierung:** um 1810 (Polsterung nach historischem Vorbild) – **Technologie:** Der Sitz ist ein Hochpolster mit Federung in Randformpolster – **Polsteraufbau:** Auf einer 2x2-Gurtung aus handgewebten Hanfgurten mit umlaufender garnierter Kantenwulst stehen vier handgedrehte Taillenfedern, die geschnürt sind; darüber ruht ein mehrfach garniertes Polster und Pikier; darüber der Lederbezug mit per Handnaht und Keder angesetztem Lederstück; Befestigung mit Porzellankopfziernägeln – **Anmerkung:** noch vorhandene originale Porzellankopfziernägel – **Objektmaße:** 87 x 45 x 47 cm; Sitzhöhe: H 48,5 x 45 x 41 cm – **Fördernde:** Torsten Otto RiH (Arbeitsleistung), Stefan Oswald RiH (Bezugsleder), Möbelrestaurierung Reinhardt Reichardt RiH (Holzergänzungen) – **Restaurierung:** Torsten Otto RiH (Untersuchung/Rekonstruktion), Möbelrestaurierung Reinhardt Reichardt (Holzergänzungen), Thomas Andersch Dipl.-Restaurator (Oberfläche des Stuhles) – **Fotografie:** LÖFFLER COLLECTION, Reichenschwand.

227
Biedermeierstuhl – **Eigentum:** Reinhardt Roßberg – **Entwurf:** unbekannt – **Herstellung:** unbekannt – **Datierung:** um 2000 (Nachbau nach Wiener Vorbild) – **Technologie:** Holzgestell mit Festpolstersitz, der eine stark garnierte Kante besitzt – **Polsteraufbau:** Im Sitz liegt auf einer 3x3(?)-Gurtung aus Leinengurten ein Federleinen aus Leinen; eine mit Brechflachs hoch aufgelegte Fasson wurde mehrfach scharf ausgarniert und mit Schweinsrückenstich an der Kante versehen; das flache Pikier besteht aus Rosshaar; der Bezug ist ein Mohairstoff mit Rosshaaranmutung und wurde mit Porzellankopfziernägeln angebracht – **Objektmaße:** 89 x 45,5 x 52 cm; Sitzhöhe: 48,5 x 44,5 x 43 cm – **Anmerkung:** Als Materialien wurden zeittypische, jetzt noch verfügbare Textilien und Werkstoffe verwendet; die Ziernägel sind Originale, die geborgen und wiederverwendet wurden – **Restaurierung/Fördernde:** Reinhardt Roßberg RiH (Polsterung), Alexander Halbeck RiH (Bezug) – **Fotografie:** LÖFFLER COLLECTION, Reichenschwand.

228/229
Bergère Confessionnal Chipier Style Louis XV (Porterchair) – **Eigentum:** LÖFFLER COLLECTION, Reichenschwand – **Entwurf:** Nayar France – **Herstellung:** Nayar France – **Datierung:** 2021/2022 (Stil Louis XV.); im 17. und 18. Jh. gebräuchlich in England, Frankreich und Nordamerika als Kaminfauteuil – **Technologie:** Buchengestell schwarz lackiert – **Polsteraufbau:** Leinengurte, 7-Gang Taillenfedern, Kantendraht, Federleinen, Afrik, Fassonleinen, Rosshaar, Baumwollwatte, Nessel, schwarzer Spannstoff, gemusterter Gobelinstoff, Borte, Quasten, Aquarellfarben, Schelllack **Objektmaße:** 177 x 81 x 84 cm; Sitzhöhe: 57 x 70 x 70 cm – **Fördernde/Restaurierung:** Elisabeth Riß Raumaus-

227
Biedermeier chair – **Property:** Reinhardt Roßberg – **Design:** unknown – **Origin:** unknown – **Date:** around 2000 (reconstructed after Viennese model) – **Technique:** wooden frame with attached upholstered seat with feather edge – **Upholstery:** seat with 3 x 3 webbing on linen straps with hessian; stitched-up flax fibre filling with blanket stitch at edge; flat second horsehair stuffing; top cover with mohair fabric of horsehair appearance, attached with porcelain-head decorative nails – **Object measurements:** 89 x 45.5 x 52 cm, seat: 48.5 x 44.5 x 43 cm – **Notes:** materials and textiles typical of the period but still available were used; original decorative nails were salvaged and reused – **Conservation/Sponsors:** Reinhardt Roßberg RiH (upholstery), Alexander Halbeck RiH (top cover) – **Photo:** LÖFFLER COLLECTION, Reichenschwand.

228/229
Bergère Confessionnal Chipier Style Louis XV (porter chair) – **Property:** LÖFFLER COLLECTION, Reichenschwand – **Design:** Nayar, France – **Origin:** Nayar, France – **Date:** 2021–22 (Louis XV style); common during the 17th and 18th century in England, France and North America as a fireside armchair – **Technique:** beech frame, black lacquer – **Upholstery:** linen straps, 7-gauge waisted springs, edge wire, hessian, palm fibre, scrim, horsehair, cotton wadding, calico, black cover, patterned Gobelin fabric, borders, tassels, watercolour, shellac – **Object measurements:** 177 x 81 x 84 cm, seat: 57 x 70 x 70 cm – **Sponsors/Conservation:** Elisabeth Riß Raumausstattermeisterin (work), Ann-Kathrin Schrodt (surface), Cammann (fabric) – **Photo:** LÖFFLER COLLECTION, Reichenschwand.

230/231
Indiscret – **Property:** Karin Semkowicz – **Design:** unknown – **Origin:** unknown – **Date:** around 1880? – **Technique:** beech and limewood frame, turned feet originally fitted with staghorn castors, making it easy to move – **Upholstery:** seat with lashed spring construction with horsehair stuffing and deep-buttoned second stuffing with horsehair and kapok cover; backrest has a horsehair first stuffing and a deep-buttoned second stuffing with horsehair and kapok cover – **Object measurements:** D: 160 cm – **Sponsors:** Karin Semkowicz RiH (work), Doris Arndt RiH, Caroline Meschter, Houlès? (passementerie), specialists Restauratoren im Handwerk e.V. (gilding material and conservation frame) – **Conservation:** Karin Semkowicz RiH, Nordheim, Doris Arndt RiH, master gilder Caroline Meschter, furniture conservator Ann-Kathrin Schrodt, Rolf Hegenbart RiH, Astrid Boeck RiH – **Photo:** LÖFFLER COLLECTION, Reichenschwand.

232/233
Armchair – **Property:** Astrid Boeck RiH – **Design:** unknown – **Origin:** unknown – **Date:** around 1900 – **Sponsors:** work Astrid Boeck – **Technique:** nut-wood frame with transparent lacquer – **Upholstery:** jute straps, wire edge, hessian, flax fibre, original first stuffing (mix of straw and flax fibre), scrim, horsehair, grey wadding, calico, linen, top cover relief velvet and epingle frisé from the Wilhelminian period and new fixed velour border – **Object measurements:** 98.5 x 63 x 67 cm, seat: 45 x 63 x 60 cm – **Sponsors:** Astrid Boeck (work), Reinhardt Roßberg (passementerie, cover fabric) – **Conservation:** Astrid Boeck RiH (retrieval of original fabric of the period for seat, backrest, back) – **Photo:** LÖFFLER COLLECTION, Reichenschwand.

stattermeisterin (Arbeitsleistung), Ann-Kathrin Schrodt (Oberfläche), Cammann (Stoff) – **Fotografie:** LÖFFLER COLLECTION, Reichenschwand.

230/231
Indiscret – **Eigentum:** Karin Semkowicz – **Entwurf:** unbekannt – **Herstellung:** unbekannt – **Datierung:** um 1880 (?) – **Technologie:** Polstergestell aus Buchen- oder Lindenholz, mit gedrechselten Füßen, die ursprünglich über Hirschhornrollen verfügten, wodurch sich das Möbel leichter versetzen ließ – **Polsteraufbau:** Der Sitz verfügt über eine geschnürte Federkonstruktion mit Rosshaarfasson und eine Capitonné-Heftung mit Rosshaar, mit einer Kapokabdeckung; die Lehne hat eine Rosshaarfasson und eine Capitonné-Heftung in Rosshaar, mit Kapokabdeckung – **Objektmaße:** D: 160 cm – **Fördernde:** Arbeitsleistung: Karin Semkowicz RiH, Doris Arndt RiH, Caroline Meschter, Posamente: Houlès (?), Vergoldung Material und Restaurierung Gestell: Fachgruppe Restauratoren im Handwerk e. V. – **Restaurierung:** Karin Semkowicz RiH, Nordheim, Doris Arndt RiH, Caroline Meschter Vergoldemeisterin, Ann-Kathrin Schrodt Möbelrestauratorin, Rolf Hegenbart RiH, Astrid Boek RiH – **Fotografie:** LÖFFLER COLLECTION, Reichenschwand.

232/233
Armlehnstuhl – **Eigentum:** Astrid Boek – **Entwurf:** unbekannt – **Herstellung:** unbekannt – **Datierung:** um 1900 – **Fördernde:** Arbeitsleistung Astrid Boeck – **Technologie:** Gestell aus Nussbaumholz mit transparentem Lack – **Polsteraufbau:** Jutegurte, Kantendraht, Federleinen, Brechflachs, ursprüngliches Fassonpolster (Mischung aus Stroh und Brechflachs), Fassonleinen, Rosshaar, graue Polsterwatte, Nessel, Feinwerg, Schechterleinen, Bezug Relief-Samt und Epinglé-Frisee aus der Gründerzeit und neuer Steh-Velours, Borte – **Objektmaße:** 98,5 x 63 x 67 cm; Sitzhöhe: 45 x 63 x 60 cm – **Fördernde:** Astrid Boek (Arbeitsleistung), Reinhardt Roßberg (Posamente und Bezugsstoff) – **Restaurierung:** Astrid Boek RiH, geborgener Originalstoff aus der Zeit für Sitz, Lehne, Spannteil – **Fotografie:** LÖFFLER COLLECTION, Reichenschwand.

234
Sofa – **Eigentum:** LÖFFLER COLLECTION, Reichenschwand – **Datierung:** Stilmöbel, 20. Jahrhundert – **Technologie:** Buchenholzgestell dunkelbraun lackiert – **Polsteraufbau:** Hanfgurte, Federleinen, Kokos, Nessel, Kapokwatte, Lehne: Hanfgurte, Federleinen, Rosshaar, Kapokwatte – **Bezug:** bedrucktes Leinen Ianthe Bloom von Liberty & Co (Entwerfer R. Beauclair ca. 1902 und erster Druck für Liberty 1967), Borte – **Objektmaße:** 100 x 136 x 65 cm; Sitzhöhe: 43,5 x 134 x 55 cm – **Fördernde/Restaurierung:** Bernhard Ziegler RiH (Polsterung) – **Fotografie:** LÖFFLER COLLECTION, Reichenschwand.

235/236
Armlehnsessel – **Eigentum:** Stefan Oswald – **Entwurf:** z. Zt. unbekannt – **Herstellung:** z. Zt. unbekannt – **Datierung:** ca. 1915–1925 – **Technologie:** Buchenholzgestell mit geschnitzten Löwenfüßen aus Eiche, dunkel gebeizt und schellackiert – **Polsteraufbau:** geschnürte Feder in Sitz, Rücken und Armlehnen, Afrikfassonpolster. Pikierung aus Rosshaar im Rücken mit Kokos. Aufgelegtes Daunensitzkissen – **Objektmaße:** 84 x 96 x 80 cm; Sitzhöhe: 40 x 62 x 76 cm – **Fördernde/Restaurierung:** Morris & Co. (Stoff), Stefan Oswald RiH (Arbeitsleistung), Ann-Kathrin Schrodt Möbelrestauratorin (Oberfläche Füße) – **Fotografie:** LÖFFLER COLLECTION, Reichenschwand.

237
Ohrensessel – **Eigentum:** Rolf Hegenbart – **Entwurf:** z. Zt. unbekannt – **Herstellung:** unbekannter Schreiner aus Weimar (Nachbau aus dem Mobiliar von Schloß Tiefurt) – **Datierung:** um 1900 (?) – **Technologie:** Holzgestell aus Kirschholz (Armlehnen massiv, Rest furniert); versehen mit Schellackoberfläche – **Polsteraufbau:** Jutegewebe (Gurte, Federgewebe, Fassongewebe),

234
Sofa – **Property:** LÖFFLER COLLECTION, Reichenschwand – **Date:** period furniture, 20th century – **Technique:** beech frame, dark-brown lacquer – **Upholstery:** hemp straps, hessian, coconut fibre, calico, kapok wadding; backrest: hemp straps, hessian, horsehair, kapok wadding – **Cover:** printed linen *Ianthe Bloom* by Liberty & Co. (designer R. Beauclair, ca. 1902, and first print for Liberty, 1967), border – **Object measurements:** 100 x 136 x 65 cm, seat: 43.5 x 134 x 55 cm – **Sponsors/Conservation:** Bernhard Ziegler RiH (upholstery) – **Photo:** LÖFFLER COLLECTION, Reichenschwand.

235/236
Armchair – **Property:** Stefan Oswald – **Design:** at present unknown – **Origin:** at present unknown – **Date:** ca. 1915–25 – **Technique:** beech frame with carved oak lion feet, stained dark, shellac – **Upholstery:** lashed springing in seat, backrest and armrest, palm fibre stuffing, second stuffing with horsehair, kapok in the backrest, loose down cushion – **Object measurements:** 84 x 96 x 80 cm, seat: 40 x 62 x 76 cm – **Sponsors/Conservation:** Morris & Co. (fabric), Stefan Oswald RiH (work), furniture conservator Ann-Kathrin Schrodt (surface feet) – **Photo:** LÖFFLER COLLECTION, Reichenschwand.

237
Wing chair – **Property:** Rolf Hegenbart – **Design:** at present unknown – **Origin:** unknown Weimar-based carpenter (replica of a furniture piece from Tiefurt Castle) – **Date:** around 1900? – **Technique:** cherrywood frame (solid armrests, rest veneered); shellac surface – **Upholstery:** jute fabric (straps, hessian, scrim), springs, tow, horsehair, wadding, cotton core, cotton fabric (1970s), passementerie (borders 1970s from the firm OPEW) – **Object measurements:** 115 x 67 x 77 cm – **Sponsors/Conservation:** Rolf Hegenbart RiH.

238
Cocktail chair – **Property:** Volker Engels – **Design:** unknown – **Origin:** unknown – **Date:** 1950s – **Technique:** beech frame, feet stained brown and lacquered – **Upholstery:** spring unit – **Cover:** jacquard fabric – **Object measurements:** 84 x 56 x 64 cm, seat: 45 x 56 x 50 cm – **Sponsors:** Volker Engels RiH (work) – **Photo:** LÖFFLER COLLECTION, Reichenschwand.

239
Stool – **Property:** Bernhard Ziegler – **Design:** unknown – **Origin:** unknown – **Date:** 21st century – **Technique:** wooden frame, visible fronts lacquered black – **Upholstery:** jute straps, hessian, edge roll: hessian, tow, deep-buttoning: horsehair and nettle – **Object measurements:** 27 x 56 x 54.5 cm – **Sponsors/Conservation:** Bernhard Ziegler RiH (work) – **Photo:** LÖFFLER COLLECTION, Reichenschwand.

240
Club chair – **Property:** Reinhardt Roßberg – **Date:** around 1925 – **Technique:** seat is a high padding with first and second stuffing, backrest turns into armrest, sprung and fluted – **Upholstery:** springs on 4 x 4 webbing with edge springs; hessian; first stuffing with palm fibre with gutter; second stuffing with palm fibre and horsehair and wadding covered in calico; seat covered with antiqued leather with piping between seat and bottom or panel; backrest and armrest are sprung and fluted in nine flutes, simple first stuffing and second stuffing with horsehair; leather cover with piping, covers are leather-covered with piping; back in leather with piping and fixated with leather-covered

Polsterfedern, Werg, Roßhaar, Watte, Baumwollkörper, Baumwollstoff (1970er Jahre), Posamente (Borte 1970er Jahre OPEW) – **Objektmaße:** 115 x 67 x 77 cm – **Fördernde/Restaurierung:** Rolf Hegenbart RiH – **Fotografie:** LÖFFLER COLLECTION, Reichenschwand.

238
Cocktailsessel – **Eigentum:** Volker Engels – **Entwurf:** unbekannt – **Herstellung:** unbekannt – **Datierung:** 1950er Jahre – **Technologie:** Buchenholzgestell, Füße braun gebeizt und lackiert – **Polsteraufbau:** Federkorb – **Bezug:** Jacquardstoff – **Objektmaße:** 84 x 56 x 64 cm; Sitzhöhe: 45 x 56 x 50 cm – **Fördernde:** Volker Engels RiH (Arbeitsleistung) – **Fotografie:** LÖFFLER COLLECTION, Reichenschwand.

239
Hocker – **Eigentum:** Bernhard Ziegler – **Entwurf:** unbekannt – **Herstellung:** unbekannt – **Datierung:** 21. Jahrhundert – **Technologie:** Holzgestell Sichtseiten schwarz lackiert – **Polsteraufbau:** Jutegurte, Federleinen, Bourlet: Federleinen, Feinwerg, Capitonné-Heftung: Rosshaar und Nessel – **Objektmaße:** 27 x 56 x 54,5 cm – **Fördernde/Restaurierung:** Bernhard Ziegler RiH (Arbeitsleistung) – **Fotografie:** LÖFFLER COLLECTION, Reichenschwand.

240
Klubsessel – **Eigentum:** Reinhardt Roßberg – **Datierung:** ca. 1925 – **Technologie:** Der Sitz ist ein Hochpolster mit Fasson und Pikier, die Lehne ist mit der Armlehne zusammen gearbeitet, gefedert und in Pfeifen bezogen – **Polsteraufbau:** Auf einer 4x4-Gurtung steht eine Federung mit hochgestellter Vorderreihe; darüber ein Jutefederleinen und eine garnierte Brechflachsfasson mit vorderem Spannboden; ein übliches Pikier in Afrik mit Rosshaar- und Watteabdeckung ist mit Nessel bezogen; der Sitz ist mit handgewischtem Leder mit jeweils Keder zwischen Sitz und Boden bzw. Blende aufwendig bezogen; Rückenlehne und Armlehnen sind gefedert und in neun Pfeifen gearbeitet; leichte Fasson und Pikier in Rosshaar; Lederbezug mit Zwischenkeder; die Blenden sind mit Leder bezogen und mit Randkeder versehen; das Spannteil ist aus Leder mit Zwischenkedern und mit lederbezogenen Ziernägeln angebracht – **Anmerkung:** Hierbei handelt es sich um eine aufwendige, zeittypische Lederbezugsarbeit in Pfeifen und mit Keder bei allen Übergängen – **Objektmaße:** 73 cm x 91 x 100 cm; Sitzhöhe: 46 x 78 x 61 cm – **Literatur:** *Polsterlehrgang: „Der Technisch-Praktische Polsterer"*, W. Engelhard. Berlin-Johannisthal 1948 – **Fördernde/Restaurierung:** Reinhardt Roßberg RiH – **Fotografie:** LÖFFLER COLLECTION, Reichenschwand.

241
Dekorationsstoff – **Eigentum:** GRASSI Museum für Angewandte Kunst Leipzig – **Inventarnummer:** 1967.97 – **Entwurf/Herstellung/Herstellungsort:** Weberhof Lübz, Gottfried Hensen, Gretel Schmitz – **Datierung:** 1967 – **Technologie:** Doppelgewebe, Wolle auf Baumwollkette – **Objektmaße:** H: 136 cm, B: 310 cm – **Beschreibung:** auf weißem Grund schwarze Quadrate in weißen, schwarz gerahmten Feldern – **Anmerkung:** Das Gewebe wurde 1967 zusammen mit 15 weiteren in anderen Farb- und Musterstellungen vom Weberhof Lübz erworben – **Fotografie:** Esther Hoyer/GRASSI Museum für Angewandte Kunst Leipzig.

242/243
Brokatell, Bezug einer Stuhllehne – **Eigentum:** GRASSI Museum für Angewandte Kunst Leipzig – **Inventarnummer:** V8307 a – **Entwurf/Herstellung/Herstellungsort:** Italien – **Datierung:** 17. Jh. – **Technologie:** Brokatell, Kette: Seide, Schuss: Leinen und Seide – **Objektmaße:** H: 40 cm, B: 60,5 cm – **Beschreibung:** Der seitlich und oben wie unten angeschnittene Musterrapport wird durch eine große Blüte auf ausladenden Blattvoluten in Rot auf gelbem Grund bestimmt. Seitliche angenähte Teilstücke sowie die an Ober- und Unterkante angebrachten Borten mit Metall-

decorative nails – **Notes:** this is a laborious contemporary piece covered in leather with piping and flutes all transitions – **Object measurements:** 73 cm x 91 x 100 cm, seat: 46 x 78 x 61 cm – **Literature:** W. Engelhard, *Polsterlehrgang: 'Der Technisch-Praktische Polsterer'*, Berlin-Johannisthal 1948 – **Sponsors/Conservation:** Reinhardt Roßberg RiH – **Photo:** LÖFFLER COLLECTION, Reichenschwand.

241
Decorative fabric – **Property:** GRASSI Museum für Angewandte Kunst Leipzig – **Inventory number:** 1967.97 – **Design/Origin:** Weberhof Lübz, Gottfried Hensen, Gretel Schmitz – **Date:** 1967 – **Technique:** double-weave, wool on cotton warp – **Object measurements:** H: 136 cm, W: 310 cm – **Description:** black squares on white ground in white fields framed in black – **Notes:** the fabric was acquired in 1967 together with fifteen other colour and pattern samples from Weberhof Lübz – **Photo:** Esther Hoyer/GRASSI Museum für Angewandte Kunst Leipzig.

242/243
Brocatelle, top cover of a chair backrest – **Property:** GRASSI Museum für Angewandte Kunst Leipzig – **Inventory number:** V8307 a – **Design/Origin:** Italy – **Date:** 17th century – **Technique:** brocatelle, warp: silk, weft: linen and silk – **Object measurements:** H: 40 cm, W: 60.5 cm – **Description:** the repeat pattern, cut to the sides as well as on top and below, is dominated by a large blossom with sprawling foliage volutes in red on a yellow ground. Elements stitched to the sides as well as borders with metal fringe (top: gold fringe – gold lamella with yellow silk core, L: 2.5 cm; below silver fringe – silver lamella with white silk core, L: 6.3 cm) make it clear that the fragment was used as the cover of a backrest – **Notes:** two further pieces with the same fabric (V8307 b,c) are in the collection, presumably also backrest covers of another chair – **Photo:** Esther Hoyer/GRASSI Museum für Angewandte Kunst Leipzig.

244/245
Brocatelle – **Property:** GRASSI Museum für Angewandte Kunst Leipzig – **Inventory number:** Gewebe I.162 – **Design/Origin:** Italy – **Date:** 16th century – **Technique:** brocatelle, warp: silk, weft: silk and linen – **Object measurements:** H: 44 cm, W: 63 cm – **Description:** pattern with opposing lions between tulip palmettes on curved, chessboard-patterned band volutes in red on yellow background. Preserved side edges establish the fabric width of 63 cm. Upper and lower edge have been cut, therefore the repeat pattern is incomplete in its height – **Notes:** acquired before 1896. In 1898 a second larger piece of the same fabric with opposite colours (yellow on red ground) was acquired by Wilhelm von Bode from Berlin (inv. no. 1898.917). No longer in the collection (loss). A piece of the same fabric (yellow on red ground) is today in the Museum für Angewandte Kunst in Cologne (inv. no. D683, acquired 1888 by Cantoni, Milan; Markowski 1976, p. 194, no. 209); another piece in the same colour composition is at the Museum of Art in Cleveland, Ohio (inv. no. 53.496) – **Photo:** Esther Hoyer/GRASSI Museum für Angewandte Kunst Leipzig.

246
Chiselled velvet – **Property:** GRASSI Museum für Angewandte Kunst Leipzig – **Inventory number:** V8302 – **Design/Origin:** Italy – **Date:** around 1600? – **Technique:** chiselled velvet, warp/weft: silk – **Object measurements:** H: 47 cm, W: 17.5 cm – **Description:** staggered vertical rows of bouquets with alternating palmette and pomegranate blossoms as well as acanthus leaves and

fransen (oben: Goldfransen – Goldlahn auf gelber Seidenseele, L: 2,5 cm; unten: Silberfransen – Silberlahn auf weißer Seidenseele, L: 6,3 cm) lassen deutlich erkennen, dass das Fragment als Bezug für eine Stuhllehne genutzt wurde. – **Anmerkung:** In der Sammlung befinden sich zwei weitere Teile desselben Gewebes (V8307 b,c), vermutlich ehemals als Lehnenbezug eines weiteren Stuhls – **Fotografie:** Esther Hoyer/GRASSI Museum für Angewandte Kunst Leipzig.

244/245
Brokatell – **Eigentum:** GRASSI Museum für Angewandte Kunst Leipzig – **Inventarnummer:** Gewebe I.162 – **Entwurf/Herstellung/Herstellungsort:** Italien – **Datierung:** 16. Jh. – **Technologie:** Brokatell, Kette: Seide, Schuss: Seide und Leinen – **Objektmaße:** H: 44 cm, B: 63 cm – **Beschreibung:** Das Muster zeigt gegenständige Löwen zwischen Tulpenpalmetten auf geschweiften, schachbrettartig gemusterten Bandvoluten in Rot auf gelbem Fond. Mit den seitlichen erhaltenen Gewebekanten ist die Gewebebreite von 63 cm bekannt. Da Ober- und Unterkante beschnitten sind, ist der Musterrapport in der Höhe unvollständig. – **Anmerkung:** Erworben wurde das Fragment vor 1896. 1898 wurde ein zweites, größeres Stück des gleichen Gewebes in umgekehrter Farbstellung (gelb auf rotem Fond) von Wilhelm von Bode aus Berlin erworben (Inv. Nr. 1898.917). Es befindet sich heute nicht mehr in der Sammlung (Verlust). Ein Stück des gleichen Gewebes (gelb auf rotem Grund) befindet sich im Museum für Angewandte Kunst Köln (Inv.-Nr. D683, erworben 1888 von Cantoni, Mailand; Markowski S. 194, Nr. 209); ein weiteres Stück in der Farbstellung des hier gezeigten Objektes befindet sich im Museum of Art in Cleveland, Ohio (Inv.Nr. 53.496) – **Fotografie:** Esther Hoyer/GRASSI Museum für Angewandte Kunst Leipzig.

246
Ziselierter Samt – **Eigentum:** GRASSI Museum für Angewandte Kunst Leipzig – **Inventarnummer:** V8302 – **Entwurf/Herstellung/Herstellungsort:** Italien – **Datierung:** um 1600 (?) – **Technologie:** Ziselierter Samt, Kette/Schuss: Seide – **Objektmaße:** H: 47 cm, B: 17,5 cm – **Beschreibung:** versetzte senkrechte Reihen von Sträußen mit wechselnd Palmett- und Granatapfelblüten sowie Akanthusblättern und je zwei gegenständigen großen Blüten – **Anmerkung:** Alter Bestand – **Fotografie:** Esther Hoyer/GRASSI Museum für Angewandte Kunst Leipzig.

247
Ziselierter Samt – **Eigentum:** GRASSI Museum für Angewandte Kunst Leipzig – **Inventarnummer:** Gewebe I.216 a – **Entwurf/Herstellung/Herstellungsort:** Venedig (?) – **Datierung:** 17. Jh. – **Technologie:** Ziselierter Samt, Kette: Seide, weiß, blau überfärbt, rot jaspé, blau überfärbt (rotviolett), Schuss: Seide, weiß, blau überfärbt, Silberlahn; Webkante: 1,2 cm – **Objektmaße:** H: 35 cm, B: 17 cm – **Beschreibung:** Das Muster in heute rotviolettem Samt zeigt verschlungene Rankenzweige mit vier verschiedenen Blatt- und Blütenmotiven in Medaillons mit aus zwei verschiedenen Musterelementen zusammengesetzter Rahmung. Der Musterrapport ist unvollständig – **Anmerkung:** Das Gewebe wurde vor 1896 aus der Sammlung des Aachener Kanonikers Dr. Franz Bock erworben – **Fotografie:** Esther Hoyer/GRASSI Museum für Angewandte Kunst Leipzig.

248
Seidengewebe – **Eigentum:** GRASSI Museum für Angewandte Kunst Leipzig – **Inventarnummer:** Gewebe I.199 – **Entwurf/Herstellung/Herstellungsort:** Italien – **Datierung:** Mitte 17. Jh. – **Technologie:** Atlas liseré, Kette: Seide, Schuss: Seide – **Objektmaße:** H: 51 cm, B: 45,6 cm Beschreibung: Auf rotem Grund stehen Reihen versetzter und in der Richtung wechselnder Blütenzweige mit drei verschiedenen Blüten, einem gezackten Blatt und kleineren Blüten. Es handelt sich um eine Variante des Mitte des 17. Jahrhunderts verbreiteten genuesischen Dreiblütenmusters *tre fiori* – **Anmerkung:** Das Gewebe wurde vor

two large blossoms facing each other – **Notes:** old inventory – **Photo:** Esther Hoyer/GRASSI Museum für Angewandte Kunst Leipzig.

247
Chiselled velvet – **Property:** GRASSI Museum für Angewandte Kunst Leipzig – **Inventory number:** Gewebe I.216 a – **Design/Origin:** Venice – **Date:** 17th century – **Technique:** chiselled velvet, warp: silk, dyed blue, red jaspé, dyed blue (red-violet), weft: silk, dyed blue, silver lamella, selvedge: 1.2 cm – **Object measurements:** H: 35 cm, W: 17 cm – **Description:** the design, today in reddish-purple velvet, depicts intertwined tendrilled branches with four different leaf and flower motifs in medallions with a frame composed of two different design elements. The pattern repeat is incomplete – **Notes:** acquired in 1896 from the collection of the Aachen canon Dr Franz Bock – **Photo:** Esther Hoyer/GRASSI Museum für Angewandte Kunst Leipzig.

248
Silk weave – **Property:** GRASSI Museum für Angewandte Kunst Leipzig – **Inventory number:** Gewebe I.199 – **Design/Origin:** Italy – **Date:** mid 17th century – **Technique:** atlas liseré, warp/weft: silk – **Object measurements:** H: 51 cm, W: 45.6 cm – **Description:** on a red ground, rows of staggered and alternating flowering branches with three different flowers, a serrated leaf and smaller flowers. This is a variant of the Genoese three-flower pattern (*tre fiori*) that was widespread in the mid 17th century – **Notes:** acquired before 1896. Comparable examples are at MAK Cologne (Markowsky 1976, p. 250, no. 370) and at Collezione Tessile Soprintendenza per i Beni Storici e Artistici della Liguria (Cataldi Gallo 2016, p. 48, fig. 1) – **Photo:** Esther Hoyer/GRASSI Museum für Angewandte Kunst Leipzig.

249
Appliqué embroidery (fragment) – **Property:** GRASSI Museum für Angewandte Kunst Leipzig – **Inventory number:** V887 a – **Design/Origin:** Italy (Genoa?) – **Date:** early 17th century – **Technique:** velvet (modified cross twill) as a ground weave; silk weaves of different colours, underlaid with paper, appliquéd; contour lines of four bundled linen threads appliquéd with white silk thread; on the three outer edges narrow red and white fabric border with loop fringes in white, yellow, red and a fourth unusual colour (green or blue) – **Object measurements:** H: 29 cm, W: 80 cm – **Description:** on blue damaged velvet ground a tendril of lily blossoms above a diagonal branch. Framed by a bar with wrapped around ribbons in different colours. – **Notes:** acquired in 1894 from the Robert Forrer Collection (Strasbourg) under the identification 'Genoa'; very similar fragment with identical motifs at Bayerisches Nationalmuseum, inv. no. T 6797 (Eikelmann/Borkopp-Restle 2002, cat. no. 33), equally assumed to be from Genoa and a fragment in the Deutsches Textilmuseum Krefeld (Bergemann 2010, Kat.-Nr.92); the border on both outer edges with loop fringe in all four colours; contour threads with red (instead of white) silk. For a comparable border, see no. 251 – **Photo:** Esther Hoyer/GRASSI Museum für Angewandte Kunst Leipzig.

250
Border – **Property:** GRASSI Museum für Angewandte Kunst Leipzig – **Inventory number:** V3180 – **Design/Origin:** Italy – **Date:** 17th century – **Technique:** fabric border in white, red, light yellow, green and blue silk; lower edge with alternating scalloped loops and small tassels – **Object measurements:** H: 2 cm, W: 31 cm –

1896 erworben. Vergleichbare Beispiele finden sich im MAK Köln (Markowsky 1976, S. 250, Nr. 370) oder in der Collezione Tessile Soprintendenza per i Beni Storici e Artistici della Liguria (Cataldi Gallo 2016, S. 48, Fig. 1) – **Fotografie:** Esther Hoyer/GRASSI Museum für Angewandte Kunst Leipzig.

249
Applikationsstickerei (Fragment) – **Eigentum:** GRASSI Museum für Angewandte Kunst Leipzig – **Inventarnummer:** V887 a – **Entwurf/Herstellung/Herstellungsort:** Italien (Genua?) – **Datierung:** Anfang 17. Jahrhundert – **Technologie:** Samt (abgewandelter Kreuzköper) als Grundgewebe; verschiedenfarbige, mit Papier unterlegte Seidengewebe appliziert; Konturlinien aus vier gebündelten Leinenfäden mit weißem Seidenfaden angelegt; an den drei Außenkanten schmale rot-weiße Gewebeborte mit Schlaufenfransen in Weiß, Gelb, Rot und vierter ausgefallener Farbe (Grün oder Blau) – **Objektmaße:** H: 29 cm, B: 80 cm – **Beschreibung:** Auf blauem, beschädigtem Samtgrund ist über diagonal gestellte gelbe Aststücke eine Blattranke mit Lilienblüten geführt. Die Rahmung bildet ein von farbigen Bändern umschlungener Stab – **Anmerkung:** 1894 aus der Sammlung Robert Forrer (Straßburg) unter Zuordnung Genua erworben; sehr ähnliches, in Motiven identisches Fragment im Bayerischen Nationalmuseum Inv.-Nr. T 6797 (Eikelmannn/Borkopp-Restle 2002, Kat.-Nr. 33), ebenfalls Entstehung in Genua angenommen, sowie im Deutschen Textilmuseum Krefeld (Bergemann 2010, Kat.-Nr. 92); bei der an zwei Außenkanten erhaltenen Borte sind die Schlaufenfransen noch in allen vier Farben erhalten; die Konturfäden sind hier mit roter (statt weißer) Seide angelegt. Für eine vergleichbare Borte siehe Nr. 251 – **Fotografie:** Esther Hoyer/GRASSI Museum für Angewandte Kunst Leipzig.

250
Borte – **Eigentum:** GRASSI Museum für Angewandte Kunst Leipzig – **Inventarnummer:** V3180 – **Entwurf/Herstellung/Herstellungsort:** Italien – **Datierung:** 17. Jh. – **Technologie:** Gewebeborte in weißer, roter, blassgelber, grüner und blauer Seide; an der Unterkante im Wechsel gebogte Schlaufengruppen und kleine Quasten – **Objektmaße:** H: 2 cm, B: 31 cm – **Anmerkung:** Eine ähnliche Borte findet sich an der Applikationsstickerei Abb. 251. Alter Bestand, Erwerb vor 1945 – **Restaurierung:** 2022 gereinigt – **Fotografie:** Esther Hoyer/GRASSI Museum für Angewandte Kunst Leipzig.

251
Applikationsstickerei – **Eigentum:** GRASSI Museum für Angewandte Kunst Leipzig – **Inventarnummer:** V886 – **Entwurf/Herstellung/Herstellungsort:** Italien oder Spanien – **Datierung:** Anfang 17. Jahrhundert – **Technologie:** Samt als Grundgewebe; verschiedenfarbige, mit Papier unterlegte Seidengewebe appliziert; Konturlinien aus zwei gebündelten Leinenfäden mit weißem Seidenfaden angelegt – **Objektmaße:** H: 48,3 cm, B: 51 cm – **Beschreibung:** Auf gelbem, stark abgeriebenem Samtgrund ist ein Fries aus großen Blattranken, Blüten und Rollwerkelementen gelegt. Mittig und aufgrund des fast vollständig ausgefallenen hellen Seidengewebes schwer ablesbar ist ein diagonal gestellter Ast eingefügt. An der Unterkante ist eine Borte mit langen Fransen in drei wechselnden Farben angenäht. Das Fragment war ursprünglich Teil einer Raumausstattung.– **Anmerkung:** Alter Bestand, Erwerb vor 1945 – **Fotografie:** Esther Hoyer/GRASSI Museum für Angewandte Kunst Leipzig.

252/253
Seidengewebe – **Eigentum:** GRASSI Museum für Angewandte Kunst Leipzig – **Inventarnummer:** V8316 – **Entwurf/Herstellung/Herstellungsort:** Frankreich (?) – **Datierung:** 1735–1750 – **Technologie:** Lampas, broschiert und lanciert, Kette: Seide, dunkelbraun, Schuss. Seide, dunkelbraun, grün, gelb, zwei Rotbrauntöne, cremeweiß; rückseitig mit einem aus acht Teilen

Notes: similar border on appliqué embroidery fig. 249; old inventory, acquired before 1945 – **Conservation:** cleaned 2022 – **Photo:** Esther Hoyer/GRASSI Museum für Angewandte Kunst Leipzig.

251
Appliqué embroidery – **Property:** GRASSI Museum für Angewandte Kunst Leipzig – **Inventory number:** V886 – **Design/Origin:** Italy or Spain – **Date:** early 17th century – **Technique:** velvet ground fabric; paper-backed silk fabrics in different colours, appliquéd; contour lines from two bundled linen threads with white silk thread – **Object measurements:** H: 48.3 cm, W: 51 cm – **Description:** a frieze of large leaf tendrils, blossoms and scrollwork elements upon on a yellow, heavily abraded velvet ground. A diagonally placed branch is inserted in the centre and on the border of the almost completely faded light silk fabric. A border with long fringes in three alternating colours is sewn onto the lower edge. The fragment was originally part of an interior decoration scheme – **Notes:** old inventory, acquisition before 1945 – **Photo:** Esther Hoyer/GRASSI Museum für Angewandte Kunst Leipzig.

252/253
Silk weave – **Property:** GRASSI Museum für Angewandte Kunst Leipzig – **Inventory number:** V8316 – **Design/Origin:** France? – **Date:** 1735–50 – **Technique:** Lampas, brocaded and patterned, warp: silk, dark brown, silk, green, yellow, two red-brown tones, creme white; back cover bound with linen fabric made from eight stitched elements – **Object measurements:** H: 44 cm, W: 49 cm – **Description:** pink and yellow blossoms and lush foliage are effectively laid on the dark-brown ground with brocaded coloured silk threads. Differentiated colour gradations and brown leaf and flower motifs, using floating warp on the brown ground achieve a sculptural quality and depth. The piece is composed of seven fabric fragments – **Notes:** fabrics of this type with a high amount of surface-level sensitive silk threads were not primarily used for covering furniture but for wall hangings. An indication of such (secondary) use for a room furnishing is the linen back cover as well as wax stains; old inventory – **Photo:** Esther Hoyer/GRASSI Museum für Angewandte Kunst Leipzig.

254
Silk damask – **Property:** GRASSI Museum für Angewandte Kunst Leipzig – **Inventory number:** Gewebe I.380 – **Design/Origin:** France – **Date:** 18th century – **Technique:** monochrome red damask, warp/weft: silk – **Object measurements:** H: 50.5 cm, W: 53 cm – **Description:** a large flower and leaf bouquet is the central motif of the fabric, which is framed by scalloped lace bands with a serrated bottom edge – **Notes:** the piece was acquired with a second fragment of the same fabric (Gewebe I.379) – **Photo:** Esther Hoyer/GRASSI Museum für Angewandte Kunst Leipzig.

255
Silk damask – **Property:** GRASSI Museum für Angewandte Kunst Leipzig – **Inventory number:** V2274 – **Design/Origin:** France – **Date:** 18th century – **Technique:** damask warp/weft: silk, light blue – **Object measurements:** H: 72 cm, W: 34.5 cm – **Description:** the pattern of this monochrome light-blue fabric is composed of large and small flowers and leaves and a steeply curved lace band with a curved bottom edge. The pattern repeat is incomplete. The fragment is composed of two pieces of fabric – **Notes:** old inventory, acquisition before 1945 – **Photo:** Esther Hoyer/GRASSI Museum für Angewandte Kunst Leipzig.

zusammengesetzten Leinengewebe hinterlegt – **Objektmaße:** H: 44 cm, B: 49 cm – **Beschreibung:** Auf dunkelbraunen Grund sind durch broschierte farbige Seidenfäden effektvoll rosafarbene und gelbe Blüten und üppiges Blattwerk gelegt. Durch differenzierte Farbabstufungen und durch flottierende Kettfäden auf den braunen Grund gelegte, braune Blatt- und Blütenmotive wurde Plastizität und Tiefenwirkung erreicht. Das Stück ist aus sieben Gewebefragmenten zusammengesetzt – **Anmerkung:** Gewebe dieser Art, mit einem hohen Anteil an auf der Oberfläche aufliegenden, empfindlichen Seidenfäden wurden in der Raumausstattung nicht vorrangig als Möbelbezüge, sondern eher für Wandbespannungen verwendet. Hinweise auf die (eventuell Zweit-) Nutzung dieses Stückes in der Raumausstattung geben die Unterlegung mit Leinengeweben sowie Wachsflecken; alter Bestand – **Fotografie:** Esther Hoyer/GRASSI Museum für Angewandte Kunst Leipzig.

254
Seidendamast – **Eigentum:** GRASSI Museum für Angewandte Kunst Leipzig – **Inventarnummer:** Gewebe I.380 – **Entwurf/Herstellung/Herstellungsort:** Frankreich – **Datierung:** 18. Jh. – **Technologie:** Monochromer roter Damast, Kette/Schuss: Seide – **Objektmaße:** H: 50,5 cm, B: 53 cm – **Beschreibung:** Hauptmotiv dieses monochromen roten Gewebes ist ein großes Blüten- und Blattbouquet, das von gewellten Spitzenbändern mit gezackter Unterkante gerahmt wird – **Anmerkung:** Das Stück wurde zusammen mit einem zweiten Fragment desselben Gewebes (Gewebe I.379) vor 1896 erworben – **Fotografie:** Esther Hoyer/GRASSI Museum für Angewandte Kunst Leipzig.

255
Seidendamast – **Eigentum:** GRASSI Museum für Angewandte Kunst Leipzig – **Inventarnummer:** V2274 – **Entwurf/Herstellung/Herstellungsort:** Frankreich – **Datierung:** 18. Jh. – **Technologie:** Damast, Kette/Schuss: Seide, hellblau – **Objektmaße:** H: 72 cm, B: 34,5 cm – **Beschreibung:** Das Muster dieses monochromen hellblauen Gewebes setzt sich aus großen und kleinen Blüten und Blättern und einem steil geschwungenen Spitzenband mit gebogter Unterkante zusammen. Der Musterrapport ist unvollständig. Das Fragment ist aus zwei Gewebestücken zusammengesetzt – **Anmerkung:** Alter Bestand, Erwerb vor 1945 – **Fotografie:** Esther Hoyer/GRASSI Museum für Angewandte Kunst Leipzig.

256/257
Rosshaargewebe – **Eigentum:** GRASSI Museum für Angewandte Kunst Leipzig – **Inventarnummer:** Gewebe I. 444 a **Entwurf/Herstellung/Herstellungsort:** Italien – **Datierung:** 18. Jahrhundert – **Technologie:** Atlasgewebe, Kette: Seide, Schuss: Seide und schwarzes Rosshaar – **Objektmaße:** H: 61,4 cm, B: 29 cm – **Beschreibung:** Den Dekor des schwarzen Gewebes bilden Zweige mit sternförmigen Blüten und Blättern in verschiedenen Formen und Größen – **Anmerkung:** zwei Fragmente desselben Gewebes; Ankauf 1889 bei Zatelli, München – **Restaurierung:** 2022 gereinigt – **Fotografie:** Esther Hoyer/GRASSI Museum für Angewandte Kunst Leipzig.

258
Musterbuch Rosshaargewebe – **Eigentum:** GRASSI Museum für Angewandte Kunst Leipzig – **Inventarnummer:** V13396 – **Entwurf/Herstellung/Herstellungsort:** Lengenfeld – **Datierung:** 1910er Jahre – **Technologie:** Gewebe, Papier und Karton geklebt – **Objektmaße:** geschlossen H: 24 cm, B: 14 cm – **Beschreibung:** Firma Mechanische Rosshaarweberei Lengenfeld Lenk und Co. gmbH, Leporello mit 28 Rosshaargewebeproben in Passepartouts in sieben verschiedenen Bindungen jeweils in unterschiedlichen Farbstellungen – **Fotografie:** Esther Hoyer/GRASSI Museum für Angewandte Kunst Leipzig.

256/257
Horsehair weave – **Property:** GRASSI Museum für Angewandte Kunst Leipzig – **Inventory number:** Gewebe I. 444 a Design/Origin: Italy – **Date:** 18th century – **Technique:** atlas, warp: silk, weft: silk and black horsehair – **Object measurements:** H: 61.4 cm, W: 29 cm – **Description:** the black fabric is decorated with branches with star-shaped flowers and leaves in various shapes and sizes – **Notes:** two fragments of the same fabric; acquired in 1889 at Zatelli, Munich – **Conservation:** cleaned 2022 – **Photo:** Esther Hoyer/GRASSI Museum für Angewandte Kunst Leipzig.

258
Sample book of horsehair fabric – **Property:** GRASSI Museum für Angewandte Kunst Leipzig – **Inventory number:** V13396 – **Design/Origin:** Lengenfeld, Saxony, Germany – **Date:** 1910s – **Technique:** fabric, paper and board, glued – **Object measurements:** closed H: 24 cm, W: 14 cm – **Description:** from Mechanische Rosshaarweberei Lengenfeld Lenk and Co. GmbH, foldout with twenty-eight horsehair fabric samples in passepartouts in seven different weaves each with different colour schemes – **Photo:** Esther Hoyer/GRASSI Museum für Angewandte Kunst Leipzig.

259
Printed fabric – **Property:** GRASSI Museum für Angewandte Kunst Leipzig – **Inventory number:** 1962.35 – **Design/Origin:** Morris & Company – **Date:** around 1885 – **Technique:** hand-printed on velvet – **Object measurements:** H: 45.6 cm, W: 64.3 cm – **Description:** the pattern repeat of the fragment is heavily cropped. A large filled poppy blossom with stalks and leaves is as the dominant motif, as well as carnation- and daisy-like blossoms and various leaf shapes that fill the ground. The motifs are printed with dark-brown outlines and white areas on a yellow ground. Company name MORRIS & COMPANY H S OXFORDSTREET on the edge – **Notes:** old inventory, 1962 newly inventoried – **Literature:** Fritz Kämpfer (ed.), *Kunsthandwerk im Grassimuseum*, Leipzig 1981, pp. 15–16; *Klassizismus, Biedermeier, Historismus und Jugendstil, Einführung: Faltblatt des GRASSI Museums für Kunsthandwerk*, Leipzig 1993 – **Conservation:** 1994 by Ingrid Pfeiffer – **Photo:** Esther Hoyer/GRASSI Museum für Angewandte Kunst Leipzig.

260
Decorative fabric with peonies – **Property:** GRASSI Museum für Angewandte Kunst Leipzig – **Inventory number:** 1901.1262 – Design/Origin: Georges de Feure (design), Deuss & Oetker, Krefeld (execution) – **Date:** around 1899 – **Technique:** atlas weave, warp/weft: silk – **Object measurements:** H: 165 cm, W: 126 cm – **Description:** axially symmetrical pattern of four peony flowers each with foliage, repeat pattern: L: 47 cm, W: 31.5 cm Notes: acquired at the World's Fair in Paris 1900, together with other woven and printed fabrics after designs by Georges de Feure, Edouard Colonna and Eugène Gaillard, from the Bing pavilion – **Literature:** Ute Camphausen in *Die Erwerbungen der Weltausstellung Paris 1900*, vol. 11 of *Mitteilungen des städtischen Museums für Kunsthandwerk zu Leipzig/Grassimuseum and seines Freundes- and Förderkreises e.V.*, Leipzig 2000, pp. 1079, 1143–1144, no. 80 – **Conservation:** 1994 by Ingrid Pfeiffer, smaller conservation measures in 2022 by Carola Berriola – **Photo:** Esther Hoyer/GRASSI Museum für Angewandte Kunst Leipzig.

259
Druckstoff – **Eigentum:** GRASSI Museum für Angewandte Kunst Leipzig – **Inventarnummer:** 1962.35 – **Entwurf/Herstellung/Herstellungsort:** Morris & Company – **Datierung:** um 1885 – **Technologie:** Handdruck auf Samt – **Objektmaße:** H: 45,6 cm, B: 64,3 cm – **Beschreibung:** Der Musterrapport des Fragmentes ist stark beschnitten. Angeschnitten, aber noch zu erkennen ist eine große gefüllte Mohnblüte mit Stilen und Blättern als bestimmendes Motiv sowie nelken- und margeritenähnliche Blumen und verschiedene Blattformen als Füllung des Grundes. Die Motive sind mit dunkelbraunen Konturen und weißen Flächen auf gelben Grund gedruckt. Am Rand Firmenbezeichnung MORRIS & COMPANY H S OXFORDSTREET – **Anmerkung:** Alter Bestand, 1962 neu inventarisiert – **Literatur:** *Kunsthandwerk im Grassimuseum*, Fritz Kämpfer (Hg.). Leipzig 1981, S. 15f.; *Klassizismus, Biedermeier, Historismus und Jugendstil, Einführung, Faltblatt des GRASSI Museums für Kunsthandwerk*. Leipzig 1993 – **Restaurierung:** 1994 durch Ingrid Pfeiffer – **Fotografie:** Esther Hoyer/GRASSI Museum für Angewandte Kunst Leipzig.

260
Dekorationsstoff mit Päonien – **Eigentum:** GRASSI Museum für Angewandte Kunst Leipzig – **Inventarnummer:** 1901.1262 – **Entwurf/Herstellung/Herstellungsort:** Georges de Feure (Entwurf), Deuss & Oetker, Krefeld (Ausführung) – **Datierung:** um 1899 – **Technologie:** Atlasbindung, Kette: Seide, Schuss: Seide – **Objektmaße:** H: 165 cm, B: 126 cm – **Beschreibung:** axial-symmetrisches Muster von je vier Päonienblüten mit Blattwerk, Rapport: L.: 47,0 cm; B.: 31,5 cm – **Anmerkung:** Erworben auf der Weltausstellung in Paris 1900, zusammen mit weiteren Geweben und Druckstoffen nach Entwürfen von Georges de Feure, Edouard Colonna, Eugène Gaillard, aus dem Pavillon Bing – **Literatur:** Ute Camphausen in: *Die Erwerbungen der Weltausstellung Paris 1900, Mitteilungen des städtischen Museums für Kunsthandwerk zu Leipzig/Grassimuseum und seines Freundes- und Förderkreises e. V.*, Heft 11. Leipzig 2000, S. 1079, S. 1143f., Nr. 80 – **Restaurierung:** 1994 durch Ingrid Pfeiffer, kleinere Konservierungsmaßnahmen 2022 durch Carola Berriola – **Fotografie:** Esther Hoyer/GRASSI Museum für Angewandte Kunst Leipzig.

261
Muster Möbelbezug – **Eigentum:** GRASSI Museum für Angewandte Kunst Leipzig – **Inventarnummer:** V3902 b – **Entwurf/Herstellung/Herstellungsort:** Deutsche Textile Kunst (DeTeKu Rudolf Hiemann) (Ausführung)/Albin Müller (Entwurf) – **Datierung:** 1920er Jahre – **Technologie:** Industrielles Maschinengewebe, Kette: Wolle, Schuss: Wolle – **Objektmaße:** H: 39 cm, B: 23,5 cm – **Beschreibung:** Möbelbezugsstoff mit stark stilisiertem floralem Muster auf schwarzem Grund. An eine blaue kelchförmige Blüte schließt sich eine Spirale aus kleineren kelchförmigen schwarzen Blüten und braunen Punkten an. Zwischen diese in senkrechten Reihen verbundenen Motive sind blaue Ranken gesetzt. – **Anmerkung:** aufgeklebtes Papierschild: „DETEKU, Original-Entwurf: Prof. A. Müller, Qualität: Gobelin, No. 12437, B: ca. 130 cm"; verwendet u. a. zur Ausstattung des Sanatoriums Dr. Barner in Braunlage. Erwerb wahrscheinlich bei einer Grassimesse in den 1920er Jahren – **Fotografie:** Esther Hoyer/GRASSI Museum für Angewandte Kunst Leipzig.

262
Muster Möbelbezug – **Eigentum:** GRASSI Museum für Angewandte Kunst Leipzig – **Inventarnummer:** V3903 c – **Entwurf/Herstellung/Herstellungsort:** Deutsche Textile Kunst (DeTeKu Rudolf Hiemann) (Ausführung)/Wilhelm Poetter (Entwurf) – **Datierung:** 1920er Jahre – **Technologie:** Industrielles Maschinengewebe, Kette: Wolle, Schuss: Wolle – **Objektmaße:** H: 39,5 cm, B: 23,5 cm – **Beschreibung:** Versetzte Reihen von großen blaugrauen Blüten mit gelb-grünem Blütenkorb und grün-grauem Stiel mit Blättern stehen auf schwarzem Untergrund – **Anmer-**

261
Sample furniture cover fabric – **Property:** GRASSI Museum für Angewandte Kunst Leipzig – **Inventory number:** V3902 b – **Design/Origin:** Deutsche Textile Kunst (DeTeKu Rudolf Hiemann) (execution), Albin Müller (design) – **Date:** 1920s – **Technique:** industrial machine weave, warp/weft: wool – **Object measurements:** H: 39 cm, W: 23.5 cm – **Description:** upholstery cover fabric with a highly stylised floral pattern on a black ground. A blue goblet-shaped blossom is followed by a spiral of smaller goblet-shaped black blossoms and brown dots. Blue tendrils are set between these motifs, which are connected in vertical rows – **Notes:** glued on paper: 'DETEKU, Original-Design: Prof. A. Müller, Qualität: Gobelin, No. 12437, W: approx. 130 cm'; used, among other things, to furnish the sanatorium of Dr Barner in Braunlage. Probably acquired at a Grassi Fair in the 1920s – **Photo:** Esther Hoyer/GRASSI Museum für Angewandte Kunst Leipzig.

262
Sample furniture cover fabric – **Property:** GRASSI Museum für Angewandte Kunst Leipzig – **Inventory number:** V3903 c – **Design/Origin:** Deutsche Textile Kunst (DeTeKu Rudolf Hiemann) (execution)/Wilhelm Poetter (design) – **Date:** 1920s – **Technique:** industrial machine weave, warp/weft: wool – **Object measurements:** H: 39.5 cm, W: 23.5 cm – **Description:** staggered rows of large blue-grey flowers with yellow-green corolla and green-grey stem with leaves on a black background – **Notes:** glued paper: 'Original-Design: Val. Petter, gesetzlich geschützt! [protected by law] No. 12461'; probably acquired at a Grassi Fair in the 1920s – **Photo:** Esther Hoyer/GRASSI Museum für Angewandte Kunst Leipzig.

263
Sample furniture cover fabric – **Property:** GRASSI Museum für Angewandte Kunst Leipzig – **Inventory number:** V3893 – **Design/Origin:** Deutsche Textile Kunst (DeTeKu Rudolf Hiemann) (execution)/Erich Kleinhempel (design) – **Date:** 1920s – **Technique:** industrial machine weave, warp/weft: wool – **Object measurements:** H: 40.3 cm, W: 23 cm – **Description:** the main division of the decor is formed by squares of black transverse and longitudinal lines with set diamonds. The areas are filled with beige on a green ground with a bird sitting on a vine in two different postures. Black, green and brown sections are highlighted by the use of a thicker thread – **Notes:** glued paper: 'Original-Design: Professor Erich Kleinhempel, gesetzlich geschützt [protected by law]! No. 12330'. Probably acquired at a Grassi Fair in the 1920s – **Photo:** Esther Hoyer/GRASSI Museum für Angewandte Kunst Leipzig.

264
Sample furniture cover fabric – **Property:** GRASSI Museum für Angewandte Kunst Leipzig – **Inventory number:** V3906 a, b; V3910 – **Design/Origin:** Deutsche Textile Kunst (DeTeKu Rudolf Hiemann) (execution)/ Herta Koch (design) – **Date:** 1920s – **Technique:** industrial machine weave, warp/weft: wool – **Object measurements:** a: H: 19.5 cm, W: 39.5 cm; b: H: 23.5 cm, W: 39.5 cm – **Description:** the surface is almost completely covered by three-pointed, ivy-like leaves. In between are a few tendrils and small circles featuring trumpet-shaped flowers. The design is shown in two colourways. V3910 is presented as a folder with wallpaper sample. Notes: glued paper: 'Original-Design: Herta Koch, gesetzlich geschützt [protected by law]! No. 12367' and 'Original-Design: Kunstmalerin Herta

kung: aufgeklebtes Papierschild: „Original-Entwurf: Val. Petter, gesetzlich geschützt! No. 12461"; Erwerb wahrscheinlich bei einer Grassimesse in den 1920er Jahren – **Fotografie:** Esther Hoyer/GRASSI Museum für Angewandte Kunst Leipzig.

263
Muster Möbelbezug – **Eigentum:** GRASSI Museum für Angewandte Kunst Leipzig – **Inventarnummer:** V3893 – **Entwurf/ Herstellung/Herstellungsort:** Deutsche Textile Kunst (DeTeKu Rudolf Hiemann) (Ausführung)/Erich Kleinhempel (Entwurf) – **Datierung:** 1920er Jahre – **Technologie:** Industrielles Maschinengewebe, Kette: Wolle, Schuss: Wolle – **Objektmaße:** H: 40,3 cm, B: 23 cm – **Beschreibung:** Die Hauptgliederung des Dekors wird durch Quadrate aus schwarzen Quer- und Längslinien mit eingestellten Rauten gebildet. Die Flächen füllen in Beige auf grünem Grund je ein auf einer Weinpflanze sitzender Vogel in zwei variierenden Haltungen. Schwarze, grüne und braune Partien sind durch Verwendung eines dickeren Fadens hervorgehoben – **Anmerkung:** aufgeklebtes Papieretikett: „Original-Entwurf: Professor Erich Kleinhempel, gesetzlich geschützt! No. 12330" Erwerb wahrscheinlich bei einer Grassimesse in den 1920er Jahren – **Fotografie:** Esther Hoyer/GRASSI Museum für Angewandte Kunst Leipzig.

264
Muster Möbelbezug – **Eigentum:** GRASSI Museum für Angewandte Kunst Leipzig – **Inventarnummer:** V3906 a,b; V3910 – **Entwurf/Herstellung/Herstellungsort:** Deutsche Textile Kunst (DeTeKu Rudolf Hiemann) (Ausführung)/Herta Koch (Entwurf) – **Datierung:** 1920er Jahre – **Technologie:** Industrielles Maschinengewebe, Kette: Wolle, Schuss: Wolle – **Objektmaße:** a: H: 19,5 cm, B: 39,5 cm; b: H: 23,5 cm, B: 39,5 cm – **Beschreibung:** Die Fläche wird fast vollständig von dreispitzigen, efeuähnlichen Blättern bedeckt. Dazwischen stehen einige Ranken und kleine Kreise und trompetenförmige Blüten. Das Muster wird in zwei Farbstellungen gezeigt. V3910 wird als Mappe mit Tapetenbeispiel präsentiert. – **Anmerkung:** aufgeklebte Papierschilder: „Original-Entwurf: Herta Koch, gesetzlich geschützt! No. 12367" und „Original-Entwurf: Kunstmalerin Herta Koch, gesetzlich geschützt! No. 12368"; Erwerb wahrscheinlich bei einer Grassimesse in den 1920er Jahren – **Fotografie:** Esther Hoyer/GRASSI Museum für Angewandte Kunst Leipzig.

265
Musterkarte mit Möbelstoff – **Eigentum:** GRASSI Museum für Angewandte Kunst Leipzig – **Inventarnummer:** V10288 a – **Entwurf/Herstellung/Herstellungsort:** D.M.W. Mitglied der Deutschen Werkstätten – **Datierung:** 1920er Jahre – **Technologie:** Industrielles Doppelgewebe, Kette: Wolle, Schuss: Wolle – **Objektmaße:** H: 12,5 cm, B: 20 cm – **Beschreibung:** Auf schwarzem Grund wechseln sich Doppelreihen ockerbrauner und blauer Zackenlinien ab – **Fotografie:** Esther Hoyer/GRASSI Museum für Angewandte Kunst Leipzig.

266
Stoffmustermappe – **Eigentum:** GRASSI Museum für Angewandte Kunst Leipzig – **Inventarnummer:** V3973 – **Entwurf/Herstellung/Herstellungsort:** Deutsche Textile Kunst (DeTeKu Rudolf Hiemann) – **Datierung:** 1920er Jahre – **Technologie:** Wolle, Textil, Karton – **Objektmaße:** geschlossen H: 32,5 cm, B: 33 cm – **Beschreibung:** Mappe aus Karton mit dem Titel „Neue Bezugsstoffe für Couch, Sofa, Sessel, mit passenden eulanisierten Uni-Plüschen als Einfassung oder für kleine Stuhlsitze, passende Vorhangstoffe dazu lieferbar". Enthalten sind Muster von Wollgeweben mit floralen Motiven aus großen, runden Blättern, die von schmalen Blättern überdeckt werden. Aufschrift auf Karton „DETEKU chenille-gobelin, ca. 130 cm breit, Rapporthöhe 35 cm", Nr. „13141" – **Anmerkung:** Erwerb wahrscheinlich bei einer Grassimesse in den 1920er Jahren – **Fotografie:** Esther Hoyer/GRASSI Museum für Angewandte Kunst Leipzig.

Koch, gesetzlich geschützt [protected by law]! No. 12368'. Probably acquired at a Grassi Fair in the 1920s – **Photo:** Esther Hoyer/GRASSI Museum für Angewandte Kunst Leipzig.

265
Sample card with furniture fabric – **Property:** GRASSI Museum für Angewandte Kunst Leipzig – **Inventory number:** V10288 a – **Design/Origin:** D. M. W. Mitglied der Deutschen Werkstätten – **Date:** 1920s – **Technique:** industrial double-weave, warp/weft: wool – **Object measurements:** H: 12.5 cm, W: 20 cm – **Description:** double rows of ochre brown and blue serrated lines alternate on a black ground – **Photo:** Esther Hoyer/ GRASSI Museum für Angewandte Kunst Leipzig.

266
Fabric sample folder – **Property:** GRASSI Museum für Angewandte Kunst Leipzig – **Inventory number:** V3973 – **Design/Origin:** Deutsche Textile Kunst (DeTeKu Rudolf Hiemann) – **Date:** 1920s – **Technique:** wool, textile, board – **Object measurements:** closed H: 32.5 cm, W: 33 cm – **Description:** carton folder with the title *Neue Coversstoffe für Couch, Sofa, Sessel, mit passenden eulanisierten Uni-Plüschen als Einfassung oder für kleine Chairsitze, passende Vorhangstoffe dazu lieferbar.* Included are patterns of woollen fabrics with floral motifs of large, round leaves overlaid with narrow leaves. Inscription on cardboard 'DETEKU chenille-gobelin, ca. 130 cm breit, Rapporthöhe 35 cm', Nr. „13141 – **Notes:** probably acquired at a Grassi Fair in the 1920s – **Photo:** Esther Hoyer/GRASSI Museum für Angewandte Kunst Leipzig.

267/268
Furniture cover fabric – **Property:** GRASSI Museum für Angewandte Kunst Leipzig – **Inventory number:** 1997.402 – **Design/Origin:** Sigmund von Weech, handwoven, Sigmund von Weech, Schaftlach – **Date:** around 1925–29 – **Technique:** weave, warp: cotton wool, viscose: weft; viscose, cotton wool (chenille) – **Object measurements:** H: 61 cm, W: 41 cm – **Description:** geometrical patterned fabric in white, black, orange and two shades of blue. The weave and colour changes create a pattern in which stripes and colour blocks are intertwined. The weave creates alternate smooth surfaces and pile sections. A selvedge has been preserved on the left edge, the irregularity of which suggests
that the fabric was woven on a hand loom – **Notes:** the fabric was probably created together with designs of tubular steel furniture for the company Junkers & Co., Dessau. See cover fabric, Sigmund von Weech, 1929, Städt. Kunstsammlung Chemnitz, in *Europäisches Textildesign der 20er Jahre*, Zurich/New York 1998, p. 46; no. 19; acquired from art dealer 1997 – **Photo:** Esther Hoyer/GRASSI Museum für Angewandte Kunst Leipzig.

269
Decorative fabric – **Property:** GRASSI Museum für Angewandte Kunst Leipzig – **Inventory number:** 1967.102 – **Design/Origin:** Weberhof Lübz, Gottfried Hensen, Gretel Schmitz – **Date:** 1967 – **Technique:** double-weave, wool on cotton warp – **Object measurements:** H: 136 cm, W: 300 cm – **Description:** staggered red rectangles and frames on a grey ground – **Notes:** the weave was acquired from the Weberhof Lübz in 1967, together with fifteen others in other colours and patterns – **Photo:** Esther Hoyer/GRASSI Museum für Angewandte Kunst Leipzig.

267/268
Möbelstoff – **Eigentum:** GRASSI Museum für Angewandte Kunst Leipzig – **Inventarnummer:** 1997.402 – **Entwurf/Herstellung/Herstellungsort:** Sigmund von Weech, Handweberei Sigmund von Weech, Schaftlach – **Datierung:** um 1925 bis 1929 – **Technologie:** Gewebe, Kette: Baumwolle, Viskose; Schuss: Viskose, Baumwolle (Chenille) – **Objektmaße:** H: 61 cm, B: 41 cm – **Beschreibung:** Geometrisch gemustertes Gewebe in Weiß, Schwarz, Orange und zwei Blautönen. Durch Bindungs- und Farbwechsel entsteht ein Muster, in dem Streifenpartien und Farbblöcke miteinander verschränkt werden. Durch die Bindung entsteht ein Wechsel aus glatten Flächen und Florpartien. Am linken Rand ist eine Webekante erhalten, deren Unregelmäßigkeit vermuten lässt, dass der Stoff auf einem Handwebstuhl entstand – **Anmerkung:** Das Gewebe entstand wahrscheinlich zusammen mit Entwürfen von Stahlrohrmöbeln für die Firma Junkers & Co, Dessau. vgl. Bezugsstoff, Siegmund von Weech, 1929, Städt. Kunstsammlung Chemnitz, in: *Europäisches Textildesign der 20er Jahre*. Zürich/New York 1998, S. 46; Nr. 19; Ankauf im Kunsthandel 1997 – **Fotografie:** Esther Hoyer/GRASSI Museum für Angewandte Kunst Leipzig.

269
Dekorationsstoff – **Eigentum:** GRASSI Museum für Angewandte Kunst Leipzig – **Inventarnummer:** 1967.102 – **Entwurf/Herstellung/Herstellungsort:** Weberhof Lübz, Gottfried Hensen, Gretel Schmitz – Datierung: 1967 – **Technologie:** Doppelgewebe, Wolle auf Baumwollkette – **Objektmaße:** H: 136 cm, B: 300 cm – Beschreibung: Versetzt angeordnete, rote Rechtecke und Rahmen auf grauem Grund – **Anmerkung:** Das Gewebe wurde 1967 zusammen mit 15 weiteren in anderen Farb- und Musterstellungen vom Weberhof Lübz erworben – **Fotografie:** Esther Hoyer/GRASSI Museum für Angewandte Kunst Leipzig.

270
Dekorationsstoff – **Eigentum:** GRASSI Museum für Angewandte Kunst Leipzig – **Inventarnummer:** 1967.98 – **Entwurf/Herstellung/Herstellungsort:** Weberhof Lübz, Gottfried Hensen, Gretel Schmitz – **Datierung:** 1967 – **Technologie:** Doppelgewebe, Wolle auf Baumwollkette – **Objektmaße:** H: 136 cm, 310 cm – **Beschreibung:** auf weißem Grund mäanderähnliche, jedoch unterbrochene Formen in Schwarz – **Anmerkung:** Das Gewebe wurde 1967 zusammen mit 15 weiteren in anderen Farb- und Musterstellungen vom Weberhof Lübz erworben – **Fotografie:** Esther Hoyer/GRASSI Museum für Angewandte Kunst Leipzig.

271
(Detail aus 289).

272
Borte mit Fransen – **Eigentum:** GRASSI Museum für Angewandte Kunst Leipzig – **Inventarnummer:** V2858 – **Entwurf/Herstellung/Herstellungsort:** Spanien – Datierung: 17. Jh. – **Technologie:** Gewebte Borte mit langen Fransen in roter, gelber und blauer Seide; je fünf Bündel einer Farbe in vier Reihen abgebunden – **Objektmaße:** H: 11,5 cm, B: 29–34 cm – **Anmerkung:** Erwerb vor 1896 (alte Inventarnummer I.2098 – Restaurierung: 2022 Carola Berriola – **Fotografie:** Esther Hoyer/GRASSI Museum für Angewandte Kunst Leipzig.

273
Borte mit Fransen – **Eigentum:** GRASSI Museum für Angewandte Kunst Leipzig – **Inventarnummer:** V1276 – **Entwurf/Herstellung/Herstellungsort:** Italien oder Spanien – **Datierung:** 17. Jh. – **Technologie:** Gewebte Borte mit langen, abgebundenen Fransen in blauer Seide und versilbertem Kupferlahn, Pompons aus grüner, roter, brauner und cremfarbener Seide – **Objektmaße:** H: 23 cm, B: 23 cm – **Anmerkung:** Erwerb vor 1896 (alte Inventarnummer I.2004) – Restaurierung: 2022 Carola Berriola – **Fotografie:** Esther Hoyer/GRASSI Museum für Angewandte Kunst Leipzig.

270
Decorative fabric – **Property:** GRASSI Museum für Angewandte Kunst Leipzig – **Inventory number:** 1967.98 – **Design/Origin:** Weberhof Lübz, Gottfried Hensen, Gretel Schmitz – **Date:** 1967 – **Technique:** double-weave, wool on cotton warp – **Object measurements:** H: 136 cm, W: 310 cm – **Description:** on white ground meander-like but interrupted shapes in black – **Notes:** the weave was acquired from the Weberhof Lübz in 1967, together with fifteen others in other colours and patterns – **Photo:** Esther Hoyer/GRASSI Museum für Angewandte Kunst Leipzig.

271
(detail from 289).

272
Border with fringe – **Property:** GRASSI Museum für Angewandte Kunst Leipzig – **Inventory number:** V2858 – **Design/Origin:** Spain – **Date:** 17th century – **Technique:** woven border with long fringe in red, yellow and blue silk; five bundles of one colour bound in four rows – **Object measurements:** H: 11.5 cm, W: 29–34 cm – **Notes:** acquisition before 1896 (old inventory number I.2098) – **Conservation:** 2022 by Carola Berriola – **Photo:** Esther Hoyer/GRASSI Museum für Angewandte Kunst Leipzig.

273
Border with fringe – **Property:** GRASSI Museum für Angewandte Kunst Leipzig – **Inventory number:** V1276 – **Design/Origin:** Italy or Spain – **Date:** 17th century – **Technique:** woven border with long, bound fringes in blue silk and silver-plated copper lamella, pompoms in green, red, brown and cream silk – **Object measurements:** H: 23 cm, W: 23 cm – **Notes:** acquisition before 1896 (old inventory number I.2004) – **Conservation:** 2022 by Carola Berriola – **Photo:** Esther Hoyer/GRASSI Museum für Angewandte Kunst Leipzig.

274
Sample of macramé borders – **Property:** GRASSI Museum für Angewandte Kunst Leipzig – **Inventory number:** V2128 – **Design/Origin:** Germany – **Date:** 17th century – **Technique:** macramé, coloured silk – **Object measurements:** sheet size: H: 16.5 cm, W: 10 cm, borders: H: approx. 6 cm, W: 1–3 cm – **Notes:** old inventory (acquisition before 1892 [published in Kusch]) – **Conservation:** single sheets bound in a book ca. 1923 – **Literature:** single samples published in Kusch 1892, plate 18; Schütte 1914, p. 13 – **Photo:** Esther Hoyer/GRASSI Museum für Angewandte Kunst Leipzig.

275
Border with fringes and tassels – **Property:** GRASSI Museum für Angewandte Kunst Leipzig – **Inventory number:** Posamenten I.127 – **Design/Origin:** Italy – **Date:** 17th century – **Technique:** wide border worked in red silk, with two layers of linen fabric backed with an intermediate layer of cardboard; pattern repeat: medallions formed by two gimps wrapped around with silk threads, crossing each other regularly; alternately filled with ballet flowers and areas with open pile; curved scalloped border with small tassels – **Object measurements:** H: 16 cm, W: 40 cm – **Notes:** acquired from Zatelli, Munich 1892 – **Conservation:** 2022 by Carola Berriola – **Photo:** Esther Hoyer/GRASSI Museum für Angewandte Kunst Leipzig.

276
Border with macramé and fringes – **Property:** GRASSI Museum für Angewandte Kunst Leipzig – **Inventory**

274
Muster von Makrameeborten – **Eigentum:** GRASSI Museum für Angewandte Kunst Leipzig – **Inventarnummer:** V2128 – **Entwurf/Herstellung/Herstellungsort:** Deutschland – **Datierung:** 17. Jahrhundert – **Technologie:** Makramee, farbige Seide – **Objektmaße:** Blattgröße: H: 16,5 cm, B: 10 cm, Bortenabschnitte: H: ca. 6 cm, B: 1–3 cm – **Anmerkung:** Alter Bestand (Erwerb vor 1892 [Publikation bei Kumsch]) – **Restaurierung:** Einzelblätter um 1923 als Buch zusammengebunden – **Literatur:** einzelne Musterbeispiele publiziert bei Kumsch 1892, Taf. 18; Schütte 1914, S. 13. – **Fotografie:** Esther Hoyer/GRASSI Museum für Angewandte Kunst Leipzig.

275
Borte mit Fransen und Quasten – **Eigentum:** GRASSI Museum für Angewandte Kunst Leipzig – **Inventarnummer:** Posamenten I.127 – **Entwurf/Herstellung/Herstellungsort:** Italien – **Datierung:** 17. Jh. – **Technologie:** Breite in roter Seide gearbeitete Borte, mit zwei Lagen Leinengewebe mit einer Zwischenlage aus Pappe hinterlegt; Musterrapport: Medaillons, die durch zwei mit Seidenfäden umwickelte, sich regelmäßig überkreuzende angelegte Gimpen gebildet werden; im Wechsel gefüllt mit Ballettenblüten und Feldern mit offenem Flor; gebogte Fransenborte mit kleinen Quasten – **Objektmaße:** H: 16 cm, B: 40 cm – **Anmerkung:** erworben v. Zatelli, München 1892 – **Restaurierung:** Carola Berriola 2022 – **Fotografie:** Esther Hoyer/GRASSI Museum für Angewandte Kunst Leipzig.

276
Borte mit Makramee und Fransen – **Eigentum:** GRASSI Museum für Angewandte Kunst Leipzig – **Inventarnummer:** V8528 – **Entwurf/Herstellung/Herstellungsort:** Italien (?) – **Datierung:** 17. Jahrhundert (?) – **Technologie:** Gewebte, geknüpfte und geflochtene Borte mit aufgesetzten Pompons und langen Fransen aus roter Seide – **Objektmaße:** H: 20,3 cm, B: 23,5 cm – **Anmerkung:** Erwerb vor 1896 (alte Inventarnummer I 2002) aus der Sammlung des Aachener Kanonikers Dr. Franz Bock – **Restaurierung:** 2022 gereinigt – **Fotografie:** Esther Hoyer/GRASSI Museum für Angewandte Kunst Leipzig.

277
Borte – **Eigentum:** GRASSI Museum für Angewandte Kunst Leipzig – **Inventarnummer:** V8519 – **Entwurf/Herstellung/Herstellungsort:** Italien (?) – **Datierung:** 17. Jahrhundert (?) – **Technologie:** Gewebeborte mit Quästchen aus roter Seide; durch die unterschiedliche Länge der Fransen und variierende Größe der Quästchen entsteht eine gebogte und räumlich ausschwingende Unterkante – **Objektmaße:** H: 5 cm, B: 22–23,5 cm – **Anmerkung:** Ankauf 1885 durch Stadtrat Hugo Scharf, Leipzig (alte Inventarnummer I 2252b) – **Restaurierung:** 2022 gereinigt – **Fotografie:** Esther Hoyer/GRASSI Museum für Angewandte Kunst Leipzig.

278
Borte – **Eigentum:** GRASSI Museum für Angewandte Kunst Leipzig – **Inventarnummer:** V8518 – **Entwurf/Herstellung/Herstellungsort:** Italien (?) – **Datierung:** Ende 17. Jahrhundert – **Technologie:** Gewebte Borte mit gedrehten Fransen und Quästchen in grüner und weißer Seide – **Objektmaße:** H: 4 cm, B: 29–31,5 cm – **Anmerkung:** Ankauf 1885 durch Stadtrat Hugo Scharf, Leipzig – **Fotografie:** Esther Hoyer/GRASSI Museum für Angewandte Kunst Leipzig.

279
Borte mit Gehänge – **Eigentum:** GRASSI Museum für Angewandte Kunst Leipzig – **Inventarnummer:** V9084 – **Entwurf/Herstellung/Herstellungsort:** unbekannt – **Datierung:** 19. Jh. – **Technologie:** Gimpenborte in weißer und grüner Seide, mit langen Gehängen aus gelben gedrehten Seidenschnüren, in weißer und hellgrüner Seide übersponnene Holzkugeln und sich nach oben verjüngende zylindrische Holzformen mit gelben, weißen, number: V8528 – **Design/Origin:** Italy? – **Date:** 17th century? – **Technique:** woven, knotted and braided border with attached pompoms and long fringe in red silk – **Object measurements:** H: 20.3 cm, W: 23.5 cm – **Notes:** acquired before 1896 (old inventory number I 2002) from the collection of the Aachen canon Dr Franz Bock – **Conservation:** cleaned in 2022 – **Photo:** Esther Hoyer/GRASSI Museum für Angewandte Kunst Leipzig.

277
Border – **Property:** GRASSI Museum für Angewandte Kunst Leipzig – **Inventory number:** V8519 – **Design/Origin:** Italy? – **Date:** 17th century? – **Technique:** woven border with tassels of red silk; through the different lengths of the fringes and the variable size of the tassels a curved and scalloped lower edge is created – **Object measurements:** H: 5 cm, W: 22–23.5 cm – **Notes:** acquired in 1885 from city councillor Hugo Scharf, Leipzig (old inventory number I 2252b) – **Conservation:** cleaned in 2022 – **Photo:** Esther Hoyer/GRASSI Museum für Angewandte Kunst Leipzig.

278
Border – **Property:** GRASSI Museum für Angewandte Kunst Leipzig – **Inventory number:** V8518 – **Design/Origin:** Italy? – **Date:** late 17th century – **Technique:** woven border with turned fringes and tassels in green and white silk – **Object measurements:** H: 4 cm, W: 29–31.5 cm – **Notes:** acquired in 1885 from city councillor Hugo Scharf, Leipzig – **Photo:** Esther Hoyer/GRASSI Museum für Angewandte Kunst Leipzig.

279
Border with pendants – **Property:** GRASSI Museum für Angewandte Kunst Leipzig – **Inventory number:** V9084 – **Design/Origin:** unknown – **Date:** 19th century – **Technique:** gimp border in white and green silk, with long pendants of yellow twisted silk cords, wooden balls spun over in white and light-green silk and cylindrical wooden forms tapering upwards with yellow, white, green and light-green ballets – **Object measurements:** H: 15.5 cm, W: 36 cm – **Notes:** with paper seal: 'Eigentum der Stadt Leipzig, Nr. 51, Leipzig, Nr. 51, Erworben 1876 auf der Kunst- und Kunstindustrie-Ausstellung, Glaspalast München [acquired 1876 at the Art and Art Industry Exhibition, Glaspalast Munich]' – **Conservation:** cleaned in 2022 – **Photo:** Esther Hoyer/GRASSI Museum für Angewandte Kunst Leipzig.

280
Border with pendants – **Property:** GRASSI Museum für Angewandte Kunst Leipzig – **Inventory number:** V8494 a, b – **Design/Origin:** unknown – **Date:** 19th century – **Technique:** woven border in salmon and yellow silk, with pendants of salmon and yellow silk cords with wooden beads, long twisted wooden forms and ballets covered with yellow and salmon silk – **Object measurements:** a: H: 11.8 cm, W: 8.5 cm; b: H: 12 cm, W: 7.5 cm – **Notes:** old inventory, acquired before 1945 – **Photo:** Esther Hoyer/GRASSI Museum für Angewandte Kunst Leipzig.

281
Border – **Property:** GRASSI Museum für Angewandte Kunst Leipzig – **Inventory number:** V3016 – **Design/Origin:** Italy – **Date:** early 19th century – **Technique:** woven border in yellow silk with white warp – **Object measurements:** H: 3 cm, W: 28.4 cm – **Notes:** acquired before 1945 from private collection, Munich – **Photo:** Esther Hoyer/GRASSI Museum für Angewandte Kunst Leipzig.

grünen und hellgrünen Balletten – **Objektmaße:** H: 15,5 cm, B: 36 cm – **Anmerkung:** mit Papiersiegel: Eigenthum der Stadt Leipzig, Nr. 51, Erworben 1876 auf der Kunst- und Kunstindustrie-Ausstellung, Glaspalast München – **Restaurierung:** 2022 gereinigt – **Fotografie:** Esther Hoyer/GRASSI Museum für Angewandte Kunst Leipzig.

280
Borte mit Gehänge – **Eigentum:** GRASSI Museum für Angewandte Kunst Leipzig – **Inventarnummer:** V8494 a,b – **Entwurf/Herstellung/Herstellungsort:** unbekannt – **Datierung:** 19. Jh. – **Technologie:** Gewebte Borte in lachsfarbener und gelber Seide, mit Gehängen aus lachsfarbenen und gelben Seidenschnüren mit Holzkugeln, langen gedrehten Holzformen und Balletten mit gelber und lachsfarbener Seide umsponnen – **Objektmaße:** a: H: 11,8 cm, B: 8,5 cm; b: H: 12 cm, B: 7,5 cm – **Anmerkung:** Alter Bestand, Erwerb vor 1945 – **Fotografie:** Esther Hoyer/GRASSI Museum für Angewandte Kunst Leipzig.

281
Borte – **Eigentum:** GRASSI Museum für Angewandte Kunst Leipzig – **Inventarnummer:** V3016 – **Entwurf/Herstellung/Herstellungsort:** Italien – **Datierung:** frühes 19. Jh. – **Technologie:** Gewebte Borte aus gelber Seide, mit weißer Kette – **Objektmaße:** H: 3 cm, B: 28,4 cm – **Anmerkung:** Erwerb vor 1945 aus Münchner Privatbesitz – **Fotografie:** Esther Hoyer/GRASSI Museum für Angewandte Kunst Leipzig.

Borte – **Eigentum:** GRASSI Museum für Angewandte Kunst Leipzig – **Inventarnummer:** V3001 – **Entwurf/Herstellung/Herstellungsort:** Italien – **Datierung:** 18. Jh. (?) – **Technologie:** Gewebte Borte aus gelber Seide, Musterung in Streifen durch aufgelegte verschieden stark gedrehte und offene Seidenfäden – **Objektmaße:** H: 2,7 cm, B: 15 cm – **Anmerkung:** Alter Bestand, Erwerb vor 1945 – **Fotografie:** Esther Hoyer/GRASSI Museum für Angewandte Kunst Leipzig.

Borte – **Eigentum:** GRASSI Museum für Angewandte Kunst Leipzig – **Inventarnummer:** V3008 – **Entwurf/Herstellung/Herstellungsort:** Italien – **Datierung:** 17./18. Jh. – **Technologie:** Gewebte Borte aus gelber Seide – **Objektmaße:** H: 2,4 cm, B: 25,2 cm – **Anmerkung:** Alter Bestand, Erwerb vor 1945 – **Fotografie:** Esther Hoyer/GRASSI Museum für Angewandte Kunst Leipzig.

282
Borte – **Eigentum:** GRASSI Museum für Angewandte Kunst Leipzig – **Inventarnummer:** V2994 – **Entwurf/Herstellung/Herstellungsort:** Italien – **Datierung:** 18. Jh. (?) – **Technologie:** Gewebte Borte aus weißer, gelber und roter Seide – **Objektmaße:** H: 2,3 cm, B: 24,8 cm – **Anmerkung:** Erwerb vor 1945 aus Münchner Privatbesitz – **Fotografie:** Esther Hoyer/GRASSI Museum für Angewandte Kunst Leipzig.

Borte – **Eigentum:** GRASSI Museum für Angewandte Kunst Leipzig – **Inventarnummer:** V3011 – **Entwurf/Herstellung/Herstellungsort:** Italien – **Datierung:** 18. Jh. (?) – **Technologie:** Gewebte Borte aus gelber, grüner und weißer Seide – **Objektmaße:** H: 2,6 cm, B: 25 cm – **Anmerkung:** Erwerb vor 1945 aus Münchner Privatbesitz – **Fotografie:** Esther Hoyer/GRASSI Museum für Angewandte Kunst Leipzig.

Borte – **Eigentum:** GRASSI Museum für Angewandte Kunst Leipzig – **Inventarnummer:** V3012 – **Entwurf/Herstellung/Herstellungsort:** Italien – **Datierung:** 17./18. Jh. – **Technologie:** Gewebte Borte aus gelber, blauer und weißer Seide – **Objektmaße:** H: 2,4 cm, B: 29,3 cm – **Anmerkung:** Alter Bestand, Erwerb vor 1945 – **Fotografie:** Esther Hoyer/GRASSI Museum für Angewandte Kunst Leipzig.

Border – **Property:** GRASSI Museum für Angewandte Kunst Leipzig – **Inventory number:** V3001 – **Design/Origin:** Italy – **Date:** 18th century? – **Technique:** woven border of yellow silk, patterned in stripes by applied silk threads, open and twisted to different degrees – **Object measurements:** H: 2.7 cm, W: 15 cm – **Notes:** old inventory, acquired before 1945 – **Photo:** Esther Hoyer/GRASSI Museum für Angewandte Kunst Leipzig.

Border – **Property:** GRASSI Museum für Angewandte Kunst Leipzig – **Inventory number:** V3008 – **Design/Origin:** Italy – **Date:** 17th/18th century – **Technique:** woven border in yellow silk – **Object measurements:** H: 2.4 cm, W: 25.2 cm – **Notes:** old inventory, acquired before 1945 – **Photo:** Esther Hoyer/GRASSI Museum für Angewandte Kunst Leipzig.

282
Border – **Property:** GRASSI Museum für Angewandte Kunst Leipzig – **Inventory number:** V2994 – **Design/Origin:** Italy – **Date:** 18th century? – **Technique:** woven border in white, yellow and red silk – **Object measurements:** H: 2.3 cm, W: 24.8 cm – **Notes:** acquired before 1945 from private collection, Munich – **Photo:** Esther Hoyer/GRASSI Museum für Angewandte Kunst Leipzig.

Border – **Property:** GRASSI Museum für Angewandte Kunst Leipzig – **Inventory number:** V3011 – **Design/Origin:** Italy – **Date:** 18th century? – **Technique:** woven border in yellow, green and white silk – **Object measurements:** H: 2.6 cm, W: 25 cm – **Notes:** acquired before 1945 from private collection, Munich – **Photo:** Esther Hoyer/GRASSI Museum für Angewandte Kunst Leipzig.

Border – **Property:** GRASSI Museum für Angewandte Kunst Leipzig – **Inventory number:** V3012 – **Design/Origin:** Italy – **Date:** 17th/18th century – **Technique:** woven border in yellow, blue and white silk – **Object measurements:** H: 2.4 cm, W: 29.3 cm – **Notes:** old inventory, acquired before 1945 – **Photo:** Esther Hoyer/GRASSI Museum für Angewandte Kunst Leipzig.

Border – **Property:** GRASSI Museum für Angewandte Kunst Leipzig – **Inventory number:** V3005 – **Design/Origin:** Italy – **Date:** 18th century? – **Technique:** woven border in pink, blue and white silk – **Object measurements:** H: 2.8 cm, W: 29.2 cm – **Notes:** acquired before 1945 from private collection, Munich – **Photo:** Esther Hoyer/GRASSI Museum für Angewandte Kunst Leipzig.

Border – **Property:** GRASSI Museum für Angewandte Kunst Leipzig – **Inventory number:** V3000 – **Design/Origin:** Italy – **Date:** 18th century? – **Technique:** woven trimming with border edge in metal; yellow and red silk; silver lamella – **Object measurements:** H: 3 cm, W: 34 cm – **Notes:** colours heavily faded on front, old inventory, acquired before 1945 – **Conservation:** cleaned in 2022 – **Photo:** Esther Hoyer/GRASSI Museum für Angewandte Kunst Leipzig.

Border – **Property:** GRASSI Museum für Angewandte Kunst Leipzig – **Inventory number:** V3013 Design/Origin: Italy – **Date:** 17th/18th century – **Technique:** woven border in yellow, blue and white silk – **Object measurements:** H: 3.5 cm, W: 29.5 cm – **Notes:** acquired before 1945 from private collection, Munich – **Photo:** Esther Hoyer/GRASSI Museum für Angewandte Kunst Leipzig.

Border – **Property:** GRASSI Museum für Angewandte Kunst Leipzig – **Inventory number:** V2980 – **Design/Origin:** Italy? – **Date:** unknown – **Technique:** small

Borte – **Eigentum:** GRASSI Museum für Angewandte Kunst Leipzig – **Inventarnummer:** V3005 – **Entwurf/Herstellung/Herstellungsort:** Italien – **Datierung:** 18. Jh. (?) – **Technologie:** Gewebte Borte aus rosafarbener, blauer und weißer Seide – **Objektmaße:** H: 2,8 cm, B: 29,2 cm – **Anmerkung:** Erwerb vor 1945 aus Münchner Privatbesitz – **Fotografie:** Esther Hoyer/GRASSI Museum für Angewandte Kunst Leipzig.

Borte – **Eigentum:** GRASSI Museum für Angewandte Kunst Leipzig – **Inventarnummer:** V3000 – **Entwurf/Herstellung/Herstellungsort:** Italien – **Datierung:** 18. Jh. (?) – **Technologie:** Gewebtes Band mit seitlichen Kanten in Metall; gelbe und rote Seide, Silberlahn – **Objektmaße:** H: 3 cm, B: 34 cm – **Anmerkung:** Farbigkeit auf der Vorderseite stark ausgeblichen, alter Bestand, Erwerb vor 1945 – **Restaurierung:** 2022 gereinigt – **Fotografie:** Esther Hoyer/GRASSI Museum für Angewandte Kunst Leipzig.

Borte – **Eigentum:** GRASSI Museum für Angewandte Kunst Leipzig – **Inventarnummer:** V3013 – **Entwurf/Herstellung/Herstellungsort:** Italien – **Datierung:** 17./18. Jh. – **Technologie:** Gewebte Borte aus gelber, blauer und weißer Seide – **Objektmaße:** H: 3,5 cm, B: 29,5 cm – **Anmerkung:** Erwerb vor 1945 aus Münchner Privatbesitz – **Fotografie:** Esther Hoyer/GRASSI Museum für Angewandte Kunst Leipzig.

Borte – **Eigentum:** GRASSI Museum für Angewandte Kunst Leipzig – **Inventarnummer:** V2980 – **Entwurf/Herstellung/Herstellungsort:** Italien (?) – **Datierung:** unbekannt – **Technologie:** Schmale gewebte Borte in gelber, grüner, roter und blauer Seide mit beidseitig nicht aufgeschnittenen Fransen in Blau, Grün, Rot, Weiß und Gelb – **Objektmaße:** H: 2 cm, B: 27,3 cm – **Anmerkung:** Alter Bestand, Erwerb vor 1945 – **Fotografie:** Esther Hoyer/GRASSI Museum für Angewandte Kunst Leipzig.

Borte – **Eigentum:** GRASSI Museum für Angewandte Kunst Leipzig – **Inventarnummer:** V2979 – **Entwurf/Herstellung/Herstellungsort:** Italien (?) – **Datierung:** unbekannt – **Technologie:** Schmale gewebte Borte in blauer, grüner, roter und gelber Seide mit beidseitig nicht aufgeschnittenen blauen Fransen – **Objektmaße:** H: 2 cm, B: 26,5 cm – **Anmerkung:** Alter Bestand, Erwerb vor 1945 – **Fotografie:** Esther Hoyer/GRASSI Museum für Angewandte Kunst Leipzig.

283
Borte – **Eigentum:** GRASSI Museum für Angewandte Kunst Leipzig – **Inventarnummer:** V12493 – **Entwurf/Herstellung/Herstellungsort:** unbekannt – **Datierung:** 17./18. Jh. (?) – **Technologie:** Metallspitze; teilweise vergoldeter Silberlahn auf Seidenseele und schmales versilbertes Kupferband durchgezogen; einseitig gebogene Unterkante – **Objektmaße:** H: 4,8 cm, B: 27,8 cm – **Anmerkung:** Alter Bestand, Erwerb vor 1945 – **Fotografie:** Esther Hoyer/GRASSI Museum für Angewandte Kunst Leipzig.

Borte – **Eigentum:** GRASSI Museum für Angewandte Kunst Leipzig – **Inventarnummer:** V12475 – **Entwurf/Herstellung/Herstellungsort:** unbekannt – **Datierung:** 18. Jh. (?) – **Technologie:** Wellenborte mit doppelseitigem Fächermotiv; Klöppelspitze; Metallfaden und -gimpe, vergoldeter Silberlahn auf Seidenseele, Kupferbänder – **Objektmaße:** H: 5,3 cm, B: 21 cm – **Beschreibung:** Wellenborte; abwechselnd ein gekipptes Rechteck mit Netz aus Metallbändern und ein Fächermotiv – **Anmerkung:** Alter Bestand, Erwerb vor 1896 (alte Inventarnummer I.2053) – **Fotografie:** Esther Hoyer/GRASSI Museum für Angewandte Kunst Leipzig.

Borte – **Eigentum:** GRASSI Museum für Angewandte Kunst Leipzig – **Inventarnummer:** V12484a – **Entwurf/Herstellung/Herstellungsort:** unbekannt – **Datierung:** 18. Jh. (?) – **Technologie:** Klöppelspitze; einseitig gebogte Klöppelspitzenborte mit Fächerformen, verbunden durch Netzgrund aus Gespinst;

woven border in yellow, green, red and blue silk with uncut fringes on both sides in blue, green, red, white and yellow – **Object measurements:** H: 2 cm, W: 27.3 cm – **Notes:** old inventory, acquired before 1945 – **Photo:** Esther Hoyer/GRASSI Museum für Angewandte Kunst Leipzig.

Border – **Property:** GRASSI Museum für Angewandte Kunst Leipzig – **Inventory number:** V2979 – **Design/Origin:** Italy? – **Date:** unknown – **Technique:** small woven border in blue, green, red and yellow silk with uncut blue fringes on both – **Object measurements:** H: 2 cm, W: 26.5 cm – **Notes:** old inventory, acquired before 1945 – **Photo:** Esther Hoyer/GRASSI Museum für Angewandte Kunst Leipzig.

283
Border – **Property:** GRASSI Museum für Angewandte Kunst Leipzig – **Inventory number:** V12493 – **Design/Origin:** unknown – **Date:** 17th/18th century? – **Technique:** metal lace; partially gilded silver lamella with silk core and small silvered copper thread pulled through; scalloped lower edge – **Object measurements:** H: 4.8 cm, W: 27.8 cm – **Notes:** old inventory, acquired before 1945 – **Photo:** Esther Hoyer/GRASSI Museum für Angewandte Kunst Leipzig.

Border – **Property:** GRASSI Museum für Angewandte Kunst Leipzig – **Inventory number:** V12475 – **Design/Origin:** unknown – **Date:** 18th century? – **Technique:** wave border with double-sided fan motif; bobbin lace; metal thread and gimp, gilt silver lamella on silk core, copper bands – **Object measurements:** H: 5.3 cm, W: 21 cm – **Description:** wave border; alternating a tilted rectangle with a net of metal bands and a fan motif – **Notes:** old inventory, acquired before 1896 (old inventory number I.2053) – **Photo:** Esther Hoyer/GRASSI Museum für Angewandte Kunst Leipzig.

Border – **Property:** GRASSI Museum für Angewandte Kunst Leipzig – **Inventory number:** V12484a – **Design/Origin:** unknown – **Date:** 18th century? – **Technique:** bobbin lace; bobbin lace border curved on one side with fan shapes, connected by a net ground of spun yarn; continuous gilded metal band at the upper edge of the net; gilded lamella, spun yarn with white silk core – **Object measurements:** H: 3.8 cm, W: 11.5 cm – **Notes:** borders with fan shapes were common in the 18th century but still produced in the 19th century; old inventory, acquired before 1945 – **Photo:** Esther Hoyer/GRASSI Museum für Angewandte Kunst Leipzig.

Gimp border – **Property:** GRASSI Museum für Angewandte Kunst Leipzig – **Inventory number:** V12477 – **Design/Origin:** unknown – **Date:** early 19th century? – **Technique:** wide gimp border with two interconnected rows; gimps: gilded lamella around silk thread?; spun yarn and gilded metal ribbon – **Object measurements:** H: 5 cm, W: 24 cm – **Notes:** acquired before 1896 (old inventory number. I.2094) – **Photo:** Esther Hoyer/GRASSI Museum für Angewandte Kunst Leipzig.

Wide gold border – **Property:** GRASSI Museum für Angewandte Kunst Leipzig – **Inventory number:** V12479 – **Design/Origin:** Germany or France – **Date:** 18th century – **Technique:** fragment with a sequence of three cartouches with net and block filling of spun yarn; metal lace in combination with inlay and appliqué technique, filling of the smaller cartouches backed with silk fabric and covered with gilded silver threads in appliqué technique; appliquéd gold gimp and motifs laid in loops;

Objekt und Bild | Objects and images **363**

durchlaufendes vergoldetes Metallband an der Oberkante des Netzes; vergoldeter Lahn, Gespinst mit weißer Seidenseele – **Objektmaße:** H: 3,8 cm, B: 11,5 cm – **Anmerkung:** Borten mit Fächerformen sind im 18. Jahrhundert verbreitet, werden aber auch noch im 19. Jahrhundert angefertigt; alter Bestand, Erwerb vor 1945 – **Fotografie:** Esther Hoyer/GRASSI Museum für Angewandte Kunst Leipzig.

Gimpenborte – **Eigentum:** GRASSI Museum für Angewandte Kunst Leipzig – **Inventarnummer:** V12477 – **Entwurf/Herstellung/Herstellungsort:** unbekannt – **Datierung:** Anfang 19. Jh. (?) – **Technologie:** Breite Gimpenborte mit zwei miteinander verbundenen Reihen; Gimpen: vergoldeter Goldlahn um Seidenfaden (?); Gespinst und vergoldetes Metallband – **Objektmaße:** H: 5 cm, B: 24 cm – **Anmerkung:** Erwerb vor 1896 (alte Nr. I.2094) – **Fotografie:** Esther Hoyer/GRASSI Museum für Angewandte Kunst Leipzig.

Breite Goldborte – **Eigentum:** GRASSI Museum für Angewandte Kunst Leipzig – **Inventarnummer:** V12479 – **Entwurf/Herstellung/Herstellungsort:** Deutschland oder Frankreich – **Datierung:** 18. Jh. – **Technologie:** Fragment mit Abfolge dreier Kartuschen mit Netzfüllung und Blöckchenfüllung aus Gespinst; Metallspitze in Kombination mit Intarsien- und Anlegetechnik, Füllung der kleineren Kartuschen u. a. mit Seidengewebe hinterlegt und flächig mit vergoldeten Silberfäden in Anlegetechnik überdeckt; angelegte Goldgimpen und in Schlaufen gelegte Motive; vergoldeter Silberlahn auf Seidenseele – **Objektmaße:** H: 8,3 cm, B: 28,6 cm – **Anmerkung:** Erwerb vor 1896 (alte Nr. I.1542) – **Fotografie:** Esther Hoyer/GRASSI Museum für Angewandte Kunst Leipzig.

Goldborte – **Eigentum:** GRASSI Museum für Angewandte Kunst Leipzig – **Inventarnummer:** V9150 – **Entwurf/Herstellung/Herstellungsort:** unbekannt – **Datierung:** 18. Jh. (?) – Technologie: Goldtresse, gewebt, mit Ausschweifbögen auf einer Seite, Musterrapport mit Blattmotiven und wellenförmiger Ranke; vergoldeter Silberlahn um Seidenseele in verschiedenen Stärken, Metallband, hellgelbe Seidenkette – **Objektmaße:** H: 2,2 cm, B: 45,8 cm – **Anmerkung:** Alter Bestand, Erwerb vor 1945 – **Fotografie:** Esther Hoyer/GRASSI Museum für Angewandte Kunst Leipzig.

Goldborte – **Eigentum:** GRASSI Museum für Angewandte Kunst Leipzig – **Inventarnummer:** V9151 – **Entwurf/Herstellung/Herstellungsort:** unbekannt – **Datierung:** um 1800 (?) – **Technologie:** Gewebte Goldborte, Randmotiv durch lange Schussfäden gebildet, gebogte Kante; Kettfäden aus heller Seide, Goldlahn um Seidenseele – **Objektmaße:** H: 1,7 cm, B: 42 cm – **Anmerkung:** Alter Bestand, Erwerb vor 1945 – **Fotografie:** Esther Hoyer/GRASSI Museum für Angewandte Kunst Leipzig.

Metallborte – **Eigentum:** GRASSI Museum für Angewandte Kunst Leipzig – **Inventarnummer:** V9149 – **Entwurf/Herstellung/Herstellungsort:** Deutschland (?) – **Datierung:** 18. Jh. (?) – **Technologie:** Gerade Silbertresse mit einseitigen Ausschweifbögen; vergoldeter Silberlahn um cremefarbene Seidenseele, gelbe Seidenkette – **Objektmaße:** H: 2,2 cm, B: 24,7 cm – **Anmerkung:** Erwerb vor 1896 (alte Nr. I.2601), nach Inventarbucheintrag Meisterstück mit Urkunde – **Fotografie:** Esther Hoyer/GRASSI Museum für Angewandte Kunst Leipzig.

284/285
Quaste – **Eigentum:** GRASSI Museum für Angewandte Kunst Leipzig – **Inventarnummer:** Posamenten I.118 – **Entwurf/Herstellung/Herstellungsort:** Italien – **Datierung:** 17. Jh./18. Jh. – **Technologie:** Kopf: Birnenförmiger Holzkörper mit rote gedrehten Seidenfäden und Silberfäden (Silberlahn auf gelber Seidenseele) im Würfelspikat umflochten, kleine silberne Knötchen zwischen den Würfelsegmenten; Corelle: rote Seiden- und Goldfäden, in kleine Schlaufen gelegt; Fransen: rote Seide und

gilded silver lamella on silk core – **Object measurements:** H: 8.3 cm, W: 28.6 cm – **Notes:** acquired before 1896 (old inventory number I.1542) – **Photo:** Esther Hoyer/GRASSI Museum für Angewandte Kunst Leipzig.

Gold border – **Property:** GRASSI Museum für Angewandte Kunst Leipzig – **Inventory number:** V9150 – **Design/Origin:** unknown – **Date:** 18th century? – **Technique:** gold braid, woven, scalloped on one side, pattern repeat with leaf motifs and wavy tendril; gilded silver lamella around silk core in various thicknesses, metal band, light-yellow silk warp – **Object measurements:** H: 2.2 cm, W: 45.8 cm – **Notes:** old inventory, acquired before 1945 – **Photo:** Esther Hoyer/GRASSI Museum für Angewandte Kunst Leipzig.

Gold border – **Property:** GRASSI Museum für Angewandte Kunst Leipzig – **Inventory number:** V9151 – **Design/Origin:** unknown – **Date:** ca. 1800? – **Technique:** woven gold border; border motif formed through long weft threads, scalloped edge; warp yarn in light silk, gold lamella around silk core – **Object measurements:** H: 1.7 cm, W: 42 cm – **Notes:** old inventory, acquired before 1945 – **Photo:** Esther Hoyer/GRASSI Museum für Angewandte Kunst Leipzig.

Metal border – **Property:** GRASSI Museum für Angewandte Kunst Leipzig – **Inventory number:** V9149 – **Design/Origin:** Germany? – **Date:** 18th century? – **Technique:** straight silver braid scalloped on one side; gilded silver lamella around cream-coloured silk core, yellow silk warp – **Object measurements:** H: 2.2 cm, W: 24.7 cm – **Notes:** acquired before 1896 (Old inventory number I.2601), according to inventory entry: master craftman's examination piece with certificate – **Photo:** Esther Hoyer/GRASSI Museum für Angewandte Kunst Leipzig.

284/285
Tassel – **Property:** GRASSI Museum für Angewandte Kunst Leipzig – **Inventory number:** Posamenten I.118 – **Design/Origin:** Italy – **Date:** 17th/18th century – **Technique:** head: pear-shaped wooden body with red twisted silk threads and silver threads (silver lantern on yellow silk core) woven around the cube, small silver nodules between the cube segments; corelle: red silk and gold threads laid in small loops; fringes: red silk and silver threads (silver lamella on yellow silk core); braided cords of alternating length placed around the fringe, loops terminated at the bottom by tassels in red silk with knotted head in gold thread; longer loops joined in the centre by ballet flowers – **Object measurements:** H: 22 cm, D: 12 cm – **Notes:** acquired in 1892 from Stefan Zatelli, Munich – **Conservation:** cleaned in 2022 – **Photo:** Esther Hoyer/GRASSI Museum für Angewandte Kunst Leipzig.

286
Tassel – **Property:** GRASSI Museum für Angewandte Kunst Leipzig – **Inventory number:** V11345 – **Design/Origin:** France – **Date:** 17th century – **Technique:** head: pear-shaped wooden form with black silk threads and silver threads (silver linen, white silk soul) woven around a mould. In the lower part of the lozenges black pile filling; corelle: black cut pile; second, cylindrical wooden form covered with black silk threads, above macramé of silver lamella on white silk core; fringe: black threads, a layer of silver thread (silver lamella, white silk core) on top – **Object measurements:** H: 37 cm W: 9 cm – **Notes:** acquired in 1885 by city councillor Hugo Scharf, Leipzig (old inventory number I 2274) – **Literature:** Kumsch

Silberfäden (Silberlahn auf gelber Seidenseele); darüber geflochtene Schnüre in alternierender Länge um die Franse gelegt, Schlaufen unten durch Spikatquästchen in roter Seide mit gestochenem Kopf in Goldfaden abgeschlossen; längere Schlaufen in der Mitte durch Ballettenblüten zusammengefasst – **Objektmaße:** H: 22 cm D: 12 cm – **Anmerkung:** Ankauf 1892 von Stefan Zatelli, München – **Restaurierung:** 2022 gereinigt – **Fotografie:** Esther Hoyer/GRASSI Museum für Angewandte Kunst Leipzig.

286
Quaste – **Eigentum:** GRASSI Museum für Angewandte Kunst Leipzig – **Inventarnummer:** V11345 – **Entwurf/Herstellung/Herstellungsort:** Frankreich – **Datierung:** 17. Jh. – **Technologie:** Kopf: Birnenförmige Holzform mit schwarzen Seidenfäden und Silberfaden (Silberlahn, weiße Seidenseele) in Fassonspikat umflochten. Im unteren Teil in den Rauten schwarze Florfüllung; Corelle: schwarzer geschnittener Flor; zweite, zylindrische Holzform überspannt mit schwarzen Seidenfäden, darüber Makramee aus Silberlahn auf weißer Seidenseele; Franse: schwarze Fäden, darüber eine Schicht Silberfaden (Silberlahn, weiße Seidenseele) – **Objektmaße:** H: 37 cm B: 9 cm – **Anmerkung:** Ankauf 1885 durch Stadtrat Hugo Scharf, Leipzig (alte Inventarnummer I 2274) – **Literatur:** Kumsch 1892, Taf. 9 – **Restaurierung:** 2022 gereinigt – **Fotografie:** Esther Hoyer/GRASSI Museum für Angewandte Kunst Leipzig.

287/288
Quaste – **Eigentum:** GRASSI Museum für Angewandte Kunst Leipzig – **Inventarnummer:** V13366 – **Entwurf/Herstellung/Herstellungsort:** Sachsen (Dresden) – **Datierung:** 17. Jh. – **Technologie:** Birnenförmiger Körper mit weißen gedrehten Leinenfäden in Fassonspikat umflochten mit vergoldeten Silberpailletten und Cantillen bestickt; Franse: äußerer Teil aus weißem Leinenfaden mit Blütenmotiven und drei Figuren in Schiffchenarbeit, mit vergoldeten Silberpailletten und Cantillen bestickt, mit zwei Drahtringen ausgesteift; am unteren Abschluss roten, verblichenen Seidenquästchen, innerer Teil aus gehäkelten Motiven aus Leinenfaden am Boden des Körpers befestigt, unten ebenfalls mit roten Seidenquästchen; – **Objektmaße:** H: 17 cm, D: 8 cm – **Anmerkung:** Alter Bestand (Erwerb vor 1892 [Publikation bei Kumsch]); weitere sehr ähnliche Quaste V1298, Vergleichsbeispiel in Dresden, Kunstgewerbemuseum, sowie Fragment im Metropolitan Museum of Art, NewYork (Ac.Nr.: 21.83.2) – **Literatur:** Kumsch 1892, Taf. 12 – **Fotografie:** Esther Hoyer/GRASSI Museum für Angewandte Kunst Leipzig.

289
Quaste – **Eigentum:** GRASSI Museum für Angewandte Kunst Leipzig – **Inventarnummer:** V1292 – **Entwurf/Herstellung/Herstellungsort:** Italien – **Datierung:** 17. Jh. – **Technologie:** Sanduhrförmiger Holzkörper mit gedrehten Seidenfäden überflochten, Dreieckmotive in verschiedenen Rottönen; Corelle: an beiden Enden der Holzform aus langem geschnittenen roten Seidenflor; Franse: gedrehte Schnürchen, durch Bindequasten aus Seide auf zwei Ebenen abgeschlossen, in verschiedenen Rottönen, einzelne in Schwarz (verblichen) – **Objektmaße:** H: 13 cm, D: 7 cm – **Anmerkung:** Farbigkeit der Seidenfäden ausgeblichen, Ankauf 1892 von Julius Böhler, München (alte Inventarnummer Posamente I.104) – **Restaurierung:** 2022 gereinigt – **Fotografie:** Esther Hoyer/GRASSI Museum für Angewandte Kunst Leipzig.

290
Quaste – **Eigentum:** GRASSI Museum für Angewandte Kunst Leipzig – **Inventarnummer:** V1308 – **Entwurf/Herstellung/Herstellungsort:** Italien od. Spanien – **Datierung:** 17. Jh. – **Technologie:** Geflochtenes Band aus vergoldetem Silberfaden zur Aufhängung; Kopf: mehrlagiges Bündel aus goldenen Balletten; Franse: Gehänge aus Crepinen, mit gelber Seide, vergoldetem Silberlahn und Metallbändern umwickelte Blattmotive einge-

1892, plate 9 – **Conservation:** cleaned in 2022 – **Photo:** Esther Hoyer/GRASSI Museum für Angewandte Kunst Leipzig.

287/288
Tassel – **Property:** GRASSI Museum für Angewandte Kunst Leipzig – **Inventory number:** V13366 – **Design/Origin:** Saxony (Dresden) – **Date:** 17th century – **Technique:** pear-shaped body braided with white twisted linen threads and embroidered with gilded silver sequins and cantillas; fringe: outer part white linen thread flower motifs and three figures in tatting embroidered with gilded silver sequins and cantillas, stiffened with two wire rings; at the lower end red, faded silk tassels, inner part of crocheted linen thread motifs attached to the bottom of the body, also with red silk tassels at the bottom – **Object measurements:** H: 17 cm, D: 8 cm – **Notes:** old inventory (acquired before 1892 [publication by Kumsch]); further very similar tassel V1298, comparative example in Dresden, Kunstgewerbemuseum, fragments at The Metropolitan Museum of Art, New York (acc. no: 21.83.2) – **Literature:** Kumsch 1892, plate 12 – **Photo:** Esther Hoyer/GRASSI Museum für Angewandte Kunst Leipzig.

289
Tassel – **Property:** GRASSI Museum für Angewandte Kunst Leipzig – **Inventory number:** V1292 – **Design/Origin:** Italy – **Date:** 17th century – **Technique:** hourglass-shaped wooden body overlaid with twisted silk threads, triangular motifs in various shades of red; corelle: at both ends of the wooden form of long red cut silk pile; fringe: twisted laces, terminated by binding tassels in silk on two levels, in various shades of red, some in black (faded) – **Object measurements:** H: 13 cm, D: 7 cm – **Notes:** silk thread colour faded, acquired in 1892 from Julius Böhler, Munich (old inventory number Posamente I.104) – **Conservation:** cleaned in 2022 – **Photo:** Esther Hoyer/GRASSI Museum für Angewandte Kunst Leipzig.

290
Tassel – **Property:** GRASSI Museum für Angewandte Kunst Leipzig – **Inventory number:** V1308 – **Design/Origin:** Italy or Spain – **Date:** 17th century – **Technique:** braided ribbon of gilded silver thread for hanging; head: multilayered bundle of golden ballets; fringe: hangings of crépine, with yellow silk, gilded silver lamella and metal bands wrapped around leaf motifs framed by cantillas, golden ballets and sequins in different sizes; silver, gilded – **Object measurements:** H: 14 cm, D: 6 cm – **Notes:** acquired in 1892 by Stefan Zatelli, Munich, an almost identical tassel was already acquired there in 1890 (inv. no. V1304) – **Literature:** Kumsch 1892, plate 12 – **Photo:** Esther Hoyer/GRASSI Museum für Angewandte Kunst Leipzig.

291/292
Tassel – **Property:** GRASSI Museum für Angewandte Kunst Leipzig – **Inventory number:** Posamenten I.121 – **Design/Origin:** Italy – **Date:** 18th century? – **Technique:** head: pear-shaped wooden form with white, yellow, pink, light-blue and black twisted silk threads braided around mould; corelle: yellow cut silk pile; fringe: yellow lace finished with yellow tassels; in the uppermost layer salmon-coloured lace finished with tassels of the same colour; above four hangings with crépines in two variations, with wooden balls, floral ballets with cantillas; finished with blue tassels – **Object measurements:** H: 13.5, D: 9 cm – **Notes:** acquired in 1892 from Zatelli, Munich – **Conservation:** cleaned in 2022 – **Photo:**

fasst von Cantillen, goldene Balletten und Pailletten in unterschiedlichen Größen; Silber, vergoldet – **Objektmaße**: H: 14 cm, D: 6 cm – **Anmerkung**: Ankauf 1892 von Stefan Zatelli, München, eine fast identische Quaste wurde dort bereits 1890 erworben (Inv.Nr. V1304) – **Literatur**: Kumsch 1892, Taf. 12 – **Fotografie**: Esther Hoyer/GRASSI Museum für Angewandte Kunst Leipzig.

291/292
Quaste – **Eigentum**: GRASSI Museum für Angewandte Kunst Leipzig – **Inventarnummer**: Posamenten I.121 – **Entwurf/Herstellung/Herstellungsort**: Italien – **Datierung**: 17. Jh. (?) – **Technologie**: Kopf: birnenförmige Holzform mit weißen, gelben, rosafarbenen, hellblauen und schwarzen gedrehten Seidenfäden in Fassonspikat umflochten; Corelle: geschnittener gelber Seidenflor; Franse: gelbe Schnürchen mit gelben Bindequasten abgeschlossen; in der obersten Lage lachsfarbene Schnürchen mit gleichfarbigen Bindequasten als Abschluss; darüber vier Gehänge mit Crepinen in zwei Varianten, mit umlegten Holzkugeln, Blütenballetten mit Cantillen; Abschluss durch blaue Bindequasten – **Objektmaße**: H: 13,5, D: 9 cm – **Anmerkung**: Ankauf 1892 von Zatelli, München – **Restaurierung**: 2022 gereinigt – **Fotografie**: Esther Hoyer/GRASSI Museum für Angewandte Kunst Leipzig.

293
Quaste – **Eigentum**: GRASSI Museum für Angewandte Kunst Leipzig – **Inventarnummer**: V1295 – **Entwurf/Herstellung/Herstellungsort**: Deutschland (?) – **Datierung**: 18. Jh. – **Technologie**: Körper und Fransen aus Seidenbändern in verschiedenen Farben; Fransen: Gehänge mit Crepinen und Blüten in verschiedenen Techniken, darunter Bündel aus roten und grünen Schleifen – **Objektmaße**: H: 15 cm, D: 5 cm – **Anmerkung**: Alter Bestand (Erwerb vor 1892 [Publikation bei Kumsch]); Farbigkeit teilweise stark verblichen – **Literatur**: Kumsch 1892,Taf. 12 – **Restaurierung**: 2022 (C. Berriola) – **Fotografie**: Esther Hoyer/GRASSI Museum für Angewandte Kunst Leipzig.

294
Quaste – **Eigentum**: GRASSI Museum für Angewandte Kunst Leipzig – **Inventarnummer**: V1283 – **Entwurf/Herstellung/Herstellungsort**: unbekannt – **Datierung**: 18. Jh. – **Technologie**: Kopf: birnenförmiger Holzkörper mit weißen, gelben und grünen gedrehten Schnüren und Balletten (Kupferstreifen mit Seide umsponnen) in Fassonspikat umflochten; Corelle: geschnittener Flor in Gelb; Fransen: gedrehte Schnürchen; Gehänge aus grünen Balletten, roten Gimpenblüten und weißen Drellierfransen – **Objektmaße**: H: 21 cm, D: 9 cm – **Anmerkung**: Alter Bestand, Erwerb vor 1945 – **Restaurierung**: 2022 gereinigt – **Fotografie**: Esther Hoyer/GRASSI Museum für Angewandte Kunst Leipzig.

295
Quaste mit Ballettengehängen – **Eigentum**: GRASSI Museum für Angewandte Kunst Leipzig – **Inventarnummer**: V11349 – **Entwurf/Herstellung/Herstellungsort**: unbekannt – **Datierung**: 18. Jh. Technologie: Kopf: zwei (?) übereinandergesetzte Holzformen mit weißem Leinenfaden gerollt, im unteren Teil mit blauen Balletten im Spikatknoten belegt; Colette: in drei Reihen aus weißen und blauen in kleine Schlaufen gelegten Fäden; Fransen: weiße Leinenfäden; darüber Crepinen aus Balletten und Gimpen in Blütenform in hellblauer Seide – **Objektmaße**: H: 18 cm, D: 9,5 cm – **Anmerkung**: Alter Bestand (Erwerb vor 1892 [Publikation bei Kumsch]) – **Literatur**: Kumsch 1892, Taf. 11 – **Restaurierung**: 2022 gereinigt – **Fotografie**: Esther Hoyer/GRASSI Museum für Angewandte Kunst Leipzig.

296
Quaste – **Eigentum**: GRASSI Museum für Angewandte Kunst Leipzig – **Inventarnummer**: V11358 – **Entwurf/Herstellung/Herstellungsort**: Frankreich (?) – **Datierung**: Ende 18. Jh. –

Esther Hoyer/GRASSI Museum für Angewandte Kunst Leipzig.

293
Tassel – **Property**: GRASSI Museum für Angewandte Kunst Leipzig – **Inventory number**: V1295 – **Design/Origin**: Germany? – **Date**: 18th century – **Technique**: body and fringes of silk ribbons in different colours; fringes: pendants with crépines and flowers in different techniques, including bundles of red and green ribbon – **Object measurements**: H: 15 cm, D: 5 cm – **Notes**: old inventory (acquired before 1892 [published by Kumsch]); colours heavily faded in parts – **Literature**: Kumsch 1892, plate 12 – **Conservation**: 2022 by Carola Berriola – **Photo**: Esther Hoyer/GRASSI Museum für Angewandte Kunst Leipzig.

294
Tassel – **Property**: GRASSI Museum für Angewandte Kunst Leipzig – **Inventory number**: V1283 – **Design/Origin**: unknown – **Date**: 18th century – **Technique**: head: pear-shaped wooden body with white, yellow and green twisted cords and ballets (copper strips spun with silk) in braided around mould; corelle: yellow cut pile; fringes: twisted cords; pendants of green ballets, red gimp flowers and white twisted drellier fringe – **Object measurements**: H: 21 cm, D: 9 cm – **Notes**: old inventory, acquired before 1945 – **Conservation**: cleaned in 2022 – **Photo**: Esther Hoyer/GRASSI Museum für Angewandte Kunst Leipzig.

295
Tassel with ballet pendants – **Property**: GRASSI Museum für Angewandte Kunst Leipzig – **Inventory number**: V11349 – **Design/Origin**: unknown – **Date**: 18th century – **Technique**: head: two? superimposed wooden forms rolled with white linen thread, the lower part covered with blue ballets in braided knots; colette: in three rows of white and blue threads laid in small loops; fringes: white linen threads; above them crépines of ballets and gimps in flower form in light-blue silk – **Object measurements**: H: 18 cm, D: 9.5 cm – **Notes**: old inventory (acquired before 1892 [published by Kumsch]) – **Literature**: Kumsch 1892, plate 11 – **Conservation**: cleaned in 2022 – **Photo**: Esther Hoyer/GRASSI Museum für Angewandte Kunst Leipzig.

296
Tassel – **Property**: GRASSI Museum für Angewandte Kunst Leipzig – **Inventory number**: V11358 – **Design/Origin**: France? – **Date**: late 18th century – **Technique**: head: narrow, conical wooden form rolled in light-blue twisted silk thread, over which salmon-coloured threads are interlaced; above this, a braided cross of white ballets and blue gimp, in between flowers with leaves of green, pink, violet, light-blue and champagne-coloured ballets, pistils of wound buttons with cantilla; corelle: at both ends of the wooden mould; of cut long pile in silk threads in all colours used; fringe: cut black threads – **Object measurements**: H: 33 cm, D: 5.5 cm – **Notes**: old inventory, acquired before 1896 (old inventory number I.2568) – **Conservation**: cleaned in 2022 – **Photo**: Esther Hoyer/GRASSI Museum für Angewandte Kunst Leipzig.

297
Tassel – **Property**: GRASSI Museum für Angewandte Kunst Leipzig – **Inventory number**: V11359 – **Design/Origin**: France? – **Date**: late 18th century – **Technique**: head: narrow, conical wooden form rolled in black twisted silk thread, over which salmon-coloured threads

Technologie: Kopf: schmale, kegelförmige Holzform in hellblauem gedrehtem Seidenfaden gerollt, darüber lachsfarbene Fäden gekettelt; darüber Spikatkreuz aus weißen Balletten und blauer Gimpe, dazwischen Blüten mit Blättern aus grünen, pinkfarbenen, violetten, hellblauen und champagnerfarbenen Balletten und Blütenstempeln aus gewickelten Knöpfen mit Cantille; Corelle: an beiden Enden der Holzfasson; aus geschnittenen langem Flor in Seidenfäden in allen verwendeten Farben; Franse: geschnittene schwarze Fäden – **Objektmaße:** H: 33 cm, D: 5,5 cm – **Anmerkung:** Alter Bestand, Erwerb vor 1896 (alte Inventarnummer I.2568) – **Restaurierung:** 2022 gereinigt – **Fotografie:** Esther Hoyer/GRASSI Museum für Angewandte Kunst Leipzig.

297
Quaste – **Eigentum:** GRASSI Museum für Angewandte Kunst Leipzig – **Inventarnummer:** V11359 – **Entwurf/Herstellung/Herstellungsort:** Frankreich (?) – **Datierung:** Ende 18. Jh. – **Technologie:** Kopf: schmale, kegelförmige Holzform in schwarzem gedrehtem Seidenfaden gerollt, darüber lachsfarbene Fäden gekettelt; darüber Spikatkreuz aus weißen Balletten und blauer Gimpe, dazwischen Blüten mit Blättern aus grünen, pinkfarbenen, hellblauen, hellrosanen, gelblich weißen und weißen Balletten und Blütenstempeln aus gewickelten Knöpfen mit Cantillen; Corelle: an beiden Enden der Holzfasson; aus geschnittenem langem Flor in Seidenfäden in allen verwendeten Farben; Franse: geschnittene mintfarbene Fäden – **Objektmaße:** H: 34, D: 5,5 cm – **Anmerkung:** Alter Bestand, Erwerb vor 1896 (alte Inventarnummer I.2567) – **Literatur:** Kumsch 1892, Taf. 11 – **Restaurierung:** 2022 gereinigt – **Fotografie:** Esther Hoyer/GRASSI Museum für Angewandte Kunst Leipzig.

298
Armlehnstuhl siehe 27.

299
Schichtmodell einer Armlehnpolsterung aus dem Klassizismus – **Eigentum:** Maximilian Busch – **Herstellung:** Maximilian Busch RiH – **Datierung:** 2021 – **Technologie:** Modell aus Buchenholz, Federleinen, Rosshaar – **Objektmaße:** 15 x 6 x 40 cm – **Fotografie:** LÖFFLER COLLECTION, Reichenschwand.

300/301
Modell einer Tonnenarmlehne aus dem Klassizismus – **Eigentum:** Maximilian Busch – **Herstellung:** Maximilian Busch RiH – **Datierung:** 2021 – **Technologie:** Modell aus Buchenholz, Federleinen, Rosshaar – **Objektmaße:** 8 x 7 x 26 cm – **Fotografie:** LÖFFLER COLLECTION, Reichenschwand.

302
siehe 39/40.

303
Lederkissen mit Feder-/ Daunenfüllung – **Eigentum:** Edmund Graf – **Entwurf:** unbekannt – **Herstellung:** unbekannt – **Datierung:** Frankreich, 1805–1810 – **Technologie:** Feder-/Daunenkissen in Lederhülle – **Polsteraufbau:** Das Sitzpolster besitzt eine Ziegen- oder Schafslederhülle, wobei die Unterseite aus festem Leinen (Inlett) besteht, um bei Benutzung das Entweichen der Luft zu ermöglichen – **Anmerkung:** Originalzustand mit Handnähten (überwendlich) – **Literatur:** Diderot / d'Alembert, Tafel IX; Edmund Graf/Albert Holtz: *Polsterungen von Barock bis Empire*, o. O. 2005 – **Restaurierung:** unrestauriert, im Originalzustand (Sicherung mit Klebestreifen) – **Fotografie:** LÖFFLER COLLECTION, Reichenschwand.

304/305
Carreau Piqué Kissen – **Eigentum:** Maximilian Busch – **Hersteller:** Maximilian Busch RiH – **Datierung:** 2021 – **Technologie:** Federleinen, Rosshaar – **Objektmaße:** 6 x 44,5 x 40 cm – **Fotografie:** LÖFFLER COLLECTION, Reichenschwand.

are warped; above it a braided cross of white ballets and blue gimp, in between flowers with leaves of green, pink, light-blue, light-pink, yellowish white and white ballets and pistils of wrapped buttons with cantilla; corelle: at both ends of the wooden form; cut long pile in silk threads in all colours used; fringe: cut mint-coloured threads – **Object measurements:** H: 34, D: 5.5 cm – **Notes:** old inventory, acquired before 1896 (old inventory number I.2567) – **Literature:** Kumsch 1892, plate 11 Conservation: cleaned in 2022 – **Photo:** Esther Hoyer/GRASSI Museum für Angewandte Kunst Leipzig.

298
Armchair, see 27.

299
Cutaway model of armrest padding from the Classicism period – **Property:** Maximilian Busch – **Origin:** Maximilian Busch RiH – **Date:** 2021 – **Technique:** model in beech, hessian, horsehair – **Object measurements:** 15 x 6 x 40 cm – **Photo:** LÖFFLER COLLECTION, Reichenschwand.

300/301
Model of bolster armrest from the Classicism period – **Property:** Maximilian Busch – **Origin:** Maximilian Busch RiH – **Date:** 2021 – **Technique:** model in beech, hessian, horsehair – **Object measurements:** 8 x 7 x 26 cm – **Photo:** LÖFFLER COLLECTION, Reichenschwand.

302
see 39/40.

303
Leather cushion with feather/down stuffing – **Property:** Edmund Graf – **Design:** unknown – **Origin:** France – **Date:** 1805–1810 – **Technique:** down cushion in leather cover – **Upholstery:** the seat cushion has a goatskin or sheepskin cover, with the underside made of strong linen (inlay) to allow air to escape during use – **Notes:** original condition with hand stitching (overedge stitch) – **Literature:** Diderot/d'Alembert, Plate IX; Edmund Graf and Albert Holtz, *Polsterungen von Barock bis Empire*, 2005 – **Conservation:** unrestored, in original condition (secured with tape) – **Photo:** LÖFFLER COLLECTION, Reichenschwand.

304/305
Carreau piqué cushion – **Property:** Maximilian Busch – **Producer:** Maximilian Busch RiH – **Date:** 2021 – **Technique:** hessian, horsehair – **Object measurements:** 6 x 44.5 x 40 cm – **Photo:** LÖFFLER COLLECTION, Reichenschwand.

306/307
Cutaway model of a carreau piqué cushion from the Classicism period – **Property:** Maximilian Busch – **Producer:** Maximilian Busch RiH – **Date:** 2021 – **Technique:** hessian, horsehair – **Object measurements:** 15 x 6 x 40 cm – **Photo:** LÖFFLER COLLECTION, Reichenschwand.

308
Upholstery materials – **workshop photo:** Cordula Fink.

309
Wooden box with tools for upholstery – **workshop photo:** Cordula Fink.

310/311
Flat padding on a drop-in seat frame – **Property:**

306/307
Schichtmodell eines Carreau Piqué Kissens aus dem Klassizismus – **Eigentum:** Maximilian Busch – **Hersteller:** Maximilian Busch RiH – **Datierung:** 2021 – **Technologie:** Federleinen, Rosshaar – **Objektmaße:** 15 x 6 x 40 cm – **Fotografie:** LÖFFLER COLLECTION, Reichenschwand.

308
Materialien für Polsterarbeiten – **Werkstattfoto:** Cordula Fink.

309
Holzkiste mit Werkzeug für Polsterarbeiten – **Werkstattfoto:** Cordula Fink.

310/311
Flachpolster auf Einlegerahmen – **Eigentum:** Reinhardt Roßberg – **Herstellung:** z. Zt. unbekannt – **Datierung:** Anfang 1920er Jahre – **Technologie:** Lederbezogener Flachpolstersitz – **Polsteraufbau:** über 2 x 2 Jutegurten befindet sich ein Jutefederleinen; darüber liegt eine Polsterung aus Holzwolle mit Feinwerkabdeckung; der Bezug ist ein handgewischtes, braunes Polsterleder (brüchig) – **Anmerkung:** Es handelt sich hierbei um einen typischen Flachpolstereinlegesitz; Polsterung mit Holzwolle als Folge der Nachwirkungen (Mangel) des Ersten Weltkriegs in Deutschland (bestimmte Materialien durften nicht verwendet werden – z. B. wurde Papier für Grundleinen verwendet) – **Objektmaße:** 32,5/40 x 38 cm – **Fotografie:** LÖFFLER COLLECTION, Reichenschwand.

312
Schichtmodell eines Kapok-Kissens – **Eigentum:** Bernd Lehmkuhl – **Herstellung:** Bernd Lehmkuhl RiH – **Technologie:** Gummikokos, Kapok, Leinen – **Objektmaße:** 7 x 50 x 50 cm – **Fotografie:** LÖFFLER COLLECTION, Reichenschwand.

313/314
Mooskissen – **Eigentum:** Reinhardt Roßberg – **Datierung:** um 1820 – **Technologie:** Festpolster, mehrfach garniert – **Polsteraufbau:** der Sitz verfügt über eine separat gearbeitete Vorderkante; die Kanten sind 2 x garniert und mit einfachem Matratzenstich versehen; Fragmente von Lasierfäden für die Pikierung sind noch vorhanden – **Anmerkung:** Als Polstermaterial wurde Moos in Ballen verwendet; das Fassonleinen ist grob handgewebt und dicht; einige handgeschmiedete Nägel befinden sich noch im Leinen – **Restaurierung:** unrestaurierter Originalbefund – **Fotografie:** LÖFFLER COLLECTION, Reichenschwand.

315
siehe 240.

316
siehe 116.

317/318
Schichtmodell eines Hocker-Kissens – **Eigentum:** Volker Engels – **Technologie:** Nadelholz, Federleinen, Rosshaar, Nessel, Leder – **Restaurierung:** Volker Engels RiH – **Fotografie:** LÖFFLER COLLECTION, Reichenschwand.

319/320
Schichtmodell eines Randformpolsters, ungarniert (Fragment) – **Eigentum:** Reinhardt Roßberg – **Datierung:** um 1800 – **Technologie:** Randformpolster mit Schnüren – **Polsteraufbau:** über einer 2 x 3-Gurtung mit handgewebten Gurten (Leinen?) liegt ein handgewebtes Leinen; das Federleinen ist an drei Seiten mit Überstand einfach ohne Unterlage am äußeren Zargenrand angenagelt (Hinterkante kein Überstand); an den drei Überstandsseiten wurde je ein Langstrohbündel einfach eingelegt und das Leinen nach innen geschlagen und mit groben, ungleich langen Heftstichen (ca. 2–5 cm) am Grundleinen angenäht; die fünf kleinen, handgedrehten Taillenfedern (Ring-

Reinhardt Roßberg – **Origin:** at present unknown – **Date:** early 1920s – **Technique:** leather-covered flat padded seat – **Upholstery:** 2 x 2 webbing with hessian cover; upholstery stuffing is wood fibre covered with fine tow; cover of antiqued brown leather (brittle) – **Notes:** typical flat padded drop-in seat; wood fibre stuffing as a result (scarcity) of the First World War in Germany (some materials could no longer be used, e.g., paper was used instead of hessian) – **Object measurements:** 32.5/40 x 38 cm – **Photo:** LÖFFLER COLLECTION, Reichenschwand.

312
Cutaway model of a kapok cushion – **Property:** Bernd Lehmkuhl – **Origin:** Bernd Lehmkuhl RiH – **Technique:** rubberised coconut fibre, kapok, linen – **Object measurements:** 7 x 50 x 50 cm – **Photo:** LÖFFLER COLLECTION, Reichenschwand.

313/314
Moose cushion – **Property:** Reinhardt Roßberg – **Date:** around 1820 – **Technique:** attached padding, stitched several times – **Upholstery:** seat with separately worked front edge; edges stitched two times with simple top stitch; fragments of brindle ties for second stuffing are still visible – **Notes:** bales of moss used as stuffing; scrim is rough, hand-woven and dense; a few hand-forged nails are still in the linen – **Conservation:** unrestored original condition – **Photo:** LÖFFLER COLLECTION, Reichenschwand.

315
See 240.

316
See 116.

317/318
Cutaway model of a stool cushion – **Property:** Volker Engels – **Technique:** softwood, hessian, horsehair, calico, leather – **Conservation:** Volker Engels RiH – **Photo:** LÖFFLER COLLECTION, Reichenschwand.

319/320
Cutaway model of an edge roll, unstitched (fragment) – **Property:** Reinhardt Roßberg – **Date:** around 1800 – **Technique:** edge roll upholstery with lashing – **Upholstery:** on top of a 2 x 3 webbing of hand-woven straps (linen?) is a hand-woven linen; hessian has been nailed to the outer frame rails on three sides without support, with overhang (no overhang on back edge); one long-straw bundle each has been placed on the three sides with overhang, the linen wrapped inside and stitched down to the hessian using rough uneven stitches (approx. 2–5 cm); the five small hand-turned waisted springs (dia. approx. 9 cm, 8 gauges) are attached unevenly with 6–7 simple stitches to the base; lashing has only survived in fragments, as have the threads used to sew in the hessian – **Object measurements:** 45/37 x 40 cm – **Notes:** an early lashing with unstitched edge roll on the used sides only – **Sponsors:** Stefan Meier Tischler (replica frame rail) – **Conservation:** Reinhardt Roßberg RiH – **Photo:** LÖFFLER COLLECTION, Reichenschwand.

321/322
Chair – **Property:** Reinhardt Roßberg – **Design:** at present unknown – **Origin:** at present unknown – **Date:** Biedermeier, around 1810 – **Technique:** sprung seat with edge roll – **Upholstery:** on a 2 x 2 webbing from hand-woven hemp straps with stitched-up edge roll on

368 Objekt und Bild | Objects and images

durchmesser ca. 9 cm, 8 Gänge) sind unregelmäßig mit einfachem Stich 6–7-fach am Grund angenäht; die Schnürung ist nur noch in Fragmenten erhalten, ebenso die Fäden vom Annähen des Federleinens – **Objektmaße:** 45/37 x 40 cm – **Anmerkung:** Es handelt sich um eine frühe Schnürung mit ungarnierter Randwulst nur an den Nutzkanten – **Fördernde:** Stefan Meier Tischler (Nachbau Zargenrahmen) – **Restaurierung:** Reinhard Roßberg RiH – **Fotografie:** LÖFFLER COLLECTION, Reichenschwand.

321/322
Stuhl – **Eigentum:** Reinhardt Roßberg – **Entwurf:** z. Zt. unbekannt – **Herstellung:** z. Zt. unbekannt – **Datierung:** Biedermeier, um 1810 – **Technologie:** Sitz mit Federung im Randformpolster – **Polsteraufbau:** auf einer 2 x 2-Gurtung aus handgewebten Hanfgurten mit umlaufender garnierter Kantenwulst stehen vier handgedrehte und geschnürte Taillenfedern; darüber sitzt ein mehrfach garniertes Polster mit Pikierung – **Bezug:** Leder mit per Handnaht und Keder angesetztem Lederstück; Befestigung mit Porzellankopfziernägeln – **Objektmaße:** 87 x 45 x 47 cm, Sitzhöhe: 48,5 x 45 x 41 cm – **Anmerkung:** Der Stuhl ist im überkommenen Zustand belassen, mit originalen Porzellankopfziernägel – **Fördernde:** Stefan Oswald RiH (Bezugsleder) – **Restaurierung:** Torsten Otto RiH (Untersuchung und Rekonstruktion), Möbelrestaurierung Reichardt (Holzergänzungen), Thomas Andersch Dipl. Rest. (Oberfläche) – **Fotografie:** LÖFFLER COLLECTION, Reichenschwand.

323
Modell einer geschnürten Federung – **Eigentum:** Torsten Otto RiH – **Entwurf:** z. Zt. unbekannt – **Herstellung:** Tischlerei Schrickel Markkleeberg, Torsten Otto RiH – **Datierung:** 2022 – **Technologie:** Buchenholzrahmen, Gurtung mit Schnürung – **Objektmaße (Rahmen):** 54 x 57 cm – **Fotografie:** LÖFFLER COLLECTION, Reichenschwand.

324–347
Serie von Filmstills zur geschnürten Federung (einem der Filme zur Ausstellung entnommen) – **Fotografie/Film:** Cordula Fink.

348–359
Serie von Filmstills zur Capitonné-Heftung (einem der Filme zur Ausstellung entnommen) – **Fotografie/Film:** Cordula Fink.

360–371
Serie von Filmstills zu Garnierarbeiten (einem der Filme zur Ausstellung entnommen) – **Fotografie/Film:** Cordula Fink.

372
Karikatur aus dem *Kladderadatsch*, Berlin, um 1850, Archiv Thomas Schriefers.

all sides, four hand-turned and lashed waisted springs; on top stitched-up padding with stuffing – **Cover:** leather with leather piece attached by hand-sewing and piping; tacked down with porcelain-head decorative nails – **Object measurements:** 87 x 45 x 47 cm, seat: 48.5 x 45 x 41 cm – **Notes:** chair in original condition, with original porcelain-head decorative nails – **Sponsors:** Stefan Oswald RiH (cover leather) – **Conservation:** Torsten Otto RiH (examination and reconstruction), furniture conservator Reinhardt Reichardt RiH (wooden add-ons), Thomas Andersch Dipl. Rest. (surface) – **Photo:** LÖFFLER COLLECTION, Reichenschwand.

323
Model of lashed springing – **Property:** Torsten Otto RiH – **Design:** at present unknown – **Origin:** Tischlerei Schrickel Markkleeberg, Torsten Otto RiH – **Date:** 2022 – **Technique:** beech frame, webbing with lashing – **Object measurements (frame):** 54 x 57 cm – **Photo:** LÖFFLER COLLECTION, Reichenschwand.

324–347
Series of still frames on lashed springing (from a video made for the exhibition) – **Photo/film:** Cordula Fink.

348–359
Series of still frames on deep-buttoning (from a video made for the exhibition) – **Photo/film:** Cordula Fink.

360–371
Series of still frames on stuffing, bridling and tufting (from a video made for the exhibition) – **Photo/film:** Cordula Fink.

372
Carricature from *Kladderadatsch* magazine, Berlin, ca. 1850, Archive Thomas Schriefers.

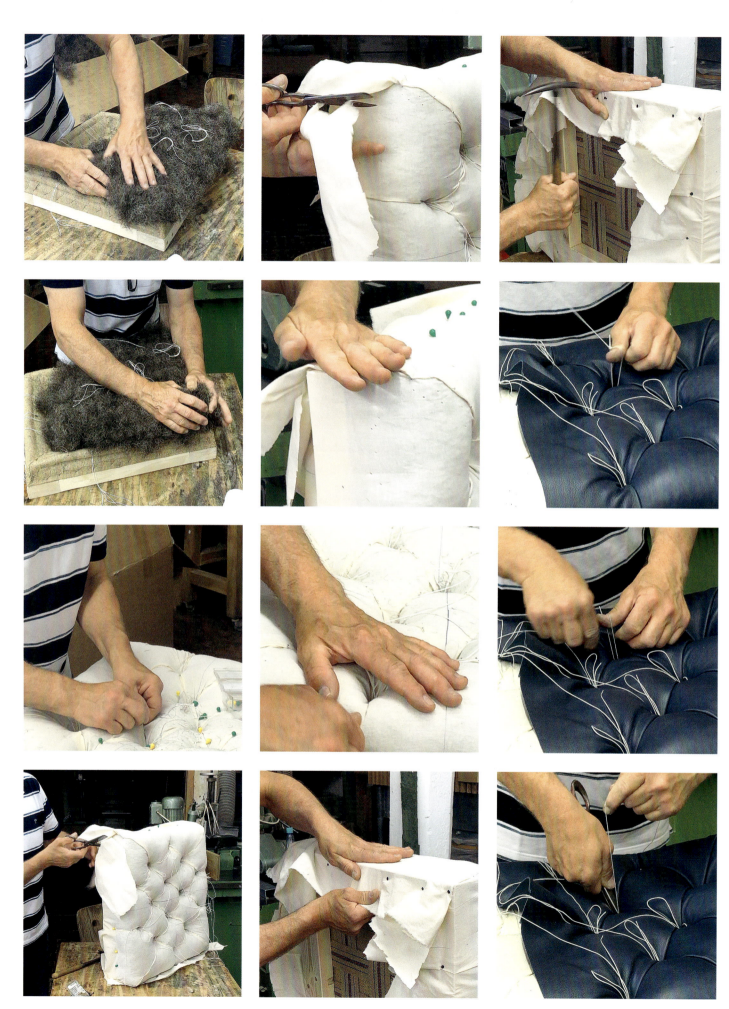

348–359
Filmstills zur Capitonné-Heftung

348–359
Stil frame showing deep-buttoning

370

Anmerkungen

1. Vgl. dazu Walter Benjamins Ausführungen zum schönen Schein, Benjamin 1961, S. 60. Benjamin 1961, S. 60.
2. Robert Maria Stieg: *Warenprobe*, in: Stieg/Hammerschmied 1979, S. 45.
3. A. a. o.
4. Die Dissertationsschrift trug den Titel: *Der Niedergang des Tapezier- und Polsterhandwerks als Produktionsgewerbe*. Vorgelegt zur Erlangung der Würde eines Doktors der wirtschaftlichen Staatswissenschaften der Rechts- und Staatswissenschaftlichen Fakultät der Martin Luther Universität Halle-Wittenberg durch Max Genath, Diplom-Kaufmann aus Dresden, bei Professor Dr. Jahn, Dresden 1935, vgl. Genath 1935.
5. Ebd., S. 40.
6. Ebd., S. 41/42.
7. Vgl. dazu eine fotografische Abbildung in: Köppen/Breuer 1904, S. 73.
8. Das Fresko wird u. a. abgebildet in: Campbell 2018, S. 208.
9. Der Typus des Pfostenstuhls verweist auf gebräuchliche Bauformen des Mittelalters und wird dadurch gekennzeichnet, dass die Beine (Pfosten) senkrecht stehen, wobei die hinteren in die Rückenlehne übergehen. Aus Stabilitätsgründen verbinden Sprossen die Beine untereinander.
10. Während Volker Bielitz, Thomas Andersch und Arnd Müller für die Konservierung und Restaurierung des Stuhlgestells verantwortlich zeichnen, realisierte Reinhardt Roßberg nach der Abpolsterung, der anschließenden Sicherung und Reinigung des Originalmaterials den Polster-Neuaufbau. Seinem Arbeitsbericht ließen sich die fachlichen Angaben zu obigen Ausführungen entnehmen.
11. Dies ermöglichten Volker Bielitz (für das Holzgestell) und Alexander Hahlbeck, der die Polsterrekonstruktion vornahm.
12. Henry Havard zeigt den Polsterstuhl von Ludwig XIV. Im 1. Band seines Lexikons über das Möbel und die Dekoration, in: Havard 1894, Bd.1 (A–C), S. 638.
13. Feulner 1927, S. 333.
14. Louis de Rouvroy, duc de Saint-Simon, lebte von 1675 bis 1755 und machte am Hof Ludwigs XIV. Karriere. In seinen Memoiren hielt er fest, was er in Versailles erlebte und sah. Vgl. dazu: Massenbach 1977.
15. Ebd., S. 336.
16. Ebd., S. 571.
17. Havard 1894, Bd. 1 (A–C), S. 651.
18. Ebd., S. 651.
19. Havard 1894, Bd. 1 (A–C), S. 542.
20. Feulner 1927, S. 397.
21. In Akt III, Szene II.
22. In deutscher Übersetzung: *Un fauteuil m'embarrasse, Un homme là dedans est tout enveloppé; Je ne me trouve bien que dans un canapé. Fais-m'en approcher un, pour m'étendre à mon aise*. Aus: Havard 1894, Bd. 1 (A–C), S. 542.
23. Bücheler/Ulmschneider 1953, S. 15.
24. Ebd., S. 17.
25. Ebd., S. 19.
26. Brief vom 18. August 1790. Dokument in: The Museum of Methodism & John Wesley's House, London. Chamber Horse. URL: https://wesleysheritage.org.uk (4.3.2022).
27. Auch John Wesley hatte im Jahr 1761 einen Ratgeber veröffentlicht: *Primitive Physick: or, an easy and natural method of curing most diseases*. Reiten, das Chamber Horse wird ausdrücklich erwähnt, aber auch

Notes

1. Cf. Walter Benjamin on beautiful semblance (Schöner Schein), Benjamin 1961, p. 60.
2. Robert Maria Stieg, 'Warenprobe', in Stieg/Hammerschmied 1979, p. 45.
3. Ibid.
4. The dissertation was titled *Der Niedergang des Tapezier- und Polsterhandwerks* als Produktionsgewerbe and was submitted by Max Genath, a trained businessman from Dresden, under Professor Dr Jahn, Dresden 1935, in order to obtain a Doctorate of Economic Sciences from the Faculty of Law and Political Science at the Martin Luther University Halle-Wittenberg; see Genath 1935.
5. Ibid., p. 40.
6. Ibid., pp. 41/42.
7. See a photographic depiction in Köppen/Breuer 1904, p. 73.
8. The fresco is depicted, among others, in: Campbell 2018, p. 208.
9. Post chair refers to a common form of construction in the Middle Ages, characterised by the fact that the legs (posts) stand vertically, with the rear ones merging into the backrest. Rungs connect the legs to each other for stability.
10. While Volker Bielitz, Thomas Andersch and Arnd Müller are responsible for the conservation and restoration, Reinhardt Roßberg realised the reupholstery, after stripping, subsequent safeguarding and cleaning of the original material. The information above was taken from his work report.
11. This was made possible by Volker Bielitz (wooden frame) and Alex Hahlbeck, who took on the reupholstery.
12. Henry Harvard shows the upholstered chair of Louis XIV in volume one of his dictionary on furniture and decoration, in Havard 1894, vol. 1 (A–C), p. 638.
13. Feulner 1927, p. 333.
14. Louis, de Rouyroy, Duc de Saint-Simon, lived from 1675 to 1755 and pursued a career at the court of Louis XIV. In his memoires he noted what he saw and encountered at Versailles. See Massenbach 1977.
15. Ibid., p. 336.
16. Ibid., p. 571.
17. Havard 1894, vol. 1 (A–C), p. 651.
18. Ibid., p. 651.
19. Havard 1894, vol. 1 (A–C), p. 542.
20. Feulner 1927, p. 397.
21. In Act III, Scene II.
22. 'Un fauteuil m'embarrasse, Un homme là dedans est tout enveloppé; Je ne me trouve bien que dans un canapé. Fais-m'en approcher un, pour m'étendre à mon aise', from Havard 1894, vol. 1 (A–C), p. 542.
23. Bücheler/Ulmschneider 1953, p. 15.
24. Ibid., p. 17.
25. Ibid., p. 19.
26. Letter from 18 August 1790. Document in the Museum of Methodism & John Wesley's House, London. 'Chamber horse' in the Online Collection at https://wesleysheritage.org.uk (accessed 4 March 2022).
27. John Wesley had also published a guidebook in 1761: *Primitive Physick: or, an easy and natural method of curing most diseases*. Horseback riding – the chamber horse – is explicitly mentioned, but a vegetarian diet was also central to the treatment of diseases. The guidebook was published in many editions. Its sphere of influence was not limited to the British upper class and nobility, but was also directed at 'men of ordinary capacities'.

diätetische vegetarische Maßnahmen standen im Zentrum der Behandlung von Krankheiten. Der Ratgeber erlebte viele Auflagen. Sein Wirkungskreis beschränkte sich dabei nicht nur auf die britische Oberschicht und den Adel, sondern richtete sich auch an *men of ordinary capacities*.

28 Batchelor 2012.
29 Fuller 1729.
30 Ebd.
31 Cheyne, George: *An essay of health and long life*, London 1724, Chap.IV of Exercise and Quiet, §5, p.99. Early English Books online Text Creation Partnership, 2011, http://name.umdl.umich.edu/004834818.0001.000.
32 Wie man sich die Benutzung des Chamber Horse vorstellen kann, zeigt eine der Anfangsszenen des 1967 gedrehten Filmklassikers *Casino Royale* mit David Niven als ehemaligem britischem Superagenten. Mit disziplinierter Körperbeherrschung und *stiff upper lip* reitet er, scheinbar völlig unangestrengt, auf einem Chamber Horse, eine heiße Tasse Tee zum Mund führend. Auf Facebook ist unter *janet doerr* ein kurzes Video zu sehen, das eine Vorstellung vom allerdings wenig professionellen Gebrauch eines Chamber Horse im Avebury Manor & Garden Museum, England, gibt. URL: https://www.facebook.com/JanetDoerrMedicalIntuitive/videos/1006013000204627 (4.3.2022).
33 Sheraton 1793, S. 14.: *Of the Chamber Horse. The upper figure shews the inside when the leather is off. Which consists of five wainscoat inch boards, clamped at the ends; to which are fixed strong wire twisted round a block in regular gradiation, so that when the wire is compressed by the weight of those who exercise, each turn of it may clear itself and fall within each other. The top board is stuffed with hair as a chair seat, and the leather is fixed to each board with brass nails, tacked all round. The leather at each end is cut in slits to give vent to the air, which would otherwise resist in the motion downwards. The workman should also observe, that a wooden or iron pin is fixed at each end of the middle board, for the purpose of guiding the whole seat as it plays up and down.This pin runs between the two upright pieces which are framed into the arms at each end, as the design shews (…).*
34 Samson 1874. URL: https://www.gutenberg.org/files/54149/54149-h/54149-h.htm (8.5.2022) *This is to answer some Objections to the Look of the Chamber-Horse (for Exercise) invented by Henry Marsh, in Clement's Inn Passage, Clare Market, London; who is well known has had the Honour to serve some Persons of the greatest Distinction in the Kingdom; and he humbly begs the Favour of Ladies and Gentlemen to try both the Chamber-Horse, which is the only way of having the best. This machine may be of great Service to Children.*
35 Bixler-Reber 1962. URL: http://researchingfoodhistory.blogspot.com/2012/08chamber-horse.htlm. Ob es sich um eine Variante des Chamber Horse handelte, ist anzunehmen: *For a neat chamber horse to carry four children at once with a mahogany frame and spring seats covered all around with Moracca[sic] Leather the top lined with fine green cloth and brass nails with four handles to hold by. Two of them supported with iron brackets finely polished and made to turn on a swivell [sic] and four foot boards made to fall down automatically for the convenience of carrying it through any doorway.*
36 Ebd.
37 Ebd.
38 Beiblatt der *Fliegenden Blätter*, München, 9. Dezember 1898, S. 24. URL: https://digi.ubuni-heidelberg.de/

28 Batchelor 2012.
29 Fuller 1729.
30 Ibid.
31 George Cheyne, *An Essay of Health and Long Life*, London 1724, Chap. IV: Of Exercise and Quiet, §5, p. 99. Early English Books online Text Creation Partnership, 2011, http://name.umdl.umich.edu/004834818.0001.000 (accessed 18 August 2022).
32 How to imagine the use of the chamber horse is shown in one of the opening scenes of the 1967 film classic *Casino Royale*, starring David Niven as the former British secret agent. With disciplined body control and *stiff upper lip*, he rid a chamber horse, seemingly without any strain, while guiding a hot cup of tea to his mouth. A short video can be seen on Facebook under 'Janet Doerr', which gives an idea of the, albeit not very professional, use of a chamber horse at Avebury Manor & Garden Museum, England. URL: https://www.facebook.com/348733878606587/videos/2149372778515563/ (accessed 4 March 2022).
33 Sheraton 1793, p. 14: 'Of the Chamber Horse. The upper figure shews the inside when the leather is off, which consists of five wainscoat inch boards, clamped at the ends; to which are fixed strong wire twisted round a block in regular gradation, so that when the wire is compressed by the weight of those who exercise, each turn of it may clear itself and fall within each other. The top board is stuffed with hair as a chair seat, and the leather is fixed to each board with brass nails, tacked all round. The leather at each end is cut in slits to give vent to the air, which would otherwise resist the motion downwards. The workman should also observe that a wooden or iron pin is fixed at each end of the middle board, for the purpose of guiding the whole seat as it plays up and down. This pin runs between the two upright pieces which are framed into the arms at each end, as the design shews.'
34 Samson 1874. URL: https://www.gutenberg.org/files/54149/54149-h/54149-h.htm (accessed 8 May 2022): 'This is to answer some objections to the Look of the Chamber-Horse (for Exercise) invented by HENRY MARSH, in Clement's Inn Passage, Clare Market, London; who it is well known, has had the Honour to serve some Persons of the greatest Distinction in the Kingdom; and he humbly begs the Favour of Ladies and Gentlemen to try both the Chamber-Horse, which is the only sure way of having the best. This machine may be of great Service to Children.'
35 Bixler-Reber 1962. URL: http://researchingfoodhistory.blogspot.com/2012/08chamber-horse.html (accessed 18 August 2022): It can be assumed that this was a variant of the chamber horse: 'For a neat chamber horse to carry four children at once with a mahogany frame and spring seats covered all around with Moracca [sic] Leather the top lined with fine green cloth and brass nails with four handles to hold by. Two of them supported with iron brackets finely polished and made to turn on a swivell [sic] and four foot boards made to fall down automatically for the convenience of carrying it through any doorway.'
36 Ibid.
37 Ibid.
38 Supplement of the *Fliegende Blätter*, Munich, 9 December 1898, p. 24. Available at https://digi.ubuni-heidelberg.de/digit/fb_bb109/0563 (accessed 4 May 2022). The Holzwarenfabrik Hildburghausen in Westphalia produced, among other things, this so-called Reitapparat. An *exercise horse* by the company, dated between 1870 and 1930, is now in the Science Museum, London, inv. no. A69185. Unlike

digit/fb_bb109/0563 (4.5.2022). Die Holzwarenfabrik Hildburghausen in Westfalen stellte u. a. diesen sogenannten *Reitapparat* her. Ein *Exercise Horse* der Firma, zwischen 1870–1930 datiert, befindet sich heute im Science Museum London, A69185. Anders als bei den britischen Modellen ist nicht zu beiden Seiten eine Armhalterung vorgesehen, sondern es konnte, wie die Zeichnung der Annonce zeigt, im Damensitz geritten werden. Das Kreisarchiv des Landratsamtes Hildburghausen konnte, aufgrund der fehlenden Bestände, keine weiteren Auskünfte erteilen.
39 Jugend 1907, S. 131. Annonce der Firma Sanitas, Berlin, mit Filialen in Düsseldorf und London (!). Das Velotrab funktionierte durch leichtes Treten der Pedale, es erinnert eher an einen modernen Hometrainer.
40 Das Velotrab (als Radfahr-Trab-Reit-Apparat beschrieben) *steht auf Gummifüssen und kann in jeden Salon gestellt werden: sein Aussehen ist höchst elegant und vornehm.* URL: https://www.ebay.de itm/Velotrab-Reitapparat-im Hause-fuer Damen-und Herren-Reklame-Ad-1907/152285340517 Velotrab-Reitapparat (4.5.2022).
41 Lot 556 versteigert am 20.10.2018 von Duggleby & Stephenson of York, The salesroom, York Auction Centre Murton, York, Y0195GF.
42 Bonnet 2009, S. 17.
43 Himmelheber 1983, S. 72.
44 Bothe/Rietz 2019, S. 165.
45 Bidlingmaier 2000, S. 186.
46 Bonnet 2009, S. 20.
47 Das Anschauungsmodell (Abb.) entstand durch Torsten Otto und Stefan Oswald, denen Stefan Kloss bezüglich der Holzbehandlung zur Seite stand. Die Beschreibung des Polsteraufbaus basiert auf den fachlichen Ausführungen der beteiligten Restauratoren.
48 Ottomeyer 1994, S. 84; Emmrich/Schroeder 2000, S. 503.
49 Ab 1787 *Journal des Luxus und der Moden*.
50 Bertuch 1786, S. 28–29. Siehe auch Valk 2012, S. 20.
51 Ottomeyer 1987, S. 116.
52 Ebd.
53 Möller 1998, S. 17: *Wegen der Beschränkung der Handels- und Transportmöglichkeiten wurden für die Möbel häufig heimische Hölzer verwendet: im Süden vor allem Kirsch- und Nussbaum, im Norden Birke und besonders in Küstennähe das importierte Mahagoni.*
54 Im Folgenden siehe Bahns 1979, S. 70–72.
55 Ebd., S. 62: *Bei ihm liegt der Sitz nicht auf dem Zargenkranz, sondern zwischen zwei seitlichen, im Extremfall mit Vorder- und Hinterbein aus einem Stück geschnitzten Brettern und wird nach vorne und hinten von zwei niedriger angesetzten Verbindungsstücken gehalten.*
56 Ottomeyer 2006, S. 47; ders. 1987, S. 112.
57 Im Folgenden siehe Witt-Dörring 2006, S. 68.
58 Im Folgenden siehe Bahns 1979, S. 72. Siehe auch Ottomeyer 1987, S. 114: *Ein Stoff allerdings, den es im 19. Jahrhundert nirgendwo und nie gab, ist der sogenannte „Biedermeierstoff" – ein vielfarbiger Streifendamast mit Streublumenmuster. Hierbei handelt es sich um eine Fiktion des „Zweiten Biedermeier", als man den Kunden zum Stilmöbel den angeblichen „Stilbezug" aufdrängte.* Zu Biedermeierstoffen im Allgemeinen siehe Völker 1996.
59 Ottomeyer 1987, S. 114.
60 Giedion 1987, S. 417.
61 Meyer 1889, S. 461.
62 Ebd., S. 210.
63 Missenharter 1926, S. 375–378.
64 Ebd., S. 375–376.
65 Ebd., S. 376.
66 Ebd., S. 375.
67 Spannagel 1937, S.17.

the British models, it did not have armrests on both sides but could be ridden in a side-saddle position, as the drawing in the advertisement shows. The archive of the Hildburghausen District Office could not provide any further information due to the lack of records.
39 Jugend 1907, p. 131. Advertisement of the Sanitas Company, Berlin, with branches in Düsseldorf and London (!). As the *Velotrab* worked by using peddles, it resembles a modern exercise bike.
40 The Velotrab (described as a cycle-trot-ride apparatus) 'stands on rubber feet and can be placed in any salon: its appearance is most elegant and distinguished'. Advert available at https://www.ebay.de itm/Velotrab-Reitapparat-im-Haus-fuer Damen-und Herren-Reklame-Ad-1907/152285340517 Velotrab-Reitapparat (4 May 2022).
41 Lot 556 auctioned on 20 October 2018 by Duggleby Stephenson of York, salesroom, York Auction Centre Murton, York, Y019 5GF.
42 Bonnet 2009, p. 17.
43 Himmelheber 1983, p. 72.
44 Bothe /Rietz 2019, p. 165.
45 Bidlingmaier 2000, p. 186.
46 Bonnet 2009, p. 20.
47 The show model (fig. 41) was created by Torsten Otto and Stefan Oswald, who were assisted by Stefan Kloss regarding the wood treatment. The description of the upholstery structure is based on the professional explanations of the restorers involved.
48 Ottomeyer 1994, p. 84; Emmric/Schroeder 2000, p. 503.
49 From 1787 *Journal des Luxus und der Moden*.
50 Bertuch 1786, pp. 28–29. See also Valk 2012, p. 20.
51 Ottomeyer 1987, p. 116.
52 Ibid.
53 Möller 1998, p. 17: 'Due to the restriction of trade and transport possibilities, domestic woods were often used for furniture: in the south mainly cherry and walnut, in the north birch and especially near the coast the imported mahogany.'
54 In the following see Bahns 1979, pp. 70–72.
55 Ibid., p. 62: 'Here, the seat does not lie on the frame rails, but between two side boards, in extreme cases with the front and back legs carved out of one piece, and is held in the front and back by two lower connecting pieces.'
56 Ottomeyer 2006, p. 47; Ottomeyer 1987, p. 112.
57 In the following, see Witt-Dörring 2006, p. 68.
58 In the following, see Bahns 1979, p. 72. See also Ottomeyer 1987, p. 114: 'However, one fabric that is nowhere and never seen in the nineteenth century is the so-called Biedermeier fabric, a multicoloured striped damask with a pattern of scattered flowers. This is a fiction of the "second Biedermeier", when the purported "style reference" for the period furniture was urged upon the customer.' On Biedermeier fabrics in general, see Völker 1996.
59 Ottomeyer 1987, p. 114.
60 Giedion 1987, p. 417.
61 Meyer 1889, p. 461.
62 Ibid., p. 210.
63 Missenharter 1926, pp. 375–378.
64 Ibid., pp. 375–376.
65 Ibid., p. 376.
66 Ibid., p. 375.
67 Spannagel 1937, p. 17.
68 Giedion 1987, pp. 629–645.
69 Benjamin 1983, p. 292.
70 See Loos' explanations for ornament and crime, in Loos 1931, pp. 79–92.
71 Giedion 1965, p. 210.

68 Giedion 1987, S. 629–645.
69 Benjamin 1983, S. 292.
70 Vgl. die Ausführungen von Adolf Loos zu *Ornament und Verbrechen*, in: Loos 1931, S. 79–92.
71 Giedion 1965, S. 210.
72 Adolf Loos: *Das Sitzmöbel (19. Juni 1898)*. Veröffentlicht in: Loos 1921, S. 53.
73 A. a. o., S. 53.
74 Stefan Üner: Friedrich Otto Schmidt, in: Ottillinger 2018, S. 149.
75 Vgl. die Ausführungen der Firma Ziegenhorn & Junker, Hoflieferanten, Kunstsalon und Ausstellungshaus für vornehme Wohnungseinrichtungen mit ausgedehntem eigenen Fabrikbetrieb in Erfurt, in: Ziegenhorn 1912, S. 3.
76 Die hier aufgeführten Bezeichnungen wurden aus Werbegründen den von Ziegenhorn & Junker produzierten Modellen vom Unternehmen selbst gegeben, ohne dass damit kunstwissenschaftlich verlässliche Zuschreibungen verbunden wären.
77 Ernst 1937, S. 10/11.
78 Behne 1930, S. 35ff.
79 Taut 1924, S. 46–54.
80 Schmidt 1930.
81 Ebd., S. 8.
82 Ebd., S. 9.
83 Ebd., S. 21.
84 Entsprechende Empfehlungen gibt auch der Architekt Bruno Taut in seinem 1924 erschienenen Ratgeber, vgl. Taut 1924, S. 56/57.
85 Giedion 1929, S. 5.
86 Ebd., S. 7.
87 Bauhaus 1928, S. 17.
88 Ebd., S. 17.
89 Otto Neustätter: *Die Geschichte auf der Gesolei*, in: Gesolei 1926, S. 69.
90 Bauhaus 1928a, S. 14.
91 Erich Dieckmann entwarf neben zahlreichen Stahlrohr- und Korbsitzmöbeln auch Klubsessel, Divan-Modelle und Sofas, die z. T. in sein Typenmöbel-Programm integriert waren. Vgl. dazu: Dieckmann 1931, S. 40–54.
92 Spiegel 1928, S. 157.
93 Ebd., S. 157.
94 Vgl. die Beschreibung des patentierten Fauteuils, *Modell Nr. KS 46*, von Anton Lorenz, in: Van Geest/Mácel 1980, S. 92.
95 Vgl. die Ausführungen von Hannes Meyer zu den Vorgaben der neuen Welt, in: Meyer-Bergner 1980, S. 29.
96 Ott-Wodni 2015, S. 268.
97 Platz 1933, S. 152.
98 Vgl. die Ausführungen von Kuno von Hardenberg: *Vom guten Sitzmöbel*, in: Innendekoration 1925, S. 220/221.
99 Ebd., S. 220.
100 Schneck 1933.
101 Ebd., S. 23.
102 Vgl. hierzu auch die Ausführungen zur Doppelfederung, in: Bücheler/Ulmschneider 1953, S. 128.
103 Ebd., S. 220.
104 Vgl. Stoffe, in: Die Form 1929, S. 658.
105 Michael Siebenbrodt: *Die Textilkollektion des frühen Bauhauses an den Kunstsammlungen zu Weimar*, in: Droste/Ludewig 1999, S. 29.
106 A. a. O.
107 A. a. O.
108 Aalto beschrieb seine kritische Haltung gegenüber Stahlrohrmöbeln in *The Humanizing of Architecture* (1940). Die entsprechende Textpassage wurde erneut abgedruckt in: Ostergard 1987, S. 154.
109 Bücheler/Ulmschneider 1953, S. 227.
110 Vgl. den 1930 erschienenen Katalog: *Warum Deutsche WK-Möbel?*, dort auf Seite 18, erneut abgebildet in:

72 Adolf Loos, 'Das Sitzmöbel [19 June 1898]', in Loos 1921, p. 53.
73 Ibid., p. 53.
74 Stefan Üner, *Friedrich Otto Schmidt*, in Ottillinger 2018, p. 149.
75 See the remarks by the company Ziegenhorn & Junker, purveyors to the court, art salon and exhibition house for distinguished home furnishings with extensive factory operations of its own in Erfurt, in Ziegenhorn 1912, p. 3.
76 The descriptions of the models produced by Ziegenhorn & Junker were given by the company as an advertisement without considering art historical accuracy.
77 Ernst 1937, pp. 10–11.
78 Behne 1930, pp. 35–37.
79 Taut 1924, pp. 46–54.
80 Schmidt 1930.
81 Ibid., p. 8.
82 Ibid., p. 9.
83 Ibid., p. 21.
84 The architect Bruno Taut also gives such recommendations in his 1924 guide; see Taut 1924, pp. 56–57.
85 Giedion 1929, p. 5.
86 Ibid., p. 7.
87 Bauhaus 1928, p. 17.
88 Ibid., p. 17.
89 Otto Neustätter, *Die Geschichte auf der Gesolei*, in Gesolei 1926, p. 69.
90 Bauhaus 1928a, p. 14.
91 In addition to numerous tubular steel and wicker chairs, Erich Dieckmann also designed club chairs, divan models and sofas, some of which were integrated into his Typenmöbel (matching standardised furniture) programme. See Dieckmann 1931, pp. 40–54.
92 Spiegel 1928, p. 157.
93 Ibid., p. 157.
94 See the description of the patented armchair model KS 46 by Anton Lorenz, in Van Geest/ Mácel 1980, p. 92.
95 See Hannes Meyer's explanations on the demands of the new world, in Meyer-Bergner 1980, p. 29.
96 Ott-Wodni 2015, p. 268.
97 Platz 1933, p. 152.
98 See explanations by Kuno von Hardenberg, *Vom guten Sitzmöbel*, Innen-Dekoration 1925, pp. 220–221.
99 Ibid., p. 220.
100 Schneck 1933.
101 Ibid., p. 23.
102 See the passages on double springing, in Bücheler/Ulmschneider 1953, p. 128.
103 Ibid., p. 220.
104 See fabrics, in Die Form 1929, p. 658.
105 Michael Siebenbrodt, *Die Textilkollektion des frühen Bauhauses an den Kunstsammlungen zu Weimar*, in Droste/Ludewig 1999, p. 29.
106 Ibid.
107 Ibid.
108 Aalto described his critical stance on tubular steel furniture in *The Humanizing of Architecture* (1940). The corresponding text passage was reprinted in Ostergard 1987, p. 154.
109 Bücheler/Ulmschneider 1953, p. 227.
110 See the 1930 catalogue *Warum Deutsche WK-Möbel?*, p. 18, reproduced in Wichmann 1992, p. 293.
111 See Thormann 2002, pp. 38–40.
112 See Arnold 1993, p. 419, and Deutsche Werkstätten 2018, p. 177.
113 See GRASSI Museum für Angewandte Kunst 2020, pp. 84, 85.
114 Seating furniture with a similar printed cover can be found

Wichmann 1992, S. 293.
111 Vgl. Thormann 2002, S. 38–40.
112 Vgl. Arnold 1993, S. 419 und Deutsche Werkstätten 2018, S. 177.
113 Vgl. GRASSI Museum für Angewandte Kunst 2020, S. 84 u. 85.
114 Ein Sitzmöbel mit gleichartig bedrucktem Bezug findet sich in Hoffmann 1932, S. 571; zu Josef Hillerbrand vgl. Arnold 1993, S. 418 und Wichmann 1992, S. 326 u. 327.
115 Vgl. Kunstsammlungen Chemnitz 1998, S. 17 u. 18 und Stöver 2018, S. 23–31.
116 Stellvertretend für die vielen Kolleginnen und Kollegen, die uns dankenswerterweise bei der Suche geholfen haben, seien hier genannt: Anja Schmidt, Architekturmuseum München; Liane Sachs, Kunstsammlungen Chemnitz; Katrin Lauterbach, Kunstgewerbemuseum Dresden; Torsten Bäz, Cammann Gobelin Manufaktur Niederwiesa.
117 Ein großer Dank gebührt Joachim Unterfrauner, Textilwerkstatt der Kunsthochschule Halle Burg Giebichenstein, für geduldige und konstruktive Gespräche zu technologischen Fragen rund um den Textildruck.
118 Fa. Textil Fab - Die Stoffdruck Manufaktur, Emmendingen.
119 Die Auswertung und digitale Bearbeitung des Fotomaterials lag in den Händen von Diplom-Restaurator Bert Müller, Dresden.
120 Linde Böttger, Textildesignerin in Naumburg, erstellte die Druckdatei und sorgte für die Umsetzung aller praktischen Arbeitsschritte bis zum vorliegenden Druckstoff.
121 Sämtliche Polsterarbeiten erledigte die Fa. Polsterei Roßberg, Leipzig-Markkleeberg, die Behandlung der Farbfassung oblag den museumseigenen Werkstätten.
122 Heinrich Geron: *Moderne Wohnlichkeit, II. Wohnform und Gesellschaftsformen*, in: Innendekoration 1925, S. 178–180.
123 Ebd., S. 178.
124 Schneck 1933, S. 7.
125 Gräff 1931, S. 45–48.
126 Ebd., S. 48.
127 Schuster 1948, S. 44.
128 1953 erschienen unter diesem Titel die Lebenserinnerungen des Designers Raymond Loewy, der in den USA einer der bedeutendsten Industriedesigner war. Vgl. Loewy 1953.
129 Ebd., S. 246.
130 Ebd., vgl. die Abbildungen und Bildunterschriften im nicht paginierten Bildteil zwischen S. 80 und S. 81.
131 Ebd., S. 228.
132 Wolfgang Heyn: *Der Mensch von Heute richtet sich ein*, in: Die Zeit 1955, S. 17.
133 Constanze 1958, ohne Paginierung.
134 Hermann Exner: *Hellerau überwindet den Bauhausstil*, in: Bildende Kunst 1956, S. 256–270.
135 Ebd., S. 270.
136 Der 8. von 11 durch Jacques Viénot formulierten Leitsätzen zur industriellen Formgebung, zusammengestellt für den *Congrès International d´Esthetique Industrielle*, der 1953 in Paris stattfand. Abgedruckt in: Werk und Zeit 1953, S. 1.
137 Neutra 1975.
138 Ebd., S. 110.
139 Ebd., S. 111.
140 Louis Jent: *Die Erzeugung des Komfortgefühls beim Sitzen*, in: Bauen + Wohnen 1961, Anhang XII-1. – Komfortgefühl.
141 A. a. O.
142 Bücheler/Ulmschneider 1953, S. 76.
143 Barth von Wehrenalp/Saechtling 1952.

in Hoffmann 1932, p. 571; on Josef Hillerbrand, see Arnold 1993, p. 418, and Wichmann 1992, pp. 326, 327.
115 See Kunstsammlungen Chemnitz 1998, pp. 17, 18, and Stöver 2018, pp. 23–31.
116 As representatives of the many colleagues who kindly helped us in our search, we would like to mention the following: Anja Schmidt, Architekturmuseum München; Liane Sachs, Kunstsammlungen Chemnitz; Katrin Lauterbach, Kunstgewerbemuseum Dresden; Torsten Bäz, Cammann Gobelin Manufaktur Niederwiesa.
117 A big thank you goes to Joachim Unterfrauner of the Textile Workshop at the Halle Burg Giebichenstein School of Art, for patient and constructive discussions on technological issues related to textile printing.
118 Textil Fab – Die Stoffdruck Manufaktur, Emmendingen.
119 The evaluation and digital processing of the photographic material was in the hands of conservator Bert Müller, Dresden.
120 Linde Böttger, a textile designer in Naumburg, produced the printing file and oversaw the implementation of each step up to the printed textile.
121 All upholstery was undertaken by the company Fa. Polsterei Roßberg, Leipzig-Markkleeberg; the painting of the wood took place in the museum workshops.
122 Heinrich Geron, *Moderne Wohnlichkeit, II: Wohnform und Gesellschaftsformen*, in Innen-Dekoration 1925, pp. 178–180.
123 Ibid., p. 48.
124 Schneck 1933, p. 7.
125 Gräff 1931, pp. 45–48.
126 Ibid., p. 48.
127 Schuster 1948, p. 44.
128 In the memoirs of the designer Raymond Loewy were published, one of the most important US-American industrial designers. See Loewy 1953.
129 Ibid., p. 246.
130 Ibid. See the illustrations and captions in the non-paginated image section between pp. 80 and 81.
131 Ibid., p. 228.
132 Wolfgang Heyn, 'Der Mensch von Heute richtet sich ein', in Die Zeit 1955, p. 17.
133 Constanze 1958, n.p.
134 Hermann Exner, *Hellerau überwindet den Bauhausstil*, in Bildende Kunst 1956, pp. 256–270.
135 Ibid., p. 270.
136 The eighth of eleven principles on industrial design by Jacques Viénot, put together for the *Congrès International d´Esthetique Industrielle*, in Paris in 1953. Reproduced in Werk und Zeit 1953, p. 1.
137 Neutra 1975.
138 Ibid., p. 110.
139 Ibid., p. 111.
140 Louis Jent, *Die Erzeugung des Komfortgefühls beim Sitzen*, in Bauen + Wohnen 1961, appendix XII-1. – Komfortgefühl.
141 Ibid.
142 Bücheler/Ulmschneider 1953, p. 76.
143 Barth von Wehrenalp/Saechtling 1952.
144 Ibid., p. 7.
145 Hans Schwippert, *Das Ende der Werkgerechtigkeit*, in Baukunst und Werkform 1953, p. 235.
146 Hans Dieter Oestereich, *Abstieg zum Anorganischen?*, in Baukunst und Werkform 1953, p. 237.
147 The text was published in Stieg/Hammerschmied 1979, pp. 9–35.
148 Ibid., p. 33.
149 Robert Maria Stieg, *Gediegen für Wenige – minder für Viele*, in Stieg/Hammerschmied 1979, p. 32.
150 Ibid., p. 32.
151 See *Die ganze Welt in unseren vier Wänden durch Radio und Fernsehen*, in Constanze 1958, p. 244.

144 Ebd., S. 7.
145 Hans Schwippert: *Das Ende der Werkgerechtigkeit*, in: Baukunst und Werkform 1953, S. 235.
146 Hans Dieter Oestereich: *Abstieg zum Anorganischen?*, in: Baukunst und Werkform 1953, S. 237.
147 Der Text wurde veröffentlicht in: Stieg/Hammerschmied 1979, S. 9–35.
148 Ebd., S. 33.
149 Robert Maria Stieg: *Gediegen für Wenige – minder für Viele*, in: Stieg/Hammerschmied 1979, S. 32.
150 Ebd., S. 32.
151 Vgl. Den Artikel: *Die ganze Welt in unseren vier Wänden durch Radio und Fernsehen*, in: Constanze 1958, S. 244.
152 Es ist die erste Strophe des Gedichtes *Der Ästhet* von Christian Morgenstern, aus: www.christian-morgenstern.de.
153 Kultur im Heim 1961, S. 15.
154 Robert d'Hooghe: *Sitzen – Sehen – Hören*, in: Werk und Zeit 1957, S. 1.
155 Gustav Hassenpflug: *Sitzmöbel in Konstruktion und Form*, in: Werk und Zeit 1957, S. 2.
156 Jürgen Klepka: *Polstermöbel. Entwicklung eines Sortiments*, in: Form + Zweck 1977, S. 33–36.
157 Ebd., S. 35.
158 Eberhard Geißler: *Polstermöbel. Instrument für Qualitätsplanung*, in: Form + Zweck 1977, S. 36–41.
159 Der Film *Playtime* entstand 1967 und kam damals unter dem Titel *Tatis herrliche Zeiten* in deutsche Kinos. Buch und Regie stammen von Jaques Tati, die Architekturausstattung von Eugène Roman, die Specta-Film-Produktion leitete Bernard Maurice, gemeinsam mit dem Co-Produzenten René Silvera. Vgl. Maddock 1993, S. 190/191.
160 Ede/Goudet 2002, S. 113.
161 Redaktion magnum: *Die Körperfreundlichkeit*, in: Magnum 1957, S. 13.
162 Werk und Zeit 1960, S.6.
163 Radice 1993, S. 248.
164 Schuster 1927, ohne Paginierung.
165 Volker Fischer: *Von der Sperrmüllmatratze zur Repariere im Blümchen-Look*, in: Deutscher Werkbund 1987, S. 100.
166 Hajo Eickhoff: *Kultur Sitzen Design. Sitzen in den 60er Jahren*, in: GH Wuppertal 1999, S. 127.
167 Ebd., S. 129.
168 Ebd., S. 100.
169 Klaus-Dieter Mädzulat: *Gesessen wird immer*, in: Form + Zweck 1973, S. 43.
170 Ebd., S. 101.
171 A. a. O.
172 Redaktion der Zeitschrift *form + zweck: Reform 74: Debüt eines Gestalters*, in: Form + Zweck 1973 a, S. 16.
173 Ebd., S. 16.
174 Werner Erhardt: *Polstermöbel – Lücken im Sortiment*, in: Form + Zweck 1973 a, S. 13.
175 Jürgen Klepka: Sitzen weich und wohlig, in: Form + Zweck 1975, S. 13.
176 Lewitzky 1962.
177 Ebd., S. 33.
178 Klaus-Dieter Mädzulat: *Gesessen wird immer*, in: Form + Zweck 1973, S. 43.
179 Die Fotografie *Oświęcim, 28.11.2006* stammt von Stefan Kraus, aus seiner Fotoreihe *Zufällige Begegnungen, Fotografien, 2006–2017*, © Stefan Kraus, Köln.
180 Robert Maria Steg: *Vorsicht: Polstermöbel!*, in: Form + Zweck 1981, S. 22–24.
181 Ebd., S. 22.
182 Ebd., S. 23.
183 Garner 1980.
184 Ebd., S. 216.
185 Max Scharnigg: *Kleine Liebe. Geschrumpftes Sofa oder

152 First verse of the poem *Der Ästhet* by Christian Morgenstern, from www.christian-morgenstern.de.
153 Kultur im Heim 1961, p. 15.
154 Robert d'Hooghe, *Sitzen – Sehen – Hören*, in Werk und Zeit 1957, p. 1.
155 Gustav Hassenpflug, *Sitzmöbel in Konstruktion und Form*, in Werk und Zeit 1957, p. 2.
156 Jürgen Klepka, *Polstermöbel: Entwicklung eines Sortiments*, in Form + Zweck 1977, pp. 33–36.
157 Ibid., p. 35.
158 Eberhard Geißler, *Polstermöbel: Instrument für Qualitätsplanung*, in Form + Zweck 1977, pp. 36–41.
159 The film *Playtime* was made in 1967 and at the time was released in German cinemas under the title *Tatis herrliche Zeiten*. It was written and directed by Jaques Tati, the architectural design was by Eugène Roman, and the Specta film production was produced by Bernard Maurice, together with the co-producer René Silvera. See Maddock 1993, pp. 190–191.
160 Ede/Goudet 2002, p. 113.
161 Editors of *Magnum, Die Körperfreundlichkeit*, in Magnum 1957, p. 13.
162 Werk und Zeit 1960, p. 6.
163 Radice 1993, p. 248.
164 Schuster 1927, n.p.
165 Volker Fischer, *Von der Sperrmüllmatratze zur Repariere im Blümchen-Look*, in Deutscher Werkbund 1987, p. 100.
166 Hajo Eickhoff, *Kultur Sitzen Design: Sitzen in den 60er Jahren*, in GH Wuppertal 1999, p. 127.
167 Ibid., p. 129.
168 Ibid., p. 100.
169 Klaus-Dieter Mädzulat, *Gesessen wird immer*, in Form + Zweck 1973, p. 43.
170 Ibid., p. 101.
171 Ibid., p. 101.
172 Editors of *form + zweck, Reform 74: Debüt eines Gestalters*, in Form + Zweck 1973a, p. 16.
173 Ibid., p. 16.
174 Werner Erhardt, *Polstermöbel – Lücken im Sortiment*, in Form + Zweck 1973a, p. 13.
175 Jürgen Klepka, Sitzen weich und wohlig, in Form + Zweck 1975, p. 13.
176 Lewitzky 1962.
177 Ibid., p. 33.
178 Klaus-Dieter Mädzulat, *Gesessen wird immer*, in Form + Zweck 1973, p. 43.
179 Photograph by Stefan Kraus from his series *Zufällige Begegnungen, Fotografien, 2006–2017*, © Stefan Kraus, Cologne.
180 Robert Maria Steg, *Vorsicht: Polstermöbel!*, in Form + Zweck 1981, pp. 22–24.
181 Ibid., p. 22.
182 Ibid., p. 23.
183 Garner 1980.
184 Ibid., p. 216.
185 Max Scharnigg, *Kleine Liebe: Geschrumpftes Sofa oder breiter Sessel? Der Loveseat ist ein Zwischending, das sich neuerdings großer Beliebtheit erfreut*, in Süddeutsche Zeitung 2019, p. 60.
186 Tillmann Prüfer, *Zum Lachen auf die Couch*, in Zeit-Magazin 2017, p. 23.
187 Maxine Naylor and Ralph Ball dedicated a book to the chair as a narrative idea, tracing the broad spectrum of diverse individual seating configurations. See Naylor 2005.
188 See explanations by Tillmann Prüfer, *Endstation Sofa*, in Zeit-Magazin 2017, p. 84.
189 Title of the report published on 23 October 2008 in Zeit- Magazin. See Zeit-Magazin 2008, pp. 20–29.
190 Van Hinte 2006, p. 116.

breiter Sessel? Der Loveseat ist ein Zwischending, das sich neuerdings großer Beliebtheit erfreut, in: Süddeutsche Zeitung 2019, S. 60.
186 Tillmann Prüfer: *Zum Lachen auf die Couch*, in: Zeit-Magazin 2017, S. 23.
187 Dem Stuhl als narrativer Idee widmeten Maxine Naylor und Ralph Ball ein Buch, indem sie dem breiten Spektrum diverser Sitzindividualitäten nachspürten. Vgl. Naylor 2005.
188 Vgl. dazu die Ausführungen von Tillmann Prüfer: *Endstation Sofa*, in: Zeit-Magazin 2017, S. 84.
189 So lautete der Titel der Reportage, die am 23. Oktober 2008 im Zeit-Magazin erschienen ist. Vgl. Zeit-Magazin 2008, S. 20–29.
190 Van Hinte 2006, S. 116.
191 Neben anderen Darstellungen vom gepolsterten Möbel zeigt Saul Steinberg diese in Strichzeichnung illustrierte Szene im 1. Kapitel seines Buches *The Art of Living*, gleich zu Beginn auf einer der ersten Seiten, in: Steinberg 1949, ohne Paginierung.
192 Jolly 2016, S. 13; Reinecke 2020, S. 49.
193 Westmann 2009, S. 35.
194 Zur Sammlungsgeschichte vgl. Thormann 2003.
195 Wichtige Grundlage für die Einordnung der Gewebefragmente sind die von Babette Küster 2004/2005 vorgenommenen, nicht publizierten Gewebanalysen. Für ihre Unterstützung auch dieses Katalogbeitrags danke ich ihr sehr.
196 Z. B. in den 1523 und 1529 in Augsburg bei Johann Schönsperger dem Jüngeren gedruckten *Furm-Oder Modelbüchlein*, https://www.metmuseum.org/art/collection/search/354650 (29.08.2022).
197 Exemplarisch dafür der Bestand bestickter Möbelbezüge der Stiftung Preußische Schlösser und Gärten Berlin-Brandenburg: Bergemann 2000.
198 Richter 1966; Anderson 2022a.
199 Englische und französische Beispiele aus dem 17. und 18. Jh. in der Sammlung des Victoria and Albert Museums, London (z. B. Armlehnstuhl um 1673, als Leihgabe aus Ham House; Westman 2019, S. 44, Fig. 3.6).
200 U. a. Wilckens 1997, S. 105–113, 120–127; Monnas 1993, S. 167–171; Monnas 2018, S. 149–186.
201 Cataldi Gallo 2016, S. 47f.
202 Jolly 2005, S. 29; Beispiele für Genua Cataldi Gallo 2016, S. 48f.
203 Vgl. Anmerkung zu Nr. 244/245.
204 Brokatelle: CIETA Vocabulaire Vocabulaire – Le vocabulaire du CIETA (17.06.2022).
205 Peter 2020, S. 9–20; Borkopp-Restle 2009, S. 191–200; Jolly 2016, S. 14; Samt: CIETA Vocabulaire Vocabulaire – Le vocabulaire du CIETA (17.06.2022).
206 Germann 1913; Jolly 2005, S. 15; Mokett (Moquette), in: Lexikon der Gewebe 2015, S. 279; Plüsch, in: Lexikon der Gewebe 2015, S. 321.
207 Cataldi Gallo 2016, S. 48–50; Browne 2009, S. 56; Jolly 2005, Kat. 14. Ein Beispiel für das *della palma*-Motiv befindet sich auch im Bestand des GRASSI MAK (Inv. Nr. V8276).
208 Bothe/Rietz 2019, S. 36–39.
209 Bothe/Rietz 2019, S. 38–41; zu Lasalle u. a. Jolly 2005, S. 34; Miller 2009, S. 79–90.
210 Glossar in: Jolly 2005, S. 246; Zitzmann 2016, S. 86f., Abb. 2.
211 Jolly 2016, S. 14.
212 Jolly 2005, S. 32f.
213 Evers 2014, S. 3f.; Zitzmann 2016, S. 85; Bothe/Rietz 2019, S. 41f.; Beard 1997.
214 Evers 2016, S. 77; Kreibich 2016, S. 132.
215 Evers 2014, S.7–54; Evers 2016, S. 73ff.; Zitzmann 2016, S. 92.
216 Döring 2016, S. 76.

191 Among other depictions of upholstered furniture, Saul Steinberg shows this scene illustrated in line drawing in the first chapter of his book *The Art of Living*, at the beginning on one of the first pages, in Steinberg 1949, n.p.
192 Jolly 2016, p. 13; Reinecke 2020, p. 49.
193 Westmann 2009, p. 35.
194 On the collection history, see Thormann 2003.
195 An important basis for the classification of the tissue fragments are the unpublished tissue analyses carried out by Babette Küster in 2004–05. I thank her very much for her support for this catalogue contribution.
196 E.g. the booklet printed in 1523 and 1529 in Augsburg by Johann Schönsperger the Younger, *Furm-Oder Modelbüchlein*, https://www.metmuseum.org/art/collection/search/354650 (29.08.2022) (accessed 31 August 2022).
197 One example is the collection of embroidered furniture covers of Stiftung Preußische Schlösser und Gärten Berlin-Brandenburg: see Bergemann 2000.
198 Richter 1966; Anderson 2022a.
199 English and French examples from the seventeenth and eighteenth centuries can be found in the collection of the Victoria and Albert Museum, London (e.g. armchair from 1673, Loan from Ham House Westman 2019, p. 44, fig. 3.6).
200 Among others Wilckens 1997, pp. 105–113, 120–127; Monnas 1993, pp. 167–171; Monnas 2018, pp. 149–186. Cataldi Gallo 2016, pp. 47–48.
201 Cataldi Gallo 2016, p. 47f.
202 Jolly 2005, p. 29; examples of Genoa: Cataldi Gallo 2016, pp. 48–49.
203 See note to figs. 244/245.
204 'Brocatelle': CIETA Vocabulaire, Vocabulaire – Le vocabulaire du CIETA (17 June 2022).
205 Peter 2020, pp. 9–20; Borkopp-Restle 2009, pp. 191–200; Jolly 2016, p. 14; 'Samt': CIETA Vocabulaire, Vocabulaire – Le vocabulaire du CIETA (17 June 2022).
206 Germann 1913; Jolly 2005, p. 15; 'Moquette', in Lexikon der Gewebe 2015, p. 279; 'Plush', in Lexikon der Gewebe 2015, p. 321.
207 Cataldi Gallo 2016, pp. 48–50; Browne 2009, p. 56; Jolly 2005, cat. 14. An example of the *della palma* motif is in the collection of GRASSI MAK (inv. no. V8276).
208 Bothe/Rietz 2019, pp. 36–39.
209 Ibid., pp. 38–41; on Lasalle, among others Jolly 2005, p. 34; Miller 2009, pp. 79–90.
210 Glossary, in Jolly 2005, p. 246; Zitzmann 2016, pp. 86–87, fig. 2.
211 Jolly 2016, p. 14.
212 Jolly 2005, pp. 32–33.
213 Evers 2014, pp. 3–4; Zitzmann 2016, p. 85; Bothe/Rietz 2019, pp. 41–42; Beard 1997.
214 Evers 2016, p. 77; Kreibich 2016, p. 132.
215 Evers 2014, pp. 7–54; Evers 2016, pp. 73-75; Zitzmann 2016, p. 92.
216 Döring 2016, p. 76.
217 https://www.leipzig-lexikon.de/biogramm/Apel_Andreas_Dietrich.htm (accessed 30 April 2022).
218 On Berlin, Evers 2014; Zitzmann 2016, pp. 85–93. On Dresden, Schneider 2016, pp. 67–68.
219 Colenbrander 2016, pp. 102–107; Browne 2009, pp. 55–56.
220 Reinecke 2020, p. 139; Jolly 2005, p. 34; Wilckens 1997, S. 42
221 Jolly 2005, p. 33.
222 Miller 2009, p. 85.
223 Browne 2009, p. 47; Thornton 1965, p. 135, note 1.
224 Jolly 2005, pp. 36–37; Jolly 2016, p. 14; Coban-Hensel 2004, pp. 116, 119–120; so-called *chambres* featuring matching curtains and state bed covers as well as

217 https://www.leipzig-lexikon.de/biogramm/Apel_Andreas_Dietrich.htm (30.4.2022).
218 Zu Berlin: Evers 2014; Zitzmann 2016, S. 85–93. Zu Dresden: Schneider 2016, S. 68.
219 Colenbrander 2016, S. 102–107; Browne 2009, S. 55f.
220 Jolly 2005, S. 34; Wilckens 1997, S. 42.
221 Jolly 2005, S. 33.
222 Miller 2009, S. 85.
223 Browne 2009, S. 47; Thornton 1965, S. 135, Anm. 1.
224 Jolly 2005, S. 36f., Jolly 2016, S. 14; Coban-Hensel 2004, S. 116, 119f.; sog. Chambres mit zusammengehörigen Vorhängen und Bezügen für ein Paradebett und Wandteppichen sind bereits vorher bezeugt, etwa das Alexandre-Chambre, das Philipp der Gute 1459 kaufte; vgl. Franke 2000, S. 121–169; zu Rechnungsbüchern im 14. Jahrhundert vgl. Bergemann 2010, S. 31.
225 Jolly 2016, S. 13.
226 Jolly 2016, S. 14; Browne 2009, S. 47–58.
227 Vgl. Nr. 242/243 und 244/245.
228 Völker 1996, S. 14; Ottomeyer 2006, S. 47.
229 U. a. Metz 2011, S. 18.
230 U. a. Metz 2011, S. 19.
231 https://www.wmgallery.org.uk/collection/artists-64/morris-co-decorators-ltd-449-oxford-street-london/initial/m/page/1/object/cherwell-printed-velveteen-f356-designed-1887 (1.5.2022).
232 Camphausen 2000, S. 1079, S. 1143f. Nr. 80; Metz 2011, S. 37; zur Weltausstellung 1900 vgl. Beitrag T. Schriefers in diesem Katalog, S. 87–89.
233 Zu Japonismus um 1900: Weisberg 2004, S. 51–71; Metz 2011, S. 19.
234 Stöver 2018, S. 22–31, 81.
235 Lindemann 2021, S. 27; Ein Beispiel eines Musterbuchs mit Druckstoffen für die Raumausstattung um 1790 befindet sich in der Sammlung des Victoria and Albert Museums (Inv. Nr. T.119-1959), https://collections.vam.ac.uk/item/O365530/manuscript-order-unknown/ (22.6.2022).
236 Völker 1996, S. 60; Lindemann 2021, S. 46–49.
237 AK Chemnitz 2006, S. 30. Zu Herta Michel-Koch: https://www.darmstadt-stadtlexikon.de/m/michel-koch-herta.html (22.5.2022).
238 Zu beiden Firmen: Schweynoch 2019, S. 146, 418f.; http://www.historisches-coswig.de/index.php?id=554; (17.06.2022); Dokumente zum Webstuhl GRASSI MAK unter Inv.Nr. V13396.
239 Schweynoch 2019, 146f. https://harvardartmuseums.org/collections/object/215666?position=10 (4.1.2022).
240 Sog. Schriever-Muster von Otti Berger in Privatbesitz, Nachwebung von Katharina Jebsen GRASSI MAK Inv. Nr. 2021.791; Heckhoff/Jebsen 2021, S. 20–25.
241 U. a. Sauer 2015, S. 112f.
242 Durch überdrehte Wollgarne lassen sich dabei Gewebe mit hoher Elastizität erzeugen.
243 Westmann 2019, S. 50; https://collections.vam.ac.uk/item/O10416/juxons-footstool-casbert-john/ (28.06.2022).
244 Lueger 1810, S. 622; Westmann 2019, S. Xii.
245 U. a. Kreibich 2014, S. 85.
246 Kumsch 1892.
247 Schuette 1912, S. 22, Taf. 65; Schuette 1914, S. 52. Leinenquasten zierten im 16. und 17. Jahrhundert vor allem Kissen, Decken und Kleidung. Im Unterschied zu Quasten aus Seide und Metall waren sie leichter zu reinigen.
248 Kreibich 2014, S. 86.
249 Kreibich 2014; Kuschel 2014; Westmann 2019.
250 Für die Unterstützung bei der Bearbeitung danke ich Messalina Mayer.
251 Z. B. drei Beutel aus dem 14. Jahrhundert bei Schuette/Müller-Christiansen 1963, Abb. 216–218, Taf. XI.

tapestries have been documented already earlier, e.g. in the *Alexandre chambre* tapestry, which was bought by Philip the Good in 1459; see Franke 2000, pp. 121–169; for account books in the fourteenth century see Bergemann 2010, p. 31.
225 Jolly 2016, p. 13.
226 Jolly 2016, p. 14; Browne 2009, pp. 47–58.
227 See p. 246, figs. 242–245.
228 Völker 1996, p. 14; Ottomeyer 2006, p. 47.
229 Metz 2011, p. 18, among others.
230 Ibid., p. 19, among others.
231 https://www.wmgallery.org.uk/collection/artists-64/morris-co-decorators-ltd-449-oxford-street-london/initial/m/page/1/object/cherwell-printed-velveteen-f356-designed-1887 (accessed 1 May 2022).
232 Camphausen 2000, pp. 1079, 1143–44 no. 80; Metz 2011, p. 37; on the World's Fair of 1900, see essay by T. Schriefers in this catalogue, pp. 87–89.
233 On Japonism around 1900, Weisberg 2004, pp. 51–71; Metz 2011, p. 19.
234 Stöver 2018, pp. 22–31, 81.
235 Lindemann 2021, p. 27; an example of a pattern book for printed textiles for room furnishing around 1790 can be found in the collection of the Victoria and Albert Museum (inv. no. T.119-1959).
236 Völker 1996, p. 60; Lindemann 2021, pp. 46–49.
237 Exhibition catalogue Chemnitz 2006, p. 30. On Herta Michel-Koch, https://www.darmstadt-stadtlexikon.de/m/michel-koch-herta.html (accessed 22 May 2022).
238 On both companies, Schweynoch 2019, pp. 146, 418–419; http://www.historisches-coswig.de/index.php?id=554 (accessed 17 June 2022); documents on the loom, GRASSI MAK, inv. no.: V13396.
239 Schweynoch 2019, pp.146–147, https://harvardartmuseums.org/collections/object/215666?position=10 (accessed 4 January 2022).
240 The so-called *Schriever Pattern* by Otti Berger in a private collection, reweave by Katharina Jebsen, GRASSI MAK, inv. no. 2021.791; Heckhoff/Jebsen 2021, pp. 20–25.
241 Sauer 2015, pp. 112–113, among others.
242 Over-twisted wool yarns can be used to create fabrics with high elasticity.
243 Westmann 2019, p. 50; https://collections.vam.ac.uk/item/O10416/juxons-footstool-casbert-john/ (accessed 28 June 2022).
244 Lueger 1810, p. 622; Westmann 2019, p. Xii.
245 Kreibich 2014, p. 85, among others.
246 Kumsch 1892.
247 Schuette 1912, p. 22, plate 65; Schuette 1914, p. 52. Linen tassels mainly adorned cushions, blankets and clothing in the sixteenth and seventeenth centuries. Unlike tassels made of silk and metal, they were easier to clean.
248 Kreibich 2014, p. 86.
249 Kreibich 2014; Kuschel 2014; Pisareva 2016; Westmann 2019.
250 I thank Messalina Mayer for her assistance.
251 e.g. three bags from the fourteenth century; Schuette-Müller-Christiansen 1963, figs. 216–218, plate XI.
252 Among others Kreibich 2014, pp. 92–94; Pisareva 2016, p. 149.
253 Wilckens 1997, p. 144.
254 On women in this field, Westmann 2019, pp. 2–15, 18–19. E.g. Alice Smythe (later Alice Mountage), mentioned as the producer of passementerie for the coronation of Elisabeth I in 1559. Westmann 2019, p. 18.
255 Fig. of the wiredrawer of 1681 in the Hausberg manuscript, Mendal Brothers, in Westmann 2019, p. 7, fig. 1.7. On production, Kuschel 2014, pp. 104–105.
256 '1681: Die Graff'sche Gold- und Silberfabrik erhält ein

252 U. a. Kreibich 2014, S. 92–94; Pisareva 2016, S. 149.
253 Wilckens 1997, S. 144.
254 Z. B. Alice Smythe (später Alice Mountage), die als Herstellerin der Posamentierarbeiten für die Krönung Elisabeth I. 1559 aufgeführt wird. Westmann 2019, S. 18. Zu Frauen in diesem Berufsstand siehe Westmann 2019, S. 2–15, 18f.
255 Abb. Drahtzieher 1681 im Hausberg-Manuskript, Mendal Brüder, in: Westmann 2019, S. 7, Abb. 1.7. Zur Herstellung siehe Kuschel 2014, S. 104f.
256 „1681: Die Graff'sche Gold- und Silberfabrik erhält ein Privilegium auf zwanzig Jahre", in: F. Th. Richter, *Jahrbüchlein zur Geschichte Leipzigs und Kalender zu den Gedenktagen seiner merkwürdigen Einwohner*, Leipzig 1863; nach: Bergemann 2006, S. 71.
257 Kreibich 2014, S. 87.
258 Pisareva 2014, S. 149, 151f.; Schneider 2016, S. 67f.
259 Grundlegende Techniken, Materialien siehe Dornbach 1894.
260 Kreibich 2014, S. 128, 132.
261 Westmann 2019, S. 8–12.
262 Beispiele in England und Dänemark in Westman 2019, S. 72.
263 Westman 2019, S. 101–104.
264 Kreibich 2014, Abb. 5 und 6.
265 National Gallery London, NG1314: https://www.nationalgallery.org.uk/paintings/hans-holbein-the-younger-the-ambassadors (18.07.2022).
266 Westmann 2019, S. 169, Fig. 7.33.
267 Vgl. Westmann 2019, S. 42 Fig. 3.4 und S. 64f.
268 Vglsbsp. Dresden, Kunstgewerbemuseum, Wilckens 1997, S. 145 sowie Metropolitan Museum of Art, NewYork (Ac.Nr.: 21.83.2).

Privilegium auf zwanzig Jahre', in F. Th. Richter, *Jahrbüchlein zur Geschichte Leipzigs und Kalender zu den Gedenktagen seiner merkwürdigen Einwohner*, Leipzig 1863; after Bergemann 2006, p. 71.
257 Kreibich 2014, p. 87.
258 Pisareva 2014, pp. 149, 151–152; Schneider 2016, pp. 67–68.
259 For basic techniques and materials, see Dornbach 1894.
260 Kreibich 2014, pp. 128, 132.
261 Westmann 2019, pp. 8–12.
262 Examples in England and Denmark, in Westman 2019, p. 72.
263 Westman 2019, pp. 101–104.
264 Kreibich 2014, figs. 5, 6.
265 National Gallery London, inv. no. NG1314: https://www.nationalgallery.org.uk/paintings/hans-holbein-the-younger-the-ambassadors (18 July 2022).
266 Westmann 2019, p. 169, fig. 7.33.
267 See Westmann 2019, p. 42, fig. 3.4 and pp. 64–65.
268 See Dresden, Kunstgewerbemuseum, Wilckens 1997, p. 145, and The Metropolitan Museum of Art, New York (acc. no. 21.83.2).

360–371
Filmstills zu Garnierarbeiten

360–371
Stil frame showing stuffing, tufting and stitching

Literaturverzeichnis | Bibliography

AK Chemnitz 2006
Fäden, Farben, Fantasien. Textildesign und Textilindustrie in Sachsen 1880 bis 1933, hrsg. von Katharina Metz, Ausst.-Kat. Kunstsammlungen Chemnitz, Chemnitz 2006.

AK Chemnitz 2011
Samt und Seide, Französische Luxus-Stoffe um 1900, anlässlich der Ausstellung „Samt und Seide. Französische Luxusstoffe aus der Epoche Pierre-Auguste Renoire" gemeinsam mit der Ausstellung „Pierre-Auguste Renoir. Wie Seide gemalt" in der Kunstsammlung Chemnitz vom 18. September 2011 bis 8. Januar 2012, hrsg. von Ingrid Mössinger und Katharina Metz, Ausst.-Kat. Kunstsammlungen Chemnitz, München 2011.

Anderson 2022
Anderson, Christina M. (Hrsg.): *A Cultural History of Furniture*, 6 Bde., London / New York / Oxford / New Delhi 2022.

Anderson 2022 a
Anderson, Christina M. (Hrsg.): *A Cultural History of Furniture. In Antiquity* Bd. 1, London / New York / Oxford / New Delhi 2022.

Arnold 1993
Arnold, Klaus-Peter: *Vom Sofakissen zum Städtebau. Die Geschichte der Deutschen Werkstätten und der Gartenstadt Hellerau*, Dresden / Basel 1993.

Bahns 1979
Bahns, Jörn: *Biedermeier-Möbel. Entstehung – Zentren – Typen*, München 1979.

Barth von Wehrenalp / Saechtling 1952
Barth von Wehrenalp, Erwin und Hansjürgen Saechtling: *Jahrhundert der Kunststoffe in Wort und Bild*, Düsseldorf 1952.

Batchelor 2012
Batchelor, Robert K.: *Thinking about the Gym: Greek Ideals, Newtonian Bodies, and Exercise in Early Eighteenth-Century England*, Statesboro 2012.

Bauen + Wohnen 1961
Bauen + Wohnen, Internationale Zeitschrift, 15. Jg., Heft 12/1961, Anhang XII–1.

Bauhaus 1928
bauhaus. Zeitschrift für Bau und Gestaltung, Dessau, 2. Jg., Heft 1/1928.

Bauhaus 1928 a
bauhaus. Zeitschrift für Bau und Gestaltung, Dessau, 2. Jg., Heft 4/1928.

Baukunst und Werkform 1953
Baukunst und Werkform, Frankfurt am Main, Heft 5/1953.

Beard 1997
Beard, Goffrey: *Upholsterers and Interior Furnishing in England 1530–1840*, New Haven / London 1997.

Behne 1930
Behne, Adolf: *Neues Wohnen – neues Bauen*, Leipzig 1930.

Beiblatt der Fliegenden Blätter 1889
Beiblatt der Fliegenden Blätter, München, 9. Dezember 1898, S. 24. URL: https://digi.ubuni-heidelberg.de/digit/fb_bb109/0563 (4.5.2022).

Benjamin 1961
Benjamin, Walter: *Goethes Wahlverwandtschaften*, in: *Illuminationen, Ausgewählte Schriften*, Frankfurt am Main 1961. Erneut abgedruckt in: *Daidalos. Transparenz und Verhüllung* Bd. 33, 15. September 1989, Gütersloh 1989, S. 60.

Benjamin 1983
Benjamin, Walter: *Das Passagen-Werk*, in: *Gesammelte Schriften*, Bd.1, hrsg. von Rolf Tiedemann, Frankfurt am Main 1983, S. 292.

Bergemann 2000
Bergemann, Uta-Christiane: *Stickereien (Stiftung Preussische Schlösser und Gärten Berlin-Brandenburg*: Bestandskatalog der Kunstsammlungen Angewandte Kunst, Textilien), Berlin 2000.

Bergemann 2010
Bergemann, Uta-Christiane: *Europäische Stickereien, 1250–1650* (Ausstellung „Stickereien des Mittelalters und der Renaissance aus der Sammlung des Deutschen Textilmuseums" 19. September 2010 bis 9. Januar 2011 Textilmuseum Krefeld), Regensburg 2010.

Bertuch 1786
Bertuch, Friedrich Justin: *Ameublement*, in: Bertuch, Friedrich Justin (Hrsg.): *Journal der Moden*, 1. Jg., Januar 1786, S. 28–30.

Bidlingmaier 2000
Bidlingmaier, Rolf: *Das Residenzpalais in Kassel. Der Architekt Johann Conrad Bromeis und die Raumkunst des Klassizismus und Empire in Kurhessen unter Kurfürst Wilhelm II.*, Regensburg 2000, S. 186.

Bildende Kunst 1956
Bildende Kunst, Dresden, Heft 5/1956.

Bixler-Reber 2012
Bixler-Reber, Patricia: *Chamber Horse*. URL: http://researchingfoodhistory.blogspot.com/2012/08chamber-horse.htlm (4.3.2022).

Bonnet 2009
Bonnet, Xavier: *Changes in Upholstery During the Empire in Pairs*, in: *Empire Furniture. Introduction, Adoption, Aadaptation and Conservation*, Amsterdam 2009, S. 17.

Bothe / Rietz 2019
Bothe, Rolf und Andreas Rietz: *Polstermöbel und textile Raumausstattungen: vom Handwerk zur Wissenschaft*, Regensburg 2019.

Borkopp-Restle 2009
Borkopp-Restle, Birgitt: *Stamped Silk Velvets – Patterns and Techniques*, in: Jolly, Anna (Hrsg.): *Furnishing Textiles. Studies on Seventeenth- and Eighteenth-Century Interior Decoration*, Riggisberger Berichte 17, Riggisberg 2009, S. 191–200.

Braun-Ronsdorf 1958
Braun-Ronsdorf, Margarete: *Dekorationsstoffe des Mittelalters und der Renaissance*, in: Ciba-Rundschau, Bd. 12 , Heft 136/1958, S. 8–16.

Browne 2009
Browne, Clare: *Silk Damask Bed Furnishings in the Early Eigteenth Century – Influences on Choice in Colour and Design*, in: Jolly, Anna (Hrsg.): *Furnishing Textiles. Studies on Seventeenth- and Eighteenth-Century Interior Decoration*, Riggisberger Berichte 17, Riggisberg 2009, S. 47–58.

Bücheler / Ulmschneider 1953
Bücheler, Robert und Otto Ulmschneider: *Neuzeitliches Polstern*, München 1953.

Campbell 2018
Caroline Campbell, Dagmar Korbmacher, Neville Rowley und Sarah Vowles (Hrsg.): *Mantegna + Bellini: Meister der Renaissance*, Ausst.-Kat., München 2018.

Camphausen 2000
Camphausen, Ute: *Die Erwerbungen auf der Weltausstellung in Paris 1900. Hrsg. im Nachgang der Ausstellung Paris – ein Fest fürs Leben. 5. Juni bis 3. Oktober 2000*, in: *Mitteilungen des städtischen Museums für Kunsthandwerk zu Leipzig, Grassimuseum und seines Freundes- und Förderkreises e. V.*, Leipzig, Heft 11/2000.

Cataldi Gallo 2016
Cataldi Gallo, Marzia: *Genoese Textiles for Interior Decoration*, in: Evers, Susanne und Generaldirektion Stiftung Preußische Schlösser und Gärten Berlin-Brandenburg (Hrsg.): *Textile Räume – Textile Spaces. Seide im höfischen Interieur des 18. Jahrhunderts. Silk in 18th Century Court Interieurs*, Dresden 2016, S. 46–53.

Cheyne, George 1724
Cheyne, George: *An Essay of Health and Long Life*. Chap. IV: *Of Exercise and Quiet*, London 1724, § 5, S. 99, in: *Eigteenth Century Collections Online. Text Creation Partnership*, 2011. URL: http://name.umdl.umich.edu/004834818.0001.000 (3.12.2021).

CIETA Vocabulaire
Online Wörterbuch des Centre Internationale d'Étude des Textiles Anciens. URL: http://vocabulaire.cieta.fr/en/ (17.06.2022).

Coban-Hensel 2004
Coban-Hensel, Margitta: *Kurfürst Moritz von Sachsen und seine Schloßausstattungen*, in: Thieme, André und Jochen Vötsch (Hrsg.): *Hof und Hofkultur unter Moritz von Sachsen (1521–1553)*, Saxonia. Schriften des Vereins für sächsische Landesgeschichte 8, Beucha 2004, S. 113–136.

Colenbrander 2016
Colenbrander, Sjoukje: *Cinese Silks imported into Europe during the Seventeenth and Eighteenth Centuries*, in: Evers, Susanne und Generaldirektion Stiftung Preußische Schlösser und Gärten Berlin-Brandenburg (Hrsg.): *Textile Räume – Textile Spaces. Seide im höfischen Interieur des 18. Jahrhunderts. Silk in 18th Century Court Interieurs*, Dresden 2016, S. 102-107.

Constanze 1958
Constanze, Hamburg, Heft 35/1958.

Daidalos 1989
Daidalos. Transparenz und Verhüllung Bd. 33, 15. September 1989, Gütersloh 1989.

Deutsche Werkstätten 2018
Deutsche Werkstätten (Hrsg.): *Eine Klasse für sich. Historischer Schiffsinnenausbau der Deutschen Werkstätten*, Dresden 2018.

Deutscher Werkbund 1987
z.B. Stühle. *Ein Streifzug durch die Kulturgeschichte des Sitzens*, Ausst.-Kat. Deutscher Werkbund e. V., Gießen 1987.

Dieckmann 1931
Dieckmann, Erich: *Möbelbau in Holz, Rohr und Stahl*, Stuttgart 1931.

Die Form 1929
Die Form. Zeitschrift für gestaltende Arbeit, Berlin, 4. Jg., Heft 24/15.12.1929.

Die Zeit 1955
Die Zeit, Ausgabe vom 3. November 1955.

Döring 2016
Döring, Detlef: *Vom Ende der schwedischen Besatzung (1650) bis zum Ende des Siebenjährigen Krieges (1763)*, in: Döring, Detlef (Hrsg.): *Geschichte der Stadt Leipzig*, 4 Bde. *Von der Reformation bis zum Wiener Kongress* Bd. 2, Leipzig 2016, S. 70–96.

Droste 1999
Droste, Magdalena und Manfred Ludewig: *Das Bauhaus webt. Die Textilwerkstatt am Bauhaus*, Berlin 1999.

Du 1986
du. Zeitschrift für Kunst und Kultur, Zürich, Heft 6/1986.

Duggleby & Stephenson of York 2018
Duggleby & Stephenson of York: *The Salesroom*, York Auction Centre Murton, York, Y0195 GF, 2018.

Ede / Goudet 2002
Ede, François und Stéphane Goudet: *Playtime*, Paris 2002.

Eikelmann / Borkopp-Restle 2002
Eikelmann, Renate und Birgitt Borkopp-Restle (Hrsg.): *Mit grossen Freuden, Triumph und Köstlichkeit. Textile Schätze aus Renaissance und Barock. Aus den Sammlungen des Bayerischen Nationalmuseums*, München 2002.

Emmrich / Schroeder 2000
Emmrich, Angelika und Susanne Schroeder: *Weimarer historische Interieurs: zum Ameublement im „Journal des Luxus und der Moden"*, in: Kaiser, Gerhard R. und Siegfried Seifert (Hrsg.): *Friedrich Justin Bertuch (1747–1822). Verleger, Schriftsteller und Unternehmer im klassischen Weimar*, Tübingen 2000, S. 501–517.

Ernst 1937
Ernst, Jupp: *Kampf dem Kitsch!* Bielefeld 1937.

Evers 2014
Evers, Susanne: *Seiden in den preußischen Schlössern. Ausstattungstextilien und Posamente unter Friedrich II. (1740–1786)*, Bestandskatalog Kunstsammlung / Stiftung Preußische Schlösser und Gärten Berlin-Brandenburg, Berlin 2014.

Feulner 1927
Feulner, Adolf: *Kunstgeschichte des Möbels*, Berlin 1927.

Fliegende Blätter 1889
Beiblatt der Fliegenden Blätter, München, 9. Dezember 1898, S. 24. URL: https://digi.ubuni-heidelberg.de/digit/fb_bb109/0563 (4.5.2022).

Form + Zweck 1973
form + zweck, Fachzeitschrift für industrielle Formgestaltung, Berlin, Heft 1/1973.

Form + Zweck 1973 a
form + zweck, Fachzeitschrift für industrielle Formgestaltung, Berlin, Heft 4/1973.

Form + Zweck 1975
form + zweck, Fachzeitschrift für industrielle Formgestaltung, Berlin, Heft 3/1975.

Form + Zweck 1977
form + zweck, Fachzeitschrift für industrielle Formgestaltung, Berlin, Heft 6/1977.

Form + Zweck 1981
form + zweck, Fachzeitschrift für industrielle Formgestaltung, Berlin, Heft 5/1981.

Franke 2000
Franke, Birgit: *Herrscher über Himmel und Erde. Alexander der Große und die Herzöge von Burgund*, in: Philipps-Universität Marburg / Forschungsinstitut für Kunstgeschichte (Hrsg.): *Marburger Jahrbuch für Kunstwissenschaft*, Marburg, Heft 27/2000, S. 121–169.

Fuller 1729
Fuller, Francis: *Medicina Gymnastica: Or a Treatise Concerning the Power of Exercise, with Respect to the Animal Oeconomy and the Great Necessity of it in the Cure of Several Distempers*, London 1704, 6. Auflage 1729, Royal Collection Trust ESTC T14628.

Garner 1980
Garner, Philippe: *Möbel des 20. Jahrhunderts. Internationales Design vom Jugendstil bis zur Gegenwart*, München 1980.

Genath 1935
Genath, Max: *Der Niedergang des Tapezier- und Polsterhandwerks als Produktionsgewerbe*, Diss. Halle-Wittenberg, Dresden 1935.

Germann 1913
Germann, Karl: *Die Deutsche Möbelplüsch- und Moquette-Industrie. Geschichtliche Entwicklung und gegenwärtige Lage*, Diss. Leipzig 1913, Leipzig 1913.

Gesolei 1926
Gesolei (Hrsg.): *Amtlicher Katalog. Grosse Ausstellung für Gesundheitspflege, soziale Fürsorge und Leibesübungen (Gesolei)*, Düsseldorf 1926.

GH Wuppertal 1999
GH Wuppertal (Lehrstuhl für Kunst- und Designgeschichte, Stiftung Design-Sammlung Schriefers), Landschaftsverband Rheinland, Rheinisches Industriemuseum Engelskirchen und Deutsches Klingenmuseum (Hrsg.): *Positionen des Designs – Die 60er*, Ausst.-Kat., Köln 1999.

Giedion 1929
Giedion, Sigfried: *Befreites Wohnen*, Zürich / Leipzig 1929.

Giedion 1965
Giedion, Sigfried: *Raum, Zeit, Architektur. Die Entstehung einer neuen Tradition*, Ravensburg 1965.

Giedion 1987
Giedion, Sigfried: *Die Herrschaft der Mechanisierung. Ein Beitrag zur anonymen Geschichte*, Frankfurt am Main 1987.

Gräff 1931
Gräff, Werner: *Zweckmässiges Wohnen für jedes Einkommen*, Potsdam 1931.

GRASSI Museum für Angewandte Kunst 2020
GRASSI Museum für Angewandte Kunst (Hrsg.): *Ständige Ausstellung. Jugendstil bis Gegenwart*, Bestandskatalog GRASSI-Museum, Leipzig 2020.

Havard 1894
Havard, Henry (Hrsg.): *Dictionnaire de l´Ameublement et de la Décoration depuis le XIIIe siècle jusqu´à nos jours*, 4 Bde., Paris 1894.

Harvard Art Museum
Online Collection des Harvard Art Museum, Artikel zu Objekt Nr. BR52.340: „*Möbel-Stoff-Doppelgewebe aus Kunstfaser. Deutsches Reichspatent. Hersteller und Vertrieb: Sächsische Rosshaarweberei Schriever & Co Dresden*". URL: https://harvardartmuseums.org/collections/object/215666?position=10 (4.1.2022).

Heckhoff / Jebsen 2021
Heckhoff, Miriam und Katharina Jebsen: *Neue Bauhaus Objekte*, in: *Textilkunst international. Informationen für kreatives Gestalten*, 49. Jg., Heft 1/März 2021, S. 20–25.

Himmelheber 1983
Himmelheber, Georg und Heinrich Kreisel: *Die Kunst des deutschen Möbels. Klassizismus, Historismus, Jugendstil* Bd. 3., München 1983.

Historisches Coswig
Privates online-Projekt Historisches-Coswig: *Roßhaarweberei*. URL: http://www.historisches-coswig.de/index.php?id=554 (17.6.2022).

Hoffmann 1932
Hoffmann, Herbert (Hrsg.): *Moderne Bauformen. Monatshefte für Architektur und Raumkunst*, 31. Jg., 1932.

Innendekoration 1925
Innendekoration, Darmstadt, 36. Jg., Heft 5/1925.

Innendekoration 1925 a
Innendekoration, Darmstadt, 36. Jg, Heft 6/1925.

Innendekoration 1926
Innendekoration, Darmstadt, 37. Jg, Heft 11/1926.

Jolly 2005
Jolly, Anna (Hrsg.): *Fürstliche Interieurs. Dekorationstextilien des 18. Jahrhunderts*, Riggisberger Berichte 12, Riggisberg 2005.

Jolly 2009
Jolly, Anna (Hrsg.): *Furnishing Textiles. Studies on Seventeenth- and Eighteenth-Century Interior Decoration*, Riggisberger Berichte 17, Riggisberg 2009.

Jolly 2016
Jolly, Anna: *„en situ" – Erscheinungsformen eines textilen Gestaltungskonzepts*, in: Evers, Susanne und Generaldirektion Stiftung Preußische Schlösser und Gärten Berlin-Brandenburg (Hrsg.): *Textile Räume – Textile Spaces. Seide im höfischen Interieur des 18. Jahrhunderts. Silk in 18th Century Court Interieurs*, Dresden 2016, S. 12–21.

Jugend 1907
Jugend. Münchner illustrierte Wochenschrift für Kunst und Leben, 1907.

Köppen / Breuer 1904
Köppen, Alfred und Carl Breuer: *Geschichte des Möbels unter Berücksichtigung der architektonischen und tektonischen Formen. Eine Stillehre für Bau-und Möbeltischler*, Berlin / New York 1904.

Kreibich 2014
Kreibich, Silke: *Posamente in der textilen Ausstattung am friederizianischen Hof*, in: *Seiden in den preußischen Schlössern. Ausstattungstextilien und Posamente unter Friedrich II. (1740–1786)*, hrsg. von Susanne Evers, Bestandskatalog Kunstsammlung / Stiftung Preußische Schlösser und Gärten Berlin-Brandenburg, Berlin 2014, S. 83–99.

Kreibich 2016
Kreibich, Silke: *Passaments in Prussian Castles. Developement and Dating of Eighteenth Century Patterns*, in: Evers, Susanne und Generaldirektion Stiftung Preußische Schlösser und Gärten Berlin-Brandenburg (Hrsg.): *Textile Räume – Textile Spaces. Seide im höfischen Interieur des 18. Jahrhunderts. Silk in 18th Century Court Interieurs*, Dresden 2016, S. 128–135.

Kultur im Heim 1961
Kultur im Heim, Berlin, Heft 3/1961.

Kumsch 1892
Kumsch, Emil: *Posamente des XVI.–XIX. Jahrhunderts*, Dresden 1892.

Kunstsammlungen Chemnitz 1998
Kunstsammlungen Chemnitz (Hrsg.): *Europäisches Textildesign der 20er Jahre*, Bestandskatalog der Kunstsammlungen Chemnitz 4, Zürich / New York 1998.

Kuschel 2014
Kuschel, Nadia: *Die Kunst der Posamentierer. Material, Technik, Restaurierung, Rekonstruktion und Kopie von Posamenten für die preußischen Schlösser*, in: *Seiden in den preußischen Schlössern. Ausstattungstextilien und Posamente unter Friedrich II. (1740–1786)*, hrsg. von Susanne Evers, Bestandskatalog Kunstsammlung / Stiftung Preußische Schlösser und Gärten Berlin-Brandenburg, Berlin 2014, S. 101–126.

Kuschel 2016
Kuschel, Nadia: *Die goldenen Posamente aus dem Tessinzimmer von 1768*, in: Evers, Susanne und Generaldirektion Stiftung Preußische Schlösser und Gärten Berlin-Brandenburg (Hrsg.): *Textile Räume – Textile Spaces. Seide im höfischen Interieur des 18. Jahrhunderts. Silk in 18th Century Court Interieurs*, Dresden 2016, S. 136–145.

Leipzig Lexikon
Online Lexikon Leipzig-Lexikon: *Apel, Andreas Dietrich*. URL: https://www.leipzig-lexikon.de/biogramm/Apel_Andreas_Dietrich.htm (30.4.2022).

Lewitzky 1962
Lewitzky, Hans: *Meine Wohnung*, Berlin 1962.

Lexikon der Gewebe
Lexikon der Gewebe. Technik – Bindung – Handelsnamen, hrsg. von Thomas Meyer zur Capellen, 5. erweit. Auflage, Frankfurt am Main 2015.

Lindemann 2021
Lindemann, Katrin: *Historische figürliche Baumwolldruckstoffe im Kontext von Erstellen, Verwenden, Sammeln, Ausstellen und Vermitteln*, KONTEXT Kunst – Vermittlung – Kulturelle Bildung 27, Diss. Paderborn 2018, Baden-Baden 2021.

Loewy 1953
Loewy, Raymond: *Hässlichkeit verkauft sich schlecht. Die Erlebnisse des erfolgreichsten Formgestalters unserer Zeit*, Düsseldorf 1953.

Loos 1921
Loos, Adolf: *Ins Leere gesprochen (1897–1900)*, Zürich 1921.

Loos 1931
Loos, Adolf: *Trotzdem 1900–1930*, Innsbruck 1931.

Lueger 1810
Otto Lueger: *Posament, das*, in: Krünitz, Johannes Georg (Hrsg.): *Oeconomische Encyclopädie oder allgemeines System, der Land-, Haus- und Staats-Wirthschaft. 115. Polypädie – 3. Post* Bd. 115, Berlin 1810, S. 622.

Maddock 1993
Maddock, Brent: *Die Filme von Jacques Tati*, München 1993.

Magnum 1957
magnum. Die Zeitschrift für das moderne Leben, Heft 15/Dezember 1957.

Markowsky 1976
Markowsky, Barbara (Hrsg.): *Europäische Seidengewebe des 13.–18. Jahrhunderts*, Kataloge des Kunstgewerbemuseums Köln 8, Köln 1976.

Massenbach 1977
Massenbach, Sigrid von: *Die Memoiren des Herzogs von Saint-Simon*, Berlin 1977.

Metz 2011
Metz, Katharina: *Samt und Seide. Französische Luxus-Stoffe um 1900*, in: *Samt und Seide, Französische Luxus-Stoffe um 1900*, hrsg. von Katharina Metz und Ingrid Mössinger, Ausst.-Kat. Kunstsammlungen Chemnitz, München 2011, S. 17–44.

Meyer 1889
Meyer, Franz: *Systematisch geordnetes Handbuch der Ornamentik zum Gebrauche für Musterzeichner, Architekten, Schulen und Gewerbetreibende sowie zum Studium im Allgemeinen*, Leipzig 1889.

Meyer-Bergner 1980
Meyer-Bergner, Lena (Hrsg.): *Hannes Meyer. Bauen und Gesellschaft. Schriften, Briefe, Projekte*, Fundus-Bücher 64/65, Dresden 1980.

Miller 2009
Miller, Lesley Ellis: *Departing from the Pheasant and the Peacock: The Role of Furnishing Textiles in the Career of Philippe de Lasalle (1723–1804)*, in: Jolly, Anna (Hrsg.): *Furnishing Textiles. Studies on Seventeenth- and Eigteenth-Century Interior Decoration*, Riggisberger Berichte 17, Riggisberg 2009, S. 79–90.

Missenharter 1926
Missenharter, Hermann: *Der bequeme Sessel*, in: *Innendekoration*, Darmstadt, 37. Jg., November-Heft/1926, S. 375–378.

Möller 1998
Möller, Renate: *Empire- und Biedermeiermöbel*, München / Berlin 1998.

Monnas 1993
Monnas, Lisa: *Italian Silks (1300–1500)*, in: Harris, Jennifer (Hrsg.): *500 Years of Textiles*, London 1993, S. 167–171.

Monnas 2018
Monnas, Lisa: *A Study in Contrasts: Silk Consumption in Italy and England During the Fifteenth and Sixteenth Centuries*, in: Schäfer, Dagmar (Hrsg.): *Threads of Global Desire: Silk in the Pre-Modern World*, Woodbridge 2018, 149–186.

Naumann 1958
Naumann, Walter Naumann: *Fachbuch für Tapezierer*, Leipzig 1958.

Naylor 2005
Naylor, Maxine und Ralph Ball: *Form Follows Idea. An Introduction to Design Poetics*, London 2005.

Neutra 1975
Neutra, Richard: *Gestaltete Umwelt. Erfahrungen und Forderungen eines Architekten*, Dresden 1975.

Ostergard 1987
Ostergard, Derek E. (Hrsg.): *Bent Wood and Metal Furniture 1850–1946*, Aust.-Kat. The American Federation of Arts, 1987.

Ottillinger 2018
Ottillinger, Eva B. (Hrsg.): *Wagner, Hoffmann, Loos und das Möbeldesign der Wiener Moderne. Künstler, Auftraggeber, Produzenten*, Ausst.-Kat., Wien 2018.

Ottomeyer 1987
Ottomeyer, Hans: *Von Stilen und Ständen in der Biedermeierzeit*, in: *Biedermeiers Glück und Ende. … die gestörte Idylle 1815–1848*, Ausst.-Kat. Münchner Stadtmuseum 1987, München 1987, S. 91–128.

Ottomeyer 1994
Ottomeyer, Hans: *Wege zur neuen Einfachheit. Arbeiten der Münchner Hofschreinerei 1800–1817*, in: *Ein Jahrhundert Möbel für den Fürstenhof. Karlsruhe, Mannheim, Sankt Petersburg 1750 bis 1850. Möbel für den Fürstenhof*, hrsg. von Rosemarie Stratman-Döhler und Wolfgang Wiese, Ausst.-Kat. Badisches Landesmuseum und Staatliche Schlösser und Gärten bei der Oberfinanzdirektion Karlsruhe 1994, Sigmaringen 1994, S. 77–85.

Ottomeyer 2006
Ottomeyer, Hans: *Die Erfindung der Einfachheit*, in: *Biedermeier. Die Erfindung der Einfachheit*, hrsg. von Hans Ottomeyer, Klaus Albrecht Schröder und Laurie Winters, Ausst.-Kat. Milwaukee Art Museum, Deutsches Historisches Museum Berlin und Albertina Wien 2006–2008, Ostfildern 2006, S. 43–55.

Ott-Wodni 2015
Ott-Wodni, Marlene: *Möbeldesign*, in: Ott-Wodni, Marlene (Hrsg.): *Josef Frank 1885–1967. Raumgestaltung und Möbeldesign*, Wien / Köln / Weimar 2015, S. 268.

Peter 2020
Peter, Michael: *Velvets of the Fifteenth Century: Art, Technique, and Business*, in: Peter, Michael (Hrsg.): *Velvets of the Fifteenth Century*, Riggisberger Berichte 24, Riggisberg 2020, S. 9–20.

Platz 1933
Platz, Gustav Adolf: *Wohnräume der Gegenwart*, Berlin 1933.

Radice 1993
Radice, Barbara: *Ettore Sottsass. Leben und Werk*, München 1993.

Reineke 2020
Reineke, Anika: *Der Stoff der Räume: Textile Raumkonzepte im französischen Interieur des 18. Jahrhunderts*, Heidelberg: art-historicum.net, 2020 (https://doi.org/10.11588/arthistoricum. 787).

Richter 1966
Richter, Gisela M. A.: *The Furniture of the Greeks, Etruscans and Romans*, London 1966.

Samson 1874
Samson, Henry: *A History of Advertising from the Earliest Times: Illustrated by Anecdotes, Curious Specimens and Biographical Notes*, London 1874.

Sauer 2015
Christiane, Sauer: *Erkundung von Potential*, in: *Textildesign. Vom Experiment zur Serie*, hrsg. von Bettina Göttke-Korgmann, Ausst.-Kat. Burggalerie im Volkspark Halle 2015, Bauhaus-Archiv und Museum für Gestaltung Berlin 2016, Halle 2015, S. 112–115.

Schmidt 1930
Schmidt, Otto: *Der alten Wohnung ein neues Gesicht*, Stuttgart 1930.

Schneck 1933
Schneck, Adolf G.: *Das Polstermöbel*, hrsg. im Auftrag des Württembergischen Landesgewerbeamtes, Stuttgart 1933.

Schneider 2016
Schneider, Sabine: *The State Apartment of August the Strong Created in Dresden Palace in 1719 – Textile Décore and Ceremonial, with Particular Focus on its Replicas*, in: Evers, Susanne und Generaldirektion Stiftung Preußische Schlösser und Gärten Berlin-Brandenburg (Hrsg.): *Textile Räume – Textile Spaces. Seide im höfischen Interieur des 18. Jahrhunderts. Silk in 18th Century Court Interieurs*, Dresden 2016, S. 62–69.

Schuette 1914
Marie Schuette: *Alte Spitzen (Nadel- und Klöppelspitzen). Ein Handbuch für Sammler und Liebhaber. Mit 172 Abbildungen*, Bibliothek für Kunst- und Antiquitätensammler 6, Berlin 1914.

Schuster 1927
Schuster, Franz: *Eine eingerichtete Kleinstwohnung*, Frankfurt am Main 1927.

Schuster 1948
Schuster, Franz: *Der Stil unserer Zeit. Die fünf Formen des Gestaltens der äußeren Welt des Menschen. Ein Beitrag zum kulturellen Wiederaufbau*, Wien 1948.

Schweynoch 2019
Schweynoch, Evelyn: *Die Rosshaarweberei Gebrüder Schriever & Co. in Dresden / Coswig*, in: *Bauhaus Sachsen / Bauhaus Saxony*, hrsg. von Olaf Thormann, Ausst.-Kat. GRASSI Museum Leipzig 2019, Stuttgart 2019, S. 146–149.

Sheraton 1793
Sheraton, Thomas: *A Cabinet-Maker and Upholsterer's Drawing Book*, London 1793.

Siegel 1892
Siegel, Eduin: *Zur Geschichte des Posamentiergewerbes mit besonderer Rücksichtnahme auf die erzgebirgische Posamentenindustrie*, Annaberg 1892.

Spannagel 1937
Spannagel, Fritz: *Unsere Wohnmöbel*, Ravensburg 1937.

Spiegel 1928
Spiegel, Hans: *Der Stahlhausbau, Wohnbauten aus Stahl*, Leipzig-Gohlis 1928.

Stadtlexikon Darmstadt
Online Lexikon Stadtlexikon Darmstadt: *Michel-Koch, Herta*. URL: https://www.darmstadt-stadtlexikon.de/m/michel-koch-herta.html (22.5.2022).

Steinberg 1949
Steinberg, Saul: *The Art of Living*, New York 1949.

Stieg / Hammerschmied 1979
Stieg, Robert Maria und Heribert Hammerschmied (Hrsg.): *Vorsicht: Polstermöbel!* Ausst.-Kat. Österreichisches Gesellschafts- und Wirtschaftsmuseum, Wien 1979.

Süddeutsche Zeitung 2019
Süddeutsche Zeitung, Wochenendausgabe, 2./3. März 2019.

Stöver 2018
Stöver, Kerstin: *Dewetex – lichtecht und farbenfroh. Textiles aus den Deutschen Werkstätten Hellerau*, in: Dresdner Kunstblätter, Heft 3/2018, S. 23–31.

Taut 1924
Taut, Bruno: *Die Neue Wohnung: Die Frau als Schöpferin*, Leipzig 1924.

Thormann 2002
Thormann, Olaf: *Stilwille und edle Materialien. Ernst Treusch – ein führender Juwelier Sachsens*, in: Leipziger Blätter, Heft 41/2002.

Thormann 2003
Thormann, Olaf: *125 Jahre Museum für Kunsthandwerk Leipzig Grassimuseum Teil 2/1. Die Museumchronik von den Anfängen bis zum Jahr 1929*, Leipzig 2003.

Valk 2012
Valk, Thorsten: *Weimarer Klassik. Kultur des Sinnlichen*, in: *Weimarer Klassik. Kultur des Sinnlichen*, hrsg. von Sebastian Böhmer und Christiane, Ausst.-Kat. Schiller-Museum Weimar 2012, Berlin / München 2012, S. 11–23.

Van Geest 1980
Van Geest, Jan und Otakar Máčel: *Stühle aus Stahl. Metallmöbel 1925–1940*, Köln 1980.

Van Hinte 2006
Van Hinte, Ed (Hrsg.): *Under Cover. Evolution of Upholstered Furniture*, Ausst.-Kat., Rotterdam 2006.

Völker 1996
Völker, Angela (Hrsg.): *Biedermeierstoffe. Die Sammlung des MAK – Österreichisches Museum für angewandte Kunst, Wien und des Technischen Museums Wien*, München / New York 1996.

Weisberg 2004
Weisberg, Gabrial P.: *Die Entstehung des Japonismus*, in: *L'art nouveau. La Maison Bing*, hrsg. von Gabriel P. Weisberg, Edwin Becker und Éveline Possémé, Ausst.-Kat. Van Gogh Museum Amsterdam 2004/05, Villa Stuck München 2005, Caixa Forum Barcelona 2005/06 und Musée des Arts Décoratifs 2006, Stuttgart 2004, S. 50–71.

Werk und Zeit 1953
Werk und Zeit, Zeitschrift des Deutschen Werkbundes, Düsseldorf, Heft 13/ März 1953.

Werk und Zeit 1957
Werk und Zeit. Zeitschrift des Deutschen Werkbundes, Düsseldorf, Heft 1/1957.

Werk und Zeit 1960
Werk und Zeit. Zeitschrift des Deutschen Werkbundes, Düsseldorf, Heft 11/1960.

Westmann 2009
Westmann, Annabel: *Extravagant Embellishment. Trimmings on State Beds in Britain. 1660–1700*, in: Jolly, Anna (Hrsg.): *Furnishing Textiles. Studies on Seventeenth- and Eighteenth-Century Interior Decoration*, Riggisberger Berichte 17, Riggisberg 2009, S. 35–46.

Westmann 2019
Westmann, Annabel: *Fringe, Frog & Tassel. The Art of the*

Trimmings-Maker in Interior Decoration in Britain and Ireland, London 2019.

Wichmann 1992
Wichmann, Hans (Hrsg.): *Deutsche Werkstätten und WK-Verband. Aufbruch zum neuen Wohnen*, München 1992.

Wilckens 1997
Wilckens, Leonie von: *Geschichte der Deutschen Textilkunst: vom späten Mittelalter bis in die Gegenwart*, München 1997.

William Morris Gallery
William Morris Gallery, Collection: *Cherwell Printed Velveteen (Designed 1887)*. URL: https://www.wmgallery.org.uk/collection/artists-64/morris-co-decorators-ltd-449-oxford-street-london/initial/m/page/1/object/cherwell-printed-velveteen-f356-designed-1887 (1.5.2022).

Witt-Dörring 2006
Witt-Dörring, Christian: *Zur Ästhetik des Biedermeiermöbels*, in: *Biedermeier. Die Erfindung der Einfachheit*, hrsg. von Hans Ottomeyer, Klaus Albrecht Schröder und Laurie Winters, Ausst.-Kat. Milwaukee Art Museum, Deutsches Historisches Museum Berlin und Albertina Wien 2006–2008, Ostfildern 2006, S. 57–69.

Zeit-Magazin 2008
Zeit-Magazin, Ausgabe vom 23. Oktober 2008.

Zeit-Magazin 2017
Zeit-Magazin, Ausgabe vom 5. Oktober 2017.

Ziegenhorn 1912
Ziegenhorn & Junker (Firma): *Rückblick auf die historischen Möbelformen im Zusammenhang mit der modernen Raumkunst*, Erfurt, ohne Jahresangabe, vermutlich 1912.

Zinnkann 2007
Zinnkann, Heidrun: *Der feine Unterschied – Biedermeiermöbel Europas 1815–1835*, in: *Biedermeiermöbel Europas 1815–1835. Der feine Unterschied*, hrsg. von Heidrun Zinnkann und Gloria Erhet, Ausst.-Kat. Museum für Angewandte Kunst Frankfurt 2007–2008, München 2007, S. 8–42.

Zitzmann 2016
Zitzmann, Christa: *Entwicklungsstand der preußischen Seidenwebkunst im 18. Jahrhundert während der Regierungszeit Friedrichs II.*, in: Evers, Susanne und Generaldirektion Stiftung Preußische Schlösser und Gärten Berlin-Brandenburg (Hrsg.): *Textile Räume – Textile Spaces. Seide im höfischen Interieur des 18. Jahrhunderts. Silk in 18th Century Court Interieurs*, Dresden 2016, S. 84–93.

No. 5. Elastische Fauteuils von Gropius.

Man erhält einen Besuch und ladet ihn zum Sitzen ein. Der Fremde bewundert die Elasticität des Stuhls, will aber nicht glauben daß derselbe 24 Federn enthalte. Man schneidet daher rasch das Polster auf und der Gast büßt durch eine rasche nicht ganz unangenehme Bewegung seine Schwergläubigkeit.

372
Karikatur aus dem *Kladderadatsch*, Berlin, um 1850, Archiv Thomas Schriefers
Carricature from *Kladderadatsch* magazine, Berlin, ca. 1850, Archive Thomas Schriefers

Abbildungsnachweis | List of illustrations

bauhaus. Zeitschrift für Bau und Gestaltung, Dessau, 2. Jg., Heft 1/1928, S. 17: 88.

Adolf Behne: *Neues Wohnen – neues Bauen*, Hesse & Becker Verlag, Leipzig 1930, Einband, Vorderseite: 85.

Berliner Illustrierte, Ausschnitt ohne Paginierung, 1920er Jahre: 145.

Caroline Campbell, Dagmar Korbmacher, Neville Rowley, Sarah Vowles (Hrsg.): *Mantegna + Bellini: Meister der Renaissance*, Ausst.-Kat., München 2018, S. 208: 5.

Deutsches Stuhlbaumuseum Rabenau: 140, 141.

Diderots Enzyklopädie. Die Bildtafeln 1762–1777, 3. Bd., Augsburg 1995, Tafeln 2246, 2256, 2257: 19, 20, 21, 22.

die LÜBECKER MUSEEN – St. Annen-Museum, Lübeck (Michael Haydn): 7/8.

Ehlenbeck & Platte, Vohwinkel (Rhld.), Annonce im Anzeigenteil der Zeitschrift Innendekoration, 41. Jg., Heft 9/1930, ohne Paginierung: 94.

Dr. Cordula Fink, Köln: 23, 24, 308, 309, 324–347, 348–359, 360–371.

Germanisches Nationalmuseum, Nürnberg: 11/12.

Sigfried Giedion: *Befreites Wohnen*, Oral Füssli Verlag, Zürich / Leipzig 1929 Titel/ Einband, Vorderseite: 87.

Werner Gräff: *Zweckmässiges Wohnen für jedes Einkommen*, Potsdam 1931, S. 48: 154.

GRASSI Museum für Angewandte Kunst Leipzig (Esther Hoyer): 9/10, 13/14, 15/16, 31, 43, 66, 98/99, 137–139, 142, 143, 144, 152/153, 163/164, 172, 199/200, 213, 241, 242/243, 244/245, 246, 247, 248, 249, 250, 251, 252/253, 254, 255, 256/257, 258, 259, 260, 261, 262, 263, 264, 265, 266, 267/268, 269, 270, 271, 272, 273, 274, 275, 276, 277, 278, 279, 280, 281, 282, 283, 284/285, 286, 287/288, 289, 290, 291/292, 293, 294, 295, 296, 297.

Henry Havard (Hrsg.): *Dictionnaire de L'Ameublement et de la Décoration depuis le XIIIe siècle jusqu'à nos jours*. Tome I–IV, Maison Quantin, Paris 1894: 18.

M. Janzen: *Le Guide du Fabricant de Meubles et du Décorateur*, Paris um 1855, ohne Paginierung: 49–54.

Kladderadatsch: Humoristisch-Satyrisches Wochenblatt: 372.

Alfred Köppen, Carl Breuer: *Geschichte des Möbels unter Berücksichtigung der architektonischen und tektonischen Formen. Eine Stillehre für Bau-und Möbeltischler*, Berlin / New York 1904, S. 73: 6.

Stefan Kraus, Köln: 214.

Kultur im Heim, Heft 1/63, Titel/Cover: 156.

Hans Lewitzky: *Meine Wohnung*, Berlin 1962, S. 185: 155.

L'Illustration, Paris, 27.5.1933: 110, 111, 112.

LÖFFLER COLLECTION, Reichenschwand: 25, 26, 29, 39/40, 44, 45/46, 47/48, 56–58, 59/60, 61, 62, 63, 64/65, 67–69, 70/71, 72–76, 77/78, 79/80, 81/82, 89–91, 92/93, 96/97, 100/101, 102, 103/104, 105/106, 107–109, 113, 114/115, 116/117, 118–121, 122/123, 124/125, 126/127, 128–130, 131/132, 133/134, 135, 149/150, 159, 160–162, 165/166, 167/168, 169/170, 171, 173/174, 175/176, 177/178, 179/180, 181/182, 183/184, 185/186, 187/188, 189/190, 191/192, 193/194, 195/196, 197/198, 201, 202/203, 204–206, 207–209, 210–212, 215–217, 218, 219, 220, 221/222, 226, 227, 228/229, 230/231, 232/233, 234, 235/236, 237, 238, 239, 240, 299, 300/301, 302, 303, 304/305, 306/307, 310/311, 312, 313/314, 315, 316, 317/318, 319/320, 321/322, 323.

© 1944 Bruno Munari. All rights reserved to Maurizio Corraini s.r.l.: 158.

Museum für Kunst und Kulturgeschichte Schloss Gottorf, Landesmuseen Schleswig-Holstein: 30.

Museumslandschaft Hessen Kassel, Möbelsammlung (Katrin Venhorst): 32, 33/34, 35/36, 37/38.

Privatbesitz: 17, 41/42, 223–225.

Juliane Rückriem: 1.

Schlaraffia-Werke Hüter & Co. GmbH., Annonce im Anzeigenteil der Zeitschrift *Innendekoration*, 41. Jg., Heft 9/1930, ohne Paginierung: 95.

Otto Schmidt: *Der alten Wohnung ein neues Gesicht*, Stuttgart 1930, im Anzeigenteil der Zeitschrift *Innendekoration*, 41. Jg., Heft 9/1930, ohne Paginierung: 83, 86.

Adolf G. Schneck: *Das Polstermöbel*, Stuttgart 1933, S. 7: 146–148.

Dr. Thomas Schriefers, Köln: 2, 93, 157.

Franz Schuster: *Der Stil unserer Zeit. Die fünf Formen des Gestaltens der äußeren Welt des Menschen. Ein Beitrag zum kulturellen Wiederaufbau*, Wien 1948, S. 111: 151.

Saul Steinberg: *The Art of Living*, New York 1949, ohne Paginierung: 3.

Stiftung Preußische Schlösser und Gärten Berlin-Brandenburg: 27/28, 298.

Hans Wichmann: *Aufbruch zum neuen Wohnen*, Birkhäuser Verlag, Basel und Stuttgart 1978, S. 293: 136.

© VG Bild-Kunst, Bonn 2022 für Andrea Branzi, Roberto Sebastián Matta, Ludwig Mies van der Rohe, Renate Müller, Richard Riemerschmid, Henry Van de Velde; © The Saul Steinberg Foundation / VG Bild- Kunst, Bonn 2022 für Saul Steinberg.

Die Geltendmachung der Ansprüche gem. § 60h UrhG für die Wiedergabe von Abbildungen der Exponate/Bestandswerke erfolgt durch die VG Bild-Kunst.

Impressum | Imprint

Die vorliegende Publikation erscheint anlässlich der Ausstellung *BESESSEN. Die geheime Kunst des Polsterns* | This publication accompanies the exhibition *DEEP-SEATED. The Secret Art of Upholstery*, GRASSI Museum für Angewandte Kunst Leipzig | Museum of Applied Arts Leipzig, 24.11.2022–26.03.2023.

KATALOG / CATALOG

Idee und Gesamtkonzept / Idea and concept
Dr. Thomas Schriefers, Köln

Herausgeber / Editor
GRASSI Museum für Angewandte Kunst Leipzig
Einrichtung der Stadt Leipzig

Autoren / Authors
Thomas Andersch, Max Busch, Dr. Cordula Fink, Dr. Thomas Rudi,
Dr. Thomas Schriefers, Xenia Schürmann, Dr. Stefanie Seeberg,
Dr. Olaf Thormann

Gestaltung / Graphic design
Dr. Thomas Schriefers, Köln

Satz und Reprografie / Typesetting and reprography
Thomas Liebscher, Passage-Verlag Leipzig

Redaktion / Editing
Dr. Thomas Rudi, GRASSI Museum für Angewandte Kunst Leipzig
Dr. Thomas Schriefers, Köln

Lektorat / Copyediting and proofreading
Anja Schrade, Stuttgart (deutsch)
Unter Mitarbeit von / With the collaboration of
Thomas Andersch, GRASSI Museum für Angewandte Kunst Leipzig
Dr. Thomas Rudi, GRASSI Museum für Angewandte Kunst Leipzig
Dr. Stefanie Seeberg, GRASSI Museum für Angewandte Kunst Leipzig

Übersetzung / Translation
Xenia Schürmann, Kassel

arnoldsche Projektkoordination / Project coordination
Julia Hohrein

Fotos / Photos
Deutsches Stuhlbaumuseum Rabenau e.V.
Germanisches Nationalmuseum Nürnberg (Monika Runge)
GRASSI Museum für Angewandte Kunst Leipzig (Esther Hoyer)
LÖFFLER COLLECTION, Reichenschwand
die LÜBECKER MUSEEN – St. Annen-Museum (Michael Haydn, Lübeck)
Museum für Kunst und Kulturgeschichte Schloss Gottorf, Landesmuseen Schleswig-Holstein
Museumslandschaft Hessen Kassel, Möbelsammlung (Katrin Venhorst)

Druck / Printing
Offizin Scheufele, Stuttgart

Papier / Paper
150 g/m² GardaMatt Art, Überzug / cover: 270 g/m² Creative Print diamant

© 2022 arnoldsche Art Publishers, Stuttgart, GRASSI Museum für Angewandte Kunst Leipzig und die Autoren / and the authors

Alle Rechte vorbehalten. Vervielfältigung und Wiedergabe auf jegliche Weise (grafisch, elektronisch und fotomechanisch sowie der Gebrauch von Systemen zur Datenrückgewinnung) – auch in Auszügen – nur mit schriftlicher Genehmigung der Copyright-Inhaber.
www.arnoldsche.com

All rights reserved. No part of this work may be reproduced or used in any form or by any means (graphic, electronic, or mechanical, including photocopying or information storage and retrieval systems) without written permission from the copyright holders.
www.arnoldsche.com

Bibliografische Information der Deutschen Nationalbibliothek
Die Deutsche Nationalbibliothek verzeichnet diese Publikation in der Deutschen Nationalbibliografie; detaillierte bibliografische Daten sind über www.dnb.de abrufbar.

Bibliographic information published by the Deutsche Nationalbibliothek
The Deutsche Nationalbibliothek lists this publication in the Deutsche Nationalbibliografie; detailed bibliographic data are available at www.dnb.de.

ISBN 978-3-89790-681-5

Made in Germany, 2022

Umschlagabbildungen / Cover illustrations
vorne / front: Armlehnstuhl, 1928–30, LÖFFLER COLLECTION, Reichenschwand (Foto / photo: Sabine Freudenberger, Nürnberg).

hinten / back: Ernst Max Jahn, Armlehnsessel, 1928, GRASSI Museum für Angewandte Kunst Leipzig (Foto / photo: Esther Hoyer/GRASSI Museum für Angewandte Kunst Leipzig).

AUSSTELLUNG / EXHIBITION

Direktor / Director
Dr. Olaf Thormann

Kurator / Curator
Dr. Thomas Schriefers, Köln

Unter Mitarbeit von / With the collaboration of
Sabine Epple
Dr. Cordula Fink, Köln
Dr. Thomas Rudi
Karoline Schliemann
Dr. Stefanie Seeberg
Dr. Olaf Thormann

Projektkoordination / Project coordination
Dr. Thomas Rudi

Gestaltung Ausstellung und Drucksachen / Exhibition design and printed matter
Dr. Thomas Schriefers, Köln

Druckvorstufe Ausstellungsgrafik / Prepress exhibition graphics
Thomas Liebscher, Passage-Verlag Leipzig

Presse- und Öffentlichkeitsarbeit / Public Relations
Anett Lamprecht

Marketing
Jasmin Braun

Konservatorische Betreuung / Restoration
Thomas Andersch
Carola Berriola
Kay Draber
Ilona Faust
Bettina Kosel

Sicherheitsmanagement und Leihverkehr / Security management and loans
Melanie Möbius

Filme und Klangtunnel / Movies and sound tunnel
Dr. Cordula Fink, Köln
Rheinklang, Köln

Übersetzung / Translation
Xenia Schürmann, Kassel

Ausstellungsaufbau, Technik / Technical support
Frank-Henning Dabels
Swen Evert
Steffen Lipp
Denis Luce

Gefördert durch / Sponsored by

SACHSEN
Staatliche Kunstsammlungen Dresden
Sächsische Landesstelle für Museumswesen

Die Maßnahme wird mitfinanziert durch Steuermittel auf der Grundlage des vom Sächsischen Landtag beschlossenen Haushaltes.

Fachgruppe der Restauratoren im Handwerk e.V.

LÖFFLER COLLECTION, Reichenschwand

Houlès, Paris

Cammann Gobelin Manufaktur, Niederwiesa

Dedar, Mailand